The media's watching Vault!
Here's a sampling of our coverage.

"For those hoping to climb the ladder of success, [Vault's] insights are priceless."
– *Money*

"The best place on the web to prepare for a job search."
– *Fortune*

"[Vault guides] make for excellent starting points for job hunters and should be purchased by academic libraries for their career sections [and] university career centers."
– *Library Journal*

"The granddaddy of worker sites."
– *U.S. News & World Report*

"A killer app."
– *The New York Times*

One of Forbes' 33 "Favorite Sites."
– *Forbes*

"To get the unvarnished scoop, check out Vault."
– *Smart Money*

"Vault has a wealth of information about major employers and job-searching strategies as well as comments from workers about their experiences at specific companies."
– *The Washington Post*

"Vault has become the go-to source for career preparation."
– *Crain's New York Business*

"Vault [provides] the skinny on working conditions at all kinds of companies from current and former employees."
– *USA Today*

VAULT
> the most trusted name in career information™

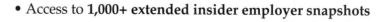

THE VAULT COLLEGE CAREER BIBLE

2009 EDITION

COLLEGE
CAREER
BIBLE

Get the BUZZ on Top Schools
Read what STUDENTS and ALUMNI have to say about:
• Admissions
• Academics
• Employment Prospects
• Quality of Life
• Social Life
Surveys on thousands of top programs
College • MBA • Law School • Grad School
VAULT
> the most trusted name in career information™
Go to www.vault.com

THE VAULT COLLEGE CAREER BIBLE

2009 EDITION

COLLEGE
CAREER
BIBLE

VAULT EDITORS

For information about permission to reproduce selections from this book, contact Vault.com, Inc. 75 Varick Street, 8th Floor, New York, NY 10013, (212) 366-4212.

Library of Congress CIP Data is available.

ISBN 10: 1-58131-623-2

ISBN 13: 978-1-58131-623-0

Printed in the United States of America

Acknowledgements

We are extremely grateful to Vault's entire staff for all their help in the editorial, production and marketing processes. Vault also would like to acknowledge the support of our investors, clients, employees, family and friends. Thank you!

Visit Vault at **www.vault.com** for insider company profiles, expert advice,
career message boards, expert resume reviews, the Vault Job Board and more.

VΛULT CAREER LIBRARY

vii

Table of Contents

Visit Vault at **www.vault.com** for insider company profiles, expert advice, career message boards, expert resume reviews, the Vault Job Board and more.

VAULT CAREER LIBRARY

ix

Visit Vault at www.vault.com for insider company profiles, expert advice,
career message boards, expert resume reviews, the Vault Job Board and more.

VAULT CAREER LIBRARY

xi

Health Care   263

High Tech   280

Hospitality and Tourism   299

Human Resources   309

Investment Management   319

Visit Vault at www.vault.com for insider company profiles, expert advice,
career message boards, expert resume reviews, the Vault Job Board and more.

VAULT CAREER LIBRARY   xiii

Visit Vault at www.vault.com for insider company profiles, expert advice,
career message boards, expert resume reviews, the Vault Job Board and more.

VAULT CAREER LIBRARY

xv

Introduction

Maybe you're facing the end of your college career; maybe you've already graduated. Either way, you're trying to answer the question you've been asked all your life: what are you going to do when you grow up? Only now, this question is no longer hypothetical. So what are you going to do?

First: relax. Whether you're a college junior, senior or recent graduate, the world will not end if you don't have a job lined up just yet. Almost everyone has difficulty figuring out what he or she wants to do with the rest of his or her life, and absolutely everyone goes through the painful process of finding that first "real" job. You're in good company. According to studies by the National Association of Colleges and Employers (NACE), less than 60 percent of college students applied for a job before graduation. But! Of those students who did apply, 80 percent had at least one job offer before graduation.

According to the NACE *Job Outlook 2009 Fall Preview*, graduates are entering a stable job market despite the recession. Respondents reported that they expect to hire 6.1 percent more college grads than in 2008. Although this is the smallest increase in recent years, employers are committed to maintaining their hiring levels.

In addition, NACE reports that more and more employers will be coming to you, the student. In its 2007 Recruiting Benchmarks Survey, almost 90 percent of employers said that they participate actively in on-campus recruiting. And they want to lock their new hires in early. In *Job Outlook*, employers reported that they are doing the majority of their recruiting (63 percent) in the fall, rather than the spring. In addition, many reported an increased use of technology as a recruiting tool, especially social networking web sites. So starting your first job search is as easy as logging on to Facebook.

Still, for most first-time job seekers, finding that first gig is never easy. This Vault guide will help you get a leg up on the competitive job search, and will assist you in narrowing your search by giving you an overview of popular industries, careers and resources.

Start with your career center

Whether you're currently enrolled or a recent graduate, your college career center is a good place to start your job search. Counselors at the career center can often provide help with resumes and interviewing, and the center also usually has job and internship listings, as well as contact information for alumni in your field of interest who are willing to provide advice to wide-eyed newbies. (Remember, you can still use your college career center even after you've graduated.)

Attend career fairs

Career fairs—veritable smorgasbords of employers and job options—are another place to test out the job market waters. Historically, employers have considered career fairs a very effective way to recruit college students. Not only are they able to get a sense of the applicant pool, but they are also able to boost their image and, hopefully, attract more applicants.

Work experience already?

The best way to get a job is to have a job. Work experience of any kind will help you get your first "real" job out of college. Working during school or over the summer, and/or participating in co-ops or internships is very valuable. Approximately 95 percent of employers in NACE's 2008 *Job Outlook* said that they factor in work experience when choosing their new hires. Remember, the perfect candidate has more than a perfect GPA; he/she also has good leadership skills, can communicate with and relate to others and is a good problem-solver.

Visit Vault at **www.vault.com** for insider company profiles, expert advice, career message boards, expert resume reviews, the Vault Job Board and more.

VAULT CAREER LIBRARY

1

Narrow your career options

Figuring out what you'd like to do is half the battle; once you've done that, your job search will automatically become more focused. After you've decided on an industry or position, look for information about the day-to-day responsibilities such a job will entail. It's tough to really understand what it's like to work at a place or position without these tips, which is why Vault provides "Days in the Life" notes and Q&As for many different occupations. Some of these are included in this book; others can be found in Vault's guides on specific industries or on www.vault.com.

Don't stress

All that said, don't stress out too much over choosing your first job. Gone are the days of working 40 years at one company and leaving with a gold watch; today's job market is much more fluid—most professionals starting their careers today will work in at least five different industries or functions before they retire. For a generation of young, curious and versatile graduates, that is an exciting prospect.

Good luck!
The Team at Vault

THE COLLEGE STUDENT JOB SEARCH

Recruiting and Internships

On-Campus Recruiting and Career Fairs

If you want to start your career at a large company, being a college student puts you in a good position to do so. Many major employers recruit college students at targeted campuses. Employers in professional services fields, such as accounting, consulting and investment banking, hire large classes of graduating students each year as analysts, while major employers in other industries often recruit new grads into management development programs. (These same employers normally hire many juniors as interns. Many students who intern at a company are extended full-time offers after graduation.)

The best place to find out which companies recruit at your school is your career services office. Companies generally visit the campus in the fall to give presentations to interested students; some colleges also hold career fairs, at which HR representatives from these companies collect resumes and speak with students. If you think you might be interested in a company, don't fail to go to these presentations!

If you're interested in a company, make sure you attend all presentations made by that company and speak to at least one company representative. Sometimes this rep will be an HR professional, sometimes a manager in the department that is recruiting, and still other times the rep will be a new hire at the company, often an alumnus of your university. Be sure that you get the business card of the representative with whom you connect the most strongly. Then follow up with an e-mail expressing your interest and perhaps making an on-target inquiry or two. This will show your motivation and initiative—and remember, companies want to hire students who are interested in them and motivated to work for them. Don't overdo it, however; writing your new contact every week is overkill.

Later in the fall, these companies hold a first round of interviews with students on campus or very near campus, often at the career center. Students who pass the first round then visit the company's offices for a second day of interviews that takes a half-day or full day. The same process is followed for internships, though recruiting for summer internships generally happens at the beginning of the spring semester.

The Importance of Interning

If you're reading this book as an underclassman or early in your senior year, you're in good shape—many college students don't begin thinking about careers until late in their senior year or (gasp) after graduation. If you're one of the early birds, make sure you take advantage of your time by getting experience through a summer and/or school-year internship.

What is an internship?

An internship is a sort of trial run at a company—and one of the best ways to test out a potential career field or employer. Internships can last two weeks or a full year, though most of them are for a three-month period or so. Most internships take place over the summer, though others may be available over the fall or spring semester or of a duration of your choosing. Similarly, the majority of internships are full time, though some are part time.

Why do an internship?

You might be tempted just to take a job to earn money. There's nothing wrong with that—but there's so much more right with doing an internship. For example, if you want to break into a field that's tough to crack, like entertainment or advertising or politics, the very best way to get a job in the field is to have interned in it. Not only will you have great experience on your resume, you'll meet plenty of contacts and potential mentors. Similarly, interning at a top company puts you on the fast track to getting a full-time offer from that firm—or one of its competitors! Most large companies are much more likely to

Visit Vault at **www.vault.com** for insider company profiles, expert advice, career message boards, expert resume reviews, the Vault Job Board and more.

VAULT CAREER LIBRARY

5

hire a former intern than someone "right off the street." Even if you don't end up working for your employer, you'll have some invaluable and difficult-to-obtain experience on your resume.

But I need to get paid!

Don't think that doing an internship means giving up on pay altogether. It's true that many internships are unpaid or only offer college credit—at the same time, these are often small, interesting organizations or companies in glamorous industries. But many others offer some kind of payment, from a stipend or travel allowance to a very generous salary. Others offer interesting perks, such as travel and the chance to attend exclusive industry events.

Tips for applying to internships

Let's say you've found an internship that interests you. That's great! The first thing you should do is to follow all the instructions. Here's a short checklist of things you need to do when applying for internships.

Apply by the deadline. A few months before the deadline is even better—a small organization might just take the first qualified intern who applies.

Follow the instructions! If you're asked to provide a writing sample, don't send your photo portfolio. If you're asked to provide a reference, start canvassing your teachers and professors.

Make sure your resume is up to date and thoroughly spellchecked. If you've never written a resume, go to your school career guidance center and ask for help. And ask an experienced professional or two that you trust to review your resume. If you are applying for internships in different fields, you may need to have more than one version of your resume highlighting different experience. Make sure that your most current contact information is on the resume.

Don't ignore the cover letter. Make a persuasive case in your cover letter, which should be tailored to each internship, that you really want to intern at the company. Do your research and be specific—and honest—about why the opportunity is right for you. Again, make sure you carefully proofread the cover letter. Let a trusted friend or teacher read it, as well.

Follow up. If you're really interested in an internship, there's nothing wrong with a quick call or e-mail a few weeks after the application to let the organization know how interested you are. But don't pepper them with phone calls every day.

Carpe diem. If you're really interested in an internship, but your qualifications aren't quite right, apply anyway and stress your real interest. Many organizations would rather have a truly excited and motivated intern than one that just meets the qualifications on paper.

Take experience over money. You can always earn money. The window of opportunity for internships isn't eternally open. If you're really broke, consider taking a part-time job in order to work at the internship you really want.

Intern any time

Most companies with internships have formal programs during the summer, when they hire a number of college or high school students. However, many companies also hire during the school year, so if you're starting your senior year, it's not too late to get that all-important professional work experience.

And, even if you've graduated from college, you can still intern to gain experience if you haven't landed a full-time job. We can't stress this enough: if you can manage it financially, interning in a profession in which you have long-term interest is almost always more preferable than taking a paying job that has nothing to do with your interests. If you're a college graduate, this may mean moving home or working a night job for fewer hours and less pay. Years down the road, we're sure you'll agree that it was worth it.

For information on internship programs, refer to the *Vault Guide to Top Internships*, which has information on more than 750 top programs, and check out the Internship Board at www.vault.com for up-to-date listings.

Make Sure You Don't Blow Your Internship

Remember that scene in *Grease* when the Rydell High kids are singing about the summer? Danny "had me a blast," while for Sandy it "happened so fast." It seems a strange comparison, but many summer interns at America's leading companies describe their summers the same way. Not all experiences are quite so rosy, but in any case, young employees get both a feel for their corporate culture and a taste of the workforce during the course of these often finely crafted programs. Whether their time is spent doing substantive work that affects the company, or just making Starbucks runs all summer, there is a goal in mind. Summer interns need to spend those precious weeks making a favorable impression in order to get that all-important full-time offer.

Granted, the reason that many summer programs are so carefully organized and lavish is so that interns will want to come back. In many programs, "you have to seriously mess up not to get [an offer]." Much more commonly, though, interns are not afforded such leeway, and need to be aware of what it takes to secure a full-time position. First and foremost, while the fate of the company may not hinge on the work interns produce, optimum effort must still be made on assignments. Simply put, no matter if it seems insignificant, "whatever work you do, make sure to do a good job," advises one recruiter. Satisfying this requirement may mean punching the clock after the summer sun has disappeared for the night. Most businesses do not take kindly to employees who leave a vapor trail out the door when the five o'clock whistle blows.

Also extremely important are the connections, however informal, made with established employees. This is especially true with mid-level and senior employees who have a say in who gets hired. Those who assume that a stellar academic record and a shiny pair of Ferragamo wing tips are a substitute for engaging conversation may be in for a rude awakening come Labor Day. Successful networking can be accomplished by working for a variety of people or through socialization inside the office. Attendance at company social events, when offered, is an "important way to build personal relationships within the company," as well. Whether cruising the halls or knocking a few back at the local pub, a gregarious persona cannot be discounted— "office wallflowers just will not cut the mustard," says one corporate insider. On the other hand, there are limits; for instance, insiders at Goldman Sachs tell a cautionary tale wherein one investment banking associate who failed to get an offer was snubbed "as a result of excessive brown nosing."

At the same time, summer interns need to be careful about exposing, or more to the point imposing, their personality on their fellow employees. At some companies, for example, "you're not allowed to be rude to anyone—secretaries, the lady in the cafeteria, or whoever it is." Even fast-paced offices with a reputation for "screamers" may be averse to bringing in new people who will perpetuate a harsh culture. "Some summer interns behave completely inappropriately," says a source at a Wall Street firm. "One recent summer associate had a big mouth and she screamed a lot. She made enemies in only eight weeks, including some managing directors."

Of course, even when interns generally play their cards right, one wrong move may stand between them and a job offer. For instance, an insider tells Vault that one would-be full-timer was not asked back to his company after "arguing with a partner at a softball game about what position to play." Another inexplicably turned over an entire assignment to an unqualified subordinate. Perhaps the most extreme example involved an overly enthusiastic intern at one firm who, while on a company retreat, stripped off his clothes and hopped into the hot tub. That's a little too much information!

Visit Vault at **www.vault.com** for insider company profiles, expert advice, career message boards, expert resume reviews, the Vault Job Board and more.

V∧ULT CAREER LIBRARY   7

How to Take Advantage of Your Internship

The internship craze is reaching new heights. Nearly three-quarters of all college students do internships today as compared to 1 in 36 in 1980. These numbers have made many employers a bit uneasy. After all, these employers are, for the most part, getting all this labor for free, or at most a small stipend. Isn't there something a little bit wrong with that? Many employers think so. That won't stop them from taking the sweet deal, but they won't feel good about. That's where you —the intern— come into the picture. The intern has an extremely receptive and grateful audience at his internship, an audience that aims to please. Consequently, if the intern plays his cards well, he or she can do extraordinary things during his two- or three-month stint.

Be there first

At most internships, especially those that take place in the summer, the company or organization will have several interns for a particular time period. If possible, arrive a week or so before the other interns. First, you will get more individual attention in the beginning and consequently can establish yourself as the "favorite" intern.

Second, you may be able to get the first pick of the assignments. Third, you may get the first pick of the desks, or wherever they will seat you. Employing this rule to its extremes, interns have been known to use this seemingly simple technique to get the later-arriving interns to become their "pseudo-interns"—farming out menial tasks to them so they can concentrate on more substantive work.

Look around

Once you get inside a company, you should not feel restrained by the department that you're working in—or even to your assigned supervisor. Figure out what you most want to do in the organization and schmooze the person who does it. A good way to do this is to ask them to lunch. A good line is: "I'm trying to absorb as much information as I can in this internship, and what you do seems particularly interesting. I wonder if you are available for lunch any time this week." They will almost always say "Yes." When they describe what they do at lunch, try to relate the skills that they employ to skills that you have. For example, if they tell you about the press release they are writing for company X, slip in how that's similar to your college newspaper writing experience. Hopefully, they will then offer you a chance to draft a press release.

If not, try to give them another nudge, but make it gently. "Oh, writing press releases seems like so much fun!" you can add, or something to that effect.

Never complain

When you are given menial errands to do, take it in good cheer. No one likes a whiner. If you feel like you must say something, couch it in humor. One State Department intern remembers telling his boss: "Although being a deputy assistant secretary of photocopying has its moments, I was wondering if I could do more substantive work here." It got his message across—and worked. Remember, as long as you do a few things that look impressive, you won't have to put on your resume that for 99 percent of the time you ran errands and photocopied stuff. So instead of complaining about your menial tasks— or even non-verbally complaining by acting dour—express an interest in doing substantive work, and be as specific as possible. Specificity shows interest.

Resumes

What can you do?

Rule number one: Employers don't really, truly care what you did at your last job. They care about what you can do for them. They wonder about your potential for future success working for them. Your resume must answer these questions.

As Shannon Heidkamp, recruiting manager for a division of Allstate Insurance says, "People need to ask themselves 'What value can I offer this prospective employer?'" Resumes should tell potential employers what skills each employee used, what tasks they accomplished and what honors they garnered—skills, tasks and honors that can be applied to future jobs. Specific job openings, whether advertised through newspaper ads, Internet sites or inter-office memos, come with specific job descriptions. If you find out about the job through a friend, ask for a copy of the job description. Your job is to meet those requirements by listing your qualifications that most closely meet these prerequisites.

10 seconds

Studies show that regardless of how long you labor over your resume, most employers will spend 10 seconds looking at it. That's it.

Because of the masses of job searchers, most managers and human resource employees receive an enormous number of resumes. Faced with a pile of paper to wade through every morning, employers look for any deficiency possible to reduce the applicant pool to a manageable number. Thus, your resume must present your information quickly, clearly and in a way that makes your experience relevant to the position in question. That means condensing your information down to its most powerful form.

So distill, distill, distill. Long, dense paragraphs make information hard to find and require too much effort from the overworked reader. If that reader can't figure out how your experience applies to the available position, your resume is not doing its job.

Solve this problem by creating bulleted, indented, focused statements. Short, powerful lines show the reader, in a glance, exactly why they should keep reading.

Think about how to write up your experience in targeted, clear, bulleted, detail-rich prose.

It's what you did, not what your name tag said

Resumes should scream ability, not claim responsibility. Employers should be visualizing you in the new position, not remembering you as "that account assistant from Chase." While some former employers can bolster your resume by their mere presence, you don't want to be thought of as a cog from another machine. Instead, your resume should present you as an essential component of a company's success.

Visit Vault at **www.vault.com** for insider company profiles, expert advice, career message boards, expert resume reviews, the Vault Job Board and more.

VAULT CAREER LIBRARY   9

Sample Resumes

Sandra Pearson

Sandypear@ivillage.com

11 Hillhouse Aavenue

New Haven, CT 06511

(203) 555-8103

SANDRA'S READY FOR A POSITION AS A PRIVATE SCHOOL TEACHER

Education:

Yale University, New Haven, CT

Bachelor of Arts, May 2008; Double Major

Psychology and History

2004 National Merit Scholar Award

2003 Micehouse National Laboratory Internship

Skills:

Microsoft Word, Excel

Editing and proofreading

Proficient Spanish

Graphic design

Work Experience:

Project Hand in Hand 2008

Consultant to teach adults an accredited course on creating curriculum based on the multiple intelligence theory

Toddling On Up 2003-2007

Teacher, day care provider; creator of art curriculum and designer of weekly programs

Yale Greenpeace Office 2007

Distributed information on recycling, made presentations; visited, advised and reorganized locations in the Yale and New Haven communities

Learning Disabilities Center at Yale 2005

Performed various clerical duties; read onto tapes and copied materials for special needs members of the Yale community

XYZ Vacuums

Sales representative for high-quality vacuum cleaners

Activities:

Kappa Beta Sorority 2004-2008; social chair 2007-2008

Community Relations Council 2006-2007

Black Alliance at Yale; publicity manager 2006-2007

Yale Gospel Choir 2004-2008

Black Caucus at Yale; co-founder 2005-2008

Roots Theatre Ensemble; costume designer 2005-2006, actress 2005-2007

Yale Antigravity Society 2007

Farley Suber

345 Fenwick Street   Elton Park, CO 79403   (750) 555-4212

Objective:

Seeking an entry-level position in sales or marketing

FARLEY CRAFTILY DISGUISES HIS GAPS IN WORK EXPERIENCE

Education:

Bachelor of Arts in Communication (Public Relations) May 2006
Minor: Business/Liberal Arts
University of Chicago, Chicago, IL
Cumulative GPA: 3.1 out of 4.0

Experience:

LONS Computing Systems

Sales and Marketing Representative

- Applied marketing skills to increase sales of Macintosh computers
- Cultivated client relationships, increasing customer satisfaction and repeat sales
- Placed advertising in magazines, including *Men's Health*, *GQ* and *Wired*
- Wrote press releases on new computer products

Broadway Master Theatre

Marketing Assistant

- Assisted with the planning, creation and distribution of theatrical press releases
- Wrote radio advertisements
- Tracked attendance based on information from reservationists and box office attendants
- Handled photo releases mailings to be distributed to the media sources

Honors and Interests:

- **Senior Honors:** Senior cumulative average of 4.0 out of 4.0
- **Terrence S. Duboff Award:** Award for academic achievement excellence in communications
- **NCAA Division 1 Golfer:** Winner of the Greenview Collegiate Classic 2006, second place finalist 2006 NCAA MidWest Cup
- **Chi Phi Sigma Fraternity:** Rush Chairman, Scholarship Chairman, Standards Board, Senior Steering Committee

Visit Vault at www.vault.com for insider company profiles, expert advice,
career message boards, expert resume reviews, the Vault Job Board and more.

VAULT CAREER LIBRARY

11

Think broadly

Applicants applying for specific job openings must customize their resume for each position. Many job hunters, particularly those beginning their careers, apply to many different jobs.

A person interested in a career in publishing, for example, might apply for jobs as a writer, proofreader, editor, copywriter, grant proposal writer, fact-checker or research assistant. The applicant may or may not have the experience necessary to apply for any of these jobs. But you may have more skills than you think.

When considering the skills that make you a valuable prospect, think broadly. Anybody who's worked a single day can point to several different skills because even the most isolated, repetitive jobs offer a range of experience. Highway toll collection, for instance, is a repetitive job with limited variation, but even that career requires multiple job skills. Helping lost highway drivers read a map means "Offering customer service in a prompt, detail-oriented environment." Making change for riders translates as "Cashiering in a high-pressure, fast-paced setting." But unless these toll-booth workers emphasize these skills to prospective employers, it'll be the highway life for them.

Selected history

A lot of things happen in everyone's day, but when someone asks "How was your day?" you don't start with your first coffee and your lost slippers. You edit. Resumes require that same type of disciplined, succinct editing. The better you are at controlling the information you create, the stronger the resume will be.

When editing your history to fit the resume format, ask yourself, "How does this particular information contribute towards my overall attractiveness to this employer?" If something doesn't help, drop it. Make more space to elaborate on the experiences most relevant to the job to which you are applying.

Similarly, if information lurks in your past that would harm your chances of getting the job, omit it. In resume writing, omitting is not lying. If some jobs make you overqualified for a position, eliminate those positions from your resume. If you're overeducated, don't mention the degree that makes you so. If you're significantly undereducated, there's no need to mention education at all. If the 10 jobs you've had in the last five years make you look like a real life Walter Mitty, reduce your resume's references to the most relevant positions while making sure there are no gaps in the years of your employment.

Cover Letters

The Cover Letter Template

Your Name
Your Street Address, Apartment #
Your City, State and Zip
Your E-mail Address
Your Phone Number
Your Fax Number

WONDERING WHAT GOES ON A COVER LETTER? HERE'S A STEP-BY-STEP GUIDE

Contact's Name
Contact's Title
Contact's Department
Contact's Company Name
Contact's Street Address, Suite #
Company City, State Zip
Company Phone Number
Company Fax Number

Date

Dear Ms./Mr. CONTACT:

The first paragraph tells why you're contacting the person, then either mentions your connection with that person or reveals where you read about the job. It also quickly states who you are. Next it wows them with your sincere, researched knowledge of their company. The goal is to demonstrate that you are a worthy applicant and entice them to read further.

The second and optional third paragraph tell more about yourself, particularly why you're an ideal match for the job by summarizing why you're what they're looking for. You may also clarify anything unclear on your resume.

The last paragraph is your goodbye: you thank the reader for his or her time. Include that you look forward to their reply or give them a time when you'll be getting in contact by phone.

Sincerely,

Sign Here

Visit Vault at **www.vault.com** for insider company profiles, expert advice, career message boards, expert resume reviews, the Vault Job Board and more.

VAULT CAREER LIBRARY   13

Date

Placement of the date, whether left justified, centered or aligned to the right, is up to your discretion, but take the time to write out the entry. If you choose to list the day, list it first, followed by the month, date and year, as follows: Tuesday, December 13, 2005. (Europeans commonly list the day before month, so writing a date only in numbers can be confusing. Does a letter written on 4/7/04 date from April 7th, or July 4th?)

Name and address

Your name and address on the cover letter should be the same as the one on your resume. Uniformity in this case applies not only to the address given, but the way the information is written. If you listed your street as Ave. instead of Avenue on your resume, do so on your cover letter, too.

Your header can be displayed centrally, just like the resume header—including your name in a larger and/or bolded font. But in most cases, the heading is either left justified or left justified and indented to the far right-hand side of the page.

If you choose to list your phone number, make sure that you don't list it somewhere else on the page.

Next comes the address of the person you are writing. In many circumstances, you'll have the complete information on the person you're trying to contact, in which case you should list it in this order:

Name of contact

Title of contact

Company name

Company address

Phone number

Fax number

However, in other cases, you have less than complete information to go on. This is particularly true when responding to an advertisement. If you have an address or phone or fax number but no company name, try a reverse directory, such as Superpages (www.superpages.com), which lets you trace a business by either its address or phone number.

When you're trying to get the name of a contact person, calling the company and asking the receptionist for the name of the recipient (normally, though not always, head of HR) may work. But usually, companies don't list this information because they don't want you calling at all. So if you call, be polite, be persistent, ask for a contact name, say thank you and hang up. Don't identify yourself. If you have questions, wait until the interview.

If you don't get all of the info, don't worry. There are several salutations to use to finesse the fact that you've got no idea who you're addressing. Some solutions are:

To whom it may concern: A bit frosty, but effective.

Dear Sir or Madam: Formal and fusty, but it works.

Sirs: Since the workforce is full of women, avoid this outdated greeting.

Omitting the salutation altogether: Effective, but may look too informal.

Good morning: A sensible approach that is gaining popularity.

Format

Unlike the resume, the cover letter offers the writer significant room for flexibility. Successful cover letters have come in various different forms, and sometimes those that break rules achieve success by attracting attention. But most don't. Here are some basic guidelines on what information the body of a cover letter should deliver.

First paragraph

To be successful, this first paragraph should contain:

• A first line that tells the reader why you're contacting him or her, and how you came to know about the position. This statement should be quick, simple and catchy. Ultimately, what you're trying to create is a descriptive line by which people can categorize you. This means no transcendental speeches about "the real you" or long-winded treatises on your career and philosophy of life.

• Text indicating your respect for the firm's accomplishments, history, status, products or leaders.

• A last line that gives a very brief synopsis of who you are and why you want the position. The best way to do this, if you don't already have a more personal connection with the person you're contacting, is to lay it out:

I am a (your identifying characteristic)

+

I am a (your profession)

+

I have (your years of experience or education)

+

I have worked in (your area of expertise)

+

I am interested in (what position you're looking for)

And thus a killer first paragraph is born.

Middle paragraph(s)

The middle paragraph allows you to move beyond your initial declarative sentences, and into more expansive and revealing statements about who you are and what skills you bring to the job. This is another opportunity to explicitly summarize key facts of your job history. The middle paragraph also offers you the opportunity to mention any connection or prior experience that you may have with the company.

Tell the employer in this paragraph how, based on concrete references to your previous performances, you will perform in your desired position. This does not mean making general, unqualified statements about your greatness, such as "I'm going to be the best you've ever had" or my "My energetic multitasking will be the ultimate asset to your company."

Comments should be backed up by specific references. Try something along the lines of "My postgraduate degree in marketing, combined with my four years of retail bicycle sales would make me a strong addition to Gwinn Cycles' marketing team."

Or, "Meeting the demands of a full-time undergraduate education, a position as student government accountant and a 20-hour-a-week internship with Davidson Management provided me with the multitasking experience needed to excel as a financial analyst at Whittier Finance."

Visit Vault at www.vault.com for insider company profiles, expert advice, career message boards, expert resume reviews, the Vault Job Board and more.

VAULT CAREER LIBRARY   15

Many advertisements ask you to name your salary requirements. Some avoid the problem altogether by ignoring this requirement, and this may be the safest route—any number you give might price you out of a job (before you have the chance to negotiate face-to-face at an interview). Alternatively, you might be pegged at a lower salary than you might otherwise have been offered. If you must give a salary requirement, be as general as possible. The safest bet is to offer a general range ("in the $40,000s"). Put the salary requirement at the end of the paragraph, not in your first sentence.

Some cover letter writers use another paragraph to describe their accomplishments. This makes sense if, for example, your experience lies in two distinct areas, or you need to explain something that is not evident on your resume, such as "I decided to leave law school to pursue an exciting venture capital opportunity" or "I plan to relocate to Wisconsin shortly." Do not get overly personal—"I dropped out of business school to care for my sick mother" is touching, but will not necessarily impress employers.

Final paragraph

The final paragraph is your fond farewell, your summation, a testament to your elegance and social grace. This should be the shortest paragraph of the letter. Here, tell your readers you're pleased they got so far down the page. Tell them you look forward to hearing from them. Tell them how you can be reached. Here's some sample sentences for your conclusion.

Thank you sentences:
Thank you for your time.
Thank you for reviewing my qualifications.
Thank you for your consideration.
Thank you for your review of my qualifications.

Way too much:
It would be more than an honor to meet with you.

A note of confidence in a callback:
I look forward to your reply.
I look forward to hearing from you.
I look forward to your response.
I look forward to your call.

Over the top:
Call me tomorrow, please.

Interviews

Getting Ready

Would a seasoned attorney stride into a courtroom on the day of an important case without having considered every angle of the case? Would a professional climber arrive in Kathmandu without provisions and maps of Mount Everest? Nope. If you want to sway the jury or reach the summit, you've got to go into the big event prepared. The same is true of going into an interview. Preparation is an essential part of the interview process and one that is easy to overlook or shortchange.

According to polls, most job candidates spend less than an hour preparing for their interviews. No one is going to make you prepare for an interview, least of all the people who will be asking the questions, so it's up to you to get ready on your own.

Unprepared interview subjects often give poor interviews, says Clift Jones, an account director at Bozell Worldwide Advertising. "One of the biggest mistakes people make is to come in with no agenda. They don't know why they want the job, anything about the unique strengths of the company or why they'd be a good match. They're eager and little else. It's much more impressive if they've put a lot of thought into what they want from a situation and what they have to offer before they come in."

By preparing for the interview you'll be doing yourself a favor. Remember, more time spent in preparation means less anxiety on the day of the interview. It's a relief to have something relevant to say, a cogent question on your tongue, a collection of stories underscoring specific elements of your prodigious competence, when the interviewer's anticipatory eyes fall on you and it's your turn to speak.

In addition to alleviating pre-interview stress, being prepared has several other benefits:

- It shows the interviewer that you care enough about the position, the company and the industry to research its current status and future.
- It suggests that once you're hired, your preparation for meetings and assignments will be equally as sound.
- It shows respect for the interviewer and the company he or she works for.
- It provides more opportunities for you and the interviewer to have a meaningful conversation in which you can find common ground.

Research

Research is a vital preparation tool. Over time, companies, like countries, develop distinct cultures and inner languages. In some cases the language of a corporation or industry can become so specialized that an outsider will have trouble understanding it. The job candidate who learns an organization's lingo well enough to speak it during the interview just might, like a long-lost relative, be embraced with a cry of, "He's one of us!" and welcomed into the fold.

Where can someone find this kind of insider knowledge? Vault produces a series of profiles and surveys on organizations that can help the information-hungry interviewee. Other user-friendly, if more company-friendly, sources of information include the packets prepared for a company's stockholders. Any stockbroker will send you these, provided you assure them of your interest in someday purchasing stocks through them. A company's human resources, treasury or public relations office will be happy to send you an annual report (which will include a company's financial, marketing and product report), a prospectus (which includes the name of the CEO and a list of major players), or a 10K report (which contains a company's historical and financial information).

Trade magazines (or "the trades"), industry insider magazines, can apprise you of current events, hirings and firings, trends and other relevant issues. Libraries, career centers and web sites can also be valuable information-gathering places. Spending a day at the library is an especially good way to get the job search going if you're just starting out.

Visit Vault at **www.vault.com** for insider company profiles, expert advice, career message boards, expert resume reviews, the Vault Job Board and more.

VAULT CAREER LIBRARY   **17**

Perhaps the most direct way of getting the real skinny on a company is to talk to someone who works there. Speaking to someone in a position similar to the one in which you're interested, can give you vital insights into the company's modus operandi and expose some of the rats in its cellar—or executive suites. If you don't know anyone who's had experience at the company, you might ask around to see if you have any less obvious connections to the industry or a parallel field.

As in other areas of the job search, it's a good idea to treat your preparation for the interview as a job. You might, for example, want to keep a notebook for observations on the companies with which you've interviewed. Or, you might collect the information you gather in an interview folder. Not only will this give you some practice—a warm-up in the organizational skills important in any job—but it will also help you focus and take the preparation process a little more seriously. Some especially important things to remember are the names, numbers and extensions of any contacts with whom you've spoken, the dates and times when those contacts occurred, lists of reasons why you're interested in a particular organization, and potential obstacles or drawbacks associated with a company.

Review your resume

Before the interview, your resume is probably going to be the only thing the interviewer knows about you. In most cases, whoever is going to interview you will have that resume close at hand and might even have memorized key elements of it, so it's important you to be totally familiar with what you've written. Take some time to review what you've done and to observe how it's represented. If you haven't updated your resume in a while, you might discover serious omissions. Maybe you've left off an important experience, or maybe you've forgotten about an experience that could take center stage during the interview. If you can't remember something on your resume, your interviewer may think you are lying.

Check the dates of past jobs for any gaps you might be asked to explain. If you were out searching for the last living grizzly bear in Arizona for those few months when you weren't working, spend some time thinking about how you can turn this to your advantage in the interview. Those tracking skills might prove your passion, bravery and tenacity, for example. Just as importantly, this offbeat experience might help you establish a connection with your interviewer and give him or her an insight into your character.

Consider doing some role playing as you review your resume. Try stepping outside yourself and look at your resume hypercritically, as an employer looking to hire you would. Based on your resume, try imagining questions you'd ask yourself and reasons for not hiring yourself. Once you've imagined the on-paper preconceptions this person likely has of you before you meet him, you can come up with an effective plan for exceeding these expectations face to face.

Because computers play such a vital role in the workplace, it's a good idea to review before the interview exactly which programs you know. If you have experience with any of the programs the company uses, you can make an immediate positive impact on the organization. If you're particularly ambitious, you can give yourself this computer advantage by finding out which programs the company uses and familiarizing yourself with them before the interview.

Emotional preparation

Even if you've made yourself into a walking tome of facts and figures, computer programs and trade lingo, you might not make a good impression unless you're emotionally prepared for the interview. In a mad rush to do whatever you have to do to land a job, you may not take the time to ask yourself how you really feel about this job.

The interview is as much a forum for you to find out if the company and the job fit your needs as it is for the company to discover whether or not you're right for them. You may have to give up some aspects of your dream job, but the goal is to sacrifice as little as possible. What do you want from a job? What are you good at doing? What do people compliment you on?

In the ideal situation, the interviewer and the interviewee are equally interested in finding a perfect fit. Look out for yourself. Ask hard questions about work conditions, drawbacks and low points. If asked tactfully and backed up with research, well-directed questions of this sort won't offend a responsible interviewer. After all, a happy employee is going to be more productive than someone who hates his job.

But if you choose unwisely the first time, don't worry—jobs are no longer forever. People change careers nowadays about as often as their hairstyles. Chances are, even the person who interviews you, if he or she hasn't been living in a cave with blind fish, will understand that you probably won't be with the company for life. Gone are the days of the 1950s "company man" who signed up after college and stayed on until he retired. Nevertheless, choosing the right job and career the first time around saves a lot of time and angst.

At the Interview

The meeting and small talk

If you're old enough to be vying for a job that requires a serious interview, you've probably met a lot of people in your life. Extend those social skills to the people in the office. Maintain solid eye contact and a firm handshake. This proven greeting combination implies strength, confidence, competence and honesty. Consider the alternative: shifty eyes and a limp handshake.

After the initial meeting and a stroll back to the interview room, the next phase begins—small talk. The interview hasn't officially begun, but make no mistake: your ability to talk about the weather is being measured up. The topic of conversation might in fact be the weather, a brief discussion of the latest media frenzy, the game last night, a round or two of the name and geography game. Small talk is meant to relax you, so allow yourself to be relaxed. Remember, though, that you're still in an interview and anything you say can be used against you in the decision process. Answer small talk questions briefly, honestly, diplomatically and tactfully. Be witty, but not obscene or clownish.

The main event

At some point, the interviewer will shift to the heart of the matter and begin to ask questions pertaining to the job and your fitness for it. Often these questions will follow a description of the available job and an explanation of the company and what it does.

Often the segue from the small talk session into the more serious portion of the interview will be marked by a description of what the company does. Your interviewer might ask you what you know about the company, and after you give your answer (astute and detailed, due to your extensive research) the interviewer will talk about the company, the job, the industry, their plans for the future. This is a good time to demonstrate your listening skills. Let them see that you're listening and interested, and pay attention to what they're saying. Take notes on the notepad you remembered to bring.

Focus

Before anything else is said it might be helpful, here, to dispense an all-purpose interviewing bromide: remember to focus. Once the middle, substance portion of the interview begins, the interviewer is primarily interested in your past job performances and possibly your life performances in as much as they relate to the open job. He or she wants to know how your experience and personality will translate into the available job. For example, when the interviewer says, "Tell me about yourself," they're interested in your work experiences, not the fact that you were born in deepest February when the moon was on the wane, and frost obscured the windowpane. Your interviewer will be thinking of little else except whether or not

Visit Vault at **www.vault.com** for insider company profiles, expert advice, career message boards, expert resume reviews, the Vault Job Board and more.

VAULT CAREER LIBRARY

19

you will be able to do the job. (This does not mean that you should purge yourself of all personality—it's fine to mention that you like ice fishing—but you should keep your eye on conveying your fitness for the job.)

During the interview you should act like a boxer in the ring. You want to land as many substantive punches as possible, and you want every one of your answers to count. If you use up a lot of your time and energy on false punches—statements that fail to focus on the job and why you're a good person to fill it—the interviewer is going to decide you're wasting time. If you feel yourself getting off topic and talking about something that's not really relevant, it's all right to mention this. Your interviewer will appreciate the fact that you reined yourself in—this demonstrates control, maturity, an understanding of the bottom line and well-developed communication skills.

Honesty

Any lies you tell about your background and accomplishments will come back to haunt you. Similarly, unless you're an experienced actor, any affectations in attitude or manner will be detected by an experienced interviewer. Interview situations are stressful enough; you don't need to add method acting to the mix. Be honest without dwelling on your weaknesses. Be the best version of yourself. Practiced interviewers will appreciate your candor. They'll know they're dealing with an honest person.

Who's doing what for whom? It is better to give than to receive

Often, an applicant will blithely run through a litany of reasons why the position fits his career paths without mentioning what skills, insights or vision he can bring to the position. It's a good idea to steer clear of this trap. Often when thinking of a position, especially one that is perfect for our career aspirations, we tend to think about it in terms of what it has to offer us. Your love for the position, however, should not be the focus of the interview. The spotlight, from beginning to end, should shine on the myriad reasons why you'll be indispensable to the company once you're in the position.

Finding common ground and bonding

Employers, being human, will often hire someone they like—someone who reminds them of themselves at the same age, or someone to whom they are connected in whatever way—instead of the person who will perform best in the job. It's far more difficult to turn a friend down for a job than it is to nix someone about whom you have no particular feeling. So try subtly and deftly (it's easy to go overboard and become an Eddy Haskell) to form a connection with the employer.

If you can discover what kind of person you're dealing with, what his or her passion is, it will be easier for you to become a bit of a chameleon for bonding purposes. Any connection you can discover with the person can help. Find a topic, such as a shared alma mater or an outside interest, upon which you can build a connection. Do what you can to size the person up. If they mention a hobby or a recent vacation, express real interest. If you can get them to like you as a person, in addition to making them feel you're the best candidate for the job, you'll have done yourself a tremendous favor.

Making an end run

Trying to use humor or other methods of endearment in an interview is risky, but so are most business ventures. Similarly, being completely straightforward in the interview holds risks, but telling the emperor he has no clothes might impress some interviewers.

We all know at least one person who has a knack for making immediate connections, one of those people who never meets a stranger. But the ability to establish an instant rapport with someone can be learned. Think about those people in your life who have a knack for meeting people. What are their secrets? How do they do it? Are they able to project a genuine enthusiasm, a guilelessness that disarms people? While it can be dangerous to try to take on someone else's personality for an interview, try to discover ways you can better connect with someone. The following is a list of things you might want to keep in mind when trying to forge a bond with your interviewer.

- **Listening**. Remember your grade school teachers. "Don't just listen. Show me you're listening." Let the interviewer see your interest and enthusiasm. Concentrate on what they're saying.

- **Read 'em and weep. Or make 'em laugh.** Try to discover what motivates your interviewers. What kind of person do they look like? How are their offices decorated? Do some research on your interviewer. Find out who they are and what they do outside of work. What are their hobbies and passions? It's amazing how much even the most reserved person will open up if you find the right subject.

- If they're trying to be funny, **don't be too nervous to laugh.**

Asking for the job

If you know you want the job, don't be afraid to let the interviewer know this, point blank. If an interviewer senses wishy-washiness, they'll offer the job to someone else. They want to hire someone who wants the job, not someone who will grudgingly accept it. Express interest in the position and the company.

Questions to Expect: The Quality Search

Interviewers, inevitably, seek the ideal candidate. To become this perfect hire, put yourself in the mind of the interviewer. Take a good look at yourself. What does this person look like? How does this person dress, and carry him or herself? Which qualities does this interviewee demonstrate in his or her answers?

Increasingly, interviewers will ask behavioral questions—questions that seek to understand you through the prism of your past behavior and accomplishments.

One cool customer

If you're the person who can step into the bloody heart of the fray with ice water in your veins when the office resembles Custer's camp on the Little Bighorn, then you'll be a valuable asset to the company. If, on the other hand, you get frazzled when someone asks for the company's address, you might be a dangerous liability when the bullets start to fly and scalps are being taken. So your interviewer is going to be watching you to see how you handle the stress of the interview and your ability to remain composed. The following are some questions you should know how to answer by the time you're sitting in the hot seat:

- You're in customer relations and an unsatisfied customer is complaining bitterly about the product or service. How do you handle the situation?
- You've been given multiple tasks. There is no way you can complete all of them on time. What do you do?
- Describe some situations that really bother you.
- You're right. You know you're right. And, yet, everyone is taking issue with what you say. How do you react?
- How well do you handle pressure in the workplace?

Visit Vault at **www.vault.com** for insider company profiles, expert advice, career message boards, expert resume reviews, the Vault Job Board and more.

VAULT CAREER LIBRARY   21

How bad do you want it and what will you do to get it?

During the interview, one quality for which your interviewer will undoubtedly be searching—in your answers, handshake, appearance and voice—is enthusiasm about the industry, the company and the particular job opening. They're counting on you to bring in a jolt of fresh-faced exuberance. You can express your energy and aggressiveness in the interview, but true excitement is difficult to fake. Here are some questions designed to measure the true level of your enthusiasm.

• What do you feel are your best and worst qualities, and how will these relate to the position?
• What interests you about this position, industry, organization?
• What are your long-term career goals?
• What motivates you?
• How important is winning to you?
• What is the most difficult thing you've ever had to do. Why?
• Has anyone ever really pushed you? How did you respond?

Where you've been and what you've done

What you've done in the past serves as the clearest indication of what you'll be able to do in the future. If you can portray yourself in your interview as someone with a string of past successes by telling honest anecdotes in which you emerge as the hero, you're on your way to winning the job at hand.

Remember, however, that an experienced interviewer will be on to you like your first grade teacher if you try to snow him or her. Here are some questions you should know how to answer in the category of past performance:

• Describe your duties at [this particular position].
• Of which of your past accomplishments are you most proud?
• What, based on your experience, have you found to be your optimal work conditions?
• What are the most valuable lessons you've learned from past work experiences?
• Which of the skills you've picked up at the positions listed on your resume do you feel will best translate into this position and why?
• What are your long-term goals in this industry and at this company?
• Describe a problem you encountered at one of your jobs and how you handled it.

Writing and rapping

These two arts form the bedrock of civilization and important skills for any job. Any experienced interviewer will be searching for soundness, if not outright eloquence, in written and oral communication. Your oral communication abilities will be on display, from the moment you meet the interviewer until the time you bid them adieu.

Your writing skills will be evaluated in the resume and cover letter, and sometimes in a formal writing sample. Those mistakes on your resume—the misspelling of your own name, the missing dot in your e-mail address—will imply a dangerous lack of attention to detail and may be viewed by a potential employer as the tip of the iceberg. If this person can't manage these small details, he or she may think, then how will they be able to handle the larger requirements of this job?

It's a good idea to remember that communication extends beyond just words. Facial expressions, gestures, style and cleanliness of dress, tone of voice, posture, scent and hairstyle send a message of one kind or another to your interviewer from the moment you stride confidently through the office door. So think about these questions.

• Compare and contrast your oral and written communication skills.

• What experience have you had with public speaking? In your view, what are the key attributes of a successful public speaker?

• Let's say someone refuses or is hesitant to embrace your ideas. How do you persuade that person you're right?

• What problems have you had with past employers and co-workers and how did you deal with these situations?

• Describe the optimal work relationship between a manager and his or her employees.

• What do you find most troubling about writing a research paper or giving a speech?

Sense of responsibility

Your interviewer is also going to be looking for a sense of accountability, a willingness to shoulder the burdens of the job. They will also be especially alert to any signs that you might not stay in the position long enough to make it worth hiring and training you.

A corollary to this sense of responsibility is whether or not you can be a self-starter. Employers are looking for self-sufficient workers—people who can produce for them from the word go. In the past, companies were interested in a worker for life. They welcomed people into the fold, trained them, nurtured them and made lifelong projects out of them. In today's climate of short-term and shifting positions, employees at every level are expected to produce, to think creatively and to make decisions about the organization's direction. Here's how your interviewer will try to determine if you have the right attitude.

• Describe some ways in which you've been a leader.

• What criteria do you use to make important personal decisions? Professional decisions?

• Under what circumstances have people depended on you?

• Describe the biggest setback you've dealt with. What was your response?

• What, so far in your life, has given you the greatest satisfaction?

• Do you prefer to have a lot of supervision or do you work well on your own?

Visit Vault at **www.vault.com** for insider company profiles, expert advice, career message boards, expert resume reviews, the Vault Job Board and more.

VAULT CAREER LIBRARY

23

Schmoozing/Networking

What does schmoozing sound like to you? Maybe it sounds smug, unctuous, oily, slimy. It sounds, quite frankly, like "oozing." Schmoozing is far from slimy, but "oozing" actually isn't a bad description of what a schmoozer does. A schmoozer slides into opportunities where none are apparent, developing friendships from the slightest of acquaintances. Through formless, oozy, schmoozy action, a schmoozer moves slowly but inexorably towards his or her goals.

What is schmoozing? Schmoozing is noticing people, connecting with them, keeping in touch with them—and benefiting from relationships with them. Schmoozing is about connecting with people in a mutually productive and pleasurable way—a skill that has taken on new importance in our fragmented, harried, fiber-optic-laced world. Schmoozing is the development of a support system, a web of people you know who you can call, and who can call you, for your mutual benefit and enjoyment. Schmoozing is the art of semi-purposeful conversation: half chatter, half exploration. Schmoozing is neither project nor process. It's a way of life.

How does schmoozing differ from networking? Conventional networking is the clammy science of collecting business cards ad infinitum, of cold-calling near strangers to grill them about possible openings in their places of work and beg them for favors. No one particularly likes to network, and no one likes to receive a call from a desperate, edgy networker either. If you've read some of those networking books and felt uncomfortable about putting their advice into practice, there's a good reason for your reluctance. Networking is awkward, it's artificial, and more often than not, it doesn't work that well.

Schmoozing, on the other hand, is natural and effective. What could be more normal that calling up new friends to let them know the latest news in your job search? Why wouldn't you let it slip to your hairdresser that you're looking for a new apartment? One of the things you'll learn as we profile schmoozers high and low is that, yes, personal contacts are important to their business and (of course) personal lives, but in the end, they are simply following their natural inclinations. They just enjoy meeting and keeping in touch with people.

Can schmoozing help bring you professional success? Of course. Most people at the top of their fields are terrific schmoozers. They understand the importance of maintaining a strong, supportive and diverse circle of contacts to call upon. People use schmoozing to find a job, schmoozing for career advancement, schmoozing the CEO that just happens to step into the same elevator. We'll also show you how schmoozing can help you even in non-workplace situations, such as cocktail parties, airport lounges and laundromats.

Schmoozing to Find a Job Through People

"I tell my clients that 15 percent of jobs are filled through the newspaper, five percent are filled through companies like mine, and 80 percent are filled through word-of-mouth," says Beth Anrig, the owner of Beth Anrig and Associates, a job placement service in Connecticut. Anrig places individuals in positions in a wide variety of industries, ranging from banking to publishing. "Do you know how most jobs are filled?" Anrig asks. "A manager asks a couple of people if they know anyone good."

We've moved past the point where we expect that jobs will be mainly filled through company recruiting and advertising. According to widely cited statistics, 75 to 80 percent of all job seekers find their new position through referrals; most openings never see the light of day (or newsprint). By schmoozing, you make word-of-mouth work in your favor. You can learn about a variety of industries and make friends and contacts upon whom you can call for career advice or assistance. Now how to do it?

Visit Vault at **www.vault.com** for insider company profiles, expert advice, career message boards, expert resume reviews, the Vault Job Board and more.

VAULT CAREER LIBRARY   25

Schmoozing to Find a Job When in School

If you're still in school, you have golden schmoozing opportunities all around you. Many students forget that there are numerous people at their university who already know them and are predisposed to want them to succeed—their professors. If you think your history professor only knows about the French Revolution, think again. He's probably pretty savvy about life in this century, as well.

Make sure you are on a first-name basis with each and every one of your professors. Even if you're enrolled in huge lecture classes and can barely see the professor, figure out when his or her office hours are (hint: they'll be printed on the syllabus or posted on the office door) and go. Most professors only see students when they're begging for extensions on papers or explaining how they slept through the midterm. Your schmoozing should come as a welcome change.

Introduce yourself to your professor at the beginning of the semester. Tell them you're looking forward to taking the class, and if you're majoring (or thinking about it) in the subject, let them know that, too. If you have any questions about something in lecture or are curious about something you've read, ask. But make sure to ask non-class-related questions, as well. How did they get interested in sociology? What research are they doing now? Can they recommend any other good classes?

Because, after all, you ultimately want to get a job after you graduate, ask your professor for advice about that, too. What have other students in his/her subject done after graduation? What does the professor recommend you do? You'd be surprised how many professors consult with companies part time. If you're at a larger university, you might want to consider taking a class at your school's business or law school, as professors at professional schools often have an even wider variety of career contacts.

Tap alumni resources

Other woefully underused routes to schmoozing for a job in school are career counselors and alumni.

Career counselors want to help you get a job. That's their job. At the same time, they also have to find jobs for the other couple of thousand students at your university. But you, smart schmoozer that you are, have an advantage—not all those students are going to bother to schmooze their career counselors. As early as possible in your school career, go to your school career center, introduce yourself and discuss your career goals. Thank your counselor for any particularly good advice or leads he gives you. Most students neglect career counselors until the spring of their senior year. Don't make the same mistake.

Alumni already have a point of similarity with you. Ron Nelson points out, "Just having that little thing like a school connection takes you from 'Who the hell are you and why are you calling me?' to 'Oh, OK, you went to Vanderbilt, too, what can I do for you?' It's not a big thing, but it's enough."

Tamara Totah, the former headhunter for the Oxbridge Group, also recommends using alumni contacts from your school, although she cautions that you should never directly ask them for a job. "The minute they hear that they get worried," she says. "Talk to them about what different opportunities may be available in the industry. People will spend 30 minutes with you. They know how tough it is."

Schmoozing for a Job Out of School

Once you're out of school, you'll have lost (sniff!) some of the support structure for which all your tuition dollars paid. What happens when you've found a job, and then realized that you're not too happy with it? Don't be afraid—most people in this age of downsizing, corporate restructuring and increasing specialization change careers at least six times during their lives.

With all the job hopping, people increasingly accept that job changing is a part of life. Your schmoozing talents will help you ease these transitions.

The informational interview

It's not a job interview—exactly. But it does get you face-to-face with someone in an industry that interests you. Informational interviews are an invaluable opportunity to learn about the inside scoop into the career field that interests you. Many people are prepared to spend 10 minutes to an hour of their time talking to those looking for a job, assessing their skills and background, and giving them some pointers in breaking into their chosen field.

Says Beth Anrig, "I tell all my clients that the best thing to do is to set up informational interviews." One caveat—"never call them that," she says. Informational interviews sound too much like interviews, and that sounds like asking for a job. Everyone is over-networked, in the official sense. No one has the time anymore to do something that is just like a job.

So don't frame the "informational interview" as any kind of interview. Instead, say that you want to talk with them, or get coffee or chat. Your goal is to have a conversation, not an interview. Ask semi-personal questions: What got you started in this industry? What other careers did you consider? Are you happy in your choice? At the same time, talk honestly and openly about your own career aspirations, and why the industry in question appeals to you. If you click, keep the person abreast of your career progress and decisions.

But never, says Totah, our erstwhile New York headhunter, ask for a job outright. "If they don't have one and you ask that, they're going to want to boot you out five minutes later," Totah says. "Believe me, if you're talking about careers, they know you want a job. If they like you and they can help you in some way they will." Schmoozing means you don't spell it out.

When calling someone for an informational interview, make it clear you are not asking for a job. The point is, if they like you, they will help you find a job. Appeal to your contact's expertise. "Everyone likes to give advice," says Anrig. "If you tell them that you are calling because a mutual acquaintance has suggested they are a real authority in their field or an inspiring example, they will be hard-pressed to turn you down."

Though the informational interview isn't a job interview (exactly), it's still important to do your research on the company and the industry. It's rude to waste someone's time during the workday, and it doesn't reflect well on you. "Most people are very generous about helping people make connections," says Wicke Chambers, our communications consultant from Atlanta. "I have a lot of business contacts and am willing to call up and set up informational interviews for people coming out of college and recent grads. I myself am approached for interviews constantly."

However, Chambers says, "What I do mind is people asking to talk to me about my job and then having absolutely no idea what they want. I've interviewed with people who don't know whether they want to be a florist, an airline pilot or a public relations executive. I don't care a hill of beans if someone hasn't at least got an idea about what they want to do and how I can help."

Visit Vault at **www.vault.com** for insider company profiles, expert advice, career message boards, expert resume reviews, the Vault Job Board and more.

VAULT CAREER LIBRARY

27

1st Annual

Asian MBA Leadership Conference & Career Expo

- Jacob Javits Convention Center
  New York City
- September 10-12, 2009

★ For more information, please visit **www.AsianMBA.net**

Asian Diversity Inc. (ADI) is privileged to present the first **Asian MBA Leadership Conference & Career Expo in 2009.** This will be the first time present and future Asian leaders from corporate, government, and the community sectors convene in such a scale. following the enormous successes of **The National Black MBA Association and National Socirty of Hispanic MBA conferences**, we hope our efforts will unite and inspire Asian leaders to take further strides not only in the corporate sector, but in the global community as well.

WORKPLACE DIVERSITY

PLAY FOR MATTEL

At Mattel, play is our core competency. Unparalleled creativity, dynamic teamwork, respect of others, integrity and rewards for excellence are how we play. We welcome every race, gender, religion to come play for us.

Learn more about Mattel and our career opportunities at www.mattel.com/careers.

play to grow • play together • play with passion • play fair

With worldwide headquarters in El Segundo, California, Mattel employs more than 30,000 employees in 43 countries and sells products in more than 150 nations throughout the world. The Mattel vision is to be the world's premiere toy brands—today and tomorrow. Mattel, Inc. (NYSE: MAT, www.mattel.com) is the worldwide leader in the design, manufacture and marketing of toys and family products, including Barbie®, the most popular fashion doll ever introduced. Learn more about our company and career opportunities at www.mattel.com/careers.

Overview

Every year, many new college and professional school grads get their first jobs as entry-level employees in Corporate America. The client service industries in particular—management consulting, investment banking, law and accounting—employ a new army of young worker bees every fall season. Lured by the opportunity to make a great deal of money and gain a broad education in the business world, recent grads often enter the corporate environment with no understanding of the written and unwritten rules of Corporate America to guide their behavior. They simply expect their new employers to train them completely.

This section of the *College Career Bible* is for the benefit of those with little practical experience with the inner workings of the corporate world. Women and minorities need to be particularly savvy in navigating the maze of office protocol and politics. The corporate world has historically been a heterosexual, white male playground. Women usually lack the prior experience, role models and mentors to guide their climb up the corporate ladder. Minorities face those and additional obstacles. Often, new female and minority hires start their jobs ready to conquer the world, only to find their enthusiasm and confidence eroded as they face each additional pitfall. And no wonder. They see few successful survivors of their kind at the top of the ladder. In 2008, only 24 Fortune 1000 companies were led by women. Among *Fortune*'s list of the Best 50 Companies for Minorities, published in 2004, only 24 percent of officials and managers that the employers honored were actually minorities.

Visit Vault at **www.vault.com** for insider company profiles, expert advice, career message boards, expert resume reviews, the Vault Job Board and more.

VAULT CAREER LIBRARY

31

A lot of diverse thinking
goes into every one of our products.

At Rockwell Collins, we believe that one of the key benefits of a highly diverse team is better, smarter solutions. That's why we're building a global workforce of men and women with different backgrounds, viewpoints and ideas. Determined to build upon our foundation of innovation. United by our singular vision — to be the most trusted source of communication and aviation electronics solutions on the planet. To find out just how far diverse thinking can take you at Rockwell Collins, visit our website.

www.rockwellcollins.com

Rockwell Collins

Building trust every day

Mentors

A Crucial Advantage

What makes the difference between a career that thrives and one that stalls? For many women and minorities, the narrow gap between failure and success is bridged by mentorships. Mentors are people who share their general business knowledge, as well as their knowledge of a specific company, with lucky mentees (someone who mentors take under their wings). Here is some advice on how to make these valuable relationships work for you.

The importance of mentors for women and minorities

Decision-makers often consciously or unconsciously bond with and champion those who remind them of themselves. Minorities in particular need in-house mentors who champion them because they usually don't have natural role models and networks at their company. Mentors will educate you about your company's office politics and cultural norms, teach you valuable job skills and pass on industry knowledge.

You mentor does not need to share your minority status. In fact, a straight white male mentor can be a major asset in your rise up the corporate ladder. It takes time, patience and investment to develop a meaningful relationship with someone who seems to be very different from yourself—but it is worth it.

Mentors can keep you with an employer

After several years at the prestigious consulting firm Booz Allen Hamilton, Cathy Mhatre had her first child. Mhatre credits her mentors at Booz Allen with keeping her at the firm. "I've now been at Booz Allen for six years, which is unusual for any consultant. One of the main reasons I am still here is because there were people who wanted to keep me here." Mhatre estimates that she has "four to six" mentors at the firm, and advises, "Because women mentors are scarce in general, find enlightened men."

Identifying Potential Mentors

Find out if your employer assigns you a mentor—then keep looking

Increasingly, employers assign mentors to incoming employees—a practice that has been common at law firms for some time and is spreading rapidly to other industries, as well. Some consulting firms have entire mentor family trees—with a "founder" mentor, his or her mentees, their mentees and so on. Make sure to take advantage of these mentors, who have specifically volunteered to serve as resources.

At the same time, the most valuable mentors are normally the ones that evolve from everyday working relationships. If someone appears willing to share their experience and skills with you and takes an interest in your career, it is likely that they would like to mentor you in some way.

Mentors can be found inside or outside your company. Look around your department, your company and the professional business organizations to which you belong. Identify people you really admire with whom you cross paths. Don't limit yourself to obvious choices (e.g., the most popular/powerful executive, the person who had your job before you, the person of the same race or gender as you). Any impressive, intelligent and insightful person you meet can evolve into a future mentor.

Visit Vault at **www.vault.com** for insider company profiles, expert advice, career message boards, expert resume reviews, the Vault Job Board and more.

VAULT CAREER LIBRARY   33

Mentors within the company can help champion or cultivate you. In your company, mentors know all the players, politics and pitfalls. Ideally, they are well respected and secure in their positions. They may be a few rungs up the corporate ladder and can help you understand different managers' personalities and preferred working styles, office politics and the lessons they have learned.

Mentors outside of work provide objectivity. Choose mentors outside of your office who know your personality and have wisdom from a wide range of experiences. Develop relationships with at least one or two people who have no impact on your career to whom you can openly vent, turn to for perspective and ask for candid feedback. You will appreciate their distance when a work issue is too controversial to discuss with a fellow colleague, even in confidence.

In many cases, you may not even need a personal relationship with these people in order to learn from them. Observe their traits from a distance, and emulate them when you get in a position of power. For example, one director at Oracle recalls that he admired a manager who recognized hard work by comping subordinates on expensive dinners and hotel rooms. This director is now implementing this practice, which breeds loyalty.

Approaching potential mentors

Be patient and build connections through regular interactions, evolving conversations in the office, over lunch or outside of the office. Don't wait for a potential mentor to invite you to lunch or coffee—you make the offer. Tell them you would love to hear about their background (people love to talk about themselves). Be direct in seeking their counsel in dealing with your own professional situations. Try to get on projects with them so you can demonstrate your personality and performance. If you do a good job with them, hopefully they will be impressed (and even see themselves in you). Bond over nonprofessional common interests. An African-American woman discovered a shared love of cooking with a senior white male executive, who often sought her out to exchange recipes.

You can try approaching speakers at seminars or classes; they may be receptive because they like working with younger, ambitious people who remind them of their younger selves and who are receptive to their wisdom.

Establish a broad group of mentors

Cultivate different mentors for different areas of your professional life. You should not expect one person to provide all of the counsel and guidance you need to get ahead. Pick and choose different people you admire for different reasons and use them as a resource in areas where they shine. Quality matters, too—one or two superstar mentors may do you more good in the end than a dozen slackers. Company and independent organizations for women and minorities are a great way to expand your network of mentors.

Getting the most from a mentor

Once you have mentors, be open to their advice. Do not be defensive—they have nothing to gain in giving you this advice. Mentors will only value and continue your relationship if you're communicative and sincerely value their counsel. Make sure you report back to them on your successes and setbacks.

How to Get a Mentor

Mary Cranston, chair of law firm Pillsbury Winthrop LLP

Mary is the chairperson of one of the largest law firms in America. She has been practicing law since 1975, and has litigated over 300 class-action cases in state and federal court, focusing on antitrust counseling and litigation, and securities litigation. She has been named to the *National Law Journal*'s list of the 100 Most Influential Lawyers in America, and *California Daily Journal*'s list of the 100 Most Influential Lawyers in California.

Her advice on how to get a mentor:

Be a good mentee. Approach individuals who have skills you want to acquire. If you just say, "Help me," they will be less likely to help. But if you say, "I had a great idea; can we work on it together?" your chances are much higher. Think about how you can contribute to the relationship, then you're more likely to get help from a mentor.

Tips for Building a Relationship with a Potential Mentor

Kristi Anderson, executive recruiter, TMP Worldwide

Show overwhelming interest in their kids! Pretend you like their kids, remember their names and ask about them often. Remembering to ask who won that high school football game will go a million miles in endearing yourself to a potential mentor.

Ask your mentor for advice often, even when you don't need it. People, especially successful people, like to hear themselves talk and to demonstrate their wisdom. Don't ask dumb or simple questions with a definitive answer, but ask your mentor open-ended questions regarding his style and experience in handling a particular business situation. Then just sit back and feign interest in the long-winded response. Even when I don't need the advice, I will pose such a question to a mentor. It makes a mentor feel like he is bringing you along in your professional development.

Tips for Mentees

It's not enough to find a good mentor—it's just as important to use them correctly. Here are a few tips to make the most of your mentor relationship.

- Find mentors at all levels of the company. The classic mentor is someone a few levels above you in an organization—close enough to your experience to guide you upwards in the ranks, experienced enough to have some pull. But you can also gain experience from mentors at your level and at other companies, as well. Your business school professors are another invaluable set of potential mentors.

- Don't approach someone and formally ask them to be your mentor. This kind of act is akin to handing your business card to someone and asking them to be your contact—it's too artificial to take root. If someone wants to be your mentor, they will indicate that fact through the interest they take in you.

- Keep in touch with your mentors. Mentorship is a relationship, and relationships are built from frequent, informal contact. This is important even when your mentor is assigned to you by your company. If you move on from a company, stay in touch with your mentor there.

- Establish trust. Everything you discuss with your mentor is between the two of you.

- Have realistic expectations. Your mentor is an advisor and advocate—not someone to do your career networking for you, or someone to cover your errors.

Visit Vault at **www.vault.com** for insider company profiles, expert advice, career message boards, expert resume reviews, the Vault Job Board and more.

VAULT CAREER LIBRARY

35

Tips for Mentees (continued)

- Don't pass up the opportunity to have a mentor. Having a mentor can make a major difference in your career path and your self-confidence.

Finding a Mentor During a Meltdown

Ashley Fieglein, director, General Atlantic Partners

During my investment banking career, I learned the importance of choosing a mentor even though I was the only woman in an all-male office. Four years into investment banking, with hundreds of hours of lost sleep under my belt, I reached a moment where I really needed to let go. A client had yelled at me. I had a stack of work on my desk guaranteeing another lost weekend. And I had gotten a call saying that two of the projects were "urgent" and needed yesterday. I felt panicked. I noticed the teardrops on my desk, even though I wasn't aware I was crying. I got up and closed the door to my office. And the hysteria set in. I sobbed. And then I suddenly realized that I really wasn't going to be OK.

I picked up the phone and called one of the senior bankers with whom I had worked very closely over the previous four years. He showed up in my office in a matter of minutes. In spite of my embarrassment, I let him rub my back while I sobbed. He closed the door, gave me a glass of water and waited until I caught my breath.

He offered to help manage the situation, to get me more support and to get me more time. And then he sent me home. No arguments allowed, though I protested that things had to get done, but he insisted that they would be OK. I think he probably stayed extra hours that night to oversee the analysts working on my projects. I was sound asleep in my bed, catching up on some long overdue rest.

When I came back in the next morning, everything seemed manageable. The client who had reamed me the night before had called back to apologize. The work was no longer insurmountable. And the urgency had subsided.

My newly-found mentor never said a word to me about the incident afterwards. I ended up calling him crying at least once or twice more, and he always supported me kindly. He always took my tears seriously. He understood that this was my way of expressing anger. And I completely trusted his support of me.

Appearance

Take extra care in your appearance. It is the first impression you make in terms of your professional credibility, and it will be easy for others to be judgmental of your looks. As a new hire at the bottom of the food chain, you should not be making any personal statements with your clothes. Nothing should distract from the quality of your work. Strive to look well-groomed and polished, a look you can achieve on any budget.

Presentation Counts

Siobhan Green, project manager

At my performance evaluation for my first job, I was shocked to be rated poorly on my professional appearance. When I asked what that meant (I had a good wardrobe and thought I was more or less fitting in with the other staff), I was told that I should "dress more like Judy." So I watched her and noticed the difference. I didn't wear makeup and she did. Her hair, face and nails were always impeccable—and mine weren't.

The president of our company, whom I often accompanied to client meetings as a note taker, was the one who gave me the low review. He didn't really know what made Judy look more professional than me, but it bothered him enough to mention it to my supervisor and note it on my evaluation. I realized that if I wanted to continue working in that company, wearing nice suits would not be enough. I would have to make sure my nails were always clean and polished, get my hair trimmed regularly, and wear some eyeliner and lipstick, at least for meetings with clients and senior managers.

- **Dress appropriately for your industry and for your position.** Dressing outside your company norm suggests a lack of judgment and cultural fit.

- **Dress well to appear older.** Often, women and minorities can look much younger than their age. Remember that you will interact with senior executives and clients who are two to three times your age. One easy way to appear older, and more professionally credible, is to dress in a more subdued, conservative style. If you are wearing a suit, you are less likely to be mistaken for the summer intern or bike messenger.

- **Women should avoid inappropriately sexy clothes.** There is no quicker way to hurt your professional credibility. If you want to be taken seriously, observe limits: don't bare your midriff, wear low-cut necklines, see-through blouses or Ally McBeal-length miniskirts. Save it for the weekend (unless you are coming into the office). Use the 50 percent rule for judgment calls: if at least half the women go without pantyhose, wear open-toed shoes or moderately short skirts, then you can.

- **Minorities can display ethnic style—in moderation.** Wearing a kente-cloth pocket square with your suit is fine, but coming to work in a full-on dashiki is not. If you wear a piece of clothing for religious reasons (a yarmulke or a headscarf, for example), select pieces in subdued colors and make sure the rest of your clothing fits company standards.

- **Geeky isn't chic in the workplace.** Does your wardrobe consist of square glasses and faded T-shirts with funny slogans? Then you'll need to invest a little bit of time and money in upgrading your look. Overhauling your image will boost your self-esteem and the respect you command from others. Unfortunately, the bottom line is that co-workers in corporate America can be even more superficial than bullies in the schoolyard.

  – No clue what to wear? Buy some fashion magazines, ask your stylish colleagues some questions about where they shop, or talk to a sales clerk in the men's department in a classy department store or chain like Brooks Brothers.

Visit Vault at **www.vault.com** for insider company profiles, expert advice, career message boards, expert resume reviews, the Vault Job Board and more.

VAULT CAREER LIBRARY   37

– Replace your glasses with simple wire frames.

– If you work in a formal dress environment, aim to have three or four tailored suits, twice as many shirts and ties, two pairs of dress shoes (one brown and one black) and four casual outfits for Fridays. If you work in a business casual environment, aim to have at least four or five nice slacks (e.g., black, gray, khaki, navy blue, olive), twice as many shirts to mix and match and two pairs of casual shoes (one brown and one black). Women should buy simple suits in neutral colors (black, brown, gray). Your mint green pantsuit may look smashing on you, but it's so memorable that you won't be able to wear it more than once a month. A simple black skirt suit, on the other hand, can be worn at least once a week. In addition, you can split up the skirt and the jacket and wear them with other items to create more work-ready looks.

– Remember that sock color needs to match shoe or pant color. And never wear athletic socks with a suit! Women, if you're wearing a skirt, wear non-shiny nude or black hose only.

Dressing Right Brings Respect
Former management consultant

When I started working, I brought with me all my clothes and shoes from college and summer jobs. I learned very quickly that while chunky heels and open-toed shoes, fitted tops and above-the-knee skirts weren't necessarily prohibited, I felt much better about myself and the respect I got from senior management by dressing more conservatively. And so my career wardrobe began with new French blue button-down shirts and conservative black pants.

• **Get your hair cut once a month** by someone other than your mother. Men, part your hair on the side instead of the middle.

• **In America, follow American standards.** Overseas, it can be quite common for corporate employees to wear the same outfit several times a week and not shower every day. Be forewarned that Americans who work in a corporate environment are typically extremely superficial about wardrobes and downright fanatical about personal hygiene. If you want to fit in as much as possible, shower and use deodorant every day, and try to have at least five fresh outfits in your wardrobe, one for each day of the week.

Dealing with Stereotyping

People stereotype others out of ignorance and convenience, not malice. As a minority in the corporate world, you may find yourself subtly or blatantly treated differently than your peers because of your assumed strengths, weaknesses and traits. This special treatment may not necessarily be unpleasant or negative. But you need to identify who is making what assumptions, and how these erroneous assumptions impact your work life. If there is any negative impact on your image at the company, and hence your long-term professional development, it is important to address the situation gracefully and request the same treatment your peers receive.

Stereotyping is often unconscious on the part of your colleagues. For example, there's an old stereotype that all Asians are good at math. And maybe you are Asian and really are quite good at math. So on, say, your first management consulting project, it seems to make sense for you to do the back office analysis while someone else interviews the client executives. But the more you do the back office number-crunching, the better you become at it, and the more it makes sense for you to do it again next time. Eventually, if you keep holing up with your calculator, you will fall behind in developing communication skills, professional presence and client relationships. Break the cycle and make sure you are learning an appropriately broad set of skills before you become pigeonholed as the "expert" of one task.

In the next section, we will outline common stereotypes for women, minorities and gay men. Specific ethnicities, age groups and sexual orientation will trigger specific stereotypes. These examples are meant to give you some idea of direct and indirect discrimination you may face based on commonly-held stereotypes. Generally, stereotypes stunt your professional development by skewing the mix of work you get, while your peers receive a more balanced training.

If you decide you are fine with the situation because it is an anomaly, is short-term or has upsides, that's fine. If you want to change the situation, you have to speak up early before the precedent is repeated too often. Whether or not you want to address the stereotype directly, at least you can inform your manager that you would like to broaden your skill set and get a good mix of challenging and diverse work. Don't approach your boss complaining. Tell him your reasoning and your proposed solutions, so that you steer the conversation toward getting his support for one option and the transition itself is assumed. The sooner you demonstrate consistent, undeniable interest and accomplishment in the areas outside of the stereotype, the sooner people will see you as a unique individual. It is not fair that it takes extra work, but the investment is worth it.

Visit Vault at **www.vault.com** for insider company profiles, expert advice, career message boards, expert resume reviews, the Vault Job Board and more.

VAULT CAREER LIBRARY 39

Common Stereotypes: Women

Assumption	Situation	Solution
You are bad at math but good at writing.	Whenever project tasks are distributed amongst the team, you always get the qualitative, not quantitative, tasks. You don't become better at math. If you are put on a quantitative task and have trouble with it, you are removed from the task instead of trained to do it better.	Make it a priority to learn new things, especially when you first start your job. Do not let yourself be removed from quantitative projects.
You are suited to detailed administrative work.	You are assigned administrative duties no one else wants: taking notes at the meetings, booking travel for the team, making copies, ordering lunch, getting coffee for clients, setting up or cleaning up a meeting.	Volunteer someone else for the task and try to get your manager's backing.
You are eye candy and probably not that bright, because you're attractive.	You are excluded from important meetings, but trotted out on fun business development outings so older male clients can flirt with you. People gossip about you.	Make sure your work stands on its own. Do not dress in a revealing or sexy manner.
You are too sensitive and emotional.	You don't get direct feedback about your performance so you don't advance. People are afraid you will cry, so they treat you gently. When you do cry, people assume you cannot handle stressful work.	Seek out truthful feedback. Remove yourself from stressful situations and control your temper and emotions.
You are timid.	People forget to ask you for your opinion because they assume you won't have one. You stop forming opinions because you are never asked about them, stunting your critical thinking and communication skills.	Practice expressing yourself. Build alliances. Emulate strong speakers.
You are a pushover.	You are asked to do work that no one else wants to do, like staying late in the office for a last-minute assignment, cleaning up other's unfinished work and delivering bad news for other people.	Learn your boundaries. Embrace the word "No," especially if these requests do not come from a manager or senior executive.
You are a token hire.	Especially in a macho environment like investment banking or sales, your peers don't believe you made it here on merit, and do not give your work and opinions equal respect.	Work twice as hard to prove yourself. Try not to be too sensitive about routine male-bonding behaviors.
Work is not as important to you as it is to your male co-workers. Your family comes first.	Co-workers will not ask you for help on tough assignments. Your manager may be reluctant to invite you on business trips or to late-night client dinners.	Meet every deadline. Do not discuss family visits or shopping excursions, especially if you take time off for these activities. Clearly state you interest in attending a client event.

The de facto secretary

Women are often unconsciously slotted into an administrative role and given routine, detail-oriented work. While these projects may be important, and it's vital to be able to pitch in during a time crunch, it's difficult to shine by doing these routine tasks. The requests may seem benign at first. Can you take the notes during the meeting? Can you prepare FedEx packages? Can you coordinate the next meeting or the next business trip? If you are the most junior person on the team, assume that status is the reason for getting these chores. In the corporate world, the guy at the bottom of the food chain takes care of all the scrub work. The more machismo-laced an environment you work in, the more pronounced the hierarchy will probably be. Check with the second-most junior person to see if he had all the same "chores" before you arrived. Make sure you pass those duties on right away when a more junior person joins the team.

If you are not the most junior teammate, you may have been designated as a secretary for the team because of your gender. How should you handle the request? If the need is legitimate and you are the most appropriate person to perform the task (e.g., because you have the time or because your piece of the work is not as time-sensitive), go ahead and do it, and don't take it personally. If the need is not legitimate, or you are not the most appropriate person for the job, do not accept the role! Ask your manager to pass the chore to a secretary or another member of your department. Or tell your manager you would like to rotate the responsibility around the team because you took the duty last time. You could simply say, "I'm sorry. I don't have time to do that and meet my other deadlines. Can someone else pitch in?"

If a client asks you to do something administrative, go ahead and do it…once. Make sure you raise the issue with your manager and get his backing before you tell the client you cannot the second time. If you are asked to do something really demeaning, like making coffee, smile sweetly or make a little joke and say you don't know how to.

If you are the only woman on the team and you are constantly performing the admin duties, you will diminish your professional credibility and stunt your professional development compared to your male peers. Address the situation politely but directly with your manager and/or other perpetrators. Here are two common scenarios women in the corporate world face and how to address them.

The note-taker

You are always asked to take notes "because you have the best handwriting." This statement could be absolutely true—some guys really have atrocious handwriting!

But when you take notes, you are busy looking down at the paper and writing down what everyone else says. As a result, you don't get to participate in the discussion as much. At review time, your manager won't recall hearing you speak in meetings, forgetting that he asked you to take notes. He'll have the impression that you are timid (playing right into another common stereotype of women). Furthermore, if you are writing madly in a future meeting that includes a client or a senior executive, you lose the opportunity to interact with and impress an important person. You may even be mistaken for a secretary yourself.

If you are the most junior person on the team, you may have to take notes until someone new is hired. If you are not the most junior person, get a reality check from a trusted peer or manager in the office who is removed from the situation at hand. "I want to ask your opinion because I'm not sure if I am being too sensitive. Who takes notes in your meetings?"

The cyclical nature of stereotyping comes from the fact that the more you do something, the better you become at it than everyone else, so then everyone wants you to continue doing it. After several meetings of being the note-taker, you learn to outline exactly how your boss likes it, type everything up with graphs and charts inserted, and distribute to the group quickly. Of course everyone will want you to keep doing it because no one else does it as well. But continuing the role compromises your professional development, self-respect and the respect of your peers, even if it is gradual and unintentional.

Visit Vault at www.vault.com for insider company profiles, expert advice, career message boards, expert resume reviews, the Vault Job Board and more.

VAULT CAREER LIBRARY   41

Talk to your manager directly, but avoid any suggestion that the offense was intentional (even if you suspect it was). Address the professional rationale behind your request and your proposed solutions. "I don't want to always be the note taker because it prevents me from participating in the discussion in a meaningful way. The issues are so interesting I'd like to share my thoughts next time. Let's rotate the responsibility, or bring a secretary into the meeting to take the notes."

Be prepared to be brushed off as being hypersensitive. "Uh oh, you're not a militant feminist are you? You are way too sensitive!" Don't back down when faced with such resistance. Stand your ground, and calmly respond. "I know it's easy for you to jump to that conclusion, but humor me, and let's rotate the responsibility. I really would like to join in the conversation next time, and I think I have proposed fair solutions." Just make sure you don't clam up in the next meeting!

The teacher

Maybe you're repeatedly asked to train new hires. Why are you singled out every time? Is it because you are friendly, patient and verbal compared to your other colleagues? Is the responsibility of training only assigned to top performers who uphold the highest standards of work quality? Is training a total pain in the neck, and your boss knows you'll be a pushover? Ask your boss or the person who trained you how the responsibility is assigned. Then you can evaluate how you want to deal with the situation.

Perhaps you don't mind this assignment because you enjoy getting to know the new hires right away, you get a break from your normal workload and you get to expense more meals on the company. Or the training assignments reflect the fact that you're a star at the company. Maybe you actually hate sitting alone in your office all day crunching numbers and you really want to be a teacher at heart, so the opportunity to train new employees is a dream niche for you.

Now for the downsides. Because training is administrative, you may be expected to carry your full load of "real" work on top, meaning that you are working much later nights than everyone else to get everything done. Is training worth compromising your personal time? On the other hand, if your manager does reduce your workload to accommodate your training assignments, over time you might fall behind your colleagues in terms of advancement because you spend your days teaching and mentoring new hires instead of getting more challenging projects and interacting with senior colleagues and clients. Is training worth compromising your professional development?

Want to get out of doing training? Tell your boss you have already conducted the training twice as many times as the last person who did it. Or point out that you have missed client meetings because of training, which is detrimental to both your development and your relationship with your client. Suggest setting up a random system to rotate the responsibility amongst your peers by drawing numbers or assigning it alphabetically by last name. Or suggest that people pair up in teams to conduct training, so it's not as time-consuming for each person.

Address and Retrain Your Manager Immediately If You Feel Singled Out

Sonja Beals Iribarren, former director at Disney

As the most junior member of the team, I accepted the fact that I drew the duty of making copies during meetings, should the need arise. That I was often the only woman in the room seemed only a coincidence until a new, younger—and male—analyst joined the team. I think we were both shocked when my boss again asked me to step out and make a few copies at the next meeting. I did so without complaint, in the name of team spirit, but did speak to my boss privately immediately afterward and told him that I wanted that duty to fall to the new junior member of the team. I tried to keep the focus on the seniority issue and away from any discussion about gender, which I felt might be interpreted as militant feminism and would not ultimately serve my purpose. I was concerned that people's perception of me would be negatively affected if I continued to accept this duty without comment. It's not about making the copies—it's that people expect you to stand up for yourself. Honestly, I wouldn't be surprised if scenarios like these aren't a test to see how you handle yourself in these situations.

Common Stereotypes: Minorities

Assumption	Situation	Solution
You are good at math but bad at communicating.	You are always given back office analyses, but never put in front of senior executives or clients to present your findings.	Don't just hand over analyses to your manager with no explanation or interpretation. If you do a good job articulating your work to your boss, you can make the next step of presenting to others.
You have a chip on your shoulder.	People assume you are difficult to work with, keep their distance and minimize interaction. You leave the job without any significant relationships, mentors or networks to help you later on.	Be careful how you express your views. Show your casual, humorous side often.
You share the same traits as everyone else of your demographic.	You are compared to the other minority of the same race as you in the department. You are called the wrong name, as if people can't tell you apart. You compete with each other for the token slot.	Establish your identity and distinguish yourself.
You do not speak English well.	You are not given time to speak in meetings or written assignments.	Work to perfect your writing and speaking skills. Ask for and excel at, writing and speaking assignments.

People naturally categorize things into convenient buckets and make assumptions about those categories. Establish your own identity, and avoid "competing" with the one other person in the office of your race. For example, let's say that you are one of two Asian-American analysts in your starting class of 12 new hires. People you don't work closely with may mix you up and call you the wrong name. As a more serious pitfall, you may be compared to each other all the time, and there may also be an assumption that only one of you will be promoted.

Don't take it personally if the other person of your ethnicity is not quick to establish a close friendship with you. She may want to establish her own identity. It is an immature reaction on her part, but an explainable one. If a friendship is meant to be, over time it will develop as you both settle in to your new jobs.

Ways of establishing your personal identity include:

- Socialize with a variety of your peers.

- Befriend the perpetrators. People will not mistake you for someone else if they get to know you. Talk about things you have in common. Let them get to know you as a person with distinct interests, rather than a token minority.

- Correct people if they call you by another name. You can do this nicely, but don't let them persist in thinking you are someone else. Correct the person on the spot, introduce yourself and laugh it off to help the perpetrator save face. "It's a big office, so I often forget names of people I've only met once or twice, too."

- Establish natural friendships with peers of your ethnicity. There is no advantage to discriminating against people who look like you, and you come off like a jerk. And you might be sacrificing a friendship with someone with whom you would otherwise really connect because of shared experiences and insights.

Visit Vault at **www.vault.com** for insider company profiles, expert advice, career message boards, expert resume reviews, the Vault Job Board and more.

VAULT CAREER LIBRARY   43

Don't Assume You Will Bond Over Race

Former strategic planning analyst

During my interviews for a competitive position at a Fortune 100 company, I continually asked about the obvious lack of African-American employees in the department. To dispel my concerns, the recruiting manager arranged for me to meet a very senior African-American officer in the company, even though I would not actually be working with him in my prospective job.

Without thinking twice, I openly asked him about the dearth of African-Americans at the company. He replied, "If you are one of those black people who needs to be around other black people, you won't find them here!"

Shocked and disappointed, I quickly learned that not all people of color view themselves as leaders or mentors of junior employees of their same race. On the contrary, many prefer to ignore ethnicity and maintain distance from other colleagues of color in order to avoid labeling.

Geography Matters

Victor Hwang, former corporate lawyer, current COO LARTA (a nonprofit think tank)

If you're a minority, geography matters. I love Austin, Texas. I spent my formative years there. I love country music, barbecue, Longhorn football and big hair. I never encountered any overt prejudice in my professional life in Austin, but one does start to feel worn down after the third time someone has confused you with your minority co-worker, every lunch at a sushi restaurant starts a talk about "other Chinese food," and people think that your parents are Thai because they're from Taiwan. It may or may not be prejudice, really it's just ignorance, but it does take a toll on your self-esteem.

So I moved to Los Angeles and never looked back. There has been such a difference in my sense of professional opportunity since I've moved to Los Angeles. Climbing the professional ladder is hard enough already; one should eliminate as many controllable obstacles as possible.

Common Stereotypes: Gay Men

Assumption	Situation	Solution
You are creative.	People come to you with more questions and projects that involve visual aesthetic, creative design or marketing, whether or not that is part of your job function.	Make it a point to shine in other areas. Make sure those areas are visible to management.
You don't have traditional masculine interests.	You are not invited to sports or bar outings. You miss out on the opportunity to network and bond out of the office.	Bring up your participation in sports, your home teams or your favorite non-gay bars and clubs. Invite yourself along.
You are checking out all the straight men in the office at all times.	Guys keep their distance. You are made to feel self-conscious.	Don't make any sexual references or jokes. Never flirt with or date co-workers.
You are flamboyant.	You are not put in front of the most conservative, stodgiest clients or senior executives.	Be mindful of corporate culture, behave conservatively and give people time to get to know you.
You are the token gay friend everyone wants.	Female colleagues want to be your best friend, talk to you about boys and fashion. Colleagues don't respect the same professional vs. personal boundaries with you. You're called "Will" from the popular show *Wiill and Grace*.	Be mindful of your interactions with others. Act professionally and conservatively, focus on work. Give people time to get to know the real you.

Visit Vault at **www.vault.com** for insider company profiles, expert advice, career message boards, expert resume reviews, the Vault Job Board and more.

VAULT CAREER LIBRARY   45

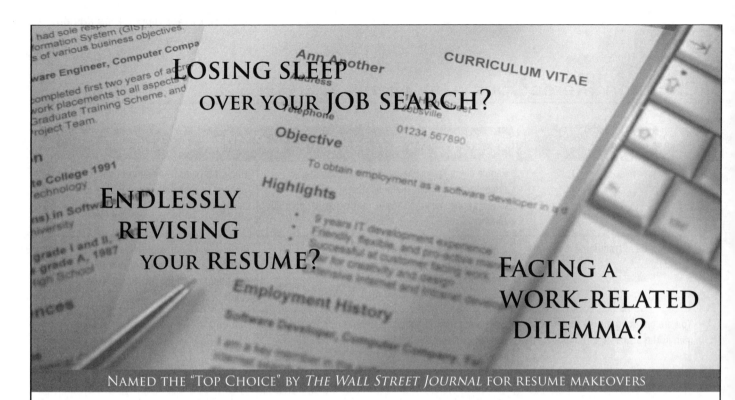

Diversity Employer Directory

Baker Hughes Incorporated

2929 Allen Parkway, Suite 2100
Houston, TX 77019-2118
Diversity Contact Phone: (713) 439-8600
www.bakerhughes.com

To be a global company, Baker Hughes is building a diverse workforce that includes men and women from more than 90 countries where we operate. Such diversity will enable us to understand local cultures and provide service that creates value for customers around the world. Baker Hughes recruiting programs reach students from universities on five continents and our development programs provide opportunities for them to advance their careers. Our ongoing effort to develop and maintain a high performance culture starts with our Core Values of Integrity, Teamwork, Performance and Learning and with our Keys to Success. We employ succession planning efforts to develop leaders across all our businesses that embody these Core Values and represent the diversity of our customer base. We constantly hire and train employees from around the world to ensure that we have a well-trained workforce in place to support our business plans.

Below are some of the schools Baker Hughes Incorporated is currently recruiting from:

Colorado School of Mines, Florida Institute of Technology, Louisiana State University, McNeese University, Michigan Tech University, Mississippi State University, MIT, Montana Tech University, New Mexico Tech University, Oklahoma State University, Southern University, Stanford University, Texas A&M University, Texas A&M Kingsville, Texas Tech University, University of Houston, University of Louisiana - Lafayette, University of Maryland; University of Oklahoma, University of Texas-Austin, University of Texas - San Antonio, University of Tulsa, University of Wyoming

Bristol-Myers Squibb

P.O. Box 4000
Princeton, NJ 08543-4000
Diversity Contact Phone: (609) 252-4000
www.bms.com/career

Different perspectives make it possible.

At Bristol-Myers Squibb, we're a diverse team of talented and creative people -- each with a different perspective. We value each person's unique contributions and inspire each other to develop the innovative solutions that extend and enhance the lives of our patients around the world.

Flexibility makes it possible.

At Bristol-Myers Squibb, our people find fulfillment in their work, extending and enhancing the lives of patients around the world. And they have fulfilling lives at home too. Bristol-Myers Squibb offers a flexible range of work/life programs that help our employees at each stage of their lives. We're proud to be ranked in the top 100 of Working Mother Magazine's "Best Companies for Working Mothers."

Opportunities make your growth possible.

Ask yourself - how far do you want to go? At Bristol-Myers Squibb, we're determined to be the company where our employees can achieve their career goals. We offer a range of opportunities to help you get there. It's simple. Your growth helps us to better extend and enhance the lives of patients around the world.

Schools Bristol-Myers Squibb Recruits from

Boston College, College of NJ, Cornell, Drexel, Lehigh, NYU, Northeastern, Michigan State, Penn State, Rutgers, Syracuse, Villanova

Visit Vault at **www.vault.com** for insider company profiles, expert advice, career message boards, expert resume reviews, the Vault Job Board and more.

VAULT CAREER LIBRARY   47

Credit Suisse

11 Madison Avenue
New York, NY 10010

Recruiting Contact:
Credit-suisse.com/careers

CREDIT SUISSE

Fostering an inclusive workplace is an integral part of Credit Suisse's business strategy. Diversity and Inclusion promotes a culture of team work which respects, values and leverages employee's differences. Diverse perspectives lead to innovative solutions for our clients. It also allows us to attract and retain top talent in a highly competitive industry. This is Credit Suisse's competitive advantage.

Global Diversity and Inclusion helps the Bank win new business, advises clients on Credit Suisse's diversity strategy and strengthens relationships our clients.

In the past year, Credit Suisse received a dozen awards from independent organizations recognizing us as a premier diversity employer.

Undergraduate Schools Credit Suisse Recruits from

Credit Suisse recruits at many of the country's top universities.

Mattel, Inc.

333 Continental Blvd.
El Segundo, CA 90245
(310) 252-2000
www.mattel.com

At Mattel, we have a vision to be The World's Premier Toy Brands - Today and Tomorrow. We understand that a culture rich in diversity is a key to business success. It allows us to better understand the business opportunities in various markets around the world, and develop products that resonate with consumers in diverse cultures. As the worldwide leader in the design, manufacture and marketing of toys and family products, including Barbie®, Hot Wheels®, American Girl® and Fisher-Price®, Mattel is not only one of the best places to work, it's also a lot of fun.

Undergraduate Schools Mattel Recruits from

UCLA; USC; UC Irvine; Loyola; Cal Poly Pomona; Claremont; California State University, Long Beach; California State University, Dominguez Hills; California State University, Fullerton; California College of the Arts; OTIS; Art Center; FIDM; RIT; FIT; Art Institute; University of Cincinnati; California Institute of the Arts

Financial Management Professional Training Program (NAVY)

520 Turner St, Suite B
Pensacola, FL 32508-5245
(850) 452-3783
www.navyfmtp.com

The Financial Management Trainee Program (FMTP) recruits high quality, prospective civilian financial managers for Department of the Navy activities. The FMTP is a 28-month program of professional development through academic and on-the-job training. Entry level positions as financial management analysts, accountants and auditors are available. Applicants may have any academic major; but those applying for accounting and auditor positions require 24 semester hours of accounting (six hours may be in business law). A minimum cumulative GPA of 2.95 in an undergraduate degree from a nationally accredited university/college is required.

Undergraduate Schools NAVY Recruits from

Nationally accredited colleges and universities

Osram Sylvania

100 Endicott St.
Danvers, MA 01923
www.sylvania.com/AboutUs/Careers/

Diversity Contact:
Leah Weinberg, Manager, Diversity Inclusion
Phone: (978) 977-1900
Recruiting Email: Diversity.recruiter@sylvania.com
If writing to this email address, the subject line must read "VAULT publications applicant".
www.sylvania.com/AboutUs/Diversity/

OSRAM SYLVANIA is honored to have received "2007 and 2008 Best Diversity Company" recognition. We are committed to developing an increasingly diverse workforce with fair and open access to career opportunities. We believe that variety of opinion, approach, perspective, and talent are the cornerstones of a strong, flexible, and competitive company. Affinity groups, a mentoring program, and strategic relationships with professional organizations and colleges all support OSRAM SYLVANIA's commitment to an inclusive environment where every talented individual can be proud to work.

Undergraduate Schools Osram Sylvania Recruits from

Bucknell; WPI; Bentley; GA Tech; Ohio; Alfred; RPI; Bryant; University of Wisconsin; Penn State; UKY; Olin; Lehigh; UFL; UNH; VA Tech; UTEP; Rose Hulman; Univ. of IL; Northeastern

Visit Vault at www.vault.com for insider company profiles, expert advice, career message boards, expert resume reviews, the Vault Job Board and more.

VAULT CAREER LIBRARY

49

LEADERSHIP DEVELOPMENT PROGRAMS

The Scoop on Leadership Development Programs

If you're looking to get an early boost for your career after graduation, consider applying to a rotational training program.

These programs, which can be found in literally every industry and type of employer, are typically offered by large employers who aim to hire recent graduates and groom them as future company leaders.

Because the programs can be found at many different types of employers, they vary widely. For starters, they can go by any number of names and labels, though they usually have the words "management," "leadership," "training" or "development" in their titles. They also vary with respect to duration, number of rotations, number of employees hired into the program each year and other details.

There are common threads that tie these programs together, however. After joining them, trainees generally rotate through many different departments/areas in order to get an overview of the different parts of an organization. Employees are also offered formal training courses and mentorship relationships as part of the program. But most importantly, these programs are all designed to train the future leaders of an organization. Because of this, employees who go through these programs not only receive the best training their organizations have to offer, but are also "tagged" as potential leaders whose progress in the organization is followed even after they graduate from the training program.

Why rotate?

The central goal of a rotational training program is to provide trainees with an overview of an organization's operations.

"The more well-rounded employees are in understanding all of the operations in a hotel, the better they'll be as a general manager," explains Nancy Vu, Manager of Field Employment and Recruiting at Hilton Hotels Corporation. Hilton hires recent graduates into what it calls its Leader-in-Training (LIT) program. In Hilton's program, a trainee rotates through about a dozen different hotel departments in a six- to eight-month period.

"We want them to understand how each department links to one another," says Vu. "We want our trainees to get their feet wet in all these areas. Then they have a better understanding of what goes on in the rest of the hotel."

Michael Danubio, Manager of College Relations for Staples agrees that the breadth of experience is the key to the retailer's Merchandise Training Program, which rotates trainees through both store and headquarters rotations over an 18-month period.

"The most valuable thing they get out of this is seeing the full cycle of the business," says Danubio. "Once they're done, they've seen a big chunk of our merchandising operation."

Formal training and mentoring

Most rotational training programs incorporate formal training and mentorship that go above and beyond what most recent graduates encounter when they join their first employers. For example, for Staples' Merchandise Training Program, trainees take seminar-type courses on everything from "pricing to negotiation skills to supply chain logistics," says Erin Egnatchik, a recent graduate of the program. "That training has been opened up to other associates [in Staples' Framingham, Mass., headquarters], but it's required for Merchandise Training Associates," says Egnatchik.

Debbie Bertan, Director of College Relations for Citigroup says that the training and mentoring offered through the company's rotational programs (called the Management Associate Programs) is one of the program's main advantages. Citigroup hires recent graduates into a two-year rotation program in its Retail Distribution Group and Citibanking Technology Solutions Group (internal information technology positions) units.

Visit Vault at **www.vault.com** for insider company profiles, expert advice, career message boards, expert resume reviews, the Vault Job Board and more.

VAULT CAREER LIBRARY   53

"It's much more structured when you join a [management associate] program," says Bertan. "There's training at various intervals. Most of the associates start with some specific training that the whole group goes through, and then there's training specific to the management associate's specific needs. There's also softer skills training—for example, training in leadership and communication skills."

But it's not just seminar-type training that new employees receive. In many cases, trainees are matched up with managers who serve as formal mentors during their time in the program. And because of an employee's status as a "future leader," he or she is also likely to pick up more informal mentors, too.

"When you enter through one of these training programs, there's more emphasis on mentorship," explains Citigroup's Bertan. "There's also greater exposure to senior leaders—partially through events and/or through networking."

Starting on the ground floor

Just because rotational management training programs are intended to groom and train recent graduates as future leaders doesn't mean that new employees have it easy. In many programs, trainees are required to pay their dues as entry-level employees.

For example, in the retail industry, trainees often start with a store-level rotation. This is the case at both Staples and TJX. In Citigroup's Retail Distribution Group Management Associate Program, trainees may start behind the teller window.

"They probably think 'What am I doing here? I just paid 100 grand for my education and I'm wearing a red shirt in a store,'" says Staples' Michael Danubio. "But the reality is once they come into the home office, they realize how invaluable that experience is."

Danubio says that a recent hire into Staples' Merchandise Training Program made a point of telling him how valuable his in-store experience turned out to be. "[Once he got to Staples' headquarters office] he was working for a senior inventory analyst that handled the furniture," recounts Danubio. "He said that from Day One, he knew what people were talking about. They were talking about specific SKUs that he learned about when he was in the store. It would have been a much longer ramp-up time if he hadn't had that experience."

At Hilton Hotels Corporation, trainees start with the unglamorous tasks related to normal hotel operations. "When they go through the housekeeping rotation," says Hilton's Vu, "They're required to make a certain number of beds, clean a certain number of rooms."

Because trainees in Hilton's program often go on to become managers at the hotel at which they train, the dues-paying is more than just a matter of learning the operations, says Vu.

Grooming leaders

From those humble entry-level rotations, however, future company leaders are created. Says Vu of Hilton's rotational program (which was established originally in 1988 as the Hilton Professional Development Program). "We have directors and VPs who came through that program and are still with us."

Because companies treat trainees as future leaders, a lot of attention is typically paid to their development. For this reason, some rotational training programs are small in size. Staples, for example, only currently hires two people a year into its Merchandise Training Program. "The organization internally can only sustain so many people at one time," says Danubio, "Because it takes a lot of internal coordination and training, and we want to make sure that we're giving them the resources they need here."

Once trainees "graduate" from rotational programs, companies usually track them through their career. Part of the reason for this is to make sure that the programs are working.

"We want to make sure that there's a reason to be supporting a program, so we track the career progression of the management associates we hire," says Citigroup's Bertan.

A consequence of tracking trainees this way, of course, is that graduates of training programs are always identified as such in the companies' human resource records, which is no small thing. "The real advantage is they are accelerated leadership programs," says Bertan. "This is our pipeline to train our future leaders."

Vault Q&A: Suzanne Rickard, Citigroup Management Associate Program

Suzanne Rickard is a graduate of New York University (the Stern School of Business undergraduate program). After graduation she joined Citigroup's Management Associate Program in the company's retail banking division. She took time out to talk with Vault about her experience with Citi's rotational program.

Vault: Tell me a little bit about Citigroup's Management Associate Program.

Rickard: The program is a two-year rotational program. The way it's set up is that you have the opportunity to rotate and train as well as perform in different functions within the retail bank. You start out with a financial associate rotation, being the person who takes deposits for clients at the teller window—handling money, etc. Then you have training as a customer service officer where you answer clients' questions and assist them with any banking related issue.

The next rotation was as an account representative, which they call Client Financial Analyst (CFA). During that rotation, I was able to open accounts for clients and also received my Series 6 and Series 63 licenses as well as my Life and Health License, so I was able to sell investment and insurance products. There's also an operations rotation, a corporate headquarters rotation, as well as a commercial, small business banking part.

Vault: How big is the program?

Rickard: In my class in the retail bank area, there are 11 associates. In total [at Citigroup], I believe it's maybe 200 or 300. I think it's been in existence for many years but has taken on a variety of structures. For the retail bank section, it could range from as small as five or so people to as large as our class, which is 11 people. They do a hiring process three times a year, in the spring, summer and fall.

There's a program for each different section of the company. For the credit card department there's a different program, for human resources there's a different program, and so on.

Vault: Where are you now in the program?

Rickard: I've already done the consumer rotation. I've also dealt with operations—that's the back office, making sure that everything balances in terms of money at the end of the day and also dealing with audits. The rotation I'm in right now is the commercial, small business banking position.

Vault: So how long is each rotation?

Rickard: The financial associate rotation was about three months, the service officer rotation was two or three months, the CFA portion is about five or six months, the operations one where you deal with audits is about three or four months. The corporate project rotation, it's supposed to be a short one, but I stayed about five months.

Visit Vault at **www.vault.com** for insider company profiles, expert advice, career message boards, expert resume reviews, the Vault Job Board and more.

VAULT CAREER LIBRARY

55

Vault: What sort of corporate project did you work on?

Rickard: I did a rotation in [Citigroup's headquarters in] Long Island City with one of the main directors of a new product. So I dealt with the marketing of the product. I dealt with the legal group. I dealt with the finance group. I dealt with other cross-functional issues. Having a product with Citibank, you have to make sure it works with everyone else and that they can sell it too.

Vault: What kind of product was it?

Rickard: It's called CitiGold. It's a premier bank product for high net worth clients. It's a type of checking account that looks to consolidate the clients' account relationships. So for example, you can open a brokerage account with that product or handle your credit card accounts through that account. We want clients to feel like they can consolidate all their finances with us, where you can have banking, borrowing, brokerage and insurance, which are all interrelated.

Vault: You mentioned other cross-functional issues in working on this project? What types of other departments did you deal with?

Rickard: I worked with our customer service group, our online system group and others. Basically everything that goes into producing and processing a financial product. It was interesting—a lot of work starting from scratch, but it's been going well.

Vault: And where were your other rotations?

Rickard: For the operations rotation, I was at a very busy branch at 34th Street that was across from Macy's. The day-to-day traffic at that branch was nonstop. They had three floors in the bank at that branch, and we dealt in the millions [of dollars]. I was there around the holidays, dealing with hundreds of people coming in and out constantly.

Vault: So what do you do in an operations role?

Rickard: I'm basically making sure transactions are being done properly, approving transactions if they're large amounts, making sure all the cash "proves" [checks out against transactions].

Vault: So with that much cash moving in and out, I'm curious as to how much slips through the cracks on a daily basis?

Rickard: That branch was really good. Everyone was pretty accurate, consistently. The operations manager had been with the bank for, I think, 20 or 30 years, and had done operations at the bank at a lot of different branches. He had a lot of experience and knew the type of people to hire and what systems to have.

So training with him, I knew what things to recognize, what to look for; it ran like a well-oiled machine. But sometimes it would get a little hectic because there were maybe 15 people or so taking clients, asking you to help them. You're constantly being asked questions, and there's not a whole lot of time to have lunch, or do other things. You're there for a couple hours after the bank closes, making sure that everything "proves out." At the end of the day you may feel like you've just gone through a frenzy but you're also happy that everything worked out for the clients as well as the staff.

Vault Q&A: Lena Davie, Staples Merchandise Training Program

After graduating from Xavier University in Cincinnati with a degree in marketing, Lena Davie was recruited into Staples' customer service rotational program. The retailer's customer service program is one of a few rotational programs Staples offers; others include a merchandise training program and a logistics training program.

Davie, who is the first Staples employee to be recruited into the rotational program, took some time out from her schedule to discus her experience at Staples—and why she finds customer service such a good fit for her.

Vault: Tell me a little bit about the program and the different positions you've rotated through.

Davie: Customer service is divided into Staples Business Delivery, which is for businesses with fewer than 20 employees, and Contracts, which is for companies with more than 20 employees. Typically our call centers service one business unit. We have two facilities for each business unit in the U.S.—in Englewood, NJ and Rochester, NY for Contracts, and Framingham, MA and Florence, KY for SBD. We also have two locations in Canada, in Halifax and Saskatchewan.

Employees in the centers are divided between order resolution, handling inquiries, and then we have our frontline sales and customer service teams that handle orders.

The program I joined is two years. I spent a year in Kentucky, where I worked in various business units in the Business Delivery organization, did QA and monitored calls. After that year, I moved to Rochester, NY with our Contracts division for six months. Now I'm in Framingham, MA at our headquarters, working on a specific organization-wide project—it's a process improvement rotation for the Business Delivery Unit.

So I got the field aspect being in Kentucky and Rochester, and since coming into Framingham, I've had the corporate experience.

Vault: And where will you be going after your current rotation?

Davie: I've actually been hired by the company, and I'll be transitioning to the Rochester Call Center where I'll be a team manager. I'll be managing front-line associates who are working with customers.

Vault: How do customers place their orders?

Davie: We have orders that come in a variety of ways. Some come in via Staples.com, some come in over the phone. We do orders by chat, we can also do orders by e-mail, and that's just for Staples Business Delivery. In the Contracts division, 90 percent of orders come through the Internet, though we also take them over the phone and then by fax.

My first rotation in the program was learning how to take calls. It helped me understand what my team was doing on the front line. I actually did three rotations in the Kentucky center—the first team was a frontline customer service sales team, the second team was the order resolution team, the third team was the quality assurance team.

I was taught the basics, starting with how to take a call. I've had that fundamental training in every location I've gone to, and it helps you build your foundation. I had one-on-one training with the trainer in the specific location. They give you that individual attention because you are going to be a future manager.

I also had management training in Kentucky. That really helped me understand what the core values are at Staples. For management training, the HR manager with the center would conduct it once a month, and every new supervisor would have to go through the course.

Vault: What sort of courses were they?

Visit Vault at **www.vault.com** for insider company profiles, expert advice, career message boards, expert resume reviews, the Vault Job Board and more.

VAULT CAREER LIBRARY   57

Davie: How to give poor performance feedback, how to get along with your peers, how to make sure you're easily approachable, those sorts of things. They're topics that are important to make sure that you're a good manager. It was very helpful. I did the management training the whole time I was there.

Vault: How did you end up with Kentucky as your first rotation?

Davie: The location was decided by the business, and it was additionally decided because I was coming from Cincinnati it would make most sense to start in Kentucky.

The second location I was able to choose—I was able to choose between Englewood and Rochester. I'm from northeast Ohio, so Rochester wasn't that far from there, and also our director of the Contracts division was located in that center, so it was opportunity for me to have that one-on-one relationship with her.

Vault: Were you set up with a formal mentor for the program?

Davie: Definitely. I have a wonderful mentor; I was assigned a mentor from our service improvement team. She's located here in Framingham, and she's been my mentor the whole program. The customer service organization is a very small, close organization. Really all of the directors have put effort and time to help my development. I can go to any of the four directors and they can help lead me where I need to go.

With my mentor, we had one-on-one sessions every two weeks, as if I was actually on her team. And then I could talk to her if I ever needed to talk to her. Once she was on pregnancy leave and wasn't in the office. I sent her an e-mail and sure enough, she responded.

Vault: How did you decide to go into customer service? Was this something you thought about when you were in school?

Davie: Coming out of school, I was thinking about going into nonprofit, so this was the other end of things.

But it has definitely been a great fit. Because I wanted to help people succeed, a customer service organization fits me. I'm really a coach. I want to help people continue to provide excellent service. I need to be one-on-one with my people. I need to talk to them. I need to be real and not always numbers-driven for them. It was a great fit for me, and it still is.

I'm expecting to stay in customer service, I think there are a lot of opportunities at Staples as we continue to grow. Because I'm very people-driven, the operations part is very close to my heart.

The people at Staples are really unique, you find people who care about the business, and focus on quality. You don't think you're in a corporate environment. I don't know how many people can say that every time you go to a new building you have a new family, I have a family Rochester, in Kentucky and in Framingham.

Vault: Have you had any issues with coming in as a recent college graduate on a "fast track" managing employees with more tenure at the company?

Davie: One thing I was always told is "You should be known for your work ethic and your quality." Most people do not know how old I am. I can be out of college and be 26 or I can come out of college and be 21. If you do great work, it doesn't matter. Not only do you have to work hard, but you do have to show an interest in people. You have to make sure that people know you want to work with them, not over them.

Vault Q&A: Young Yuk, Intuit's Rotational Development Program

As he was graduating from the University of California at Berkeley with a degree in electrical engineering and computer science, Young Yuk knew for sure he didn't want to be an engineer or programmer. Beyond that, though, he wasn't too sure. He found a good chance to explore possible career paths as part of the first class of Intuit's Rotational Development Program.

Vault: How did you find out about Intuit's rotational program and why did it appeal to you?

Yuk: Coming out of college, I knew I didn't want to do engineering and programming anymore, so I wanted a transition job. The Rotational Development Program, even the phrase, got me excited. I randomly learned about it just through the career center e-mail list, luckily.

I didn't know such programs existed until senior year of college, but now I think there's more buzz around these types of programs. I'm heavily involved in college recruiting, so I go to most events and share my perspective on the program. People are very interested. I think people think of the program as a means to rise up the corporate ladder faster. I don't necessarily like that correlation, but it's there.

When you get out of college, most people still don't know what they want to do. This is a good way to accelerate your career development. You get hands-on experience rather than just hearing about it or doing informational interviews. You also learn to think like a person in that job and can ask the right questions.

And with the people I work with who are in their 30s and 40s, when I talk to them, they always say they wish they had done something like this.

Vault: So you explored other similar programs?

Yuk: Yes. I think the difference between our program and others is that other companies are focused on one function like marketing and you get to rotate within that function. With our program, you rotate across multiple functions that are core to the business and mostly focused on delivering for customers.

Vault: How is the program structured?

Yuk: It's a 27-month program, so two years and three months. Every six months, we rotate into a different core business function: marketing, product management, product development—which is optional, if you're qualified, process excellence—which is like operations and strategy.

Everyone starts off in Tucson, AZ for three months at our call center. This is not necessarily one of our rotations, but we go there to learn about our products and learn about our customers by providing technical phone support. That period in Tucson serves as a springboard for our first rotation. Intuit has a very high attention to customer-driven innovation, it's one of our buzzwords, having that perspective is very important

Vault: So everyone does that rotation together?

Yuk: Yeah, it's almost like *The Real World*, everyone gets an apartment that they share with a person in the program, and you get a car. The apartment and car are provided by Intuit. You get to know each other for three months. That's one of the things I'll look back on most fondly, that I made 11 good friends in the boot camp, which is what we call it.

Vault: So then where do you rotate to?

Yuk: The rest of the rotations are primarily in Mountain View, our headquarters. There are occasional rotations elsewhere.

Generally there's a big list of opportunities available, and we get to talk to leaders and managers on what our top three or five rotations would be. Then the leaders and all of our advisors get into a room and make decisions, combining business need and personal desires. There's no interviewing or anything like that.

Visit Vault at **www.vault.com** for insider company profiles, expert advice, career message boards, expert resume reviews, the Vault Job Board and more.

VAULT CAREER LIBRARY   59

Everyone hits marketing and product management. If you have a background in it, you can do programming. There's a process excellence rotation, which is Six Sigma related, improving internal business processes. There's also a strategy rotation, but only a few of us have done that so far.

Vault: What rotations did you do?

Yuk: Product development, marketing, product management, and strategy.

I did programming because I wanted to prove to myself that I can do that at Intuit, and learn how it's done at our company, even though I knew coming in that I didn't want to do that long term. Marketing, that was a stretch of my brain, because it's thinking in a totally different way than engineers do. At the highest level, marketers are selling the product, you can't just blast them with all the details up front. Engineers like to be specific with how things work. While I enjoyed my marketing rotation, I don't think I could be as successful at it.

Product management was an easier transition given my technical background.

I enjoy strategy because it's very being in the front end of things, looking for new businesses, and also I like the fact that we Intuit has a focus on not just the market but looking at the customer problems, which I enjoy.

All the rotations have given me a tremendous amount of self-awareness, we explicitly have discussions with managers and advisors and among each other about what we like to do, what we don't like to do, all the time.

Vault: What happens after you finish your last rotation?

Yuk: I'll be done in December. It's a new process, so what they're going to do is have us talk to hiring managers for about three weeks. Shouldn't be much a surprise as to what the offer should be. Some of us know they want to go into product management, some know they want to go into marketing. I would be content with a full-time strategy job.

I think there might be a job outside for me that might be better. One thing that's great is I can have honest discussions with our managers and leaders about what I want to be doing five to 10 years out. We think it's important that people are happy and doing work that they are passionate about. One of our leaders thinks that if Intuit helps someone recognize their passion and supports them in finding that dream job, he/she would leave as a promoter of the company as a great place to work, with a focus on individuals' goals.

Vault: Do you have events with the others in the program regularly?

Yuk: We meet up all the time. After every six months, we have two to three days for development and fun. We have a full day on something around leadership, or maybe something around effective written communication, and then we'll have a whole day of group bonding activities. During the rotation we have monthly meetings, and also there are a slew of courses that they offer to all employees that we tap into.

Vault: Anything else you'd like to talk about?

Yuk: There's one aspect of my job that I would like to mention. We get the opportunity to do white space projects where you get to drive a project with 10 percent of your time and run with it. The project that I've been driving, with a team of eight to 10 people, has as its goal trying to accelerate people's development.

So far, what we've done is interview leaders across the company for an hour—we go to all levels of the organization from managers to executives—we ask them questions about leadership, career and personal development. Then we document this all and share it across the company through a wiki. Each person has a profile and there's a diagram of their journey of their career inside and outside Intuit. So employees in the company are getting to know their leaders and where they're coming from, and are getting exposed to different career paths. It helps us understand what paths might be available for us looking forward.

Leadership Employer Directory

Osram Sylvania

100 Endicott Street
Danvers, MA 01923
www.sylvania.com/AboutUs/Careers

Diversity Contact:

Leah Weinberg, Manager, Diversity Inclusion
Phone: (978) 977-1900
Recruiting Email: Diversity.recruiter@sylvania.com
If writing to this e-mail address, the subject line must read "VAULT publications applicant".
www.sylvania.com/AboutUs/Diversity/

OSRAM SYLVANIA is honored to have received "2007 and 2008 Best Diversity Company" recognition. We are committed to developing an increasingly diverse workforce with fair and open access to career opportunities. We believe that variety of opinion, approach, perspective, and talent are the cornerstones of a strong, flexible, and competitive company. Affinity groups, a mentoring program, and strategic relationships with professional organizations and colleges all support OSRAM SYLVANIA's commitment to an inclusive environment where every talented individual can be proud to work.

Undergraduate Schools Osram Sylvania Recruits from

Bucknell; WPI; Bentley; GA Tech; Notre Dame; Ohio; Alfred; RPI; Bryant; University of Wisconsin; Penn State; UKY; Olin; Lehigh; UFL; UNH; Arizona State; VA Tech; UTEP; Rose Hulman; Univ. of IL; Northeastern

Visit Vault at **www.vault.com** for insider company profiles, expert advice,
career message boards, expert resume reviews, the Vault Job Board and more.

VΛULT CAREER LIBRARY 61

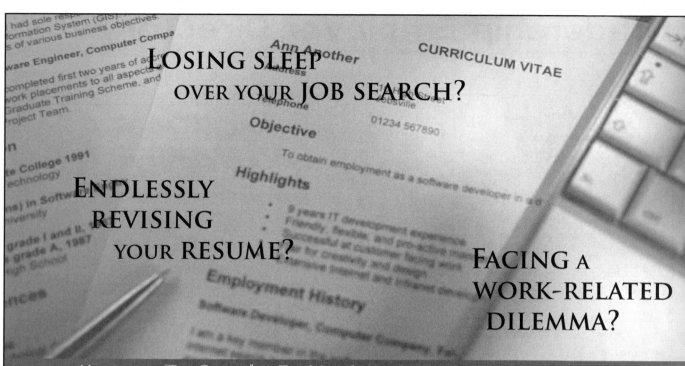

GRADUATE EDUCATION

COLLEGE
CAREER
BIBLE

Graduate School

To Go or Not To Go

When it comes to graduate school, there are two main schools of thought. The first (led by anxious parents everywhere) says, "Go right away! Otherwise, you'll forget what it's like to be in school, and you won't be able to study! And you'll never get a decent job in the real world anyway!" If this voice is the one currently pounding in your brain, tell it to be quiet and go take a nap. Then, listen to the more rational side of the debate, often specified in small print on graduate school applications: most graduate students are in their late 20s, as schools like it if you have both life and professional experience before pursuing a higher degree.

Of course, not all graduate degrees are created equal. First there are professional degrees (law, teaching, medicine) versus academic degrees (literature, art history). Some programs take only a year, others seem to take the rest of your life. Also, certain professions essentially require you to have more than a B.A. before even considering them (particularly in academia). Other fields are more willing to take a chance on a brash young thing, such as yourself.

Ultimately, the best thing to do is to ask people who are experienced in your chosen field. Ask them if they think you would be best off going to grad school right away, or if they feel you should wait awhile. Ask them about the best schools, and the best degrees for what you want to do. Don't forget to ask them if their companies ever pay for employees to get more education. Frequently, a company will chip in and give an employee flexible hours, in return for a guarantee of work for a certain period of time after he or she has graduated.

One thing graduate school should not be is a last resort. It is too expensive and time consuming to do without really knowing that it's what you want to be doing—at least for the time being.

Certification vs. Degree

There are a multitude of factors you need to take into consideration when deciding whether to pursue an advanced degree, attend local classes towards a certificate, or study for and take your certification exam. The following factors will aid in your decision-making:

- **Stage in life.** Don't let an arbitrary and subjective detail like your age get in the way of your education or professional advancement. If you really want to do it, it doesn't matter whether you're 25 or 125.

- **Stage in career.** Will the degree help you in your career progression? If you have already broken into a field and have amassed experience in it, probably not. If you're looking to change jobs to another company, you may want to consider it. If you're an independent consultant and want to ensure that new clients find you credible, you may want to go back to school.

- **Impact on income.** Can you afford to go to school full time? Can you find a good part-time program while you continue to work? Is it worthwhile to take out a loan? Will your employer help you out with a tuition assistance program?

- **Impact on relationships.** How will your time away from your friends and family impact your relationships? What's more important to you right now and in the future?

- **Volatility of field.** Is this field going to be around in the future—or are there tell-tale signs that it will be replaced by technological advancements or radically altered so that your specialty won't be needed? Check out trends and professional forecasts on web sites like Vault.com and SHRM.org for more insight.

- **Return on investment.** What are the benefits of each option?

Visit Vault at **www.vault.com** for insider company profiles, expert advice, career message boards, expert resume reviews, the Vault Job Board and more.

VAULT CAREER LIBRARY

65

- **Time and money.** Do you need this education by a certain deadline, for a certain reason and on a certain budget? If so, certification will be much quicker and cheaper to attain than a degree. If time and money are of no concern, do both.

- **True motive.** Are you looking to make more money? Then, depending on your current employer's compensation system, you may have to change jobs to a company that rewards its employees based on education rather than tenure. Also, if you are over 40, it probably won't make a difference if you have another degree if you already have over 15 years of career-relevant experience.

- **Theoretical education.** If you want this, school is often a better option.

- **Practical application.** Certification might make more sense here.

It's no secret that having an advanced degree will make you more marketable in the job market, should you need to change employers. If you're just starting out or trying to break into a field, you should definitely pursue a relevant degree; it will open up doors for you and get you more money from the get-go. If you're already established in the field and have a wide array of experience, you'll probably be OK without a degree for future internal advancement—although getting a degree certainly wouldn't hurt you for credibility and possible job changes. Furthermore, achieving a professional certification (e.g., PHR/SPHR) is a boon for degreed professionals and seasoned ones alike.

Attending local college-run certificate programs can give you some added, high-level insight into areas of interest, but won't substitute for a degree or certification. And as far as which school to attend, research all the possibilities and select the one that's right for you. The right program may not be at a "big name" university, but at a smaller institution that offers you the perfect education and training. Be sure to check out the alumni association and career placement office to find out where the school's graduates have landed jobs and which companies actively recruit from the school. The decision to pursue either an advanced degree or certification all comes down to what you feel more comfortable with and your personal career goals.

The Application

Applying to graduate school can sometimes be a daunting task. Even after completing thorough research, selecting the college or university and submitting the application, applicants are frequently left with unanswered questions and legitimate concerns about the evaluation process.

Some of the commonly asked questions students have at this stage of the process are: "How much emphasis is placed on my undergraduate grades?" "Are my standardized test scores strong enough?" "How important are my written essay and work experience to my application?" and "Who makes the final admission decision?"

International students, required in almost all cases to submit a test score or documentation indicative of their ability to study in English, are faced with additional criteria by which their application will be judged, and may therefore find the evaluation process that much more intimidating. It should help to know that the application and evaluation process is relatively straightforward.

Regardless of the program, the evaluations are based on two main criteria:

- Academic background
- Personal background

In order to determine if one's academic background is admissible, the applicant is asked to submit official undergraduate and or graduate transcripts indicating one's coursework, showing credits and grades in these courses; a standardized test score (such as the GRE or GMAT) specifically requested by the program; and a TOEFL or TOESL test score report, if applicable.

To determine if one's personal or professional background is admissible, an applicant is asked to submit two or more letters of recommendation, preferably from academic or professional references; a written essay(s), which may pertain to a specific topic or reflect the applicant's objective in pursuing the degree program; and a resume or curriculum vitae summarizing the applicant's work experience to date.

In addition, some programs may request a portfolio or sample of one's work. Many schools will request a personal interview after evaluating the application. This may be done in person or over the telephone.

Academic background

The admission committee will begin by reviewing the main indicators of how well one will do in a graduate degree program: undergraduate grades, standardized test scores and TOEFL or TOESL score.

When reviewing the undergraduate or graduate grades, the committee will look closely at the overall grade point average, as well as grades in the major or concentration. The standardized test score is examined, and depending on the type of program, special consideration may be given to a particular section of the test.

Personal background

While the grades and test scores are the most objective measure of the applicant's ability, the personal and professional criteria can do much to enhance an applicant's profile. The written essay, which for some schools may take the place of a personal interview, provides evidence of an applicant's writing ability and his or her motivation to pursue the program.

Letters of recommendation describe an applicant's skills and abilities in the workplace or the classroom. The resume informs of areas outside the classroom where a student may demonstrate competence or knowledge. The combination will provide a clear picture of an applicant's admissibility and subsequent selection for the program.

Application tips

There are a few things you can do to ensure the smooth processing and evaluation of the application. The overall appearance of your application indicates your professionalism and organizational abilities, so be sure to write neatly or type your application, essay and resume (checking for any spelling or grammatical errors). International students should keep in mind any cultural differences such as the order of first and last names. Also, make sure to complete and send in your application in a timely manner—try not to leave it all for the last minute—especially if you're hoping for financial aid. Give ample notice to the people writing your recommendations, and leave yourself time to correct mistakes or find any additional information that might be required. You might even consider making a schedule for yourself so you don't cram all of your preparation into the week or two before the deadline.

Answer all questions on the application completely and, if necessary, attach any additional information on separate sheets of paper. Make every effort to have official transcripts and translations sent directly from your previous university. Lastly, try to have standardized test scores sent to the university in advance, so they arrive at about the same time as your application.

The most important piece of advice that a prospective graduate student could receive is this: do not hesitate to ask questions. There are many ways to obtain answers to specific questions about admissions policies: you can search the Web, attend university information sessions, and e-mail, write, fax or telephone the admissions office. Knowing the answers to your questions will help you discover whether your academic and personal profiles match your school of choice and allow you to go through the admission process with greater confidence. Good luck.

Visit Vault at **www.vault.com** for insider company profiles, expert advice, career message boards, expert resume reviews, the Vault Job Board and more.

VAULT CAREER LIBRARY

67

Law School

Choosing a Law School

Which law school should you attend? In some ways, this question seems simplistic: you want to go to the best law school that will admit you. But what defines a good law school? There are many books about law schools and surveys that rank them, notably the annual issue published by *U.S. News & World Report*, and it is a good idea to review these publications. Even to the uninitiated, some names pop up immediately: Harvard, Yale, Stanford, Columbia. By reputation and stringent academic requirements, schools like these claim to take only the cream of the crop. And a prestigious law school, with its higher profile, might lead to better employment opportunities after graduation than a less well-known school. But there are considerations other than reputation.

Admittedly, it's hard to wade through the volumes of press materials each law school will send you. Review the course catalogs, certainly, but also look for statistics about the percentage of graduates who go on to litigation, corporate law or other areas of the law, and the kinds of practices they join to get an idea of the kind of training the school focuses on. It's also a good idea to visit the school in person and, if possible, sit in on some classes. "I think it's important to meet with the students at the school," says one recent graduate, "because you get the real facts about what the school is like. Go to whatever mixers they set up for their applicants, if you can."

Another element you should consider is location. Not all of the best law schools are in big cities, but being in an urban setting has a number of advantages. You will have direct contact with many law firms, city agencies and government offices with the resources to hire interns and law students. "Going to a law school in a big city meant that I could have a variety of internships and summer jobs without worrying about housing or moving," says one junior corporate litigator. Many firms also prefer to hire summer associates from local schools. If you have your eye on practicing in New York, for example, it's often a good idea to go to a New York school. You'll be in closer proximity to interview at local firms and some classes (such as criminal law or professional responsibility) may focus on New York State law.

And then there are more practical considerations. Will the school provide housing? If you live off campus, what will your daily commute be like? Are you ready to pick up and move alone or to take your family to a new city or state? Can you afford the tuition? Do you share the school's philosophy and emphasis? Is there a particular professor with whom you want to work?

Ultimately, the decision of which law school to go to is as personal as it is practical. Even if it's important to know school statistics and rankings, your choice needs to be a school that will teach the skills you want to learn, in a location where you can live comfortably. This is especially true if you are embarking on a second career and hesitate to uproot your whole life.

Law School Reputation

Reputation is a subjective quality, usually based on other subjective qualities and usually measured in national rankings and local prestige.

Every year, *U.S. News & World Report* publishes an issue devoted to ranking the colleges and universities of the United States. This is the ranking that people talk about for law schools. The magazine looks at subjective factors like ratings by academics, lawyers and judges, as well as statistical data like LSAT (Law School Aptitude Test) scores, bar passage rates, and acceptance and rejection rates. It conducts opinion polls and gathers statistics on average LSAT scores and undergraduate grade point averages (GPAs). Employers often use the rankings to determine which schools merit an on-campus interviewing visit. And, in a chicken and egg way, the fact that the law firms are paying more attention to those law schools leads to better applicants at those schools, since that's where law students see good career prospects. If you've missed the latest print issue, you can review the rankings online at www.usnews.com.

National ranking systems like those published by *U.S. News* have been criticized for subjectivity and an overdependence on reputation without considering issues like who gets jobs, what graduates think of their law school and so on. Some critics,

Visit Vault at **www.vault.com** for insider company profiles, expert advice, career message boards, expert resume reviews, the Vault Job Board and more.

VAULT CAREER LIBRARY   69

including a coalition of law school deans, have come up with alternative rankings. For more information about alternative rankings and criticism of subjective national rankings, refer to Judging the Law Schools, an "unauthorized ranking" of law schools by Thomas E. Brennan, a former Chief Justice of the Michigan Supreme Court (www.ilrg.com/rankings), and The Ranking Game, from Indiana University School of Law-Bloomington (monoborg.law.indiana.edu/lawrank/index.html).

In 2008, Vault released its own law school rankings based on the performance of law school graduates. We surveyed nearly 400 hiring partners, hiring committee members, associate interviewers and recruiting professionals across the country on which law schools best prepare their graduates to achieve in the firm environment. The respondents—who represent over 100 law firms—were advised to consider the following factors in their rankings: research and writing skills; knowledge of legal doctrine; possession of other relevant knowledge (e.g., science for IP lawyers); and ability to manage a calendar and work with an assistant. By limiting the scope of our survey, we highlight an important part of the law school decision—the value of law school graduates in the real world once they enter the workforce. However, most lawyers and clients still use the *U.S. News* rankings as a yardstick of prestige.

A school that ranks in the top of the *U.S. News* list, a "national" law school, offers advantages in the form of portability of degree. Students who attend national schools typically have an easier time finding jobs in different geographical regions than do those coming from lower-ranked schools. A national school may also have highly regarded faculty. "I went to the best law school I got into and would encourage everyone to do the same," says a Harvard alum working in a large Boston firm. "Law school is about getting a credential and access to the career, not an experience unto itself. It's called a professional school for a reason."

Of course, many successful corporate lawyers haven't gone to Harvard or Yale. A local school can be an excellent strategic and financially sound decision, especially for someone who knows the geographic area in which he wants to practice. And all firms hire from the top of their local school class. "I have realized that if you don't get into a top-10 national school, it is sometimes better to go to a local school with many local connections to firms than to go to a second-tier national school in a state in which you won't practice," says a Boston associate. "For example, people in Boston who went to Boston College Law School have good luck landing jobs in firms even though there are a lot of second-tier national schools ranked above them."

If you're lucky enough to get into several schools with good programs in areas of law that interest you, then you just need to think about personal comfort. This is where money and location come into play.

Advice for the 1L

Work steadily

Even if you've been a last-minute, overnight crammer your whole life, that system will not serve you well in law school. There is just too much material for that to be humanly possible. "Don't ever expect to cram," says one graduate, "or leave things to the last minute. You'll drown." Not only will you be memorizing an enormous amount of information, but you will also need to be so familiar with legal principles and reasoning as to be able to use them in a new context on exam questions. You have to work steadily from the very beginning of your first year so that you don't get overwhelmed at the end.

Interact

Set up study groups with serious students and attend them regularly. Go to your professors during their office hours with issues you don't understand. And, as scary as it is, ask questions in class and be prepared to participate. You are not merely being social. Everyone has different strengths and discussing your questions with fellow students can help you understand often complex issues. Yes, it's tempting to see classmates as rivals—why do you want to help others when the tests are graded on a curve? "It's easy to get caught up in the competitiveness, so be careful," says one third-year lawyer. Warns another graduate, "If you're overly competitive, the other students will avoid you like a plague." In reality, a good litigator engages in discussion and a good law student will get used to this at an early stage. Furthermore, law school can be intense, lonely and isolating. A support system can help you keep your sanity in the worst moments.

Don't panic

Law school grades can be brought up in your second and third years. If you feel lost at sea in the beginning, rest assured— the odds are that most of your classmates don't know what they're doing either. And there's no way to tell who's going to get the best grade. The student who speaks confidently in class may not have the skills to analyze issues on paper, while the quiet, insecure student who takes copious notes and studies on weekends might get the only A in the course. So don't spend time worrying about other students' skills—concentrate on your own.

Make use of study guides

There are many study guides available to the first-year law student. You can listen to tapes, study from flash cards, buy professional outlines, attend lectures and even take additional courses. Find what works for you and most accurately emphasizes what your professor emphasizes (she's putting the test together, after all).

Be prepared in class

Do your reading and be prepared to answer questions. Some professors are ruthless inquisitors; others are more interested in fostering general class discussions. Either way, you'll lower your stress level if you are prepared to be called on and give intelligent answers. One litigator offers this tip: "I usually reviewed what I studied right before class, so it was fresh."

Review

You might have done the reading for class and taken good notes, but just because you read or wrote it down once doesn't mean you know it cold. Set aside time regularly to review your notes and previous materials to build up that store of accessible knowledge you'll need to call on for the final exam. Repetition is the key.

Don't get sucked in

Try to keep up with your friends outside law school and engage in some extracurricular activities, even if it's just going to the movies occasionally or playing a game of basketball. The advantage of interacting with your fellow law students is also its disadvantage: you're all in the same boat. Talking about law 24 hours a day can be exhausting and counterproductive; you can get immersed and caught up in your fellow students' panic attacks or intense competitiveness. "I made a lot of friends in law school," says one former law student, "but I lost some friends, too, because I didn't keep in touch with all my friends from before law school." You will likely have more time and feel less pressure in your second and third years and you will be glad not to have alienated your non-law school friends. Escaping from the law once in a while will actually make you a better student in the long run, and it is an important lesson to keep in mind when you actually become an attorney.

Visit Vault at www.vault.com for insider company profiles, expert advice, career message boards, expert resume reviews, the Vault Job Board and more.

VAULT CAREER LIBRARY

71

LSAT 101

For many prospective students, few things are more dreaded than standardized testing, and the Law School Admissions Test (LSAT) is among the most fearsome tests of all. Unlike other standardized tests, like the SAT or GRE, the LSAT does not test the taker's current knowledge set, but instead tests his/her ability to logically deduce the answer based on given information. The LSAT is used to evaluate a candidate's logical and reasoning skills, as well as his/her analytical thinking. The exam can be arduous and exhausting, requiring months of dedicated preparation. The LSAT is administered by the Law School Admissions Council four times a year and most schools require that you have taken the LSAT before you apply to law school. The test is roughly three and a half hours long and the limited time allotted for each section tends to be the greatest challenge for success. The test breaks down into the following six sections:

- **Logical reasoning (two sections, 35 minutes each, 48 to 52 questions total).** This section tests your ability to dissect an argument. The questions each consist of an argumentative passage of three or four sentences. There is usually a flaw with the argument, and your job is to find out what it is. Occasionally the argument is valid, and your job is to determine the conclusion. This section is pretty dense, so be prepared to do some thorough reading. Year after year, the LSAT tends to re-use similar wording and questions molds. When studying for this section, it is important to review the main categories of questions of which the LSAT is fond. An important test-taking tip is that this section tends to begin and end with relatively manageable questions and intentionally includes the hardest questions in the middle of the section to trick the taker into wasting unnecessary time. Since each and every question on the LSAT is worth the same amount, skipping the harder questions and then returning to them if you have time is essential to gaining as many points as possible in this section.

- **Logic games (one section, 35 minutes, approximately 24 questions).** This is traditionally one of the hardest sections of the LSAT; however, it also the easiest to improve upon with dedicated practice. The best description of these "games" is that they involve logical reasoning of a system of relationships. You'll usually have to draw a diagram or create mapping sequences to figure out the relationships based on the rules given to you. There are four games with five to eight questions for each game.

- **Reading comprehension (one section, 35 minutes, approximately 24 to 28 questions).** As a lawyer, you're going to read through hundreds of cases, statutes, documents and memoranda. Reading comprehension is extremely important. This section includes four passages, each roughly 400 to 500 words long and followed by five to eight questions. As of the June 2007 LSAT, one of the sections now includes comparative reading with two separate yet related passages (still totaling 400 to 500 words combined). Typically, the passages are timely and cover topics including science, history, art and law. Don't let this scare you though—the LSAT never requires you to have prior knowledge of any of the reading comprehension subjects, just the ability to analyze the passages and comprehend the main objective.

- **Un-scored test section (one of the above sections, 35 minutes).** This section is used by the LSAC to test out prospective questions and formats for future LSAT tests. Fortunately for the test taker, this section is un-scored; unfortunately, this section is not labeled as the test section, so it is important to work equally as hard on every section of the exam. Although unconfirmed by the LSAC, based on every LSAT test ever administered, the test section always appears as one of the first three sections of the test.

- **Writing sample (30 minutes).** The writing sample will be on a topic chosen by the test committee. The topic usually presents a situation and pertinent details and asks the test taker to write a brief argument and defend his/her position. The essay does not affect your LSAT score in any way but it is forwarded to all of the schools to which you are applying. Although the essay is un-scored, a black page or blatant lack of effort will reflect poorly on the applicant when the admissions committee reviews the application package. According to an admissions official at an accredited law school, his office relies more on the applicant's personal statement than the LSAT essay to evaluate a candidate's writing abilities; however, the LSAT writing sample may be compared to the personal statement to gage consistency of writing ability.

Scoring

The LSAT is graded on a matrix that converts the raw score (0 to 100) to a 120 to 180 scale. The scores are also broken down into percentiles, with the average score (50th percentile) being a 152. There is no passing score, but it becomes increasingly harder to move up in the matrix. You don't necessarily need to get all the questions right in order to get a perfect score, but your score can drop based on the answer to a single question.

LSAT help

There are many books and courses designed help you to "beat" the LSAT, including Kaplan, the Princeton Review and the LSAT Center Course. These courses teach specific strategies for tackling each section. The LSAT doesn't change that much from year to year, so if you study older tests and practice a lot, you'll improve your chances of doing well on the real thing. The most important aspect is time management and endurance, so always make sure to take practice tests within the time allotted so you don't burn out in the middle the real thing.

Visit Vault at **www.vault.com** for insider company profiles, expert advice, career message boards, expert resume reviews, the Vault Job Board and more.

V/\ULT CAREER LIBRARY

73

Business School

Why Get an MBA?

Is it a quant boot camp where students find themselves chained to their laptops and their spreadsheets? Is it a country club where students mix and mingle, discussing future business plans over cocktails? Or is it a mandatory two years that would-be CEOs must serve in order to get that bump in salary and that chance to rise into upper management?

The school part

Business school is definitely school. Particularly in the first year, when students in many programs take "core" classes in fields like accounting and corporate finance, the workload at business school is often described as "overwhelming." In class, students learn marketing strategies and management theories, negotiation tactics, the heavy quantitative lifting of valuing a company and other useful business concepts. Many business schools utilize "business cases" to illustrate concepts the students learn. Through these cases, students study the way these concepts have played out in real-world situations.

Recently, business schools have re-vamped their curricula. Since 2002 when business schools looked like they were headed for disaster in the wake of managerial debacles perpetrated by MBA graduates, MBA programs have done much to improve their reputations, in particular adding ethics classes and programs. For example, the Yale School of Management reorganized its curriculum for fall 2007, focusing on teaching fundamentals in an integrated way in order to create well-rounded leaders and problem solvers, rather than quant jocks.

The business part

But business school is often as much about careers as it is than books and learning. While at school, future MBAs often have one foot in the classroom and the other in the working world. For starters, unlike their graduate, law or medical school counterparts, very few business school students enroll in the programs without having first gained experience in the working world. (Most programs require some work experience and are developing specific "young applicant" programs for students without it.) The program itself is also shorter—the traditional full-time MBA program is two years, which serves as less of a hiatus from working life than other graduate programs. In fact, some students in full-time MBA programs continue to consult or work part-time with their former employers throughout their time at business school.

For some students, business school is a necessary step in their career path. In the financial services and consulting industries, many large employers will not promote employees past the analyst level until they have received their MBA. It is common practice for these budding bankers and consultants to attend business school after a two- to three-year stint as an analyst following college; some of them return to their firms as associates.

Many other students earn their MBA degrees through evening classes while working full-time. For many of these part-time, evening and executive MBA students, getting an MBA is especially attractive because their employers are footing the bill for their degrees.

Going global

Unlike law school, business school is becoming increasingly international. With MBA programs like those at INSEAD and IE Business School climbing the rankings, going to business school outside of the U.S. is a veritable option, not only for students looking to work in another country. While historically, international MBA students left their country of origin to study in the U.S., more and more are looking closer to home, no matter where that may be. In addition, more and more U.S. students are looking to study abroad, as international MBA programs are only one year long and gaining prestige.

Visit Vault at **www.vault.com** for insider company profiles, expert advice, career message boards, expert resume reviews, the Vault Job Board and more.

VAULT CAREER LIBRARY 75

Moreover, you don't have to study abroad to work abroad. Business schools like NYU's Stern School of Business, which offers a TRIUM Global MBA with the London School of Economics and Political Science and HEC School of Management, Paris, and the Hult International Business School, which has locations in Boston, Dubai and Shanghai, are offering global programs. Study abroad isn't just for undergrads any more!

MBA diversity

MBA programs have been historically un-diverse. In 2008, the percentage of women MBA students hovered at about 30, and minority MBA students around 15, according to the 2008 *Global MBA® Graduate Survey* published by the Graduate Management Admission Council (GMAC—the organization that administers the GMAT business schools admissions test). Luckily, there are organizations and foundations focused on promoting MBA diversity by helping women and minority students apply and succeed in MBA programs. For example, the Consortium for Graduate Study in Management and Ten School Diversity Alliance work with top business schools to sponsor events and programs that focus on minority students. The Forté Foundation is committed to promoting women in MBA programs, as well as their business careers. Many of these organizations offer scholarships to help you fund your business education.

Check out the new *Vault/CGSM Guide to Business School Diversity* to learn more about diversity initiatives at top business schools.

Career-minded

More so than students at other graduate programs, students at business school enroll to accomplish specific objectives related to their careers. According to GMAC's 2008 *Global MBA® Graduate Survey*, about half (52 percent) of business school students use the MBA degree to enhance opportunities in their current occupation or industry; the other half (48 percent) seek to switch careers. Often, career switchers are experienced professionals who have worked in the corporate world in a non-business function (engineering, for example), who wish to transition to a business-oriented management track.

And on the whole, MBAs are satisfied with their degrees. Most MBA-holders say getting their degree was personally rewarding. According to the *Global MBA® Graduate Survey*, almost two-thirds (63 percent) say that they would definitely recommend their MBA program to prospective students.

The good news

Most business school students expect to make more money once they graduate. In fact, according to the *Global MBA®* *Graduate Survey*, most full-time MBA students expect a 67 percent increase in salary. This opportunity certainly exists, even in a recession. In general, having an MBA on your resume puts you in a better position to negotiate and command a higher salary (even if you return to the same industry or even the same company at which you worked previous to business school).

There are other reasons to get the degree other than a bump in salary. Many recruiters and managers find MBAs to be more polished professionals in certain respects. According to the 2008 *Corporate Recruiters Survey* published by GMAC, recruiters find the following skills both highly attractive and well developed in MBA graduates:

- Managing strategy and innovation
- Knowledge of general business functions
- Strategic and system skills
- Interpersonal skills

The bad news

Landing a six-figure job is no guarantee. During recessions, MBA hiring takes a larger hit than undergraduate hiring or direct-from-industry hiring. According to the 2008 *Corporate Recruiters Survey*, hiring projections were down in 2008 from 2007, and are expected to continue their downward trajectory.

With the finance industry bearing the brunt of this economic downturn, thousands of bankers are out of a job, many of whom are prospective MBA students. According to GMAC, GMAT takers are already up 12 percent for 2008. With so many people applying to MBA programs, 2008 and 2009 will be competitive years for admission. And when these students graduate starting in 2011, the market will be flooded with highly qualified grads.

Luckily, MBA hiring has been rising for the past few years and continued to do so through the housing bubble burst. GMAC notes that more 2008 MBA graduates are being recruited directly out of school than they were in the past six years. In addition, MBAs will still be in demand at investment banks, as many are choosing to limit their undergraduate hires in lieu of more qualified hires. GMAC reported that 2008 salaries may start at an average base of $80,511 with most employers adding other compensation and benefits. Students will have to wait and see what will happen in the next few years once the dust clears and we look at our new financial landscape.

The GMAT

Like other academic institutions, business schools have their own standardized test to rank applicants. Unlike other graduate programs that require the GRE, business schools almost exclusively require that you sit for the Graduate Management Admissions Test®, or GMAT®. Your score on the GMAT is extremely important to your admission to business school. Like the SAT or ACT in high school, the GMAT provides an easy-to-understand score that ranks your aptitude against every other candidate. While a lower GMAT isn't going to assure that a rejection letter will be in your future, you will make yourself a much more attractive candidate if you can fill in a strong GMAT score in your application.

What is the GMAT?

The GMAT is a computer adaptive standardized test designed to measure how successful a person will be in a graduate program in business. The exam is comprised of three parts: the analytical writing assessment, a quantitative section and a verbal section, all of which are to be completed in three-and-a-half hours. The exam currently costs $250 per sitting and is hosted in computer-enabled testing centers around the world. You may only take the exam once per calendar month and weekend tests tend to fill up early, so make sure to plan ahead.

So what does computer adaptive test mean? Computer adaptive means that unlike some other standardized tests, the questions on the quantitative and verbal sections of the GMAT will change based on how you are doing on the exam. For example, if you begin the quantitative section with five correct answers, the sixth question will likely be harder than the first five. The same is true in the opposite direction. If your first three answers are incorrect, the fourth question will be easier than the first three. So you may ask yourself, why would I want harder questions? The answer is that the harder the questions you are able to answer, the higher your score on the GMAT will be.

Analytical writing

The GMAT begins with analytical writing assessment comprised of two 30-minute essays covering both an analysis of an issue and an analysis of an argument. The section is scored out of 6, with a percentile score attached. Current topics are available on GMAC's web site, mba.com.

Visit Vault at **www.vault.com** for insider company profiles, expert advice, career message boards, expert resume reviews, the Vault Job Board and more.

V/\ULT CAREER LIBRARY 77

Quantitative section

The second piece of the GMAT is the quantitative section. This section is comprised of 37 multiple choice questions of two types: data sufficiency and problem solving. Data sufficiency questions will typically be comprised of a question with two statements that follow. The test taker must then determine if each statement alone is sufficient to answer the given question, if they are sufficient together, or if they are not sufficient at all. Problem-solving questions are more typically multiple-choice questions that can be designed to test different mathematical concepts.

Sample Quantitative Questions	
Data sufficiency	**Problem solving**
If a business school requires you to pay a student contribution of 10% of your first year expenses, with the remaining 90% covered by student loans, how much will you be responsible for paying? (1) Your student loan amount for the first year will be $54,000 (2) You contribution is equal to 15% of your current $40,000 salary (A) Statement (1) ALONE is sufficient, but statement (2) alone is not sufficient. (B) Statement (2) ALONE is sufficient, but statement (1) alone is not sufficient. (C) BOTH statements TOGETHER are sufficient, but NEITHER statement ALONE is sufficient. (D) EACH statement ALONE is sufficient. (E) Statements (1) and (2) TOGETHER are NOT sufficient. The correct answer is D.	Kerri, Heather and Jenny go shopping at the campus bookstore. Heather buys 8 items, Jenny buys 6 items, and Kerri buys 1 item, with each item costing $10. Once they get home, they all decide to share what they purchased. Kerri has to pay $40 to the other two girls, how much does she give to Jenny? (A) $30 (B) $10 (C) $20 (D) $40 (E) None of these The correct answer is B.

Verbal section

The final piece of the GMAT is the verbal section. There are 41 multiple choice questions in this section, consisting of three question types: reading comprehension, critical reasoning and sentence correction. Like the quantitative section, you will have 75 minutes to complete the verbal section. The reading comprehension questions will feature a passage of up to 350 words, with multiple questions testing your understanding of the passage to follow. Critical reasoning questions will test your ability to understand an argument and evaluate a plan of action through the analysis of a short paragraph. The final question type, sentence correction, tests your knowledge of the conventions and rules of written English by providing alternatives to an underlined passage.

Sample Verbal Questions	
Critical reasoning	**Sentence correction**
Adrian's broker Bill calls him about buying the stock of a leading pharmaceutical company. Bill explains that he expects the stock to appreciate by 20% in the next year. With a weak economic outlook, Adrian is skeptical. Which of the following, if true, would most help William's argument? (A) The pharmaceutical company is currently overvalued by 10%. (B) The pharmaceutical company's profits are expected to increase by 50% in each of the next three years. (C) The pharmaceutical company's leading prescription drug will be going off patent this year. (D) The pharmaceutical company's peer group is expected to appreciate by 15% in the next year. (E) The S&P 500 Index is expected to grow by 10% next year. The correct answer is B.	The recent decline in the housing market <u>make me feel fortunate that I didn't spend all of my savings on that condominium in Miami.</u> (A) make me feel fortunate that I didn't spend all of my savings on that condominium in Miami. (B) make me feel fortunate that I haven't spend all of my savings on that condominium in Miami. (C) make me feel fortunate that I haven't spent all of my savings on that condominium in Miami. (D) makes me feel fortunate that I didn't spend all of my savings on that condominium in Miami. (E) makes me feel fortunate that I didn't spent all of my savings on that condominium in Miami. The correct answer is D.

Scoring

Both the quantitative and the verbal sections of the GMAT are scored out of 60 points, with percentiles that are determined based on the scores from the previous three-year period. These scores are then combined to generate the more familiar total GMAT score, which can range from 200 to 800. This score will be immediately available to you after completing the verbal section, once you are prompted on whether or not you would like to see your score. If you select yes, the score will be displayed and the results will be sent to the schools that you previously selected. If you choose no, the test will be cancelled and no scores will be sent. However, schools will be able to see that you cancelled your test. The analytical writing section of the GMAT is the only portion of the test in which you won't know your score immediately; your analytical writing score will be delivered with your official score report, which generally takes three weeks. Scores are valid for up to five years, so many admissions officers actually recommend taking the GMAT while you are still in undergraduate as some of the concepts tested may be fresher in your mind.

What is the GMAT used for?

The GMAT is the one opportunity that business school admissions committees have to rate your application objectively. Unlike the rest of your application, which focuses on essays and work experience, there are no subjective elements to the GMAT, and a high score provides a great opportunity to distinguish yourself from other applicants.

Admissions committees use the official score for easy comparisons across applications, as well as to determine if you are likely to be successful at the graduate level (undergraduate course work aside). If, for example, you have a below average GPA during your undergraduate years, or went to a less prestigious institution, the GMAT is one way of easing any concerns that the admissions committee may have.

While there is no particular score that will guarantee access to your program of choice, schools generally give such guidance on their web sites. Most schools will post both a mean GMAT score, while also publishing data on the range of scores for admitted students. For example, the mean GMAT score for admitted students in 2008 for Wharton was 714, with the middle 50 percent of students having scores between 680 and 740. Although it obviously isn't necessary to score above the posted

Visit Vault at **www.vault.com** for insider company profiles, expert advice, career message boards, expert resume reviews, the Vault Job Board and more.

VAULT CAREER LIBRARY

79

mean, your focus should be on whether or not you fall within the published range of scores, generally the 25th to 75th percentiles. If you fall below this level, consider retaking the exam. While the GMAT is just one portion of the overall application, a very low score is an easy way of eliminating an otherwise promising application.

Percentiles

One other metric to focus on, beyond the headline score, is the percentile ranking given for all sections of the exam. Most schools look for strength across each of the three parts of the exam. Scores below a given percentile can draw red flags. These measures are particularly important for schools with stringent quantitative curriculum. "We look for quantitative scores above the 80th percentile," an admissions committee member said. "Any score below that level causes concern and we pay closer attention to their quantitative course load as undergraduates."

Starting the Application

Now that you've decided to go to business school, and have visited a few prospective schools and mastered the GMAT, it's time to focus on the application. Unlike a job application, a business school application is going to require a significant time commitment to make certain that you are presented in the best way possible. Expect to spend weeks, if not months completing your application. While it may seem like a long time, consider that a life-changing decision rests on the quality of your application. The application is so fundamentally important because it is your way to talk to the admissions committee. Admissions officers should be able to see all of your most meaningful accomplishments, as well as understand why you chose the school to which you're applying. The application is also your opportunity to address any potential weaknesses. If you spend two months putting together a polished application that wows an admissions officer, all that time will have been well spent.

Timeline

There are two types of admissions cycles for business schools. The first is the much more common round-by-round application process and the second is the less common rolling admissions process.

Round-by-round admissions cycles generally open in July with the announcement of that year's essay questions. Schools are cognizant of the time required to complete the application, so they give you more than enough time to complete your application before the first application deadline.

Most schools have three application deadlines. The first deadline is generally in the fall at the end of October to the beginning of November. The deadline for the second round is usually in January, with the final round deadline in March. After you submit your application, most schools offer interviews by invitation. Some schools interview all applicants roughly four to six weeks after the initial deadline. After the interviews, admissions decisions are reported in late December, early March, and finally in May for each of the first, second and third rounds, respectively.

So in which round should you apply? If you ask an admissions officer, she will tell you to wait until your application is as good as it can be, with the caveat that you should make every effort to apply before the final round. The majority of candidates wait until the second round to apply. This allows them additional time to prepare their application while heeding the advice of admissions officers to avoid the final round. Waiting until you have a polished application is certainly good advice, though there are distinct advantages to applying in the first available round.

Applying during the first round has several benefits. The first is that fewer people have planned far enough ahead to apply during this round. Lower numbers not only have fewer applicants competing, but they also mean application readers are able to spend more time evaluating each application. Business schools do adjust for the lower number of applicants by accepting a slightly smaller number of candidates than the second round. However, if you end up on a waiting list after the first round, you will have two chances—the second and third rounds—to be selected off of the waitlist. This means waitlisted candidates are effectively reapplying for both the second and third round, as their applications are compared to the candidates of both of these rounds.

Besides the round-by-round process, some schools have decided to employ a rolling admissions process. For these schools, candidates will have their applications reviewed in the order in which they are received, and admissions decisions made throughout. Many schools will promise to review the file and make a decision within a given time frame—usually anywhere from eight to 12 weeks—without the need for a specific deadline. The time line is similar to round-by-round schools, with essay questions being released a little earlier in the spring with an ultimate deadline of April when the process starts again for the next school year.

Visit Vault at **www.vault.com** for insider company profiles, expert advice,
career message boards, expert resume reviews, the Vault Job Board and more.

V/\ULT CAREER LIBRARY

81

Medical School

The History of Medical Schools in the U.S.

The very first medical school in the original 13 colonies was founded in 1765 by John Morgan at the University of Pennsylvania, which at the time was known as the College of Philadelphia. The faculty had been trained at the University of Edinburgh and used British medical education as the model. Thus, the first medical school in the United States was built within an institution of higher learning. It promoted bedside learning that was to supplement medical lectures. The medical school was within a few blocks from the Pennsylvania Hospital that was founded by Benjamin Franklin.

Medical education in that era included formal lectures for a semester or two and several years of apprenticeship. There was no formal tuition, no prerequisite academic preparation and written exams were not mandatory. With the progress of science in the 19th century started the new era of medical education calling for full-time investigators and teachers in biochemistry, bacteriology, pharmacology, etc. In the 1870s, the first teaching hospital, the Hospital of the University of Pennsylvania, was built. Teaching hospitals are those that teach future physicians the art of medicine, and thus have residents and medical students working alongside the main doctors (known as attendings).

Medical school in the 20th century

The birth of modern medical education in the United States and Canada is often attributed to Abraham Flexner, a professional educator, who in 1910 published the Flexner Report for the Carnegie Foundation. The report was a commentary of the state of medical education at the time. It criticized the fact that there were too many medical schools, many of which were substandard. At the time the report was published there were 155 medical schools in the United States and Canada and only 16 of these required two or more years of college work as an admission requirement. (Many of the others came into being simply to make money from tuition as opposed to actually providing a quality education.) Flexner proposed a four-year medical school curriculum—two years of basic science education followed by two years of clinical training. He also proposed the requirements for admission to include the high school diploma and a minimum of two years of college science. The report resulted in the closure of many medical schools that were not incorporated within a university; this way, medical education would be associated with institutions known for academic excellence. In 1935 there were 66 MD granting institutions that survived the reform, 57 of which were part of a university.

These improvements in medical education were followed by the birth of standardized testing for medical school admissions. The Medical College Admission Test (MCAT) was developed in 1928. It was implemented to improve attrition rates that at the time ranged from 5 to 50 percent. By 1946 attrition rates at medical schools in the U.S. decreased to 7 percent.

The student body

As for the student body in these early medical schools, it will come as no surprise that the students were white and male. Medical schools were closed to African-Americans, except for a few older medical schools in the north. The first African-American to graduate from a northern medical school was Dr. David J. Peck, who graduated from Rush Medical School in Chicago in 1847. Between 1868 and 1904 seven medical schools for African-Americans were established. Unfortunately, by 1923 only Howard University Medical School in Washington and Meharry Medical School in Nashville remained open. Things were not much better for women. The first medical school for women, The Women's Medical College of Pennsylvania, was founded in 1850, and eventually came to be known as the Medical College of Pennsylvania. Drexel University eventually took over the school, and it is now known as Drexel College of Medicine. The first woman to graduate from a medical school in the U.S. was Dr. Elizabeth Blackwell. She graduated first in class from Geneva Medical College (now SUNY Upstate Medical University College of Medicine) in New York in 1849. The first African-American woman to

Visit Vault at **www.vault.com** for insider company profiles, expert advice, career message boards, expert resume reviews, the Vault Job Board and more.

V∧ULT CAREER LIBRARY 83

graduate from a medical school in the U.S. was Dr. Rebecca Lee Crumpler who graduated from the New England Female Medical College in Boston in 1846.

Med school today

In 2008, there are 125 MD granting institutions, most of which still follow the curriculum that was proposed by Flexner and all of which require the MCAT. Things have changed, however, most notably the student and medical school faculty body. Each year, a little over 17,000 students start their first year of medical schools, close to 30 percent of whom are minorities. In 2006, 48.4 percent of the entering class of medical students and 48.6 percent of the graduating class were women.

A Brief Overview: Applying to Medical School

The application process begins long before you start filling out your med school applications. You've got to do your homework. Your academic requirements, grades, MCAT scores and interviews will determine where you apply and were you attend medical school.

Undergraduate academic requirements

One of the biggest myths surrounding the medical school application process is that the applicant must be a science major, particularly a biology or chemistry major. In actuality, a medical school applicant may major in any subject area he or she chooses. Regardless of the major one chooses, an applicant only needs to complete medical school admission prerequisites. Prerequisites differ from school to school, but the standard usually consists of eight semester-long classes broken down as follows:

- Two semesters of basic chemistry
- Two semesters of organic chemistry
- Two semesters of biology
- Two semesters of physics

Most medical schools also require one to two semesters of basic college English or writing courses. The good news is that most undergraduate institutions have similar requirements in order to graduate, and fulfilling these requirements will typically also take care of the medical school prerequisite. But be aware that some medical schools will not accept Advance Placement (AP) English credit to satisfy this requirement, and will expect at least another semester of English. Also, some schools require one to two semesters of mathematics, particularly calculus. You should research your schools of interest to find out what prerequisites to complete in order to be considered for admission. This information is usually readily available on the medical school's web site or through your pre-medical advisor.

With only eight to 10 semester classes devoted to the prerequisites required for admission, students can use the rest of their time to major in any subject area they choose. Many students end up choosing biology or chemistry anyway because the common medical school prerequisites coincide with the prerequisites for a biology or chemistry major. Also, many students feel that a strong background in biology or chemistry will help prepare them for the MCAT. But if one examines the data provided by the Association of American Medical Colleges (AAMC) showing the correlation between MCAT score and undergraduate major, there is no evidence indicating a background in biology or chemistry will provide a higher MCAT score (data available at http://www.aamc.org/students/mcat/examineedata/char99.pdf).

If a biology or chemistry major doesn't affect MCAT scores, which major should you choose and why? Pick a major that you will enjoy. Not only do students usually do better in subject areas they enjoy, but college only lasts four years. If you don't enjoy your major for those four years, you'll probably be miserable and regret the decision in the long run.

The MCAT

The Medical College Admission Test (MCAT) was designed to assess knowledge of scientific principles and concepts through the use of problem solving, critical thinking and writing. In short, the MCAT tests both aptitude and knowledge. One could think of it as a synthesis of the SAT, which tests aptitude, and the ACT, which tests outside knowledge. First developed in 1928 as a way to decrease attrition rates in medical school, the MCAT has undergone several revisions, the most recent of which was to change the subject material to emphasize the skills and concepts identified by physicians and medical educators as prerequisite for the practice of medicine. The paper form of the test was also converted to a completely computerized format in 2007. The test is developed by the Association of American Medical Colleges (AAMC) in conjunction with its member U.S. medical schools. The MCAT is an unavoidable challenge that must be faced when applying to any medical school. It is one of the critical factors that medical schools use to evaluate an applicant, so it must be taken seriously.

In 2007, the MCAT will be offered on 22 separate testing dates, 20 of which are between April and September, with the other two test dates in January. The test is administered in Thomson Prometric Testing Centers, which are facilities set up throughout the country for the administration of various computer-based standardized exams. It is usually recommended that students take the MCAT about 18 months before they plan to enter medical school, though they can take as far in advance as needed and up to three times total without needing special permission. For instance, if you plan on entering medical school in the fall of 2008, you should plan to take the test around April of 2007. The bottom line is that a medical school needs your MCAT scores to evaluate your application and it takes about 30 days for scores to be released after the test date, so plan accordingly.

The only way to register for the MCAT is online at: www.aamc.org/mcat. You will be able to register at this web site six months prior to the test date. It is highly recommended that you submit your registration early to ensure that you will be able to take the test at your first choice test center and to avoid any late fees. This will help to alleviate the additional stress of having to travel to an unfamiliar location to take the test. It is important to note that there is absolutely no walk-in registration.

You can take the MCAT up to three times each year, although you must complete an exam before registering to take another. Please note that when your scores are reported to medical schools, all of your previous scores are sent. Therefore, it is best to feel fully prepared before attempting to take the test. Never take the official test for mere practice.

Taking the MCAT is expensive! In 2006, the regular examination fee was $210 with a late registration fee of $50. There is no indication that these prices will be reduced in the future, so be prepared to pay at least this much at the time you register for the test.

Content of the MCAT

The MCAT is composed of four sections: physical sciences, biological sciences, verbal reasoning and the writing sample. All of the sections consist of multiple choice questions except for the writing sample, which consists of two essays. The number of test questions for each section, the order of the exam sections and the time allotted are as follows:

Section	Number of Questions	Time (minutes)
Physical Sciences	52	70
Verbal Reasoning	40	60
Writing Sample	2	60
Biological Sciences	52	70

Visit Vault at www.vault.com for insider company profiles, expert advice, career message boards, expert resume reviews, the Vault Job Board and more.

VAULT CAREER LIBRARY

85

The **verbal reasoning section** consists of several passages, each about 500 to 600 words long, taken from the "humanities, social sciences, and areas of the natural sciences," which are loosely defined areas. These topics are often not tested elsewhere on the MCAT. Each passage is followed by five to 10 questions based on the information presented in the passage. All of the information needed to answer each question is provided in the accompanying passage so you should not need to apply any outside information you may have studied.

The **physical sciences section** is designed to assess your reasoning in general chemistry and physics. The **biological sciences section** is designed to assess your reasoning in biology and organic chemistry. For a complete list of specific topics covered in each section, check the official MCAT web site at www.aamc.org/mcat. Each section contains 10 to 11 problem sets, each about 250 words in length that describe a situation or problem. Each problem set is followed by four to eight questions. There are also approximately 10 questions found in each section not accompanied by a passage. Unlike the verbal reasoning section, the Physical and Biological Sciences sections do expect you to have a background in these areas and use information you have studied before the test to answer the questions.

The **writing sample** consists of two 30-minute essays. This section of the MCAT is designed to assess your ability to develop a central idea, synthesize concepts and ideas, write clearly, and use proper grammar, syntax and punctuation. Each writing sample item provides a specific topic that you must respond to by typing your response. The topics vary widely from your opinions on global warming to whether or not you agree with a common adage, but do not include religious or emotionally charged issues or issues related to the application process or your decision to pursue a career in medicine.

The MCAT is truly a grueling test, but luckily, the total exam length has decreased significantly with the implementation of the computerized format. The overall length of the test day is about five-and-a-half hours. There are three optional 10-minute breaks.

How the MCAT is scored

Your total score on the MCAT is a composite of the score for each of the four sections. For each multiple choice section, your raw score is calculated by adding the number of questions you answer correctly. It is important to note that there is no penalty for incorrect answers, unlike some of the other standardized tests. Since there are multiple versions of the MCAT given at any one time, it is necessary to convert the raw scores to a scale to take this difference into consideration. For the three multiple choice sections of the test, the scaled scores range from a low of 1 to a high of 15. For the writing sample, each of your essays is read by two different individuals. Each individual score ranges from 1 to 6 and the total raw score is then converted to an alphabetic scale ranging from J (lowest) to T (highest). The alphabetic score is obtained from the summation of the scores received on each of your essays.

MCAT resources

It is critical for you to be proactive when preparing for this ever-important test. You should talk to students who have taken the test before you and stay in touch with your pre-medical advisor, if available, to be aware of all upcoming deadlines. The best place to check out the nitty-gritty details of the MCAT is at the official MCAT web site, www.aamc.org/mcat. A online practice test is offered at www.e-mcat.com.

The AMCAS Application

For most applicants, the formal application process for medical school starts with filling out the AMCAS application, which can be accessed through the Association of American Medical Colleges web site at www.aamc.org. This electronic application is typically known as the "primary" application, and is a common application that goes out to all of the medical schools to which you are applying. Almost every medical school in the country requires you to send them this initial application so that they can screen applicants for their individual or "secondary" applications. The primary AMCAS application requires that you fill out personal information, record grades for your classes, describe extracurricular activities and write a personal statement. You must also send them an official copy of your transcript. Along with your primary application, AMCAS will also send your MCAT scores to medical schools. Secondary applications are sent by individual schools after they screen your primary application. These often require you to write several additional essays and fill out more personal information, but this is highly dependent on the school, so you should be prepared for the extra time commitment and pay close attention to the unique deadlines for these supplemental applications.

Please note that there are a few schools that do not require AMCAS, and you must apply to these schools directly. Most of these schools take part in the Texas Medical and Dental Schools Application Service, including the University of Texas Southwestern, Texas A&M University and Texas Tech University. Further information about this process can be found at www.utsystem.edu/tmdsas/HomepageMS&Pre-HlthAdv.htm.

There are several key points to consider when deciding what schools to apply to. No matter the credentials you possess, you should apply to at least one school where your chances for admittance are higher than at most other schools, often called a "safety." The chance of getting into your state school is often better than your chances for getting into a private school because your state schools are required to accept more applicants from your state. Typically, 80 to 90 percent of a state school's student body consists of in-state residents. It is always wise to apply to your state schools, even if you prefer not to go there now; you may change your mind if they are the only schools you are accepted to. However, just because the odds are in your favor at state schools, do not think that admission is guaranteed at any medical school. The disclaimer here is that even so-called "perfect" applicants get rejected from medical schools, so be aware that the process is imperfect and thus can be unfair to even the most deserving candidates.

It is always a good idea to apply as early as possible. Some schools have a rolling admissions process in which they send out acceptances throughout the interview season, and as the number of acceptances goes up, it gets more competitive for the late interviewees. There is also an early decision program in which certain medical schools participate. This program requires that you apply to only one participating school, which requires filling out the AMCAS by August 1st, and then waiting to hear back.

If accepted, you will know by October 1st, and you must attend this medical school. You can only apply to other medical schools once you have been rejected from you early decision school or received an official release from them allowing you to apply elsewhere. Check with individual schools to see if they participate in this program.

There is no magic number of schools to apply to, but the majority of students send their AMCAS application to between 10 and 30 different schools. If you get more interviews than you care to attend, you can always withdraw your application from individual programs, so it is better to apply to a lot of medical schools and get plenty of interviews, rather than apply to a few schools and get a small number of interviews. With that said, it is important to realize that AMCAS charges an application fee of $160 for one medical school designation, and then charges an additional $30 for each additional medical school. Individual schools often charge an additional fee for their secondary applications, most of them around $50, so be aware of this additional cost of applying.

Visit Vault at **www.vault.com** for insider company profiles, expert advice, career message boards, expert resume reviews, the Vault Job Board and more.

VAULT CAREER LIBRARY   **87**

INDUSTRY OVERVIEWS

Day one

and the possibilities
are endless

Day one. It's when you take charge, meet new challenges and stretch yourself.
It's where you discover fresh opportunities around every corner. And it's
where you find the freedom to explore different services and industry sectors.
From your very first day, we're committed to helping you achieve your potential.
So, whether your career lies in assurance, tax, transaction or advisory services,
shouldn't your day one be at Ernst & Young?

What's next for your future?
Visit ey.com/us/eyinsight and our Facebook page.

ERNST & YOUNG
Quality In Everything We Do

Accounting

Why Accounting?

What exactly is accounting, and why do we need it? Accounting is a system by which economic information is identified, recorded, summarized and reported for the use of decision makers.

So what does that mean?

Put simply, accounting is the language of business. An accounting system essentially tracks all of the activities of an organization, showing when and where money has been spent and commitments have been made. This aids decision making by allowing managers to evaluate organizational performance, by indicating the financial implications of choosing one strategy over another and by highlighting current weaknesses and opportunities. It allows managers to take a step back, look at the organization, assess how it is doing and determine where it should be going.

Accounting, however, is not the exclusive domain of Big Business. In all likelihood, you have been managing your own personal accounting system for years—it's called your checking account. Every time you record an entry in your check ledger, you are acting like an accountant. Your check ledger is an accounting log of all of your deposit and withdrawal activities, helping you identify your cash inflows and outflows and letting you know how much money you have left in the bank. It lets you know where your money went and helps you make decisions on how to plan your future purchases and expenses. If this log is not regularly balanced for accuracy, you would have an inaccurate picture of your cash position and might spend more than you have (a common situation, given the popularity of overdraft protection features offered by banks).

You get the picture. Now, imagine these functions performed on more complicated items and on a much larger scale. While you might have 500 checkbook transactions in a year, many organizations might have that many transactions every minute. This is what an accountant does. And, just as you would eventually be lost without a relatively accurate checkbook, organizations would not be able to make useful decisions without an accurate accounting system. Anyone who has pulled out his or her hair trying to balance his or her checkbook should have an appreciation for both the importance and challenges of accounting.

Why choose accounting as a career?

So why would anyone choose a career in accounting as opposed to another business profession, like investment banking or management consulting? Isn't accounting boring and tedious?

Accounting has always had an image problem, stuck in the public consciousness as a profession populated by math geeks who love crunching numbers but little else. While this stereotype may have been accurate at one point in history, it no longer presents an accurate picture of what the career is like. While the basic mechanics of accounting can certainly become tedious, such functions are increasingly becoming automated, with accountants focusing more on analysis, interpretation and business strategy.

In fact, accounting has been rated one of the most desirable professions available. According to *The 2002 Jobs Rated Almanac*, "accountant" was the fifth-best job in terms of low stress, high compensation, lots of autonomy and tremendous hiring demand. Furthermore, the National Association of Colleges and Employers' summer 2004 salary survey ranked the accounting services industry first among the top 10 employers with job offers for graduating college students.

Visit Vault at **www.vault.com** for insider company profiles, expert advice, career message boards, expert resume reviews, the Vault Job Board and more.

VAULT CAREER LIBRARY   91

Accounting Uppers and Downers

Uppers

- **Collegial work environment.** Public accounting firms, particularly the Big Four firms (Deloitte Touche, Tohmatsu, Ernst & Young, KPMG and PricewaterhouseCoopers; see sidebar on p. 10), tend to hire large classes of newly graduated accountants. Being surrounded by so many people with similar interests and concerns makes acclimation to the firm and the job much more agreeable. It also provides fertile ground for networking opportunities. According to one public accountant, "I started with a class of almost 100 other college graduates, and we bonded quickly through all of the training and client work. While most of these people have since left the firm, I still keep in touch with most of them, which is great since they've all fanned out to dozens of interesting companies. I've already turned some of them into clients and am working on many others. The networking opportunity is tremendous."

- **Applicability to many functions.** A strong knowledge of accounting is applicable across all management functions, including purchasing, manufacturing, wholesaling, retailing, marketing and finance. It provides a base from which to build broad knowledge about virtually all business functions and industries. As the collectors and interpreters of financial information, accountants develop comprehensive knowledge about what is occurring and close relationships with key decision makers, and are increasingly being called upon to offer strategic advice. Senior accountants or controllers are often selected as production or marketing executives because they have acquired in-depth general management skills.

- **Exposure to different companies.** Public accounting offers rapid exposure to a number of different clients and activities, accelerating the attainment of skills and experience. According to one Big Four audit senior who specializes in entertainment industry clients, "I've been with the firm for less than three years, but I've become intimately involved in work for large industry players like Sony, Viacom and Disney, as well as for a good number of smaller entertainment and media companies. Being able to learn about the business of entertainment from the industry's benchmark companies has really sped up my professional development. Few professions would have offered me such a great learning opportunity."

- **Better hours and less stress than investment banking and management consulting.** The hours and travel required by the accounting profession are much less stressful and more predictable than that found in investment banking and consulting. In public accounting, you generally know you'll be very busy for a few months out of the year and then settle in to a manageable 40- to 45-hour workweek, whereas I-bankers and consultants are notorious for regularly pulling 60- to 80-hour weeks (at least) and hopping on planes at a moment's notice. "As hard as I worked as an accountant, my life has truly been swallowed by my I-banking job," says one former auditor who, after attaining an MBA, is now an investment banker. "I pretty much work six days a week, with at least part of my Sunday spent on some work item or another. I actually had a life when I was an auditor—not anymore."

- **Hobnobbing with executives.** Public accountants spend a great deal of time visiting clients' offices and communicating with senior client personnel. They have a unique opportunity to venture inside some of the world's most successful companies and to interact with high-level client executives such as controllers, CFOs and CEOs. As a result, public accountants gain intimate familiarity with various companies' internal processes and operations as well as increase their network of senior industry contacts. Frequently these senior individuals will offer jobs to the auditors they dealt with.

- **Great for women.** The profession has taken great strides to implement flexible work arrangements and other initiatives to provide lifestyle choices for women. According to the Bureau of Labor Statistics, women now account for approximately 60 percent of the accounting profession, with the outlook for women accountants looking bright. According to a CFO survey by Robert Half International, 58 percent of CFOs believe that the number of women accountants in management-level positions (such as vice president or chief financial officer) will increase in the next five years. According to one partner who has worked for several large firms, "At the risk of sounding politically incorrect, my 17 years of experience have shown me that women tend to make better accountants than men. In my observation, men often tend to be focused on the big picture, while women are more acutely aware of intricate detail. Well, accounting demands a detail-oriented approach more than any other skill, so you do the math."

Downers

• **Lower pay than investment banking and consulting.** The more manageable lifestyle has its trade-off: lower pay. On average, starting base salaries in accounting are 15 to 20 percent lower than investment banking or consulting, not including the bonus incentives that can significantly increase a banker's or consultant's overall pay package. According to the same former auditor/current investment banker from above, "I do make a lot more money as an I-banker—I mean a LOT—which does make up somewhat for losing my personal life, but it doesn't feel that way all the time. Sometimes it seems that, if you divided my I-banking compensation by the number of hours I spend working, I would be making about minimum wage." Bonus incentives are much smaller in public accounting, if they exist at all. "You'll never become 'stinkin' rich' on an accountant's wage," adds one Big Four tax partner, "but I like to think that, since we are supposed to be conservative and intelligent in matters pertaining to money, we know best how to take care of our money and make it work for us. You will definitely lead a comfortable life."

• **Many bosses with different priorities.** Accountants, particularly public accountants, are usually assigned to multiple projects at any given time and must prioritize and, when needed, learn to say "no." This is particularly true in public accounting, where multiple, simultaneous projects for different clients are commonplace. According to one auditor, juggling projects "has honestly been the hardest part of my job. Forget the clients, they're relatively easy to deal with—it's the partners on those clients that get you. They all want you to focus on their projects first. On more than one occasion, a partner has screamed my head off, really got down and cursed, because of a perceived 'lack of focus' on my part. You just have to try to explain your situation, try to demonstrate that you have everything covered and move on." This premium on time management is also present in investment banking and consulting.

• **Relatively conservative, conformist cultures.** Accountants are generally looking to see if reported numbers conform to one set of regulations or another (Generally Accepted Accounting Principles, the Internal Revenue Code, SEC regulations, etc.). This emphasis on regulations (in fact, one might say that the entire accounting industry exists because of regulations) translates into a generally risk-averse culture and ethos that emphasizes conformity

• **Pressure to stay "chargeable."** This is one of the subtler, yet highly sensitive parts of being an accountant. Like attorneys, public accountants generally work under billable hour arrangements (they are paid by clients for each hour billed). This means that they must account for every single hour they work and accurately allocate them to each project they work on, whether client-related or otherwise. Being "chargeable" means billing a high percentage of your hours to work performed for paying clients as opposed to non-billable projects. This tracking of billable hours, while often tedious, is absolutely crucial to the profession—it is the basis for how public accounting firms determine revenues, expenses, profitability, efficiency, performance and a host of other metrics. With such vital items at stake, timesheets and chargeability often are the subject of much stress and consternation. "Yeah, we can work 60 hours in a week," says one audit senior, "but not all of those hours are chargeable to a client. Some days, you can spend time on a proposal for new business, some time on developing a new product or service and some time on performing general research on a specific issue. All of these activities are important to continued success, but they hurt you because none of them are chargeable to a specific client. In other words, the firm isn't getting paid for this work. While the firm values this non-chargeable work, it doesn't want you doing too much of it—it wants you out there making money for the firm. So when you find yourself doing this stuff, your chargeability goes down and your performance numbers suffer, which can hurt your reviews, your paycheck and ultimately your future at the firm. However, you can't err on the other side either—you bill too many hours to your clients and you run the risk of going over budget and having the client give you the third degree on why the job is taking you so long. It can be pretty stressful."

Visit Vault at **www.vault.com** for insider company profiles, expert advice, career message boards, expert resume reviews, the Vault Job Board and more.

VAULT CAREER LIBRARY   **93**

- **Accountants frequently perform back-office work and, as a result, have no decision-making ability.** Most financial companies are steered by the front office executives who determine and execute transactions needed to maximize revenue. Accountants are rarely consulted regarding the merits of these decisions, as their job is simply to compute and record the financial impact of these transactions.

- **Private sector accountants work on the cost side and as a result receive relatively low compensation.** In other words, accountants who are performing internal functions do not generate revenue for the company. Typically, in order to command a high salary in the corporate world, an individual needs to generate revenue for the firm. Since most accounting roles are non-revenue generating, accountants' salaries are lower than those of Wall Street's finance jocks.

Public vs. Private Accounting

Just as there are types of accounting, there are also types of accountants. While there are many ways to classify accountants, the most common division is between public and private accountants.

Public accountants mainly deal with financial accounting (the preparation of financial statements for external parties such as investors). Private accountants deal with both financial and management accounting.

Public accountants

Public accountants receive a fee for services provided to individuals, businesses and governments. Public accounting firms vary greatly in size and the type of services provided. Most public accounting firms provide some combination of auditing, tax and management consulting services. Small firms mainly provide tax or bookkeeping services for smaller companies and organizations that do not have internal accounting departments. Larger firms usually provide these services to firms that have internal accounting departments. Because all public companies are required to have yearly audits, the large public accounting firms are extremely important for fulfilling this requirement.

The four largest accounting firms are known as the "Big Four," and are among the most well-known organizations throughout the world. (Previously, it was the Big Eight, which became the Big Six and then the Big Five when PriceWaterhouse and Coopers & Lybrand merged to form PricewaterhouseCoopers. Because of the collapse of Arthur Andersen, we're now down to the Big Four. See p. 10 for basic information on the Big Four.) The Big Four is made up of:

- Deloitte & Touche
- Ernst & Young
- KPMG
- PricewaterhouseCoopers

Many students pursuing accounting careers aim to start their careers at one of the Big Four firms. The Big Four have offices throughout the United States, as well as in many other countries. These firms recruit at a majority of the top schools throughout the world.

In addition to the Big Four, there are thousands of other accounting firms ranging from small proprietorships to large international partnerships. The difference between these firms and the Big Four is size, often measured in terms of billings. The Big Four have billings in excess of $16 billion a year. A large majority (97 percent) of companies listed on the New York Stock Exchange are clients of the Big Four.

Regional accounting firms represent clients that do most of their business within the U.S., although they may also have a few international clients. The largest regional firms can be thought of as somewhat smaller versions of the Big Four. And as the category name suggests, these practices tend to be stronger in certain regions. If you're considering working for a regional public accounting firm, be sure to research the quality of the firm's practice in your area. The large regional players include Grant Thornton, BDO Seidman and Jackson Hewitt.

Local accounting firms operate in a small number of cities and tend to focus on small businesses and individuals. These organizations conduct more tax and tax planning engagements and traditionally handle more of the bookkeeping responsibilities for their clients.

While most people start their careers at a public accounting firm, many gain valuable experience in public accounting and switch to the private sector after two years (or however long it takes them to get certified as a CPA). Accountants with public accounting experience are well positioned to take financial officer positions at corporations, government agencies or nonprofits.

Furthermore, the workload in public accounting is seasonal. Traditionally, individuals in this industry have had easier summers due to low work loads. However, these days, public accounting firms use summer time to provide SOX and other consulting services to their clients. The recent trend in the industry has been to perform substantive testing as early as in August. This development has added intensity to the previously laid-back summer schedule.

Private accountants

Private accountants work for businesses, the government or nonprofit agencies.

Corporations—Most corporations have an internal accounting group that prepares the financial information (both tax and audit) for the public accountants, tracks company performance for internal evaluation and works with management on issues related to acquisitions, international transactions and any other operational issues that arise in the running of the company. Within corporations, there are several roles that an accountant can take on. These include, but are not limited to the following:

• Internal auditors perform financial accounting tasks within an organization. Typically, these employees will perform audits of specific divisions or operational units of a company. Also, it is important to note that Sarbanes-Oxley, Section 404 has been implemented to prevent or detect fraud. Under its provisions, public companies are required to have strong controls, which should be monitored on an annual basis. The implementation and monitoring of these controls is charged to each firm's internal auditors. As a result, there has been growing demand for internal auditors over the past few years, which has created a lucrative exit opportunity for public accountants working for the Big Four and other public accounting firms.

• Management accountants can work in several different areas of a corporation. On the finance side, accountants can work in the financial planning and analysis or treasurer's group, analyzing potential acquisitions and making funding decisions for the company. On the accounting side, there are opportunities within the accounting group to handle tax issues and to work with external auditors to prepare financial statements such as SEC filings. Additionally, on the accounting side, opportunities exist to work within specific divisions to track costs and analyze operational performance.

Government agencies—Government accountants can work at the federal, state or local level. Many government organizations have large accounting departments to analyze the performance and allocation of their funds. The Department of Defense (DOD), the General Accounting Office (GAO), the Internal Revenue Service (IRS) and the Securities and Exchange Commission (SEC) typically hire large numbers of accountants for services and evaluations within the organization. Accountants at the IRS typically review individual and corporate tax returns. The SEC hires experienced accountants to evaluate filings made by public companies. These accountants ensure that firms are complying with SEC regulations.

Nonprofit organizations—Accounting for nonprofits is very similar to for-profit accounting; they both follow Generally Accepted Accounting Principles (GAAP). In addition to understanding GAAP, nonprofit accountants must also understand the FASB standards written specifically for these organizations as well as the tax regulations specific to those organizations. (For example, nonprofit organizations are typically exempt from federal taxation.)

Visit Vault at www.vault.com for insider company profiles, expert advice, career message boards, expert resume reviews, the Vault Job Board and more.

VAULT CAREER LIBRARY   95

The accounting groups in these organizations are typically smaller than those in for-profit companies, so an employee may be responsible for more than one area of accounting (e.g., both financial statements and tax issues).

Public or private?

According to many college professors and career services counselors, most college students interested in accounting should try to start their careers in public accounting. This route carries a number of benefits, including higher salaries, more interesting and diverse work, exposure to many different industries and the ability to fulfill a requirement for certification.

One senior manager at a Big Four firm captures the general opinion of the majority of people we spoke with: "For someone just out of college, public accounting is really the only way to go," he says. "You gain experience and get up the learning curve much more quickly. A public accountant will perform three or four audits of entire companies in a year, whereas a private accountant could be stuck monitoring cash ledgers—one account—for a year. Even in the long term, there are benefits. You have more control over your career progression. In private, you'll often see highly productive and talented individuals mired in their jobs or limited to lateral career moves because they have to wait for the people above them to retire or otherwise leave the company. Public accounting is much more of a meritocracy—you'll advance as fast and as high as you want to."

However, public accounting life is not for everyone. Private accountants generally don't travel nearly as much as public accountants, and their work schedules are much more stable—they rarely have to pack a briefcase and go to a client at a moment's notice. Private accountants also do not have to deal with the chargeability issue (the pressure on public accountants to work on billable projects as much of the time as possible). Finally, they are not required to get their CPA and thus do not have to deal with the rigors of fulfilling the grueling certification requirements.

Job opportunities

Long gone are the days when public accountants were generalists being exposed to projects in audit, tax and consulting fields. These days, most accounting jobs (especially those at the Big Four) provide specific industry training. Accountants who spend many years working within one department of any given company develop niche competencies needed to succeed within the industry in which they are employed or to whom they provide services. As a result of this specialization, accountants can demand higher salaries within the industry of their expertise. Yet there are fewer job opportunities available to them since their specialized skill set results in a very narrow job search parameter. This is especially true for senior-level accountants.

Most people anticipate this pigeonholed effect and try to expand their expertise by switching jobs every few years. Doing so prevents them from being stuck within a particular industry, as well as increases their knowledge base and provides for a new intellectual challenge. Most importantly, switching jobs within the accounting industry frequently results in a significant bump up in salary. Yet job-hopping accompanied by short duration of employment can be perceived to be a poor reflection of a candidate's overall commitment or dedication and might be viewed as a red flag on a resume.

Historically, public accounting firms have faced roughly 25 percent turnover ratio, which means that one quarter of their staff leave the firm every year. This is still the case, since most accountants working for the Big Four stay with them for only a few years. Newly-minted college graduates employed by the public accounting firms will frequently stay with the company for about three years, which is sufficiently long to progress from staff accountant to senior accountant. Those who have worked as senior accountants for at least one year had a chance to supervise staff and to lead engagements, so they can leverage this leadership experience to get a better position and higher pay at a different company. Furthermore, three years at the Big Four is more than enough time to obtain work experience necessary to receive the CPA license.

Working for a public accounting company (especially for one of the Big Four) places individuals on a very lucrative career path. There is a high demand for well-trained accountants; those working for the Big Four will receive multiple calls on a weekly basis from recruiter offering to place them with a different firm. Some of these job offers may be hard to resist, despite the fact that raises in public accounting typically range between 8 to 14 percent.

The CPA

Becoming a CPA is no easy task. It demands a higher education commitment than most other career paths. To qualify for certification, you must meet the requirements of the state or jurisdiction where you wish to practice. The state requirements are established by the state board of accountancy and vary from state to state. Because of these variations, first determine where you are planning to practice accounting and then review that state's certification requirements on the web site for the state's CPA society or board of accountancy.

Becoming a certified public accountant entails the successful completion of the following: (a) 150 credit hours of college-level education, which translates to five years of college and graduate-level work; (b) achievement of passing grades on all four parts of the Uniform Certified Public Accountants Exam (the CPA exam); and (c) the requisite amount of accounting work experience as mandated by each state, often two years or so.

What you can do without becoming a CPA

You most certainly can perform accounting functions without being certified, and there are many successful people in the profession who have taken this route. Noncertified accountants are not required to fulfill the five-year requirement; they aren't even required to have a degree in accounting (although, obviously, it helps). A traditional four-year degree is all that is necessary to be a noncertified accountant. The actual functions of an accountant are not, as the saying goes, rocket science, and complicated mathematics is rarely needed; thus, advanced certification might not seem necessary. Internal auditors, management accountants and tax personnel may all practice their professions without the CPA or any other professional designation.

Furthermore, many accounting professionals (CPAs and otherwise) contend that the CPA exam is nothing more than a rite of passage, an intense exercise in memorization that adds little actual value to your technical development as an accountant. These people generally feel that all of the information you crammed into your brain disappears once the exam is over. Many of them even said that this "brain drain" should happen since much of this information will never be seen in your actual practice; if you ever do need it, you can quickly look it up.

Finally, CPAs have to comply with the continuing professional education requirements. Most states require attendance for a minimum number of hours annually (often 40 hours annually or 80 hours biannually) for appropriate continuing professional education (CPE) to maintain a CPA license.

What you can't do

However, not being certified has a few significant drawbacks. Foremost among these is that it can be career limiting—most public accounting firms will not promote an auditor above a certain level (senior associate; these levels are discussed later in this guide) without at least passing the exam.

There are a couple of important reasons for this. First, only a CPA may sign an audit opinion. This signature is crucial, as it signifies that the auditor believes that the financial statements reasonably represent the company's actual financial position, giving the users of these statements more confidence that they can rely on them to make their decisions. Thus, an auditor without a CPA can not perform one of the most important activities of the profession.

Visit Vault at www.vault.com for insider company profiles, expert advice, career message boards, expert resume reviews, the Vault Job Board and more.

VAULT CAREER LIBRARY   97

Furthermore, a failure to pursue certification is often interpreted by public accounting firms as a lack of commitment to the profession, and few firms are willing to invest resources in someone who might leave the profession altogether (especially when there are so many others out there who are willing to pursue certification).

Another downside of not having a CPA is that you would miss out on the credibility that the certification carries. As with other advanced professional certifications, the CPA tends to give the stamp of "expert" in the eyes of the public and thus more perceived confidence in the accountant's abilities. Such credibility could mean the difference to a recruiter who's deciding between two otherwise comparable job candidates.

One final, ever-so-important downside of not having a CPA: you'll make less money. According to the staffing agency Robert Half International, the CPA can, on average, increase a candidate's base salary by 10 percent, with specialized fields (such as forensic accounting) commanding even higher salaries.

Now, this is not meant to scare you into pursuing the CPA, nor is it meant to suggest that you are a slacker if you don't pursue the CPA. You can still have a successful career in accounting without it. For example, public tax accountants generally do not sign off on audit opinions, and tax returns generally do not require the signature of a CPA. However, pursuing the CPA opens you up to many more opportunities and can only help a career in accounting. Thus, plans for certification should be seriously considered by anyone looking to break into the accounting field.

A Day in the Life: Staff Auditor

9 a.m. I get into the office around the same time that everybody else does. From previous experience, I don't expect to hear from my superiors (i.e. senior auditor and/or manager) until at least 10:00 a.m. Based on my workload, I anticipate having two hours of availability today. Consequently, in accordance with the firm's policy, I email the HR representative and inform her of my schedule. She e-mails me back, stating that one of the senior managers might need my help in the afternoon.

For the next hour I read my e-mails, tie up loose ends from the day before and come up with the plan for the day. When working in the office, I usually sit with the other staff auditors, as the cubicles can only be used by the senior auditors and managers.

10 a.m. Still have not heard back from my superiors. So I email them the status of my work. Half an hour later the senior auditor calls me inquiring whether I have any questions and wondering how soon I will be done.

11 a.m. The senior auditor stops by and asks me to put aside my current project. For the next 30 minutes, he wants me to make photocopies and deliver envelopes to the mailroom. Once these tasks are completed I continue the original project, which entails tying the quantity amounts on the holdings report to those found on the broker statement. I also have to foot (i.e. total) the holdings report and ensure that all the numbers in this report add up to the total holdings amount shown at the bottom of this statement.

12 p.m. I e-mail other staff auditors wondering what they are doing for lunch. Most of us know each other from the summer internship (which took place between our junior and senior years in college). Turns out that half of my friends are at clients' sites and others are swamped with work. However, two of my buddies are heading to the local diner at 1 p.m. and I agree to join them.

The work is monotonous, but the time is flying by. Once I finish working on the holdings report, I start working on the cash statement. For some reason the total amount on the cash statement does not tie to the total on the bank statement, differing by $3 million. I call the senior auditor about this issue. He explains that the difference is due to timing. In other words, the bank statement does not reflect the $3 million deposit made at month end.

1 p.m. Lunch.

2 p.m. I check my voice messages and e-mails. One of the e-mails is from the client and is addressed to the entire team. Two weeks after requesting the documents, the client finally provided us with the necessary reports. This means that my workload is about to get heavier. Sure enough, 10 minutes later, I receive a call from the manager. He wants to meet with the entire team in order to come up with the plan of action and allocate the work. The meeting is scheduled to take place tomorrow at 10:30 a.m. I program it into my calendar and resume my activities from the morning.

3 p.m. Receive a call from the HR representative. She wants to find out my availability for the rest of the day. I should be done with the current project by 4:00 and tell her so. She provides me with the name and phone number of a manager who is in need of assistance. I promptly call him. Turns out there is an Excel file that needs to be modified. The manager provides me with detailed instructions on what to do. This is an urgent project which needs to be completed by the end of the day. Once I get off the phone, I wrap up the morning project and commence work on the new assignment.

5 p.m. I run into difficulty with the Excel file. The assignment requires me to use the "vlookup" function in Excel but I am not sure how to properly use this feature. I call the manager and he guides me through this issue.

6:30 p.m. I finish the Excel project and e-mail it to the manager. I also e-mail the completed project from the morning to my senior for review and final sign-off. Before heading home I still need to update my hours in the system. Since I worked on two different projects today, I carefully allocate the proper number of hours worked to each of these projects. I organize my desk, turn off my laptop and start to head out. Glancing at my watch, the time reads 7 p.m. I am fortunate that this is not the busy season, when my departure time might be as late as 11 p.m.

Visit Vault at **www.vault.com** for insider company profiles, expert advice, career message boards, expert resume reviews, the Vault Job Board and more.

V∧ULT CAREER LIBRARY

99

Employer Directory

Amper, Politziner & Mattia
2015 Lincoln Highway
P.O. Box 988
Edison, NJ 08818
Phone: (732) 287-1000
Fax: (732) 287-3200
www.amper.com

Anchin, Block & Anchin LLP
1375 Broadway
New York, NY 10018
Phone: (212) 840-3456
Fax: (212) 840-7066
www.anchin.com

Beers & Cutler PLLC
Tysons Corner
8219 Leesburg Pike, Suite 800
Vienna, VA 22182
Phone: (703) 923-8300
Fax: (703) 923-8330
www.beersandcutler.com

Berdon LLP
360 Madison Avenue
New York, NY 10017
Phone: (212) 832-0400
Fax: (212) 371-1159
www.berdonllp.com

BKD LLP
Hammons Tower
901 East St. Louis Street, Suite 1800
Springfield, MO 65801-1900
Phone: (417) 831-7283
Fax: (417) 831-4763
www.bkd.com

CBIZ & Mayer Hoffman McCann P.C.
6050 Oak Tree Boulevard South
Suite 500
Cleveland, OH 44131
Phone: (216) 447-9000
Fax: (216) 447-9007
www.cbiz.com

Cherry, Bekaert & Holland
1700 Bayberry Court, Suite 300
Richmond, VA 23226-3791
Phone: (804) 673-4224
Fax: (804) 673-4290
www.cbh.com

Citrin Cooperman & Company
529 Fifth Avenue, 2nd Floor
New York, NY 10017
Phone: (212) 697-1000
Fax: (212) 697-1004
www.citrincooperman.com

Clifton Gunderson LLP
301 SW Adams Street, Suite 600
Peoria, IL 61602
Phone: (309) 671-4560
Fax: (309) 671-4576
www.cliftoncpa.com

Crowe Horwath LLP
330 East Jefferson Boulevard
South Bend, IN 46624-0007
Phone: (574) 232-3992
Fax: (574) 236-8692
www.crowehorwath.com

Deloitte & Touche USA LLP and its subsidiary
1633 Broadway
New York, NY 10019
Phone: (212) 489-1600
Fax: (212) 489-1687
www.deloitte.com

Dixon Hughes PLLC
1829 Eastchester Drive
High Point, NC 27261-2612
Phone: (336) 889-5156
www.dixon-hughes.com

Eide Bailly LLP
4310 17th Avenue South
Fargo, ND 58103
Phone: (701) 239-8500
Fax: (701) 239-8611
www.eidebailly.com

Eisner LLP
750 Third Avenue
New York, NY 10017
Phone: (212) 949-8700
www.eisnerllp.com

Elliott Davis, LLC
200 East Broad Street
P.O. Box 6286
Greenville, SC 29606
Phone: (864) 242-3370
Fax: (864) 232-7161
www.elliottdavis.com

Ernst & Young LLP
5 Times Square
New York, NY 10036-6530
Phone: (212) 773-3000
Fax: (212) 773-6350
www.ey.com

Goodman & Company, LLP
1 Commercial Place
Norfolk, VA 23510-2119
Phone: (757) 624-5100
Fax: (757) 624-5233
www.goodmanco.com

J.H. Cohn LLP
4 Becker Farm Road
Roseland, NJ 07068
Phone: (973) 228-3500
Fax: (973) 228-0330
www.jhcohn.com

KPMG LLP
345 Park Avenue
New York, NY 10154-0102
Phone: (212) 758-9700
Fax: (212) 758-9819
www.us.kpmg.com

Larson, Allen, Weishair & Co., LLP (LarsonAllen)
220 South Sixth Street, Suite 300
Minneapolis, MN 55402-1436
Phone: (612) 376-4500
Fax: (612) 376-4850
www.larsonallen.com

Visit Vault at **www.vault.com** for insider company profiles, expert advice,
career message boards, expert resume reviews, the Vault Job Board and more.

VAULT CAREER LIBRARY

101

Employer Directory, cont.

McGladrey & Pullen, LLP
3600 American Boulevard West
3rd Floor
Bloomington, MN 55431-4502
Phone: (952) 835-9930
Fax: (952) 921-7702
www.mcgladrey.com

Moss Adams LLP
999 3rd Avenue, Suite 3300
Seattle, WA 98104
Phone: (206) 302-6800
Fax: (206) 652-2098
www.mossadams.com

Parente Randolph LLC
2 Penn Center Plaza, Suite 1800
Philadelphia, PA 19102-1725
Phone: (215) 972-0701
Fax: (215) 563-4925
www.parentenet.com

Lattimore, Black, Morgan and Cain, P.C.
5250 Virginia Way
P.O. Box 1869
Brentwood, TN 37024-1869
Phone: (615) 377-4600
www.lbmc.com

Marcum & Kliegman, LLP
10 Melville Park Road
Melville, NY 11747
Phone: (631) 414-4000
Fax: (631) 414-4001
www.mkllp.com

Novogradac & Company LLP
246 First Street, 5th Floor
San Francisco, CA 94105
Phone: (415) 356-8000
Fax: (415) 356-8001
www.novoco.com

Plante & Moran PLLC
27400 Northwestern Highway
Southfield, MI 48034
Phone: (248) 352-2500
Fax: (248) 352-0018
www.plantemoran.com

PricewaterhouseCoopers LLP
300 Madison Avenue, 24th Floor
New York, NY 10017
Phone: (646) 471-4000
Fax: (646) 471-4444
www.pwc.com

Reznick Group, PC
7700 Old Georgetown Road, Suite 400
Bethesda, MD 20814-6224
Phone: (301) 652-9100
Fax: (301) 652-1848
www.reznickgroup.com

Rothstein, Kass & Co.
4 Becker Farm Road
Roseland, NJ 07068
Phone: (973) 994-6666
Fax: (973) 994-0337
www.rkco.com

Schneider, Downs & Co., Inc.
1133 Penn Avenue
Pittsburgh, PA 15222-4205
Phone: (412) 261-3644
Fax: (412) 261-4876
www.sdcpa.com

SMART Business Advisory and Consulting, LLC
80 Lancaster Avenue
Devon, PA 19333
Phone: (610) 254-0700
Fax: (610) 254-5292
www.smartgrp.com

Tofias PC
350 Massachusetts Avenue
Cambridge, MA 02139
Phone: (617) 761-0600
Fax: (617) 761-0601
www.tofias.com

UHY Advisors
30 South Wacker Drive, Suite 2850
Chicago, IL 60606
Phone: (312) 578-9600
Fax: (312) 346-6500
www.uhyadvisors-us.com

Virchow, Krause & Company, LLP
10 Terrace Court
Madison, WI 53718
Phone: (608) 249-6622
www.virchowkrause.com

Vitale Caturano & Company
80 City Square
Boston, MA 02129
Phone: (617) 912-9000
www.vitale.com

Weiser LLP
135 West 50th Street
New York, NY 10020
Phone: (212) 812-7000
Fax: (212) 375-6888
www.weiserllp.com

Wipfli LLP
11 Scott Street
Wausau, WI 54403
Phone: (715) 845-3111
Fax: (715) 842-7272
www.wipfli.com

WithumSmith+Brown
5 Vaughn Drive
Princeton, NJ 08540
Phone: (609) 520-1188
Fax: (609) 520-9882
www.withum.com

Advertising

An Introduction to Advertising

The concept of advertising existed long before we had a term for it. In 981 A.D., the great Viking explorer Eric the Red left Norway to survey an island west of Iceland. Except for the southern coast, this new land was little more than a gigantic iceberg. But Eric was a natural at advertising. To persuade immigrants to leave Norway and settle the island, he painted a picture of temperate climate, rolling meadows and lush farmland; to top it all off, he named it Greenland. Eric created a brand, and hundreds of land-starved Vikings boarded longships and headed west for this so-called "greenland."

These days advertisers don't (usually) have to resort to lies to get their audience to take notice of Brand X. They do, however, have to produce creative, clever, informative and visually arresting campaigns that stand out in an increasingly cluttered world of instant information and fleeting images. The mission is exceedingly difficult when it's so easy to ignore an advertisement or commercial. Print ads can "disappear" with the flip of a page. And on television (or TiVo), a 30-second commercial ceases to exist with the click of the remote control.

Brandyland

Advertising is defined as the art of positioning and creating brands, and persuading consumers to buy them through messages in mass media. The clothes you wear, the cars you drive, your insurance company and your choices in entertainment are all brands. (Even an intangible like a country can be branded—Eric the Red's canny tactics presaged recent efforts in branding countries to attract travelers and business investment.) In fact, the "brand" is the core concept of advertising. David Ogilvy, founder of Ogilvy & Mather, who built up icons like the American Express card and Rolls Royce, described a brand as: "The intangible sum of a product's attributes: its name, packaging and price, its history, its reputation and the way it's advertised." Implicit within is a unique promise of value and trust that distinguishes it from its competitors. The job of an advertising agency is to use every tool at its disposal to clothe the brand with substance and endow it with personality that fits a consumer's personal values and aspirations. The product is now a trusted friend, and other items are merely strangers.

If done effectively, a consumer develops an emotional relationship with a brand. Smart advertisers can tap into this well of feeling, and attach value to the product by creating the anticipation of a superior experience. (Just take a look, for example, at the Herbal Essences shampoo television ads, which strongly imply that women will be brought to the heights of ecstasy merely by shampooing their hair with the product.) Yes, customers do buy products and services for sheer functionality, but purchasing decisions go far beyond that.

This link, properly built, leveraged and translated into an emotionally involving and gratifying experience, will produce an intensely loyal, committed customer. His or her lifetime value to the brand is significant, since the best customers often become brand advocates and recruit new customers. In a recent Nielsen survey, 78 percent of Internet users said they trusted word-of-mouth consumer recommendations, versus 61 percent for consumer opinions posted online, about 55 percent for magazines, TV or radio, and 34 percent for search engine ads. (Brand haters have the same power—the industry calls them "badvocates.")

The antidote to "jaded"?

Over the past few decades, the average consumer has become a bit cynical and is savvier when it comes to recognizing traditional advertising gambits. Institutions, from the presidency to churches to Ivory soap, are no longer instinctively trusted. And the increasing saturation of advertising messages—before feature films, on mini-billboards on grocery carts and micro-screens in bathroom stalls—is contributing to information overload, forcing consumers to unconsciously tune out most advertising. As they become harder to reach, an integrated marketing plan becomes more important. All aspects of a unified communications plan (advertising, sales promotion, public relations, digital and direct marketing) work together as one rather

Visit Vault at **www.vault.com** for insider company profiles, expert advice, career message boards, expert resume reviews, the Vault Job Board and more.

V/\ULT CAREER LIBRARY 103

than each working in isolation. In a successful campaign, every customer contact with the brand reinforces and extends its basic message. The basic proposition of integrated marketing is to surround customers with the brand, and the look, feel and tone of all messages must convey the essential brand image. However, in an age when advertising, media and marketing are farmed out in all directions, this has become increasingly difficult.

Clash of the (advertising) titans

"Advertising agencies are idea stores, and just about everyone gets in on the act," says Chuck Bachrach, media director of the Los Angeles-based, full-service agency Rubin Postaer and Associates. Those stores posted their best financial results in five years in 2007, with industry revenue of $31.1 billion bumped up 9 percent from the previous year's total of $28.2 billion.

The industry is dominated by a handful of huge holding companies dubbed the Big Four—Omnicom, WPP, the Interpublic Groupe and Publicis—each of which contains dozens of subsidiaries. (The 1980s represented the grand age of empire-building in advertising, as each group acquired companies at will.) The largest members of the quartet—Omnicom and WPP—are comparably sized, with annual revenue of $12.7 billion and $12.4 billion, respectively; significantly smaller are Interpublic ($6.6 billion) and Publicis ($6.4 billion). Two relatively tiny entities, Dentsu ($2.4 billion) and Havas ($2.3 billion) round out the pack.

Looking forward

No matter how insiders want to spin it, the advertising landscape is definitely changing. The shift may be referred to in different terms: push vs. pull; brand control is moving from the manufacturer to the individual; the "interruption" model is now the "invitation" model. But everyone agrees that the Internet (or, more appropriately, digital connectivity) is reshaping how advertisers reach their audience. The industry needs a new business model.

This advertising revolution will not be televised; it will appear on computer screens, yes, but also on cell phones and BlackBerries. Marketers are now all but required to promote their brands on every platform of the digital continuum: blogs, YouTube, search engines, Second Life, widgets, social networks, RSS feeds, text messages. Digital advertising, which generated $3.4 billion or 27 percent of ad industry revenue in 2007, is far and away the fastest growing of all disciplines. ("Interactive" marketing is another term used to describe the segment.) For each of the past several years, the sector swelled about 20 percent, and during that time, individual company reports of annual increases on the order of 50 percent or more were not uncommon.

Advertising shops, like the main players in other industries, have been somewhat slow to adapt to the environmental change. But there have been signs that companies are now ready to react. Publicis announced recently that it expects 25 percent of its revenue to be digitally originated by 2012. And even the larger, less flexible networks (that's you, WPP) have been busy buying up independent agencies or forming their own by harvesting in-house personnel (Tribal DDB). At the same time, something unexpected is happening: traditional agencies are competing with digital ones for digital work, and vice versa. Insiders have speculated that within five or 10 years, a separate category for digital advertising will cease to exist as it is integrated into every other aspect of the game.

Besides the pace of innovation, there's another incentive for moving online: cost. Compared to a spot on the big three networks during primetime—and certainly compared to the $2 million a company would spend for one 30-second ad broadcast during the Super Bowl—digital is cheap (so far). But it also draws in smaller amounts of revenue. For a standout production, there's the added potential of a "viral" breakout, which can function like a larger, second wave of media attention with no additional investment. When an item or idea goes viral, online fans of the product/service/advertisement/mascot/slogan embrace it, share it with friends and create their own brand-related stories and experiences, often reaching hundreds of thousands of people.

Those already on the digital bandwagon are quick to point out that the elements that matter most to advertisers, like how many people are exposed to a product's commercial, can be much better tracked electronically. Yet there's still a fog around those seemingly hard-to-fudge basic statistics like unique site visitors and page views. There's no industrywide "standard" for tabulating those numbers. As a result, figures supplied by online "hosts" and measurement companies, such as ComScore and Nielsen/NetRatings, which rely upon "representative" user panels, can vary widely. In a recent evaluation of Style.com, ComScore said the site had 421,000 visitors while the site's owner, Condé Nast, put the number at 1.8 million. Site owners complain that certain visitors (i.e., those who access from within business networks or university mainframes) are not counted properly, and also posit that the panel members surveyed are not so representative after all.

At an industry conference in Austin titled "Chaos: New Agendas in Advertising," Roy Spence, president of GSD&M playfully offered: "By the way, people still watch TV." Through the first three quarters of 2007, ad spending on "the box" was pegged at $47.2 billion, as opposed to $7.2 billion for online endeavors. However, growth for TV was just 5.2 percent over the prior year, much smaller than growth in digital. Industry lifers still think the best quality product is delivered via television. It's also the most visible and most instantly accessible platform, and presents the best way for the industry to view and celebrate its collective work (it's harder to show an interactive project on the screen behind the winner at award time).

Working in Advertising

How, what, where

An agency can specialize in one field or another, or act as a "full-service" destination that houses a variety of disciplines. The industry idea of "traditional" advertising is what most people think of as advertising—mainly commercials for television (or sometimes radio broadcast) and print work found in magazines and newspapers. An adjunct to this area is "media," or the specific plan that defines how, where and when a client's ad dollars are spent—from which magazines or TV stations will carry the message, at what times of day and how often, or how large a print spread.

It's at marketing communications firms that one finds the most variety and the most contemporary approaches to promoting a product. There are companies that deal exclusively in outdoor advertising (i.e., billboards), direct mailing, sales and retail promotion (in-store sampling, contests, rebates), the somewhat recently developed area of "advertrying" and, of course, Internet and digital efforts. But it's the Internet that is fueling industry growth: revenue from marketing services rose 13.1 percent in 2006 (to $15.1 billion) compared to only 4.2 percent for advertising and media. As such, marketing's share of total industry revenue increased 2.1 percent to 53.6 percent. However, the amount of worldwide income derived from marketing services differs markedly among the Big Four firms.

Public relations (PR) firms are sometimes considered outside the scope of advertising/marketing, but the two fields certainly overlap in their intent. Public relations experts try to sway public opinion (in regard to companies) or governmental legislation (for trade groups) through a program of activities—think fund raisers and sponsorships, "news" releases or other actions. They're especially useful in managing a crisis (like the recall of ConAgra-produced Peter Pan peanut butter in summer 2007). Besides, many full-service agencies or networks incorporate one or more PR companies.

Step into the ring ...

The industry fosters a huge amount of competition, both self-imposed and market driven. Three or four main networks live within each advertising conglomerate and battle each other for business (like Saatchi & Saatchi, Leo Burnett and Publicis within Publicis Group). Of course, these companies are also vying with others outside the holding company. Furthermore, the selection of TBWA, say, by client Z, is likely judged on a number of factors in addition to the creative and financial attributes of the proposal. Previous working relationships with the company or its parent, competition from other products

Visit Vault at www.vault.com for insider company profiles, expert advice, career message boards, expert resume reviews, the Vault Job Board and more.

VAULT CAREER LIBRARY   105

in its field, the client's ability to contribute to the process all come into play. The whole arrangement is further complicated by two features of the environment. The industry is in a constant state of flux—seemingly every week a new agency is born ("whole" or split off from a network) or suddenly owned by a different corporate parent. Also, members of the advertising workforce—who chiefly lie in two camps: the "creatives" and the account managers—change employers at an alarming pace. There's also the ongoing debate as to whether a monster firm or a tiny creative shop is the best way to go. An independent startup often has the benefit of a fresh perspective, younger staff (who may have better facility with today's media), greater flexibility and responsiveness. It also holds the possibility of a more intense, interpersonal relationship with the client, or more of a partnership dynamic. A larger agency has the overwhelming advantage of access to resources. It can draw in affiliated firms that specialize in digital or direct marketing, for example, or provide extra creative input, or consider more media planning and buying options. A midsized company that's a part of a large advertising family possibly combines the best of both worlds. Many in the industry would agree that, aside from gigantic multinational businesses, which usually contract with the biggest networks, there has been a noticeable trend toward the selection of smaller, edgy shops.

Clients frequently choose not to keep all their eggs in one advertising basket, whether for creative variety or security. So it's equally possible that PepsiCo, for example, could use an integrated advertising network like McCann WorldGroup, or several agencies within the Omnicom Group, or a seemingly haphazard mix-and-match collection of firms to handle its business. But most often, that PepsiCo contract isn't all-encompassing. Account responsibilities for Pepsi, like other multinationals, are usually fragmented into pieces defined by geographic region, product line or specific promotion.

Major Career Paths in Advertising

Account services

Account services professionals manage the relationship between the agency and the client. They are the first line of contact with the client—and the first line of defense. Essentially, they are the project managers for advertising client accounts.

The account services hierarchy ranges from account coordinator at the entry level, to account directors (also called management supervisors) who oversee one or more client relationships in their entirety. Account services people are marketing and communications consultants; they must know as much about the brand as the client, and more about how to advertise it.

Successful account services pros must be all of the following.

- **Integrators.** Account people craft the communications marketing plan and insure that all of the agency's resources are working together to make the plan a reality.

- **Organized.** Account services professionals are detail-oriented, and masters of multitasking and following up. They are keepers of the overall timetable for ad production, placement and communication.

- **Generalists.** They must have a working knowledge of every agency discipline ranging from evaluating copy and art to media and production.

- **Advocates.** They are the client's advocate within the agency, and the agency's advocate to the client. Diplomacy and eloquence are key.

- **Students and lovers of advertising.** They must immerse themselves in advertising and marketing and learn the lessons of past and current successes and failures.

- **Cheerleaders.** As leaders of the team, account people must be superb "people" people, exhibiting grace under pressure. "When everyone's walking around moping because the client hates the new campaign, or there's been a screw up somewhere, it's my job to get everyone back on track. In account services, the glass is always half full," an account supervisor at a large agency notes (cheerfully).

Media services

Broadly, media services is responsible for the planning and buying of print, broadcast, out-of-home (billboards) and interactive media in the most effective and efficient way possible. Media planners are the strategists—they determine when and where it's most advantageous to buy advertising space for any given campaign. Buyers actually negotiate for, and purchase, the media space.

But that's hardly the whole story. These media specialists are also key members of the advertising branding team. They must find environments that extend and reinforce the brand image of their clients—and buy space for advertising those brands. Armed with consumer research, both proprietary and purchased, media professionals not only know the target audience's media habits—the programs they watch and listen to, the magazines and newspapers they read—they also know what influences consumers to make purchasing decisions. Purchase decision influencers are people who have a lot of influence over the purchase but aren't the "target market." For example, while men may purchase suits, women have significant influence over which suits their male partners and companions buy.

The result of the media specialists' research and work is the media plan for the advertising campaign. Major media outlets will then compete to get on the plan (that is, to secure a portion of the client's ad budget for their magazine or television network or newspaper). The plan itself contains recommendations on where the client should spend their media budget to achieve the campaign's goals in the most efficient way. The plan outlines how many people the media recommendation reaches, how many times the commercial or print ad will run, and the total audience impressions the plan will attract.

Once the plan is approved, media vehicles like television stations, newspapers and magazines that weren't included in the plan fight to get included. So, in the midst of a buy, buyers not only have to contend with the job of purchasing media, they also have to entertain presentations from disappointed media sales reps. Media buyers, especially, frequently socialize with sales representatives from media organizations on a regular basis.

Creative services

Many people outside of the industry view creative as the "romantic" part of the business. Romantic and exciting though it may seem, copywriting and art direction is hard work. Creative services jobs are indeed exciting, but failure is easy to come by.

Once the creative strategy is set (by the account services folks) and approved by the client, and once the consumer research has been transformed into a media plan, it's time for the Big Idea—a creative translation of the strategy into a compelling and persuasive ad. And there is nothing more difficult than facing a hard deadline and sitting at a desk, well into the night, staring at a blank sheet of paper, in an office littered with balled up sheets of paper, while thinking, "Lord, send me an idea!"

Copywriters, who write the copy (words, script, whatever) and art directors, who visually design the ads, work as a team. Together, they create ads, not only for the current campaigns but for "back up"—campaigns that are continually tested in the event that the current advertising loses its effectiveness—or "wears out" campaigns, as well.

The creative process, for new ads, is initiated by the client. Let's say the client calls the account executive and requests a four-color ad for *Modern Maturity* magazine. The account executive writes a creative strategy statement for the ad (obviously aimed at an older audience) and takes it to the creative supervisor. The creative supervisor assigns the ad to a copywriter and art director team with a due date. Once the ad is completed and approved internally, the copy and layout are presented to the client.

Visit Vault at www.vault.com for insider company profiles, expert advice, career message boards, expert resume reviews, the Vault Job Board and more.

VAULT CAREER LIBRARY   107

Account planning/research

Account planning, an import from British advertising agencies, is a relatively new discipline in the United States. Most of the larger agencies and many of the smaller ones have embraced it. Account planning uses qualitative research to determine why consumers behave the way they do. Planners function as the voice of the consumer within the agency, and their main goal is to gain a deeper understanding of the way consumers react to their clients' product or service. Planners burrow into the consumer's mind, plumbing for insights about the product, its position and competition, and research is their tool. They live with the brand and its consumers. The insights they gain are considered the target market's psychographics—their attitudes, opinions and values. These consumer psychographics help copywriters and art directors create more effective advertising.

Traffic

Traffic managers are the keepers of the creative process—schedules and approvals reside in their domain. If account services professionals are like the generals, setting and managing the overall strategy, traffickers are the foot soldiers and work with creative, media and the account group to insure that all deadlines are met. Print publications and broadcast stations have unchangeable closing dates. In addition, it's traffic's responsibility to see that the ads are approved at every stage of their development and forwarded to the media on time. Successful traffic managers are organized, detail-oriented and able to work under pressure. It is a difficult, highly stressful job.

Production

There are two types of production specialists at advertising agencies—print and broadcast. Print production specialists are schooled in every aspect of the print production process and are experts at making ads look great in magazines, newspapers and out-of-home venues. Most print production advertising professionals are hired from printing companies and other graphic design outlets.

Broadcast producers are in charge of the actual production of TV and radio commercials. They work closely with the creative department to select directors, production facilities, talent, music and just about every other aspect of broadcast production. Like their sisters and brothers in print production, broadcast producers are well-organized, able to work well under pressure, and experts at their craft.

Employer Directory

24/7 Real Media
132 West 31st Street
New York, NY 10001
Phone: (212) 231-7100
Fax: (212) 760-1774
Toll free: (877) 247-2477
www.247realmedia.com

Aegis Group plc
180 Great Portland Street
London W1W 5QZ
United Kingdom
Phone: +44-20-7070-7700
Fax: +44-20-7070-7800
www.aegisplc.com

Arnold Worldwide Partners
101 Huntington Avenue
Boston, MA 02199
Phone: (617) 587-8000
Fax: (617) 587-8070
www.arnoldworldwidepartners.com

Bartle Bogle Hegarty
60 Kingly Street
London W1B 5DS
United Kingdom
Phone: +44-20-77-34-16-77
Fax: +44-20-74-37-36-66
www.bbh.co.uk

BBDO Worldwide
1285 Avenue of the Americas
New York, NY 10019
Phone: (212) 459-5000
Fax: (212) 459-6645
www.bbdo.com

Campbell Mithun
222 South 9th Street
Minneapolis, MN 55402
Phone: (612) 7347-1000
Fax: (612) 7347-1515
www.campbellmithun.com

Cliff Freeman and Partners
36 West 20th Street, 5th Floor
New York, NY 10011
Phone: (212) 710-8660
Fax: (212) 201-5777
www.clifffreeman.com

Crispin Porter + Bogusky
3390 Mary Street, Suite 300
Miami, FL 33133
Phone: (305) 859-2070
Fax: (305) 854-3419
www.cpbgroup.com

DDB Worldwide Communications Group Inc.
437 Madison Avenue
New York, NY 10022
Phone: (212) 415-2000
Fax: (212) 415-3414
www.ddb.com

Dentsu Inc.
1-8-1, Higashi-shimbashi, Minato-ku
Tokyo, 105-7001
Japan
Phone: +81-3-6216-5111
Fax: +81-3-5551-2013
www.dentsu.co.jp

Deutsch Inc.
111 8th Avenue
New York, NY 10011
Phone: (212) 981-7600
Fax: (212) 981-7525
www.deutschinc.com

Digitas Inc.
33 Arch Street
Boston, MA 02110
Phone: (617) 369-8000
Fax: (617) 369-8111
www.digitasinc.com

Fallon Worldwide
901 Marquette Avenue, Suite 2400
Minneapolis, MN 55402
Phone: (612) 758-2345
Fax: (612) 758-2346
www.fallon.com

Goodby Silverstein & Partners
720 California Street
San Francisco, CA 94108
Phone: (415) 392-0669
Fax: (415) 788-4303
www.goodbysilverstein.com

Grey Group Inc.
777 Third Avenue
New York, NY 10017
Phone: (212) 537-3700
Fax: (212) 537-3533
www.greydirect.com

Havas
2 allée de Longchamp
92281 Suresnes Cedex
France
Phone: +33-1-58-47-90-00
Fax: +33-1-58-47-99-99
www.havas.com

Interpublic Group of Companies
1114 Avenue of the Americas
New York, NY 10036
Phone: (212) 704-1200
Fax: (212) 704-1201
www.interpublic.com

JWT
466 Lexington Avenue
New York, NY 10017
Phone: (212) 210-7000
Fax: (212) 210-7770
www.jwt.com

Leo Burnett Worldwide, Inc.
35 West Wacker Drive
Chicago, IL 60601
Phone: (312) 220-5959
Fax: (312) 220-3299
www.leoburnett.com

Visit Vault at www.vault.com for insider company profiles, expert advice,
career message boards, expert resume reviews, the Vault Job Board and more.

VAULT CAREER LIBRARY   109

Employer Directory, cont.

Lowe & Partners Worldwide
60 Sloane Avenue
London SW3 3XB
United Kingdom
Phone: +44-20-7584-5033
Fax: +44-20-7823-8429
www.loweworldwide.com

McCann Worldgroup
622 3rd Avenue
New York, NY 10017
Phone: (646) 865-2000
Fax: (646) 487-9610
www.mccann.com

Ogilvy & Mather Worldwide, Inc.
Worldwide Plaza
309 West 49th Street
New York, NY 10019-7399
Phone: (212) 237-4000
Fax: (212) 237-5123
www.ogilvy.com

Omnicom Group Inc.
437 Madison Avenue
New York, NY 10022
Phone: (212) 415-3600
Fax: (212) 415-3530
www.omnicomgroup.com

Publicis Groupe S.A.
133, Avenue des Champs-Elysées
75008 Paris
France
Phone: +33-1-44-43-70-00
Fax: +33-1-44-43-75-25
www.publicisgroupe.com

Saatchi & Saatchi
375 Hudson Street
New York, NY 10014
Phone: (212) 463-2000
Fax: (212) 463-9855
www.saatchi-saatchi.com

TBWA Worldwide, Inc.
488 Madison Avenue
New York, NY 10022
Phone: (212) 804-1300
Fax: (212) 804-1333
www.tbwa.com

Wieden + Kennedy
224 NW 13th Avenue
Portland, OR 97209
Phone: (503) 937-7000
Fax: (503) 937-8000
www.wk.com

WPP Group plc
27 Farm Street
London W1J 5RJ
United Kingdom
Phone: +44-20-7408-2204
Fax: +44-20-7493-6819
www.wpp.com

Young & Rubicam Brands
285 Madison Avenue
New York, NY 10017
Phone: (212) 210-3000
Fax: (212) 210-4680
www.youngandrubicam.com

Zimmerman Advertising
2200 West Commercial Boulevard, Suite 300
Fort Lauderdale, FL 33309
Phone: (954) 731-2900
Fax: (954) 731-2977
www.zadv.com

Aerospace and Defense

Industry Overview

The Wright stuff

The aerospace industry consists of companies which produce aircraft, spaceships and the jets, engines and rockets that propel them. The defense industry produces a complementary group of goods, including satellites, ships and submarines, tanks and armored vehicles, and guns, bullets, explosives and other weapons. These industries are closely allied, with companies frequently participating in both spheres.

The aerospace industry makes most of its money by supplying individuals and commercial airlines with planes for business or pleasure. The commercial airline industry is notoriously cyclical, operating at the mercy of the business cycle; factors like the price of airline tickets and terrorism (or the threat thereof) also affect the number of people who travel by air, and hence the rate at which airline companies purchase new planes.

The lucrative nature of defense contracts shouldn't be underestimated, either: the U.S. government budgeted a whopping $480 billion for defense in 2008, give or take the odd hundred million allotted for special items during the year. Since making fighter jets and cargo planes require largely similar skill sets, and defense contracts are a generally recession-proof form of revenue, many aerospace and defense companies have arms that handle both commercial and military production. Major manufacturers of engines for planes include Pratt & Whitney, a subsidiary of United Technologies, Westinghouse and GE, Rolls Royce, and Daimler-Benz, which put the "vroom" in more than just cars.

Take it to the skies

The commercial aircraft market is dominated by archrivals Boeing and Airbus, who also have interests in defense contracts—Boeing derived nearly half its revenue from government contracts in 2007, while archrival Airbus is partly owned by EADS, the European Aeronautic Defense and Space Company. Smaller players, like Textron (which owns Cessna), Embraer and Bombardier also have interests in both commercial and military aircraft and technology. Other major defense contractors include contract leader Lockheed Martin, ship- and submarine-builder Northrop Grumman, General Dynamics, Raytheon, BAE Systems and United Technologies.

Plane dealing

The biggest rivalry in the industry is between U.S.-based Boeing and European-owned Airbus. These companies are the two largest suppliers of large jets to airlines, and the summer of 2007 saw them battling it out with their newest offerings. Airbus hoped to tempt buyers from the airlines that ferry large numbers of people between major airports with its A380, a double-decker plane of Brobdingnagian proportions. It seats 500 passengers, give or take, but has been plagued by problems with its assembly and wiring, which delayed its release by two years, and drove Airbus into the red—and its customers to Boeing's offerings, like the proven 747, which seats about 400. Boeing's newest offering, the 787 Dreamliner, was introduced in July 2007, but encountered its own fleet of production setbacks and delays. (There were also problems with its flight-test program, delivery schedule and its subcontracted and outsourced elements.) It's now expected to formally debut during 2009, by different accounts either "early" in the year or at the end of the third quarter.

The 787 has been designed to transport comparatively smaller numbers of passengers—only about half as many as the A380—but its carbon-composite construction offers several advantages. The plane is lighter, and hence more fuel efficient; the construction also mean that the plane requires less maintenance and isn't as prone to metal fatigue—a boon to airlines, whose margins have been falling as customers become more savvy about comparison-shopping for tickets. The composite

Visit Vault at www.vault.com for insider company profiles, expert advice, career message boards, expert resume reviews, the Vault Job Board and more.

VAULT CAREER LIBRARY   111

structure also means passenger-pleasing features like larger windows and higher cabin pressure and humidity. As of January 2008, Boeing had received 817 orders for the new model, making the plane the fastest-selling commercial airliner ever.

A new player enters the game

Boeing and Airbus may face a third competitor, however. China is reveling in its newfound industrial might, and plans to launch its own aircraft manufacturer. China Aviation Industry Corporation (AVIC) has already produced the ARJ-21, a short-haul plane tailored to the vagaries of air travel in China that can carry about 80 people; it is scheduled to enter service in 2009. The Chinese government is loath to see its rapidly growing market for air transport—which is expected to create a demand for 1,500 planes by 2010—farmed out to foreign companies, however, and AVIC has its sights set on producing large jets for the international market.

DE-fence!

Speaking of international relations, the defense portion of the industry has been affected by a wave of large mergers, as well as other factors. The industry inked deals worth some $31 billion in 2007 (including GE's $4.8 billion acquisition of Smiths Aerospace); almost half of the 43 transactions outside the U.S. involved the BRIC countries (Brazil, Russia, India, China). During the 2008 presidential election, industry watchers waited to see the impact on aerospace. While some pundits saw a democratic president as bad for the industry, others thought that spending levels would be consistent through 2010 or so, and then funding for war-related expenditures would simply slide under the Homeland Security umbrella. Almost all the experts believe the rapid pace of industry consolidation will continue.

And aside from all that getting and spending, the defense industry has had to cope over the past few years with changes in the methods of warfare. Modern battles are unlikely to be fought on a traditional battlefield against a professional army fielded by a government, and to be more like the agonizing and protracted conflict going on in Iraq and Afghanistan. Of course, this means that enormous tanks are out—and smaller, faster and lighter equipment is in. Automation is also a growing trend. Machines, unlike humans, never need to sleep or eat, are always paying attention and can be easily repaired or replaced in the event they are damaged.

Industry innovations show up in a variety of different guises. In 2007, Honeywell's MAV (Micro Air Vehicle) was sent to Iraq in order to help troops identify and defuse bombs and other threats. The device, which is about the size of a breadbox, consists of a fan in a cylindrical housing (which provides lift) as well as a small payload of wireless cameras and other sensors. The MAV can hover inches above a suspected bomb, allowing it to be more closely examined, or climb to about 10,000 feet for surveillance of a larger area. Remotely operated sensors are also the latest trend in border surveillance. Also in 2007, Boeing set up its first 27-mile stretch of monitored border between the U.S. and Mexico. Aimed at preventing smuggling and illegal immigration, the border security consists of a series of towers outfitted with radar, cameras, loudspeakers and data links. The towers are tall enough to see over trees and other obstacles, and allow rangers to monitor the movements of people as far away as several miles.

Spatial relations

Then, of course, there's space, the final frontier, which is soon to become as crammed with tourists as Times Square the weekend before Christmas. After Richard Branson, scion of the Virgin Group, announced that he would be offering space tours via Virgin Galactic in 2004, EADS Astrium, the space wing of the European defense giant, announced in 2007 that it would be offering 1.5 minute stints in a weightless environment on a space ship for €200,000. The spacecraft, which has yet to be built, would take off like an ordinary jet before lighting its rocket.

More prosaically, most effort in the space division of aerospace is devoted to the design, launching and maintenance of satellites for GPS devices, communications, weather prediction and research, and television and radio broadcast. Specialized leaders in this field include Alcatel Space, Astrium, Orbital Sciences and Arianespace, a division of EADS. Government and military demand for satellite bandwidth is expected to quadruple in the next decade—and, as such, companies in this group (which can't seem to launch satellites fast enough) have been attaching their tech to civilian birds. Major aerospace and defense companies continue to build space activities into their long-term investment plans, even though shooting for the stars won't turn cash flow positive in any time frame outside of a science fiction novel.

Working in the Indusry

Who, how, and how many

According to the AIA (Aerospace Industries Association), as of 2008, about 650,000 people were employed in the aerospace industry, and about two-thirds of those jobs were in aircraft and parts manufacturing. According to the Bureau of Labor Statistics, the industry has a higher-than-average number of people with advanced degrees in subjects like mechanical and electrical engineering. Besides engineers, defense industry employers are perennially seeking employees with security clearances. In order to obtain one, an employee must be a U.S. citizen, submit to a thorough investigation of his background, and be sponsored, either by a corporation or the government.

Giving the kids their wings

Companies are trying to recruit the latest crop of young'uns, as a quarter of their workforce will be retirement-ready by 2010. In order to woo their newest hires, major aerospace firms like Boeing and Lockheed Martin are getting all Web 2.0. Boeing lured in potential job seekers with the promise of a shot at winning an iPod, as well as sponsoring a Facebook group for former interns. Lockheed, on the other hand, allows potential job seekers to IM recruiters, while Rolls Royce's engine department instituted a fast-track management program that will promote new hires into management positions after a few years.

Roger, niner

So you've electronically networked your way into an interview. Now what? Insiders report that questions include behavioral questions—"Tell me about a time when you were working in a group and something when wrong. What went wrong? What was your role in the situation? What was the outcome?" Some engineers likewise report they're being given technical questions to test their expertise: "Have you ever had to resolve a complex technical challenge without all of the necessary information? If so, how did you find out what you needed to know?" Companies can give as little as one interview, or as many as three and these vary from an informal chat on the phone with a recruiter to a panel interview. Another common question relates to the interviewee's eligibility for security clearance, a necessary attribute when working in many defense sectors. Only U.S. citizens can be granted security clearances, and must submit to having their backgrounds thoroughly searched in order to obtain it.

Looking up

In the long term, both the aerospace and defense industries are poised to grow. Worldwide, passenger air traffic is forecast to increase by 5 percent a year through 2027 to 9 billion passengers—well over twice the number that fly the skies today, and someone's got to build all those planes. Growth in this sector might be depressed by lower consumer spending, brought about by rising prices, in the U.S. or Europe (which still account for the majority of airline customers), but it will be tempered by expansion in Asia.

Visit Vault at www.vault.com for insider company profiles, expert advice, career message boards, expert resume reviews, the Vault Job Board and more.

VAULT CAREER LIBRARY 113

In addition, with the debacles in Afghanistan and Iraq, not to mention the increase in religious fanaticism in general, terrorism is a continuing concern, so the defense industry looks as if it's got its hands full for the time being. The U.S. defense budget is up about 60 percent over its 2001 levels, and politicians are unlikely to reduce it lest they appear to be neglecting domestic security.

Employer Directory

AAR Corp.
1100 North Wood Dale Road
Wood Dale, IL 60191
Phone: (630) 227-2000
Fax: (630) 227-2039
Toll free: (800) 422-2213
www.aarcorp.com

Alliant Techsystems Inc.
7480 Flying Cloud Drive
Minneapolis, MN 55344
Phone: (952) 351-3000
Fax: (952) 351-3009
www.atk.com

BAE Systems
6 Carlton Gardens
London, SW1Y 5AD
United Kingdom
Phone: +44-12-52-37-32-32
Fax: +44-12-52-38-30-00
www.baesystems.com

Ball Aerospace & Technologies Corporation
1600 Commerce Street
Boulder, CO 80301
Phone: (303) 939-4000
Fax: (303) 939-5100
www.ballaerospace.com

The Boeing Company
100 North Riverside Plaza
Chicago, IL 60606
Phone: (312) 544-2000
Fax: (312) 544-2082
www.boeing.com

C&D Zodiac, Inc.
5701 Bolsa Avenue
Huntington Beach, CA 92647
Phone: (714) 934-0000
Fax: (714) 934-0088
www.cdzodiac.com

Cessna Aircraft Company
I Cessna Boulevard
Wichita, KS 67215
Phone: (316) 517-6000
Fax: (316) 517-5669
Toll free: (800) 423-7762
www.cessna.com

Cubic Corporation
9333 Balboa Avenue
San Diego, CA 92123
Phone: (858) 277-6780
Fax: (858) 277-1878
www.cubic.com

Curtiss-Wright Corporation
4 Becker Farm Road, 3rd Floor
Roseland, NJ 07068
Phone: (973) 597-4700
Fax: (973) 597-4799
www.curtisswright.com

DRS Technologies, Inc.
5 Sylvan Way
Parsippany, NJ 07054
Phone: (973) 898-1500
Fax: (973) 898-4730

DynCorp International Inc.
3190 Fairview Park Drive, Suite 700
Falls Church, VA 22042
Phone: (571) 722-0210
Fax: (571) 722-0252
www.dyn-intl.com

Esterline Technologies Corporation
City Center Bellevue
500 108th Avenue NE, Suite 1500
Bellevue, WA 98004
Phone: (425) 453-9400
Fax: (425) 453-2916
www.esterline.com

GenCorp, Inc.
Highway 50 and Aerojet Road
Rancho Cordova, CA 95742
Phone: (916) 355-4000
Fax: (916) 351-8668
www.gencorp.com

General Dynamics Corporation
2941 Fairview Park Drive, Suite 100
Falls Church, VA 22042-4513
Phone: (703) 876-3000
Fax: (703) 876-3125
www.gendyn.com

General Electric Company
3135 Easton Turnpike
Fairfield, CT 06828-0001
Phone: (203) 373-2211
Fax: (203) 373-3131
www.ge.com

Goodrich Corporation
4 Coliseum Centre
2730 West Tyvola Road
Charlotte, NC 28217
Phone: (704) 423-7000
Fax: (704) 423-5540
www.goodrich.com

Hamilton Sundstrand Corporation
1 Hamilton Road
Windsor Locks, CT 06095
Phone: (860) 654-6000
www.hamiltonsundstrand.com

Honeywell International Inc.
101 Columbia Road
Morristown, NJ 07962
Phone: (973) 455-2000
Fax: (973) 455-4807
Toll-Free: (800) 601-3099
www.honeywell.com

ITT Corporation
4 West Oak Lane
White Plains, NY 10604
Phone: (914) 641-2000
Fax: (914) 696-2950
www.itt.com

Jacobs Technology Inc.
600 William Northern Boulevard
Tullahoma, TN 37388
Phone: (931) 455-6400
Fax: (931) 393-6389
www.jacobstechnology.com

Visit Vault at **www.vault.com** for insider company profiles, expert advice, career message boards, expert resume reviews, the Vault Job Board and more.

VAULT CAREER LIBRARY   115

Employer Directory, cont.

L-3 Communications Holdings
600 3rd Avenue
New York, NY 10016
Phone: (212) 697-1111
Fax: (212) 805-5477
www.L-3Com.com

Lockheed Martin
6801 Rockledge Drive
Bethesda, MD 20817-1877
Phone: (301) 897-6000
Fax: (301) 897-6704
www.lockheedmartin.com

Moog Inc.
Plant 4, Jamison Road
East Aurora, NY 14052
Phone: (716) 687-4567
Fax: (716) 687-5969
www.moog.com

Northrop Grumman Corporation
1840 Century Park East
Los Angeles, CA 90067-2199
Phone: (310) 553-6262
Fax: (310) 553-2076
www.northropgrumman.com

Orbital Sciences Corporation
21839 Atlantic Boulevard
Dulles, VA 20166
Phone: (703) 406-5000
Fax: (703) 406-3502
www.orbital.com

Parker Hannifin Corporation
6035 Parkland Boulevard
Cleveland, OH 44124-4141
Phone: (216) 896-3000
Fax: (216) 896-4000
www.parker.com

Pratt & Whitney
400 Main Street
East Hartford, CT 06108
Phone: (860) 565-4321
Fax: (860) 565 5442
www.pratt-whitney.com

Raytheon Company
870 Winter Street
Waltham, MA 02451-1449
Phone: (781) 522-3000
Fax: (781) 522-3001
www.raytheon.com

Rockwell Collins, Inc.
400 Collins Road NE
Cedar Rapids, IA 52498
Phone: (319) 295-1000
Fax: (319) 295-1523
www.rockwellcollins.com

Rolls-Royce Corporation
2001 South Tibbs Avenue
Indianapolis, TN 46206
Phone: (317) 230-2000
Fax: (317) 230-4020
www.rolls-royce.com

Sequa Corporation
200 Park Avenue
New York, NY 10166
Phone: (212) 986-5500
Fax: (212) 370-1969
www.sequa.com

Teledyne Technologies Incorporated
1049 Camino Dos Rios
Thousand Oaks, CA 91360
Phone: (805) 373-4545
Fax: (805) 373-4775
www.teledyne.com

Textron Inc.
40 Westminster Street
Providence, RI 02903-2596
Phone: (401) 421-2800
Fax: (401) 457-2220
www.textron.com

Triumph Group, Inc.
1550 Liberty Ridge Drive, Suite 100
Wayne, PA 19087
Phone: (610) 251-1000
Fax: (610) 251-1555
www.triumphgroup.com

United Space Alliance
1150 Gemini Street
Houston, TX 77058
Phone: (281) 212-6200
Fax: (281) 212-6177
www.unitedspacellliance.com

United Technologies Corporation
1 Financial Plaza
Hartford, CT 06103
Phone: (860) 728-7000
Fax: (860) 565-5400
www.utc.com

Wyman-Gordon Company
16801 Greenspoint Park Drive
Suite 355
Houston, TX 77060
Phone: (281) 856-9900
Fax: (281) 856-3601
www.wyman-gordon.com

Agriculture

Industry Overview

Feed me

The agriculture industry's broad scope includes everyone from farmers and ranchers to scientists who devise new and better foods and the businesspeople who keep it all running. The various disciplines within the industry seek ways to more efficiently feed Earth's ever-growing population while improving profit margins for food-related businesses. Allied industries provide the infrastructure that makes this possible, including rail and road transportation, pesticides and fertilizers, and processors that transform raw products into comestibles.

Looking at the numbers, the agriculture industry is a massive undertaking. In 2008, more than 87 million acres of land—an area slightly larger than that of Germany—were devoted to planting corn, with wheat production taking up 60 million acres and soybeans another 75 million acres. Soybean production is up 17 percent over 2007's harvest, while corn production is down nearly 10 percent, which will still produce the second-largest harvest in U.S. history (the largest crop was produced in 2007, the largest since 1944). To feed the protein-ravenous masses, more than 100,000 cattle and 378,000 hogs are slaughtered every day in the U.S. Agriculture's not just about edibles, though; rather it covers everything that is grown or raised for consumption. Cotton and wool are agricultural products, as are animal byproducts, ornamental plants, tobacco, lumber and the various fruits and grains used to produce alcohol. The industry, unsurprisingly, is huge, accounting for 1 percent of U.S. gross domestic product (GDP). That might seem like small potatoes, but 1 percent of the 2007 GDP—$13,843,825,000,000, according to the International Monetary Fund—is a hefty chunk of change.

The farmer's dilemma

Despite its significant contribution to the GDP, agriculture is very risky and often unprofitable. Profit margins, especially for crops such as soybeans, wheat and corn, are very low, so these plants are frequently grown on large, industrial farms, as tiny returns per acre make small-scale farming economically unfeasible. Fruits and vegetables offer higher returns on lower acreage, but the investment in plants, soil preparation and the necessary labor-intensive harvesting makes the likelihood of farmers breaking even in the first few years unlikely.

Farmers are also at the mercy of pests, plant diseases and weather, the king of all X-factors. While insecticides and pest- and disease-resistant strains of plants can mitigate these risks, they of course cannot be entirely controlled. Heat, drought, flooding, storms and other "acts of God" wreak havoc on yields and, in extreme circumstances, can even lead to famine. The weather doesn't even have to be especially dramatic to drive up prices: the per-bushel cost of 2006 corn went gone up 28 percent, a two-year high, due to a hot, dry spell in the Midwest in July of that year. The flooding of during the summer of 2008 destroyed about 10 percent of the harvest.

Further complicating matters is the fact that commodities such as corn, soybeans, and wheat are subject to market forces. To wit: a good harvest suppresses the price of a commodity and lowers profits, while a poor one raises prices but causes shortages. This inverse relationship between productivity and profit has plagued agribusiness for decades. Government subsidies for corn, wheat, milk, cotton and a number of other farm products also affect the equation. Designed to hedge risks and lessen farmers' financial burden, these subsidies keep agricultural commodity prices artificially low in domestic markets and around the world.

All of the issues detailed above have forced the consolidation of farms and processing firms. Today, the real players in the industry are all big companies such as Cargill, Archer Daniels Midland, Tyson, Perdue, Bunge and Pilgrim's Pride. ConAgra, at one time a major farming firm, is currently divesting its agricultural business to focus on branded and value-added

Visit Vault at **www.vault.com** for insider company profiles, expert advice, career message boards, expert resume reviews, the Vault Job Board and more.

VAULT CAREER LIBRARY 117

packaged foods. Meanwhile, Bayer, Dow and DuPont all have a stake in biotech, fungicides and pesticides, each with its own crop sciences division. Monsanto, meanwhile, is a leader in the genetic engineering field.

Little. Yellow. Different.

When you think of corn, what initially comes to mind is probably something edible: creamy corn on the cob dripping with golden butter, or crisp, salty corn chips or sweet sodas. It's unlikely that you would consider postage stamps, aspirin or imitation silk, but all of these goods are manufactured using corn byproducts. Archer Daniels Midland is one of the largest agricultural processors in the world, turning oilseeds (like soybeans), corn, wheat and nuts into food products like flour, sweeteners and emulsifiers, as well as plant-derived wood preservatives, industrial starches (which become everything from wallboard to glue) and ethanol. Bunge is the world's largest processor of oilseeds, turning them into such products as biofuels, livestock meal and mayonnaise, while Cargill is a highly diversified agricultural products processor, making such items as soy waxes, vitamins, pharmaceutical coatings, flavoring agents, dairy and meat products.

Fueling a greener future

Demand for biofuel has made the past few years a boom time for corn producers like Archer Daniels Midland. Ethanol—the alcohol-based fuel produced from fermenting corn, beets, wheat, or any other sugar-bearing feedstock—has quickly become the poster child for America's solution to gas shortages and the greenhouse effect. Mixed with gasoline to create E85 (85 percent ethanol, 15 percent gasoline), ethanol promises to replace America's reliance on foreign oil with a renewable, homegrown resource. The flurry of activity around the hot new fuel has caused corn prices to spike and corn production to swell—farmers planted 92.9 million acres of corn in 2007, a high not reached since 1944, when 95.5 million acres of corn were planted to supply depleted allies in Europe.

Another biofuel seeing growth is biodiesel, which can be produced from vegetable oils, animal fat and even leftover, artery-clogging grease used in restaurants. In its purest form, biodiesel releases 75 percent less carbon dioxide than petroleum diesel. Additionally, there's no conversion or new technology involved to scare off new consumers—as long as it runs on diesel, it'll run on biodiesel. The growing popularity of biodiesel has increased demand for soybeans (whose oil is commonly used for biodiesel), as production of the fuel tripled from 2004 to 2005 and doubled between 2006 and 2007; about 900 million gallons are produced annually.

Bean there, done that

Biodiesel aside, soybeans have taken a bit of a beating as of late, due to the sudden and resounding condemnation of trans fats in American foods. The process of hydrogenation that soybean oil undergoes to lengthen its shelf-life (and that of the products it's used in, including some brands of crackers, cookies and fish sticks) produces the much-loathed trans fats, which are believed to clog arteries and raise cholesterol levels when consumed in excess. Fast food restaurants and junk food manufacturers are cutting trans fats out of their products in response to growing consumer concern and outright bans—like New York's December 2006 decision to cut trans fats from its restaurants. Soybean farmers are being pressured to grow beans low in linolenic acid (a substance that causes soybean oil to go rancid), thereby eliminating the need for hydrogenation while keeping the soybean oil flavor intact. However, the conversion to low-linolenic soybeans isn't far enough along to replace the traditional, high-linolenic beans, although production of the coveted bean is expected to triple in 2008.

Not exactly American Pastoral

You're in for a shock if "agriculture" brings to mind amber waves of grain and fruited plains. Rather, agribusiness is as tech-focused and cutting-edge as every other industry these days. Steroids, hormones and antibiotics, for example, are routinely administered to U.S. meat and dairy animals. Steroids up the rate at which meat animals transform feed into muscle, while hormones, when administered through slow-release pellets implanted in the animal's ear, cause it to gain weight and, in cows, improve milk production. Hormones are also applied to fruits and vegetables. In order to ship fruit long distances, it must be picked before it is fully ripe to withstand the journey. Once it reaches its destination, it is treated with ethylene, the chemical which, in nature, causes fruits to ripen.

Antibiotics are given to animals to cure illnesses—a frequent occurrence when stock is kept in close conditions and fed an unnatural diet. Modern poultry flocks, for instance, are so large that sick animals frequently cannot be isolated, so producers treat all the birds that may have come into contact with the infected individual by adding antibiotics to the animals' drinking water. Feed lot-fattened, corn-fed cattle must be given antibiotics too; the feedlot diet of corn can distress their digestive tracts and lead to fatal infections. Antibiotics are more widely used in subtherapeutic doses, or doses not large enough to cure an infection, a practice that encourages the proliferation of antibiotic-resistant bacteria (much as with a human who takes antibiotics at the first sign of every sniffle). Without competition, resistant bacteria can spread rapidly throughout a population and subsequently be transferred to people who eat raw or undercooked meat.

Begun, this clone war has

Beyond antibiotics and hormones, recent biotech advances have become major issues in the agriculture industry. While farmers have been selecting crops for higher yield, greater disease resistance, better flavor and other desirable qualities for the last 12,000-odd years, we are now able to manipulate individual genes in order to express specific traits. Genetic engineering has produced Golden Rice, designed to accumulate vitamin A in the edible portion of the grain, a boon for cultures where rice is the staple crop and a varied diet is often a luxury. Insufficient quantities of vitamin A can cause blindness and even death in children.

Researchers are looking into growing oral vaccines for hepatitis B and HIV in tomatoes, potatoes and even tobacco. Embedding drugs in plants promises a less expensive method than traditional vaccine production, which would make large-scale vaccination of the populations of poorer countries possible. Genetic tinkering has produced plants such as Monsanto's Roundup Ready corn, canola, soybeans and cotton, and Bayer CropScience's Liberty Link corn, which are, respectively, resistant to the proprietary herbicides Roundup and Liberty. Today, nearly all soy and half of the corn grown in the U.S. is genetically modified, as is 75 percent of cotton.

Scientists are also beginning to explore these methods for use on animals, seeking to increase egg and milk production, change fat content and speed maturity. Genetically modified varieties of catfish and tilapia, designed to grow faster, are already for sale in some countries, while bulls are being cloned in order to improve the breeding stock of cattle. Pet fish implanted with genes that produce luminescent proteins have been available for purchase since 2003.

However, such tinkering has spawned a number of advocacy groups that fear unforeseen consequences. Many groups argue that direct genetic manipulation could produce harmful side effects that simple hybridization and crossbreeding would not, while others warn that herbicide residue might remain in the tissues of resistant plant varieties, or that engineered genes might cross into wild plant populations. Environmental advocacy groups won a small victory in March 2007, when a federal judge halted the planting of Monsanto's Roundup Ready alfalfa, on the grounds that the plant had not undergone complete environmental impact testing before its 2005 release. The debate rages on, on a global scale: Mexico barred biotech companies from planting genetically-modified corn within its borders in October 2006. That same month, Japan increased its testing of rice imported from the U.S., sniffing out unapproved genetically modified rice in the 1.1 million tons of short- and medium-grain rice in its warehouses.

Visit Vault at **www.vault.com** for insider company profiles, expert advice, career message boards, expert resume reviews, the Vault Job Board and more.

VAULT CAREER LIBRARY 119

The organic green giant

Consumers, motivated by concerns about the above, as well as factory farming, animal cruelty and the health of the environment, are increasingly demanding organic, ethically-treated, free-range, and antibiotic- and hormone-free food products. And apparently they are willing to pay the premium price: according to the Organic Trade Association, Americans spent $17 billion on organic products in 2006, an increase of 22 percent over 2005. That year, organics accounted for 2.5 percent of all retail foods sold.

Many businesses are taking advantage of this surge in organic interest. The supermarket chain Whole Foods, one of the more popular purveyors of organic produce, has the highest profit margin per square foot of any grocery store. At the other end of the spectrum, Wal-Mart began offering organic products in 2006. While such produce's widespread availability will certainly have tangible benefits for the environment and for customers, there are some drawbacks. Faced with price competition, retailers will inevitably demand lower prices from organic farmers, which could put them out of business. In addition, though organic produce can be sourced from foreign countries—China, for instance—regulations stipulating what "organic" means are certain to differ from country to country, or could even be absent altogether.

You just can't get good help these days...

Despite the increasing reliance on machinery to do the grunt work of the agriculture industry, there are still some jobs that require that human touch. Unskilled migrant and immigrant laborers have provided this necessary muscle power for relatively low pay for decades, often filling positions that more prosperous Americans don't want. However, as the sanctity of the nation's borders has come to the fore in this era of homeland security, the agriculture industry has struggled to find and keep cheap labor. In December 2006, immigration raids at Swift & Company's meat processing plants (Swift is the third-largest meatpacker in the nation, behind Cargill and Tyson Foods) netted more than 1,200 illegal immigrants—the replacement of which, coupled with lost production, cost the company $45 million. A solution to the problem remains elusive; an immigration bill that would give illegal immigrants a chance to obtain legal status was defeated in the Senate in June 2007, making meatpackers and farmers worry about increased raids and dwindling applicants.

Picking up the bill

Every so often Uncle Sam takes a look at the current policies aimed at aiding the agriculture industry in the form of the highly contentious Farm Bill. In terms of controversy, the 2008 incarnation (also known as the Food, Conservation and Energy Act of 2008) lived up to expectations, only becoming law when Congress overturned a Presidential veto of the bill. In many ways, the Farm Bill provides a snapshot of how politics work in Washington, pitting special interest groups and lobbyists against legislators (and one another), as each attempts to get the best possible deal out of the legislation. And, although easily ignored, the decisions of what to include within the bill have serious ramifications not only in the U.S., but all around the world. This is only exacerbated by the fact that the provisions of the bill shape the ag-industry for years to come; the 2008 bill, for example, will be in effect until 2013 (and possibly longer, given the length of time it can take to pass such a gargantuan piece of legislation).

One of the most controversial issues at stake in the 2008 bill was that of farm subsidies. Given the bumper crop prices being reaped by farmers due to record food prices and an ever-increasing demand for biofuel crops, there was a substantial body of feeling that farm subsidies should be cut, both to ease the cost for the U.S. taxpayer, and to encourage free trade around the globe. When the bill was passed by Congress, however, the subsidies were included within it, and even increased in some cases. The reasons for that are several-fold, and include a desire to keep agricultural jobs within the U.S., as well as security concerns, and the influence of lobbyists.

One example of how government subsidies affect the U.S. is in the ubiquity of junk food, much of which has ingredient lists that are heavily based on wheat, soybeans, corn, and corn-derived sugars and fats. All of those crops are subsidized by the

Government, making them less expensive to grow, meaning that they'll pop up more often in the American diet than non-subsidized crops.

Another bone of contention in the battle over the farm bill had to do with the influx of imported food. According to The New York Times, the U.S. is importing $65 billion in food a year, or double the amount it imported ten years ago. Consumer groups want clear labeling on imported food, arguing that Joe American has a right to know if the beef on his plate was slaughtered on foreign soil. Opponents (namely, the meat lobby) say that the cost of such labeling would overburden the industry, and have successfully limited such labeling to seafood despite 2002 legislation requiring country-of-origin labeling on meat, produce and nuts. However, in light of recent scares regarding imported foods—including the massive pet food recall in March 2007 due to tainted wheat gluten from China, and the subsequent closing of 180 Chinese food plants in June after a nationwide inspection—those calling for enforced labeling of imported food found more sympathetic ears in Congress, and a provision was included in the bill to place the country of origin on all meats, produce and certain types of nut.

Other provisions in the bill, meanwhile, included extensions to the food stamps program, and a pilot food aid program that involves buying locally-sourced food overseas to donate to poor countries rather than shipping American crops. On the "green" side, the bill included extra funding for research in organic farming, and the establishment of incentives and grants to encourage farms to increase energy efficiency and put renewable energy systems in place.

That wasn't the only eco-friendly piece of legislation, though. The bill also contained a raft of measures—including grants, subsidies and loan guarantees—for driving the biofuel industry forward. A significant amount of money was set aside for research and production of advanced biofuels (i.e. non-corn-based biofuels).

While the bill caused controversy within the U.S., the drubbing it received abroad was perhaps even more significant. Criticized as being anti-free trade, the bill has met a significant amount of opposition from foreign leaders who complain that it takes global agricultural policy in the wrong direction. The problem? Subsidies (surprise!), which allow U.S. products a price advantage in the marketplace, disadvantaging poorer countries.

From farmhand to finance

An enormous range of man- and womanpower is required to keep the culture of agri- humming along. The agriculture industry is exceptionally diverse when you consider the number of different segments it encompasses. Operations include fish hatcheries, apple orchards, flower nurseries, slaughterhouses and more. Farm workers (who account for 90 percent of industry employees) require minimal training, but the Bureau of Labor Statistics (BLS) expects that more efficient machinery will reduce the number of such jobs in the future. However, small-scale farming, especially of the organic variety, is expected to grow. Managers, meanwhile, include farm and ranch owners, as well as those who operate ripening facilities or cold storage. Agricultural graders sort products, such as fruits and eggs, and inspectors evaluate the cleanliness of processing facilities. These professionals generally require both an agriculture degree and a background in the field.

The agriculture industry has plenty of opportunities for those who want to avoid getting their hands dirty, as well. Commodities merchants are needed to buy and sell grain, cocoa and other articles of commerce to ensure a consistent supply. Ecologists consult for the farming world as consumers and the government grew more concerned about the environmental impact of factory farming on the land and ecosystems. Agronomists (researchers in the many disciplines involving agriculture) start at the bachelor degree level, and many have doctorates to perform "pure" research. Logistics experts get the stuff from where it is to where it's going, while veterinarians keep the livestock healthy (until its time to kill it). Along with the usual jobs in HR, sales and IT, lawyers and MBAs are needed to keep good business practices and make sure everyone plays by the rules.

Although agriculture has been around since, oh, say, the dawn of modern man, the industry is constantly trolling for advanced technologies and the scientists who create them. Chemists come up with coloring and flavoring agents and new uses for agricultural byproducts. Agricultural scientists devise new food-processing methods, study soil and animal management and

Visit Vault at www.vault.com for insider company profiles, expert advice, career message boards, expert resume reviews, the Vault Job Board and more.

VAULT CAREER LIBRARY 121

frequently consult for the government or food processing companies. Bioengineers tweak genetic codes to create herbicide-resistant plants, Mexican jumping beans that can do the Lindy hop, or whatever other special function is required of an organism. Agricultural engineers design farm equipment for increased efficiency and reduced environmental impact. Depending on the career path they wish to pursue, these people generally have advanced degrees. The BLS reports that the agricultural scientist and engineer industries, specifically, are expected to grow by 14 percent between 2004 and 2014.

Vault Q&A: Bettye Hill, Archer Daniels Midland Company (ADM)

As director of compliance in employment in the office of compliance and ethics at Archer Daniels Midland Company (ADM), Bettye Hill is responsible for ensuring that the agriculture leader is compliant with a wide variety of standards when it comes to employment. The owner of a bachelor's degree with a concentration in management from Southwest Texas State in San Marcos, Hill collected a wide variety of educational and career experience before arriving at ADM. Her educational background includes an MBA, a JD and an LLM; her career path has been similarly wide-ranging, and includes HR positions in the insurance and grocery industries, as well as running her own private law practice. She took some time out to speak with Vault about her current position.

Vault: Can you explain what your office's main responsibilities are?

Hill: The office of compliance and ethics oversees ADM's operations and employees to ensure that as a company we act with integrity. We perform compliance audits and also investigate complaints. Some of the compliance issues we look at could very well be things that are regulated—that is, legal regulations—but they're also best practices, too.

We also develop policies and guidelines, implement and review training programs and interact with government entities on government inquiries, for example, the Department of Labor. We manage the affirmative action plans of the company.

We also interact with ADM locations outside the United States to ensure that we're compliant with the labor laws for those particular countries.

There's also government-required reporting that we make sure we file (for example, the EEO-1 report), which is a required report related to equal opportunity.

Vault: Of your many degrees, which do you think is most relevant to your current position?

Hill: Obviously the bachelor's degree is necessary without any others. I am able to utilize my MBA and law degree in this position.

Vault: In what way do you use your MBA?

Hill: I would say it provides me with the ability to make decisions from a much broader business perspective because it enhances my critical and strategic thinking. This comes into play with strategic long-term planning—looking at what strategic processes you have to have in place to get the desired end result. The MBA gives me the skills I need to align what I am doing to the business objectives of the company.

Vault: Can you give me an example of what this means on a day-to-day basis?

Hill: Let's take as an example training needs. We would make an assessment of what those needs are, then we would determine how best to provide the training that is needed.

That includes all the business considerations that are required when providing the training, including frequency, and how the training would be provided—by this, I mean the medium—the cost of the training, and which people will receive it. All of this has to be determined once you identify the need.

Vault: And how would you say your law degree comes into play?

Hill: We certainly assist management with questions they may have on employment, such as the Fair Labor Standards Act, FMLA and so on. We deal with employment law every day.

Vault: Having worked in a variety of industries, how would you say working in the agriculture industry compares?

Hill: It's an industry you can be proud to be a part of. You know it's an industry that deals with the necessities of life, food, feed, fuel and industrial products. I think it's a great industry from that standpoint.

Vault: How would you characterize the corporate culture at ADM?

Hill: I think at ADM you have an opportunity to work with colleagues that are bright, definitely driven and committed to ADM's continued success.

Visit Vault at **www.vault.com** for insider company profiles, expert advice, career message boards, expert resume reviews, the Vault Job Board and more.

V/\ULT CAREER LIBRARY   **123**

Employer Directory

A. Duda & Sons, Inc
1200 Duda Terrace
Oviedo, FL 32765
Phone: (407) 365-2111
Fax: (407) 365-2010
www.duda.com

ADM Alliance Nutrition, Inc.
1000 North 30th Street
Quincy, IL 62301
Phone: (217) 222-7100
Fax: (217) 222-4069
www.admani.com

Ag Processing Inc
12700 West Dodge Road
Omaha, NE 68154
Phone: (402) 496-7809
Fax: (402) 498-2215
Toll free: (800) 247-1345
www.agp.com

Agri Beef Co.
1555 Shoreline Drive, 3rd Floor
Boise, ID 83702
Phone: (208) 338-2500
Fax: (208) 338-2605
Toll free: (800) 657-6305
www.agribeef.com

**Alabama Farmers
Cooperative, Inc.**
121 Somerville Road SE
Decatur, AL 35601
Phone: (256) 353-6843
Fax: (256) 350-1770
www.alafarm.com

The Andersons, Inc.
480 West Dussel Drive
Maumee, OH 43537
Phone: (419) 893-5050
Fax: (419) 891-6670
www.andersonsinc.com

**Archer Daniels Midland
Company (ADM)**
4666 Faries Parkway
P.O. Box 1470
Decatur, IL 62525
Phone: (217) 424-5200
Fax: (217) 424-6196
Toll free: (800) 637-5843
www.admworld.com

Associated British Foods plc
Weston Centre
10 Grosvenor Street
London, W1K 4QY
United Kingdom
Phone: +44-20-7399-6500
Fax: +44-20-7399-6580
www.abf.co.uk

Blue Diamond Growers
1802 C Street
Sacramento, CA 95814
Phone: (916) 442-0771
Fax: (916) 446-8461
www.bluediamond.com

Bunge Limited
2 Church Street
Hamilton, HM 11
Bermuda
Phone: (914) 684-2800
Fax: (914) 684-3497
www.bunge.com

Cargill
15407 McGinty Road West
Wayzata, MN 55391
Phone: (952) 742-7575
Fax: (952) 742-7393
Toll free: (800) 227-4455
www.cargill.com

**Chiquita Brands, International,
Inc.**
250 East 5th Street
Cincinnati, OH 45202
Phone: (513) 784-8000
Fax: (513) 784-8030
www.chiquita.com

CHS Inc.
5500 Cenex Drive
Inver Grove Heights, MN 55077
Phone: (651) 355-6000
www.chsinc.com

ConAgra Foods, Inc.
1 ConAgra Drive
Omaha, NE 68102-5001
Phone: (402) 595-4000
Fax: (402) 595-4707
www.conagra.com

**Corn Products International,
Inc.**
5 Westbrook Corporate Center
Westchester, IL 60154
Phone: (708) 551-2600
Fax: (708) 551-2570
Toll free: (800) 443-2746
www.cornproducts.com

D'Arrigo Bros. Company
383 West Market Street
Salinas, CA 93908
Phone: (831) 424-3955
Fax: (831) 424-3136
www.andyboy.com

Dunavant Enterprises, Inc.
3797 New Getwell Road
Memphis, TN 38118
Phone: (901) 369-1500
Fax: (901) 369-1608
www.dunavant.com

Golden Peanut Company, LLC
100 North Point Center East, Suite 400
Alpharetta, GA 30022
Phone: (770) 752-8205
Fax: (770) 752-8306
www.goldenpeanut.com

Griffin Industries, Inc.
4221 Alexandria Pike
Cold Spring, KY 41076
Phone: (859) 781-2010
Fax: (859) 572-2575
www.giffinind.com

Employer Directory, cont.

J.G. Boswell Company
101 West Walnut Street
Pasadena, CA 91103
Phone: (626) 583-3000
Fax: (626) 583-3090
www.jgbowelltomato.com

Iowa Turkey Growers Cooperative
207 West 2nd Street
West Liberty, IA 52776
Phone: (319) 627-2126
Fax: (319) 627-6334
Toll free: (888) 511-4500

Land O'Lakes Purina Feed LLC
1080 County Road
Shoreview, MN 55126
Phone: (651) 481-2222
www.lolfeed.com

MFA Incorporated
201 Ray Young Drive
Columbia, MO 65201
Phone: (573) 874-5111
Fax: (573) 876-5430
www.mfaincorporated.com

Monsanto Company
800 North Lindbergh Boulevard
St. Louis, MO 63167
Phone: (314) 694-1000
Fax: (314) 694-8394
www.monsanto.com

Murdock Holding Company
10900 Wilshire Boulevard, Suite 1600
Wayzata, MN 55391
Phone: (952) 742-7575
Fax: (952) 742-7393
Toll free: (800) 227-4455

Murphy-Brown LLC
2822 Highway 24 West
Warsaw, NC 28398
Phone: (910) 293-3434
Fax: (910) 289-6400
www.murphybrownllc.com

National Grape Cooperative Association, Inc.
2 South Portage Street
Westfield, NY 14787
Phone: (716) 326-5200
Fax: (716) 326-5494
www.nationalgrape.com

Orscheln Farm and Home LLC
101 West Coates Street
Moberly, MO 65270
Phone: (660) 263-4335
Fax: (660) 269-3500
www.orscheln.com

Perdue Farms Incorporated
31149 Old Ocean City Road
Salisbury, MD 21804
Phone: (410) 543-3000
Fax: (410) 543-3292
Toll free: (800) 473-7383
www.perdue.com

Pilgrim's Pride Corporation
4845 U.S. Highway 271 North
Pittsburg, TX 75686-0093
Phone: (903) 855-1000
Fax: (903) 856-7505
www.pilgrimspride.com

Pioneer Hi-Bred International, Inc.
7100 NW 62nd Avenue
Johnston, IA 50131
Phone: (515) 270-3200
Fax: (515) 334-4515
Toll free: (800) 247-6803
www.pioneer.com

Smithfield Foods, Inc.
200 Commerce Street
Smithfield, VA 23430
Phone: (757) 365-3000
Fax: (757) 365-3017
www.smithfieldfoods.com

Southern States Cooperative, Incorporated
6606 West Broad Street
Richmond, VA 23230
Phone: (804) 281-1000
Fax: (804) 281-1413
www.southernstates.com

Sun World International, LLC
16350 Driver Road
Bakersfield, CA 93308
Phone: (661) 392-5000
Fax: (661) 392-5092
www.sun-world.com

Syngenta Corporation
2200 Concord Pike
Wilmington, DE 19803
Phone: (302) 425-2000
Fax: (302) 425-2001
www.syngenta.com

Tyson Foods, Inc.
2210 West Oaklawn Drive
Springdale, AR 72762-6999
Phone: (479) 290-4000
Fax: (479) 290-4061
www.tysonfoodsinc.com

Western Farm Service, Inc.
3705 West Beechwood Avenue
Fresno, CA 93711
Phone: (559) 436-2800
Fax: (559) 436-2949
www.westernfarmservice.com

Wm. Bolthouse Farms, Inc.
7200 East Brundage Lane
Bakersfield, CA 93307
Phone: (661) 366-7270
Fax: (661) 366-9236
www.bolthouse.com

Wilbur-Ellis Company
345 California Street, 27th Floor
San Francisco, CA 94104
Phone: (415) 772-4000
Fax: (415) 772-4011
www.wilburellis.com

Visit Vault at **www.vault.com** for insider company profiles, expert advice, career message boards, expert resume reviews, the Vault Job Board and more.

VAULT CAREER LIBRARY

125

Airlines

Industry Overview

A volatile industry

The airline industry consists of companies that move people and cargo with planes. The International Air Transport Association (IATA) claims that this $470 billion worldwide industry stimulates 8 percent of global GDP through tourism, shipping and business travel. But despite its enormous contribution to world commerce, the industry has historically gone through dizzying booms and alarming busts as it reacts to regulatory changes and economic factors. Airlines are just starting to dig themselves out of the hole caused by September 11th. The IATA says the implementation of security measures has cost the industry $5.6 billion per year. Spats with labor unions, troubles with underfinanced pensions, high jet fuel prices and a string of bankruptcies, from which some carriers are still emerging, have caused further havoc. The July 2007 attack on Glasgow's airport is a reminder that the airline industry is still a target for terrorists. Nevertheless, *The Economist* thinks that once these issues have been resolved (no easy task), the airlines will be in a position to expand.

Cleared for takeoff

The airline industry took to the skies following the Wright brothers' first successful flight in 1905. As with many new technologies, airplanes were first used extensively by the military—namely, during World War I, for reconnaissance, bombing and aerial combat. Following the war, when the U.S. found itself with a surplus of military aircraft and pilots without much to do, the postal service opted in 1918 to start a transcontinental airmail service, which ran from New York to San Francisco. To keep costs down, 12 spur routes were spun off to independent contractors. Thus the familiar scions of the friendly skies—American Airlines, United Airlines, TWA and Northwest—were born.

Passenger flights didn't become a reality until Ford introduced a 12-seat plane in 1925. The Ford Trimotor made carrying people potentially profitable. Pan American Airways, the first airline with international destinations, was founded in 1927. Remarkably, airlines remained generally profitable during the Great Depression. Under the New Deal, the government subsidized airlines to carry mail. In 1934, however, postal reforms reduced the amount of money airlines earned for carrying the mail. By 1938, over a million Americans were flying on airplanes. This industry's rapid growth prompted new government policies. In 1938, Congress enacted the Civil Aeronautics Act. The airlines were happy that an independent agency was in charge of aviation policy. Before 1938 Civil Aeronautics Act passed, numerous government agencies and departments pushed and pulled airlines in many directions.

World War II brought many advances to the civilian air transport sector. Innovations initially intended for bombers made passenger planes larger, faster, and able to carry heavier payloads and to fly at higher altitudes. The 1970s saw the introduction of supersonic air travel with the advent of the Concorde. Due to the Concorde's only crash in 2000, as well as world economic effects after the September 11, 2001 attacks, the supersonic airliner stopped flying in October 2003.

Big trouble for the Big Six

After September 11th, Congress gave well over $20 billion to the airline industry in the form of reimbursements for losses incurred while planes were grounded following the attacks, monetary help for new passenger and plane security requirements, and pension funding relief. But many of the industry's major players were forced to shoulder massive debt loads to continue their operations; this was on top of debt they had been accumulating since even before the terrorist attacks. Of the "Big Six"—United, US Airways, American, Northwest, Continental and Delta—all but two, Continental and American, have been forced to file for Chapter 11. Smaller airlines, including Great Plains, Hawaiian, Midway, National, Sun Country and Vanguard, have also shown up in bankruptcy court.

Visit Vault at www.vault.com for insider company profiles, expert advice, career message boards, expert resume reviews, the Vault Job Board and more.

VAULT CAREER LIBRARY 127

Though passenger confidence continued to grow in the years following the terrorist attacks, the industry's red ink kept on flowing. The SARS scare in Asia, the Iraq war and a slowdown in the economy also hurt airlines. According to a June 2004 Senate report, the industry carried combined debts of more than $100 billion. Thus, major carriers continued to lobby the feds for financial support in the form of subsidies and loans.

Looking up?

The industry has struggled with profitability due to a combination of factors. Air carriers have been hit hard by rising fuel costs, with jet fuel prices in 2007 averaging about $80 per barrel. The high cost of oil remains a huge challenge to the airline industry. The IATA projected that in 2007, the industry's fuel bill will grow to $119 billion, an increase of $8 billion from 2005, when fuel costs totaled $111 billion. Labor disputes and underfinanced pensions have also been expensive problems for many carriers. Even JetBlue, which had strong profits for several years, suffered loses recently as it continues to grapple with rapid growth and rising expenses.

Overall, however, costs associated with air travel have dropped significantly over the past five years, resulting from price competition and attempts to keep ticket prices low despite high fuel costs. In early 2007, IATA Director General and CEO Giovanni Bisignani said the industry's distribution costs (the cost of selling tickets, such as ticket processing, credit card processing fees, etc.) are down 13 percent. Bisignani added that non-fuel unit costs, the cost per seat mile excluding the price of fuel, have declined 15 percent. Industry belt-tightening seems to be working. The IATA reports that the industry break-even fuel price went from $22 per barrel in 2003 to $65 per barrel in 2006.

Recently, the airline industry has started to show other signs of recovery. According to the IATA, a stronger world economy saw passenger traffic rise by 7 percent between 2005 and 2006, and air freight experienced a 5 percent gain. In order to accommodate this increased demand for air travel and to lower their fuel expenditures, airlines began snapping up new, more fuel-efficient planes. The airline industry's profitability has improved, and the IATA predicts that the industry will see $5 billion in profits in 2007. However, IATA Director General Bisignani pointed out that the airlines still have $200 billion dollars of debt. Moreover, he warned that an event like another terrorist attack or a pandemic scare could put many carriers back in the red.

A global network

Around the world, many airlines still are heavily subsidized—or owned outright—by their home nations. While this has been a successful setup for many, others haven't been so lucky. Swissair and Belgium's airline, Sabena, both crumbled when their respective governments couldn't keep up with demands for subsidies. Subsidized international and U.S. carriers have formed global alliances to avoid some regulatory issues and to maximize profits by sharing resources, including routes and marketing strategies. Well-known alliances include Oneworld—an alliance between American Airlines, British Airways and several other carriers—and SkyTeam, a partnership made up of Delta Air Lines, Air France, AeroMexico and other airlines. Such partnerships aren't always successful. An alliance between Dutch carrier KLM and Alitalia fell apart, for instance, after the Italian airline had trouble securing funding from its government patrons.

Partnerships aside, the airline industry remains remarkably competitive, and in today's tough climate, it's everyone for themselves. Tight regulatory controls in the U.S. make it difficult for major domestic carriers to merge. For example, a plan to join United Airlines and US Airways was shot down due to antitrust regulations. The US Airways name showed up again in merger talks, linked to America West for $1.5 billion, and the two companies made it official in September 2005. Then, in November 2006, US Airways made an offer for Delta. However, in early 2007, Delta's creditors rejected US Airways' $10 billion bid. Even if US Airways had purchased Delta, size (large or small) is no guarantee of profit. Four of the Big Six have gone into bankruptcy since 2001, and smaller budget airlines have also started struggling to make a profit.

Going regional

Regional airlines, which benefit from smaller, newer jets and lower operating costs than the domestic giants, have gained ground in recent years, becoming the fastest growing segment of the airline market. Approximately 25 to 30 regional, or commuter, carriers operate in the industry today, according to the Bureau of Labor Statistics. Recent statistics from the Regional Airline Association reveal that one in five domestic airline passengers travel on a regional airline, and that planes serving regional markets make up one-third of the U.S. commercial airline fleet on the whole. The big carriers have taken notice, and many now have controlling interests in newer regional airlines—Delta controls Comair, for instance, while American has American Eagle. In April 2006, Compass Airlines became a subsidiary of Northwest. The trend is reflected in Europe, too. Both globally and domestically, alliances with major carriers give the upstart regionals access to major airport hubs. In some cases, however, regional and low-budget airlines have skirted the hub question altogether by choosing to operate out of slightly out-of-the-way airports—Southwest's use of Islip airport, in a suburb of New York, and JetBlue's adoption of Long Beach, near Los Angeles, are two examples. And in other instances, regional airlines have decided to spread their wings and join the burgeoning low-cost boom. Some regional airlines now do longer haul flights. For example, Midwest Airlines (formerly Midwest Express) connects several cities in the Midwest to destinations like Boston, New York and San Francisco.

The budget boom

The budget airline sector—consisting of top performers like Southwest Airlines and JetBlue, plus a growing number of upstarts—has gotten a good deal of attention lately. But budget flight isn't a new phenomenon in the industry. In fact, Southwest has been around since 1971. The difference is in the branding and public acceptance of these carriers, fueled in part by Southwest's customer-centric approach, and by customers' reduced service expectations post-September 11th. Expanded routes have helped, too. Where once low-budget carriers limited their flights to relatively short hauls in regional markets, today's top discount airlines regularly offer cross-country, and even international, flights.

The budget carrier phenomenon has rocked Europe, too, where about 60 low-cost carriers operated in 2006, compared to just four in 1999. European customers have warmed up to the budget boom as well. British-based easyJet increased its passenger flow more than eightfold between 1999 and 2004, while low-cost carrier Ryanair, operating out of Ireland, ranked as one of the top performers in the industry worldwide. Some of the larger airlines have decided to take advantage of the low-cost boom, such as United's Ted and Delta's Song, but to not much avail; Song, in fact, was reabsorbed into Delta in 2006, three years after its first plane took off.

The boom in low-budget carriers isn't limited to North America and Europe. There are also low-fare carriers in Asia, where there are now about 45 discount airlines. Examples are Singapore-based Tiger Airways, Pakistani carrier Aero Asia and Jakarta-headquartered Adam Air. In June 2007, South Korea's largest airline, Korean Air Lines, announced plans to start a low-fare unit to compete with discount carriers in Asia. Some budget airlines are also branching out into long-haul flights across the Atlantic and Pacific.

Cutting costs

Above all, cost-savings are seen as key to the success of low-budget carriers. One way air carriers measure their fiscal health through cost per available seat mile (or CASM), a complex formula involving airplane capacity, operating costs, route lengths and other factors. Whereas American Airlines spends about 9.4 cents for each seat on each mile flown, budget competitors like Southwest and JetBlue lighten their loads with CASMs of 7.6 cents and 6.4 cents, respectively, according to an MSNBC article from December 2003. Those pennies add up over time, and so-called "legacy" carriers are under pressure to pinch them ever harder. But with more liberal work rules and a less-senior workforce overall, low-cost carriers beat their established rivals in terms of labor costs.

Visit Vault at www.vault.com for insider company profiles, expert advice, career message boards, expert resume reviews, the Vault Job Board and more.

VAULT CAREER LIBRARY   129

Other cost-cutting measures in the airline industry overall include streamlining fleets and retiring older planes, canceling unprofitable routes, greater efficiency in procurement processes involving suppliers and slashing commissions once paid regularly to middlemen such as travel agencies. Airlines have saved money through online booking, and they encourage customers to book directly through airlines web sites by offering incentives such online bonus miles. According to a 2006 *International Herald Tribune* article, online booking saves the airline industry $2 billion a year.

These airlines have also realized that consumers prefer to pick and choose their perks. An in-flight cocktail on JetBlue will still set you back $5, but XM radio and DIRECTV are free. Charging for amenities that previously came gratis allows carriers to keep ticket prices low, yet still turn a profit. Many airlines now charge passengers for meals and snacks. On Air Canada, customers now pay $2 for a pillow and a blanket. Moreover, some airlines now charge people for extra legroom. On Northwest, a bigger exit-row seat costs an additional $15. United's flyers can sign up an Economy Plus subscription, which is $299 a year. Subscribers get seats with five inches of extra legroom.

How low can you go?

Low-fare carriers, such as Southwest and JetBlue, were once the darlings of the airline industry. Recently, however, Southwest and JetBlue have had troubles of their own. When an ice storm hit JetBlue's hub at JFK airport in New York in February 2007, passengers were trapped on the tarmac for eight or more hours. It took JetBlue nearly a week to resume normal operations. JetBlue's founder and CEO David Neeleman apologized publicly for what happened and also introduced a "passenger's bill of rights." In May 2007, Neeleman stepped down as the airline's CEO.

In June 2007, *The Wall Street Journal* reported on a growing profit squeeze at Southwest. Over the past four years, Southwest's unit costs—the expenses to fly each seat one mile—have risen almost 20 percent due to increased labor costs and higher fuel prices. The airline's hedges to lock in low fuel prices have become less successful, and passengers have resisted increases in fares. Low-cost carriers are also facing greater competition from other airlines, which copied budget airlines' low-cost model during the post-September 11 industry downturn. Southwest has said it will respond to these pressures by reining in its rapid growth.

The lap of luxury

Some of the newest carriers attempt to attract the super-wealthy and business travelers instead of the budget-minded traveler. Upscale airlines MaxJet, SilverJet and Eos fly between New York and London. On Eos, which was launched in 2005, the airline's "guests" travel in style—they sleep on 6'6" beds and dine on gourmet meals. L'Avion, a business-class airline that offers service between Paris and New York, boasts that passengers can enjoy comfy seats and French food. In the Middle East, luxury airline Al Khayala aims to attract well-heeled customers by providing service that's somewhere between first class and a private jet. The airline uses specially modified Airbus A319s, which the company has configured to seat just 44 people instead of the usual 170 passengers. The wealthy also have the option of the Eclipse 500. Eclipse Aviation makes this "very light jet," which sells for about $1.5 million. Florida-based company DayJet owns several of the small jets and runs an air taxi service for business travelers.

Established airlines are also trying to cater to the luxury market. For example, Lufthansa is expanding the airline's first-class lounge in the Munich airport. New additions to the lounge will include day beds, showers, a gourmet restaurant and a bigger bar. Lufthansa is also spending millions of dollars to upgrade luxe lounges in Paris, New York's JFK, Berlin and Düsseldorf. In addition, Singapore Airlines is upgrading its business and first-class cabins on certain flights. The airline announced that, on some flights, it was rolling out 35-inch wide seats in first class. According to Singapore Air, the seats, which fold into beds, are "the largest seat in the sky" and are "exquisitely upholstered in fine-grained leather with mahogany wood trimming."

Investing in a dream(liner)

Major carriers hope to save money in the future by investing in new planes that offer a lower cost of ownership and operation. In late 2003, Boeing's board of directors gave the company the go-ahead to offer the 787 Dreamliner for sale. The following April, Japan's All Nippon was the first airline to order Boeing's new passenger jet, which promises fuel savings of up to 20 percent. By December 2006, Boeing had nearly 450 orders for the new Dreamliner, and the number had soared to more than 580 by June 2007.

Meanwhile, Airbus, the French firm and Boeing's rival for No. 1 aircraft maker in the world, unveiled a brand new high-scale jumbo-jet, the A380, at the start of 2005 at a gala event during the Le Bourget air show in Toulouse, France. Designed to comfortably seat 555, the A380 rocked the airline industry and represented a joint effort with France, Britain, Germany and Spain, all of whom contributed to the 10-year, $13 billion program that designed the plane. The double-decker leviathan, the largest plane ever built, boasts a 262-foot wingspan and extra space companies can use to install bedrooms, gyms, bars and lounges.

The conservation end, though, is where the A380 packs its biggest punch: its carbon fiber components and fuel-efficient technology are estimated to match or exceed Boeing's 20 percent fuel savings, and slash cost per passenger. However, in October 2006, Airbus announced that the delivery of the new jet would be delayed until the second half of 2007, with the industrial ramp-up finished in 2010. As of June 2007, Airbus had 13 signed contracts from two airlines for the A350, and another five customers had agreed to purchase 148 A350s.

It's not easy being green

Global warming is a hot topic, and airplanes are one of the biggest contributors to carbon emissions. Environmentalists have also criticized the airline industry for planes' air pollution in general. In 2006, Al Gore's documentary *An Inconvenient Truth* was a surprise hit, and a number of businesses have started going "carbon-neutral." Members of the airline and aviation industries are finally starting to address concerns about airplanes' emissions. In June 2007, the IATA has asked the aerospace industry to build zero-emissions airplanes within the next 50 years. Later that month, Louis Gallois, the CEO of Airbus, called on aircraft makers to work together to invent more environmentally-friendly technology. In addition, the European Commission proposed a $2.13 billion public-private plan, dubbed the Clean Sky program. The program, which would start in 2008, would help Europe's air-transportation sector develop technologies to reduce planes' pollution.

Labor pains

According to the Bureau of Labor Statistics, labor costs make up roughly 38 percent of many airlines' operating costs—that's around 40 cents for every dollar spent by an air carrier. Passenger safety regulations and a workforce made up of highly specialized and rarely cross-trained professionals, half of whom are unionized, make it tough for airlines to trim costs from their labor budgets. One way they've done this is by cutting staffs to the bare bones. Following September 11th, Continental Airlines and US Airways were the first to make dramatic cuts, laying off about 20 percent of their respective workforces and paring flight schedules. Most other carriers followed suit.

Cuts in salaries and benefits

At many airlines, employees have agreed to salary and benefit cuts to help keep airlines from going bankrupt. For example, in June 2006, Delta's pilots union agreed to a 14 percent pay cut. Other employees at Delta also agreed to pay cuts, including CEO Gerald Grinstein, whose pay was chopped by 25 percent. In May 2007, Northwest Airlines departed bankruptcy protection following a 20-month reorganization. The restructuring attempted to make the airline competitive for future years.

Visit Vault at **www.vault.com** for insider company profiles, expert advice, career message boards, expert resume reviews, the Vault Job Board and more.

VAULT CAREER LIBRARY   131

Among other things, Northwest's new labor contracts pay employees less. Flight attendants for the airline used to make as much as $44,190, but now their pay tops out at $35,400.

Although American Airlines posted an annual profit for the first time in six years, many workers were angry during the airline's annual stockholder meeting in May 2007. These employees, who agreed to salary cuts in recent years to keep the airline flying, were unhappy because top executives got bonuses worth millions of dollars. At Northwest, the airline cut pilots' wages by 40 percent and increased their hours. In protest, pilots regularly call in sick to take days off, which results in more cancelled flights.

In order to save money, airlines have also started outsourcing many jobs that used to be filled with airline employees. For example, in 2005, Alaska Airlines replaced its baggage handlers with lower-paid outside contractors. In 2006, Northwest hired non-union employees to clean airplanes. In some cases, airlines have also replaced people with machines—just think of the self-service check-in kiosks that have sprung up at airports in recent years.

Not just plane jobs

One manager for a major airline says, "This is not a place for the faint of heart. The airline industry is chaotic, and [it has been] particularly brutal for the traditional or legacy carriers since 2001." This source feels career development opportunities are extremely limited. The contact adds, "There is a glut of MBAs that have never moved up due to the incredibly heavy toll exacted by several world events (the dot-com bust, September 11th, SARS, the Iraq war). However, work hours are pretty light, and the travel benefits can be fantastic." An insider at American Airlines agrees that working for the airline industry is tough, explaining, "If making lots of money, getting big bonuses and securing promotion opportunities are important to you, AA may not be the best place to work. However, if you value work/life balance, enjoy solving challenging business problems and love flying first class to any destination across the globe, American really isn't that bad."

The airline industry hires a wide variety of employees ranging from pilots and flight attendants to ticket agents, sales people and managers. Although flight crews are the most visible in the industry, most airline employees don't fly the friendly skies. Rather, they work in airport terminals or in offices. Due to the fact the flights leave at all hours, many who work in the industry have schedules that are variable or irregular. Most jobs with the airline industry are in or near the cities that serve as major airlines hubs. For example, many of Northwest Airlines' jobs are in Minneapolis-St. Paul.

In the airline industry, most recieve standard benefits, such as health insurance and paid vacation—and many also have benefits like retirement plans and profit sharing. One perk that attracts many people to the industry is free or reduced-fare flights for airline employees and sometimes even their family members.

Many airline jobs are also unionized. Unions include the Air Line Pilots Association International (ALPA), the International Association of Machinists and Aerospace Workers (IAM), and the Association of Flight Attendants-CWA (AFA-CWA). The AFA, which represents 55,000 flight attendants at 20 airlines, claims it is the largest flight attendant union.

Navigating airline interviews

Most sources at airlines, regardless of their position, say the interview process can be long and usually involves multiple meetings. A reservations agent for Continental says, "The hiring process was very long. It took about six months from resume submitted to being hired." The contact says there were two rounds of interviews. One HR person with American Airlines says, "The interview process can be lengthy and meeting with a number of people the norm." A mechanic with Continental says getting the job entailed three interviews. Flight attendants for various airlines say a group interview is part of the hiring process.

An airline agent says interview questions included "Where do you see yourself 10 years from now?", "How do you deal with difficult people?", "Do you work better by yourself or in a group?", "Do you loose you temper easily?" and "How important it is to spend the holidays with your loved ones?" Another ticket agent says one question was, "Describe the most difficult problem you dealt with at a previous job and how you handled it." A manager says questions included "What is your greatest accomplishment?" Some say they also needed to pass a medical examination or psychological tests.

The future of airline careers

Industry employment is largely at the mercy of the economy, though the BLS expects jobs to increase somewhat independently due to a growing population and greater demand for air travel. The BLS predicts employment growth initially in low-cost and local carriers. After larger airlines recover from bankruptcy, the BLS says, larger airlines will start hiring again. However, the airline industry is often as turbulent as the skies it flies, and salaries and perks aren't what they used to be.

Flying High: Airline Careers

Here are overviews of some professions in the airline industry. We begin with information about flight crews and move on to airline jobs for aviophobics who would prefer to stay on the ground.

Flight attendants

They are not all pneumatic babes, they're not called stewardesses anymore and, no, they don't want to hear about your cockpit. Flight attendants are both male and female, they vary in appearance, age (age restrictions were recently abolished) and ethnicity, and they can make the difference between a comfortable flight and a nightmarish one. And while you may think that getting your bag of pretzels is of paramount importance, the primary responsibility of a flight attendant is the safety of the passengers. Competition for the few attendant jobs at the "Big Six" carriers is stiff, but smaller regional carriers and airlines are a good place to start a career in the skies. According the U.S. Bureau of Labor Statistics, the median salary for flight attendants was $43,470 in 2004, the most recent year for which data is available. Bucking industry trends, Southwest pays its flight attendants per trip.

Tested and trained

Flight attendants are trained and tested professionals: they undergo weeks of (often unpaid) training; most large airline companies require them to pass a grueling exam that tests them on every nut and bolt of the aircraft on which they serve. In the wake of the September 11 hijackings, many flight attendants have also undergone training in self-defense.

Flight attendant training lasts about four to six weeks, during which trainees learn emergency procedures, such as how to operate an oxygen system and give first aid. Trainees for international routes get additional instruction in passport and customs regulations and terrorism coping techniques. The training is rigorous and not all trainees pass the examinations. The lure of free travel to exotic locales attracts applicants, but the often unglamorous process of being cloistered with 100 trainees at a budget hotel in Houston or Cleveland weeds many would-be flight attendants out of the group.

At home and away

The hours for flight attendants vary widely, and many flight attendants work at night, on weekends and on holidays. They spend about 75 to 80 hours a month on the ground preparing planes for flights, writing reports following completed flights and waiting (just like passengers) for planes that arrive late. In-flight work can be strenuous because of demanding passengers and crowded flights. Attendants are on their feet during much of the flight and must remain helpful and friendly regardless of how they feel or how obnoxious their passengers are. As a result of scheduling variations and limitations on flying time, many flight attendants have 11 or more days off a month. Attendants can be away from their home base—often the hub city

Visit Vault at www.vault.com for insider company profiles, expert advice, career message boards, expert resume reviews, the Vault Job Board and more.

VAULT CAREER LIBRARY   133

of the airline they work for—a great deal of the time, and are compensated by the airlines with hotel accommodations, meal allowances and, of course, discounted or free tickets for both themselves and their immediate families.

Save yourself

It takes a patient, extroverted personality to become a flight attendant. It also takes steady nerves and a sense of duty. In the event of an emergency, atttendants must take the passengers' safety into account before their own. This can entail anything from simple reassurance to directing passengers during evacuation following an emergency landing. Though the chances of a plane crash are small, flight attendants must be undaunted by the prospect of disaster. Airlines that serve international destinations also look for individuals who are fluent in foreign languages, such as Spanish, French, German, Chinese, Japanese, Greek, Italian and Russian.

Pilots

Senior pilots are among the best-paid employees in the United States. According to the Bureau of Labor Statistics, the median salary for pilots, co-pilots and flight engineers was $137,160 in 2004, the most recent year for which data was available. Because pilots have such good incomes, competition for these jobs is understandably intense. Pilots need a commercial pilot's license with an instrument rating. They also must have a medical certificate. Pilots need to have 20/20 vision, with or without corrective lenses; good hearing; and be in excellent health overall. In addition, they have to be certified to fly the types of aircraft the airline operates. In early 2007, the FAA said the agency would allow pilots, who previously had been allowed to fly until they were 60 years old, to keep working in the cockpit until age 65.

Most planes have a pilot and co-pilot. Generally, the captain, who is the most experienced pilot, supervises all other crew members. The pilot and co-pilot share the job of flying. They also split other duties, such as monitoring instruments and communicating with air traffic controllers. In a handful of airplanes, there's a third pilot—called a second officer or flight engineer—who helps the other pilots.

Calling Ted Striker

The more FAA licenses a pilot has—that is, the more flying time he has on complex, modern equipment—the more in demand his services will be. For this reason, military-trained pilots are particularly desirable. However, recent military actions mean they are in short supply.

If you don't want to become an Air Force fighter pilot, there are other ways to get experience flying planes. Civilians can learn to fly at a private flight school and gain practice flying on progressively larger aircraft; they may work their way up from private jets to regional carriers and from there to the larger airlines. One pilot, who is now the captain of an Airbus A320 passenger airline, says he "first spent several years flying for charter and mail contract carriers." Before a major U.S. airline hired the pilot, he flew for a smaller regional airline.

Initially, a newly hired pilot will be a flight engineer or co-pilot, assisting the captain with communications with control towers, instrument readings and flight duties. Work assignments for flight attendants and pilots are frequently given on a seniority basis, with the most senior employees having the pick of the litter. New hires, therefore, must be prepared to receive less desirable assignments initially.

Jobs on the ground

If you're afraid of flying, there still might be a job for you in the airline industry. Positions on the ground vary greatly. They include a wide range of jobs, such as mechanics, baggage handlers, ticket agents, customer service representatives and reservations agents. Airlines also hire people to work in information technology, marketing and sales, finance and administration and more.

The skills and education you need depend on the on-the-ground position for which you are applying. For most administrative positions, employees need strong computer skills. A recent posting for a finance associate with United required an MBA and two years of related work experience in an area such as banking, consulting or accounting. Mechanics need to have licenses. Often, airlines are seeking reservations representatives who speak languages other than English, including Spanish, Japanese, Mandarin Chinese, Creole, French and German.

Salaries for these jobs vary as well. According to the BLS, the 2004 median salary for aircraft mechanics and service technicians was $54,890. Reservation ticket agents and travel clerks' median salary was $31,450, and customer service representatives typically earned $28,420.

Some airlines also need temporary and seasonal workers, usually in jobs such as customer service and ramp service. Working in a temporary job can sometimes give you a foot in the door for a more permanent position. In addition, airlines including United and Northwest have paid and unpaid internships.

Visit Vault at www.vault.com for insider company profiles, expert advice, career message boards, expert resume reviews, the Vault Job Board and more.

VAULT CAREER LIBRARY   135

Employer Directory

Air Canada
Air Canada Centre
7373 Côte-Vertu Boulevard West
Dorval, Quebec H4Y 1H4
Canada
Phone: (514) 205-7856
Fax: (514) 205-7859
www.aircanada.com

Air France-KLM Group
45, Rue de Paris
75747 Roissy, Cedex-CDG
France
Phone: +33-1-41-56-78-00
Fax: +33-1-41-56-56-00
www.airfranceklm-finance.com
www.klm.com

Alitalia—Linee Aeree Italiane S.p.A.
Viale Alessandro Marchetti, 111
Rome 00148
Italy
Phone: +39-06-6562-21
Fax: +39-06-6562-4733
www.alitalia.com

All Nippon Airways Co., Ltd.
Shiodome City Center
1-5-2 Higashi-Shimbashi
Minato-ku, Tokyo 105-7133
Japan
Phone: +81-3-6735-1000
Fax: +81-3-6735-1005
www.ana.co.jp

AMR Corporation (American Airlines)
4333 Amon Carter Boulevard
Fort Worth, TX 76155
Phone: (817) 963-1234
Fax: (817) 967-9641
www.aa.com

British Airways Plc
Waterside, Harmondsworth
London, UB7 0GB
United Kingdom
Phone: +44-87-08-50-85-03
Fax: +44-20-87-59-43-14
www.british-airways.com

Continental Airlines, Inc
1600 Smith Street
Department HQSEO
Houston, TX 77002
Phone: (713) 324-2950
Fax: (713) 324-2687
www.continental.com

Delta Air Lines, Inc
1030 Delta Boulevard
Atlanta, GA 30320-6001
Phone: (404) 715-2600
Fax: (404) 715-5042
www.delta.com

Deutsche Lufthansa AG
Von-Gablenz-Straße 2-6
D-50679 Cologne, 21
Germany
Phone: +49-0221-826-3992
Fax: +49-221-826-3646
www.lufthansa.com

Japan Airlines Corporation
4-11 Higashi-shinagawa 2-chome
Shinagawa-ku, Tokyo 140-8605
Japan
Phone: +81-3-5460-6600
www.jai.com

JetBlue Airways Corporation
118-29 Queens Boulevard
Forest Hills, NY 11375
Phone: (718) 286-7900
Fax: (718) 709-3621
www.jetblue.com

Korean Air Lines Co., Ltd.
1370, Gonghang-dong, Gangseo-gu
Seoul 157-712
Korea
Phone: +82-2-2656-7857
Fax: +82-2-2656-5709
www.koreanair.com

Iberia, Líneas Aéreas de España, S.A.
Velázquez 130
Madrid 28006
Spain
Phone: +34-902-400-500
Fax: +34-91-587-47-41
www.iberia.com

Northwest Airlines Corporation
2700 Lone Oak Parkway
Eagan, MN 55121
Phone: (612) 726-2111
Fax: (612) 726-7123
www.nwa.com

Sabre Holdings Corporation
3150 Sabre Drive
Southlake, TX 76092
Phone: (682) 605-1000
Fax: (682) 605-8267
www.sabre-holdings.com

Singapore Airlines Limited
Airline House
25 Airline Road
Singapore 819829
Phone: +65-6541-4885
Fax: +65-6542-9605
www.singaporeair.com

UAL Corporation (United Airlines)
77 West Wacker Drive
Chicago, IL 60601
Phone: (312) 997-8000
www.united.com

US Airways Group, Inc.
111 West Rio Salado Parkway
Tempe, AZ 85281
Phone: (480) 693-0800
Fax: (480) 693-5546
www.usairways.com

Architecture and Interior Design

The Architecture Career Path

Much like interior design companies, architectural firms often have specialties: residential, commercial or institutional. Residential architects plan all manner of private residences, including multifamily residential buildings, such as condominiums or semi-attached dwellings. Commercial architects design public spaces, such as office buildings and country clubs. Institutional architects work on structures such as public libraries and municipal buildings. Some firms include inhouse services such as structural, mechanical and electrical engineering, or design-related services like landscape and interior design. Depending on the size and geographic location of the firm, work may focus only on one area or cover all three. Company size varies widely—the number of employees ranges anywhere from one person to over 100, but the average is nine or 10 people. Since most people have limited knowledge of the construction process, they'll enlist an architect as the first step in developing a new residence or public building. A successful architect, like an interior designer, pays careful attention to the wants and needs of his/her client, turning ideas into tangible drawings and offering assistance in many aspects of the project, including site studies, securing planning and zoning approvals, and helping to select a contractor.

Clients select architectural firms in the same manner they choose a designer, gathering names from friends and associates who have developed similar projects, through publications, such as *Architectural Digest*, and researching which architects designed the buildings or homes they admire. They can also contact the American Institute of Architects (AIA) for lists of local architects. Many design publications list architects as resources, and architects also self-promote in trade publications. As in any industry, certain icons are so well known that they can be very selective about the projects they accept. Some current well-known architects include Frank Gehry, Santiago Calatrava and Richard Meier. One of Meier's recent famous works is the Getty Center in Los Angeles. Two of Gehry's latest notable structures are the Guggenheim Museum Bilbao in Spain and the Walt Disney Concert Hall in Los Angeles. Calatrava's projects include an addition to the Milwaukee Art Museum, the recently completed Chords Bridge in Jerusalem and a skyscraper in Sweden known as the Turning Torso tower. The number of famous architects taking on residential projects has increased; for example, Calatrava is working on the Chicago Spire, a residential superstructure planned to be the tallest building in the U.S., and Frank Gehry is developing ideas for a luxury tower in Manhattan. The phenomenon of prominent architects working on residential projects is not entirely new; after all, famed architect Frank Lloyd Wright is often most remembered for his private dwellings such as Fallingwater, a residential home in Bear Run, Penn. One reason architects take on private residences is the increased level of creativity those projects engender. As Richard Meier has said, "Individuals aren't afraid to take risks. You don't get that level of collaboration with many corporate clients."

Architects are usually brought on board shortly after the land or existing property has been acquired, ultimately selected based on some combination of price, qualification and personal fit. Owners usually interview several prospective applicants, getting a chance to see examples of the firms' work and how they organize projects for completion. The interview also provides an opportunity for potential clients to interact with the person or people who will be working on the job before committing to anything. Many firms, too, exercise their own judgment, careful not to take every opportunity that crosses their path. As one principal of a midsized architectural firm says, "We have made a concerted effort to filter our client base so that we don't accept projects from potential clients who we sense may not be a good fit."

Architecture jobs

Depending on the size of the firm, positions vary. At smaller firms, job descriptions and responsibilities tend to overlap, as each person is expected to wear more than one hat. A small to midsized firm (four to 10 people) tends to offer the following positions:

Administrative: This position focuses on providing administrative support and office management: filing, answering phones, scheduling, ordering—anything that helps the office run smoothly. Administrative positions require no background in

Visit Vault at www.vault.com for insider company profiles, expert advice, career message boards, expert resume reviews, the Vault Job Board and more.

VAULT CAREER LIBRARY   137

architecture and provide a good way for a person with an interest in architecture to safely test the waters and observe the actual operations of an architecture firm.

Draftsperson: There are often two categories within this title, junior and senior, differentiated by level of experience and responsibility. A draftsperson drafts the drawing for a project, directed by the project architect or project manager. She should have the requisite degree in architecture, but is not necessarily licensed, and she should have a solid understanding of computer aided design (CAD) in addition to good hand-drawing and hand-lettering skills. A wide range of experience is acceptable for this position.

Job captain: This person coordinates and works on the drawings for a project. She organizes and updates the drawings and directs staff as necessary. A job captain has a degree in architecture but is not necessarily licensed. She should have a minimum of about five years' work experience.

Project manager: The person in this position is responsible for day-to-day management, coordination of staff on projects, scheduling of tasks and consultant coordination. This job requires educational and work experience similar to what a job captain requires.

Project architect: A project architect is responsible for the overall supervision of the project: design and coordination of details for the drawings, consultation coordination, decision making for field issues, etc. (in small offices some responsibilities overlap with the project managers). Production of specifications (what types of materials are to be used) and overall review of project documents are also responsibilities of a project architect. This position requires licensing in the state of employment. Attaining this position typically requires 10 years of work experience.

Principal or partner: This person runs the firm. Some firms with more than one head person have a design principal or partner and a business partner. At others, the principal might do everything: design, marketing, overall administrative and strategic planning, client contact and meetings, project scheduling, and administration and business planning.

Salaries and corporate culture

Similarly to interior design, architecture is often misunderstood, and as a result, glamorized. Some top architects have the opportunity to work on famous buildings and landmarks, and express great creativity. But there are scores of others working on much more mundane projects, and not being well compensated either. In fact, architecture careers have a reputation for being underpaid, particularly relative to the amount of education required. Asked to describe a drawback to her job, one architect says, "The pay, in comparison to other professions, such as law and medicine, tends to be lower."

Salary ranges in a small to medium-size firm are usually anywhere from $30,000 for lower-level positions to $80,000 for positions higher up the food chain. Employees at larger firms can make more money, and certainly, well-known architects can command more also. Average architectural salaries range from $25,000 to $80,000, depending on a person's experience and the size of the company they work for. Partners can earn well into six figures, particularly at large firms. Salary.com states the national average for architectural salaries as $49,381 on the low end, $56,637 for the middle bracket and $66,427 on the high end.

Though architecture is known for long hours and late nights, this is more accurate at some firms than others. Some firms maintain fairly stable 9-to-5, 40-hour workweeks, while others are more stressful. Hours worked often depend on the type of projects the firm undertakes and the deadlines it agrees to; some companies take on publicly funded or other institutional projects and face contract provisions that require absolute deadlines on certain phases of the process. This requires the architect to meet deadlines, no matter the overtime involved.

Corporate culture varies depending on the size of the firm, larger leaning toward more conservative and hierarchical, smaller ones usually allowing greater freedom. Architecture certainly allows for more creativity than professions, such as banking or accounting, but it is still business-focused and requires one to turn an artistic vision into something useful and functional.

Asked if architecture is creative, one architect responded, "I would say yes, but not in the same way school is creative. Clients generally don't give us free rein and some firms also separate their staff into design and production groups, the former being more freely creative on a conceptual level and the latter being more technical. The production staff figures out how to build what the design staff creates."

Like fashion, entertainment and other creative professions, certain industry stars glamorize the profession and create misunderstanding about the reality of working in the business. The Frank Gehrys and I.M. Peis (architect of Hancock Place, the tallest building in Boston, not to mention the controversial Louvre Pyramid) of the world are rare; much more common are architects who love their job but work on average projects and receive average paychecks.

Pay fluctuates depending on firm size and an architect's area of specialization. Small to midsized firms offer greater freedom in terms of creativity and structure, but generally do not compensate employees as well. Unlike interior design, architecture is more of a necessity than a luxury. Any person or company that needs to create a structure has to enlist the help of an architect, so clients don't tend to have as much expendable income across the board as those enlisting interior decorators. Perks include travel and social invitations; architects attend many of the same events frequented by interior designers and other professionals in the design arena. Although architects may not need to be as image-conscious as their interior design colleagues, they still must maintain knowledge of trends and culture. Appearing knowledgeable and speaking eloquently on historical architecture and famous buildings is essential. Being published in trade magazines is extremely helpful for raising awareness about a particular firm and the talented individuals it employs.

Employment options

Architects are not limited to working only at traditional architectural firms. The AIA provides a list of the many options available within four main categories: corporate architecture, public architecture, facility management and "other options." Corporate architects are employed within the retail, office, manufacturing, medical and hospitality industries, and there are numerous job choices available at such companies, ranging from entry-level planners to high-level executives. Public architects work for government agencies from federal to local levels. The government recruits architects to serve on capital projects planning, design and construction programs; the architect may be a direct government employee or hired as a consultant. Projects might include civic buildings, government offices, military facilities, courts and research facilities. Facility management uses architects to integrate architecture, engineering and environmental sciences for public and private corporations, architecture and consulting firms. Facilities management, as explained by the Facility Management Association of Australia, "coordinates the strategic and operational management of facilities in public and private sector organizations. They range from those making very high-level decisions within an organization and contributing to strategic planning, to those managing the operations of the facilities. Facility managers are key decision-makers in the areas of communications, utilities, maintenance and other workplace services. They often control the spending in these areas and are responsible for the outcomes." In terms of "other" career options, architects can serve as writers, critics and educators. For instance, Michael Graves served as an architecture professor at Princeton for nearly 40 years, and Robert A.M. Stern is the dean of the Yale School of Architecture.

A Day in the Life: Principal, Architecture Firm

9 a.m. Arrive at the office. Check with the administrative staff for messages and the day's schedule. Return e-mails and phone calls, particularly regarding East Coast projects, so they get any information they need before the close of business (considering the three-hour time difference). Deal with any pressing administrative issues and make task lists for the day.

10 a.m. Since it's Monday, conduct a project meeting with all the managers to review pending and upcoming issues on all projects. Afterwards, have meeting with administrative staff to review the coming week and all scheduling and administrative

Visit Vault at www.vault.com for insider company profiles, expert advice, career message boards, expert resume reviews, the Vault Job Board and more.

VAULT CAREER LIBRARY   139

issues. On other weekday mornings, attend construction meetings at project sites with the clients, contractor, decorator and any necessary subcontractors. These meetings can last several hours or consume the majority of the day.

12 p.m. Break for lunch with Brian. We usually go "off campus" and discuss any urgent issues, calendar issues or projects, potential clients, etc.

1 p.m. Address project issues. Conduct client meetings.

3 p.m. Deal with paperwork of various kinds: memos, project correspondence, billing. Read all mail, review accounts payable. Spend time directing staff on both administrative and design issues. Deal with contracts and proposal packages for new clients. Some days, have to pick up daughter from school and spend the afternoon with her; when this occurs, work from the home office, which is connected electronically with the office server.

Interior Design Basics

Designer or decorator?

The terms interior designer and interior decorator are often used interchangeably by both design industry professionals and laypeople; however, the difference between the two is distinct and important. An interior designer is likely to be offended if referred to as a decorator, but a decorator probably won't correct you if mistaken for a designer.

The primary distinction between the two is that a designer has more responsibility and is formally trained and educated, whereas a decorator may be self-taught and have no formal schooling. Designers, who have been trained in many areas, including drafting, space planning, furniture design and history, ergonomics and business practices, are involved in all facets of a project. They are expected to have in-depth knowledge of safety and building codes and many construction-related issues. On the other hand, a decorator tends to be limited to working primarily with surface decorations like paint, furnishings and fabrics. Numerous designers and decorators practice interior design, with decorators primarily concentrating on residential design and designers more evenly dispersed through residential and contract design. In an *Architectural Digest* interview, interior designer Mariette Himes Gomez explains, "I hate to generalize, and I don't want to set up stereotypes, but decorators usually are individuals who prefer to reupholster and do new draperies and pick out furniture." On the other hand, Gomez describes her interior design practice as "coordinat[ing] our services with an architect from the time the building is under construction."

The role of a designer

Interior designers are hired to plan the interiors, and to some extent, exteriors of private homes, hotels, restaurants, cruise ships, hospitals, offices and countless other spaces. They work with clients, contractors, architects and any number of specialists to create functional and pleasing living and working environments. They make decisions about flooring materials, wall and ceiling paints and treatments, lighting, window treatments, appliances, furnishings and accessories.

Good taste and visuals are only a part of the elements a designer must consider when creating a space. Designers must also address functionality and compliance with safety codes and standards. Educated interior designers should be aware of how all these components relate to codes and guidelines and ensure they are in compliance with regulations.

Designers must have a wide range of skills. While creativity is probably the most widely acknowledged asset, designers must also have the ability to multitask and work effectively on several projects at one time; time management and organizational abilities are key. Designers must also be effective communicators, able to work with clients, contractors, architects and vendors, to name a few. As Betty Sherrill, president of legendary design firm McMillen, Inc., says, "Part decorator, part architect, the interior designer today must have a head for business and budgets, as well as a command of materials and marketing."

Interior Design Accreditations

Accreditations and education

In almost every state, there is more than one accredited interior design education program. The Council for Interior Design Accreditation posts a list of accredited programs on its web site (www.accredit-id.org). In New York, there are nine approved programs, the most notable being the Pratt Institute in Brooklyn. Parsons is not council-accredited, but it does have a considerable reputation in the field. The number of accredited programs available in a geographic region depends on the size of the state, as well as the profile of design there. Well-known design hubs, such as California (Los Angeles and San Francisco) and Illinois (Chicago), have 14 and seven programs respectively, but smaller states without a real design hub, such as Iowa and Nevada, each have one.

Formal schooling

The need for formal schooling in interior design is debatable. According to the American Society of Interior Designers, at least 50 percent of all practicing designers in the United States have completed two or more years of college or vocational training; 40 to 45 percent have completed a four-year college program. Of the four-year college graduates, 40 percent received a degree in interior design. The remaining 60 percent have degrees in architecture, fine arts, liberal arts, industrial design, education and business administration, among other subjects. Depending on whether you are interested in contract or residential design, the requirements will vary. Residential design is less likely to require formal schooling and a specific background, whereas contract design is more restrictive, often necessitating a design degree. There are many, many successful residential decorators (who might call themselves designers, depending on their location) who have absolutely no formal schooling in design. However, many of these individuals have other outstanding characteristics and qualities that have made them a success. They probably have a very strong work ethic, outstanding taste and an eye for beauty. They most likely have very strong people skills. They probably have excellent presentation skills and are well versed in the art of sales. "Design isn't so much about decorating as sales. You have to sell yourself, your image, your ideas and the products," says one top residential designer.

Young would-be designers have plenty of options. With some serious networking and hard work, you can probably get in the door in a support position at a residential design firm and work your way up from there, taking night courses in design to increase your pace up the ladder. If you are switching careers and don't have years to spend climbing the corporate ladder, a degree or at least certificate in design is very beneficial. Having a degree will open you up to working at both residential and commercial firms and will get you a better position than someone with zero design education—but you will definitely still have to put in many years of hard work to get to head designer. Going out on your own is usually not an option for most brand-new design graduates or those with little concrete experience. Most clients will want to see a portfolio of a designer's work, which won't add up to much if a designer only has school projects or pictures of his/her own living room to show.

The main thing to keep in mind is that interior design is not the glamorous job it may appear to be. If you envision days spent shopping for fabrics and picking out furnishings, that's really only about 10 percent of the job. "Be prepared to work very hard when you first start out," says one designer. "A lot will be expected of you and you will need to pay your dues. Be very sure that this is what you want to do. Design, particularly if you work for one of the big firms, is not always as creative or glamorous as you might think. It is a business and it is about business. On the other hand, if you are good, there are great opportunities out there."

Visit Vault at **www.vault.com** for insider company profiles, expert advice, career message boards, expert resume reviews, the Vault Job Board and more.

VAULT CAREER LIBRARY   141

Licensing

The field of interior design is still evolving, and what designates an interior designer varies by location. ASID provides a list (www.asid.org/legislation/state) of requirements by state. Twenty-two states, as well as the District of Columbia, have some regulations regarding what qualifications an interior designer must meet. Other states not on that list either don't have any requirements or are in the process of defining them. It's important to make sure you know the requirements for the state where you intend to practice. It is also important to remember that decorators (as opposed to designers) do not have to meet the same requirements. Currently, designation requirements are still under debate in many localities. For example, the October 2004 issue of *Interior Design* details the efforts of Ruth Lynford, the legislative chair of Interior Designers for Legislation in New York, encouraging a bill that would reserve the title of interior designer "for those who meet certain educational and professional qualifications and pass an examination on fire, safety and building codes." (Anyone practicing for 15 years or more would have been able to apply for an exemption.) After two years, the bill was finally passed, only to be overturned by the governor. Only time will tell how successful future legislative measures will be.

States that do register and license designers typically require some combination of education and work experience, and possibly passing a qualifying exam. The most popular exam is offered by the National Council for Interior Design Qualification (NCIDQ). This organization, founded in the early 1970s, was created to establish the necessary qualifications for designating a professional interior designer. The NCIDQ administers a qualifying exam that entitles successful candidates to become certified in interior design and a professional member in interior design-related organizations such as the American Society of Interior Designers (ASID). The exam tests knowledge of safety and health issues, space planning, historical styles, fabric selection and math. Requirements for taking the NCIDQ are: four to five years of interior design education plus two years of full-time work experience in interior design, or three years of interior design education plus three years of full-time work experience in interior design, or two years of interior design education plus four years of full-time work experience in interior design.

Membership in ASID or other professional groups such as the International Interior Design Association (IIDA), while not necessary to function in the industry, does hold weight and can be beneficial in acquiring clients. These organizations have various types of memberships, such as student, professional, allied and industry. They provide opportunities for networking and further education in addition to being great sources of information. ASID has over 40 chapters throughout North America. To become a professional member, an interior designer must have passed the NCIDQ exam in addition to having a course of accredited education or relevant work experience. Allied members are not required to have passed the NCIDQ exam but must either have acquired a four- or five-year bachelor's degree in interior design or architecture, or two- or three-year degree or certificate in interior design, or six years of full-time work in interior design or architecture. The ASID web site (www.asid.org) provides its members valuable information for networking and industry information. It even has an area for posting resumes and searching for candidates.

It is imperative for designers in contract design to be licensed. In this portion of the industry, designers work primarily on large commercial properties such as hotels, resorts and cruise ships, and it's critical that designers in these areas have knowledge of safety regulations and codes. In residential design, it is not as important, since the design space is mostly private and not required to meet such stringent regulations.

Just as the American Bar Association (ABA) reviews and accredits educational programs for the legal profession, the interior design industry has the Council for Interior Design Accreditation. The council, formerly known as FIDER, was established in 1970 to develop standards for interior design education. It is responsible for accrediting interior design programs and ensuring a program meets the qualifications of the industry. Attending a council-approved school is not required to practice interior design or to take the NCIDQ, but the accreditation suggests that the institution and its graduates are concerned with meeting industry standards. The council provides a list of its approved programs by state. Whether to pursue a formal degree in interior design or to take a more general approach is an important decision that will affect future employment. If you're interested in pursuing a career in commercial or hospitality design, it's highly advisable to complete a formal degree.

According to a recent interior design graduate of Parsons School of Design in New York City, her first job with a hospitality firm would not have been possible without such a degree. In fact, her firm would not have even contemplated her resume without the requisite design degree.

On the other hand, if residential design is more appealing, then a less traditional approach is acceptable. Many employees and even principals at well-recognized design firms hold no formal qualifications in interior design. It is not unusual for highly successful residential interior designers (or decorators) to have no formal background in the field; instead, they often hold degrees in art history, architecture or fine arts. If a degree is the chosen path, there are several methods for acquiring it. Many schools offer a bachelor's of interior design (BID) or bachelor's of fine art with a concentration in interior design (BFA). Others provide associate's degrees and continuing education courses, which are also a means of gaining some formal training. Some schools also offer interior architecture degrees. These are architecturally based degrees with an emphasis on interior design, but they are not exact substitutes for an interior design education.

One residential interior designer who attended Parsons School of Design says that she finds her formal training and education in the field to be a huge asset. "It trained me how to think a certain way and be aware of all the elements that go into making great design," she says.

A typical curriculum for a degree in interior design varies according to program. Associate's degree and certificate programs are less time-consuming, and therefore more concentrated. If you are already enrolled in a school that does not offer a program in interior design, your next best alternative is to take courses in the arts, both studio and history classes. Education in art history is the backbone of many noncertified designers and decorators. Drawing and sculpture, or whatever art courses appeal to you, can only benefit your visual growth and understanding. Other recommended areas of study are business and marketing. As Rhonda Layton, an interior designer and business owner, says, "Interior design is about 90 percent networking, marketing, selling, knowing the right people and this little thing called chutzpah, 7 percent paperwork and 3 percent design."

A Day in the Life: Design Assistant

8 a.m. Arrive at the office before the rest of the staff, brew coffee and ensure the office is in order. Wash dishes left over from yesterday's client meeting.

8:30 a.m. Check voicemail and e-mail for messages. Review calendar for day's appointments and call for confirmations. Adjust schedule as necessary and print revised schedule for head designer.

9 a.m. Other employees arrive. Operate switchboard for all incoming calls and take messages for staff who are unavailable. Field calls from sales representatives requesting appointments with designers. Interface with clients and vendors.

10 a.m. Speak with the head designer. Receive instructions on several tasks, such as picking up fabric samples from design center, contacting dealers regarding memo items (pieces on loan for display only) for a client meeting and dictation of a letter for a potential client that must be messengered by noon.

11 a.m. Work on projects assigned by head designer while continually operating switchboard. Letter is first priority; complete it and give to head designer to proof. Contact dealers regarding memo items and arrange shipment with local delivery service.

12 p.m. Send revised letter to potential client. Once messenger arrives, escape for lunch. Pick up fabric samples while picking up lunch—a reprieve from the switchboard for at least an hour. Visit several fabric houses and leave design center loaded down with bags. Pick up lunch for yourself and other office mates at nearby café.

1:30 p.m. Check voicemail and e-mail for messages while you were out. Open and sort mail. Address envelopes for bookkeeper. Prepare office for client meeting at 2:30. Run up the street to purchase a new orchid for entryway. Brew more coffee and tea. Ensure conference room is organized and clean. Gather any last minute information head designer needs for meeting.

Visit Vault at www.vault.com for insider company profiles, expert advice, career message boards, expert resume reviews, the Vault Job Board and more.

VAULT CAREER LIBRARY 143

2:30 p.m. Show clients to conference room, offer drinks and snacks. Work on additional projects other staff members have requested: errands, scheduling of appointments, shipments of furniture. Keep track of money in meters and ensure clients do not get parking tickets while in meeting.

4:00 p.m. Clients leave. Clean conference room, wash dishes. Empty trash throughout office. Return calls on behalf of designer and schedule additional appointments for remainder of week.

5:00 p.m. Since there is nothing urgent to complete, you get to leave on time!

Employer Directory

AECOM Technology Corporation
555 South Flower Street, Suite 3700
Los Angeles, CA 90071-2300
Phone: (213) 593-8000
www.aecom.com

Bechtel Group, Inc.
50 Beale Street
San Francisco, CA 94105
Phone: (415) 768-1234
Fax: (415) 768-9038
www.bechtel.com

Callison Architecture, Inc.
1420 5th Avenue, Suite 2400
Seattle, WA 98101
Phone: (206) 623-4646
Fax: (206) 623-4625

Cannon Design
2170 Whitehaven Road
Grand Island, NY 14072
Phone: (716) 773-6800
Fax: (716) 773-5909
www.cannondesign.com

Fxfowle Architects Pc
22 West 19th Street
New York, NY 10011
Phone: (212) 627-1700
www.fxfowle.com

Gresham, Smith and Partners
1400 Nashville City Center
511 Union Street
Nashville, TN 37219-1733
Phone: (615) 770-8100
Fax: (615) 770-8494
www.gspnet.com

HDR, Inc.
8404 Indian Hills Drive
Omaha, NE 68114
Phone: (402) 399-1000
Fax: (402) 399-1238
www.hdrinc.com

Heery International, Inc.
999 Peachtree Street NE
Atlanta, GA 30309
Phone: (404) 881-9880
Fax: (404) 892-8479

H+L Architecture
1621 18th Street, Suite 110
Denver, CO 80202
Phone: (303) 295-1792
Fax: (303) 292-6437
www.hlarch.com

HOK Group, Inc.
211 North Broadway, Suite 600
St. Louis, MO 63102
Phone: (314) 421-2000
Fax: (314) 421-2152
www.hok.com

HKS, Inc.
1919 McKinney Avenue
Dallas, TX 75201
Phone: (214) 969-5599
Fax: (214) 969-3397
www.hksinc.com

Leo A Daly Company
8600 Indian Hills Drive
Omaha, NE 68114
Phone: (402) 391-8111
Fax: (402) 391-8564
www.leoadaly.com

M. Arthur Gensler Jr. & Associates, Inc.
2 Harrison Street, Suite 400
San Francisco, CA 94105
Phone: (415) 433-3700
Fax: (415) 836-4599
www.gensler.com

NBBJ
223 Yale Avenue North
Seattle, WA 98109
Phone: (206) 223-5555
Fax: (206) 621-2300
www.nbbj.com

RMJM Hillier
500 Alexander Park
Princeton, NJ 8543
Phone: (609) 452-8888
Fax: (609) 452-8332
www.hillier.com

RTKL Associates Inc.
901 South Bond Street
Baltimore, MD 21231
Phone: (410) 537-6000
Fax: (410) 276-2136
www.rtkl.com

Skidmore Owings & Merrill LLP
224 South Michigan Avenue
Suite 1000
Chicago, IL 60604
Phone: (312) 554-9090
Fax: (312) 360-4545
www.som.com

SmithGroup, Inc.
500 Griswold Street, Suite 1700
Detroit, MI 48226
Phone: (313) 983-3600
Fax: (313) 983-3636
www.smithgroup.com

URS Corporation
600 Montgomery Street, 26th Floor
San Francisco, CA 94111
Phone: (415) 774-2700
Fax: (415) 398-1905
www.urscorp.com

Zimmer Gunsul Frasca Architects LLP
320 SW Oak Street, Suite 500
Portland, OR 97204
Phone: (503) 224-3860
Fax: (503) 224-2482

Visit Vault at www.vault.com for insider company profiles, expert advice, career message boards, expert resume reviews, the Vault Job Board and more.

VAULT CAREER LIBRARY   145

limitless potential

[MERRILL LYNCH]

growth and momentum

inspiring colleagues

Merrill Lynch offers you unparalleled opportunities to build your career. Our premier brand and global capabilities create a strong foundation for you to explore a range of diverse career options. Working within a dynamic environment, you will contribute to our company's business growth and momentum. It's a great time to join us.

Work alongside industry-leading professionals to deliver exceptional solutions to our clients. Expect to be a contributor, a collaborator, and a colleague.

For more information or to apply online, visit **ml.com/careers**

Merrill Lynch is an equal opportunity employer.

ml.com/careers

 **Merrill Lynch**

Banking

Investment Banking

What is investment banking? Is it investing? Is it banking? Really, it is neither. Investment banking, or I-banking, as it is often called, is the term used to describe the business of raising capital for companies and advising them on financing and merger alternatives. Capital essentially means money. Companies need cash in order to grow and expand their businesses; investment banks sell securities (debt and equity) to investors in order to raise this cash. These securities can come in the form of stocks, bonds or loans. Once issued, these securities trade in the global financial markets.

Generally, an investment bank comprises the following areas:

Corporate finance

The bread and butter of a traditional investment bank, corporate finance generally performs two different functions: 1) mergers and acquisitions advisory, and 2) underwriting. On the mergers and acquisitions (M&A) advising side of corporate finance, bankers assist in negotiating and structuring a merger between two companies. If, for example, a company wants to buy another firm, then an investment bank will help finalize the purchase price, structure the deal and generally ensure a smooth transaction. The underwriting function within corporate finance involves raising capital for a client. In the investment banking world, capital can be raised by selling either stocks or bonds to investors.

Sales

Sales is another core component of an investment bank. Salespeople take the form of: (1) the classic retail broker, (2) the institutional salesperson or (3) the private client service representative. Brokers develop relationships with individual investors and sell stocks and stock advice to the average Joe. Institutional salespeople develop business relationships with large institutional investors—those who manage large groups of assets, like pension funds or mutual funds. Private client service (PCS) representatives, often referred to as private wealth managers, lie somewhere between retail brokers and institutional salespeople, providing brokerage and money management services for extremely wealthy individuals. Salespeople make money through commissions on trades made through their firms.

Trading

Traders also provide a vital role for the investment bank. Traders facilitate the buying and selling of stock, bonds or other securities, either by carrying an inventory of securities for sale or by executing a given trade for a client. Traders deal with transactions, large and small, and provide liquidity (the ability to buy and sell securities) for the market—often called making a market. Traders make money by purchasing securities and selling them at a slightly higher price. This price differential is called the "bid-ask spread."

Research

Research analysts follow stocks and bonds and make recommendations on whether to buy, sell or hold those securities. Stock analysts (known as equity analysts) typically focus on one industry and will cover up to 20 companies' stocks at any given time. Some research analysts work on the fixed-income side and will cover a particular segment, such as high-yield bonds or U.S. Treasury bonds. Salespeople within the investment bank utilize research published by analysts to convince their clients to buy or sell securities through their firm. Corporate finance bankers rely on research analysts to be experts in the industry in which they are working. Reputable research analysts can generate substantial corporate finance business and substantial trading activity, and thus are an integral part of any investment bank.

Visit Vault at **www.vault.com** for insider company profiles, expert advice, career message boards, expert resume reviews, the Vault Job Board and more.

VAULT CAREER LIBRARY 147

Syndicate

The hub of the investment banking wheel, syndicate provides a vital link between salespeople and corporate finance. Syndicate exists to facilitate the placing of securities in a public offering, a knock-down-drag-out affair between and among buyers of offerings and the investment banks managing the process. In a corporate or municipal debt deal, syndicate also determines the allocation of bonds.

Commercial Banking

Commercial banks, unlike investment banks, generally act as lenders, putting forth their own money to support businesses as opposed to investment advisors who rely on other folks—buyers of stocks and bonds—to pony up cash. This distinction, enshrined by fundamental banking laws in place since the 1930s, has led to noticeable cultural differences (exaggerated by stereotype) between commercial and investment bankers. Commercial bankers (deservedly or not) have a reputation for being less aggressive, more risk-averse and simply not as "mean" as investment bankers. Commercial bankers also don't command the eye-popping salaries and prestige that investment bankers receive.

There is a basis for the stereotype. Commercial banks carefully screen borrowers because the banks are investing huge sums of their own money in companies that must remain healthy enough to make regular loan payments for decades. Investment bankers, on the other hand, can make their fortunes in one day by skimming off some of the money raised in a stock offering or invested into an acquisition. While a borrower's subsequent business decline can damage a commercial bank's bottom line, a stock that plummets after an offering has no effect on the investment bank that managed its IPO.

We'll take your money

Commercial bankers make money by their legal charter to take deposits from businesses and consumers. To gain the confidence of these depositors, commercial banks offer government-sponsored guarantees on these deposits on amounts up to $100,000. But to get FDIC guarantees, commercial banks must follow a myriad of regulations (and hire regulators to manage them). Many of these guidelines were set up in the Glass-Steagall Act of 1933, which was meant to separate the activities of commercial and investment banks. Glass-Steagall included a restriction on the sale of stocks and bonds (investment banks, which could not take deposits, were exempt from banking laws and free to offer more speculative securities offerings). Deregulation—especially the Financial Services Modernization Act of 1999—and consolidation in the banking industry over the past decade have weakened these traditional barriers.

The lending train

The typical commercial banking process is fairly straightforward. The lending cycle starts with consumers depositing savings or businesses depositing sales proceeds at the bank. The bank, in turn, puts aside a relatively small portion of the money for withdrawals and to pay for possible loan defaults. The bank then loans the rest of the money to companies in need of capital to pay for, say, a new factory or an overseas venture. A commercial bank's customers can range from the dry cleaner on the corner to a multinational conglomerate. For very large clients, several commercial banks may band together to issue "syndicated loans" of truly staggering sizes.

Commercial banks lend money at interest rates that are largely determined by the Federal Reserve Board (currently governed by Ben Bernanke). Along with lending money that they have on deposit from clients, commercial banks lend out money that they have received from the Fed. The Fed loans out money to commercial banks, which in turn lend it to bank customers in a variety of forms—standard loans, mortgages and so on. Besides its ability to set a baseline interest rate for all loans, the Fed also uses its lending power to equalize the economy. To prevent inflation, the Fed raises the interest rate it charges for the money it loans to banks, slowing down the circulation of money and the growth of the economy. When it wants to encourage economic growth, the Fed will lower the interest rate it charges banks.

Making money by moving money

Take a moment to consider how a bank makes its money. Commercial banks in the U.S. earn 5 to 14 percent interest on most of their loans. As commercial banks typically only pay depositors 1 percent—if anything—on checking accounts and 2 to 3 percent on savings accounts, they make a tremendous amount of money in the difference between the cost of their funds (1 percent for checking account deposits) and the return on the funds they loan (5 to 14 percent).

Corporate Finance

Stuffy bankers?

The stereotype of the corporate finance department is stuffy, arrogant (white and male) MBAs who frequent golf courses and talk on cell-phones nonstop. While this is increasingly less true, corporate finance remains the most white-shoe department in the typical investment bank. The atmosphere in corporate finance is, unlike that in sales and trading, often quiet and reserved. Junior bankers sit separated by cubicles, quietly crunching numbers.

Depending on the firm, corporate finance can also be a tough place to work, with unforgiving bankers and expectations through the roof. Although decreasing, stories of analyst abuse run rampant and some bankers come down hard on new analysts simply to scare and intimidate them. The lifestyle for corporate finance professionals can be a killer. In fact, many corporate finance workers find that they literally dedicate their lives to the job. Social life suffers, free time disappears and stress multiplies. It is not uncommon to find analysts and associates wearing rumpled pants and wrinkled shirts, exhibiting the wear and tear of all-nighters. Fortunately, these long hours pay remarkable dividends in the form of six-figure salaries and huge year-end bonuses.

Personality-wise, bankers tend to be highly intelligent, motivated, and not lacking in confidence. Money is very much a driving motivation for bankers, and many anticipate working for just a few years to earn as much as possible, before finding less demanding work. Analysts and associates tend also to be ambitious, intelligent and pedigreed. If you happen to be going into an analyst or associate position, make sure to check your ego at the door but don't be afraid to ask penetrating questions about deals and what is required of you.

Investment bankers generally work in deal teams which, depending on the size of a deal, vary somewhat in makeup. In the paragraphs below, we will provide an overview of the roles and lifestyles of the positions in corporate finance, from analyst to managing director. (Often, a person in corporate finance is generally called an I-banker.) Because the titles and roles really do not differ significantly between underwriting to M&A, we have included both in this explanation. In fact, at most smaller firms, underwriting and transaction advisory are not separated, and bankers typically pitch whatever business they can scout out within their industry sector.

Analysts

Analysts are the grunts of the corporate finance world. They often toil endlessly with little thanks, little pay (when figured on an hourly basis), and barely enough free time to sleep four hours a night. Typically hired directly out of top undergraduate universities, this crop of bright, highly motivated kids does the financial modeling and basic entry-level duties associated with any corporate finance deal.

Visit Vault at www.vault.com for insider company profiles, expert advice, career message boards, expert resume reviews, the Vault Job Board and more.

VAULT CAREER LIBRARY 149

Modeling every night until 2 a.m. and not having much of a social life proves to be unbearable for many an analyst. Furthermore, when not at the office, analysts can be found feverishly typing on their BlackBerries. Not surprisingly, after two years, many analysts leave the industry. Unfortunately, many bankers recognize the transient nature of analysts, and work them hard to get the most out of them they can. The unfortunate analyst that screws up or talks back too much may never get quality work, spending his days bored until 11 p.m. waiting for work to come, stressing even more than the busy analyst. These are the analysts that do not get called to work on live transactions, and do menial work or just put together pitchbooks all of the time. The very best analysts often get identified early by top performing MDs and VPs, thus finding themselves staffed on many live transactions.

When it comes to analyst pay, much depends on whether the analyst is in New York or not. In the City, salary often begins for first-year analysts at $55,000 to $70,000 per year, with an annual bonus of approximately $60,000 to $85,000. While this seems to be quite a lot for a 22-year-old with just an undergrad degree, it's not a great deal if you consider per-hour compensation. Bonuses at this level are also force-ranked, thus identifying and compensating top talent. At most firms, analysts also get dinner every night for free if they work late, and have little time to spend their income, often meaning fat checking and savings accounts and ample fodder to fund business school or law school down the road. At regional firms, pay typically is 20 percent less than that of their New York counterparts. Worth noting, though, is the fact that at regional firms (1) hours are often less, and (2) the cost of living is much lower. Be wary, however, of the small regional firm or branch office of a Wall Street firm that pays at the low end of the scale and still shackles analysts to their cubicles.

Regardless of location, while the salary generally does not improve much for second-year analysts, the bonus will dramatically increase for those second-years who demonstrate high performance. At this level, bonuses depend mostly on an analyst's contribution, attitude and work ethic, as opposed to the volume of business generated by the bankers with whom he or she works.

Associates

Much like analysts, associates hit the grindstone hard. Working 80- to 100-hour weeks, usually fresh out of top-tier MBA programs, associates stress over pitchbooks and models all night, become experts with financial modeling on Excel, and sometimes shake their heads wondering what the point is. Unlike analysts, however, associates more quickly become involved with clients and, most importantly, are not at the bottom of the totem pole. Associates quickly learn to play quarterback and hand-off menial modeling work and research projects to analysts. However, treatment from vice presidents and managing directors doesn't necessarily improve for associates versus analysts, as bankers sometimes care more about the work getting done, and not about the guy or gal working away all night to complete it.

Usually hailing directly from top business schools (sometimes law schools or other grad schools), associates often possess only a summer's worth of experience in corporate finance, so they must start almost from the beginning. Associates who worked as analysts before grad school have a little more experience under their belts. The overall level of business awareness and knowledge a bright MBA has, however, makes a tremendous difference, and associates quickly earn the luxury of more complicated work, client contact and bigger bonuses.

Associates are at least much better paid than analysts. A $95,000 to $100,000 salary generally starts them off, and usually bonuses hit $35,000 to $55,000 or more in the first six months. (At most firms, associates start in August and get their first prorated bonus in January.) Newly minted MBAs cash in on signing bonuses and forgivable loans as well, especially on Wall Street. These can amount to another $35,000 to $55,000, depending on the firm, providing total first-year compensation over $200,000 for top firms. Associates beyond their first year begin to rake it in, earning $250,000 to $500,000 and up per year, depending on the firm's profitability and other factors.

Vice presidents

Upon attaining the position of vice president (at most firms, after four or five years as associates), those in corporate finance enter the realm of real bankers. The lifestyle becomes more manageable once the associate moves up to VP. On the plus side, weekends sometimes free up, all-nighters drop off, and the general level of responsibility increases—VPs are the ones telling associates and analysts to stay late on Friday nights. In the office, VPs manage the financial modeling/pitchbook production process in the Corporate Finance office. On the negative side, the wear and tear of traveling that accompanies VP-level banker responsibilities can be difficult. As a VP, one begins to handle client relationships, and thus spends much more time on the road than analysts or associates. As a VP, you can look forward to being on the road at least two to four days per week, usually visiting current and potential clients. Don't forget about closing dinners (to celebrate completed deals), industry conferences (to drum up potential business and build a solid network within their industry), and, of course, roadshows. VPs are perfect candidates to baby-sit company management on roadshows.

Directors/managing directors

Directors and managing directors (MDs) are the major players in corporate finance. Typically, MDs set their own hours, deal with clients at the highest level, and disappear whenever a drafting session takes place, leaving this grueling work to others. (We will examine these drafting sessions in depth later.) MDs mostly develop and cultivate relationships with various companies in order to generate corporate finance business for the firm. At this point in a banker's career, the job completes the transition from managing a process to managing a relationship. MDs typically focus on one industry, develop relationships among management teams of companies in the industry, and visit these companies pitching ideas on a regular basis. These visits are aptly called sales calls.

Mergers and Acquisitions

Mergers & Acquisitions (M&A) transactions can be roughly divided into either mergers or acquisitions. These terms are often used interchangeably in the press, and the actual legal difference between the two involves arcana of accounting procedures, but we can still draw a rough difference between the two.

Acquisition: When a larger company takes over another (smaller firm) and clearly becomes the new owner, the purchase is typically called an acquisition on Wall Street. Typically, the target company ceases to exist post-transaction (from a legal corporation point of view) and the acquiring corporation swallows the business. The stock of the acquiring company continues to be traded.

Merger: A merger occurs when two companies, often roughly of the same size, combine to create a new company. Such a situation is often called a "merger of equals." Both companies' stocks are tendered (or given up), and new company stock is issued in its place. For example, both Chrysler and Daimler-Benz ceased to exist when their firms merged, and a new combined company, DaimlerChrysler was created.

M&A advisory services

For an I-bank, M&A advising is highly profitable, and there are many possibilities for types of transactions. Perhaps a small private company's owner/manager wishes to sell out for cash and retire. Or perhaps a big public firm aims to buy a competitor through a stock swap. Whatever the case, M&A advisors come directly from the corporate finance departments of investment banks. Unlike public offerings, merger transactions do not directly involve salespeople, traders or research analysts, although research analysts in particular can play an important role in "blessing" the merger. In particular, M&A advisory falls onto the laps of M&A specialists and fits into one of either two buckets: seller representation or buyer representation (also called target representation and acquirer representation).

Visit Vault at **www.vault.com** for insider company profiles, expert advice, career message boards, expert resume reviews, the Vault Job Board and more.

VAULT CAREER LIBRARY 151

Representing the target

An I-bank that represents a potential seller has a much greater likelihood of completing a transaction (and therefore being paid) than an I-bank that represents a potential acquirer. Also known as sell-side work, this type of advisory assignment is generated by a company that approaches an investment bank (also an investment bank may also make the initial approach and "pitch" the idea of the company being sold or merged) and asks the bank to find a buyer of either the entire company or a division. Often, sell-side representation comes when a company asks an investment bank to help it sell a division, plant or subsidiary operation.

Generally speaking, the work involved in finding a buyer includes writing a Selling Memorandum and then contacting potential strategic or financial buyers of the client. If the client hopes to sell a semiconductor plant, for instance, the I-bankers will contact firms in that industry, as well as buyout firms that focus on purchasing technology or high-tech manufacturing operations. In the case of many LBO transactions, a sell-side firm might even hold an "auction" in which it will accept bids for the company, in order to get the seller the best price possible for its property.

Representing the acquirer

In advising sellers, the I-bank's work is complete once another party purchases the business up for sale, i.e., once another party buys your client's company or division or assets. Buy-side work is an entirely different animal. The advisory work itself is straightforward: the investment bank contacts the firm their client wishes to purchase, attempts to structure a palatable offer for all parties, and makes the deal a reality. (Again, the initial contact may be from the acquiring company. Or the investment bank may "pitch" the idea of an acquisition of Company X to the acquiring company.) However, most of these proposals do not work out; few firms or owners are readily willing to sell their business. And because the I-banks primarily collect fees based on completed transactions, their work often goes unpaid. However, this doesn't stop investment banks from dreaming up new proposals.

Consequently, when advising clients looking to buy a business, an I-bank's work often drags on for months. Often a firm will pay a nonrefundable retainer fee to hire a bank and say, "Find us a target company to buy." These acquisition searches can last for months and produce nothing except associate and analyst fatigue as they repeatedly build merger models and pull all-nighters. Deals that do get done, though, are a boon for the I-bank representing the buyer because of their enormous profitability. Typical fees depend on the size of the deal, but generally fall in the one-two percent range. For a $100 million deal, an investment bank takes home $1 to $2 million. Not bad for a few months' work.

Sales and Trading

The war zone

If you've ever been to an investment banking trading floor, you've witnessed the chaos. It's usually a lot of swearing, yelling and flashing computer screens: a pressure cooker of stress. Sometimes the floor is a quiet rumble of activity, but when the market takes a nosedive, panic ensues and the volume kicks up a notch. If you haven't been to a trading operation, imagine a football-field sized floor with people sitting nearly on top of one another, televisions blaring CNN news, and a decibel level that resembles a sporting event, not a library. It's highly social, tense and loud. The atmosphere is what makes the trading floor unique. Traders rely on their market instincts to move millions of dollars, and salespeople spend hours on the phones, schmoozing with clients and yelling for bids from their traders. Deciding what, when and how much to buy or sell is difficult with millions of dollars at stake.

However, salespeople and traders work much more reasonable hours than research analysts or corporate finance bankers. Rarely does a salesperson or trader venture into the office on a Saturday or Sunday; the trading floor is completely devoid of life on weekends. Any corporate finance analyst who has crossed a trading floor on a Saturday will tell you that the only noises to be heard on the floor are the clocks ticking and the whir of the air conditioner.

Blurring the line between corporate finance and S&T: Structuring

Although there are vast differences between S&T and Corporate Finance, with the recent emergence of more complex derivatives trading, the line has been blurred. One such area is Structured Credit. Unlike regular trading of equity or debt, structured credit instruments (such as CDOs and CLOs) take months to structure (much like a corporate finance deal), before they can be traded in the markets. These instruments are usually exceptionally profitable.

Although the products they structure are eventually sold and traded, the lifestyle of those in structuring is very similar to corporate finance. These individuals work long hours, building models, visiting with clients and writing offering memorandums. However, due to the market-based nature of their products, structurers usually sit on the trading floor and work intricately with sales and trading professionals.

S&T: A symbiotic relationship?

Institutional sales and trading are highly dependent on one another. The propaganda that you read in glossy firm brochures portrays those in sales and trading as a shiny, happy integrated team environment of professionals working for the client's interests. While often that is true, salespeople and traders frequently clash, disagree and bicker.

Simply put, salespeople provide the clients for traders, and traders provide the products for sales. Traders would have nobody to trade for without sales, but sales would have nothing to sell without traders. Understanding how a trader makes money and how a salesperson makes money should explain how conflicts can arise.

Traders make money by selling high and buying low (this difference is called the spread). They are buying securities for clients, and these clients filter in through sales. A trader faced with a buy order for a buy-side firm could care less about the performance of the securities once they are sold. He or she just cares about making the spread. In a sell trade, this means selling at the highest price possible. In a buy trade, this means buying at the lowest price possible.

The salesperson, however, has a different incentive. The total return on the trade often determines the money a salesperson makes, so he wants the trader to sell at a low price. The salesperson also wants to be able to offer the client a better price than competing firms in order to get the trade and earn a commission. This of course leads to many interesting situations, and at the extreme, salespeople and traders who eye one another suspiciously.

The personalities

Salespeople possess remarkable communication skills, including outgoing personalities and a smoothness not often seen in traders. Traders sometimes call them bullshit artists while salespeople counter by calling traders quant guys with no personality. Traders are tough, quick and often consider themselves smarter than salespeople. The salespeople probably know better how to have fun, but the traders win the prize for mental sharpness and the ability to handle stress.

Visit Vault at www.vault.com for insider company profiles, expert advice, career message boards, expert resume reviews, the Vault Job Board and more.

VAULT CAREER LIBRARY   153

Shop Talk

Here's a quick example of how a salesperson and a trader interact on an emerging market bond trade.

SALESPERSON: Receives a call from a buy-side firm (say, a large mutual fund). The buy-side firm wishes to sell $10 million of a particular Mexican Par government-issued bond (denominated in U.S. dollars). The emerging markets bond salesperson, seated next to the emerging markets traders, stands up in his chair and yells to the relevant trader, "Give me a bid on $10 million Mex Par, six and a quarter, nineteens."

TRADER: "I got 'em at 73 and an eighth."

Translation: I am willing to buy them at a price of $73.125 per $100 of face value. As mentioned, the $10 million represents amount of par value the client wanted to sell, meaning the trader will buy the bonds, paying 73.125 percent of $10 million plus accrued interest (to factor in interest earned between interest payments).

SALESPERSON: "Can't you do any better than that?"

Translation: Please buy at a higher price, as I will get a higher commission.

TRADER: "That's the best I can do. The market is falling right now. You want to sell?"

SALESPERSON: "Done. $10 million."

Research

If you have a brokerage account, you have likely been given access to research on stocks that you asked about. This research was probably written by an investment banks' research department or by an independent research arm of the brokerage firm..

To the outsider, it seems that research analysts spend their time in a quiet room poring over numbers, calling companies and writing research reports. The truth is an entirely different story, involving quite a bit of selling on the phone and on the road. In fact, research analysts produce research ideas, hand them to associates and assistants, and then man the phone talking to buy-side stock/bond pickers, company managers and internal salespeople. (In the world of research, the "analyst" is the highest ranking position.) They become the managers of research reports and the experts on their industries to the outside world. Thus, while the lifestyle of the research analyst would initially appear to resemble that of a statistician, it often comes closer to that of a diplomat or salesperson.

It All Depends on the Analyst

Insiders stress that the research associate's contribution entirely depends on the particular analyst. Good analysts (from the perspective of the associate) encourage responsibility and hand off a significant amount of work. Others communicate poorly, maintain rigid control and don't trust their assistants and associates to do much more than the most mundane tasks.

Being stuck with a mediocre analyst can make your job miserable. If you are considering an entry-level position in research, you should carefully evaluate the research analyst you will work with, as this person will have a huge impact on your job experience.

Note that in research, the job titles for analyst and associate have switched. In corporate finance, one begins as an analyst, and is promoted to associate post-MBA. In research, one begins as a research associate, and ultimately is promoted to the research analyst title.

The Year in Review

Crisis marks the end of an era

During summer 2007, the phrase "credit crisis" took center stage. The nation watched helplessly as the subprime housing market imploded, affecting nearly every sector imaginable. Among the first to feel the crunch were the U.S. banking giants, some of which had seemed infallible. The crisis set off instability in financial markets both international and stateside, resulting in skittish investors. The crisis continued into 2008, and within the first quarter, more write-downs (reductions in book values of assets due to their being overvalued compared to their market values) at financial institutions only made investors wary, setting off drops in market liquidity. By March 2008, conditions were explosive, setting off the demise of global investment bank Bear Stearns. A few months later, the crisis took down another investment bank, as the U.S. government took control of the leading but ailing home mortgage companies, Fannie Mae and Freddie Mac. U.S. Treasury Secretary Henry Paulson indicated that allowing either of the giants to fail would "cause great turmoil" for domestic and international financial markets. To this end, his predictions seemed accurate; stocks rallied after the takeover announcement was made.

But the market gains were short-lived, and not long after, the credit crisis claimed its second investment bank, as Lehman Brothers filed for Chapter 11 bankruptcy in September 2008 after the federal government refused to support a takeover of the bank as it did for Bear. However, a few days after the filing, British giant Barclays stepped in, agreeing to purchase Lehman's U.S. investment banking operations, saving 10,000 jobs in the process. This was followed by Japan's Nomura agreeing to buy Lehman's Asian operations, which included about 3,000 employees.

On the same day that Lehman filed Chapter 11, Merrill Lynch—attempting to avoid a bankruptcy filing—agreed to be bought by Bank of America for $44 billion. The combination of BofA and Merrill Lynch—which was worth about $100 million not too long before the deal was announced—will create the country's largest brokerage house and consumer banking franchise. Merrill's 17,000 brokers and BofA's wealth managers will combine to form a powerful unit that will be known as Merrill Lynch Wealth Management.

And this was just the beginning of the changes on Wall Street. Two days after Lehman's bankruptcy filing and Merrill's acquisition of BofA, the crisis hit another boiling point, as the U.S. government seized control of American International Group, the monstrous insurance giant commonly known as AIG. The deal was a monumental one, putting a private insurance firm into the hands of the government and thus placing U.S. taxpayer dollars on the hook. The deal sent $85 billion to AIG in the form of a federal loan and handed the U.S. government an approximate 80 percent stake in the insurance company. The deal also sent banking stocks plummeting, as investors feared that more banks than were thought had huge liquidity issues. Included in those financial firms were the last two large independent investment banks still standing: perennial league table leader Goldman Sachs and perennial runner-up Morgan Stanley. Both firms' shares took nosedives when the AIG rescue was announced, with Morgan Stanley's shares falling about 24 percent and Goldman's slipping 19 percent (at one point, Morgan's shares were down an astounding 44 percent and Goldman's were in the hole by as much as 26 percent). Although both firm's shares rebounded a day later, they would soon make moves that would significantly change the face of investment banking as we know it.

On the heels of its seizing control of Fannie Mae, Freddie Mac and AIG, the Feds stepped in again to try to help curtail the financial crisis plaguing bank's and other financial institution, temporarily banning short selling and backing $50 billion in money market funds as well entering talks to buy up distressed mortgages, putting the U.S. government on the hook for up to $1 trillion. This was indeed good news for banks in distress, and the U.S. stock market reacted with making a huge leap. But this also underscored just how bad the situation was for everyone, including the top dogs on Wall Street. And on September 21, 2008, Goldman Sachs and Morgan Stanley decided to take matters into their own hands. In the midst of Congress endeavoring to pass a $700 billion rescue package for big Wall Street players, Goldman and Morgan both requested

Visit Vault at www.vault.com for insider company profiles, expert advice, career message boards, expert resume reviews, the Vault Job Board and more.

VAULT CAREER LIBRARY   155

to become bank holding companies. The requests were granted by the Federal Reserve, giving them the backing of bank deposits instead of relying on high-risk forms of financing.

By becoming bank holding companies—which gives the two venerable Wall Street firms a similar status as commercial banking behemoths Citi, BofA and JPMorgan Chase—Goldman and Morgan Stanley will now be closely regulated by several federal supervising organizations, and not only overseen by the SEC. The holding company status also means Goldman and Morgan will have to lower the amount they can borrow versus their capital, resulting in financially safer institutions with limited upside potential with respect to profits.

On the same day it became a bank holding company, Morgan Stanley also entered into an agreement with Mitsubishi UFJ Financial Group, which will buy 10 to 20 percent of Morgan Stanley's common stock. The Japanese bank has been making a big move in the U.S. recently. In August 2008, it acquired the remaining one-third of San Francisco-based UnionBanCal that it did not already own.

The fall of Bear

Though the effects of the credit crisis were felt throughout the industry, Bear Stearns—the investment house with the highest exposure to overvalued mortgage-backed securities—was harder hit than most. In October 2007, the bank announced that it would let go more than 310 staffers and combine its separate mortgage businesses into one. Its two home loan-related hedge funds—the High Grade Structured Credit Strategies Fund and its similarly named Enhanced Leverage counterpart—had imploded in July, turning $1.6 billion of investors' funds to dust (this was seen by some as the beginning of the credit crisis). Bear Stearns was forced to write off $200 million with the stroke of a pen—and fired the executive responsible for the asset management department, co-president Warren Spector.

Despite the lingering cloud and a disastrous third quarter (in which its revenue in fixed income declined 88 percent), Bear Stearns management asserted in October that it was cautiously optimistic, asserting that "most of our businesses are beginning to rebound." This cautious optimism proved unfounded, and in December 2007, the firm revealed its quarterly results, including a staggering $854 million loss—the first quarterly loss in Bear Stearns' history. Most of the losses came from write-downs, which the firm reported were $700 million greater than expected. Despite the quarterly results, Bear CEO James Cayne claimed his confidence in the company was "rock solid." In response to the disappointing results, Cayne and other Bear executives noted that they were foregoing their holiday bonuses—"as it should be," according to Cayne himself. In January 2008, when Bear's future took a turn for the worse, Cayne resigned.

In March 2008, facing collapse, Bear received a temporary reprieve when JPMorgan Chase & Co. and the New York Federal Reserve moved in to provide the firm with emergency funding. Bear, whose shares immediately fell 53 percent on the news, admitted that its financial situation had "significantly deteriorated" after it fell prey to a cash shortage brought on by the credit crisis. But within a matter of days, the situation turned even more dire. Fearing Bear's cash shortage, the firm's clients withdrew approximately $17 billion over two days, leaving the 85-year-old Bear with no choice (other than claiming bankruptcy) but to sell. And on Monday, March 16th, that sale became official when JPMorgan Chase announced it would buy Bear for $2 a share—just $236 million, or approximately 97 percent less than Bear's value in the previous week. (After much grumbling from Bear shareholders, the deal was cut at a higher value: $10 a share.) To help finance the deal, the Federal Reserve agreed to provide J.P. Morgan with about a $30 billion credit line, "believed to be the largest Fed advance on record to a single company," according to *The Wall Street Journal*.

Aftershocks of the buyout were felt all around the world. In Japan, stocks immediately sunk to the lowest they'd been in two years. Analysts in the U.K. predicted a depression on the scale of that which occured in the 1930s. Swiss-based UBS announced it would likely cut another 8,000 jobs. And in the U.S., financial stocks plummeted during the first few hours of trading on March 17th.

JPMorgan Chase, meanwhile, stepped forward to answer questions about what would become of Bear Stearns' employees. The bank stated that about 50 percent of job offers extended by Bear Stearns would be rescinded. Summer interns had it a little better—the firm assured summer interns that they "will be offered 10 weeks of pay if they work for a certain nonprofit organization and will get an early chance to apply for fall positions." Graduates denied full-time jobs were allowed to keep their signing and relocation bonuses, and given access to career services. The cuts came mostly in areas where there was overlap, such as M&A, equity underwriting and corporate finance. Offers in investment management and other areas such as commodities, merchant banking and prime brokerage (Bear's jewel) were unaffected.

Plenty of pink slips

For others in the banking trenches, the situation didn't look much rosier. Credit Suisse was one of the first big finance firms to downsize in response to the credit crisis, slashing about 150 jobs in September 2007. By the beginning of 2008, Credit Suisse confirmed that market conditions had caused the company to cut about 500 investment banking positions—a total of about 20 percent of the group. Goldman Sachs, which had estimated job cuts to be around 10 percent earlier in the year, said in June 2008 that 25 percent of its investment banking employees (about 1,500) at the vice president level had been cut. Morgan Stanley didn't fare much better, announcing in February 2008 that it would cut 1,000 jobs in its operations, technology and asset management units, in addition to shutting down its U.K. home loan business and decreasing the size of its U.S. counterpart. And in reaction to a $6 billion write-down in the first quarter of 2008 and its third quarterly loss in a row, Merrill Lynch announced in April 2008 that it would cut 3,000 positions (adding to the 1,100 the firm slashed in the first quarter of 2008).

Deutsche Bank, meanwhile, announced in April 2008 that it was cutting nearly 1,000 investment banking jobs in mortgage banking and other areas. Though the number was not in the realm of some its banking brethren, it still spelled trouble for Deutsche, which reported its first quarterly loss in five years—a €131 million net loss for the first quarter of 2008, contrasted with a €2.12 billion profit in the first quarter of 2007. UBS felt the pinch of the credit crunch, too, announcing in May 2008 that it would be cutting approximately 5,500 jobs, in addition to the 1,500 positions it eliminated in 2007. No doubt the news had just a little bit to do with UBS's first quarter loss of $10.9 billions.

Citi fared the worst of all the big banks, announcing at the beginning of 2008 that it was cutting 4,200 jobs, bringing its ultimate total number of layoffs close to 20,000 to 24,000. A few months later, it slashed another 2,000 positions. (Citi, perhaps in a damage control move, announced that it was simply culling the "bottom 5 percent of performers" each year.)

Though no bank was able to remain truly impervious to the credit crunch, some firms had it worse than others. In March 2008, Lehman Brothers announced that it was laying off about 5 percent of its total workforce of 28,600 employees. The cuts, which affected all of its business units, were hardly the first wave of cutbacks for Lehman—in 2007, the company slashed about 4,000 jobs, mostly in its mortgage operations arm. In the second quarter of 2008, some analysts were predicting that Lehman would be the next firm to fall—in a July 2008 poll on the financial site Motley Fool, more than 40,000 respondents chose Lehman Brothers as the next firm to have a "Bear Stearns-style implosion." (As of mid-July, Lehman's stock price was hovering around $20 per share, well below its 52-week high of $70, but higher than its 52-week low of $12 per share, which the stock traded at in early July.)

Cuts at all levels

All in all, estimated layoffs for the banking industry since its mortgage-related downfall were a staggering 79,000 jobs, the Bureau of Labor Statistics reported in January 2008. And those at the top were hardly exempt from the axe. In addition to the resignation of Bear Stearns' Cayne, there were quite a few shake-ups at the top of banking pyramids.

In July 2007, UBS's CEO Peter Wuffli was cut from the firm, and replaced by deputy CEO Marcel Rohner. Wuffli's removal was largely attributed to the collapse of a hedge fund the firm managed. In November 2007, Merrill Lynch took drastic action

Visit Vault at www.vault.com for insider company profiles, expert advice, career message boards, expert resume reviews, the Vault Job Board and more.

VAULT CAREER LIBRARY   157

after posting a $8.4 billion write-down and a $2.3 billion loss for the third quarter of 2007 (its largest quarterly loss ever), forcing CEO Stan O'Neal to step down. In his place Merrill substituted New York Stock Exchange Chief John Thain, after BlackRock CEO Larry Fink declined the position, insisting on full transparency of Merrill's exposure to the subprime market.

In December 2007, Citi had a full-time search on its hands after CEO Charles Prince resigned in November. The firm settled on Vikram S. Pandit to take over the reins. Pandit had only spent six months at the firm, but still managed to beat out such candidates as Robert B. Willumstad, Citi's former president, and Michael A. Neal, the head of GE Capital's commercial finance division. Wachovia also made a major change, asking CEO Ken Thompson to retire in June 2008. The request followed Wachovia's significant losses (including $707 million in the first quarter of 2008) due to failure to successfully integrate A.G. Edwards and buying mortgage lender Golden West not long before the subprime mess. A month later, Wachovia found Thompson's replacement, naming Robert K. Steel—former undersecretary of the U.S. Treasury—as its new chief executive and president.

Tough times for the top women of Wall Street

In April 2008, Morgan Stanley co-president Zoe Cruz—heir-apparent to Morgan's CEO throne and the 16th most powerful woman in the world, according to *Forbes* magazine—was summarily dismissed by CEO John Mack. Some argue that Cruz took the fall for Mack, who lobbied for her firing as a preemptive move to save his own job.

Lehman Brothers' Erin Callan—considered the most powerful woman on Wall Street after Cruz—suffered a similar fate in June 2008, when she was demoted from her position as chief financial officer, a spot she only held for a few short months. In July 2008, Callan left Lehman to head up Credit Suisse's global hedge fund unit. Callan's departure came as little surprise for Lehman Brothers, which had suffered a net loss of $2.8 billion in the second quarter of 2008. (Throughout her term as financial officer at Lehman, Callan argued for more transparency in financial reporting.) Callan's move to the Swiss giant's hedge fund arm was a coming home of sorts—she worked for Lehman's hedge fund unit at the start of her 13-year career with the firm.

The ballad of Fannie and Freddie

Although the departure of CEOs and other top executives certainly made good drama, virtually nothing made the credit crisis more pronounced than the consumer fear surrounding the uncertainty of the future of mortgage giants Freddie Mac and Fannie Mae. The mortgage agencies' stocks both lost half their value in July 2008—an event that some analysts said was worse for the financial markets than the collapse of Bear Stearns. (Fannie has lost about $7.2 billion since mid-2007 and Freddie has lost about $4.6 billion.) Following the stock nosedives, the U.S. Treasury finagled a few favors from Congress on behalf of the two agencies: a temporary increase in a credit line for Fannie and Freddie, along with temporary authority to purchase equity in one or both of the mortgage companies.

After much negotiation regarding the fate of Fannie and Freddie, House and Senate heads reached a tentative agreement within a few weeks. The Congressional Budget Office reported that a temporary plan to bail out Fannie and Freddie could cost the government $25 billion, including a $4 billion provision that would let local governments purchase and restore previously foreclosed houses.

You can run, but you can't hide

In early 2008, the FBI announced that it had begun a criminal investigation into 14 companies, as part of a larger inquiry into what had gone wrong with the mortgage industry. Goldman Sachs, Morgan Stanley and famously-defunct Bear Stearns received requests for information about subprime mortgage-linked securities. The FBI investigation, which is being carried out in cooperation with the Securities and Exchange Commission, has also targeted mortgage lenders and loan brokers.

By June 2008, effects of the investigation finally began to trickle down. Former Bear Stearns hedge fund managers Ralph Cioffi and Matthew Tannin were taken into custody—the first two arrests in conjunction with the probe. Cioffi and Tannin each face nine counts of conspiracy, securities fraud and wire fraud for purportedly deceiving investors about the stability of Bear's hedge funds. More arrests—at additional firms—are expected to follow as the query into the $396.6 billion fraud deepens.

The tables don't lie

Despite the rocky second half of 2007, investment banking league tables looked much as they did in 2006. In total global debt, equity and equity-related underwriting volume, Citi ranked No. 1 for the second consecutive year, according to Thomson Reuters. Citi, which worked on 1,740 deals worth a total of $617.6 billion, had its hands in two of the world's largest deals of the year: Blackstone's $4.75 billion IPO, underwritten by Citi, Morgan Stanley and 15 other banks; and MF Global Ltd.'s $2.92 billion IPO, underwritten by Citi, J.P. Morgan, Lehman Brothers, Merrill Lynch and UBS Investment Bank.

In worldwide announced M&A deal volume, perennial powerhouse Goldman Sachs again ranked No. 1, with Morgan Stanley in second place and Citi in third. Goldman also again took the top spot in the U.S., with Morgan in second and Lehman Brothers in third. As far as the largest worldwide transactions, BHP Billiton's acquisition of Rio Tinto down under in Australia for $192.7 billion came in at No. 1, followed by ABN-AMRO Holding's $99.4 billion sale and the $61.4 billion spinoff of Kraft Foods. By industry sector, financial services was the busiest when it came to merging, acquiring and divesting in 2007, with about 5,000 announced deals worth a total of $700 billion. In the U.S., overall M&A deal volume for the year hit a record $1.57 trillion, a 5.5 percent increase versus 2006.

The Fortune-ate ones

The 2008 Fortune 500 list included in its top 40 a number of big banking players, including Citi (No. 8), Bank of America (No. 9), JPMorgan Chase (No. 12), Goldman Sachs (No. 20), Morgan Stanley (No. 21), Merrill Lynch (No. 30), Lehman Brothers (No. 37) and Wachovia (No. 38). Goldman Sachs also ranked No. 2 on *Fortune*'s Best Companies to Work For list.

Small goes big time

Since the credit crunch began, it's been a big time for smaller boutique banks such as Moelis & Co., which advised on a number of big-ticket deals, including Yahoo!'s $44.6 billion unsolicited proposal from Microsoft, Allied Waste's pending $12.7 billion sale to Republic Services and Anheuser-Busch's $61.2 billion sale to InBev.

There has also recently been a good deal of jockeying for status between big name banking players. For years, J.P. Morgan Chase was the third-biggest bank in the U.S., trailing just behind Citi (Bank of America being No 1.). This rankled J.P. Morgan CEO Jamie Dimon, who spent many years at Citi under Sanford Weill. But Weill turned on Dimon in the late 1990s, ousting him and installing former CEO Charles Prince in his place. Dimon went on to a career at Bank One, which he then merged with JPMorgan Chase. In January 2008, Dimon had reason to cheer (despite the fact that his firm had taken a $1.3 billion subprime write-down and posted lower-than-expected earnings for 2007): for the first time, JPMorgan Chase's market value surpassed that of Citigroup's—$136 billion to $129.8 billion, to be exact. Although Citi still holds more assets, Dimon won bragging rights, declaring his firm the second-largest bank in America by market value.

Final completion

The long-awaited ABN AMRO transaction was finally completed in October 2007 after many months of anticipation and talks with Barclays, which ultimately bowed out of the deal. In April 2007, ABN AMRO received a letter from a consortium made up of Banco Santander, the Royal Bank of Scotland and Fortis—an invitation to start exploratory merger talks. The three-

Visit Vault at **www.vault.com** for insider company profiles, expert advice, career message boards, expert resume reviews, the Vault Job Board and more.

VAULT CAREER LIBRARY

159

bank consortium ultimately offered about $90 billion for ABN AMRO—$10 billion more than Barclays was offering. In October 2007, Barclays withdrew its bid for ABN AMRO and received break-up fees of €200 million from ABN AMRO. ABN AMRO was then officially purchased by the consortium.

Other high-profile (but less pricey) banking buys include Jefferies' June 2007 purchase of the Putnam Lovell investment banking business from Canada's National Bank Financial Group, and Oppenheimer Holdings' January 2008 acquisition of most of CIBC World Markets' U.S. investment banking business.

Down and out on Wall Street

Following the onslaught of the credit crisis, job security for those working in the industry became shaky at best. And a 2008 report by the National Association of College & Employers concerning the job outlook for several industries confirmed the gloomy career picture: For jobs in the financial sector—including banking and other fields—hiring was down overall by 7 percent.

Compensation will also be down in 2008. At a news conference in Albany in July 2008, New York Governor David Paterson said that Wall Street banks could end up slashing bonuses by approximately 20 percent in 2008. Paterson also scoffed at economists who believe the U.S. will not experience a recession: "This has finally confirmed to me that flying saucers have landed and that people from outer space are in our midst, influencing policy."

Whether alien life forms are trying to infiltrate legislative bodies or not, it's highly probable that, given the hits that most banks have already taken, bankers will close 2008 with significantly lighter wallets.

More failures ahead?

Analysts have predicted more bank failures in the industry's immediate future. *The New York Times* reported in July 2008 that federal regulators are steadying themselves for more bank closures, and analysts predict that some 150 of 7,500 small and mid-sized banks may fail over the next year to year-and-a-half.

Meanwhile, in 2007, the Federal Deposit Insurance Corporation flagged 76 "problem" banks, up from 50 at the end of 2006. Still, the FDIC has also assured customers that the state of the industry has been much worse—there were more than 1,000 banks on the same list toward the end of the last banking crisis, in 1992.

The final chapter in Lehman's history: 11

After being unsuccessful in its efforts to find a corporate buyer, Lehman announced on September 15, 2008, that it would file for Chapter 11 bankruptcy, a form of bankruptcy under which the firm would have its assets protected. The bankruptcy filing did not apply to Lehman Brother Asset Management or Neuberger Berman, LLC, whose portfolio management, research and operating functions will remain intact.

Over the course of the weekend leading up to the bankruptcy decision, potential buyers Bank of America and Barclays Plc both pulled out of talks to acquire Lehman (in parts or as a whole). As far as the possibility of a government loan goes, it looks like the U.S. Treasury may be using Lehman as an example. Treasury Secretary Henry Paulson said in a briefing regarding the firm's demise that he "never once considered it appropriate to put taxpayer money on the line" to save Lehman Brothers. On September 15th, the firm's stock was down to a mere 21 cents a share—quite a tumble from the high of $67 a share it had traded at within the past 12 months.

One day after it filed bankruptcy, Lehman Brothers found a financial savior in the form of Barclays, which agreed to purchase parts of the struggling firm for $2 billion. The transaction will include Lehman's equity, fixed income and M&A advisory units. In addition to avoiding bankruptcy, the Barclays takeover prevented about 10,000 Lehman investment banking jobs from being cut (for the time being, at least).

Merrill's surprise selloff

After witnessing the demise of Lehman Brothers and deciding to take matters into its own hands, Merrill Lynch agreed to be acquired by Bank of America in an all-stock transaction for $29 a share (about $44 billion in total) in September 15, 2008. Some Street insiders speculated that the Federal Reserve might have played a part in helping to arrange the sale as a way to attempt damage control. The deal, which is expected to close in early 2009, has received approval from directors of Merrill Lynch and Bank of America. Shareholder and regulatory approvals are also needed before the transaction is finalized.

Meanwhile, Bank of America CEO Ken Lewis appeared confident regarding the bank's acquisition of Merrill. In a statement, Lewis said that BofA "could have rolled the dice and possibly got it at a cheaper price," but added that "the long-term benefits" and "a strategic opportunity" were attractive for the bank. Once Merrill is officially incorporated with Bank of America, Merrill will become the biggest brokerage house in the U.S., employing more than 20,000 financial advisers. The combined entity will also be the largest consumer banking company. At the end of the day on which the transaction was announced, Merrill sold for $17 a share (compared with the $29 a share it was purchased for). Merrill can only back out of the agreement if its shareholders vote against the transaction, but if Bank of America's shareholders oppose the deal, Bank of America or Merrill can terminate the agreement.

An end of an era

On September 21, 2008, while Morgan Stanley and Goldman Sachs—the last two large independent investment banks still standing—were granted requests to become bank holding companies, giving them the backing of bank deposits instead of relying on high-risk forms of financing (as of August 31, 2008, Morgan Stanley had $36 billion in retail deposits and Goldman had $20 billion). Morgan Stanley and Goldman will now be similar in status and will soon directly compete with the likes of Bank of America, Citi and JPMorgan Chase. The moves changed the face of Wall Street, ending the reign of the large independent brokerage house. Many analysts and industry observers expect both Goldman and Morgan Stanley to acquire commercial banking firms to beef up deposits, so in the near future, the banking landscape will likely look a lot different than it does now.

Visit Vault at www.vault.com for insider company profiles, expert advice, career message boards, expert resume reviews, the Vault Job Board and more.

VAULT CAREER LIBRARY   161

THE WORLD NEVER SLEEPS.

Dreams.   **Realities.**

In Harvard Square, Jackson has just cracked an equation. Meanwhile, in Austin, Texas, Rita - the woman who will soon give Jackson an analyst position - is on her way to give a presentation on microfinance. And in Singapore, a team of Global Capital Markets Associates are projecting the impact of the growth of the global middle class.

Working in more than 100 countries means being open-minded in every way: how we do business, how we find solutions, and how we choose our colleagues. To us, inclusion isn't a rule to follow; it's a way of life. Because we're all different, and we're proud to be. That's why at Citi, the world never sleeps. **oncampus.citi.com**

Citi never sleeps™

Employer Directory

Citi

388 Greenwich St.
New York, NY 10013

Recruiting Contact:
www.oncampus.citi.com
Phone: (212) 559-1000

Your ambitions are more than plans for the future. They're your hopes and dreams. They're a part of who you are and who you aspire to be. When you join Citi you'll cultivate those aspirations with market-leading training and exposure to the most complex and groundbreaking transactions around the world. You'll join a company with an impressive, far-reaching heritage. Among our proud alumni are finance ministers, Nobel Prize winners, and even New York's mayor. While ambitions have taken them in different directions, their business foundation began with Citi.

Whatever your dreams Citi can make them a reality.

Undergraduate Schools Credit Suisse Recruits from

Boston College; CMU; Columbia; Cornell; Georgetown; Harvard; Howard; Michigan; Morehouse/Spelman; NYU; Rutgers; UPenn; Dartmouth; Duke; University of Illinois; Johns Hopkins; MIT; Princeton; UVA; FAMU; American; Barnard; Baruch; Berkeley; Boston University; BYU; Cal Polytechnic; Canisius; Cincinnati; Claremont; Dakota State; University of Delaware; Drexel; Duke; Emory; Florida State; Florida A&M; Fordham; George Mason; Georgia Tech; University of Georgia; Hofstra; University of Indiana; Iona; Jacksonville; Maryland; U of Miami; Niagara; Northeastern; Notre Dame; Penn State; Pomona; Purdue; Rice; RPI; SMU; South Florida; Stanford; Stevens; Stony Brook; SUNY Buffalo; Syracuse; Tampa; Temple; Texas A&M; UT Austin; UCLA; USC; Villanova; Wake Forest; Washington University; Yale

Credit Suisse

11 Madison Avenue, 10th Floor
New York, NY 10010-3629
USA

Recruiting Contact:
Credit-suisse.com/careers

Active in over fifty countries and employing more than 48,000 people, Credit Suisse provides investment banking, private banking and asset management services to companies, institutional clients and high-net-worth individuals. There are exceptional opportunities for growth in new product areas and emerging markets; there are equally exceptional opportunities for people who can help deliver that growth.

Undergraduate Schools Credit Suisse Recruits from

We recruit from top undergraduate programs. For more information, please visit our website: www.credit-suisse.com/careers.

Visit Vault at **www.vault.com** for insider company profiles, expert advice, career message boards, expert resume reviews, the Vault Job Board and more.

VAULT CAREER LIBRARY

163

Employer Directory, cont.

Goldman, Sachs & Co.

85 Broad Street
New York, NY 10004

Recruiting Contact:
Phone: (212) 902-1000
www.gs.com/careers

Undergraduate schools Goldman Sachs recruits from:
The firm hires from a number of schools on a divisional basis, and welcomes online applications from all colleges and universities. The following is a list of our primary cross-divisional target schools:

Barnard, UC Berkeley, Brown University, Carnegie Mellon, University of Chicago, Columbia University, Cornell University, Dartmouth College, Duke University, Emory University, Georgetown University, Hampton University, Harvard University, Howard University, Indiana University, Lehigh University, University of Michigan, MIT, Morehouse College, University of North Carolina, Northwestern University, University of Notre Dame, New York University, Pace University, Princeton University, Rutgers University, Spelman College, Saint John's University, Stanford University, SUNY Binghamton, Syracuse University, University of Texas at Austin, UCLA, USC, University of Pennyslvania, University of Puerto Rico, Vanderbilt University, University of Virigina, Wellesley College, Yale University

Goldman Sachs is a leading global investment banking, securities and investment management firm that provides a wide range of services worldwide to a substantial and diversified client base that includes corporations, financial institutions, governments and high-net-worth individuals. Founded in 1869, it is one of the oldest and largest investment banking firms. The firm is headquartered in New York and maintains offices in London, Frankfurt, Tokyo, Hong Kong and other major financial centers around the world. Please visit our careers site for information about applying online and our recruiting process.

Employer Directory, cont.

Allen & Company
711 Fifth Avenue, 9th Floor
New York, NY 10022
Phone: (212) 832-8000
Fax: (212) 832-8023
Firm does not have a web site.

Bank of America
100 North Tryon Street
Charlotte, NC 28255
Phone: (704) 388-2547
Fax: (704) 386-6699
www.bankofamerica.com

Bank of New York Mellon
1 Wall Street
New York, NY 10286
Phone: (212) 495-1784
Fax: (212) 809-9528
www.bnymellon.com

Barclays Capital
5 The North Colonnade
Canary Wharf
London, E14 4BB
United Kingdom
Phone: +44-20-7623-2323

200 Park Avenue
New York, NY 10166
Phone: (212) 412-4000
Fax: (212) 412-7300
www.barcap.com

The Blackstone Group
345 Park Avenue
New York, NY 10154
Phone: (212) 583-5000
Fax: (212) 583-5712
www.blackstone.com

BNP Paribas
16, boulevard des Italiens
Paris 75009
France
Phone: +33-1-4014-4546
Fax: +33-1-40-14-69-73

787 Seventh Avenue
New York, NY 10019
Phone: (212) 841-2000
Fax: (212) 841-2146
www.bnpparibas.com

Brown Brothers Harriman
140 Broadway
New York, NY 10005-1101
Phone: (212) 483-1818
Fax: (212) 493-8545
www.bbh.com

CIBC World Markets
MG Corporate Finance
300 Madison Avenue
New York, NY 10017
Phone: (212) 856-4000
www.cibcwm.com

Citi Consumer Banking
399 Park Avenue
New York, NY 10043
Phone: (800) 285-3000
Fax: (212) 793-3946
www.citi.com

Citi Institutional Clients Group
388 Greenwich Street
New York, NY 10013
www.citigroup.com

Citi Markets & Banking
388 Greenwich Street
New York, NY 10013
Phone: (212) 816-6000
www.citigroupcib.com

Citigroup Inc. (Citi)
399 Park Avenue
New York, NY 10043
Phone: (800) 285-3000
Fax: (212) 793-3946
www.citi.com

Cowen and Company LLC
1221 Avenue of the Americas
New York, NY 10020
Phone: (646) 562-1000
Fax: (646) 562-1741
www.cowen.com

Deloitte & Touche Corporate Finance LLC
600 Renaissance Center, Suite 900
Detroit, MI 48243-1704
Phone: (313) 396-3000
Fax: (313) 396-3618
www.investmentbanking.deloitte.com

Deutsche Bank
60 Wall Street
New York, NY 10003
Phone: (212) 250-2500
www.db.com

Dresdner Kleinwort
30 Gresham Street
P.O. Box 52715
London, EC2V 2XY
United Kingdom
Phone: +44-20-76-23-80-00

1301 Avenue of the Americas
New York, NY 10019
Phone: (212) 969-2700
www.dresdnerkleinwort.com

Evercore Partners
55 East 52nd Street, 43rd Floor
New York, NY 10055
Phone: (212) 857-3100
Fax: (212) 857-3101
www.evercore.com

Visit Vault at **www.vault.com** for insider company profiles, expert advice, career message boards, expert resume reviews, the Vault Job Board and more.

VAULT CAREER LIBRARY

165

Employer Directory, cont.

FBR Capital Markets
1001 19th Street North
Arlington, VA 22209
Phone: (703) 312-9500
Fax: (703) 312-9501
www.fbrcapitalmarkets

Gleacher Partners
660 Madison Avenue, 19th Floor
New York, NY 10021
Phone: (212) 418-4200
Fax: (212) 752-2711
www.gleacher.com

Greenhill & Co.
300 Park Avenue
New York, NY 10022
Phone: (212) 389-1500
www.greenhill.com

Houlihan Lokey
1930 Century Park West
Los Angeles, CA 90067
Phone: (310) 553-8871
Fax: (310) 553-2173
www.hl.com

HSBC North America Holdings Inc.
26525 North Riverwoods Boulevard
Mettawa, IL 60045
Phone: (224) 554-2000
Fax: (224) 552-4400
www.hsbcnorthamerica.com

Jefferies & Company
520 Madison Avenue, 12th Floor
New York, NY 10022
Phone: (212) 284-2300
www.jefferies.com

JMP Securities
600 Montgomery Street, Suite 1100
San Francisco, CA 94111
Phone: (415) 835-8900
Fax: (415) 835-8910
www.jmpsecurities.com

J.P. Morgan Chase Commercial Bank
270 Park Avenue
New York, NY 10017
Phone: (212) 270-6000
Fax: (212) 270-2613
www.jpmorganchase.com

J.P. Morgan Investment Bank
270 Park Avenue
New York, NY 10017
Phone: (212) 270-6000
Fax: (212) 270-2613
www.jpmorgan.com

Keefe Bruyette & Woods, Inc.
The Equitable Building
787 Seventh Avenue, 4th Floor
New York, NY 10019
Phone: (212) 887-7777
Fax: (212) 541-6668
www.kbw.com

KPMG Corporate Finance
120 Broadway, 23rd Floor
New York, NY 10271
Phone: (888) 957-5764
www.kpmgcorporatefinance.com

Lazard
30 Rockefeller Plaza
New York, NY 10020
Phone: (212) 632-6000
www.lazard.com

Macquarie Group
125 West 55th Street
New York, NY 10019
Phone: (212) 231-1000
www.macquarie.com/us

Moelis & Company
245 Park Avenue, 32nd Floor
New York, NY 10167
Phone: (212) 880-7300
Fax: (212) 880-4260
www.moelis.com

Morgan Keegan
Morgan Keegan Tower
50 Front Street, 17th Floor
Memphis, TN 38103
Phone: (901) 524-4100
Fax: (901) 579-4406
www.morgankeegan.com

Morgan Stanley
1585 Broadway
New York, NY 10036
Phone: (212) 761-4000
Fax: (212) 762-0575
www.morganstanley.com

Nomura Holdings, Inc.
1-9-1, Nihonbashi, Chuo-ku
Tokyo 103-8645
Japan
Phone: +81-3-52-55-10-00
Fax: +81-3-32-78-04-20

2 World Financial Center, Building B
New York, NY 10281-1198
Phone: (212) 667-9300
Fax: (212) 667-1058
www.nomura.com

Oppenheimer & Co.
125 Broad Street
New York, NY 10004
Phone: (212) 668-8000
www.opco.com

Perella Weinberg Partners
767 Fifth Avenue
New York, NY 10153
Phone: (212) 287-3200
Fax: (212) 287-3201
www.pwpartners.com

Piper Jaffray & Co.
800 Nicollet Mall, Suite 800
Minneapolis, MN 55402
Phone: (612) 303-6000
Fax: (612) 303-8199
www.piperjaffray.com

Employer Directory, cont.

Raymond James Financial
880 Carillon Parkway
St. Petersburg, FL 33716
Phone: (727) 567-1000
Fax: (727) 567-5529
www.rjf.com

RBC Capital Markets
Royal Bank Plaza
200 Bay Street
Toronto, ON M5J 2W7
Canada
Phone: (416) 842-2000

1 Liberty Plaza
165 Broadway
New York, NY 10006-1404
Phone: (212) 428-700
www.rbccm.com

Robert W. Baird & Company
777 East Wisconsin Avenue
Milwaukee, WI 53202
Phone: (414) 765-3500
Fax: (414) 765-3633
www.rwbaird.com

Rothschild
Rothschild North America
1251 Avenue of Americas, 51st Floor
New York, NY 10020
Phone: (212) 403-3500
Fax: (212) 403-3501
www.us.rothschild.com

Royal Bank of Scotland
36 St Andrew Square
Edinburgh, EH2 2YB
Scotland
Phone: +44-13-15-56-85-55
www.rbs.com

Thomas Weisel Partners
1 Montgomery Street
San Francisco, CA 94104
Phone: (415) 364-2500
Fax: (415) 364-2695
www.tweisel.com

U.S. Bancorp
800 Nicollet Mall
Minneapolis, MN 55402
Phone: (800) 872-2657
www.usbank.com

UBS Investment Bank
299 Park Avenue
New York, NY 10171
Phone: (212) 821-3000
www.ibb.ubs.com

Wachovia Corporation
301 South College Street, Suite 4000
1 Wachovia Center
Charlotte, NC 28288-0013
Phone: (704) 374-6161
Fax: (704) 383-0996
www.wachovia.com

Wells Fargo
420 Montgomery Street
San Francisco, CA 94163
Phone: (866) 249-3302
www.wellsfargo.com

William Blair & Company LLC
222 West Adams Street
Chicago, IL 60606
Phone: (312) 236-1600
Fax: (312) 368-9418
www.williamblair.com

Visit Vault at **www.vault.com** for insider company profiles, expert advice,
career message boards, expert resume reviews, the Vault Job Board and more.

VAULT CAREER LIBRARY 167

Consumer Goods/Marketing

Industry Overview

Ask for it by name

The consumer products industry produces and markets practically every item an individual can possibly purchase: from canned soup to shaving cream, chewing gum to washing machines—and everything in between.

To get a handle on the market, analysts often divide it into two categories, durable and nondurable goods. As the names imply, the former comprises items with (relative) staying power, like home furnishings, jewelry and electronics. The latter includes more ephemeral merchandise, with a life expectancy of fewer than three years, like soap, clothing, personal care items and cleaning supplies. Others, however, break the industry down into products that are staples and those that are discretionary—the difference between what consumers need and what they'd like to have. But however long they're intended to last, and whether consumers need them or not, these disparate products all have one thing in common: the overwhelming majority are sold under a brand name.

Brands exist ostensibly as a way for consumers to differentiate one manufacturer's goods from another—but of course, they mean so much more. A "brand" has two components. First, there's the association with the brand that the marketers and advertisers wish to cultivate in the minds of consumers, called the brand identity, where the brand promises (among other things) to make the consumer feel happier, more successful, more efficient or more popular. Then there's the idea of the brand that actually exists in the minds of consumers, called the brand image, which depends on how well it delivers on those promises. Effective brands communicate with consumers on an emotional level through advertising, and a buyer's feelings are also colored by previous experiences with the product. Of course, there can be considerable disconnect between the brand identity and the brand image, since a brand's image can be affected by all manner of scandal, rumor and negative press. There can also be a disconnect when the target audience fails to respond to the brand or finds it undesirable.

Internationalists

Regardless, branding these days drives an enormous amount of consumption. The numbers are staggering: spending on consumer products accounts for two-thirds of the volume of trade in the economy, and yearly spending on consumables hovers around $7 trillion in the U.S. alone. In addition, consumer products are making inroads into the furthest reaches of the globe: as American and European markets become increasingly saturated and competitive, manufacturers of consumer products are turning toward emerging markets in boom nations like those in the so-called BRIC (Brazil, Russia, India, China), Turkey and Eastern Europe.

These growing markets are like honey for consumer products manufacturers. Between 2003 and 2007, an index compiled by Morgan Stanley of the value of public companies in 25 developing nations increased nearly 250 percent. One reason for this phenomenal growth is tied to the World Bank's estimate that, by 2030, what it defines as the middle class will triple to include 1.2 billion people—and the overwhelming majority will live in the developing world.

Reaching customers in these dynamic economies is not simply a matter of shipping products to stores and advertising that they're ready to be taken home. There are a number of factors that companies must consider before taking on an emerging economy. Doing so is a risky endeavor, and is not a route to guaranteed gains. Emerging economies are unstable and prone to sudden financial crises, as in Russia in the late 1990s and Argentina in 2002. To further complicate matters, emerging economies often play by different rules than developed ones. Governments in these countries can be prone to cronyism and corruption, impeding the profitability and functions of businesses. Developing countries' infrastructure may be poorly maintained or absent entirely: utilities necessary for the smooth operation of business—such as electricity, clean water and reliable modes of transport—may be sporadically or entirely absent, leading to manufacturing difficulties and fragile supply

Visit Vault at www.vault.com for insider company profiles, expert advice, career message boards, expert resume reviews, the Vault Job Board and more.

VAULT CAREER LIBRARY 169

chains. While China's economic liberalization may have spurred a surprisingly high growth rate, it's still a communist country, operating under the dubious premise that bureaucracy can harness the market.

In addition, regulation of consumer products in developing markets may be notably absent, as in early 2007 when food products from China contaminated with melamine killed housepets in the U.S. In addition, cute toys coated in lead paint, counterfeit toothpaste full of lethal chemicals and defective tires that allegedly caused fatal accidents led to multiple recalls of Chinese-made imports and brought heavy media and legislative scrutiny to the issue.

The economic climate in a particular country is another hurdle that consumer products companies must sometimes overcome. While the elite in developing nations enjoy spending power and a standard of living roughly on par with that of Western countries, the majority of the population—95 percent, by some estimates—live on about $2,000 per year or less. Still, they are just like consumers everywhere: they desire products that make their lives easier and more pleasant, and are willing to shell out (within their means) for little luxuries. So, to tap this huge, profitable and underserved market, consumer products companies sell products like toothpaste, laundry detergent, shampoo, deodorant and moisturizer in small packets for a few pennies apiece. While the profit on such items might be mere fractions of a cent, they sell in large enough volumes to make serving this market a very profitable endeavor.

Of course, as branding guru Martin Lindstrom once noted, "A global brand-building strategy is, in reality, a local plan for every market." And when the markets are as disparate as Guangzhou and Cincinnati, what customers want will differ greatly. For instance, Crest toothpaste comes in flavors like tea and salt in China, flavors a Midwesterner would find mildly bewildering, to say the least. Lower-income consumers in China prefer to wash their clothes by hand, rather than pay for the excess water and electricity a washing machine consumes, and so they need washing detergent formulated specially for the task. In India, Whirlpool sells microwaves that can shallow-fry and sauté—cooking methods for a country that hasn't yet embraced convenience foods to the extent that the U.S. has.

Plan of ad-tack

That said, despite the developing world's growing importance in the consumer products industry, product sales in Western countries still account for the majority of these companies' income. But diverting new customers from Europe and the U.S. away from other products is increasingly difficult, as the people of developed nations are inundated with advertising. It's estimated that Americans, for example, see between 600 and 3,000 ads per day, and that most ignore them completely or view them as a nuisance, as users of ad-blocking software and fast-forwarding TiVo owners will attest. While traditional marketing techniques—catchy jingles, clever patter, happy housewives, etc.—have worked in years past, consumers are becoming increasingly immune to their effects.

In order to overcome consumers' jaded attitudes, marketers try to find new and clever ways to attract eyeballs to Product X, making the consumer products industry a cutthroat world. One recent trend has found companies running Internet contests in which audiences create their own ads for the product, with mixed results. Chevrolet gave Internet denizens stock footage of the Tahoe to craft into ads in 2006, and amateur muckracking documentarians promptly returned commentary on the cars' gas mileage and effect on the environment. A contest sponsored by Malibu Rum sparked participants' ire when it altered the rules of its contest. Unilever's Dove and Pepsi's Frito Lay had better luck with entries submitted to run in coveted slots during the 2007 Super Bowl and the Oscars, respectively. And Heinz chose a winner in April 2008 from over 2,000 entries responding to call on its web site for homemade ads for its world-famous ketchup.

Companies now also customarily enter the public's space—MySpace, that is. Scores of companies have set up campaigns on social networking sites to draw the attention of bright young things with plenty of disposable income. Procter & Gamble began using social networking site Facebook to promote tooth whitening strips in 2006, while Unilever promoted its Axe brand of men's body spray on MySpace. Several other firms, including American Apparel, adidas and Dell, have set up presences in the virtual world Second Life, hoping to communicate with consumers wherever they go.

Trading up

It's a time-honored adage that the rich are getting richer and the poor are getting poorer. In the U.S., incomes at the high end have been growing dramatically, and the number of millionaires has doubled in the past 10 years. As a result, more consumers are demanding products with an aura of luxury about them. Brands cultivate such an image in a number of ways. Louis Vuitton, whose logo-splashed bags are more common than litter on some New York City streets, manages to maintain its high profile by sponsoring America's Cup races, and only sells its wares through a small group of stores.

Several other high-end brands—Gucci, Rolex, Nokia's Vertu—clamp down on the number of stores that sell their wares so that only the select few can buy them. Polo maintains its strong whiff of upper-crust appeal, even while expanding some lines into decidedly midmarket—even (gasp) discount—retail channels JCPenney and Kohl's by allowing the lower-priced brands to feed off the halo of their higher-end cousins. However, readily available objects can still be considered luxury items: Whirlpool's sleekly designed Duet washer (priced at about $1,000 more than your run-of-the-mill white box) was the best-selling front-loading washer in 2006.

As the midmarket becomes increasingly saturated with luxury products, some brands have moved into pricking consciences in order to make consumers shell out. In 2006, Apple, Armani, Gap and Converse all embarked on a co-branding initiative with Product (Red), a humanitarian campaign co-founded by the musician Bono. The deal with Product (Red) is that a portion of profits from certain items (T-shirts, MP3 players, sneakers) are sent to a charity that then funds the distribution of AIDS medication in Africa. Needless to say, the campaign sparked some backlash, especially in regards to its $100 million marketing budget. One site, Buylesscrap.org, launched in 2007, pointed out that charities would be better off if people donated money directly to them instead of shopping, and that Product (Red) hardly makes it clear exactly how much money is going towards charity and how much towards its strong marketing push.

It's a natural

Philanthropy isn't the only way that brands are grabbing consumers' attention. The overwhelming interest in all things green, organic and natural is currently a major force driving consumptive activity, and even Wal-Mart's gotten on the green wagon. The green energy division of GE was its fastest-growing segment in 2006, and in 2006, Levi's brought out jeans made from organic cotton—a smooth move, considering sales of organic cotton clothing will top $2.5 billion in 2008. The Hain Celestial Group and Dean Foods, segment leaders when it comes to organic, natural and/or soy-based products, have both been around for several decades and are now reaping the benefits of earlier investments. (Even companies that appeal to the sweet tooth have leaned towards the "nutritional" if not the "natural"; Nestlé acquired the medical nutrition business of drug company Novartis in July 2007, around the same time Coca-Cola came out with a vitamin-enhanced Diet Coke and bought the parent of Vitaminwater, Glaceau.) The significance of the trend hasn't been lost on the top consumer products companies; most consumers don't realize that Cascadian Farms (frozen fruits and vegetables) and Kashi (cereals) are actually cogs in the larger machinery of General Mills and Kellogg's, respectively.

However, as consumer interest in products designated as "natural" and "organic" increases, there's some fudge factor about what these terms actually mean. In 2007, a number of poultry processors, including Sanderson Farms, objected to the use of the word "natural" on chicken products that had been treated with such substances as salt water, chicken broth and carrageenan, a thickener derived from seaweed that is added to prevent the chicken from drying out when cooked. The processors petitioned the U.S. Agriculture Department to update its definition of "natural," which at present excludes only the use of artificial colors, flavors and ingredients.

This occurred only a few months after natural cosmetics company Burt's Bees introduced an initiative calling for manufacturers of natural cosmetics to voluntarily ban certain ingredients from items sold as "natural," like sodium laureth sulfate and p-thalates. (Its initiative, called The Greater Good, promotes a list of natural ingredients, such as "black currant oil" and buttermilk, which is praised for being "richer in fats and emollients than whole cow's milk.") The topic came up

Visit Vault at www.vault.com for insider company profiles, expert advice, career message boards, expert resume reviews, the Vault Job Board and more.

VAULT CAREER LIBRARY 171

again in 2008: Dr. Bronner's Magic Soaps (officially named All One God Faith) accused 13 companies of false advertising by claiming their personal care products are organic; it subsequently filed a lawsuit in California on May 1, 2008 against the likes of consumer products groups Hain Celestial, Kiss My Face, Stella McCartney America, Estée Lauder and Whole Foods. Dr. Bronner's claims that certain components are made by treating them with petrochemicals, and others are suspected carcinogens.

The main problem is that there are a number of entities that certify products as organic, but no one definitive authority. In contrast to the food industry, there is no governmental body that governs lipsticks and face creams. However, the end of May 2008 did bring one authoritative statement: The California Attorney General filed suit against four companies (including Hain subsidiary Avalon Naturals) in an attempt to force them to append warning statements on their products about possible carcinogens.

As goes the economic climate, so goes consumer products

What may someday be referred to as "The Great Economic Turmoil of 2008" has affected a number of industries, perhaps none more so than consumer products. Escalating energy costs have raised shipping expenses, and petroleum-related products—integral to the process for making diapers, plastics, cleaners and packaging—have also driven costs. The price of basic ingredients, from peanuts to fruit, has climbed as well. Del Monte, Newell Rubbermaid, Kimberly Clark and Smucker's were just a few of the army of companies raising prices during the summer of 2008. Kellogg's sneakily kept cereal prices where they were while it made its boxes smaller.

Research showed that consumers, to save on gas, began to actively curtail their driving, which translated to fewer shopping trips, fewer products rung up and similarly poor results in the retail sector. They also cut out impulse buys, and bigger-ticket purchases such as food and other basic needs took up a larger slice of the take-home-pay pie. In the spring of 2008, the beauty market (which includes biggies L'Oreal and Estée Lauder), usually immune to the effects of financial stress, showed the largest one-quarter sales decline since 1997.

Marketing and Brand Managers

Marshaling the troops

Since it is such an important part of the industry, there are many job opportunities associated with branding and marketing. While each company organizes its people in a slightly different manner, consumer goods companies generally have a team of people specializing in each of their brands, in order to coordinate the efforts of the various departments whose work affect them, like research and development, advertising, manufacturing, product design, packaging design and sales, among others.

Typically, a team consists of a brand manager who heads up the operation, more junior associate brand managers and entry-level assistant brand managers. The team works with the aforementioned departments to drive brand awareness and consumption. These brand teams are then organized by region and function—for instance, all the personal care brands for the Americas might be grouped together, and all the food brands for Europe and so on. Since consumer goods companies are frequently large, multinational concerns, they often shuttle people from place to place, which allows workers to gain valuable experience in foreign markets.

Branding is also a fertile field for consultants, for those who would prefer to work with a wider variety of products or companies. Related job functions include market research, which determines why people buy the things they do (and how to get them to buy more), public relations and product management, which aims to develop new products in response to consumer demand. Other job functions at consumer goods companies include positions in manufacturing and quality control, HR, IT, legal and accounting.

Forging ahead

While some marketing departments hire students straight out of college, advancing in this line of work usually requires an MBA, especially if one intends to reach the post of brand manager. To gain more experience, it's advisable to start at smaller companies and smaller brands. While it may seem cool when everyone knows what you're working on, it may be difficult to make much of a difference to the brand.

In addition, marketers should gain as much experience as possible in a wide variety of products—and experience in working abroad will help give a new perspective, as well. Students fresh out of college usually start out as assistant brand managers, and are generally promoted to associate brand managers within a year or two. After 12 months as an associate brand manager, hires can head up their own smaller brand for a year or so before being moved onto a more important and profitable brand. Beyond that, he or she can be promoted to the position of category manager, developing strategies for a whole clutch of brands.

Brace yourself for the interrogation

Ready for the interview? Vault sources agree that job seekers in the consumer goods industry should come armed with a good idea of why they're seeking a particular position at a particular company, and be able to articulate that reason clearly. Having a good grasp of the company's situation in the industry and history will help, as well (good thing you're holding this guide!).

Be prepared for several rounds of interviews—sources reported undergoing as few as two to as many as seven interviews. Behavioral questions were the most common sort reported by hires: the type of questions that begin, "Tell me about a time when …" Interviewees should also be able to field questions about their skills and past job experience. Some marketing positions will ask potential hires (especially MBAs) to analyze an advertisement or answer a case question.

Keeping up the goods work

Marketing is well known as a cyclical industry that rises and falls in step with the state of the economy. Market corrections may slow things down temporarily, but since the economy, by definition, consists of people buying and selling things, as the economy grows, so will companies' marketing efforts. What shape these efforts might take in the future, however, remains to be seen. As consumers are increasingly intolerant of (or immune to) traditional modes of advertising, marketers will increasingly rely on cleverer ways to make products stand out in an overstaturated marketplace.

Some suggestions bandied about in a February 2007 article about the future of the industry on Brandchannel.com included celebrity endorsements (because if Lindsay Lohan does it, it's clearly worth imitating), product placement on TV and in movies, and "branded experiences" (like the Apple stores) to get consumers engaged with the brand. Other trends that are forecasted to grow include leveraging social issues to allow people to interact with the brand, such as Product (Red). Internet advertising has a long way to go, and leveraging the power of such a now-ubiquitous media outlet without making people tune out remains a challenge to be tackled by a new generation of marketers.

What is a marketer? The allure of brand management

Marketing encompasses a wide variety of meanings and activities. Some marketing positions are very close to sales, while others set overarching marketing strategy. What marketing positions have in common is the sense of ownership over the product or service, as well as the drive to understand customer needs and desires and translate those into some kind of marketing communication, advertising campaign or sales effort. The manager of product or service marketing is called the brand manager—he or she is the ruler of that marketing universe.

Visit Vault at **www.vault.com** for insider company profiles, expert advice, career message boards, expert resume reviews, the Vault Job Board and more.

VAULT CAREER LIBRARY **173**

Careers within the marketing/branding arena are high profile. The business world is now realizing that strong brands and solid marketing programs drive shareholder value, and that companies can no longer make fundamental strategy decisions without truly understanding how to market a product. Today's business challenges—the quest for company growth, industry consolidation and deregulation, economic webs, and the emergency of new channels and technologies—make marketers even more valuable.

The titles of brand manager, product manager and, to a lesser extent, marketing manager are often used to describe the same function—some companies use one title, others use another. Marketing managers tend to be used in industries other than consumer packaged goods; product managers are often used in tech industries. "Brand management" implies more complete supervision of a product. The typical brand management framework gives a brand "group" or "team"—generally comprised of several assistant brand or assistant marketing managers and one supervising brand manager—responsibility for all matters relevant to their product or products. Whether this responsibility is, in fact, complete depends somewhat on the size of the company relative to the number of brands it has, the location of the brand group and most importantly on the company's attitude toward marketing.

How important is the individual brand manager?

Consider the company to determine the level of brand manager responsibility. The first factor is the size of the company relative to its number of brands. For a company with hundreds of different brands—Nabisco, for example—brand managers, or even assistant brand managers, may have a great deal of power over a specific brand. At companies with a few core products, brand managers will focus on narrower aspects of a brand. As one recently hired assistant brand manager at Coca-Cola comments: "They're not going to take an MBA and say, 'Okay, you're in charge of Sprite.'" Brand managers at such companies will instead be focused on marketing to a particular demographic or geographic group, or perhaps handling one aspect of the product's consumption (plastic bottles, cases of aluminum cans and so forth).

International brand managers have historically held more sway than managers in the company's home market, but keep in mind that the daily tasks of international brand managers often lean more toward questions of operations, rather than questions of strategy or marketing. ("How much should we produce?" or "How is our distribution network affecting sales?" rather than "What do we want our brand identity to be?") International brand management is sometimes split into two positions. Global brand managers are more strategic, concentrating on issues such as protecting brand equity and developing product offerings that can be rolled out into subsidiaries. Local brand managers are more tactical. Local managers focus on executing global plans that are delivered to them, and tweak them for local consumers. Also know that with the increasing trend toward globalization and the truly global presence of certain brands, companies have sought to impose more centralization and tighter controls on the marketing of those brands from country to country. In the past, individual country managers have had more discretion and leeway to make decisions about a brand's packaging, advertising, etc. Now, companies have established tighter guidelines on what can be done with regard to a brand around the world, with the goal of protecting and enhancing the value of the brand, and ensuring a consistent product and message worldwide.

Finally, consumer goods companies place varying levels of importance on their brand or marketing departments. Some, such as the Ford Motor Company, are driven as much by financial analyses of production costs or operations considerations as by marketing. The level of emphasis on finance or operations matters at a firm will influence not only the independence and authority of marketing managers, but also potential marketing career paths. At some companies, marketing is the training ground for general management. At General Mills, marketing is considered so important that employees in other functions who show promise are plucked from their positions and put into the department.

Careers in Marketing

Taking charge of a brand involves tackling many diverse job functions—and different subspecialties. Decide where you'd like your main concentration to lie.

Brand management

In a typical brand management organizational structure, positions are developed around responsibility for a particular product rather than a specific functional expertise (e.g., you're an assistant brand manager for Cheerios). This structure enables you to be the "master of all trades," acquiring an expertise in areas such as manufacturing, sales, research and development, and communications. In brand management, the marketing function is responsible for key general management decisions, such as long-term business strategy, pricing, product development direction and, in some cases, profit and loss responsibility. Brand management offers a terrific way to learn intensively about a particular product category (you could be a recognized expert on tampons!) and to manage the responsibility of running a business and influencing its performance.

The core of brand work is brand strategy. Brand managers must decide how to increase market share, which markets and demographic groups to target and what types of advertising and special promotions to use. And at the very heart of brand strategy is identifying a product's "brand identity." Brand groups then figure out how to exploit brand strategy or, in some cases, how to change it. PepsiCo's Mountain Dew has built its popularity among youth as a high-caffeine beverage into a "brand identity" of cutting-edge bravado that has boosted market share, while the Banana Republic chain underwent a transformation from an outdoor adventure store that sold actual Army-Navy surplus to an upscale, chic clothing store. In both cases, the brands have benefited from a shift in brand identity, and consequently, a shift in their market. Brand identity is normally created and confirmed through traditional print, radio and TV advertising. Advertising is usually produced by outside agencies, although brand insiders determine the emphasis and target of the advertising.

Some liken a brand manager to a hub at the center of a hub and spoke system, with the spokes going out to departments like finance, sales, manufacturing, R&D, etc. It is the brand manager's job to influence the performance of those groups—over whom he or she has no direct authority—in order to optimize the performance of his or her brand or product line.

Advertising

If you enjoy watching commercials more than television programs, then consider the advertising side of marketing. As an account executive, your role is to serve as a liaison between your brand management client and the departments within your agency. Account executives manage the creative production process from beginning to end, from researching what benefits a product offers, to writing the strategy for a typical commercial. Account executives must also handle matters such as briefing the creative department on how to execute the advertising strategies, working with the media department to buy ad time or space and determining how to spend the marketing budget for advertising. (Will potential consumers be best reached via TV, outdoor billboards, print or radio—or through a general saturation campaign?) Along with managing the creative process, account executives at ad agencies are increasingly becoming strategic experts in utilizing traditional media, digital media, direct marketing and other services.

Direct marketing

Ever wonder who is responsible for making those coupons you receive in the mail? Or the Saab videotape you've received every two years since you bought your car in 1993? You can thank direct marketers. Direct marketers are masters in one-to-one marketing. They assemble databases of individual consumers who fit within their target market, go after them with a personal approach and manage the production process from strategy inception to out-the-door distribution.

Visit Vault at www.vault.com for insider company profiles, expert advice, career message boards, expert resume reviews, the Vault Job Board and more.

VAULT CAREER LIBRARY   175

Direct marketers have two main objectives: to stay in touch with their current consumer base and to try to generate more business by finding individuals who fit a target set of criteria but are not currently using their particular product. For instance, if you've ever checked out of the supermarket and got a coupon for Advil after buying a bottle of Tylenol, chances are a direct marketer is trying to convince you to switch brands by offering you a monetary incentive.

It's important to note that direct marketing isn't just done through snail mail. It operates in multiple media, such as the Web, telemarketing and in-store promotions. Direct marketers have a powerful new tool in their arsenal—the Internet. Marketers are able to track the online habits and behavior of customers. They can then serve up customized banner advertisements that are much more likely to be relevant to them. Many consumers have agreed to receive promotional offers on certain subjects— marketers can then send them targeted e-mail messages that allow for much easier access to purchase or action (clicking on a link, for example) than a conventional mail direct marketing programs.

Affiliate/property marketing

If you're working with a major brand company like Nike, Disney, Pepsi or L'Oreal, chances are you'll do a lot of cross-promotion, or "affiliate marketing." For instance, Nike has marketing relationships with the NBA, NFL and a variety of individual athletes and athletic teams. Disney has a strong relationship with McDonald's; cute toys from the entertainment company's latest flick are often packaged with McDonald's Happy Meals upon the release of each new movie. L'Oreal works with celebrities, like Heather Locklear, and sponsors events, such as the annual Academy Awards.

Marketers must manage the relationship between any two entities. If Disney wants to promote the cartoon *du jour* with McDonald's, or Pepsi wants to make sure that all Six Flags theme parks have a Pepsi ride, then marketers need to ensure both parties get what they need out of the deal and stay true to their own brand images.

Price marketing/sales forecasting

Pricing is largely driven by market pressure. Most people, for example, won't pay more than $2 for a hamburger in a fast-food restaurant. On the other hand, brand managers always have some pricing leeway that can greatly affect market share and profitability. An increase of a nickel in the price of a product sold by the millions can make huge differences in revenue— assuming the price rise doesn't cause equivalent millions less of the products to be sold. Brand managers need to figure out the optimal pricing strategy for their product, though it's not always a case of making the most money. Sometimes it makes more sense to win market share while taking lower profits. How do brand managers justify their prices? Through extensive research. Paper towels, for example, may be much more price-sensitive than a luxury item like engagement rings or smoked salmon.

Brand and marketing managers don't always have free reign over pricing. At some companies, such as those that sell largely through mail order, or those with complex pricing systems, pricing and promotional offers may be limited to what the operational sales system can handle. Explains one marketing manager at a long-distance phone company (an industry with notoriously tangled pricing plans): "It's very easy to offer something to the customer. It's very difficult to implement that in the computer system."

Another large part of the general management duties of brand managers is forecasting product sales. This means not only keeping track of sales trends pertaining to one's product, but also anticipating responses to marketing campaigns and product launches or changes. The forecasts are used to determine production levels. Once a year, brand groups draw up budgets for their production, advertising and promotion costs, try to convince the finance folks that they absolutely need that amount, get less than they ask for, and then rework their budgets to fit the given budget. As one international brand manager at one of the world's biggest consumer goods companies puts it: "You don't determine the production and then get that budget; you get the budget, and then determine the production."

High-tech marketing

Not everyone markets applesauce for a living. Many people choose to enter the world of high-tech marketing because they want to work with products and technologies that reshape and improve the world around us. These marketers feel that they would rather change the way a person interacts with the world in a sophisticated way, rather than spend time understanding what hair color teenagers find most appealing. High-tech marketers spend much of their time understanding research and development issues, and working on new product launches.

Technology companies like Intel, Dell and Microsoft have recognized the power of branding and are utilizing traditional marketing tactics more and more. Amazon's extensive marketing campaign in 1998 helped brand that company in the mind of consumers still new to e-commerce as the company to purchase books (and other products) online. Intel became perhaps the first semiconductor company readily identifiable to the public through its heavily branded "bunny people." Marketing in the high-tech world will continue to grow in importance over the next decade, as technology companies become more consumer-oriented (see Microsoft's X-Box). Marketing a service or software product versus a more tangible product is a bit different. It may be more challenging to understand how consumers relate to the product. Inventory and distribution issues may be tracked differently.

Market research

If you are an analytical person who likes numbers and analysis, and enjoys tracking consumer behavior, then market research may be the field for you. A product is much more effective when a company understands the consumer it is targeting. That's where market researchers come in. They employ a variety of different qualitative and quantitative research techniques to understand consumers. Surveys, tracking systems, focus groups, satisfaction monitors, psychographic and demographic models, and trial/repurchase estimations are all methods researchers use to understand how consumers relate to their products. Researchers who find that consumers associate lemon scents with cleanliness, for example, may suggest that cleansers could drive up sales by adding a lemon aroma.

Public relations

Public relations professionals manage company communications and relations with the outside world. You can work for an internal PR firm (large companies have their own departments that manage the public relations for all of their brands) or you can work for a PR agency and be placed on a brand account. Public relations executives write public releases to local and national publications and develop ideas that will increase the buzz surrounding their brand. Some PR firms have excellent reputations for pulling off stunts that get their products in the news and increase their brand recognition. Public relations executives may also be forced to defend a brand in the face of public scrutiny—such as the Tylenol brand during the rash of poisonings in the 1980s. While event-driven functions like press releases and stunts are significant, perhaps the most important function of a PR professional is to establish strong relationships with media representatives and to persuade them to cover an interesting story about the company they represent.

Marketing consulting

Although most well-known consulting firms are known for their expertise in general strategy, many consulting firms now hire industry or functional experts that focus on marketing issues. These firms need people with expertise in the areas of branding, market research, continuous relationship marketing, pricing strategy and business-to-business marketing—they tend to hire people with previous marketing experience and value consultants who have been successful marketing managers and have lived through the full range of business issues from the inside. McKinsey and Monitor are two general strategy firms that have begun to hire marketing specialists. Other boutique marketing consulting firms, such as Kurt Salmon, focus on certain

Visit Vault at **www.vault.com** for insider company profiles, expert advice, career message boards, expert resume reviews, the Vault Job Board and more.

VAULT CAREER LIBRARY   **177**

product categories like beverages, health care and retail. All major ad agencies are also attempting to reinvent themselves as marketing partners focused on marketing strategy beyond simple advertising.

What is a Brand?

Marketing analysis is primarily concerned with identifying a market, understanding it and developing a product to fill a need in the market. (There are of course, other logistical details, such as understanding what is required to make the product profitable.)

But a product is just a physical object or service. A brand, on the other hand, is a product that has consistent emotional and function benefits attached to it. Products are interchangeable—a brand builds value. Brands engage the consumer, inspire an emotional reaction and are consistent in their appearance. What attributes create brands?

Consistent strategy

Products that are constantly changing their strategies/market positions will never hold a consistent place in the consumer's mind. Owning a piece of the consumer's mind makes a brand a brand. When you think of a coffee shop, you now think of Starbucks—that's because Starbucks is a successful brand.

Consistent appearance

What do people think of visually when they think of your brand? Everyone knows Nike's logo—an elegant, high-speed swoosh.

Positioning

Good brands must stand for different things than their category competitors. Volvo cars, for example, are associated with safety, while Corvettes stand for sporty speed, and Saturns for value and good customer service.

Connection with target audience

A brand must build an emotional connection with the consumers who use it. The consumer must feel that there are no substitutes in the marketplace. Consumers may choose Pepsi or Coke in a blind taste test—but that "preference" has little to do with the drink they actually buy in the supermarket.

Top 12 Ways to Revitalize a Brand

Despite the fact that product categories are becoming more complex every day and marketing budgets are down, brand managers are constantly feeling pressure to increase sales, profits and market share. This list is adapted from an article in *Brandweek* and provides excellent examples of how companies improved the marketing of brand name products.

1. Create new usage occasions. (Wednesday is Prince Spaghetti Day; Orange juice is not just for breakfast anymore.)

2. Find customers outside your existing target group. (The Bank for Kids; Gillette for Her product line; and Pert for Kids shampoo.)

3. Discover a new way of using the product. (Lipton Recipe Soup Mix; Baking soda can be used as toothpaste; Jell-O pudding can be used as cake filling; Comet disinfecting powder not only cleans surfaces in your house, but also is great to use on old garden tools and old sneakers.)

4. Position your product as the one used by professionals and experts. (Chapstick and Picabo Street; Tide and its "professional launderettes.")

5. Tell a compelling story about your product's origins. (Jack Daniels; Nantucket Nectars; Ben & Jerry's.)

6. Create a jingle that relates to your product's unique feature. (Heinz ketchup's "Anticipation"; Wisk's "Ring around the Collar"; Alka Seltzer's "Plop, Plop, Fizz, Fizz.")

7. Develop a new delivery vehicle or packaging convenience. (Lysol toilet bowl cleaner's "angle neck"; the Colgate "pump.")

8. Create a character to personify your product, ingredient or attribute. (Post's California Raisins; Kraft's Cheesasaurus; Dow's Scrubbing Bubbles.)

9. Use media vehicles in a new way. (P&G created the "soap opera" to advertise their brands; the "Got Milk" campaign effectively uses mouth-watering billboards; newspapers as a means of distributing product samples.)

10. Look for effective tie-ins/partnerships. (United Airlines serving Starbucks Coffee; McDonald's distributing Disney toys; Gillette distributing razors at Boston Red Sox baseball games.)

11. Promote your product as benign addiction. (Lay's "Bet You Can't Eat Just One"; Snackwell's "Won't be able to say no.")

12. Become a reason for family and friends togetherness. (M&M's Make Friends; Kodak Golden Moments; McDonald's after the big baseball game; "Celebrate the Moments of Your Life" with Folgers.)

Visit Vault at www.vault.com for insider company profiles, expert advice, career message boards, expert resume reviews, the Vault Job Board and more.

VAULT CAREER LIBRARY   179

Employer Directory

Procter & Gamble

2 P&G Plaza
Cincinnati, OH 45202

Recruiting Contact:
Phone: (513) 983-1100
E-mail: Careers.im@pg.com
www.pg.com/careers

Undergraduate schools Procter & Gamble recruits from:

• Carnegie-Mellon; Case Western; Clarkson; Cornell; Duke; Florida A&M; Florida International; Florida State; Georgia Institute of Technology; Harvard; Indiana; Iowa State; Kansas State; Massachusetts Institute of Technology; Miami of Ohio; North Carolina A&T State; Northern Kentucky; Northwestern; Ohio State; Pennsylvania State; Purdue; Rensselaer Polytechnic; Tennessee State; Tulane; Tuskegee; Cincinnati; Colorado; Dayton; Florida; Illinois; Kentucky; Michigan; Missouri; North Carolina; Notre Dame; Puerto Rico; South Florida; Tennessee; Texas; Virginia; Wisconsin

Three billion times a day, P&G brands touch the lives of people around the world. Our corporate tradition is rooted in the principles of personal integrity, respect for the individual and doing what's right for the long-term. A career at P&G offers a chance to touch someone's life. Our people get involved — with their workplace, their community, their neighbors and each other. If you want a company whose actions reflect their ethics and whose people live their values, then you should consider a career at P&G. A New Challenge Every Day ™

Employer Directory, cont.

3M Company
3M Center
St. Paul, MN 55144
Phone: (651) 733-1110
Fax: (651) 733-9973
www.3m.com

adidas AG
Adi-Dassler-Strasse 1-2
91074 Herzogenaurach
Germany
Phone: +49-9132-84-0
Fax: +49-9132-84-2241
www.adidas-group.com

Anheuser-Busch Companies, Inc.
1 Busch Place
St. Louis, MO 63118
Phone: (314) 577-2000
Fax: (314) 577-2900
www.anheuser-busch.com

Avon Products, Inc.
1345 Avenue of the Americas
New York, NY 10105-0196
Phone: (212) 282-5000
Fax: (212) 282-6049
www.avoncompany.com

Bose Corporation
The Mountain
Framingham, MA 01701
Phone: (508) 879-7330
Fax: (508) 766-7543
www.bose.com

Cadbury plc
Cadbury House, Uxbridge Business Park
Sanderson Road
Uxbridge UB8 1DH
United Kingdom
Phone: +44-18-95-61-50-00
Fax: +44-18-95-61-50-01
www.cadbury.com

Campbell Soup Company
1 Campbell Place
Camden, NJ 08103-1799
Phone: (856) 342-4800
Fax: (856) 342-3878
www.campbellsoup.com

The Clorox Company
1221 Broadway
Oakland, CA 94612-1888
Phone: (510) 271-7000
Fax: (510) 832-1463
www.thecloroxcompany.com

The Coca-Cola Company
1 Coca-Cola Plaza
Atlanta, GA 30313
Phone: (404) 676-2121
Fax: (404) 676-6792
www.thecoca-colacompany.com

Coach Incorporated
516 West 34th Street
New York, NY 10001-1394
Phone: (212) 594-1850
Fax: (212) 594-1682
www.coach.com

Colgate-Palmolive Company
300 Park Avenue
New York, NY 10022
Phone: (212) 310-2000
Fax: (212) 310-3284
www.colgate.com

Columbia Sportswear Company
14375 NW Science Park Drive
Portland, OR 97229-5418
Phone: (503) 985-4000
Fax: (503) 985-5800
www.columbia.com

ConAgra Foods Incorporated
1 ConAgra Drive
Omaha, NE 68102-5001
Phone: (402) 595-4000
Fax: (402) 595-4707
www.conagra.com

Del Monte Foods Company
1 Market at The Landmark
San Francisco, CA 94105
Phone: (415) 247-3000
Fax: (415) 347-3565
www.delmonte.com

Diageo PLC
8 Henrietta Place
London, ENG W1G 0NB
United Kingdom
Phone: +1-21-28-15-51-33
Fax: +1-21-25-71-30-50
www.diageo.com

Eastman Kodak Company
343 State Street
Rochester, NY 14650
Phone: (585) 724-4000
Fax: (585) 724-0663
www.kodak.com

The Estée Lauder Companies, Inc.
767 Fifth Avenue
New York, NY 10153
Phone: (212) 572-4200
Fax: (212) 572-3941
www.elcompanies.com

Fortune Brands, Inc.
520 Lake Cook Road
Deerfield, IL 60015
Phone: (847) 484-4400
Fax: (847) 478-0073
www.fortunebrands.com

General Electric Company
3135 Easton Turnpike
Fairfield, CT 06828
Phone: (203) 373-2211
Fax: (203) 373-3131
www.ge.com

General Mills Incorporated
1 General Mills Boulevard
Minneapolis, MN 55426
Phone: (763) 764-7600
Fax: (763) 764-7384
www.generalmills.com

Visit Vault at **www.vault.com** for insider company profiles, expert advice,
career message boards, expert resume reviews, the Vault Job Board and more.

VAULT CAREER LIBRARY

181

Employer Directory, cont.

H. J. Heinz Company
600 Grant Street
Pittsburgh, PA 15219
Phone: (412) 456-5700
Fax: (412) 456-6015
www.heinz.com

Hasbro, Inc.
1027 Newport Avenue
Pawtucket, RI 02862-1059
Phone: (401) 431-8697
Fax: (401) 727-5544
www.hasbro.com

Henkel KGaA
Henkelstrasse 67
D-40191 Düsseldorf
Germany
Phone: +49-21-17-97-0
Fax: +49-21-17-98-24-84
www.henkel.com

The Hershey Company
100 Crystal A Drive
Hershey, PA 17033-0810
Phone: (717) 534-4200
Fax: (717) 534-7873
www.thehersheycompany.com

Hormel Foods
1 Hormel Place
Austin, MN 55912-3680
Phone: (507) 437-5611
Fax: (507) 437-5489
www.hormelfoods.com

The J.M. Smucker Company
1 Strawberry Lane
Orrville, OH 44667
Phone: (330) 682-3000
Fax: (330) 684-3026
www.smuckers.com

Jockey International, Inc.
2300 60th Street
Kenosha, WI 53141
Phone: (262) 658-8111
Fax: (262) 658-1812
www.jockey.com

Johnson & Johnson
1 Johnson & Johnson Plaza
New Brunswick, NJ 08933
Phone: (732) 524-0400
Fax: (732) 214-0332
www.jnj.com

Kellogg Company
1 Kellogg Square
Battle Creek, MI 49016
Phone: (269) 961-2000
Fax: (269) 961-2871
www.kelloggcompany.com

Kimberly-Clark Corporation
351 Phelps Drive
Irving, TX 75038
Phone: (972) 281-1200
Fax: (972) 281-1435
www.kimberly-clark.com

Kraft Foods, Inc.
3 Lakes Drive
Northfield, IL 60093
Phone: (847) 646-2000
Fax: (847) 646-6005
www.kraft.com

L'Oréal
41, rue Martre Centre Eugene Schueller
Clichy, 92117
France
Phone: +33-47-56-82-65
Fax: +33-47-56-86-42
www.loreal.com

Land O'Lakes, Inc.
4001 Lexington Avenue North
Arden Hills, MN 55112
Phone: (651) 481-2222
Fax: (651) 481-2000
www.landolakesinc.com

Levi Strauss & Co.
1155 Battery Street
San Francisco, CA 94111
Phone: (415) 501-6000
Fax: (415) 501-7112
www.levistrauss.com

Liz Claiborne, Inc.
1441 Broadway
New York, NY 10018
Phone: (212) 354-4900
Fax: (212) 626-1800
www.lizclaiborneinc.com

LVMH Moët Hennessy Louis Vuitton SA
22 Avenue Montaigne
75008 Paris
France
Phone: +33-44-13-22-22
Fax: +33-44-13-21-19
www.lvmh.com

MARS, Incorporated
6885 Elm Street
McLean, VA 22101
Phone: (703) 821-4900
Fax: (703) 448-9678
www.website.com

Mary Kay Inc.
16251 Dallas Parkway
Dallas, TX 75001
Phone: (972) 687-6300
Fax: (972) 687-1642
www.marykay.com

Mattel, Inc.
333 Continental Boulevard
El Segundo, CA 90245-5012
Phone: (310) 252-2000
Fax: (310) 252-2179
www.mattel.com

McCormick & Company, Inc.
18 Loveton Circle
Sparks, MD 21152
Phone: (410) 771-7301
Fax: (410) 527-8214
www.mccormick.com

MillerCoors LLC
1225 17th Street
Denver, CO 80202
Phone: (303) 279-6565
Fax: (303) 277-5415
www.millerbrewing.com

Employer Directory, cont.

Molson Coors Brewing Company
311 10th Street
Golden, CO 80401-0030
Phone: (303) 279-6565
Fax: (303) 277-5415
www.molsoncoors.com

Nestlé SA
Avenue Nestle 55
Vevey, 1800
Switzerland
Phone: +41-924-2111
Fax: +41-924-4800
www.nestle.com

New Balance Athletic Shoe, Inc.
Brighton Landing
20 Guest Street
Boston, MA 02135-2088
Phone: (617) 783-4000
Fax: (617) 787-9355
www.newbalance.com

Newell Rubbermaid, Inc.
10B Glenlake Parkway, Suite 300
Atlanta, GA 30328
Phone: (770) 407-3800
Fax: (770) 407-3986
www.newellrubbermaid.com

NIKE, Inc.
1 Bowerman Drive
Beaverton, OR 97005
Phone: (503) 671-6453
Fax: (503) 671-6300
www.nike.com

Nintendo Co., Ltd
11-1 Kamitoba Hokotate-cho Minami-ku
Kyoto-shi, KYT 601-8116
Japan
Phone: +81-35-820-22-51
Fax: +81-75-601-85-01

Nintendo of America Incorporated
4820 150th Avenue NE
Redmond, WA 98052
Phone: (425) 882-2040
Fax: (425) 882-3585
www.nintendo.com

PepsiCo, Inc.
700 Anderson Hill Road
Purchase, NY 10577
Phone: (914) 253-2000
Fax: (914) 253-2070
www.pepsico.com

Perry Ellis International, Inc.
3000 NW 107 Avenue
Miami, FL 33172
Phone: (305) 592-2830
Fax: (305) 594-2307
www.pery.com

Polo Ralph Lauren Corporation
650 Madison Avenue
New York, NY 10022
Phone: (212) 318-7000
Fax: (212) 318-7690
www.ralphlauren.com

Quiksilver, Inc.
15202 Graham Street
Huntington Beach, CA 92649
Phone: (714) 889-2200
Fax: (714) 889-3700
www.quiksilver.com

Revlon Inc.
237 Park Avenue
New York, NY 10017
Phone: (212) 527-4000
www.revlon.com

Royal Philips Electronics
Breitner Center, Amstelplein 2
1096 BC Amsterdam
Netherlands
Phone: +31-20-597-77177
Fax: +31-20-597-70710
www.philips.com

S.C. Johnson & Son, Inc.
1525 Howe Street
Racine, WI 53403-5011
Phone: (262) 260-2000
Fax: (262) 260-6004
www.scjohnson.com

Sara Lee Corporation
3500 Lacey Road
Downers Grove, IL 60515
Phone: (630) 598-6000
Fax: (630) 598-8482
www.saralee.com

Skechers USA, Inc.
228 Manhattan Beach Boulevard
Manhattan Beach, CA 90266
Phone: (310) 318-3100
Fax: (310) 318-5019
www.skechers.com

Sony Corporation
1-7-1 Konan
Minato-Ku, TKY 108-0075
Japan
Phone: +1-813-5448211
Fax: +1-813-5448224
www.sony.net

The Timberland Company
200 Domain Drive
Stratham, NH 03885
Phone: (603) 772-9500
Fax: (603) 926-9239
www.timberland.com

Tupperware Brands Corporation
14901 South Orange Blossom Trail
Orlando, FL 32837
Phone: (407) 826-5050
Fax: (407) 826-8874
www.tupperwarebrands.com

Visit Vault at www.vault.com for insider company profiles, expert advice, career message boards, expert resume reviews, the Vault Job Board and more.

VAULT CAREER LIBRARY   183

Employer Directory, cont.

Tyson Foods, Inc.
2210 West Oaklawn Drive
P.O. Box 2020
Springdale, AR 72762-6999
Phone: (479) 290-4000
Fax: (479) 290-4061
www.tyson.com

Unilever PLC
Unilever House
PO Box 68
Blackfriars
London, ENG EC4Y 0DY
United Kingdom
Phone: +44-20-78-22-52-52
Fax: +44-20-78-22-69-07
www.unilever.com

Whirlpool Corporation
2000 M63
Benton Harbor, MI 49022
Phone: (269) 923-5000
Fax: (269) 923-5154
www.whirlpoolcorp.com

Wm. Wrigley Jr. Company
410 North Michigan Avenue
Chicago, IL 60611
Phone: (312) 644-2121
Fax: (312) 644-0015
www.wrigley.com

Energy/Oil and Gas

What is the Energy Sector?

Besides mc², what is energy?

The energy sector produces, converts and distributes fuels for heat, light and propulsion. Oil, natural gas and coal are burned to make heat and electricity. Wind, flowing water and sunlight are converted into electricity. Oil is refined to propel cars, planes and industrial machines. And to achieve these things, the companies who are producing, transporting, converting and distributing these energy sources are supported by a variety of service firms, investors and equipment providers.

There is a great divide between the oil and gas industries and the network of companies that produce electrical power, even though each side accounts for about half of the business jobs across both the sector. "Oil and gas" refers to the exploration for, and extraction and processing of oil and natural gas. In contrast, the electric power business revolves around converting fuel to electricity in power plants and distributing that electricity to consumers. The economics of the two fields, and the regulations that govern them, are quite distinct. Generally, people make their energy careers in one camp or the other, without too much crossover.

Just how big is the industry that comprises all those diverse activities? Companies in the energy sector take in over $1 trillion in revenue annually, out of the $20 trillion earned by all U.S. businesses. Energy-related businesses employ about three million people—or 2 percent of the U.S. workforce—far more than banking, high tech or telecommunications.

Big oil

The price of oil sends a ripple effect throughout the world's economy, affecting not only drivers who have to shell out at the pump, but other forms of transportation, the cost of all goods and services, and the availability of basics like food and shelter. Nearly half of petroleum production in the U.S. goes toward gasoline, according to the NPRA. Other products include asphalt, solvents, and even the wax used in things like chewing gum and crayons. Leading companies, ranked according to sales, are ExxonMobil, Royal Dutch/Shell, BP, TOTAL S.A., ChevronTexaco, Gazprom (Russia) and ConocoPhillips, according to *Forbes*. In terms of oil-equivalent reserves, they're dwarfed by the Middle East's nationalized energy companies, as well as those of Venezuela and Nigeria.

Oil companies engage in exploration and production of oil ("upstream" activities), oil transportation and refining ("midstream"), and petroleum product wholesale and retail distribution ("downstream"). The largest companies, known as the "majors," are vertically integrated, with business operations along the entire spectrum from exploration to gas stations. Smaller oil companies, known as "independents," are often exclusively involved in exploration and production. Upstream is considered the glamorous place to be, where all the big decisions are made. Upstream jobs also involve heavy international work, with many employees sent off to new postings around the world every three years or so. Some companies focus exclusively on midstream and downstream activities. They operate refineries to distill crude oil into its many commercially useful petroleum derivatives, like gasoline, jet fuel, solvents and asphalt. Refineries are, in theory, built to last 40 years, but some have been around for as long as 80 years. That means that new refineries are rarely built, and the refinery business is mostly about managing the razor-thin margins between purchased crude oil inputs and revenue from refined product outputs.

Aside from these are the sectors and businesses that feed off of oil. Oil services companies provide a range of outsourced operational support; for instance, they may rent out oil rigs, conduct seismic testing or transport equipment. Working for one of these probably means working in Texas or abroad, and can feel very much like working for an oil company, given the similarity in issues and activities. Equipment manufacturers make turbines, boilers, compressors, pollution control devices, well drilling and pipeline construction equipment, software control systems, and some provide engineering services and construction/installation of their equipment. Pipeline operators own and manage tens of thousands of miles of petroleum (and

Visit Vault at **www.vault.com** for insider company profiles, expert advice, career message boards, expert resume reviews, the Vault Job Board and more.

V∧ULT CAREER LIBRARY 185

natural gas) pipelines. Many also operate oil intake terminals, engage in commodities trading and energy marketing, (and own natural gas storage facilities) or petroleum refineries as well. Pipeline companies are not household names; nonetheless, the largest ones take in several billion in annual revenue, comparable to the scale of a medium-sized oil company. The fortunes of these companies follow the price of oil: when oil is expensive, oil companies drill a lot and make a lot of money, so business volume and revenue increase for their contractors.

Industry History

Richer Rockefellers

The modern oil industry in the U.S. was born in the late 19th century, when, after investing in a Cleveland oil refinery during the Civil War, John D. Rockefeller founded Standard Oil in 1870. As of 1880, Standard refined 95 percent of all oil in the U.S. Branded an illegal monopoly in 1911, Standard was divided into 34 companies, including many whose descendants are still around today, like Mobil, Chevron, Shell and Esso (later renamed Exxon).

As public works projects in the 1930s improved the country's transportation infrastructure, Americans took to the road and demand for oil gushed ever higher. Also during that time, the oil giants turned to Texas to seek their fortunes. Soon thereafter, Chevron, Texaco, Exxon and Mobil went overseas to expand their reserves, buying up rights to oil fields in Saudi Arabia (a bargain at $50,000).

Oil gets organized

In 1960, top oil-producing countries Iran, Iraq, Kuwait, Saudi Arabia and Venezuela met in Baghdad to form the intergovernmental organization OPEC, or the Organization of the Petroleum Exporting Countries. OPEC nations collectively supply just above 43 percent of the world's oil exports and control more than three-fourths of total crude oil reserves in the world. In addition to its founding member countries, the current roster includes Algeria, Indonesia, Libya, Nigeria, Qatar and the United Arab Emirates; in 2007, Angola was added and Ecuador rejoined the group after withdrawing in 1992. (Indonesia will exit the group at the end of 2008.) The members meet twice a year to decide on their total output level of oil, considering actions to adjust it if necessary in response to oil market developments. OPEC countries seek to ensure that oil producers get a good rate of return on their investments and that consumers continue to be able to access steady supplies of oil. Basically, it's all about supply and demand—if oil production rises faster than demand, prices fall, a situation which OPEC claims hurts both producers and, eventually, consumers (in the form of inflation). Surely, consumers would beg to differ.

Oil stateside

Oil is certainly a slippery subject in the U.S., where high prices at the gas pump and environmental issues associated with extraction and production always garner plenty of attention. The issue of drilling in the Arctic National Wildlife Refuge, for instance, was a huge topic in the election of 2000, and continues to surface at semi-regular intervals. (Drilling there was proposed as a means to relieve pressure on gas prices in the spring of 2008; more on that later.) Many of these decisions rest on politics and power: While the Clinton administration had proposed selling some six million acres in the Gulf of Mexico, off the coast of Florida, this amount was reduced at the behest of Florida Gov. Jeb Bush in 2001. But at other times, true environmental concerns hold sway; take as a case in point the fact that the last oil refinery built in the U.S. was completed in 1976. And although a handful more could help deliver lower gas prices, the risks and controversy surrounding their construction—refineries need to be built near water, and disasters like the Exxon Valdez oil spill have contributed to what, according to industry pundits, translates into a NIMBY ("Not in my backyard") attitude among the public—have all but scuttled the possibility of any new refineries any time soon.

In the U.S., according to the National Petrochemicals and Refiners Association (NPRA), there are 155 refineries, owned by 60 companies, with aggregate crude oil processing capacity of 17.6 million barrels per day (a barrel is 42 gallons). Total U.S. demand for finished petroleum products in 2007 was 18.5 million barrels per day. Back in 1981, there were 325 refineries, capable of producing 18.6 million barrels per day. OPEC estimates the world demand for oil will close on 90 million barrels per day by 2010, predicted to rise to more than 103 million barrels per day by 2020. For a variety of reasons, most obviously pricing concerns and the fact that U.S. demand outstrips supply, the nation imports a portion of its oil from other nations. In fact, according to NPRA for 2006, while 96 percent of refined petroleum product is produced domestically, the U.S. imports 60 percent of the crude oil it uses in the refining process.

Troubled times lead to alliances

The 1970s saw two crises in oil pricing—an Arab oil embargo in 1973 and the outbreak of the Iranian revolution in 1979. In both cases, oil prices rose sharply. After a peak in prices in the early part of the 80s, the market saw a sharp decline followed by a collapse in 1986. By the 90s, prices had recovered, though they never regained the high levels of the previous decade. Another collapse occurred in 1998 following economic instability in Asia—prices sank to $10 a barrel. By 2000, they had climbed back up to over $30 a barrel.

At the end of the 1990s, following the Asian crisis, the industry witnessed several mega-mergers among major international oil companies, including the well-known Exxon-Mobil and Chevron-Texaco marriages. (British Petroleum also merged with Amoco and Arco to form BP, and Conoco joined with Phillips Petroleum to become ConocoPhillips). Many small independent companies weren't so lucky, and went into bankruptcy.

Though the industry has recovered—oil prices have risen sky high as the Iraq war drags on (hitting $135 a barrel in May 2008)—producers will continue to see pressure as environmental concerns became more pronounced. Supply may also become an issue as continued unrest in Iraq (not to mention instability in pockets of the Middle East) has prevented the exporting of crude oil from that country.

Russia, rebels rising

With oil resources naturally limited, the industry constantly has to search for new supplies. Since the collapse of the Soviet Union, Russia has been taking steps to modernize its oil infrastructure. With proven oil reserves of 60 billion barrels, mostly situated in Western Siberia, Russia also holds the world's largest natural gas reserves (and is also its largest exporter). International oil services companies like Halliburton and Baker Hughes have begun working with the major Russian oil companies in recent years, and the country's economy is becoming increasingly reliant on oil exports—in 2007, the energy sector accounted for just over 20 percent of Russia's GDP. In February 2003, BP invested $6.8 billion in Russia, creating a new joint venture company with Russia's fourth-largest oil company, TNK. (That investment, now worth $45 billion, is a presently a tad unsteady; during the summer of 2008, after some BP staffers' visas were not renewed, the venture's Russian investors forced out the BP-supported chief executive and other management personnel in a bid, some said initially, that signaled a state takeover of the concern.) Analysts say the country has great potential, and could eventually produce 10 million barrels of oil per day by 2010, and President Putin has made energy the centerpiece of Russia's growth strategy in the coming decades. But this promise is dampened by an inefficient infrastructure, including government corruption and the legacy of the Soviet collapse. Russia poses a geographical challenge, as well. Exports are limited by the capacity of the pipeline system crisscrossing the vast tundra, though new networks, such as the Baltic Pipeline System, have been developed in recent years and negotiations are underway for others. Similar measures are under consideration for natural gas.

Africa is another source of oil reserves. In February 2004, Exxon Mobil began a $3 billion development project off the coast of Angola, and in July 2003, crude oil production began for the first time in the nation of Chad, the result of the World Bank's single largest investment in sub-Saharan Africa. And it's also becoming a more significant source of U.S. oil supply, with

Visit Vault at www.vault.com for insider company profiles, expert advice, career message boards, expert resume reviews, the Vault Job Board and more.

VAULT CAREER LIBRARY   187

imports increasing more than 40 percent in the first half of the decade. But companies doing business on the continent are sometimes vulnerable to dramatic political unrest and violence. Royal Dutch/Shell has been plagued with difficulties at its operations in Nigeria's Niger Delta due to clashes between soldiers and militant groups in the area and attacks on its installations. In May 2008, Royal Dutch calculated that it was losing the equivalent of 30,000 barrels of crude oil (translation: almost $3.5 million) every day due to such attacks. (About half of Nigeria's output of 2.1 million barrels a day is processed by the company.)

"Classical" gas

Natural gas is one source that bridges the oil and gas versus electricity divide: it is extracted from the earth together with oil and can be used in much the same way, but it has also gained importance as a primary fuel for generating electricity. Today, about a third of the energy used in the U.S. is fueled by natural gas. As demand for electricity boomed in the 1990s, the market revved up, and with it came the entry of "energy merchants" like the infamous Enron, which set out to purchase natural gas cheaply, convert it into electricity, and reap profits from the "spark spread"—the markup on the sale of power. These merchants eventually manufactured a "shortage" in electricity that sent prices soaring, which in turn affected the price per cubic foot of natural gas. But the U.S. has limited domestic resources for natural gas production. As the supply shrinks, U.S. production falls by roughly 2 percent a year. Importing gas from other countries, including Russia, Qatar and Trinidad, and building pipelines in places like Alaska and Canada are touted as options, but they're expensive and unwieldy ones.

Big sparks

Public utilities, which are involved in power generation, transmission (from generator to substation) and distribution (from substation to residential or commercial consumer) are, by definition, located all over the country—everyone has to get their electricity and (natural) gas from somewhere, of course. "Utility" is actually a loose term that refers to all types of companies: investor-owned utilities, government-owned utilities, municipal power companies, rural electric co-ops and independent power producers (IPPs) or non-utility generators (NUGs). Utilities may differ greatly in terms of their lines of business. Some have sold off most of their generation assets and are primarily distribution companies with power lines as their primary assets, while others may own large amounts of regulated power plants, and may also own non-utility generators or individual independent power plants. As the electricity market fell apart starting in 2001, most IPPs sold off their assets piecemeal to large utility holding companies or financial institutions. Thus, there's been a massive consolidation among utility holding companies. There are presently about 50 investor-owned utilities in the country, but industry insiders predict that in a few years mergers may result in as few as 10.

Companies produce electricity in a variety of ways, from the simple and natural to the complex. Solar sources (and photo-voltaic cells), water (hydroelectric plants), and below-ground stores of heat and steam (geothermal) are used in the most environmentally uncomplicated methods. Coal can be used as well, although it's messy and contributes to polluting greenhouse gases. Nuclear plants, also relatively clean, are regaining ground, but they still suffer the NIMBY effect; the word "nuclear" still conjures up danger signals in the minds of most Americans.

Green concerns

So-called "greenhouse gases," produced through the burning of fossil fuels, are increasingly acknowledged to be a major factor behind the global warming phenomena, a trend that threatens major environmental repercussions in coming decades. The Kyoto protocol, developed by a group of nations over the last decade to limit greenhouse gas emissions, was a hot topic as the Bush administration came into power in 2000. The administration decided not to sign on to the protocol, which would have required the U.S. to reduce its 1990 levels of greenhouse gas emissions by 7 percent by the years 2008-2012. That administration's response to the global warming problem has raised the ire of many environmentalists, who see U.S.'s energy policy as too accommodating to corporate interests. Nonetheless, "clean energy" is a growing trend. San Francisco's Clean Edge, which monitors such activity, finds that revenue growth for companies involved in power generated by wind, solar cells, bio fuels and fuel cells is up 40 percent for 2007, and is on track to triple to $254 billion over the next ten years.

Meanwhile, corporations have taken their own baby steps to ease the environmental impact of their products. In January 2003, 14 U.S. oil corporations and subsidiaries launched the Chicago Climate Exchange, a trading program allowing participating members to earn redeemable credits for exceeding emissions reduction goals. Even automobile companies are starting to come around; Ford and GM have begun make their automobiles more fuel-efficient—note the increasing news accounts on hybrid and ethanol-powered vehicles, and the battery-powered Volt, GM Chevrolet's work-in-progress—as consumers are abandoning gas-guzzling trucks and SUVs at an alarming rate (which is just as much a factor of inflated gas prices).

Today, the U.S. oil industry spends a lot of time lobbying Congress for a "comprehensive energy policy." According to the NPRA, such a policy could include tax incentives for new and existing refinery capacity, reasonable environmental regulations that balance the need for cleaner fuel with market demand, and a clearer policy toward individual states adopting requirements for fuel formulations (California, Connecticut and New York, for instance, have tougher restrictions on what can go into fuel in order to reduce potentially harmful emissions, restrictions that companies say cost them millions). But that's just one way to go—other players are pushing for carbon caps which would limit carbon-dioxide emissions and force companies to purchase offset credits in "payment" for excess emissions (the scheme is sometimes referred to as "cap-and-trade"). Such a move would greatly benefit the electricity-making nuclear plant operators—especially the two largest, Exelon and Entergy—and to a lesser extent, natural gas-fired generators, since their facilities don't send out large quantities of CO_2, which puts them at a distinct price advantage over firms that will have to buy credits. Further, it would pave the way for advances in the number of nuclear facilities (since energy will be cheaper to produce). Lastly, it would drive up electricity prices for the consumer while creating the possibility of what *The Wall Street Journal* called "supernormal profits for nuclear operators in markets where rates are deregulated and have more ability to rise." (Assuming an offset price of $25 per million metric tons of carbon output, Exelon estimated that the system could bring it some $2 billion extra each year in profit before interest, taxes, depreciation and amortization.)

Gone with the windfall?

That last proposal could bring the same kind of legislative scrutiny to certain power traders that the oil company sees all the time. As gasoline prices were beginning to take off for good in 2005, Exxon Mobil came under increasingly hostile fire for its 2005 financial results—they were much too high. The company reported a whopping profit of $36.1 billion—the largest single-year profit ever for an American firm—and had to hold an electronic news conference to "explain" its robust earnings to budget-challenged consumers in a tightening economy. Politicians started tossing around the idea of a "windfall profits" tax on the oil industry, a suggestion which gained force as the company continued to reset records in 2006 and 2007 (with a profit of $40.6 billion). The issue of oil company earnings became a major talking point for 2008 Democratic presidential candidate Barack Obama, and Big Oil's top five execs were raked over the coals by Democratic members for the Senate Judiciary Committee in May. While some sort of governmental "input" may be inevitable, it's not clear how or whether such a measure will help bring down costs for the average citizen.

Before the committee, for their part, the oil men called for permission for more exploration and drilling in the Atlantic, Pacific, the Gulf of Mexico and the Arctic National Wildlife Refuge in Alaska (always a topic of controversy). They also floated the idea that high prices were a result of market forces and OPEC, and were not under their control (that same argument doesn't quite work when talking about astronomical profits, though). However, the representatives were not so easily distracted. Committee chair Patrick Leahy of Vermont asked the execs to reveal the amount of their annual compensation; when ConocoPhilips' EVP John Lowe said he wasn't sure, Leahy fired back "I wish I made enough money that I didn't even have to know how much I make." And California Senator Dianne Feinstein had harsher words. "(It seems)

Visit Vault at **www.vault.com** for insider company profiles, expert advice, career message boards, expert resume reviews, the Vault Job Board and more.

VAULT CAREER LIBRARY

189

that you are all just hapless victims of a system, you blame one thing or another, which most people would say is just simply the cost of doing business. Yet you rack up record profits quarter after quarter after quarter, and apparently have no ethical compass about the price of gasoline."

The reply of Chevron's vice chairman Peter Robertson? "I don't feel like a victim at all."

Tick, tick, tick...

But the bottom line is that oil is a non-renewable resource, and experts warn that there is an urgent need for a large-scale alternative energy infrastructure. In addition to alternatives already in use, such as solar, wind and geothermal energy systems, new technologies are constantly in development, but it's a race against time. According to the Alternative Energy Institute, the world's supply of oil will reach its maximum of production, and the midpoint of its depletion, around 2010. Already, about 65 percent of known oil reserves in the U.S. have been used up. Soon, the AEI warns, more than half of the world's petroleum reserves will be owned and controlled by countries in the Middle East, a fact that could only heighten the problems wrought by political instability in the area.

Employment Prospects

The Bureau of Labor Statistics classifies jobs in the industry under its "mining" segment as "oil and gas extraction," including both oil and natural gas. This category offers something for everyone: There are management and administrative jobs for white-collar types (about 20 percent of the industry in 2006, the last year for which statistics are available); hardier souls might choose to toil directly in construction/extraction or production—a total of 45 percent of the workforce—as derrick and rotary drill operators or roustabouts, electricians or refinery operators. There are also plenty of opportunities for the scientifically-minded, with jobs in geology and engineering (about 8 percent). According to the BLS, about 75 percent of the U.S. workforce concentrated in California, Louisiana, Oklahoma and Texas. Coal mining and associated activities take place almost wholly in three states: Pennsylvania, Kentucky and West Virginia.

Though earnings are relatively high in the industry, BLS predicts a drop-off in overall employment in coming years, with an anticipated wage and salary decline of 2 percent by 2016 (compared to overall growth in all industries of 11 percent). The industry is known for its fluctuations—as prices skyrocket, companies invest in new technologies and expand their explorations, while lower prices have the opposite effect. Still, new technologies for exploration, including 3-D and 4-D seismic exploration methods, new drilling techniques, and technologies for exploring deep under the sea, will continue to produce a demand for skilled workers. The "graying" of the utility industry is another well-documented trend; 60 percent of current utility employees are expected to retire by 2015—meaning there's lots of opportunity today for young job seekers.

Energy sector positions capture about 2 percent of new MBA graduates, an amount roughly proportional to the industry's size. In contrast, the investment banking and investment management sectors together capture 40 percent of graduates, and consulting absorbs another 20 percent. Even the significantly smaller high tech industry takes on three times the number of new MBAs as does the energy sector. What this means for you as a job seeker is that the energy sector is not as dominated by people with graduate business degrees as some other popular arenas. There is plenty of opportunity for smart, well-trained college graduates to rise through the ranks without necessarily going back to school. Additionally, energy companies as a whole employ a high percentage of production workers (the people who drive local utility repair trucks, laborers on oil rigs and gas station attendants), compared to other industries; about 90 percent of jobs in the energy sector are blue-collar jobs or technical positions.

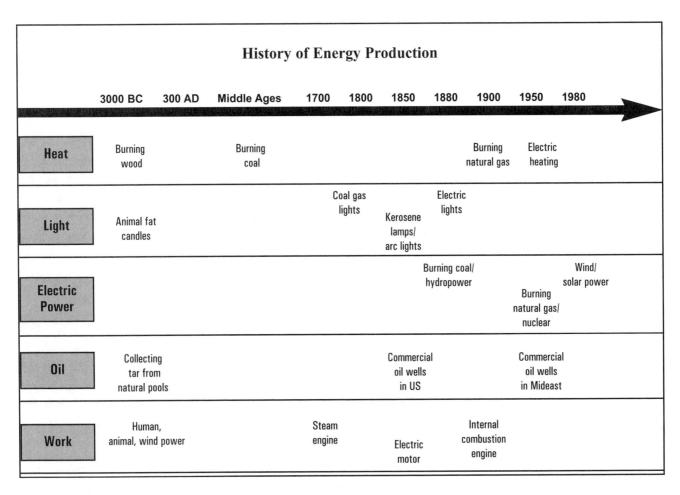

History of Energy Production

	3000 BC	300 AD	Middle Ages	1700	1800	1850	1880	1900	1950	1980
Heat	Burning wood		Burning coal					Burning natural gas	Electric heating	
Light	Animal fat candles				Coal gas lights	Kerosene lamps/ arc lights	Electric lights			
Electric Power							Burning coal/ hydropower		Burning natural gas/ nuclear	Wind/ solar power
Oil	Collecting tar from natural pools					Commercial oil wells in US			Commercial oil wells in Mideast	
Work	Human, animal, wind power			Steam engine		Electric motor		Internal combustion engine		

Technology Frontiers

People in the energy sector are passionate about the high tech nature of their industry. Although the basic process of gathering fuels and burning them to produce electricity, light, heat and work is fairly set, how efficient that process is and how much pollution it generates are the subjects of some pretty hard-core science and revolutionary changes.

In order to be a compelling job candidate, it helps to be knowledgeable and passionate about new technologies appearing on the horizon. Below are just a handful of examples of the cutting-edge research and development happening in different parts of the energy world:

• One company has developed a very low-tech alchemy to turn pollution into fuel: letting algae "eat" NOx (nitrogen oxide) and CO_2 (carbon dioxide) emissions from fossil plants. Algae thrive on these abundant feedstocks in power plant exhaust streams—pollution is reduced, the algae grows and can later be dried and burned as fuel.

• An important emerging power plant pollution-control technology involves burning fuel without using a flame. The recently commercialized Xonon combustor turns natural gas into energy by bringing it into contact with a catalyst. In flameless combustion, no NOx is formed at all, thus preventing smog and acid rain.

• High-temperature superconducting transmission lines are currently in testing. Traditional copper wires cause enough resistance to lose some 10 percent of the electricity they carry. Superconducting niobium-titanium alloy wires cooled by a tiny liquid nitrogen core eliminate line losses and thus effectively increase our electricity supply.

• We have used the principal of piezoelectricity for decades to generate electricity from motion. Certain types of miniature crystals spontaneously generate a high-voltage current when moved—portable gas grill lighters that don't use a flint work

Visit Vault at www.vault.com for insider company profiles, expert advice, career message boards, expert resume reviews, the Vault Job Board and more.

VAULT CAREER LIBRARY 191

in this way. Now companies are looking into more advanced applications, like using piezoelectric generators embedded in the sole of a soldier's boot to power battlefield equipment.

• Did you know there's a gasoline-powered car with a fuel efficiency of 10,000 MPG? Such impressive efficiency comes from using a tiny, one-cylinder engine with little internal resistance, thin hard tires and a super-light car body to reduce road friction, a bubble-shaped aerodynamic design and a lightweight child driver on a smooth and level indoor track. While these extreme design elements may not be practical for commercial vehicles, fuel efficiency R&D (research and development) is an active and promising space.

• Data transmission over electrical wires is a little-known, older technology that is finding exciting new applications. The current in an electrical wire can also carry data—street lights have been remotely controlled this way for decades, and in the past few years home automation via the wires in the wall has proliferated. (Did you know that you can turn your dishwasher on from your computer at work?) Companies have recently started marketing modems that send and receive more complex data over power lines: Internet access, voice and video.

• Battery technology is one of the real stumbling blocks of technological innovation these days—how much does it help you to have a supercomputer the size of a pad of paper if it dies after being unplugged for two hours? Companies are bringing better rechargeable lithium ion batteries to market, and actively developing laptops and cell phones powered by fuel cells with mini onboard tanks of hydrogen or methanol fuel.

• If you think wireless electricity is impossible, think again! We will soon be seeing desk surfaces and other furniture manufactured with embedded electrical chips—when you put a portable device down on the surface, the chip activates and recharges your laptop, phone, television, blender, razor, vacuum cleaner or whatever. Less realistically, people have also thought about wireless electricity in the form of "space solar power," in which huge solar-paneled satellites would collect energy from the sun and beam it to earth in the form of radio frequencies, which would then be converted into electricity.

• Bringing the fabled hydrogen economy to reality requires an inexpensive source of free hydrogen. Development-stage hydrogen production techniques include harnessing the sun to release hydrogen from pure sugar, and using high-temperature catalysis (rather than energy-intensive electrolysis) to split water into H_2 and O_2.

Energy Career Opportunities

In order to pursue a job in the energy sector, your first decision is what type of position you want—in other words, what functional role you want to play. Your function has a lot more impact on the nature of your job than does the type of company in which you work.

You can have a wide variety of business jobs in the energy sector:

• Asset development
• Corporate finance
• Quantitative analytics, risk management
• Trading, energy marketing
• Investment analysis
• Consulting
• Business development
• Banking
• Strategy and planning
• Economics and policy analysis

Different companies can have widely varying names by which they refer to these roles. For example, "marketing" in one company involves advertising and product promotion, whereas "marketing" in another can mean commodities trading. Similarly, "business development" can be more akin to sales in one company, or synonymous with strategic planning in another.

What Type of Company?

Job functions and company types intersect in numerous ways—for example, you can do corporate finance in a large oil company or with a small fuel cell manufacturer, or choose between asset development and trading within a given utility. (See chart "Employer Types by Job Function" on page 171.) Below, we have summarized the characteristics of each of the major energy sector employer types:

Oil companies

As we've discussed, oil companies engage in exploration and production of oil, oil transportation and refining, and petroleum product wholesale and retail distribution. The largest companies are vertically integrated, with business operations along the entire spectrum from exploration to gas stations. Smaller oil companies are often exclusively involved in exploration and production.

Oil services companies

Oil services companies provide a very wide range of outsourced operational support to oil companies, such as owning and renting out oil rigs, conducting seismic testing and transporting equipment. The fortunes of these companies follow the price of oil: when oil is expensive, oil companies drill a lot and make a lot of money, so business volume and revenue increase for their oil services contractors. Working for an oil services company probably means working in Texas or internationally, and can feel very much like working for an oil company, given the similarity in issues and activities.

Pipeline operators

Pipeline operators own and manage tens of thousands of miles of petroleum products and natural gas pipelines. Many of them also operate oil intake terminals, engage in commodities trading and energy marketing, and own natural gas storage facilities or petroleum refineries, as well. Unlike the major oil companies, pipeline operation companies are not household names— nonetheless, the largest ones take in several billion dollars in annual revenue, comparable to the scale of a medium-sized oil company.

Utilities

Utilities are, by definition, located all over the country—everyone has to get their electricity and gas from somewhere, of course. However, as a result of massive consolidation among utility holding companies, the corporate offices for your local utility may not necessarily be that local. There are presently about 50 investor-owned utilities in the country, but industry insiders predict that in a few years mergers may leave us with as few as 10. The "graying" of the utility industry is a well-documented trend; 60 percent of current utility employees are expected to retire by 2015, meaning there's lots of opportunity today for young job seekers.

"Utility" is actually a loose term that we use to succinctly refer to gas utilities and all types of power generation companies: investor-owned utilities, government-owned utilities, municipal power companies, rural electric co-ops and independent power producers (IPPs) or nonutility generators (NUGs). Utilities differ greatly in terms of their lines of business: some have

Visit Vault at www.vault.com for insider company profiles, expert advice, career message boards, expert resume reviews, the Vault Job Board and more.

VAULT CAREER LIBRARY 193

sold off most of their generation assets and are primarily distribution companies with power lines as their primary assets. Others may own large numbers of regulated power plants, and may also own nonutility generators or individual independent power plants. As the electricity market fell apart starting in 2001, most IPPs sold off their assets piecemeal to large utility holding companies or financial institutions.

Transmission grid operators

Transmission grid operators, known as independent system operators (ISO) or regional transmission operators (RTO), provide a power generation dispatch function to a regional electricity market. They don't own the transmission lines, but coordinate how much power is generated when and where, such that supply and demand are equal at every moment. This is an extremely complex process, and necessitates the analytical skills of electrical engineers and other generally quantitative and analytical operations staff.

Equipment manufacturers

Equipment manufacturers make turbines, boilers, compressors, pollution control devices, well drilling and pipeline construction equipment, software control systems, pumps and industrial batteries. Many of them also provide engineering services and construction/installation of their equipment. The major gas turbine manufacturers, for example, also offer engineering, procurement and construction of entire power plants. Oil-related equipment makers are often characterized as "oil services" firms. The equipment manufacturers in the energy industry are not particularly concentrated in one geographic area, though of course many of the oil business-oriented ones have major offices in Texas.

Investment funds

Investment funds are a diverse bunch: mutual funds, private equity funds and hedge funds. As a whole, the investment fund world is fairly concentrated in Boston, New York and San Francisco, but there are small funds dotted all over the country, as well.

Mutual funds hire stock analysts primarily out of MBA programs to track, value and recommend stocks in a particular sector (e.g., energy, natural resources, consumer goods) to the fund managers. However, there are a lot of other finance-related positions inside these massive firms for which graduating undergrads are sought.

The number of hedge funds in the U.S. has been growing at a phenomenal rate in the past few years, but they are still notoriously difficult places to get jobs. Hedge funds often hire people out of investment banking analyst programs. They tend not to hire people out of the mutual fund world, given that their valuation approach is so different, their investing horizon is so much shorter, and their orientation many times is towards short-selling, as well as buying stocks. While some hedge funds may focus exclusively on energy, most are generalist and opportunistic with respect to their target sectors.

Private equity funds invest money in private (i.e., not publicly traded) companies, often also obtaining operating influence through a seat on the portfolio company's board of directors. As a result, an analyst's work at a private equity fund is vastly different from that at a mutual fund or hedge fund. You are not following the stock market or incorporating market perception issues into your valuations and recommendations; instead, you are taking a hard look at specific operating issues, identifying concrete areas where the portfolio company can lower costs or enhance revenue. A few private equity firms specialize in energy investing, and many more do occasional deals in the energy space as part of a broader technology or manufacturing focus. Private equity firms hire just a few people straight out of college or MBA programs, and many others from the ranks of investment banking alumni.

Banks

Banks are primarily involved in lending money to companies, but they also have their own trading operations, private wealth management and investment analysis groups. Commercial and investment banks arrange for loans to energy companies, as well as syndicate loans for them (i.e., find other people to lend the money). Investment banks manage IPOs, and mergers and acquisitions (M&A) activities, as well. The banking world is overwhelmingly centered in New York (and London), with some smaller branches in Chicago and San Francisco.

Consulting firms

Consulting firms offer rich opportunities for those interested in the energy industry. Consulting on business issues (rather than information technology or technical, scientific issues) is done at three types of firms: management consultancies, risk consulting groups and economic consulting shops. Consulting firms are often interested in hiring people with good functional skills rather than requiring specific industry expertise and provide a broad exposure to energy sector business issues, as well as good training. Business consulting firm offices are located in most major cities, but much of the energy sector staff may be located in Houston, Washington, D.C. and New York.

Nonprofit groups

Nonprofit groups are tax-exempt corporations (pursuant to IRS code 501(c)3) engaged in issue advocacy or public interest research. Advocacy groups may focus on developing grassroots support for public policy changes, publicizing public interest issues or problems through direct actions, or working to influence politicians to enact or change legislation. Most of the energy-related advocacy groups focus on environmental topics, though some also cover corporate financial responsibility and investor protection issues. Think tanks are public policy research institutes, staffed mainly by PhDs who generate research and opinion papers to inform the public, policy-makers and media on current issues. Interestingly, the think tank is primarily a U.S. phenomenon, although the concept is slowly catching on in other countries. Some think tanks are independent and nonpartisan, whereas some take on an explicit advocacy role. Nonprofits are funded by individual donations and grants from foundations, and accordingly a substantial portion of their staffs are dedicated to fundraising. Most energy nonprofits are based in Washington, D.C., where they have access to the federal political process, but many of them have small regional offices or grassroots workers spread out across the country.

Government agencies

Government agencies at the federal and state levels regulate the energy markets and define public energy and environmental policy. Federal agencies are mostly located in Washington, D.C., and each state has staff in the state capital. Jobs can include policy analysis, research project management or management of subcontractors. The energy agencies tend to hire people with environmental or engineering backgrounds, and are lately following a policy of hiring people with general business and management education and experience.

Energy services firms

Energy services firms help companies (in any sector) reduce their energy costs. Working for an energy services firm is similar in many respects to consulting—except that you go much further down the path of implementation. Typically, an energy services firm first conducts an energy audit to understand where a company spends money on energy: electricity, heat and industrial processes. Then, the firm actually implements energy-saving measures "inside the fence" of the client company. This can involve investments and activities such as putting lightbulbs on motion sensors, upgrading the HVAC (heating, ventilation, air conditioning) system, negotiating better rates with the utility suppliers, or developing a cogeneration power

Visit Vault at www.vault.com for insider company profiles, expert advice, career message boards, expert resume reviews, the Vault Job Board and more.

VAULT CAREER LIBRARY   195

plant adjacent to the factory. Often, the energy services firm receives payment for these services in the form of a share in the net energy cost savings to the client. These firms are located across the country, with a few of the largest clustered in Boston.

Employer Types by Job Function

Job Function	Possible Employer Types
Asset Development	Utility; Oil Company; Pipeline Operator; Energy Services Firm
Corporate Finance	Utility; Pipeline Operator; Oil Company; Equipment Manufacturer
Quantitative Analytics, Risk Management	Utility; Oil Company; Transmission Grid Operator; Pipeline Operator; Investment Fund; Bank
Trading, Energy Marketing	Utility; Oil Company; Pipeline Operator; Investment Fund; Bank
Investment Analysis	Investment Fund; Bank
Consulting	Consulting Firm; Oil Services Company
Business Development	Equipment Manufacturer; Utility; Oil Services Company; Pipeline Operator; Energy Services Firm
Banking	Bank
Strategy and Planning	Utility; Oil Company; Pipeline Operator; Oil Services Company; Equipment Manufacturer
Economic and Policy Analysis	Government Agency; Nonprofit Group; Consulting Firm

Employer Directory

The AES Corporation
4300 Wilson Boulevard, 11th Floor
Arlington, VA 22203
Phone: (703) 522-1315
Fax: (703) 528-4510
www.aes.com

ALLETE, Inc.
30 West Superior Street
Duluth, MN 55802
Phone: (218) 279-5000
Fax: (218) 720-2502
www.allete.com

Alliant Energy Corporation
4902 North Biltmore Lane
Madison, WI 53718
Phone: (608) 458-3311
Fax: (608) 458-4824
www.alliantenergy.com

American Electric Power Company, Inc.
1 Riverside Plaza
Columbus, OH 43215-2372
Phone: (614) 716-1000
Fax: (614) 716-1823
www.aep.com

Anadarko Petroleum Corporation
1201 Lake Robbins Drive
The Woodlands, TX 77380-1046
Phone: (832) 636-1000
Fax: (832) 636-8220
www.anadarko.com

Baker Hughes Incorporated
2929 Allen Parkway, Suite 2100
Houston, TX 77019-2118
Phone: (713) 439-8600
Fax: (713) 439-8699
www.bakerhughes.com

BJ Services Company
4601 Westway Park Boulevard
Houston, TX 77027
Phone: (713) 513-3300
Fax: (713) 513-3456
www.bjservices.com

BP p.l.c.
1 St James's Square
London SW1Y 4PD
United Kingdom
Phone: +44-20-7496-4000
Fax: +44-20-7496-4630
www.bp.com

Cameron International Corporation
1333 West Loop, Suite 1700
Houston, TX 77027
Phone: (713) 513-3300
Fax: (713) 513-3456
www.c-a-m.com

Chevron Corp.
6001 Bollinger Canyon Road
San Ramon, CA 94583
Phone: (925) 842-1000
Fax: (925) 842-3530
www.chevrontexaco.com

ConocoPhillips Company
600 North Dairy Ashford Road
Houston, TX 77079
Phone: (281) 293-1000
Fax: (281) 293-1440
www.conocophillips.com

Consolidated Edison, Inc.
4 Irving Place
New York, NY 10003
Phone: (212) 460-4600
Fax: (212) 982-7816
www.conedison.com

Duke Energy Corporation
526 South Church Street
Charlotte, NC 28202
Phone: (704) 594-6200
Fax: (704) 382-3814
www.duke-energy.com

Eaton Corporation
Eaton Center
1111 Superior Avenue
Cleveland, OH 44114-2584
Phone: (216) 523-5000
Fax: (216) 523-4787
www.eaton.com

Edison International
2244 Walnut Grove Avenue
Rosemead, CA 91770
Phone: (626) 302-1212
Fax: (626) 302-2517
www.edison.com

Entergy Corporation
689 Loyola Avenue
New Orleans, LA 70113
Phone: (504) 576-4000
Fax: (504) 576-4428
www.entergy.com

Exelon Corporation
10 South Dearborn Street, 37th Floor
Chicago, IL 60680-5379
Phone: (312) 394-7398
Fax: (312) 394-7945
www.exeloncorp.com

Exterran Holdings, Inc.
4444 Brittmoore Road
Houston, TX 77041
Phone: (713) 335-7000
Fax: (281) 854-3051
www.exterran.com

Exxon Mobil Corporation
5959 Las Colinas Boulevard
Irving, TX 75039-2298
Phone: (972) 444-1000
Fax: (972) 444-1350
www.exxonmobil.com

FirstEnergy Corp.
76 South Main Street
Akron, OH 44308
Phone: (800) 646-0400
Fax: (330) 84-3866
www.firstenergycorp.com

Visit Vault at www.vault.com for insider company profiles, expert advice, career message boards, expert resume reviews, the Vault Job Board and more.

VAULT CAREER LIBRARY   197

Employer Directory, cont.

Florida Power & Light Company
700 Universe Boulevard
Juno Beach, FL 33408
Phone: (561) 694-4000
Fax: (561) 694-4620
www.fpl.com

FMC Technologies, Inc.
1803 Gears Road
Houston, TX 77067
Phone: (281) 591-4000
Fax: (281) 591-4102
www.fmctechnologies.com

GE Energy
4200 Wildwood Parkway
Atlanta, GA 30339
Phone: (678) 844-6000
Fax: (678) 844-6690
www.gepower.com

Halliburton
5 Houston Center
1401 McKinney, Suite 2400
Houston, TX 77020
Phone: (713) 759-2600
Fax: (713) 759-2635
www.halliburton.com

Hess Corporation
1185 Avenue of the Americas
New York, NY 10036
Phone: (212) 997-8500
Fax: (212) 536-8593
www.hess.com

Koch Industries, Inc.
4111 East 37th Street North
Wichita, KS 67220
Phone: (316) 828-5500
Fax: (316) 828-5739
www.kochind.com

Marathon Oil Corporation
5555 San Felipe Road
Houston, TX 77056
Phone: (713) 629-6600
Fax: (713) 296-2952
www.marathon.com

MDU Resources Group, Inc.
1200 West Century Avenue
Bismarck, ND 58506
Phone: (701) 530-1000
Fax: (701) 530-1698
www.mdu.com

Nabors Drilling USA, LP
515 West Greens Road, Suite 1000
Houston, TX 77067
Phone: (713) 232-7500
Fax: (713) 232-7027
www.nabors.com

National Oilwell Varco, Inc.
7909 Parkwood Circle Drive
Houston, TX 77036
Phone: (713) 346-7500
Fax: (713) 435-2195
Toll free: (888) 262-8645
www.nov.com

Occidental Petroleum Corporation
10889 Wilshire Boulevard
Los Angeles, CA 90024
Phone: (310) 208-8800
Fax: (310) 443-6690
www.oxy.com

Pacific Gas and Electric Company
77 Beale Street
San Francisco, CA 94177
Phone: (415) 973 7000
Fax: (415) 267 7268
www.pge.com

PPL Corporation
2 North 9th Street
Allentown, PA 18101
Phone: (610) 774-5151
Fax: (610) 774-4198
www.pplweb.com

Progress Energy, Inc.
410 South Wilmington Street
Raleigh, NC 27601
Phone: (919) 546-6111
Fax: (919) 546-2920
www.progress-energy.com

Puerto Rico Electric Power Authority
Avenida Ponce de León 17½
Santurce, PR 00909
Phone: (787) 289-3434
Fax: (787) 289-4120
www.prepa.com

Schlumberger Limited
5599 San Felipe, 17th Floor
Houston, TX 77056
Phone: (713) 513-2000
www.slb.com

Sempra Energy
101 Ash Street
San Diego, CA 92101
Phone: (619) 696-2000
Fax: (619) 696-2374
Toll free: (877) 736-7721
www.sempra.com

Shell Oil Company
1 Shell Plaza
910 Louisana Street
Houston, TX 77002
Phone: (713) 241-6161
Fax: (713) 241-4044
www.shellus.com

Smith International, Inc.
16740 East Hardy Road
Houston, TX 77032
Phone: (281) 443-3370
Fax: (281) 233-5199
Toll free: (800) 877-6484
www.smith.com

Employer Directory, cont.

Southern Company
30 Ivan Allen Jr. Boulevard NW
Atlanta, GA 30308
Phone: (404) 506-5000
Fax: (404) 506-0455
www.southernco.com

Sunoco, Inc.
1735 Market Street, Suite LL
Philadelphia, PA 19103-7583
Phone: (215) 977-3000
Fax: (215) 977-3409
Toll free: (800) 786-6261
www.sunocoinc.com

Transocean Inc.
4 Greenway Plaza
Houston, TX 77046
Phone: (713) 232-7500
Fax: (713) 232-7027
www.deepwater.com

Valero Energy Corporation
1 Valero Way
San Antonio, TX 78249
Phone: (210) 345-2000
Fax: (210) 345-2646
Toll free: (800) 531-7911
www.valero.com

Weatherford International, Ltd.
515 Post Oak Boulevard
Houston, TX 77027
Phone: (713) 693-4000
Fax: (713) 693-4323
Toll free: (800) 257-3826
www.weatherford.com

The Williams Companies Inc.
1 Williams Center
Tulsa, OK 74172
Phone: (918) 573 2000
Fax: (918) 573 6714
www.williams.com

Xcel Energy Inc.
414 Nicollet Mall
Minneapolis, MN 55401
Phone: (612) 330-5500
Fax: (800) 895-2895
Toll free: (800) 328-8226
www.xcelenergy.com

Visit Vault at **www.vault.com** for insider company profiles, expert advice,
career message boards, expert resume reviews, the Vault Job Board and more.

VAULT CAREER LIBRARY

199

Engineering

Overview of Engineering Careers

They're everywhere!

Engineers are involved in any industry where a product is made, designed or repaired. They design software, create and develop mechanical systems, improve civil infrastructure, design and develop aircraft and spacecraft, and evaluate industrial systems. Engineering is the art of applying scientific and mathematical principles, experience and judgment to design, build and repair a technical product or system to meet a specific need.

In good company

Engineering has a long and storied history—after all, who do you think figured out how to build the Pyramids or send men to the moon? Its ranks are also filled with such historical luminaries as Leonardo Da Vinci, Thomas Edison and Henry Ford.

Wide variety of work

The five largest fields of engineering are chemical, civil, electrical, industrial and mechanical engineering. There are also many more specialized engineering fields, including nuclear, biomedical, aerospace and environmental engineering. Professional societies recognize more than 25 engineering specialties, and new ones continue to develop along with advances in science and technology. Engineers are problem solvers; and if you're considering a career in engineering, it's probably because you have a love of math and science and have a knack for dissecting complex mechanical or logistical problems.

Specialized knowledge

A fundamental aspect of engineering is the practical application of scientific or mechanical knowledge. A civil engineer, for example, might be assigned a project to build or improve roads and bridges, dams and irrigation systems, water treatment processes or public transportation systems. Civil engineers also test buildings to make sure they are structurally sound, particularly large institutional ones. The term "civil engineering" essentially indicates projects related to public works; the work itself may involve principles of mechanical engineering, electrical engineering or other specialized fields.

Making it, and making it work

Manufacturers employ engineers to design and develop products such as consumer and industrial electronics, fabricated metals, machine tools, chemical compounds, transportation equipment, aircraft, communication equipment and space vehicles. Engineers also develop the production processes necessary to create those products, from designing the machinery to designing the factories where the machinery is operated.

Other avenues

With so many separate disciplines within the engineering field, it's not surprising that there is some overlap. Some of the most common fields of engineering are:

Visit Vault at **www.vault.com** for insider company profiles, expert advice,
career message boards, expert resume reviews, the Vault Job Board and more.

VAULT CAREER LIBRARY   201

Electrical engineering

As members of the largest engineering field, electrical engineers deal with anything from power systems and transmission, circuitry and communication, to industrial robots, microprocessors and digital broadcasting. They might also design circuit boards for audio equipment, broadcast systems for cell phones and television or power stations and citywide electric utility services. Other projects might include radar and navigation systems, electric motors, machinery controls, lighting and wiring in buildings, automobiles and aircraft.

Software engineering (programming), web engineering, IT engineering

Software engineers (also called programmers) create programs for use on various computer platforms such as Windows, Macintosh or Unix. Web engineers are essentially programmers who develop applications specifically for the Web. Specialists in information technology (IT) focus on creating and maintaining information networks, often within companies or government agencies. IT engineers make sure that networks stay secure and run smoothly, both within an office (known as a local area network, or LAN) and between remote locations (known as a wide area network, or WAN).

Mechanical engineering

Mechanical engineers create, develop and run manufacturing systems, engines, pipelines, robots, refrigeration equipment and other mechanical tools. Mechanical engineers focus on how machines work by researching, developing, designing, manufacturing and testing tools, engines, machines and other mechanical devices. They work on power-producing machines, such as electric generators, internal combustion engines, and steam and gas turbines. They also develop power-using machines, such as refrigeration and airconditioning equipment, machine tools, material handling systems, elevators and escalators, industrial production equipment and robots used in manufacturing.

Mechanical engineers work in many industries, and their jobs vary by industry and function. Some specialties include: applied mechanics; computer-aided design and manufacturing; energy systems; pressure vessels and piping; and heating, refrigeration and airconditioning systems. Mechanical engineering is one of the broadest engineering disciplines. Mechanical engineers may work in production operations in manufacturing or agriculture, maintenance or technical sales; many are administrators or managers.

Chemical engineering

It is true that chemical engineers are comfortable with chemistry, but they do much more with this knowledge than just make chemicals. In fact, the term "chemical engineer" is not even intended to describe the type of work a chemical engineer performs. Instead, it is meant to reveal what makes the field different from the other branches of engineering. Chemical engineers apply the principles of chemistry and engineering to solve problems involving the production or use of chemicals, building a bridge between science and manufacturing.

The knowledge and duties of chemical engineers overlap many fields. They apply principles of chemistry, physics, mathematics, and mechanical and electrical engineering. They frequently specialize in a particular operation, such as oxidation or polymerization. Others specialize in a particular area, such as pollution control, or the production of specific products, such as fertilizers and pesticides, automotive plastics or chlorine bleach. They must be aware of all aspects of chemical manufacturing and how it affects the environment, the safety of workers and customers. Because chemical engineers use computer technology to optimize all phases of research and production, they need to understand how to apply computer skills to process analysis, automated control systems and statistical quality control.

Environmental engineering

Using the principles of biology and chemistry, environmental engineers develop methods to solve problems related to the environment. They are involved in water and air pollution control, recycling, waste disposal and public health issues. Environmental engineers conduct hazardous waste management studies, evaluate the significance of the hazard, offer analysis on treatment and containment and develop regulations to prevent mishaps. They design municipal sewage and industrial wastewater systems. They analyze scientific data, research controversial projects and perform quality control checks. Many environmental engineers work as consultants, helping their clients comply with regulations and clean up hazardous sites, including brownfields, which are abandoned urban or industrial sites that may contain environmental hazards.

Careers in Electrical Engineering

America's dependence on electronics is so great that most people can't get through a day without using a product that has a microcontroller or other electronic circuitry. And this is all part of electrical engineering. Digital alarm clocks, automotive controls, computer networks, TVs, cell phones and MP3 players were all designed in large part by clever people who studied electronic engineering in college. Indeed, many of the products we take for granted today, from the smallest chip to the large supercomputers that help predict weather, stemmed from the minds of electronic engineers who wanted to build something new and different.

From ideas that range from seemingly crazy to really nifty, to just plain useful, engineers come up with working products. Marketing people might come up with concepts and software developers play an important role in design, but engineering is where it all begins. The digital revolution that's changing the world wouldn't be possible without it—electronic engineers are developing the hardware that is truly changing the world.

Entering this fast-paced field requires an inquisitive mind, and an ability to understand difficult technical principles that are often mathematically based. A creative bent and the ability to analyze problems from different angles also help. If you have these traits, you'll find that you'll always be challenged by a career as an electrical engineer and particularly by the fast rate of technical change.

There are a number of other beneficial paybacks for those who choose electrical engineering. Electronic engineers earn good salaries while getting to work with interesting technologies. And because many products require electronic technologies, it's fairly easy to find a field you can understand and enjoy.

On the downside, staying abreast of technology in a global economy is a challenge. Technologists must keep up to date so they don't lose their job to cheaper offshore workers. The impact of international competition from low-wage countries is being hotly debated throughout the electronics industry.

The scoop

Since electronic engineers are the men and women responsible for developing concepts for new technologies, they play an integral part in the digital revolution. Among other advances, electrical engineers made the Internet a vehicle for communicating freely to people anywhere on Earth. They devised techniques for sending data, the methods for making sure everything gets to its destination. They designed the PCs, servers and other equipment that let people see images from around the globe in a matter of seconds.

When people talk about smart appliances, smart phones and other so-called smart products, they're unknowingly complimenting the intelligent people who made those products. Electrical engineers are responsible for making cell phones small enough to fit in your pocket, and they also figured out how to put cameras into a mobile phone that can last for hours without recharging.

But electrical engineers have been changing the world for most of the 20th century. The term electronics didn't exist at the dawn of the 1900s. But the engineers of the day quickly realized that the science of moving electrons had enough potential to have its own name.

Visit Vault at www.vault.com for insider company profiles, expert advice, career message boards, expert resume reviews, the Vault Job Board and more.

VAULT CAREER LIBRARY   203

Some history

During the first half of the 1900s, engineers made radios with tubes (glass enclosures surrounding large, fragile electronic circuits, often assembled by hand). The first TVs also had many tubes besides the picture tube, which is still widely used as the television's screen. These tubes were so large and bulky that Eniac, the first real digital computer, weighed 30 tons when it started churning data in 1944.

The stage for the era of electronics was set by research scientists at Bell Labs, who did the work of electrical engineers, even though many didn't hold what was then a new degree. In 1947, Bell researchers figured out how to make a transistor, which became the basic building block of the silicon chips now used in millions of products.

In the 1950s, a transistor radio the size of a cigarette pack was a marvel. Today, there are literally millions of transistors on a chip. The size benefits of digital electronics over tubes are obvious: for example, compare the bulky cathode ray tube computer screens that have been used for decades to the sleek flat panel displays of today. The CRT, which is also the technology used for conventional television screens, is the last of the tube technologies to become obsolete, falling victim to replacements that were developed by electronic engineers.

This act of replacement is a mainstay of engineering. The nature of the field involves tinkering—looking at something and figuring out how to make a better version. Whether an engineer is looking at equipment on a factory floor, in an airplane or in his office, he's likely to take the shell off a product, see how it works and then come up with something better.

This kind of tinkering forms the basis for new technologies. The scope is staggering—everything from compact disk players, airbags and antilock braking systems, to computer networks and calculators derive from new technologies developed by electrical engineers who thought there was a better way to do something.

The history of electronics is loaded with people who had a novel idea and then worked diligently to bring their products to life. Hewlett-Packard was started by a couple of guys working in a garage, where they created a novel instrument first used by sound engineers making Disney's *Fantasia*.

Decades later, an HP engineer worked nights to come up with a new product that contained a new technology—some referred to this product as a personal computer. Steve Wozniak wasn't the first to make an affordable computer, but he helped found Apple Computers, the first company to make computers available to the average family.

There are many other companies that have significantly impacted the electronics industry; as a matter of fact, electrical engineers at IBM have led the country in patents for decades, providing breakthrough after breakthrough. And engineers at Texas Instruments invented the integrated circuit—commonly known as a microchip—and also popularized compact calculators.

Electrical Engineering Employment Opportunities

Electrical engineering is an exploding field. If you have an electronic engineering degree, it's hard to think of a field that provides more choices. The boom of smart equipment has created many jobs for engineers, and the push to come up with the next new thing keeps engineers busy across many fields. Cars, trains, robots and refrigerators all have electronic controls; even lightbulbs and dog collars now employ electronic components.

Among the largest employers of electrical engineers are computer, telecommunications and consumer electronics companies. These fields are pretty much the domain of electrical engineer, though a few mechanical engineers are needed for package design. There are almost always job openings at the giants within these fields, such as IBM, Motorola, Cisco, Sharp, Qualcomm, Texas Instruments and Dell. These huge corporations employ hundreds of engineers at their home offices, but many also have remote engineering sites scattered around the country.

Most major corporations also have international offices. Though there is some chance for transferring overseas, the bulk of engineers in a region tend to be from that area.

Finally, there are a number of smaller companies that produce many different types of basic computing and telecommunications equipment.

The mainstays

The majority of electrical engineers go into what might be considered traditional job categories (if anything can be considered traditional in an industry that really didn't start to mature until 1981, when the first IBM PC was introduced).

The declining costs of electronics mean chips and systems will continuously find new applications. As computer chips become cheaper, clever electrical engineers can design electronic controls that are cheaper than mechanical switches.

And that's bound to continue. Semiconductor manufacturers make exponentially more chips every year. Though the first microchip was made by Texas Instruments' Jack Kirby in 1958, it wasn't until 1994 that worldwide sales cracked $100 billion. In the following six years, the industry matched growth that had previously taken 36 years, as sales surpassed $200 billion in 2000, according to the Semiconductor Industries Association.

Common appliances like refrigerators and stoves have benefited from plenty of electrical technologies, but it's only been in recent years that they have incorporated electronic components like microcontrollers. Today, it's possible to buy a refrigerator that links to the Internet and uses bar code readers to determine whether it's time to buy milk or mustard.

Diverse industries

While this kind of growth creates many new job opportunities, job growth doesn't rise at nearly the same rate as market shipments. Corporations contend there aren't enough skilled engineers, and many are hiring engineers from foreign countries or contracting with designers abroad.

Nevertheless, the industry has not suffered a decline in the number of jobs worldwide. That's partly because the electronics industry is predicated on providing new, improved products in increasingly shorter development cycles. In some industries, like those of mobile phones and PCs, new products come out every few months, making older products obsolete in a hurry. Throughout the electronics industry, more than half of a company's revenue typically comes from products that were introduced within the past 18 months.

All these products require some level of design expertise. Complex products obviously require skilled engineers who understand leading-edge technologies, but someone has to design even the simplest products. New electrical engineers can often find a home with companies that need some design expertise for these simpler products.

But engineers can ply their craft in many different fields. Many engineers start out in conventional areas of electronics, but remain on the lookout for openings in fields that particularly interest them. Guitar amplifiers, race cars and medical instruments all have electronic components. Trains and planes make extensive use of electronic controls. A few lucky engineers are able to blend their hobby, whether that's music or racing, with their career.

Not everyone wants to combine their hobby and their job. Sometimes that takes the fun out of things. But for those who do, it is a possibility, as electronics is an area that holds almost unlimited career opportunities for engineers who want to work in areas that might be considered "out of the mainstream."

While the dominant firms in many fields are well known, there are far more opportunities at the hundreds of smaller firms around the country. Throughout the electronics industry, there are often customers who want something a bit different from

Visit Vault at **www.vault.com** for insider company profiles, expert advice, career message boards, expert resume reviews, the Vault Job Board and more.

VAULT CAREER LIBRARY   205

what mainstream companies can provide. Smaller companies can carve out a niche in these specialized areas, which are often too minor for large corporations to address. Most of these so-called contract design houses have fewer than 50 engineers.

Civil Engineering Careers

What is civil engineering?

Civil engineering is just one of many types of engineering, which includes chemical, computer/software, mechanical, electrical, agricultural, aerospace, biomedical/bioengineering, mining, systems, engineering management, nuclear and industrial. Unlike other forms of engineering, civil engineering deals with the practical aspects of everyday life. Because there is a range of design and technology issues within the civil field, programs of study in civil engineering tend to incorporate information from other areas to develop engineering solutions. In this sense, programs of study in civil engineering tend to be more comprehensive than those of other engineering fields.

As defined by the American Society of Civil Engineers (ASCE), "Civil engineering is about community service, development and improvement. It involves the conception, planning, design, construction and operation of facilities essential to modern life, ranging from transit systems to offshore structures to space satellites. Civil engineers are problem solvers, meeting the challenges of pollution, traffic congestion, drinking water and energy needs, urban redevelopment and community planning."

The word civil is derived from the Latin word civilis, which derives from civis, or citizen. Engineering is defined by the Accreditation Board for Engineering and Technology (ABET) as "the profession in which a knowledge of the mathematical and natural sciences gained by study, experience and practice is applied with judgment to develop ways to utilize economically the materials and forces of nature for the benefit of mankind." Thus, civil engineering is applying learned scientific knowledge to the creation of processes, information, technology and solutions that make everyday life easier for the average citizen, meaning all of us. It is a profession that significantly affects the life of our global environment.

Examples of civil engineering: past and present

Traditionally, civil engineering is most often associated with roads, bridges, buildings and dams. But civil engineering has always been a major facet of society and culture. Examples of civil engineering designs abound throughout history, from the construction of the Pyramids in ancient Egypt to the Parthenon in Athens, to the Great Wall of China. And in the relatively short history of the United States, great civil engineering has characterized our most distinguished national treasures. From highways to skyscrapers, great feats have been achieved within the field in the past 150 years.

Transportation didn't become a major issue in the United States until automobiles were commercially available. Roads that were once designed for horses and buggies were insufficient for modern cars. In 1908, the first concrete road was laid in Detroit, Michigan, which was to become the home of automobile manufacturing, and some 30 years later the Federal Interstate Highway System was created and eventually authorized in 1956. This highway system, originally named the Dwight D. Eisenhower System of Interstate and Defense Highways, is comprised of over 45,00 miles of interconnecting roads. Though modern roads were crucial for effective transportation, structurally sound bridges were also necessary. As industry grew, the need for wider and stronger bridges to accommodate railroad commerce and increased traffic forced engineering methods to change. The Romans constructed magnificent stone bridges throughout the European empire, some of which are still in use. But it was not until the Industrial Revolution that bridge construction changed dramatically. With new materials such as iron, bridge design became more technologically advanced. In the 20th century, steel and concrete became the materials of choice for bridges. One of the best examples of this is the Golden Gate Bridge, which was completed in 1937.

The incredible architectural achievements of the early 20th Century caused civil engineering to begin to attract greater recognition than its sister fields. The Woolworth Building, the Sears Tower and the Chrysler Building exemplified these modern architectural designs, and the public became fascinated with these larger-than-life structures that combined art and engineering. The collective American imagination was also captured during the building of the concrete Hoover Dam in 1931. In the midst of the Great Depression, flooding and water shortages affected the adjoining area. Not only were thousands of jobs provided, but a major hydroelectric innovation was created to address irrigation, power and water supply needs in the neighboring area.

Civil Engineering in Detail

All basic engineering studies begin at the same point, with general courses in math and science. But for those who choose to pursue civil engineering, a specialty area needs to be determined. There are six major disciplines: structural, geotechnical, environmental, transportation, water resources and construction. Though the disciplines are related, the differences are significant enough that a civil engineering degree with a specialization in structures does not mean you are qualified to design a water treatment facility.

Structural

A structural engineer focuses on the design and analysis of structures, such as buildings and bridges, to determine how well these structures will hold up to various environmental factors, including earthquakes, hurricanes and excessive wind. Structural engineering research has focused on developing technology to protect buildings during earthquakes, of critical concern since there were over 30,000 reports of seismic activity worldwide in 2003. If a structure is badly designed, it will eventually fail, which could potentially harm to the people who live or work in or around it. In 1940, the original Tacoma Narrows Bridge in Washington collapsed, as excessive winds created vibrations and caused the steel and concrete bridge to give way, as if it was made from rubber. More recently, the failure of New Orleans' levees during Hurricane Katrina led to extensive investigations on the structural integrity and design of the levee system.

Other structural projects on which an engineer might focus are amusement park rides, sporting arenas and even the International Space Station. Many people are confused about the difference between architecture and structural engineering, particularly the role each plays in the construction of commercial and residential projects. Though the architect may provide artistic elements to the structure, the engineer makes sure it can stand. Structural engineers are also learned in the properties and behavior of the various materials used in construction, such as steel, concrete, aluminum, timber and plastics. Without the work of structural engineers, how we travel, where we work and even how we entertain ourselves would be vastly different.

Geotechnical

Geotechnical engineering incorporates science and technology to create projects and solve problems relating to geology. Geology is more than the study of rocks and volcanoes, and geotechnical engineering requires knowledge of not only geology, but chemistry, physics and earth science, as well. Technology involving the Earth and its natural resources has an effect on a global scale. Some components of geotechnical engineering are soil mechanics, earthquake engineering, foundation engineering, coastal and offshore engineering, rock mechanics, applied seismology, petroleum engineering, drilling and hydrogeology. Construction projects involve tunnels, pipelines, mines, levees, embankments, stable slopes and structural foundations. The engineer must also consider soil conditions in all of these scenarios, as the project might not succeed if the soil is unsuitable. In turn, during environmental disasters, soil remediation is developed by geotechnical engineers. Petrolatum, natural gas and mineral exploration are all major industries involved in geotechnical engineering. The necessary analysis involved in geotechnical engineering requires extensive field tests and laboratory work.

Visit Vault at www.vault.com for insider company profiles, expert advice, career message boards, expert resume reviews, the Vault Job Board and more.

VAULT CAREER LIBRARY 207

Environmental

Environmental protection has become a significant problem in the last 30 years or so. As the public has become increasingly aware of environmentalism and pollution, the development of technology to preserve and improve the environment has become necessary. Environmental engineering analyzes environmental problems and develops solutions to those problems. This discipline combines the study of environmental science, mathematics, atmospheric science, biology, hydrology, chemistry and engineering technology. Improving air and water quality, locating and treating underground water sources, solid waste management, rehabilitating contaminated industrial and residential areas, and treating non-hazardous and hazardous substances are all tasks undertaken by environmental engineers. Providing safe drinking water, reducing air emissions, understanding global warming and treating waste water are all critical to a safe and clean environment. Because environmental problems are so widespread, this specialty is essential to several industries, and in some cases, the work of an environmental engineer may overlap with that of a geotechnical or water resources engineer.

Water resources

The average human male body is composed of 60 percent water. Water comprises 70 to 75 percent of the Earth's surface. In short, water is one of our most essential natural resources. However, it is also one of the most threatened. Water scarcity is not a new phenomenon; over 2,000 years have passed since the times of Biblical droughts and the availability of clean water continues to be a concern. Diminishing water resources are the cause of many potential conflicts. A water resources engineer finds ways to improve the quality and quantity of water and water sources. Hydrology, meteorology, fluid dynamics and environmental science all play a part in water resources engineering. These specialists concentrate on flood and storm water analysis, wetland protection, groundwater remediation, water supply planning and management, wastewater treatment and beach erosion control. In 2007, severe flooding in the Mexican state of Tabasco caused over 20,000 people to evacuate their homes. Water resources engineers are trained to assess flood risk and develop technology to prevent flooding. Knowledge of water quality and groundwater modeling, remote sensing of precipitation, and awareness of how pollutants travel in surface and groundwater are essential to this field. The design, construction and maintenance of canals, dams, pumping stations, and water storage and treatment facilities are all responsibilities of water resources engineers. Many university programs in environmental engineering incorporate water resources as a subcategory.

Construction

Every single civil engineering project involves construction—a structure needs to be erected, a tunnel needs to be dug, a road needs to be laid, a treatment plant needs to be built. Construction engineers manage these projects. Once a given project is designed by an engineer of the appropriate specialty, the construction engineer will oversee day-to-day responsibilities. Once a contractor is awarded a project, he/she assigns the construction engineer to the project site. This engineer then works with various engineers involved in the project design, such as electrical, structural, chemical or geotechnical engineers. The construction engineer is also responsible for implementing and maintaining the project schedule and the budget, incorporating technical and managerial knowledge to bring the project to a successful close. Construction engineers have the most complete understanding of construction projects, and have strong command of various engineering disciplines not just their own. The construction industry is one of the largest in the world; a present day example would be the rebuilding of Iraq, most of which is being carried out by American corporations. This field is also known as engineering management.

Transportation

Getting stuck in a traffic jam may not be the highlight of your day; nor is waiting for a train after you missed an earlier one. The development of an efficient and reliable transportation system is crucial in maintaining a functioning society and daily movement, whether by car, bus, train, airplane, boat or truck, can either adversely or constructively affect commerce.

Transportation engineers are responsible for designing, constructing and maintaining highways, railways, airfields and ports. Besides researching and improving traffic control, these engineers develop new methods of transportation and find ways to improve mass transportation. Some of their research also includes pedestrian accidents. Transportation innovations improve the quality of life throughout the word. In Hong Kong, an integrated pedestrian walkway and escalator system allows commuters to shorten their travel time while alleviating road congestion. Transportation engineers also plan and maintain pipelines for gas, water and oil.

Vault Q&A: Jay Wilkins, BASF's Rotational Development Program

After graduating with a degree in chemical engineering from the University of Texas at Austin, Jay Wilkins admittedly had "no idea" what type of engineering position he wanted to pursue. He ended up joining BASF's Professional Development Program (PDP) for chemical engineers, which gave him the opportunity to work and gain experience in several different positions.

Vault: How did you find out about BASF's PDP program?

Jay Wilkins: BASF posted on the career site through the engineering center at my school.

Vault: Did you know what sort of engineering position you were looking for when you graduated and started the program?

Wilkins: I really had no idea. That's what I think is so great about this program. When I came out of school, I really didn't know what kind of chemical engineering career I wanted to pursue. For example, there's process engineering, project engineering, product development, operations engineering, instrumentation, control systems engineering, environmental health and safety, and many other derivatives. In addition to the various job functions, there are also many different industries in which to perform them. Just within BASF alone, there are divisions for polymers, agricultural products, such as fertilizers and pesticides, cosmetics, catalysts, inorganics, nutritional products, coatings and textures, textiles, pharmaceuticals and many other chemical groups, such as oxo-alcohols and specialty amines.

What I really liked about the rotational program is that not only did you get experience in several different job functions, but also in several different industries within the same company. By the time I got done with the program, I knew exactly what I wanted to do and where I wanted to do it.

When I went through the program, there were three six-month assignments; since then, it's been changed to two nine-month assignments. I rolled off the program a month ago.

Vault: So where did you start out?

Wilkins: I started out as an operations engineer in Port Arthur, Texas. There, I was dealing with issues in the plant on a day-to-day basis—solving problems that arose in the plant and implementing small capital projects. For example, I designed and implemented a control loop to regulate the concentration in a furnace feed line. I also monitored the performance of over 300 process safety valves in order to determine which ones were leaking into the flare header.

The Port Arthur site is a chemical plant. It produces ethelyne, propylene and other chemical derivatives. It's the largest steam cracker in the world. A steam cracker takes long chains of hydrocarbons and heats them up, "cracking" the chains and forming double bonds.

Vault: Where did you go next?

Wilkins: My second rotation was at a smaller site, a manufacturing plant in Sparta, Tennessee, in the Upper Cumberland Mountains. It was a site that produced performance polymers or hard plastics. Every brand of hand tool, such as Black and Decker, DeWalt and Bosch, uses plastics from the Sparta BASF site.

Visit Vault at **www.vault.com** for insider company profiles, expert advice, career message boards, expert resume reviews, the Vault Job Board and more.

VAULT CAREER LIBRARY 209

Sparta was a manufacturing site rather than a chemical plant. It was very different from the Port Arthur site. For example, there weren't as many on-site engineers in Sparta. As a PDP participant at that site, I got to experience a combination of process, operations and product engineering. In a smaller site, you wear many hats, because there are not 10 to 12 engineers with all different job functions. There's just a handful of engineers and all share duties. As a result, I had a lot of responsibility and opportunity to do a lot of capital projects, day-to-day improvement projects and also some design work. It was a good chance to do lots of different things within the same job.

Vault: So where are you now?

Wilkins: Geismar, Louisiana. It's a town close to Baton Rouge. I recently accepted a permanent position here, but it was also my third rotational assignment. I picked this position because I really enjoyed the work I was doing during my assignment. When it was time to roll off of the program, I applied to an open position here.

It's a process engineering position, which is a bit different from operations and project engineering. It's more design work, working on projects that are a long time in the future, even a couple years off. I'm doing a lot of sizing and simulation work. It's a lot of what I like to call pencil-and-paper engineering. It's similar to the type of engineering you do in school.

Vault: What sort of products are you working on?

Wilkins: Geismar is our largest North American site, and is a very large chemical plant. It's almost what you would call seven or eight chemical plants in one. So at this site we make many chemicals—we make specialty amines, polyalcohols, ethylene oxide, isocyanates, aniline, diols, surfactants and a few others. As a PDP, I was working mostly on projects in ethylene oxide and TDI, which is an isocyanate used for foams that go into products such as seat cushions.

Vault: Did you get to choose your rotations?

Wilkins: The first assignment was chosen for me when I signed up for the program. PDP participants are placed depending on business needs. Halfway through my first assignment, I was able to choose the second one. BASF has a database set up and there's a list of job openings for PDP participants only. I checked the database the other day and there were 50 to 60 openings all over the company.

You basically apply to whichever positions you are interested in, and it's a first come, first serve basis. Assignments must be at different sites. The process begins three months before your rotation ends, and you usually go through a phone interview.

Vault: Was your relocation paid for?

Wilkins: Everything that is associated with the move is paid for, including a house-hunting trip.

Vault: Is there much communication among the different employees in the program?

Wilkins: We have teleconferences about once a month to discuss what each PDP participant is working on and maintain contact with all participants. A lot of times, it's just more of keeping details straight, hearing about what other people are doing in the sites and their roles, and hearing about other assignments so you can make the decision about whether you want to rotate to that assignment.

Vault: Is there a formal mentor program set up?

Wilkins: With this program, at your first site you have a mentor that's assigned to you, basically to kind of guide you along. Usually it's somebody who's not in your department.

Vault: How often did you meet with your mentor?

Wilkins: Really as often as I wanted to. I knew where his office was, and we'd talk maybe about once every other week. We'd try to have lunch every two weeks.

Also, it's remarkable how many people you come across who graduated from the program. These former PDP participants can relate to where you're at; they've been in your shoes, and you can always ask them questions. It's good to have so many engineers around you who have gone through the same program.

Visit Vault at **www.vault.com** for insider company profiles, expert advice, career message boards, expert resume reviews, the Vault Job Board and more.

VAULT CAREER LIBRARY

211

Employer Directory

Agilent Technologies, Inc.
5301 Stevens Creek Boulevard
Santa Clara, CA 95051
Phone: (408) 345-8886
Fax: (408) 345-8474
Toll free: (877) 424-4536
www.agilent.com

Bechtel Group, Inc.
50 Beale Street
San Francisco, CA 94105-1895
Phone: (415) 768-1234
Fax: (415) 768-9038
www.bechtel.com

The Boeing Company
100 North Riverside Plaza
Chicago, IL 60606-1596
Phone: (312) 544-2000
Fax: (312) 544-2082
www.boeing.com

Bridgestone Americas Holding, Inc.
535 Marriott Drive
Nashville, TN 37214
Phone: (615) 937-1000
Fax: (615) 937-3621
www.bridgestone-firestone.com

Caterpillar Inc.
100 NE Adams Street
Peoria, IL 61629
Phone: (309) 675-1000
Fax: (309) 675-1182
www.cat.com

CH2M HILL Companies, Ltd.
9191 South Jamaica Street
Englewood, CO 80112
Phone: (303) 771-0900
Fax: (720) 286-9250
www.ch2m.com

Chevron Corporation
6001 Bollinger Canyon Road
San Ramon, CA 94583
Phone: (925) 842-1000
Fax: (925) 842-3530
www.chevron.com

ConocoPhillips
600 North Dairy Ashford Road
Houston, TX 77079
Phone: (281) 293-1000
Fax: (281) 293-2819
www.conocophillips.com

Crown Holdings, Inc.
1 Crown Way
Philadelphia, PA 19154
Phone: (215) 698-5100
Fax: (215) 676-7245
www.crowncork.com

Danaher Corporation
2099 Pennsylvania Avenue NW
12th Floor
Washington, DC 20006
Phone: (202) 828-0850
Fax: (202) 828-0860
www.danaher.com

Deere & Company
1 John Deere Place
Moline, IL 61265
Phone: (309) 765-8000
Fax: (309) 765-5671
www.deere.com

Dover Corporation
280 Park Avenue, Floor 34W
New York, NY 10017
Phone: (212) 922-1640
Fax: (212) 922-1656
www.dovercorporation.com

Emerson Electric Co.
PO Box 4100
8000 West Florissant Avenue
St. Louis, MO 63136
Phone: (314) 553-2000
Fax: (314) 553-3527
www.emerson.com

Federal Prison Industries, Inc.
320 1st Street NW, Building 400
Washington DC 20534
Phone: (202) 305-3500
Fax: (202) 305-7340
www.unicor.com

Fluor Corporation
6700 Las Colinas Boulevard
Irving, TX 75039
Phone: (469) 398-7000
Fax: (469) 398-7255
www.fluor.com

Foster Wheeler Ltd.
Perryville Corporate Park
Clinton, NJ 08809-4000
Phone: (908) 730-4000
Fax: (908) 730-5315
www.fwc.com

General Dynamics Corporation
2941 Fairview Park Drive, Suite 100
Falls Church, VA 22042
Phone: (703) 876-3000
Fax: (703) 876-3125
www.gendyn.com

The Goodyear Tire & Rubber Company
1144 East Market Street
Akron, OH 44316
Phone: (330) 796-2121
Fax: (330) 796-2222
www.goodyear.com

Guardian Industries Corp.
2300 Harmon Road
Auburn Hills, MI 48329
Phone: (248) 340-1800
Fax: (248) 340-9988
www.guardian.com

Halliburton Company
5 Houston Center
1401 McKinney, Suite 2400
Houston, TX 77010
Phone: (713) 759-2600
Fax: (713) 759-2635
www.halliburton.com

Employer Directory, cont.

Honeywell
Honeywell International Inc.
101 Columbia Road
Morristown, NJ 07962
Phone: (973) 455-2000
Fax: (973) 455-4807
www.honeywell.com

Illinois Tool Works Inc.
3600 West Lake Avenue
Glenview, IL 60026
Phone: (847) 724-7500
Fax: (847) 657-4261
www.itw.com

International Paper Company
6400 Poplar Avenue
Memphis, TN 38197
Phone: (901) 419-7000
Fax: (901) 214-9682
Toll free: (800) 223-1268
www.internationalpaper.com

Kimley-Horn and Associates, Inc.
3001 Weston Parkway
Cary, NC 27513
Phone: (919) 677-2000
Fax: (919) 677-2050
www.kimley-horn.com

Lockheed Martin Corporation
6801 Rockledge Drive
Bethesda, MD 20817
Phone: (301) 897-6000
Fax: (301) 897-6704
www.lockheedmartin.com

The Marmon Group, LLC
181 West Madison Street, 26th Floor
Chicago, IL 60602
Phone: (312) 372-9500
Fax: (312) 845-5305
www.marmon.com

MeadWestvaco Corporation
11013 West Broad Street
Glen Allen, VA 23060
Phone: (804) 327-5200
Fax: (404) 897-6383
www.meadwestvaco.com

Michelin North America, Inc.
1 Parkway South
Greenville, SC 29615
Phone: (864) 458-5000
Fax: (864) 458-6359
Toll free: (800) 847-3435
www.michelin-us.com

Mohawk Industries, Inc.
160 South Industrial Boulevard
Calhoun, GA 30701
Phone: (706) 629-7721
Fax: (706) 624-3825
Toll free: (800) 241-4494
www.mohawkind.com

Northrop Grumman Corporation
1840 Century Park East
Los Angeles, CA 90067-2199
Phone: (310) 553-6262
Fax: (310) 553-2076
www.northropgrumman.com

Otis Elevator Company
1 Farm Springs Road
Farmington, CT 06032
Phone: (860) 676-6000
Fax: (860) 676-5111
Toll free: (800) 233-6847
www.otisworldwide.com

Owens-Illinois, Inc.
1 Michael Owens Way
Perrysburg, OH 43551
Phone: (567) 336-5000
Fax: (419) 247-7107
www.o-i.com

Parker Hannifin Corporation
6035 Parkland Boulevard
Cleveland, OH 44124
Phone: (216) 896-3000
Fax: (216) 896-4000
www.parker.com

Parsons Corporation
100 West Walnut Street
Pasadena, CA 91124
Phone: (626) 440-2000
Fax: (626) 440-2630
www.parsons.com

Precision Castparts Corp.
4650 SW Macadam Avenue, Suite 440
Portland, OR 97239
Phone: (503) 417-4800
Fax: (503) 417-4817
www.precast.com

Raytheon Company
870 Winter Street
Waltham, MA 02451
Phone: (781) 522-3000
Fax: (781) 522-3001
www.raytheon.com

Rockwell Automation, Inc.
1201 South 2nd Street
Milwaukee, WI 53204
Phone: (414) 382-2000
Fax: (414) 382-4444
www.rockwellautomation.com

Shaw Industries, Inc.
616 East Walnut Avenue
Dalton, GA 30722
Phone: (706) 278-3812
Toll free: (800) 441-7429
www.shawfloors.com

Siemens AG
Wittelsbacherplatz 2
D-80333 Munich
Germany
Phone: +49-89-636-00
Fax: +49-89-636-52-000
www.siemens.com

Visit Vault at **www.vault.com** for insider company profiles, expert advice,
career message boards, expert resume reviews, the Vault Job Board and more.

VAULT CAREER LIBRARY   213

Employer Directory, cont.

Sonoco Products Company
1 North 2nd Street
Hartsville, SC 29550
Phone: (843) 383-7000
Fax: (843) 383-7008
Toll free: (800) 377-2692
www.sonoco.com

Smurfit-Stone Container Corporation
150 North Michigan Avenue
Chicago, IL 60601
Phone: (312) 346-6600
Fax: (312) 580-2272
www.smurfit.com

Terex Corporation
200 Nyala Farms Road
Westport, CT 06880
Phone: (203) 222-7170
Fax: (203) 222-7976
www.terex.com

The Timken Company
1835 Dueber Avenue SW
Canton, OH 44706
Phone: (330) 438-3000
Fax: (330) 471-3452
www.timken.com

United Technologies Corporation
1 Financial Plaza
Hartford, CT 06103
Phone: (860) 728-7000
Fax: (860) 565-5400
www.utc.com

W.W. Grainger, Inc.
100 Grainger Parkway
Lake Forest, IL 60045
Phone: (847) 535-1000
Fax: (847) 535-0878
www.grainger.com

Fashion

Do you thrill to the thought that gray might—just might—be the new black? Do you tire of fashion trends before they even hit the stores? Then a career in fashion could be the right choice for you. Those who truly love the field say that the perks—fabulous clothes, exposure to famous people and brands, extraordinary diversity, awareness of upcoming trends and cool job status—are worth the struggle. Still, fashion is not all glitz and glamour. Even more than talent, an understanding of the industry is what lands the job.

Even though the fashion industry is difficult to break into, opportunities abound there—creative jobs in design and marketing; retail sales and buying positions; corporate careers in finance, planning and distribution.

Yet whether you are seeking a place on the catwalk or in the haute couture clubhouse, the fashion business is just that—a business. Insiders from all over the fashion world say that their jobs are high on stress and low on pay. Moreover, insiders conclude, people are often judged as much on looks as on performance. With its rigorous hours, capricious culture and wobbly corporate ladder, the fashion industry certainly isn't for everybody. Yet for a dedicated minority, there is no more exciting and inspiring place. Lecturing at a forum hosted by the Fashion Group Foundation, designer Isaac Mizrahi characterized fashion this way: "I hope you all adore what you're doing. It's really got to be this obsession. You have to love cloth. You have to love chalk. You have to love pins. You do it because you love to do it and can't stop doing it."

Designers create and produce garments, textiles and accessories. Some have formal training and some do not. Almost all designers begin as assistant designers for a few years and eventually become designers. In a large company, a designer may move up the ladder to be a design director. A design director manages the designers from each group. For example, at a company like Bebe, there may be a designer for each group (such as dresses, suits, knits and denim), but a design director will coordinate the efforts of all the designers so the brand presents a cohesive image. Product development usually refers to retailers that develop their own product in conjunction with manufacturers. Product development differs from design in that it usually doesn't require as many technical skills. In fact, product developers may work with designers from other companies to create products for their own brand.

Fashion Design Jobs

Assistant Designer: Helps the designer create new designs. May help with sketches and research.

Designer: Creates plans for clothes that fit the image, season and price point of the brand.

Assistant Technical Designer: Assists designer or technical designer in all aspects of quality and fit procedures. Must have strong computer skills.

Technical Designer: Follows design direction to develop garments through technical sketches, specific measurements for garments, receiving and reviewing samples, and sketching and measuring garments for technical packages.

Sample Pattern Maker: Translates designers' sketches into wearable works of art by draping and making patterns to create sample garments. Almost all pattern makers draft patterns on computers.

Textile Designer: Creates textiles by using various fibers and knitting or weaving techniques for industries ranging from apparel to upholstery.

Visit Vault at **www.vault.com** for insider company profiles, expert advice, career message boards, expert resume reviews, the Vault Job Board and more.

VAULT CAREER LIBRARY   215

The Scoop on Design Careers

Most fashion experts would agree that design, one of fashion's most competitive and exciting fields, requires technical and art training, leadership, ingenuity, highly developed patternmaking skills and a keen understanding of the aesthetic, as well as the practical and cost-effective. Design also calls for absolute dedication. Some of the most successful designers refer to their vocation as an "obsession" or a "way of life." Given the hardships, designers have to be crazy about what they do. How else would they be able to survive the grueling hours, low entry-level pay and lack of success guarantees?

The first step toward becoming a designer is reconsidering your decision. Our insiders say there is no shame in being a realist: "Fashion students often come in bright-eyed and idealistic. They think they are ready for the hard work and difficult hours so long as they can have the glamour, too. What they don't realize is that very, very few designers hit it big." Aspiring designers also err when it comes to focus. "You have to think about what consumers really want," advises another source. "It's vital to know the realities of the job market. Pay attention to what people are going to buy rather than what you want to create." And it never hurts to look at your other options. "Students don't know that there are a hundred other jobs in fashion besides design," says an insider from a New York fashion school. "There are trim buyers, pattern makers, sample makers, quality control experts and fashion consultants. Often, these jobs are not only better-paying, they are 100 percent more secure."

For those who have listened to the naysayers and still want to be designers, the advice is: go for it. Insiders from such famous New York City fashion schools as Pratt, Parsons and FIT all concede that someone has to be the next Karl Lagerfeld or Diane von Furstenberg. Why not you? If you think you have the guts, the talent and the backbone, "go global and go for the top," declares one enthusiastic source.

The climb may take some time, however. "It's very rare for a young fashion designer to set up his own label immediately after graduation," confesses a source. In reality, most graduates will spend five or more years working for a designer, gaining experience, earning a reputation and making contacts. Some fashion professionals will even start a design career outside of the industry in order to break into the field. Internships at major fashion houses or other jobs, like pattern work or retail, can sometimes launch you into design. The bottom line: don't be too hasty. Think of each job as a stepping stone in your career, so that you will always know what options you have.

Our Survey Says: Fashion Industry Culture

Image

In the fashion industry, your image is an important factor in your career. In some fields, such as modeling, a certain "type" is required. In other fields, such as public relations, good looks are preferred. Evidence of fashion's obsession with appearance is everywhere. Many retail employees must sport the clothing of their company. Designers serve as walking examples of their work. Even employees at fashion magazines "dress accordingly." Appearance is more important for fashion professionals who interact with the public and who work for high-end employers. (If you work in finance or planning, your dress matters less. And if you work at Kohl's versus Bloomingdale's, being "fashionable" is not as important.)

The "beauty prerequisite" is a source of pride, but also of contention. "You're often judged by what you wear and what you look like," says a designer who specializes in women's couture. Noverto Gonzalez, who worked as an assistant buyer at Saks Fifth Avenue says, "You have to represent whom you work for. The industry can be pretentious. They look at your shoes, bag and watch to check out the label." Certainly, appearance alone probably won't make or break a fashion career. Most fashion employers are looking for traditional skills and abilities. Nevertheless, in the fashion industry, appearance may count more than it does in other industries.

Read the magazines and follow celebrities if you want to keep up with the latest trends. Consider magazine staples like *Vogue*, *Elle*, *Harper's Bazaar* and *W*. You may also want to look at the French, English or Spanish editions of these magazines.

Do good and be beautiful

Fashion is home to glamour, beautiful people and, of course, celebrities. Everyone knows the name of at least one supermodel; most people could name quite a few more. In fashion, namedropping and networking are the norm. But another common, if less known, aspect of the fashion world is philanthropy. "Philanthropy," designer Kenneth Cole said at a fashion charity event, "has been part of our corporate culture from the beginning."

This warm-and-fuzzy consciousness isn't simply motivated by the heart: the wallet has something to do with it. Specifically, mixing philanthropy with commerce is a sales tool called cause-related marketing. Since public service is an ideal conduit for sales, many famous designers embrace one cause or another. However, these causes are often as changeable as the industry itself. Points out one fashion insider: "Fashion may embrace fur-wearing one day and protest it the next. Its loyalties are superficial." There are drawbacks to here-today-gone-tomorrow activism. Nevertheless, public service organizations can benefit by the media attention given to "fashionable causes."

Melting pot

The glass ceiling is not much of a problem in an industry where "women outnumber men." "Race is rarely, if ever, an issue" and "a large number of the men in design are gay," says an insider at an upscale department store. In fact, an insider at The Gap is happy to report, "Gender and ethnicity are just not an issue." In almost all aspects of the industry, the pervasion of different cultures, races, religious faiths and sexual orientations is common. "I expected to see a lot of white upper-class yuppies," remarks one J. Crew insider, "but this wasn't what I envisioned. The proverbial New York City melting pot boils over into the [J. Crew] corporate office."

L'Oreal is one brand that prides itself on its international flavor. In fact, it boasts that many of its employees are multilingual. Nike is also sound in the diversity department. At this company, different ethnic groups gather for "informal meetings." One member of the company's "Hispanic caucus" finds Nike "a fun place to meet other Latinos and network." Of course, not all employees are content with their company's heterogeneity. At companies like Lands End and L.L. Bean, some employees complain of a lack of diversity. But others argue that the predominately white demographics simply reflect the surrounding communities. "Maine and Wisconsin are not exactly known for large mixes of ethnic communities," says one. "It would follow that the minority headcount is proportional to the community and state." An Asian-American L.L. Bean insider agrees, "I have always felt that the employee makeup simply reflects the general population [in Maine]." As production continues to grow overseas, fashion industry employees are becoming more accustomed to a global marketplace. Companies may buy their fabric from Korea, cut and sew in Sri Lanka, pack and ship in Hong Kong, warehouse in the U.S. and sell in Canada and Mexico.

While the fashion industry is one of the most ethnically diverse around, insiders still complain of "a herd mentality." Complains one: "At my last job, everyone had a blonde bob. Fortunately, my new job is more diverse. It doesn't seem that race or sexuality is that important—it's all about how you look. Class and style are what are most important." Speaking of blondes, one celebrity dresser "can't wait to dress Gwyneth Paltrow." Why? "Because everyone wants to dress her!" He continues, "I enjoy meeting celebrities on a personal level, although not everything about my job is glamorous. It's not glamorous running around buying shoes at the last minute and sitting around a seating chart at 3 a.m., guessing who will be happy sitting next to each other." An assistant designer agrees that the industry is, at best, unpredictable. "I'm not doing what I thought I'd be doing," she says. "There are some people [in this industry] with high-profile jobs, but most of us end up working for other famous people."

Visit Vault at **www.vault.com** for insider company profiles, expert advice, career message boards, expert resume reviews, the Vault Job Board and more.

VAULT CAREER LIBRARY

217

Networking

Ask around the fashion industry and you'll find people who dreamed of working there all their lives and people who stumbled into their positions by chance. One associate designer maintains, "To get into the creative end of the industry, you need a proper education. You need to study design. Technical people, such as buyers and inventory planners, on the other hand, are more likely to have 'fallen' into their jobs." No matter how they got there, however, fashion professionals admit that having industry contacts is often more important than having talent. "To find a job," reveals an employee from Macy's Inc., "it's important to use the people you know. I found my first job through contacts, the next by sending an exploratory note and the third was luck—I got it out of a newspaper advertisement. I'd say my first job was the easiest to find."

While many people—and fashion students in particular—might feel dismayed by this need to know the "right people," one insider says worry is unnecessary. "Students often think they cannot make connections while confined within college walls," says a career counselor from a top New York fashion school. "This is a myth. Connections is just another word for relationships. You have relationships with other students, professors, career counselors, the school administration and many others. At fashion schools, most of the teachers have previous experience in the fashion industry." What does that mean? An acquaintance at your school or workplace might already have valuable job information!

It all comes down to networking. To find the right fashion job for you, it is necessary to discuss your job search with the people you know—and with the people they know. Ask questions, inquire about openings and request informational interviews. Fashion students should attend as many college-sponsored events as possible and seek relevant internships. After a fashion internship has ended, they should keep in touch with their managers. A fashion career counselor confirms, "Those who serve as intern advisors often grow very fond of their interns. They want to know that you've graduated; they want to help and advise you."

Internships

Most fashion internships are in design, marketing and production—and unpaid. Like the entertainment industry, actual education isn't as important as work experience. You will need some education to get in the door, but after that, your resume or connections will get you farther. If you want to go into fashion or retail, get an internship or even a part-time job in sales or merchandising to get started. Each experience on your resume will help land a better internship or full-time job the next time. Although some internships are posted in the trade papers, many internship searches are self-directed because many are never publicized. If the position is at a popular company or designer, the internship will never be posted since everyone will want it on his or her resume.

Make sure to express your desire to learn and help the company—even if you think your level of responsibility is not as high as you would like. Once you are in the company, you can find out about other positions before they may even be open. Build your resume, and you can get the interviews and introductions. Of course, your initial job in the fashion industry may not pay well. There are several options here—you work to get the experience or to learn enough to start your own business. If you are thinking of the latter, take any experience you can. It will pay off later.

A Day in a Life: Assistant Product Manager, Macy's, Inc. Merchandising Group

Noverto Gonzales graduated from the University of North Texas with a BA in merchandising in 1999. His first summer internship was at JC Penney in Texas. It was a 10-week program: five weeks as assistant department manager on the retail floor and five weeks as an assistant buyer. He knew he wanted to live in New York City, so the summer before he graduated, Noverto landed another internship in the city. He was offered an internship at Barney's and Saks Fifth Avenue but chose the one at Saks since a salary came with it. The Barney's internship paid a small stipend at the end of the summer. His New York City job search was entirely self-directed.

After graduation, he was offered a position at JC Penney (in Texas) and Saks Fifth Avenue. JC Penney was very supportive and knew he wanted to go to New York. He began his career as an assistant buyer at Saks Fifth Avenue Catalog. He moved on to Macy's, Inc. as an assistant product manager. Macy's operates Bloomingdale's and Macy's department stores. At Macy's, Inc.'s Merchandising Group, he worked with other product managers, buyers, the design team and the technical design team. The group, a division of Macy's, Inc. (formerly Federated Department Stores), is responsible for the conceptualization, design, sourcing and marketing of private brands that are exclusive to Macy's and Bloomingdale's. These private labels include: INC, Style & Co., Alfani, Tools of the Trade, Charter Club, JM Collection, Tasso Elba, Club Room and Greendog.

Noverto Gonzalez's Day

9 a.m. Get into office and check e-mail. Our overseas office in Turkey has left me some notes. Update production time and action plans. The approvals for fit samples, lap dips and trims are managed by product development. For example, if our designer doesn't like a button on a sample, we have to find a replacement.

10:30 a.m. Fit model comes in. We have fittings three times a week. I keep a "Fit" book and take notes of things that were changed. The designer and assistant designer are also in the meeting.

11:30 a.m. I go back to my office to update the open purchase orders. If the parameters of the order change, I have to update it and make sure the legal documents are correct, as well. Some of essential information is color, style number, vendor, country of origin, first cost and landed cost. I also deal with quota issues.

12:30 p.m. Get back to the office and work on design samples. Go over current season sales and look through styles and colors. Look at different types of bodies or fabrication. Often, I have to address costing issues. If we want our cost of production to be something specific, like $5, we might have to negotiate with our vendors. Or we would look at the price of a set and then increase the price of the pant and decrease the shirt. Every year we are pressured to reduce cost from last year.

2 p.m. Grab a quick and late lunch.

2:30 p.m. Attend line development meeting. We're always working on three seasons at once. Develop fall, go into meeting for holiday and check spring production calendar. The seasons [Macy's] followed were fall, holiday, spring and summer.

4 p.m. Check e-mail and update my calendar. Once a week, I track all shipments. I reconcile the shipping logs, purchase orders and sales. If the shipment does not have a corresponding receipt number, I ask someone in the DC (distribution center) or e-mail a vendor and ask for proof of shipment.

5:30 p.m. Track advertising samples. These samples are used for our ads. The buyers request ad samples.

6: p.m. Go home!

Visit Vault at **www.vault.com** for insider company profiles, expert advice, career message boards, expert resume reviews, the Vault Job Board and more.

VAULT CAREER LIBRARY   **219**

4 p.m. Check e-mail and update my calendar. Once a week, I track all shipments. I reconcile the shipping logs, purchase orders and sales. If the shipment does not have a corresponding receipt number, I ask someone in the DC (distribution center) or e-mail a vendor and ask for proof of shipment.

5:30 p.m. Track advertising samples. These samples are used for our ads. The buyers request ad samples.

6: p.m. Go home!

Gonzalez comments: "My favorite part of the industry is working with fashion forecasting offices. You know what's going on next year. The ironic thing is that there are so many trends but most things end up looking the same! Every company does similar things. The worst part of the industry is that it is pretentious. You always have to stay on top. If something doesn't sell then you're responsible for it."

A Day in a Life: Dress Buyer, Victoria's Secret Catalog

Sylvia Dundon graduated from the Fashion Institute of Technology with a BA in marketing (concentration merchandising management) and an AAS in buying and merchandising in December 1998. It took two years to obtain her AAS and another three years for her BA since she was working at the Gap and Victoria's Secret while she was attending school. She began her career as an assistant buyer at Victoria's Secret Catalog and was later promoted to associate buyer.

Sylvia Dundon's Day

9 a.m. Check e-mail and voicemail. Prioritize who gets called back first based on what time zone they're in.

9:30 a.m. Check sales on computer—especially dress sales for the items I bought most recently. If the catalog just dropped (that is, was sent out), wait a few days for the sales to hit. Work with the planner. ("At Victoria's Secret, the planner is the buyer's partner. The planner executes the actual purchase order, financial planning, stock models and markdowns.")

10:30 a.m. Decide how to allocate five pages of the catalog. For example, how many dresses should I feature per page? Do I think I'll sell more dresses with three per page or should I focus on one large picture of a single dress? I have to justify my decisions to management and work with the merchandise manager. Some of my decisions are based on what sold in the catalog last year.

11:30 a.m. Sample fitting. Go to the fit room and work with your technical specialist and fit model. The fit model tries on samples and we make sure the garment is the right specifications and fit. If the garment is not correct, we send our corrections to the vendor. A sample garment usually goes through one to three rounds of corrections.

12 p.m. Layout and film review. I go visit the creative department and look at a layout of our catalog. The point is to review the actual photography and layout (for colors). If the color of the garment is wrong, I cut a swatch from the garment as a sample so the creative dept. can fix the photo to match. If the skirt in the photo is too long, they can fix the length, too. If everything looks great, I just approve the layout.

12:45 p.m. Run out to buy a sandwich so I can eat at my desk and check voicemail.

2 p.m. Roll out my sample rack. Send out samples for a photo shoot. Work with in-house model for shoot samples to make sure they fit and look right according to Victoria's Secret standards.

3 p.m. Meet a few vendors. I cut a few fabric swatches for product development. Sometimes I go out into the market or vendor showrooms to look at their lines. If I really like something, I will ask them to send samples for me the next day.

4 p.m. Go to a fashion forecast meeting. This meeting includes both the fashion and design departments and is intended to make sure that we're all aware of the trends and direction that Victoria's Secret wants to take that season. Even though we're buying different categories (dresses, shirts, etc.), we all want to have the same mindset. I also see slide shows of samples bought in Europe. All the buyers get to see the main themes for the season—which include a color palette and the general trends.

6 p.m. Address production issues. Approve a button or lab dip. The lap dip is the color intended for production. Quite often, the manufacturer hasn't produced the correct color, so I have to ask them to do another lab dip.

7 p.m. Address the e-mails I didn't get to during the day. Go home!

Visit Vault at **www.vault.com** for insider company profiles, expert advice, career message boards, expert resume reviews, the Vault Job Board and more.

VAULT CAREER LIBRARY

221

Employer Directory

Abercrombie & Fitch Co.
6301 Fitch Path
New Albany, OH 43054
Phone: (614) 283-6500
Fax: (614) 283-6710
www.abercrombie.com

Alstyle Apparel, LLC
1501 East Cerritos Avenue
Anaheim, CA 92805
Phone: (714) 765-0400
Fax: (714) 765-0450
Toll free: (800) 225-1364
www.alstyle.com

Ann Taylor Stores Corporation
7 Times Square, 15th Floor
New York, NY 10036
Phone: (212) 541-3300
Fax: (212) 541-3379
www.anntaylor.com

Carter's, Inc.
The Proscenium
1170 Peachtree Street NE, Suite 900
Atlanta, GA 30309
Phone: (404) 745-2700
Fax: (404) 892-0968
www.carters.com

Chanel S.A.
135, Avenue Charles de Gaulle
92521 Neuilly-sur-Seine Cedex
France
Phone: +33-1-46-43-40-00
www.chanel.com

Coach, Inc.
516 West 34th Street
New York, NY 10001
Phone: (212) 594-1850
Fax: (212) 594-1682
www.coach.com

Crocs, Inc.
6328 Monarch Park Place
Niwot, CO 80503
Phone: (303) 848-7000
Fax: (303) 468-4266
www.crocs.com

Delta Apparel, Inc.
2750 Premiere Parkway, Suite 100
Duluth, GA 30097
Phone: (678) 775-6900
Fax: (678) 775-6992
Toll free: (800) 285-4456
www.deltaapparelinc.com

Dolce & Gabbana SPA
Via Santa Cecilia, 7
20122 Milan
Italy
Phone: +39-02-77-42-71
www.dolcegabbana.it

Donna Karan International Inc.
550 Seventh Avenue
New York, NY 10018
Phone: (212) 789-1500
Fax: (212) 921-3526
www.donnakaran.com

Eddie Bauer, Inc.
15010 NE 36th Street
Redmond, WA 98052
Phone: (425) 755-6100
Fax: (425) 755-7696
www.eddiebauer.com

Fruit of the Loom, Inc.
1 Fruit of the Loom Drive
Bowling Green, KY 42103
Phone: (270) 781-6400
Fax: (270) 781-6588
www.fruit.com

Gap Inc.
2 Folsom Street
San Francisco, CA 94105
Phone: (650) 952-4400
Fax: (415) 427-2553
www.gapinc.com

Guess?, Inc.
1444 South Alameda Street
Los Angeles, CA 90021
Phone: (213) 765-3100
Phone: (213) 744-7838
www.guess.com

Hanesbrands Inc.
1000 East Hanes Mill Road
Winston-Salem, NC 27105
Phone: (336) 424-6000
Fax: (336) 424-7631
www.hanesbrands.com

J. Crew Group Inc.
770 Broadway
New York, NY 10003
Phone: (212) 209-2500
Fax: (212) 209-2666
www.jcrew.com

Jockey International, Inc.
2300 60th Street
Kenosha, WI 53141
Phone: (262) 658-8111
Fax: (262) 658-1812
Toll free: (800) 562-5391
www.jockey.com

Jordache Enterprises, Inc.
1400 Broadway, 15th Floor
New York, NY 10018
Phone: (212) 944-1330
Fax: (212) 239-0063
www.jordachecorporate.com

Jones Apparel Group, Inc.
1411 Broadway
New York, NY 10018
Phone: (212) 642-3860
Fax: (215) 785-1795
www.jonesapparel.com

Tommy Hilfiger
25 West 39th Street, 14th Floor
New York, NY 10018
www.tommy.com

Kellwood Company
600 Kellwood Parkwway
Chesterfield, MO 63017
Phone: (314) 576-3100
Fax: (314) 576-3460
www.kellwood.com

Employer Directory, cont.

Kenneth Cole Productions, Inc.
603 West 50th Street
New York, NY 10019
Phone: (212) 265-1500
Fax: (212) 830-7422
www.kennethcole.com

L'Oreal USA
575 5th Avenue
New York, NY 10017
Phone: (212) 818-1500
Fax: (212) 984-4999
www.lorealusa.com

Levi Strauss & Co.
1155 Battery Street
San Francisco, CA 94111
Phone: (415) 501-6000
Fax: (415) 501-7112
www.levistrauss.com

Limited Brands
3 Limited Parkway
Columbus, OH 43216
Phone: (614) 415-7000
Fax: (614) 415-7440
www.limited.com

Liz Claiborne, Inc.
1441 Broadway
New York, NY 10018
Phone: (212) 354-4900
Fax: (212) 626-3416
www.lizclaiborneinc.com

Louis Vuitton North America, Inc.
19 East 57th Street
New York, NY 10222
Phone: (212) 318-7000
Fax: (212) 888-5780
Toll free: (800) 377-7656

Macy's, Inc.
7 West Seventh Street
Cincinnati, OH 45202
Phone: (513) 579-7000
Fax: (513) 579-7555
www.federated-fds.com

Nike, Inc.
1 Bowerman Drive
Beaverton, OR 97005-6453
Phone: (503) 671-6453
Fax: (503) 671-6300
Toll free: (800) 344-6543
www.nikebiz.com

Nine West Group Inc.
1129 Westchester Avenue
White Plains, NY 10604
Phone: (914) 640-6400
Fax: (914) 640-1676
Toll free: (800) 999-1877
www.ninewest.com

Nordstrom, Inc.
1617 Sixth Avenue
Seattle, WA 98101-1742
Phone: (206) 628-2111
Fax: (206) 628-1795
www.nordstrom.com

Oxford Industries, Inc
222 Piedmont Avenue NE
Atlanta, GA 30308
Phone: (404) 659-2424
Fax: (404) 653-1545
www.oxfordinc.com

Polo Ralph Lauren Corporation
650 Madison Avenue
New York, NY 10222
Phone: (212) 318-7000
Fax: (212) 888-5780
Toll free: (800) 377-7656
www.ralphlauren.com

OshKosh b'Gosh, Inc.
112 Otter Avenue
Oshkosh, WI 54901
Phone: (920) 231-8800
Fax: (920) 231-8621
www.oshkoshbgosh.com

Phillips-Van Heusen Corporation
200 Madison Avenue
New York, NY 10016
Phone: (212) 381-3500
Fax: (212) 381-3950
www.pvh.com

Polo Ralph Lauren Corporation
650 Madison Avenue
New York, NY 10022
Phone: (212) 318-7000
Fax: (212) 888-5780
www.polo.com

Reebok International Ltd.
1895 J.W. Foster Boulevard
Canton, MA 02021
Phone: (781) 401-5000
Fax: (781) 401-7402
www.reebok.com

Renfro Corporation
661 Linville Road
Mt. Airy, NC 27030
Phone: (336) 719-8000
Fax: (336) 719-8215
Toll free: (800) 334-9091
www.renfro.com

Samsonite Corporation
575 West Street, Suite 110
Mansfield, MA 02048
Phone: (508) 851-1400
Fax: (508) 851-8715
www.samsonite.com

The Timberland Company
200 Domain Drive
Stratham, NH 03885
Phone: (603)772-9500
Fax: (603) 773-1640
www.timberland.com

V.F. Corporation
105 Corporate Center Boulevard
Greensboro, NC 27408
Phone: (336) 424-6000
Fax: (336) 424-7631
www.vfc.com

The Warnaco Group, Inc.
501 7th Avenue
New York, NY 10018
Phone: (212) 563-2000
Fax: (212) 971-2250
Toll free: (800) 759-4219
www.warnerco.com

Visit Vault at **www.vault.com** for insider company profiles, expert advice, career message boards, expert resume reviews, the Vault Job Board and more.

VAULT CAREER LIBRARY   223

THE WORLD NEVER SLEEPS.

Dreams.   **Realities.**

In Harvard Square, Jackson has just cracked an equation. Meanwhile, in Austin, Texas, Rita – the woman who will soon give Jackson an analyst position – is on her way to give a presentation on microfinance. And in Singapore, a team of Global Capital Markets Associates are projecting the impact of the growth of the global middle class.

Working in more than 100 countries means being open-minded in every way: how we do business, how we find solutions, and how we choose our colleagues. To us, inclusion isn't a rule to follow; it's a way of life. Because we're all different, and we're proud to be. That's why at Citi, the world never sleeps. **oncampus.citi.com**

Citi never sleeps

Financial Services and Insurance

State of the Industry

Like a bazaar that offers something to satisfy every customer's potential needs, the financial services industry presents a little bit of everything to prospective clientele. But while the trade is a vast one, its subdivisions are specialized to meet individuals' fiscal needs. Many of these specialized financial categories are covered in this guide.

The firms we chose to profile as the top financial services firms primarily operate in one of the following categories: credit cards, insurance, mortgages, auto financing, ratings, financial data services or diversified financials. (Noticeably missing categories include accounting, investment banking, commercial banking and investment management—all of which are covered in other Vault guides.)

Although the evolution of the financial services business has been a long and storied one, its development and expansion continues well into this century. What follows is a brief overview of the financial services fields covered in this guide.

Credit Card Services

Looming large

Issuing credit cards is one of the most common ways in which financial services firms provide credit to individuals. Via the credit card, firms provide individuals with the funds required to purchase goods and services, and in return, individuals repay the full balance at a later date, or make payments on an installment basis. Via the debit card, people avoid debt by withdrawing the purchase amount from their bank accounts and transferring it to the seller. Though you're most likely familiar with how credit and debit cards work, you might not be familiar with just how large the industry is. According to Reuters, as of 2007, there were more than 640 million credit cards in circulation in the U.S. And according to CreditCards.com, Visa had a 46 percent U.S. market share based on credit card receivables outstanding in 2007, followed by MasterCard with 36 percent, American Express with 12 percent and Discover with 6 percent. On a global scale, Visa accounted for 65 percent of the market, MasterCard had a 30 percent share, followed by American Express and Japan-based JCB card (both of which had unknown shares).

A bumpy ride

In the first quarter of 2008, Visa and MasterCard spent $860,000 and $720,000 apiece in order to attempt to combat proposed federal regulations, which would shield consumers from high interest rates and let merchants who take credit cards negotiate their transaction fees. The proposed legislation, called the "Credit Card Fair Fee Act of 2008," as spearheaded by the Federal Reserve, the Office of Thrift and Supervision, and the National Credit Union Administration.

Potential legislation against Visa and MasterCard was only the tip of the iceberg of credit card companies' difficulties in 2008. MasterCard posted a $746 million loss for the second quarter of the year, due in no small part to the $1.8 billion the company ended up paying American Express in a settlement stemming from a 2004 lawsuit contending that MasterCard—along with competitor Visa—had barred some financial companies from distributing cards through American Express. In the third quarter of 2008, MasterCard will make its first $150 million payment to American Express—a practice that will continue for 12 quarters. Meanwhile, Visa, in its settlement, is paying American Express a total of $2.25 billion.

Visit Vault at **www.vault.com** for insider company profiles, expert advice, career message boards, expert resume reviews, the Vault Job Board and more.

VAULT CAREER LIBRARY 225

 # ODDS ARE, YOU'RE NOT GOING TO HAVE A TOP TEN SONG.

BUT YOU CAN HAVE A TOP TEN INTERNSHIP.

Northwestern Mutual's internship program has been named one of America's top ten internships for 12 straight years. To see if you qualify, just go to nminternship.com. No matter what kind of voice you have, it's your chance to be in the top ten.

 **Northwestern Mutual**®
the quiet company®
insurance / investments / ideas™

Consumer credit purgatory

Credit card companies were hardly the only ones to feel the pinch of the credit crunch. Consumers worldwide felt the breakdown of the subprime market in many ways, and those in the U.S. took the brunt of the fallout. In late 2007, International Monetary Fund Director Rodrigo Rato predicted the U.S. would be the hardest hit throughout 2008. Sadly, his predictions seemed to be fulfilled quickly—by June 2008, *The Guardian* reported on the trend of more and more middle-class citizens being forced to live in their cars due to the foreclosures brought on by the subprime crisis. And that wasn't the end of the market backlash. In July 2008, the Senior Loan Officer Opinion Survey on Bank Lending Practice reported that 65 percent of U.S. banks admitted to stiffening their overall lending practices over the course of the year as a result of the credit crisis, a 30 percent jump versus its April 2008 report.

Heavy metal

The credit card traces its roots back to 1914 when Western Union began doling out metal cards, called "metal money," which gave preferred customers interest-free, deferred-payment privileges. Ten years later, General Petroleum Corporation issued the first metal money for gasoline and automotive services, and by the late 1930s, department stores, communication companies, travel and delivery companies had all began to introduce such cards. Then, companies issued the cards, processed the transactions and collected the debts from the customer. The popularity of these cards grew until the beginning of World War II, when "Regulation W" restricted the use of cards, and as a result, stalled their growth.

After the war, though, cards were back on track. Modes of travel were more advanced and more accessible, and more people were beginning to buy expensive modern conveniences such as kitchen appliances and washing machines. As a result, the credit card boomed in popularity, as consumers could pay for these things on credit that otherwise they couldn't afford to buy with cash.

Charge-it

In 1951, New York's Franklin National Bank created a credit system called Charge-It, which was very similar to the modern credit card. Charge-It allowed consumers to make purchases at local retail establishments, with the retailer obtaining authorization from the bank and then closing the sale. At a later date, the bank would reimburse the retailer and then collect the debt from the consumer. Acting upon the success of Franklin's Charge-It, other banks soon began introducing similar cards. Banks found that cardholders liked the convenience and credit line that cards offered, and retailers discovered that credit card customers usually spent more than if they had to pay with cash. Additionally, retailers found that handling bank-issued cards was less costly than maintaining their credit card programs.

The association and the Master

Bank of America masterminded credit card innovations in the 1960s with the introduction of the bank card association. In 1965, Bank of America began issuing licensing agreements that allowed other banks to issue BankAmericards. To compete with the BankAmericard, four banks from California formed the Western States Bankcard Association and introduced the MasterCharge. By 1969, most credit cards had been converted to either the MasterCharge (which changed its name to MasterCard in 1979) or the BankAmericard (which was renamed Visa in 1977).

Cutting the cost of transaction processing and decreasing credit card fraud were the next innovations introduced to the industry. Electronic authorizations, beginning in the early 1970s, allowed merchants to approve transactions 24 hours a day. By the end of the decade, magnetic strips on the back of credit cards allowed retailers to swipe the customer's credit card through a dial-up terminal, which accessed the issuing bank cardholder's information. This process gave authorizations and

Visit Vault at **www.vault.com** for insider company profiles, expert advice, career message boards, expert resume reviews, the Vault Job Board and more.

VAULT CAREER LIBRARY

227

Department of the Navy

If you would like to join more than 7,800 diverse employees, we have a financial management career opportunity for you!

Program Description

▶ Entry Level Analyst, Accountant, and Auditor positions.

▶ 28 months of professional development through academic and on-the-job training.

▶ Starting salary between $38,000 and $40,000.

▶ Successful trainees' salaries increase more than $17,000 over a 28-month period.

Federal Benefits

▶ Career Development

▶ Health and Life Insurance

▶ 10 Paid Holidays

▶ 13 Paid Vacation and Sick Days

▶ Performance-Based Pay Increases During The 28-month Training Program

▶ Thrift Savings Plan (Tax Deferred Contributions)

▶ Federal Retirement System (Pension Plan)

Financial Management Career Program
520 Turner Street, Suite B
Pensacola, FL 32508-5245

Telephone: (850) 452-3785 or -3783

www.navyfmcp.com

Civilian Careers in Financial Management

On-the-Job-Training

Classroom Training

Rotational Work Assignments

processed settlement agreements in a matter of minutes. In the 1980s, the ATM (Automatic Teller Machine) began to surface, giving cardholders 24-hour access to cash.

The debut of the debit, the climb of the cobrand

The 1990s saw the debit card rise in popularity. The debit card grew from accounting for 274 million transactions in 1990 to 8.15 billion transactions in 2002. (According to the Packaged Facts report "Debit Cards in the U.S.," there were 28 million debit card transactions in the U.S. in 2007, worth a total of $1.4 trillion.) The 1990s also witnessed the surge of cobranded and affinity cards, which match up a credit card company with a retailer to offer discounts for using the card (think Citibank's AAdvantage cards and American Express' Mileage Rewards program). Although cobranded cards took a dip in the late 1990s—according to some industry experts, this was because issuers had exhausted the most lucrative partners—they returned in full force during the early part of the new millennium. In 2003 alone, MBNA—called "The King of the Plastic Frontier" by *BusinessWeek*—struck some 400 new deals with various companies such as Merrill Lynch, Royal Caribbean and Air Canada. Additionally, it renewed deals with another 1,400 organizations, including the National Football League and the University of Michigan. In 2004, MBNA signed agreements with numerous other companies and organizations such as A.G. Edwards & Sons, the Massachusetts Institute of Technology, Arsenal Football Club (U.K.), Charles Schwab and Starwood Hotels and Resorts. (In 2005, MBNA was acquired by Bank of America.)

And then there were four

In September 2003, a federal court upheld a lower court ruling that cost credit card powerhouses Visa and MasterCard a combined $3 billion. The court found Visa and MasterCard rules preventing the companies' member banks from also issuing American Express and Morgan Stanley's Discover cards to be illegal and harmful to competition. MasterCard was forced to pay $2 billion in damages and Visa paid $1 billion.

In October 2004, the U.S. Supreme Court decided not to hear Visa and MasterCard's appeal in the government's antitrust suit against them, effectively ending the two companies' rules that had prevented banks from issuing cards on rival networks. As a result, Amex and Discover became free to partner with the thousands of banks that issue Visa and MasterCard. This allows Amex and Discover to gain ground on the two credit powerhouses that, together, control at least 80 percent of the U.S. credit card purchase volume (as of July 2007), according to the National Retail Federation.

Re-Discovering the possibilities

In the midst of Morgan Stanley's great personnel exodus of March 2005, the firm announced plans to spin off its Discover credit card unit. Former Morgan Stanley CEO Philip Purcell reasoned that Discover "will be more properly valued as a stand-alone entity" than as a piece of Morgan Stanley. Soon after the announcement, analysts began estimating the Street value of the huge credit card unit. The range fell between $9 billion and $16 billion. Analysts also disagreed over whether or not the spin-off would maximize shareholder value.

However, new CEO John Mack's first big after taking over the reins in mid-2005 was to reverse course on the Discover business, which predecessor Purcell had talked of selling off. "Discover is not only a strong business, but also an attractive asset for Morgan Stanley," Mack said in a statement. "It is a unique, successful franchise with growth opportunities that gives Morgan Stanley a consistent stream of stable, high-quality earnings and substantial cash flow, diversifies the company's earnings and broadens our scale and capital base."

But despite the kind words, there was ultimately a change of heart for Morgan Stanley. Although Discover delivered record before-tax earnings of $16 billion in 2006, Morgan Stanley announced the same year that it planned to spin off Discover,

Visit Vault at **www.vault.com** for insider company profiles, expert advice, career message boards, expert resume reviews, the Vault Job Board and more.

VAULT CAREER LIBRARY

229

which some analysts said would allow both businesses to grow more quickly. The deal was finally completed in June 2007, and though financial terms weren't disclosed, analysts estimated Discover's worth to be $13 billion at the time.

As an autonomous firm, Discover is now led by CEO David W. Nelms, and as of August 2008, its stock was trading at $15.52 a share. Net income for the second quarter 2008 was $234.15 million, up from $209.24 million in the second quarter 2007. Being its own entity has hardly exempted Discover from dealing with a few roadblocks. In August 2008, a lawsuit from Discover asserting a conspiracy between MasterCard and Visa was deemed limited in reach by a judge who also rejected allegations from Discover that MasterCard was excluding Discover from distributing debit cards.

The big buy

In June 2005, BofA announced its acquisition of credit card behemoth MBNA in a $35 billion deal, following closely on the heels of its $49 billion purchase of FleetBoston Financial in 2003. The MBNA purchase made Bank of America one of the largest card issuers in the U.S., with $143 billion in managed outstanding balances and 40 million active accounts. Bank of America added more than 20 million new customer accounts as well as affinity relationships with more than 5,000 partner organizations and financial institutions. It achieved overall expense efficiencies of $850 million after-tax, fully realized in 2007, and a restructuring charge of $1.25 billion after-tax. Cost reductions came from a range of sources, including layoffs. (In unrelated cuts, the bank announced plans to slash 7,500 jobs in its mortgage, home-equity and insurance groups in summer 2008).

In November 2006, BofA announced that it had agreed to acquire US Trust, the wealth management subsidiary of Charles Schwab Corporation. The $3.3 billion acquisition, completed in July 2007, helped BofA strengthen its capabilities in serving high net worth clients and increase its assets under management.

The big IPOs

At the end of August 2005, MasterCard, which became a private share corporation in 2002, announced plans to become a publicly-traded company. On May 25, 2006, MasterCard finally went public, and began trading on the New York Stock Exchange (NYSE) under the ticker 'MA.' "Listing on the NYSE marks a major milestone for MasterCard and reinforces our commitment to continued growth and building value for our customers and stockholders," Robert Selander, the company's president and chief executive officer, told the Associated Press. The market had expected the issue to open in the $40 to $43 range, but MasterCard was at $39 after a series of setbacks delayed the process. But by most accounts, the IPO has been a huge success. As of August 2008, the stock had zoomed to over $234 per share, thanks in part to solid growth rates. During the second quarter 2008, 951 million MasterCard cards were issued, up 11 percent. MasterCard's worldwide purchase volume went up 12.8 percent to $655 billion, while transactions processed went up 13.6 percent to 5.2 billion.

MasterCard wasn't the only piece of plastic that's dazzled IPO investors. On March 19, 2008, Visa set a record for stateside IPOs when it raised $17.9 billion in its initial public offering. (The deal got even bigger when Visa's underwriters decided to exercise their option to buy 40.6 million more shares at $44 each for about $1.8 billion.) The firm's shares were initially valued at $44 per share—higher than the expected $37 to $42 range—and increased 35 percent to $59.50 almost immediately upon going public. At the end of the first day of trading, Visa's shares (which trade on the NYSE under the symbol 'V') closed at $56.50, a 28.4 percent increase from its opening price. As of September 2008, Visa's stock was still going strong, trading for around $74 a share.

The road, however, has been rocky as MasterCard and Visa have recently weathered some storms. In November 2007, MasterCard and Visa announced that they would be paying American Express $1.8 billion and $2.25 billion, respectively, in a settlement stemming from a 2004 lawsuit contending that the companies had barred some financial companies from distributing cards through American Express.

Visit Vault at **www.vault.com** for insider company profiles, expert advice, career message boards, expert resume reviews, the Vault Job Board and more.

VAULT CAREER LIBRARY   231

No contact credit

"Contactless" cards and finger-swiping systems are the latest advances in the world of plastic purchasing. According to CreditCards.com, by mid-2007, banks had issued about 27 million debit and credit cards that could be scanned via a radar-like beam, rather than having to be run through a machine. The popularity of contactless credit and debit cards—which can be used at numerous retailers such as McDonald's, 7-Eleven and CVS—is only expected to skyrocket. According to market research firm Packaged Facts, there will be approximately 109 million cards in circulation by 2011. Other than not having to run the cards through a machine, another benefit is that no signature is required for purchases less than $25.

Another no-contact credit payment system is now in place: the pay-by-finger system, in which individuals' fingers are scanned and linked to their payment information. All you have to do is press your finger (its print) against a device, enter some personal information, such as your phone number on a keypad and your payment is made; fingerprints are linked up with credit or debit cards. The system is already in place at hundreds of U.S. supermarkets such as Albertsons and Piggly Wiggly.

A worrying trend

There's been a number of reports detailing the disturbing trend of cash-strapped homeowners declining to pay their mortgages as the U.S. economy has continued to tank. Maybe because of this trend—or in spite of it—American Express and Visa began a rewards program that allows customers to pay their monthly mortgage or rent with a credit card. Although the companies said that customers have the potential to earn exponentially more bonus points than they had before, some analysts pointed out that the main concern with such a program is that credit card owners who are already in debt will only continue to fall deeper into credit issues. And those debt issues already run deep with Americans to begin with. A Sallie Mae/Gallup poll released in August 2008 revealed that parents of college students who borrowed on credit cards put an average of more than $5,800 on their cards while students put about $2,500 on their plastic. Besides big-ticket items like education, other accouterments of wealth are also frequently put on Americans' credit cards without a second thought—swimming pools and car payments are no longer a rarity to charge.

But is it preferable to put college payments on a credit card rather than luxury items that would otherwise be out of reach? It may be, according to some credit card companies. CompuScore, which markets Visa cards, came under fire from the Federal Trade Commission in August 2008 for profiling cardholders' transactions, reducing the credit limits of customers who used their cards at marriage counselors, tire shops, billiard halls and pawn shops. The FTC hasn't called the company's actions illegal, but it did allege that the company wasn't upfront about its actions. Either way, it may pay for consumers to watch where they use their cards.

Insurance

Risky business

The insurance industry combines to form a multi-trillion-dollar market dealing in risk. In exchange for a premium, insurers promise to compensate, monetarily or otherwise, individuals and businesses for future losses, thus taking on the risk of personal injury, death, damage to property, unexpected financial disaster and just about any other misfortune that could occur.

The industry is often divided into categories such as life/health and property/casualty. Life insurance dominates the mix, making up about 60 percent of all premiums. The bigger categories can be subdivided into smaller groups; property insurance, for instance, may cover homeowner's, renter's, auto and boat policies, while health insurance is made up of subsets including disability and long-term care.

But these days, you can find insurance for just about anything, including weddings and bar mitzvahs, policies for the chance of weather ruining a vacation and policies for pets (a market that grew 342 percent from 1998 to 2002, had sales of $160 million in 2005 and exploded to $195 million by 2007, according to the industry publication Small Business Trends). Even insurance companies themselves can be insured against extraordinary losses—by companies specializing in reinsurance.

Although insurance isn't the sexiest business around, celebrity policies always get a lot of press. While rumors that Jennifer Lopez had insured her famous asset for $1 billion proved to be unfounded, other such policies do indeed exist. In fact, the phrase "million dollar legs" comes from Betty Grable's policy for that amount (a similar policy is held by TV's Mary Hart); other notable contemporary policies include Bruce Springsteen's voice, reportedly covered at around $6 million.

The world's top five

Though the U.S. is well ahead of the rest of the world in terms of insurance coverage, insurance is a truly global business. The industry is the biggest in the world, raking in more than $4 trillion in revenue annually, according SocialFunds, an investment news site. Ranked by sales, the top five insurance companies are Germany's Allianz, the Netherlands' ING, New York-based American International Group (AIG), France's AXA and Japan's Nippon Life Insurance Company. Other leading U.S. insurers include State Farm, MetLife, Allstate, Prudential, Aetna and Travelers.

Consolidation is the name of the game—Hoovers reports that the top 10 property/casualty insurers account for nearly half of all premiums written. Perhaps the most notable example of the mergers and acquisitions mania in the industry was the $82 billion merger in 1998 between Citicorp and the Travelers Group, which created Citigroup (now known as Citi). Some insurance companies have also begun to reconfigure themselves from mutual insurers, or those owned by policyholders (e.g., State Farm), to stock insurers, or those held by shareholders (e.g., Allstate). This process, known as "demutualization," promises to raise even more capital for insurance companies to indulge in more acquisitions.

The last 25 years have seen a shift in the industry away from life insurance toward annuity products, focusing on managing investment risk rather than the (inevitable) risk of mortality. With increasing deregulation in the U.S. and Japan, these insurers are moving ever closer to competition with financial services firms. Indeed, the business of the insurance industry doesn't end with insurance. The world's top insurance companies have broadened their array of financial services to include investment management, annuities, securities, mutual funds, health care management, employee benefits and administration, real estate brokerage and even consumer banking. The move towards financial services followed the 1999 repeal of the Glass-Steagall Act, which barred insurance companies, banks and brokerages from entering each other's industries, and the Gramm Leach-Bliley Act of 1999, which further defined permissible acts for financial holding companies. Now insurance companies are free to partner with commercial banks, securities firms and other financial entities.

At the speed of the Internet

Like many other industries, the insurance market has been transformed in recent years by the Internet. Traditionally, insurance products have been distributed by independent agents (business people paid on commission) or by exclusive agents (paid employees). But insurers who sell over the Web reap the benefits of lower sales costs and customer service expenses, along with a more expedient way of getting information to consumers, which is transforming traditional methods by cutting costs and increasing the amount of information available to consumers. Celent Communications estimates that the online insurance market takes in over $200 billion in sales each year. Of course, an automated approach to doing business means fewer sales people are needed—Celent reported that insurance giant Cigna, for instance, eliminated 2,000 jobs in 2002 because of increased efficiencies.

With more IT comes a greater need for IT security—Celent estimates that U.S. insurers spend about 2.5 to 3 percent of premium on security. Aside from the threat of viruses, hackers and the like, regulations have made security a top priority—

Visit Vault at **www.vault.com** for insider company profiles, expert advice, career message boards, expert resume reviews, the Vault Job Board and more.

VAULT CAREER LIBRARY

233

the Health Information Portability and Accountability Act (HIPAA), for instance, which went into effect in 2003, sets strict standards for the privacy and security of the patient information transferred between health insurers and providers.

Recovering from September 11th

The September 11 terrorist attacks sent shockwaves through the industry. Not only did they constitute perhaps the largest insured loss in U.S. history—with estimates ranging between $40 billion and $50 billion in claims for loss of life and property, injuries and workers' compensation—but they also caused insurers and re-insurers to take a hard look at how they would handle the risks associated with possible future terrorist acts. The Terrorism Risk Insurance Act, signed into law by President Bush in November 2002, aimed to deal with the nearly incalculable risk posed by this threat. Among other things, the law defines a terrorism-related event as one with a minimum of $5 million in damages. It provides for the sharing of risk between private insurers and the federal government over a three-year period, with each participating company responsible for paying a deductible before federal assistance is available. If losses are incurred above the insurer's deductible, the government is obliged to pay 90 percent. While the measure met with a considerable amount of grumbling from all parties involved, for the most part the industry acknowledged that the plan at least allows for the potential risk to insurers from terrorism-related disasters to be quantified.

Property insurance stalemate?

In parts of the U.S. such as California and Louisiana, which have dealt with rampant wildfires and Hurricane Katrina in recent years, another trend has arisen. More and more, property insurers are requiring homeowners to take precautions to protect their houses or confront the possibility of being dropped—a trend that has continued into 2008 with precautions from companies encouraging homeowners to guard against floods and winter freezing.

Some insurance companies in California are requiring homeowners to replace their roofs with fire-resistant ones, and other companies in hurricane-prone coastal areas are requiring policyholders to install storm-resistant shutters. Still, since the requirements are following three years of record profits for the property insurance industry, the Associated Press reported in June 2007 that many homeowners are up at arms about the potential cost. But the insurance industry isn't backing down on their requirements, and some companies have even decided to pull out of certain states altogether. For example, Farmers Insurance said in August 2008 that it would pull out of the North Carolina homeowners' market by the end of the year.

Despite the deluge of flood-related insurance claims in the Midwest in 2008, many companies are surprisingly weathering the financial storm. In July 2008, rating agency Standard & Poor's (S&P) said that the Midwest floods were unlikely to impact the ratings of many insurance companies. S&P added that the Midwest flooding was likely to have fairly little impact on insurance companies in general, although financial consequences are expected to vary across Midwest states that have experienced particularly vigorous flooding.

Unhealthy health care

Medical malpractice remained a hot topic through 2008. Health insurers generally get a bad rap from the public, and the media and politicians give plenty of air time to horror stories about managed care companies slighting critically ill patients, and insurers refusing to cover necessary treatments or technologies. Is this reputation deserved? Depends on who you ask, but the industry has its own battles in health care—for example, it sees medical malpractice claims, which have skyrocketed in recent years, as a true crisis. Indeed, according to the Insurance Information Institute, some insurers have quit writing malpractice policies entirely rather than shoulder the risk (the median malpractice award in 2001, the latest year for which this figure is available, was $1 million). And it looks like costs keep increasing—a report by reinsurance company Aon said that malpractice awards tend to go up by 6 percent each year. Insurance company Farmers, which racked up more than $100 million in malpractice-related losses in 2003, finally got out of malpractice overage in September of the same year. But by

August 2008, there was more brewing on the medical malpractice front. New York Governor David Paterson signed a bill that gives a little financial relief to doctors with high premiums. The bill also deferred the possibility of a surcharge for doctors. Those backing the bill said that doctors were likely to have to pay a 30 percent hike in insurance rates without the passage of the proposal.

Lots of jobs

In the U.S., the insurance industry employs around 2.36 million people, according to industry trendwatcher Plunkett Research. Of these jobs, 62 percent are with insurance carriers, while 38 percent are with insurance agencies, brokerages and providers of other insurance-related services, as reported by the U.S. Bureau of Labor Statistics in its most recent survey. Most insurance agents specialize in life and health insurance, or property and casualty insurance. But a growing number of "multi-line" agents sell all types of insurance. An increasing number of agents also work for banking institutions, non-depository institutions, or security and commodity brokers.

Ratings

Making the grade

Credit rating is another sector of the financial services industry that serves a highly specific purpose. Founded by John Knowles Fitch as the Fitch Publishing Company in 1913, Fitch was one of the early leaders in providing financial statistics. The Fitch rating system of "AAA" to "D," introduced in 1924, has become the standard for the financial community. Fitch, one of the four major credit-rating agencies (the others are Moody's Investors Service, Standard & Poor's and DBRS), is the leader in providing ratings on debt issued by companies, covering entities in more than 80 countries.

Moody's, founded in 1900, is one of the most prominent and widely utilized sources for credit ratings, research and risk analysis on debt instruments and securities. In addition, Moody's provides corporate and government credit assessment and training services, credit training services and credit software to financial institutions, with 9,000 accounts at 2,400 institutions worldwide. The firm's ratings and analyses track 100 sovereign nations, 11,000 company insurers, 25,000 public finance issuers and 70,000 structured finance obligations. Moody's ratings business consists of four groups: structured finance, corporate finance, financial institutions and sovereign risk and public finance. The firm's primary clients include corporate and government issuers as well as institutional investors, banks, creditors and commercial banks.

Standard & Poor's operates through six main divisions: credit ratings, data services, equity research, funds, indices and risk solutions. Nearly $1.5 trillion in investor assets was directly tied to S&P indices as of June 2008, more than all other indices combined. The firm has the world's largest network of credit ratings analysts, and its equity research division is the world's largest producer of independent equity research. More than 1,000 institutions—including 19 of the top 20 securities firms, 13 of the top 20 banks, and 11 of the top 20 life insurance companies—license its research for their investors and advisors.

DBRS, an international ratings agency, is headquartered in Toronto and gives ratings to borrowing entities. The company is split into corporate, financial institutions, public finance and structured finance divisions. The firm prides itself on being "the leading rating agency in Canada" as well as being the first rating agency to have a full-service web site for customers.

Suspect practices

Rating agencies have recently come under severe scrutiny for their ratings of mortgage-backed securities—specifically, whether or not these ratings helped contribute to the subprime mortgage crisis. In late 2007, the Securities and Exchange Commission (SEC) began an inquiry into whether appropriate procedures were followed for ratings companies like Moody's

Visit Vault at **www.vault.com** for insider company profiles, expert advice, career message boards, expert resume reviews, the Vault Job Board and more.

VAULT CAREER LIBRARY   235

and S&P. The SEC has alleged that some ratings agencies gave unnaturally high rankings to mortgage-backed securities and some debt products.

The problems for the rating agencies didn't end with the SEC. In July 2008, Connecticut Attorney General Richard Blumenthal filed a lawsuit against Fitch, Moody's and S&P, alleging that the firms gave municipal bonds falsely low ratings and, consequently, caused customers to pay for unneeded bond insurance as well as elevated interest rates. Additionally, Blumenthal said the agencies ran afoul of the Connecticut Unfair Trade Practices Act by neglecting to mention "material facts that caused bond insurers in Connecticut to purchase bonds at higher interest rates."

Actuaries

Once considered an esoteric niche for accountants at insurance companies, actuaries are now some of the most respected and essential employees in the corporate world. They wield a combination of solid mathematics and out-of-the-box thinking to assess risk and project outcomes for a variety of businesses. They are the wizards of the corporate world, and are increasingly used to determine the course of the future for numerous companies.

Most actuaries can be found at insurance companies, where they model the risks associated with paying out insurance premiums for a variety of unforeseen or unknowable events. They also help manage pensions, government entitlement programs and college endowments, which rely on future assumptions. And increasingly, they're being called upon to assess risk throughout the corporate world, from hedge fund investments to new product launches.

Beyond insurance

In recent years, actuarial careers have grown well beyond the insurance industry, though insurers remain a major employer of actuaries and also help further the thinking behind actuarial science. Pension funds, another traditional standby for actuarial careers, are evolving and giving actuaries new challenges and opportunities. Actuaries are also finding new directions elsewhere in the finance sector, some at traditional Wall Street firms, as well as hedge funds. Other corporations, ones not necessarily involved in finance, often employ actuaries, either on a consulting basis or full time, to help make important business decisions. And governments at the federal, state and even local levels are finding actuaries an important piece of their budget and planning processes.

Outside finance, however, there's a variety of risks and rewards that can be measured by actuaries. These can be as simple as running numbers on vendor bids and their potential services or as complex as determining whether a product line will be profitable.

Career decisions

The most recent edition of the *Jobs Rated Almanac*—which rates jobs by salary, intellectual stimulation, opportunity for advancement, hours and job-related stress—had "actuary" in second place behind "biologist." In fact, the vast majority of job surveys also have actuarial careers at or near the top.

As actuaries well know, there are lots of factors to consider when building a career. Some actuaries are very business-oriented and can thrive under the pressure-cooker of Wall Street. Others may be more introverted and prefer simply to let their work speak for itself. Either way, actuarial science provides plenty of options and a great deal of choice in balancing lifestyles.

Actuarial careers are also generally quite secure. Demand for actuaries remains strong and, despite the falloff in pension work, is only expected to grow in the coming years. The job requires a deep knowledge of finance and mathematics, and the certification process is strenuous. If you can manage that, you won't have many problems finding and keeping a job.

Your career as an actuary can take many forms. The role of actuaries has grown well beyond insurance and pension industries. Actuaries are a growing, dynamic force in the business world. That's not to say that the life of a working actuary is glamorous. Few actuaries are managing Trump-style deals, leading companies or saving corporations from financial ruin. Of course, few businesspeople, in general, do that anyway.

Being an actuary means, for the most part, a 9-to-5 office job. As your expertise and responsibilities grow, that may change somewhat, just as any job advancement would alter one's lifestyle. But in the end, you'll go in, have meetings, define goals, crunch numbers, write reports and implement your work, then come home. Maybe you'll do some catch-up at the end of the day with e-mail or some work-related reading.

Office drone, you say? Hardly. You're going to be dealing with very important issues that not only affect the company you work for but also the thousands, even millions, of customers of that company and its competitors. Your hard work can save billions of dollars and jobs, and can help others prepare for and mitigate the worst risks that can befall a company.

"Not bad for a mathematician, right?" said one pension actuary who's currently working to make sure that a major corporation's now-closed pension fund can still pay off its surviving beneficiaries. "I've got 15,000 or so people who will need this fund, maybe for the next 30 years. Without this fund, they have nothing. It's nice to feel like you're helping people."

And don't pooh-pooh the 9-to-5 thing, either. You'll work hard, but you'll also have the opportunity to have a life— something quite rare in the business world. Furthermore, your expertise, training and certifications all mean that you'll earn a very comfortable salary. You'll start in the $50,000 annual salary range, and make 10 times that in a surprisingly short amount of time.

A Day in the Life: The Researcher

7 a.m. Get on the train and head into the city with a sheaf of research notes from the night before.

8 a.m. Arrive at work. If it's Monday, prepare for the weekly meeting. "The Monday meeting tends to last most of the day. Everyone talks about everything the company's doing, the state of every investment or potential target. And everyone chips in. People come in and out as needed, but for the executive committee, it's a 9-to-5 thing." Since it's not Monday, gather the latest research from Wall Street on potential takeover targets.

9 a.m. Present updates, if needed, to the executive committee on previously discussed targets. Generally done through e-mail.

9:30 a.m. Hit the phones. There's always more to find out beyond what you read in the papers or in the research notes. I'll call clients, suppliers, anybody that the target deals with to see how they do things and what their problems might be.

11 a.m. Previously scheduled interview with a representative of a target company. This is purely informational, and both our guys and their guys know we're doing it. We're just saying we want a stake, they're saying they don't want to sell, but that's how the dance begins. So we meet and get a sense of each other at a lower level before we hand it off to the managing directors and the C-level executives.

12 p.m. Lunch, target company rep in tow.

1:30 p.m. Back in the office, writing up the report on the meeting along with potential follow-up questions and research.

2 p.m. More phone work and computer research.

Visit Vault at **www.vault.com** for insider company profiles, expert advice, career message boards, expert resume reviews, the Vault Job Board and more.

VAULT CAREER LIBRARY   237

3:30 p.m. Meeting with the deal team on a current negotiation. They seem to think they're overpaying, and they want us to take a look at a piece of the target's business again. Turns out we hadn't revisited the topic in a few months, and it was easy to find out what was going on. Probably saved a few million there.

5 p.m. Conference call with portfolio company managers about the latest in supply chain research.

6 p.m. Order dinner while going over the day's activity on portfolio and target companies. Write up developments for directors as needed.

8 p.m. Home.

Private Wealth Management

The private wealth management industry integrates the varied and complex business of managing wealth by accounting for income needs, taxes, estate preservation and asset protection for the wealthy. Typically, private wealth management is a smaller division of a much larger investment firm or bank. The private wealth manager leverages the expertise of the various departments inside the firm, such as the trust department, to present clients with solutions to wealth management issues. Though not required to be expert in one particular area of wealth management, private wealth managers must know enough about each area to expertly represent their clients' best interests and, where appropriate, offer advice.

The job

It is the first job of private wealth managers to help create, from among various investment strategies, income or growth sufficient for the everyday needs of their clients. In addition, they must provide enough excess growth to account for inflation in order that their client's purchasing power does become eroded over time. Let's face it, $1 doesn't buy as much as it used to for Jed and Granny. In addition, hopefully, the wealth manager will continue to grow the clients' assets so that they become richer.

Because the rich often need to live solely off of their investments, today's private wealth managers must use a variety of investment techniques to help clients create enough income every year to live off of. Sounds easy enough right? Not really. When you consider that someone who invests $1 million in a conservative corporate bond returning 5 percent creates a modest $50,000 a year in income, it becomes obvious that having a million dollars or so just isn't as a big a deal as it used to be. Sure $50,000 is a lot of money for doing nothing. But living on champagne and caviar is out of the question. With average wages in the U.S. at a little over $35,000 per year as of 2004, according to the Social Security Administration, the average typical family with two income-earners can earn more than someone with $1 million in the bank who lives off of his or her investments. Indeed, because of inflation, the portfolio with a $1 million must return in excess of 7.5 percent just to keep up with the two-worker household that can possibly expect to get raises every year. With rates of return in the stock market sometimes as high 20 percent or more, 7.5 percent may not seem a very high return, but when you consider that the S&P 500 has returned less than 1 percent annually over the last six years you'll see that the job of private wealth managers in creating income for their clients isn't always easy.

Another problem wealthy clients often encounter is taxes. None of us like paying taxes. For most of us, however, we would willingly pay additional taxes if it meant that we were making additional income. For the wealthy it isn't quite as simple. When managing large pools of assets, small differences in tax rates can translate into big changes in after-tax returns. Various types of investments used by the wealthy are treated and taxed differently by the IRS. For example, income derived from the interest rates of bonds is taxed differently than long-term capital gains derived from selling stock. It is the private wealth manager's job to balance assorted types of investments to create the most tax efficient combination for the client.

In today's society, people with money are sometimes targeted with lawsuits just because they happen to have money. So, an increasingly popular area of practice for private wealth managers is called "asset protection," which helps the wealthy guard against losing their money in civil lawsuits. There are several techniques used to protect assets, including U.S. trusts laws and foreign, offshore banks. Advocates of asset protection methods contend that making their clients impervious to lawsuits doesn't just protect assets, but also prevents lawsuits from even happening.

Career paths

The primary role in private wealth management is the private banker, also called the investment or financial advisor. This is the person who evaluates a client's financial position, recommends solid investments, helps with the fiduciary aspects of their client's accounts (regularly consulting tax and accounting experts within the firm), and even sets up a family office for wealthier clients to pay bills, staff and make sure family members are appropriately taken care of, or "given their allowances" as one banker put it.

Analysts

The career track for the private banker is fairly cut and dry at the major corporate banks and the Wall Street brokerage firm. Undergrads coming in are called analysts, just as they are in the sales and trading division and the investment banking arm and everywhere else within the corporation. They're the ones who do all the researching, number crunching, report writing and, yes, coffee fetching on occasion, for the higher-ups who are actually working for the clients.

Being an analyst at a private bank is very much akin to similar roles in trading and investment banking. If a private banker needs an analysis done on a client's tax status, you'll tap the appropriate expertise within the firm to draw up the report. If a client is looking for a hedge fund investment with a specific strategy, you'll provide the banker or relationship manager with the best options. And while the banker can be called at any time to address a client's needs, you'll be called by the banker to assist and will probably keep longer hours on top of that, as well.

The rewards can be fairly standard for the financial industry, with starting salaries ranging around $45,000 to $60,000 annually. Bonuses can be lighter than those given to investment bankers, however, anywhere from the $15,000 to $30,000 range. At smaller firms, that bonus range can vary from analyst to analyst, depending on how useful they were in addressing client needs. The same goes for larger firms, of course, but the range is smaller, especially if there's an entire analyst class to consider.

Associates

The next rank up is associate, or just plain old private banker at the smaller firms. These are the guys who work with the clients and attract new business, the real face of the private bank for most clients. This is considered a very entrepreneurial job, in that you'll be expected to not only serve clients but also attract new clients, as well. At many firms, you'll also be expected to attempt to sell your clients on the company's proprietary financial products, though the practice is starting to be curtailed at some firms.

Associates will work closely with clients to create an overall financial strategy that encompasses not only investment but also income management, budget, real estate holdings, taxes, small business partnerships, estate planning and even paying the day-to-day bills of the household, all depending on the level of service the client wants (and the fees he or she is willing to pay, but at this level, fees are a secondary consideration to impeccable service and peace of mind).

Associate pay generally mirrors other Wall Street positions, with a newly minted associate making about $75,000 to $85,000 per year. Bonuses can vary, however, depending on how the firm structures compensation. Some private bankers receive bonuses solely on selling the client new services and the company's investment products, getting a percentage of the business the private bank brings in from that client. Others have more complex metrics, measuring performance against the client's stated goals. For example, some private wealth management clients may not want anything more complex than safe fixed-

Visit Vault at **www.vault.com** for insider company profiles, expert advice, career message boards, expert resume reviews, the Vault Job Board and more.

VAULT CAREER LIBRARY   239

income investments that generate income with little or no risk, with a stated goal of 5 percent yield each year. If the private banker reached that goal, he would get a larger bonus than he would have if the investment only yielded 4.85 percent. Or if the banker managed to get 5.35 percent—without altering the client's risk profile or otherwise deviating from the state goals—the bonus would be higher.

Some private wealth managements eschew commission bonuses altogether, preferring to grant bonuses that do not give clients the appearance that their banker is simply interested in selling them on products. These firms' bonus metrics are primarily based on fulfilling the clients' goals—a few firms even ask clients to review their bankers each year. Of course, firms will always appreciate it when associates convince their clients to use the private bank's estate planning services instead of someone else's, and in that sense, selling a non-investment service is seen as very bonus-worthy.

Likewise, associates are expected to drum up new business, and bonuses can come if you manage to gain new clients. Sometimes this will come from word-of-mouth, as current clients recommend the associate to their high-net-worth peers. It also comes from good, old fashioned networking, which means an investment on the associate's part in both time and, at times, money—especially when belonging to the right club or attending the right charitable event can mean a room full of potential clients. Some private banking firms organize cultural events or sports outings for their clients, as well, with the hopes that they'll bring well-moneyed colleagues or friends for associates to network with.

Vice presidents

In time, salaries and bonus money for motivated, skilled and trusted associates can top $500,000, usually anywhere from five to eight years, depending on the firm and opportunities that have presented themselves, and up to $1 million within 10 to 13 years of private banking. At that level, however, an associate has often already been promoted to the level of vice president. As such, he or she can be placed in a position overseeing a number of associates, or even a regional office. Alternatively, an associate who has specialized in spotting unique investment opportunities or has helped come up with new products can branch off from the client business and into an investment specialty. They may end up as market strategist or in-house portfolio consultants, gaining a smaller piece of individual clients' business, but making up for it by consulting with larger numbers of clients.

Managing directors

Finally, after years of service—and income that can top $2 million or more for the best performing vice presidents—a successful, entrepreneurial, client-driven VP can be named a managing director. In these positions, an MD can expect to be in charge of associates in a major branch office, or even in the headquarters city. They can be given the highest-net-worth clients, or the problem clients whose money is just too valuable for the firm to lose. In specialty positions, they may end up as the private bank's chief investment officer, chief fiduciary officer or general counsel. There are generally only a handful of MDs within any private wealth management firm, and they are often on the executive committees of the firm. At this level, salaries enter a realm in which the MD may want to find a private banker of his own—and are generally high enough that firms don't discuss them, though still nowhere near the level where they have to be reported to the Securities and Exchange Commission!

Private Equity

In its broadest sense, private equity is an investment derived from a nonpublic entity. Of course, under that definition, any individual who owns a single share of stock is, indeed, a private equity investor. The kind of private equity we're talking about is much bigger; these individuals don't just invest in stock—they buy whole companies.

In modern private equity, a pool of capital is created from private investors, ranging from university endowments and pension funds to hedge funds, Wall Street investment banks and high-net-worth individuals. The managers of these private equity pools, or funds, then try to put that capital to work, generally by purchasing private or public companies, "fixing" them so they generate more revenue, cash and earnings, and then "flipping" them by selling the improved company to another buyer or taking it public on the equity markets.

Private equity investments aren't just about buying and selling companies, however. Many private equity firms invest in debt, helping a company salvage itself by loaning it money in exchange for an equity position or another form of return. Some private equity firms target funds at startup companies—these are called venture capital firms, though a diversified private equity management company will often include venture capital activity alongside acquisitions and debt purchases. Venture capital investments are often made in exchange for equity in the private company that, the firm hopes, will turn into big profits should the startup go public or get sold.

Who are private equity investors?

The institutions and people who invest in private equity funds are some of the wealthiest in the world. Major pension funds, such as the California Public Employees Retirement Systems (CalPERS), place some of their money with private equity funds to boost returns. Major Wall Street investment banks also place investments in private equity funds—unless, of course, they create their own in-house private equity funds as did Goldman Sachs and Morgan Stanley. Hedge funds often invest in private equity funds due to the outstanding performance these funds have amassed through the years. Indeed, a few hedge funds have blurred the line between themselves and private equity firms by taking part in public company buyouts either on their own or in partnership with more traditional private equity firms.

And finally, the firms themselves are often heavily invested in their own private equity funds. The private—and, recently, public—companies that manage private equity pools ensure their interests are aligned with those of their investors by placing a large chunk of their own wealth in the mix. This has, of course, resulted in the creation of a breed of private equity deal makers that have joined the billionaires' club, most famously Henry Kravis at KKR or current industry poster boy Steve Schwarzman of Blackstone.

The modern private equity firm

Today, private equity firms are primarily dedicated to the purchase of companies or stakes therein. Yet some, including Bain Capital and the Blackstone Group most notably, have entered other businesses, including distressed debt and real estate. At the same time, hedge funds have started dabbling in private equity as well, mostly through placements, but occasionally through their own, active efforts as well.

Yet the average private equity firm remains dedicated to the concept of the buyout. Over the long haul, the returns from a private equity placement have yet to be rivaled consistently by any other asset class, including hedge funds. There simply aren't any other investments where returns can reasonably be as high. And even with questions arising about the current M&A and LBO environments, private equity funds have proven their worth to investors time and again.

Private equity in the U.S.

There are only about 200 private equity companies operating at any one time in the United States, and that number can vary due to openings and closures on the small end of the scale. But the money they manage is impressive. According to the newly created Private Equity Council—formed by firms in response to increasing pressure from Washington on their activities and profits—private equity firms were responsible for $406 billion in transactions in 2006. They had already eclipsed that mark by mid-2007.

Like their venture capital cousins, private equity firms generally find specialties within the industry. Some firms will focus on middle-market, mid-cap transactions, while others take aim at overseas purchases. Still others look at small, public companies or those within a specific sector.

Visit Vault at www.vault.com for insider company profiles, expert advice, career message boards, expert resume reviews, the Vault Job Board and more.

VAULT CAREER LIBRARY 241

And then there are the big ones. They have the money and clout to go after the biggest deals in a variety of sectors. Here's a list of the biggest and most noteworthy firms in private equity today:

> The Blackstone Group
> Kohlberg Kravis Roberts & Co. (KKR)
> The Carlyle Group
> Texas Pacific Group
> Bain Capital
> Providence Equity Partners
> Apollo Advisors
> Warburg Pincus Cerberus Capital Management
> Thomas H. Lee Partners

Auto Financing

Revving up the payments?

Essentially the first on the scene, Ford Motor Credit was the forerunner when it came to auto financing. An indirect, wholly owned subsidiary of Ford Motor Company, Ford Motor Credit was incorporated in Delaware, in 1959, so that Ford dealers could provide competitive financing services to individuals and businesses interested in buying cars. The company's true origins, however, were about 40 years earlier, when founder Henry Ford sought to discourage excessive consumer borrowing by devising layaway plans in order to keep his $265 Model Ts rolling off the lot; this tactic sowed the seeds for Ford Motor Credit to later make ownership possible for customers unable or unwilling to meet the entire upfront cost of a car.

Other giants in the business include Chrysler Financial and GMAC, which have been making headlines lately. In May 2007, Cerberus Capital Management purchased 80 percent of Chrysler from DaimlerChrysler. (In late 2007, Daimler shareholders decided to drop the Chrysler after the sale to Cerberus, renaming the company "Daimler AG.") A few months later, Cerberus bought 51 percent of GMAC.

Chrysler and GMAC aren't the only big fish in the industry. GE Capital Auto Financial Services (the financing unit of General Electric) and Honda Financial Services are contenders as well, along with a plethora of banks' auto financing divisions, including HSBC Auto Finance, Wells Fargo Auto Financing and Capital One Auto Financing.

Lower resale values, longer leases

The auto financing business has existed for decades, but some recent developments have proven fairly tumultuous for the industry. In July 2008, Chase Auto Finance announced that it would stop financing Chrysler car and truck leases in the wake of leased vehicles having less value. Loans for retail vehicle sales will still take place, but Chrysler, Dodge and Jeep products won't get leases from Chase. Ford Motor, in the meantime, increased the prices on some of its vehicle leases due to the firm's lending unit experiencing heavy losses.

Additionally, *The Wall Street Journal* reported in June 2007 that loan financing plans for car owners have been extended longer and longer, due mostly to the rise of small monthly payments and arrangements that involve no money down. According to the *Journal*, this trend has resulted in consumers becoming blind to the full cost of a product, looking only at the monthly payments involved instead of the overall cost of the vehicle—often adding thousands of dollars to the overall cost.

USA Today reported on a similar trend in 2008, revealing that car loans now tend to average seven years or longer. Typically, consumers keep deciding to refinance the outstanding balance of their old car loan in order to lock in low monthly payments—but lengthen their loan term in the process. This trend has only seemed to worsen. In March 2008, the Cleveland Plain Dealer reported that Americans take an average of two years longer to pay off their car loans than consumers from 30 years ago. The newspaper, analyzing data from the Federal Reserve, reported that the average car loan stretches over five years—and many extend to seven years.

The Big Three are in big trouble

Many industry observers have speculated that life may get even tougher for the Big Three automakers, a group that has been through a rough ride recently. Some analysts are even speculating that General Motors, Ford and Chrysler may be headed for bankruptcy. Their latest results have not looked good, to say the least. GM reported a 2008 second quarter net loss of $15.5 billion, Ford endured a $8.7 billion loss for the same period and analysts believe that Chrysler (which doesn't report its financial results) doesn't have international sales to reinforce itself in tough times. Although the auto financial services companies won't be going out of business any time soon, they are increasingly seeking to get out of leasing. Chrysler Credit has been rumored to be on its way out of the business, while Ford Motor's credit unit and GMAC are stiffening their borrowing rules, the Financial Post reported in August 2008. Elevated borrowing expenses and write-downs on companies' lease portfolios have crippled the industry.

Mortgages

Before the crisis

Home mortgages were the turf of commercial banks at the outset of the century. But shortly after the Depression, the government created the Federal Housing Administration, which offered insured home loans. Fannie Mae, originally part of the FHA, was established in 1938 to help provide affordable homeownership. In 1968, it officially became a shareholder-financed company, but its mission remains the same. Similarly, Freddie Mac, founded in 1970, helps Americans finance homes and provides assistance in financing rental housing. Other major mortgage providers in the U.S. include Regions, Capital Home Loans and SunTrust. And on the Internet, online companies such as LendingTree connect potential homeowners with hundreds of lenders.

Enter the crisis

The subprime mortgage crisis that hit the U.S. in 2007 affected not only the lending industry but also sent aftershocks across a number of business sectors—with some analysts predicting that the financial disaster will ultimately lead the U.S. into a recession.

The crisis began when a number of subprime borrowers—consumers with low credit ratings paying interest rates above the prime rate—began to default on their home loans. As these lendees began to default in record numbers, subprime lenders began to go out of business. According to the Mortgage Lender Implode-o-Meter (a web site devoted entirely to tracking the collapse of the mortgage lending industry), between late 2006 and mid-2008, 277 major lending companies have folded.

The reverberations of the crisis have been felt everywhere, from domestic and international stock markets to government agencies.

Visit Vault at **www.vault.com** for insider company profiles, expert advice, career message boards, expert resume reviews, the Vault Job Board and more.

VAULT CAREER LIBRARY   **243**

Fannie and Freddie feel the heat

In July 2008, after losing billions in the previous year following a flood of homeowner defaults, Freddie Mac and Fannie Mae's stocks lost half their value—an event that some analysts said was worse for the financial markets than the collapse of Bear Stearns, the 85-year-old investment bank that crumbled as a result of the subprime crisis.

Following the stock nosedives, the U.S. Treasury finagled a few favors from Congress on behalf of the agencies: a temporary increase in a credit line for Fannie and Freddie, along with temporary authority to purchase equity in one or both of the mortgage companies. U.S. Treasury Secretary Henry Paulson was resolute that any plan to save the agencies does not benefit their shareholders.

But Paulson led a plan to save Freddie Mac and Fannie Mae nearly two weeks before their financial plight came to light, *The Wall Street Journal* reported in July 2008. In an attempt to help curtail the consequences of the housing crisis, Paulson assured the Fed and the Federal Reserve Bank of New York that any loans to Fannie or Freddie would serve only as an "interim step," not a permanent solution.

In August 2008, with its stock down 90 percent since the beginning of the year, Fannie Mae endured a few management changes as the firm's chief financial officer, chief business officer and chief risk officer all stepped down. (Fannie CFO Stephen Swad had only been with the firm for a year before a replacement stepped in.)

Presidential hopefuls on the fate of Mae and Mac

In early September 2008, speaking about the agencies' fates, Democratic presidential nominee Barack Obama said in a news conference that if elected in November 2008, he first plans to decipher whether or not the companies are public or private. If the companies are determined to be public, he said "they have to get out of the profit-making business," but if they're private, the government won't "bail them out." Republican candidate John McCain, meanwhile, has pledged support for Fannie and Freddie. He has called them "vital to Americans' ability to own their own homes" and said that "we cannot allow them to fail."

Fannie and Freddie's new boss: Uncle Sam

On September 7, 2008, the U.S. government seized control of Fannie Mae and Freddie Mac in a drastic attempt to stop their ongoing losses. U.S. Treasury Secretary Henry Paulson said the government will take control of the firms and supplant each of the firm's CEOs with new heads. (After staying on for a transition stage, Fannie's current head Daniel H. Mudd will be replaced by former TIAA-CREF chairman Herbert M. Allison Jr., while Freddie's current head Richard F. Syron will be succeeded by Carlyle Group Senior Adviser David M. Moffett.) Additionally, the Treasury will obtain $1 billion in preferred shares for both Fannie and Freddie and will provide about $200 billion in funding. Paulson indicated that allowing either of the giants to fail would "cause great turmoil" for domestic and international financial markets. To this end, his predictions seemed accurate; stocks rallied after the takeover announcement was made.

As far as the big funding picture goes for the future, the Treasury will also restrict the size of each firm's mortgage portfolio to $850 billion. As of September 2008, Fannie had approximately $758 billion in mortgages and securities while Freddie had about $798 billion.

Financial Data Services

Big shots

The financial data services industry provides retirement and payroll services to screening services and credit monitoring. According to Fortune's 2008 Most Admired Companies in the U.S. list, the top five most admired firms in the financial data services sector are (in this order): Dun & Bradstreet, Automatic Data Processing, MasterCard, DST Systems and Paychex. "Contenders" to these, according to *Fortune*, include First Data, Western Union, Alliance Data Systems, Fiserv and SunGard Data Systems. The firms made the list after receiving high rankings in factors such as innovation, people management, social responsibility, quality of management, financial soundness and quality of products and services.

Fortune also ranked top financial data services companies according to their profits. On that list, First Data came in as No.1, followed by Fiserv, SunGard Data Systems, Western Union, Fidelity National Information Services and MasterCard. An upswing in credit card transactions lifted First Data to its top ranking, and the August 2007 acquisition of electronic bill payment company CheckFree Corp. helped Fiserv secure the No. 2 ranking. Overall, *Fortune* ranked financial data services the 15th most profitable industry.

Visit Vault at **www.vault.com** for insider company profiles, expert advice, career message boards, expert resume reviews, the Vault Job Board and more.

VAULT CAREER LIBRARY   245

Employer Directory

Citi

388 Greenwich St.
New York, NY 10013

Recruiting Contact:
www.oncampus.citi.com
Phone: (212) 559-1000

Your ambitions are more than plans for the future. They're your hopes and dreams. They're a part of who you are and who you aspire to be. When you join Citi you'll cultivate those aspirations with market-leading training and exposure to the most complex and groundbreaking transactions around the world. You'll join a company with an impressive, far-reaching heritage. Among our proud alumni are finance ministers, Nobel Prize winners, and even New York's mayor. While ambitions have taken them in different directions, their business foundation began with Citi.

Whatever your dreams Citi can make them a reality.

Undergraduate Schools Credit Suisse Recruits from

Boston College; CMU; Columbia; Cornell; Georgetown; Harvard; Howard; Michigan; Morehouse/Spelman; NYU; Rutgers; UPenn; Dartmouth; Duke; University of Illinois; Johns Hopkins; MIT; Princeton; UVA; FAMU; American; Barnard; Baruch; Berkeley; Boston University; BYU; Cal Polytechnic; Canisius; Cincinnati; Claremont; Dakota State; University of Delaware; Drexel; Duke; Emory; Florida State; Florida A&M; Fordham; George Mason; Georgia Tech; University of Georgia; Hofstra; University of Indiana; Iona; Jacksonville; Maryland; U of Miami; Niagara; Northeastern; Notre Dame; Penn State; Pomona; Purdue; Rice; RPI; SMU; South Florida; Stanford; Stevens; Stony Brook; SUNY Buffalo; Syracuse; Tampa; Temple; Texas A&M; UT Austin; UCLA; USC; Villanova; Wake Forest; Washington University; Yale

Financial Management Professional Training Program (NAVY)

520 Turner St, Suite B
Pensacola, FL 32508-5245
(850) 452-3783
www.navyfmtp.com

The Financial Management Trainee Program (FMTP) recruits high quality, prospective civilian financial managers for Department of the Navy activities. The FMTP is a 28-month program of professional development through academic and on-the-job training. Entry level positions as financial management analysts, accountants and auditors are available. Applicants may have any academic major; but those applying for accounting and auditor positions require 24 semester hours of accounting (six hours may be in business law). A minimum cumulative GPA of 2.95 in an undergraduate degree from a nationally accredited university/college is required.

Undergraduate schools NAVY recruits from:

Nationally accredited colleges and universities

Northwestern Mutual Financial Network

720 East Wisconsin Avenue
Milwaukee, WI 53202-4797

Recruiting Contact:
Phone: (414) 271-1444
E-mail: tammybrudnicki@northwesternmutual.com
www.nmfn.com

Undergraduate schools Northwestern Mutual recruits from:
Nationwide

NORTHWESTERN MUTUAL FINANCIAL NETWORK ...
has been named a "Top 10 Internship" in America's Top Internships by the Princeton Review eight consecutive times since 1996 and named America's 2000 Top Sales Force co-winner (with Cisco Systems) by *Sales & Marketing Management Magazine*. The internship program provides career opportunity to college students who want to "test drive" a career in sales. Financial representative positions are also available. Reps provide guidance and innovative solutions to clients to develop a customized plan that meets long-term financial goals. The position is an opportunity to build your own business while providing financial security for your clients.

Employer Directory, cont.

Aflac (American Family Life Assurance Company)
1932 Wynnton Road
Columbus, GA 31999
Phone: (706) 323-3431
Fax: (706) 324-6330
www.aflac.com

Alliance Data (Alliance Data Systems Corporation)
17655 Waterview Parkway
Dallas, TX 75252
Phone: (972) 348-5100
Fax: (972) 348-5335
www.alliancedata.com

The Allstate Corporation
2775 Sanders Road
Northbrook, IL 60062-6127
Phone: (847) 402-5000
Fax: (847) 326-7519
Toll free: (847) 402-5000
www.allstate.com

American Express
World Financial Center
200 Vesey Street
New York, NY 10285
Phone: (212) 640-2000
www.americanexpress.com

American Family Insurance Group
6000 American Parkway
Madison, WI 53783-0001
Phone: (608) 249-2111
www.amfam.com

AmeriCredit
801 Cherry Street, Suite 3900
Fort Worth, TX 76102
Phone: (817) 302-7000
Toll free: (800) 284-2271
www.americredit.com

Aon Corporation
Aon Center
200 East Randolph Street
Chicago, IL 60601
Phone: (312) 381-1000
Fax: (312) 381-6032
www.aon.com

Arthur J. Gallagher & Co.
The Gallagher Centre
2 Pierce Place
Itasca, IL 60143-3141
Phone: (630) 773-3800
Fax: (630) 285-4000
www.ajg.com

Assurant
1 Chase Manhattan Plaza
New York, NY 10005
Phone: (212) 859-7000
Fax: (212) 859-5893
www.assurant.com

Berkshire Hathaway Inc.
1440 Kiewit Plaza
Omaha, NE 68131
Phone: (402) 346-1400
Fax: (402) 346-3375
www.berkshirehathaway.com

Capital One Financial
1680 Capital One Drive
McLean, VA 22012
Phone: (703) 720-1000
www.capitalone.com

CB Richard Ellis Group, Inc.
100 North Sepulveda Boulevard
Suite 1050
El Segundo, CA 90245
Phone: (310) 606-4700
Fax: (949) 809-4357
www.cbre.com

Visit Vault at **www.vault.com** for insider company profiles, expert advice, career message boards, expert resume reviews, the Vault Job Board and more.

V/\ULT CAREER LIBRARY   247

Employer Directory, cont.

The Chubb Corporation
15 Mountain View Road
Warren, NJ 07059
Phone: (908) 903-2000
Fax: (908) 903-2027
www.chubb.com

CIT Group
505 Fifth Avenue
New York, NY 10017
Phone: (212) 771-0505
www.cit.com

Citigroup
399 Park Avenue
New York, NY 10043
Phone: (212) 559-1000
Fax: (212) 793-3946
www.citigroup.com

Countrywide Financial Corp.
4500 Park Granada
Calabasas, CA 91302-1613
Phone: (818) 225-3000
Fax: (818) 225-4051
www.countrywide.com

Daimler Financial Services
Eichhornstraße 3
10875 Berlin
Germany
Phone: +49-30-2554-0
Fax: +49-30-2554-2525

36455 Corporate Drive
Farmington Hills, MI 48331
Phone: (248) 991-6700
Fax: (248) 957-2997
www.daimler-financialservices.com

Discover Financial Services
2500 Lake Cook Road
Riverwoods, IL 60015
Phone: (224) 405-0900
Fax: (224) 405-4993
www.discoverfinancial.com

DST Systems
333 West 11th Street
Kansas City, MO 64105
Phone: (816) 435-1000
Fax: (816) 435-8618
www.dstsystems.com

The Dun & Bradstreet Corporation
103 JFK Parkway
Short Hills, NJ 07078
Phone: (973) 921-5500
Fax: (973) 921-6056
www.dnb.com

Equifax
1550 Peachtree Street NW
Atlanta, GA 30309
Phone: (404) 885-8000
Fax: (404) 885-8055
www.equifax.com

Fidelity National Financial
601 Riverside Avenue
Jacksonville, FL 32204
Phone: (888) 934-3354
www.fnf.com

First American Corp.
1 First American Way
Santa Ana, CA 92707
Phone: (800) 852-3643
Fax: (714) 250-3000
www.firstam.com

First Data Corporation
6200 South Quebec Street
Greenwood Village, CO 80111
Phone: (303) 967-8000
Fax: (303) 967-6701
www.firstdata.com

Fiserv
255 Fiserv Drive
Brookfield, WI 53045
Phone: (262) 879-5000
Fax: (262) 879-5013
www.fiserv.com

Fitch Ratings
1 State Street Plaza
New York, NY 10004
Phone: (212) 908-0500
Fax: (212) 480-4435
www.fitchratings.com

Genworth Financial Inc.
6620 West Broad Street
Richmond, VA 23230
Phone: (804) 281-6000
Fax: (804) 662-2414
www.genworth.com

GMAC Financial Services
200 Renaissance Center
Detroit, MI 48265
Phone: (313) 556-5000
Fax: (313) 556-5108
www.gmacfs.com

Guardian (The Guardian Life Insurance Company of America)
7 Hanover Square
New York, NY 10004-2616
Phone: (212) 598-8000
Fax: (212) 919-2170
www.guardianlife.com

Hartford Financial Services
Hartford Plaza
690 Asylum Avenue
Hartford, CT 06115-1900
Phone: (860) 547-5000
Fax: (860) 547-2680
www.thehartford.com

Leucadia National Corporation
315 Park Avenue South
New York, NY 10010-3607
Phone: (212) 460-1900
Fax: (212) 598-4869
www.leucadia.com

Liberty Mutual
175 Berkeley Street
Boston, MA 02117
Phone: (617) 357-9500
Fax: (617) 350-7648
www.libertymutualgroup.com

Employer Directory, cont.

Lincoln Financial Group
1500 Market Street, Suite 3900
Philadelphia, PA 19102
Phone: (215) 448-1400
Fax: (215) 448-3962
www.lfg.com

Loews Corporation
667 Madison Avenue
New York, NY 10021-8087
Phone: (212) 521-2000
Fax: (212) 521-2525
www.loews.com

Marsh & McLennan Companies, Inc.
1166 Avenue of the Americas
New York, NY 10036-2774
Phone: (212) 345-5000
Fax: (212) 345-4838
www.marshmac.com

MassMutual
1295 State Street
Springfield, MA 01111-0001
Phone: (413) 744-1000
Fax: (413) 744-6005
www.massmutual.com

MasterCard Worldwide
2000 Purchase Street
Purchase, NY 10577
Phone: (914) 249-2000
Fax: (914) 249-4206
www.mastercard.com

Moody's Investors Services
99 Church Street
New York, NY 10007
Phone: (212) 553-0300
Fax: (212) 553-4820
www.moodys.com

Nationwide
1 Nationwide Plaza
Columbus, OH 43215-2220
Phone: (614) 249-7111
Fax: (614) 854-5036
www.nationwide.com

New York Life Insurance Company
51 Madison Avenue
New York, NY 10010
Phone: (212) 576-7000
Fax: (212) 576-8145
www.newyorklife.com

Pacific Life Insurance Company
700 Newport Center Drive
Newport Beach, CA 92660
Phone: (949) 219-3011
www.pacificlife.com

The Progressive Corporation
6300 Wilson Mills Road
Mayfield Village, OH 44143
Phone: (800) 766-4737
www.progressive.com

Prudential Financial, Inc.
751 Broad Street
Newark, NJ 07102-3777
Phone: (973) 802-6000
Fax: (973) 802-4479
www.prudential.com

Sallie Mae
12061 Bluemont Way
Reston, VA 20190
Phone: (703) 810-3000
Fax: (703) 984-5042
www.salliemae.com

Scottrade
12800 Corporate Hill Drive
St. Louis, MO 63131-1834
Phone: (314) 965-1555
Fax: (314) 543-6222
www.scottrade.com

Standard & Poor's
55 Water Street
New York, NY 10041
Phone: (212) 438-2000
Fax: (212) 438-7375
www.standardandpoors.com

State Farm
1 State Farm Plaza
Bloomington, IL 61710
Phone: (309) 766-2311
Fax: (309) 766-3621
www.statefarm.com

SunGard Data Systems
680 East Swedesford Road
Wayne, PA 19087-1586
Phone: (800) 825-2518
www.sungard.com

Thornburg Mortgage
150 Washington Avenue, Suite 302
Santa Fe, NM 87501
Phone: (505) 989-1900
Fax: (505) 989-8156
www.thornburgmortgage.com

Toyota Financial Services
19001 South Western Avenue
Torrance, CA 90509
Phone: (310) 468-1310
Fax: (310) 468-7829
www.toyotafinancial.com

The Travelers Companies, Inc.
385 Washington Street
St. Paul, MN 55102
www.travelers.com

Unum
1 Fountain Square
Chattanooga, TN 37402
Phone: (423) 294-1011
Fax: (423) 294-3962
www.unum.com

USAA
9800 Fredericksburg Road
San Antonio, TX 78288
Phone: (210) 498-2211
Fax: (210) 498-9940
www.usaa.com

Visa USA
900 Metro Center Boulevard
Foster City, CA 94404
Phone: (650) 432-3200
Fax: (650) 432-3631
www.usa.visa.com

Visit Vault at **www.vault.com** for insider company profiles, expert advice,
career message boards, expert resume reviews, the Vault Job Board and more.

VAULT CAREER LIBRARY

249

Department of the Navy

If you would like to join more than 7,800 diverse employees, we have a financial management career opportunity for you!

Program Description

► Entry Level Analyst, Accountant, and Auditor positions.

►28 months of professional development through academic and on-the-job training.

►Starting salary between $38,000 and $40,000.

►Successful trainees' salaries increase more than $17,000 over a 28-month period.

Federal Benefits

► Career Development

► Health and Life Insurance

► 10 Paid Holidays

► 13 Paid Vacation and Sick Days

► Performance-Based Pay Increases During The 28-month Training Program

► Thrift Savings Plan (Tax Deferred Contributions)

► Federal Retirement System (Pension Plan)

Financial Management Career Program
520 Turner Street, Suite B
Pensacola, FL 32508-5245

Telephone: (850) 452-3785 or -3783

www.navyfmcp.com

Civilian Careers in Financial Management

On-the-Job-Training

Classroom Training

Rotational Work Assignments

Government and Politics

Life on Capitol Hill

Working hard or hardly working?

A government employee sits in his office. He's bored and decides to find out what's inside his old filing cabinet. The worker rifles through the cabinet's contents and finds an old brass lamp. The employee thinks the lamp will look nice as a decoration, and he decides to take it home. While he's polishing the lamp, a genie appears and says he'll grant the worker three wishes. "I wish for an ice cold Coke right now!" The employee gets his Coke and drinks it. After knocking back the soft drink, the government worker states his second wish. "I wish I were on a tropical island." Suddenly, he's on an island with beautiful beaches and palm trees. Then the employee tells the genie his third and final wish. "I wish I never had to work ever again." Poof! The employee is transported back to his government office.

As the above joke demonstrates, many people believe that public employees are lazy. Recent studies, however, say government employees might actually work harder than many people in the private sector. For example, a 2004 study by Sue A. Frank and Gregory B. Lewis, two researchers from Georgia State University, found that government employees reported slightly higher work effort than private-sector workers.

Another common public perception is that government employees are incompetent. In May, 2007, Senator John McCain, who was addressing the Oklahoma State Legislature on the topic of government reform, brought up the idea of inept federal employees who can never be fired. McCain said, "The civil service has strayed from its reformist roots and has mutated into a no-accountability zone, where employment is treated as entitlement, good performance as an option, and accountability as someone else's problem. Our current system isn't fair to the many good workers who must pick up the slack of those who aren't doing their jobs. The failings in our civil service are encouraged by a system that makes it very difficult to fire someone even for gross misconduct." It is hard for the federal government to fire employees who are performing poorly. However, a study by the U.S. Office of Personnel Management found that supervisors branded only a small percentage of workers—fewer than 4 percent—as poor performers.

Not just paper-pushing bureaucrats

Misconceptions of government extend beyond the stereotype of the lazy, inept employee. When you think about working for the government, you might imagine a job where you work in an office with lots of red tape and a clock to punch. In fact, there are a wide variety of government jobs, which include positions in local, state and federal government. The *Vault Guide to the Top Government & Nonprofit Employers* mostly describes federal government agencies, so this overview focuses primarily on federal jobs. Not all of these positions are in offices. Although the federal government hires office clerks and secretaries, it also needs air traffic controllers, health care workers, criminal investigators, scientists and attorneys. There are dozens of job categories, which run the gamut from able seaman to zoologist.

Many public servants believe strongly in their work, serving the American people and the missions of their particular agencies. Office culture varies depending on the agency and the office's location. One insider, who works for the Environmental Protection Agency, says, "Working for the federal government is a unique experience. Each federal agency has a specific culture developed as a result of its mission." The contact adds the each agency's culture is also influenced by the region in which it is located.

Another common notion is that federal government employees are dissatisfied with their work, but this is not generally the case. In March 2007, the Merit Systems Protection Board released a report. The board found that, in spite of perceptions of decreased organizational stability and worries about changes to pay systems, most federal employees were content with their jobs.

Visit Vault at **www.vault.com** for insider company profiles, expert advice, career message boards, expert resume reviews, the Vault Job Board and more.

VAULT CAREER LIBRARY   251

Moreover, the level of satisfaction varies from agency to agency. A 2006 survey of 221,000 federal workers found that the folks at the Federal Emergency Management Agency (FEMA) were among the least happy. Also, it's important to keep in mind that different agencies are better for different categories of employees. In a 2007 survey, Federal Computer Week ranked the top agencies for information technology employees in terms of job satisfaction. The publication put the Social Security Administration, the Justice Department and the Army at the top of the list. The General Services Administration, the Agriculture Department and the Homeland Security Department/Federal Emergency Management Agency were at the bottom of the barrel.

In case you slept through Government 101

The federal government has three branches: the executive branch, the judicial branch and the legislative branch. The government's legislative branch, which includes the House of Representatives and the Senate, forms and amends the country's legal structure. The judicial branch interprets the laws that the legislative branch passes. Finally, the executive branch includes the Executive Office of the President, the Cabinet departments and nearly 90 independent agencies. In 2004, the executive branch employed 96 percent of federal civilian workers.

Each executive Cabinet department runs programs related to a facet of life, such as transportation or agriculture. The 15 Cabinet departments are Agriculture, Commerce, Defense, Education, Energy, Interior, Health and Human Services, Homeland Security, Housing and Urban Development, Justice, Labor, State, Transportation, Treasury and Veterans Affairs. A secretary, who belongs to the president's Cabinet, heads up each Cabinet department.

The most recent Cabinet department is the Department of Homeland Security (DHS), which was formed after the terrorist attacks of September 11, 2001. Officially established in March 2003, the DHS became the government's largest department, and signaled the largest government transformation since the 1949 establishment of the Department of Defense. The DHS is composed of 22 formerly separate federal agencies.

A brief history of government employment

The history of some parts of the government goes back before the United States was even a country. This is particularly true of branches of the armed forces. The U.S. Army, for example, traces its roots back to June 14, 1775, when the Second Continental Congress created the "American continental army." The U.S. Navy found its beginnings in the Continental Navy, established several months before the writing of the Declaration of Independence. Some nonmilitary entities have also been around for centuries. For instance, the U.S. Postal Service's history stretches back more than 200 years to the days when colonists traded mail between each other and across the Atlantic.

During America's early days, the president filled government jobs, and an employee could be fired at will. This process, known as the "spoils system," meant that federal jobs were used to bolster political parties. The federal government was a fraction of the size it is today, and most jobs were administrative and clerical positions in Washington, D.C., Philadelphia, Boston and New York. Many of the first presidents, including George Washington and Thomas Jefferson, had high expectations for federal employees. During the presidency of James Monroe, the Tenure of Office Act of 1820 passed. Under this act, many officials' terms were limited to four years, the same length of time as the president's term.

John Quincy Adams refused to remove officials solely for political reasons, but subsequent presidents used the spoils system to reward their supporters. Some presidents, such as Andrew Jackson, argued that the system was better for the country. Jackson felt trained officials in Washington posed a threat, and he thought bureaucracy was dangerous. The country grew, and the government—which expanded as well—became more complex. By the mid-1800s, individuals were starting to see the negative effects of the spoils system, which placed people with little knowledge in specialized jobs. The system led to inefficiency, corruption and sometimes even theft. For instance, Samual Swartwout, collector of customs for the Port of New

York, took off for Europe with more than a million dollars in embezzled public money. The spoils system had also extended into some branches of the military, and it may have impaired forces' effectiveness in certain campaigns.

The Pendleton Civil Service Reform Act as well as subsequent laws changed the spoils system. President Chester Arthur signed the Pendleton Civil Service Reform Act into law in 1883. The act established the tradition and means of permanent federal employment based on merit instead of political party affiliation. The Civil Service Reform Act created the U.S. Civil Service Commission. In the beginning, only about 10 percent of the civil service positions were part of the competitive civil service system. By 1909, however, almost 64 percent of the U.S. federal employees were appointed based on merit. (Certain positions in government, such as some ambassadorships and heads of federal agencies, are still filled by political appointees.)

In 1940, the Hatch Act prohibited campaign contributions by officeholders. The goal of the act was to separate the civil service from politics. (Through a 1993 revision to the Hatch Act, most federal employees can now participate in political activities during their free time.) In 1978, President Jimmy Carter's administration established the U.S. Office of Personnel Management (OPM). This independent agency of the U.S. government is in charge of administering a nationwide merit system for federal employment. The OPM's duties include examination, recruitment and training.

Why Capitol Hill?

Who works for the government today?

The federal government employs nearly two million civilian workers, excluding people who work for the U.S. Postal Service. This makes the federal government the largest single employer in the country. Most federal employees (more than 80 percent) work outside of Washington, D.C. The states that boast the largest number of federal jobs are Florida, Texas, California, Maryland and Virginia. A number of agencies hire Americans to work overseas.

According to the Office of Personnel Management (OPM), the average full-time government employee is 46.7 year old. The OPM says 55.5 percent of federal workers are men, and 44.5 percent are women. About 31 percent of these men and women are ethnic minorities. More than 41 percent of federal employees have a college degree or higher.

Some federal workers are unionized. The American Federation of Government Employees (AFGE), which acts on behalf of about 600,000 federal and D.C. government workers, is the largest federal employee union. Another union that represents federal employees is the National Federation of Federal Employees (NFFE). The American Federation of State, County and Municipal Employees (AFSCME) stands up for librarians at the Library of Congress. The Congressional Research Employees Association (CREA) represents many of the professional and nonprofessional employees who work for the library's Congressional Research Service.

Considering Working on the Hill?

If your considering working on the Hill, you should make sure you know what you're getting into. Here, we give you a quick self-assessment test to see if a career on Capitol Hill seems like a good fit for you.

The Hill is probably for you if:

• You like excitement and the idea that every day can bring something different.

• You enjoy following public affairs and reading the newspaper.

• You like talking about politics ... a lot.

Visit Vault at **www.vault.com** for insider company profiles, expert advice, career message boards, expert resume reviews, the Vault Job Board and more.

VAULT CAREER LIBRARY   253

- You don't mind starting off paying your dues by answering the phone, writing letters and taking calls from angry constituents.

- You don't care what your workspace looks like, so long as you have a desk and a computer.

- You work well under pressure.

The Hill is probably not for you if:

- You'd rather be doing anything other than talking about politics.

- You prefer stable, predictable environments.

- You don't like talking to random people during the course of your day.

- You want the security of a distinct career path.

- You don't like long, unpredictable hours.

The pros and cons of working for Uncle Sam

Often, government wages are competitive with the private sector salaries. Many federal jobs use the GS pay scale. The GS scale starts at GS-1 ($16,620 to $20,798 base salary in 2007) and goes up to GS-15 ($93,062 to $120,981 base in 2007). The typical starting level for someone with an undergraduate degree is a GS-5, which begins around $25,600. People with master's degrees generally start out at the GS-9 level ($38,824 to $50,470 in 2007). There's a separate scale for executives, which ranges from Level I (the highest) to Level V (the lowest). In 2007, the base pay for executives ranged from $136,200 to $186,600. To complicate things further, some agencies have their own pay scales. The Peace Corps, for example, has FS levels instead of GS levels for employees.

Federal employees say excellent benefits are one of the big perks when it comes to working for Uncle Sam. One respondent says that even if government salaries are slightly lower than in the private sector, "the small monetary difference is easily offset by job security, flexibility and advancement opportunities." Typically, benefits for full-time federal workers include medical and dental coverage, life insurance, vacation, sick leave, tuition assistance and retirement benefits. According to a February 2007 article in *USA Today*, retired government employees are twice as likely to get pensions as their equals in the private sector. Moreover, the article adds, the typical government pension is much more generous.

When it comes to schedules and working from home, the government may offer more flexibility than the corporate world. A 2007 CDW Government study found that telework adoption in the federal government outpaced that in the private sector. The survey discovered that 44 percent of federal employees had the option to telework, an alternative that only 15 percent of private-sector employees enjoy.

A September 2007 article in *The Washington Post* discusses how some federal agencies are increasingly offering bonuses to recruit and retain employees for hard-to-fill positions. According to a report that the Office of Personnel Management prepared for Congress, 47 government agencies paid more than $140 million in bonuses to recruit, retain and relocate employees during 2006. Departments that offered such incentives to employees included Defense, Agriculture, Commerce and Veterans Affairs. The OPM report added that the average recruitment bonus was more than $8,000, the average retention bonus was more than $5,000 and the typical relocation incentive was about $11,500.

Many federal workers also like the security of working for the government. One source at the USDA says, "The Federal government is extremely stable. If they restructure and eliminate jobs, then they make every effort to relocate displaced workers. It is the ultimate in job security."

Sources who work for the government, like those who work for any large organization, often complain about the amount of red tape they encounter. A doctor for the Department of Veterans Affairs, for example, says, "This medical center is in tension between the desire for excellent professional care and the limited budget, between innovation that has achieved the highest levels of quality of care and the burden of unmotivated bureaucracy." Sometimes working for the government can also be political. One insider at the FCC says, "I've generally enjoyed working here, but frequently politics overwhelms the mission of the agency." Another common gripe about working for the government is that it can be difficult to advance. Some insiders say it's impossible to move up in the ranks unless you change jobs, become a manager or move, and a few government insiders say it is impossible to get promoted period. One civilian staffer with the Air Force, for example, feels, "Opportunities for advancement are not there."

Finding a position with the federal government

A U.S. Department of Agriculture insider says, "The one tip that I have for someone seeking federal employment for the first time is to forget all the preconceived stereotypes. Federal employees are the hardest working, [most] caring and most satisfied people that I know."

Within the federal government, there are two classes of jobs. Competitive service jobs fall under the OPM's jurisdiction, and some service agencies establish their own qualification requirements. Most government agencies post job openings on USAJOBS (www.usajobs.gov), the federal government's official careers site. When you're applying for a position with the federal government, it's essential to read the vacancy announcement carefully and fill out the application forms properly. You'll have to submit an application form or a resume containing information that your existing resume probably doesn't have. Often, agencies also want applicants to send written knowledge, skills and abilities assessments called KSAs.

The Department of Agriculture employee says, "It is extremely important to read the job announcement and provide everything requested in a complete package with the correct formatting before the announcement expires ... The next most important and difficult part of the hiring process is answering the Knowledge, Skills and Abilities (KSA) well enough to get an interview. Address every KSA in the affirmative, and provide as much supporting evidence as possible."

Some government departments and agencies also have special entrance exams or other requirements. For example, the U.S. Postal Service has a number of written examinations for different positions such as motor vehicle operator or city carrier. Applicants for temporary jobs with the postal service don't need to take exams, but they still need to pass a pre-employment drug test. Becoming a Foreign Service Officer for the U.S. Department of State is extremely difficult, and studying for the Foreign Service examination can be a grueling exercise. Successfully completing the exam (and then the subsequent oral interviews) requires extensive and intensive knowledge of U.S. and world history, international relations and major political issues. Foreign Service Officers also have to pass a security background check and a medical exam.

Getting a taste of government service

The government also has a number of internship and job opportunities for students. Some programs that are offered across the federal government include the Presidential Management Fellows (PMF) Program, the Workforce Recruitment Program For College Students With Disabilities (WRP) and the Student Education Employment Program, which includes the Student Temporary Employment Program (STEP), and the Student Career Experience Program (SCEP). More information about the Student Education Employment Program is available online at www.opm.gov/employ/students/index.asp. The OPM also has a special web site for students, www.studentjobs.gov.

In addition, many agencies have their own internship and job programs for undergraduate and graduate students. The U.S. Department of Justice, for example, has job and internship opportunities for law students. Programs include the Attorney General's Honors Program and the Summer Law Intern Program. The White House has a highly selective fellowship program. White House Fellows spend two years working in the White House as assistants to senior officials.

Visit Vault at **www.vault.com** for insider company profiles, expert advice, career message boards, expert resume reviews, the Vault Job Board and more.

VAULT CAREER LIBRARY

255

Where the jobs are going to be

According to the Bureau of Labor Statistics (BLS), between 2004 and 2014 government employment—including that in hospitals and public schools—is expected to grow by 10 percent. The BLS projects that during this period local government educational services will increase 10 percent, and state government educational services will increase by more than 19 percent. The bureau expects that employment with the federal government, including the U.S. Postal Service, will increase by less than 2 percent as the federal government continues to contract out government positions to private businesses.

Already, the government has started to outsource more activities. As a result, there's a shortage of people who can oversee and monitor contracts. The federal government is looking for individuals who have project management skills. Additionally, many federal workers plan to retire by 2009. This means that federal agencies are hiring new employees as part of the government's succession planning strategy.

A recent study by the nonprofit Partnership for Public Service says that, over the next couple years, federal agencies will hire more than 190,000 employees in a wide range of occupational fields. The nonprofit organization expects about 83,000 of these jobs to be at the Department of Homeland Security. By 2010, Homeland Security plans to hire 22,000 airport screeners and more than 15,000 Border Patrol agents and Customs and Border Patrol officers.

Other federal agencies will also hire employees in categories such as computers, science, accounting and auditing, engineering, program management, medicine and public health. The Department of Veterans Affairs will need large a numbers of doctors and nurses, and the Department of Defense plans to hire thousands of engineers. During the next several years, as air traffic controllers retire, the FAA will be hiring a large number of air traffic controllers. The FAA has said that it plans to take on 12,500 new air traffic controllers by 2014.

Capitol Hill Internships

Some of the most powerful people in Washington have never run for office, yet they command as much power as many of Members of Congress. And many of them began their careers answering phones or writing letters as interns on Capitol Hill.

Traditionally seen as the starting point to a career in government and politics, Capitol Hill offices are flooded with resumes every year from undergraduates eager to gain experience and contacts to begin their ascent to Washington powerbroker. Internships are available in the personal offices of Members of Congress—both Senators and Representatives. Additionally, Committees on both the House and Senate side offer internships.

"Interning is the best way to get your foot in the door," said one former intern who used the experience to find a full-time position. "The minute I walked in on the first day of my internship, I knew that I wanted to work on Capitol Hill. The office was buzzing with activity, the televisions were tuned to the House floor, and everyone in the office was young and dedicated. Interning allows you to experience the excitement of Capitol Hill and build the skills and contacts you will need to start a career."

There are two important considerations to make in applying for internships on Capitol Hill: where you want to work and what you want to do. Most of the internships offered by Congress will be with Members' personal offices. The Congressional committees and House and Senate leadership offices all offer internship opportunities, as well. The following descriptions provide some of the differences and advantages of each type of internship.

Personal offices

Personal offices of both Senators and Members of the U.S. House of Representatives reflect the individual personality and management style of the Members. Representatives' Washington, D.C. offices usually employ eight to 10 employees.

Senators' Washington offices are much larger in terms of employees and the staff sizes are based on the population of the state each Senator represents.

In general, House offices will feel more intimate (some might say cramped) than the Senate offices. In the House, interns generally work on a variety of topics, depending where the staff feels their skills can be best utilized. Due to their larger staffs, Senate offices may be able to provide a greater degree of specialization in an area of interest to the intern, such as the legislative process or media relations. Despite these differences, much of the experience will be the same regardless whether one chooses the House or Senate; answering the phone, responding to constituent inquiries, processing requests for flags flown over the U.S. Capitol and helping visitors are all part and parcel of the intern experience.

In applying for internships, students should definitely consider the Members of Congress who represent their home towns and their college's or university's location. To find information on a Member of Congress, including an internship application, visit the Member's personal web site. Web sites for House Members can be accessed at www.house.gov, and Senators sites can be found at www.senate.gov.

Committees

The committees of the U.S. Congress offer internships. The committees are where much of the legislative process takes place. Internships with a committee provide the opportunity to learn about specific areas of legislation (e.g., tax policy or the annual appropriations process) and to dig deeper into the legislative process than a similar internship in a Member's personal office. Since committee staffs do not answer to constituents as Members' staffs do, interns will spend much less time writing letters. However, they most likely will not get the same level of interaction with a Member of Congress and the senior staff as interns do in a personal office.

Leadership offices

The Republican and Democrat Members of the House and Senate elect leaders to organize their parties, set their agendas, count votes and communicate their messages. The top elected leaders in each party are given separate offices and staffs to carry out their responsibilities. These leadership offices are another source of Capitol Hill internships for students. Since there are fewer leadership offices and staff members, and since members of the leadership enjoy high-profile positions, internships with these offices will be very competitive.

Outside the Washington Beltway

While most students focus on internships inside the Beltway, there are opportunities where they live and study to build experience and make contacts. One of the best ways to become involved in the process is to volunteer for a political campaign. Closely contested Senate and House races require an army of unpaid labor to help achieve a victory on Election Day. Volunteers will often have the opportunity to work closely with the candidate and his or her top campaign staff. Moreover, a victory by their candidate provides a ready-made path to an internship or position on Capitol Hill. Contacting the appropriate local or national party committees can help turn up races that need assistance.

Additionally, many Members of Congress offer internships in their district offices. While the work focuses more on constituent aid than on the legislative process, the schedule may be more flexible to accommodate school hours and the experience could provide entry into the Washington, D.C. office after graduation.

Visit Vault at www.vault.com for insider company profiles, expert advice, career message boards, expert resume reviews, the Vault Job Board and more.

VAULT CAREER LIBRARY 257

When to intern

The busiest time in Washington for interns is during the summer. The streets of Washington literally seem to be teeming with undergraduates. Summer internships provide a good opportunity to network with other interns and enjoy a wide range of social activities. Furthermore, Congress tends to be very busy during the early summer months of June and July. Congress takes an August recess during Washington's hottest month, and the pace of life slows down greatly on the Hill and across the city. Internships at times other than the summer can be a very good option since there will be fewer interns and more work to go around. Often, they are combined with college programs for credit. However, students should work to ensure that Congress is in session while they are in Washington; interning during November and December of an election year will greatly reduce the value of the experience since Congress rarely has any official activities scheduled during this time.

Advocacy Organizations

For students more interested in a cause than a specific political agenda, or for those students who want to broaden their Washington, D.C. experience beyond Capitol Hill, nearly every organization and every cause is represented in some form or another within the nation's capital. Many of these are large organizations that provide internships for students. However, please be aware that internships will vary from organization to organization: Some will be well structured, others less so; many will offer pay or stipends, but many more will not; some will be smaller organizations while others will be larger and more bureaucratic. It is imperative for students to do their research.

While the list of advocates within Washington is too numerous to cover in great detail, there are many organizations on the right, left and even in the center that students may wish to explore.

For example, students interested in the issue of gun control could apply for internships on either side of the debate, depending on their philosophy, and still work with some of the most influential organizations in Washington. The National Rifle Association and the Brady Campaign to Prevent Gun Violence both offer legislative internships in their Washington area headquarters.

Students interested in environmental issues should consider the liberal-leaning World Wildlife Federation or Sierra Club, while those who favor a conservative philosophy on the environment could look into opportunities with a think tank or the Council of Environmental Republican Advocacy or a business organization.

There are many organizations that are also nonpartisan, and that represent a professional group or other point of view. For example, the American Medical Association represents the interests of doctors before Congress and works closely with members of both parties.

Please note that it is very common for organizations with distinct agendas on both the left and the right to describe themselves as "non-partisan." While this is true in a legal sense, the fact is that many of these organizations do favor the left or the right in their activities. Students who aren't sure about an organization's true nature should cast a critical eye on its issue advocacy efforts, board of directors and web site to determine its true leanings.

For a comprehensive list of advocacy organizations in Washington, as well as White House and Congressional staff, corporate offices and trade associations, check out the *Capitol Source*, which is published by the National Journal Group. It is available in Washington area bookstores and can be ordered online at www.njdc.com/about/capitolsource.

Examples of advocacy organizations

While many advocacy organizations are legally nonpartisan, their politics can be considered different shades of liberal, conservative or middle of the road. Below are some examples of various types of advocacy organizations and their ideological leanings.

American Heart Association: While headquarters in Dallas, the American Heart Association, like many medical groups, maintains an advocacy office in Washington, D.C. to lobby for greater research funding and promote legislation that encourages healthy lifestyles, such as anti-tobacco measures. It is considered a moderate organization. www.americanheart.org

AARP: The nation's leading seniors organization is also one of the most influential advocates in the nation's capital, making its presence felt on a number of high-profile issues, including Social Security, Medicare and health care issues. It is generally considered a moderate organization. www.aarp.org

Brady Campaign to Prevent Gun Violence: The Brady Campaign, named after the former White House press secretary wounded during the attempted assassination of President Ronald Reagan, works to enact gun control laws and regulation through grassroots organization and campaign support to similar-minded candidates. It is considered a liberal organization. www.bradycampaign.org

Citizens for a Sound Economy: CSE fights for lower taxes, less government and fewer regulations. It recruits and trains grassroots activists across the country to influence the economic agenda on the national, state and local levels. It is considered a conservative organization. www.cse.org

Christian Coalition: The Christian Coalition supports policies on the federal, state and local levels that reflect its moral values. Examples include opposition to abortion and gambling, and support for lower taxes, among many social and economic issues. It is considered a conservative organization. www.cc.org

Concord Coalition: The Concord Coalition advocates for fiscal responsibility while ensuring Social Security, Medicare and Medicaid remain secure. It was founded by the late former Senator Paul Tsongas (D-MA) and former Senator Warren Rudman (R-NH) and is considered a moderate organization. www.concordcoaltion.org

National Resources Defense Council: The NRDC supports environmental protections and engages in advocacy on issues ranging from global warming to nuclear waste. It is considered a liberal organization. www.nrdc.org

National Rifle Association: The National Rifle Association provides an array of services to gun owners and is a well-known legislative advocate in the nation's capital. The NRA opposes legislation that regulates gun ownership and supports candidates who agree with its positions on gun issues. It is considered a conservative organization. www.nra.org

Common Cause: Common Cause is a strong proponent of campaign finance reform and actively lobbies to reduce the amount of money in the political process. It is considered a liberal organization. www.commoncause.org

The Staff Assistant

If you are coming out of an undergraduate program or are a recent graduate, and want to start your career on the Hill, your first position will most likely be as a staff assistant (or possibly as a legislative correspondent).

The staff assistant role is viewed as the traditional entry-level position for those with little to no Capitol Hill or legislative experience. It is not glamorous and the pay is low, but it does provide the first important entrée to Capitol Hill.

The primary responsibilities of the staff assistant tend more toward administrative work. On the surface, a staff assistant is often seen as a glorified, college-educated receptionist. As a staff assistant, you will usually be the first person a visitor sees upon entering the office. Your responsibilities include greeting guests, arranging tours of the Capitol, opening and sorting the mail, and answering the phone.

However, as a staff assistant, you will also have the opportunity to assist the more senior staff in a variety of areas and learn the ropes on Capitol Hill. As you learn the fundamentals of your position, you will have more time to put your education to

Visit Vault at **www.vault.com** for insider company profiles, expert advice, career message boards, expert resume reviews, the Vault Job Board and more.

VAULT CAREER LIBRARY   259

use. Staff assistants often have the chance to work with legislative assistants to research legislation and other issues, take on special projects for the chief of staff, or help the press secretary by proofreading speeches and organizing media lists.

Moreover, the position of staff assistant reinforces one of the foremost truisms of work in Washington: proximity to power is key. As a staff assistant, you will perform many mundane tasks. You will be paid far less than you could command in an entry-level position elsewhere. You will also work directly for a Member of Congress and position yourself for far more interesting jobs in the future. Therefore, newcomers to Washington are hungry for an entry-level spot on Capitol Hill. It is the proximity that provides experience and opens doors to bigger opportunities.

"Getting started on the Hill means lots of time doing stuff they didn't teach you in college, like answering the phones and spending a lot of time dealing with constituents. But I wouldn't give up this job for anything. A lot of my friends off the Hill make more money, but in the long run my time on the Hill will open a lot more doors for me down the road," says one staff assistant.

"Working as a staff assistant is both frustrating and exciting," another explains. "Frustrating because some of the work can be tedious and some of the people you deal with can be quite rude. It's exciting because our office moves so fast. The Senator is very involved on many high-profile issues and is always being asked to appear on television. I've been able to meet many high-profile Washington dignitaries and leaders."

The Foreign Service

The Foreign Service is often the first thing that comes to mind when people think of a global government career. And unlike many of the other opportunities covered in this book, a Foreign Service career is indeed that—a career. Joining the Foreign Service means accepting a professional (and personal) life spent overseas, with constant rotations every few years. It can be very rewarding, exciting and occasionally glamorous work.

While the salary generally does not match what you can make in the private sector, generous allowance perks and subsidies help make up the difference. For example, there is a hardship "bonus" for postings in difficult areas of the world, up to 25 percent above your base salary. One Foreign Service Officer commented on the pay: "There's a lot of internal grumbling about the salary, but it's really not that bad. When you look at the remuneration, you have to look at the whole package, including subsidized housing and unlimited access to American military exchanges and the American-priced foodstuffs."

Applicants enter the Foreign Service in one of five career tracks: management affairs, consular affairs, economic affairs, political affairs and public diplomacy. Which career track you enter as a beginning FSO (Foreign Service Officer) will influence the nature of your assignments and your career, and there is little crossover between the tracks once you have made your decision. FSOs often undergo intensive training before being posted to their first overseas assignment, including, in some cases, up to two years full-time language study. Check out www.state.gov for more information on the application procedure, and also www.afsa.org, the American Foreign Service Organization, for more information on what life is like in the Foreign Service.

Qualifications

While potential FSOs come from all backgrounds, being accepted is extremely competitive—roughly 40,000 applicants apply for the Foreign Service exam every year, only about 400 are eventually accepted. If you are serious about joining the Foreign Service, be prepared to do your homework!

The exam is offered once a year, and studying for it can be a grueling exercise. Successfully completing the exam (and then the subsequent oral interviews) requires extensive and intensive knowledge of U.S. and world history, international relations and major political issues. Says one foreign service officer who joined in the mid 1990s: "The applicants who do best on the test are those who have literally spent a lifetime preparing for it. They're naturally interested in foreign affairs and world events, have often done their degree in that area, and have followed the news their whole life. This type of background will be invaluable." Check out www.state.gov for more information on the exam, study hints and guides.

Potential FSOs come from a wide variety of backgrounds, and knowledge of a foreign language is not required (though it will make you a more attractive candidate). In addition to deep knowledge of world affairs, the State Department looks for personal characteristics and traits that will best represent America overseas.

Uppers and downers

The Foreign Service is an excellent training ground and a superior way to see the world. As the world is a constantly changing place and an increasingly wide array of international issues—think medical, environmental, social and religious, as well as economic and political—on the agenda, the Foreign Service can provide an exciting and stimulating career path.

The lifestyle and constant rotations have a downside, too, and that is the impact on your personal life. While picking up and exploring a new city and a new job every few years can be exciting in your 20s, the lack of stability can be more problematic as you get older. Having a spouse or partner who is willing to rotate with you is a plus. The State Department is gradually lengthening the time of each rotation, expanding the average to three or four years.

Visit Vault at **www.vault.com** for insider company profiles, expert advice, career message boards, expert resume reviews, the Vault Job Board and more.

VAULT CAREER LIBRARY   261

Employer Directory

Central Intelligence Agency (CIA)
1423 Chain Bridge Road
McLean VA 22101
Phone: (703) 482-1100
Fax: (703) 482-1739
www.cia.gov

Democratic National Committee
430 South Capitol Street SE
Washington, DC 20003
Phone: (202) 863-8000
www.democrats.org

Environmental Protection Agency (EPA)
Ariel Rios Building
1200 Pennsylvania Avenue NW
Washington, DC 20460
Phone: (202) 272-0167
www.epa.gov

Executive Office of the President of the United States
1600 Pennsylvania Avenue NW
Washington, DC 20500
Phone: (202) 456-1414
Fax: (202) 456-2461
www.whitehouse.gov

Federal Bureau of Investigation
J. Edgar Hoover Building
935 Pennsylvania Avenue, NW
Washington, DC 20535
Phone: (202) 324-3000
www.fbi.gov

Federal Reserve System
20th Street and Constitution Avenue NW
Washington, DC 20551
Phone: (202) 452-3000
www.federalreserve.gov

Federal Trade Commission (FTC)
600 Pennsylvania Avenue NW
Washington, DC 20580
Phone: (202) 326-2222
www.ftc.gov

Internal Revenue Service (IRS)
1111 Constitution Avenue NW
Washington, DC 20224
Phone: (202) 622-5000
Fax: (202) 622-4355
www.irs.gov

National Security Agency
9800 Savage Road
Fort Meade, MD 20755
Phone: (301) 688-6524
Fax: (301) 688-6198
www.nsa.gov

Republican National Committee
310 First Street SE
Washington, DC 20003
Phone: (202) 863-8500
Fax: (202) 863-8820
www.rnc.org

U.S. Department of Defense
The Pentagon
Washington, DC 20301
Phone: (703) 428-0711
www.defenselink.mil

U.S. Department of Education
400 Maryland Avenue SW
Washington, DC 20202
Phone: (202) 401-2000
Fax: (202) 401-0689
www.ed.gov

U.S. Department of Homeland Security
245 Murray Drive
Washington, DC 20528
Phone: (202) 282-8000
Fax: (703) 235-0442
www.dhs.gov

U.S. Department of the Interior
1849 C Street NW
Washington, DC 20240
Phone: (202) 208-3100
www.doi.gov

U.S. Department of Justice
950 Pennsylvania Avenue NW
Washington, DC 20530
Phone: (202) 514-2000
Fax: (202) 307-6777
www.usdoj.gov

U.S. Department of Labor
200 Constitution Avenue NW
Washington, DC 20210
Phone: (202) 693-6000
Fax: (202) 693-6111
www.dol.gov

U.S. Department of State
2201 C Street NW
Washington, DC 20520
Phone: (202) 647-4000
Fax: (202) 647-1558
www.state.gov

U.S. Department of the Treasury
1500 Pennsylvania Avenue NW
Washington, DC 20220
Phone: (202) 622-2000
Fax: (202) 622-6415
www.ustreas.gov

U.S. Department of Transportation
4000 7th Street SW
Washington, DC 20590
Phone: (202) 366-4000
www.dot.gov

U.S. Department of Veterans Affairs
810 Vermont Avenue NW
Washington, DC 20420
Phone: (202) 273-5400
www.va.gov

U.S. Securities and Exchange Commission (SEC)
200 F Street NE
Washington, DC 20549
Phone: (202) 551-6551
Fax: (202) 772-9295
www.sec.gov

Health Care

Industry Overview

An industry in flux

You can't live with it and you can't live without it—this pretty much sums up the attitude many Americans have toward today's health care industry. The sector is a veritable Rube Goldberg machine of providers of patient care, manufacturers, middlemen and insurance companies. It's no secret that the sector is a volatile one despite making up around 16 percent of the nation's gross domestic product (GDP). U.S. health care spending totaled $2.3 trillion in 2007, more than what people spent on housing or food. Despite the awesome quantities of money involved in the industry, industry players have a tough time figuring out how to turn a profit in such a way that benefits both providers and patients—not to mention shareholders. Economists predict health care spending will make up 20 percent of the country's GDP in 2016, a percentage considered unsustainable by many analysts. It is estimated that the public sector will pay for nearly half of all health spending in the U.S. by that year—not a healthy number.

Big trouble

Another unhealthy number is the growing number of people who will need medical attention in the coming decades due to the increasing prevalence of bariatric and geriatric patients. In 2007, census data revealed that Americans were the fattest people on the planet. One quarter of adults are classified as clinically obese. Carrying a few extra pounds won't be listed as a cause of death, but it also doesn't just mean that one's trousers are a tad snug: overweight and obese people are increasingly at risk for disorders like heart disease, stroke, osteoarthritis, type II diabetes, certain types of cancer and a number of other long-term (and expensive) conditions. Economists are continually trying to figure the economic impact of overweight and obese Americans. In 2006, researchers estimated that obesity cost insurers around $80 billion per annum, and the number is rising. However, the term "overweight" is difficult to define consistently; additionally, there are a number of subtle effects, like depressed wages from weight discrimination and missed productivity due to disability, that can have profound economic consequences. More worryingly, the incidence of obesity in children has tripled since the 1970s, according to data from the Centers for Disease Control and Prevention; studies have shown that children who were overweight had an 80 percent chance of growing up to be obese adults.

Having a senior moment

Speaking of adults, according to the American Association of Retired Persons (AARP), by the year 2050, seniors will outnumber children for the first time ever. With approximately one million people turning age 60 each month worldwide, the phenomenon known as "global aging" promises to have a profound effect on the demand for and delivery of health care services. This shift is sparking interest in all issues affecting senior health, from preventive care to programs promoting home care and assisted living as alternatives to merely shunting the elderly to oft-dreaded nursing home care.

The United States' aging population is also putting pressure on the nation's reimbursement system for seniors and low-income patients. The Medicaid program is funded by the federal government but administered by the states, serving low-income individuals who do not have access to health care through their employers, while the Medicare program serves people over the age of 65. Because of this, the federal government looms large in health care. In fact, ranked by sales, the government's own Centers for Medicare & Medicaid Services (CMS) is the No. 1 provider in the insurance industry, covering around one in four people, and distributing $554 billion in benefits in 2006—more than a fifth of the spending of the federal government. Expenditures from the program are expected to rise to 11 percent of GDP through 2008.

Visit Vault at www.vault.com for insider company profiles, expert advice,
career message boards, expert resume reviews, the Vault Job Board and more.

VAULT CAREER LIBRARY   263

As the 77 million members of the baby boomer generation reach age 65 and sign up for Medicare, the government will foot an even larger share of the health care bill. In 2007, Ben Bernanke, chairman of the Federal Reserve, warned in a Senate hearing that the spiraling costs of Social Security and government-funded health care could precipitate a budgetary crisis if not swiftly addressed. He predicted that the programs, burdened by the baby boomers, could increase publicly held government debt from 37 percent of the GDP in 2007 to 100 percent of GDP in 2030, and that it would increase astronomically thereafter, requiring large increases in taxes and deep cuts in government spending.

Let's go to Part D

The solution to this problem, of course, is to expand the benefits offered by Medicare. In 2006, Part D, a prescription drug benefit plan, was rolled out. (Medicare parts A, B and C govern hospital stays, doctor's visits and plans offered through other insurers, respectively.) The Bush administration has made several attempts to tweak the program, with mixed results. The revised Medicare drug plan, known as Medicare Part D, which came into effect in 2006, provided seniors with a flurry of plan options provided by various private insurance companies. But the Byzantine regulations for the program left many seniors confused and worried they were not getting the coverage they needed. Befuddled seniors notwithstanding, insurance companies have posted record profits from administering Part D.

In 2007, new regulations refigured the rates at which Medicare compensates hospitals and physicians for various procedures. Compensation for surgeries, such as hip and knee replacements and various cardiac procedures, will be cut by as much as a third. In response, the American Medical Association (AMA) announced that if compensation for Medicare patients is reduced, physicians will be forced to restrict the number of such cases they can handle. This legislation represents the opening salvo in a series of laws that will try to rein in Medicare spending by 34 percent over the next decade. Further economic fallout may include hospitals seeking higher reimbursement from insurance companies, which will then raise premiums, further increasing the cost of health care.

Flying without a net

Then there is the problem of the remaining 86 percent of the population, who aren't eligible for Medicare or Medicaid and either must buy private insurance on their own, get it through an employer or just go without and hope for the best. An alarming number of Americans, including many children, are uninsured—15.8 percent of the population at last count, or some 48 million people.

What's more, this number, along with the number of those who must purchase insurance on their own, will grow. As generally healthy people opt not to pay for health insurance—the cost of which increased at twice the rate of inflation in 2006—the pools of people buying insurance increasingly consists of people with expensive, chronic conditions or those who think they will imminently need expensive medical care—an actuarial nightmare that's driving up premiums. At such high costs, employers are increasingly unwilling or unable to pay to insure their employees, further enlarging the ranks of the uninsured.

Uninsured individuals increase pressure on the price of health care in other ways, as well. They are less likely to get regular checkups and treat minor medical problems before they become major issues, causing many to end up seeking treatment in the emergency room. Since many of the uninsured don't have the financial reserves to buy health insurance in the first place, a hospital stay can be devastating, and many default on their debts or are forced into bankruptcy by medical bills. In order to defray the costs of essentially providing free medical care, hospitals must charge higher prices. Reports also indicate that health care is more expensive overall for the uninsured. For example, hospitals bill uninsured clients a higher rate for the same procedures provided to those with health coverage, since big insurance companies are able to negotiate discounts with providers.

The solution to America's health care woes is not as simple as forcing everyone to purchase insurance, however. The fragmented nature of the industry, with so many different players jockeying for their slice of profits, has played a role in increasing the amount that patients must pay for care, since administrative costs only drive up the price of services.

The situation isn't so rosy for consumers fortunate enough to have coverage, either. As the cost of providing health care coverage continues to rise, many employers are finding they can no longer afford this benefit, and are passing more of the costs on to employees in the form of higher premiums, deductibles and stingier reimbursement plans.

Instead of pointing fingers or complaining about the situation, some people are doing something about high health care costs. Seattle's Virginia Mason Medical ran into trouble when the insurance companies that referred patients there pointed out that, despite the stellar quality of the care it delivered, it cost significantly more than other hospitals in the area. Virginia Mason went on a cost-cutting campaign, eliminating pricey medical equipment and specialists. Oddly, the hospital kept losing money, due to the skewed way insurers reimburse procedures. High-tech options, like MRI scans, net big checks from insurers, while simple, equally effective procedures, which cost far less, may cause hospitals to lose money.

In short, insurers are paying caregivers based on how much they do to a patient, as opposed to how effective—or even necessary—the treatments are. The doctors at Virginia Mason and the insurance companies reworked the payment scheme for the hospital so that patients were treated more efficiently. Instead of seeing scads of specialists for back pain, getting an MRI, and finally going to physical therapy, patients are now sent directly to physical therapy, which costs much less, and immediately starts to alleviate the patient's pain.

The quest for reform

The health care crisis had been a hot topic throughout the Presidential primaries, but the issue is taking a back seat to broader economic woes. Still, the health care system is a problem that the newly-elected President, whether it be Obama or McCain, will have to revisit regardless. Legislators have been notably reluctant to deal with the issue ever since Hillary Clinton's attempt to create a universal coverage plan was shot down early in her husband's tenure as president. In 2007, however, California Governor Arnold Schwarzenegger outlined a plan to insure the 36 million residents of his state. Individuals would be required to purchase insurance, either privately or through their employers, and health insurance companies would be obliged to cover them. Employers not offering insurance would pay 4 percent of payroll into a state fund for coverage; government assistance in purchasing this insurance would be given to people below a certain income level. To defray future costs, the state will sponsor initiatives against obesity and diabetes, and will levy a fee of 4 percent of gross revenue on hospitals and 2 percent on doctors to pay for it all. Needless to say, many groups oppose the plan: business owners say that mandated coverage is a sneaky form of tax and will stunt economic growth in the state; a nurses' group says it panders to insurance companies; conservatives cry socialism and liberals claim Schwarzenegger stole their idea. With so few groups happy with the plan, it just might work.

The need for heath care reform was also addressed by President Bush in his State of the Union address in January 2007. He proposed a tax break for people who have to purchase their own insurance, in order to make it more affordable, while taxing employer-provided plans as income. The plan is expected to make coverage affordable for a few million people at best. Critics have rushed to point out the flaws in the proposal. It does not take into account that smaller groups of people, or worse yet, groups of elderly or sick people, are a greater actuarial risk than larger groups, and premiums increase to reflect that. They also point out that this tax scheme would have the effect of driving people towards less expensive plans (which offer skimpier coverage, naturally) in order to reduce spending on unnecessary procedures. Furthermore, it dangerously destabilizes the system under which workers receive health insurance through their employers, the only part of the nation's health insurance plan that could be remotely described as functional. The President also proposed federal funding for states that are creating ways to cover their uninsured populations.

Visit Vault at **www.vault.com** for insider company profiles, expert advice, career message boards, expert resume reviews, the Vault Job Board and more.

VAULT CAREER LIBRARY   **265**

CDHC—the new wave of care?

Another plan for health care that has generated a buzz in the Bush administration is the idea of "consumer-driven health care," or CDHC. The idea is elegant in theory: If consumers can control their own health care spending, providers and insurers will be forced to compete for business, thus (hopefully) increasing quality of care while driving down costs. At the crux of CDHC are health savings accounts (HSAs), or tax-free accounts offered along with low-cost, high-deductible insurance plans. Either employee or employer (or both) stow away a certain amount of money in the HSA each year, which consumers can spend on virtually any health treatment or medication they want; whatever is unused remains in the account for any future health-related expenses.

Proponents of CHDC point out that the cost of plastic surgery and other elective procedures not covered by insurance has effectively kept pace with inflation, since consumers can shop around and find the best care for the best price. Since 1998, the average price of a tummy tuck has risen 19 percent, only slightly higher than inflation, and far below the 49 percent rise in per capita spending on health care for the same period. Opponents of the plan suggest that employers will use CDHC as a cover to reduce employee compensation. What CDHC plans do not take into account is that the bulk of the cost of health care spending is not from overconsumption of medical care by people who can afford it, but rather from treating people with chronic conditions, which can easily require in excess of thousands of dollars per year to manage. CDHC also fails to take into account that competitive pricing only works when one is in a position to make rational, informed decisions about which doctors to visit; in the event of a medical emergency, a severely wounded, unconscious or similarly incapacitated person is in no position to comparison shop.

Liability looms

Another type of reform that gets plenty of congressional buzz is medical malpractice liability, which the powerful AMA has made its top priority. The association has taken to identifying states that are in a "medical liability crisis" owing to exploding insurance premiums and the aftereffects of those costs—namely, that some providers are limiting or halting certain services because of liability risks. As of July 2006, there were 22 states on the AMA's list. One such state, Massachusetts, is a case in point: According to Massachusetts Medical Society research, 50 percent of the state's neurosurgeons, 41 percent of orthopedic surgeons and 36 percent of general surgeons had been forced to limit their scopes of practice due to insurmountable medical liability costs.

The Bush administration said an end to "junk lawsuits" was one of its primary goals for the president's second term, calling for "medical liability reform that will reduce health care costs and make sure patients have the doctors and care they need." In the early months following his January 2005 inauguration, Congress passed Bush-backed legislation to restrain class-action lawsuits and overhaul bankruptcy laws. However, Bush's influence has not fared as well for the "med-mal" bill, which was passed through the House but not the Senate. Bush's proposal would have limited the amount a health provider could be required to pay a patient for "pain and suffering" to $250,000 beyond actual cost of medical services; the proposal also provided for payout of judgments over time instead of in a lump sum.

It's a seemingly unending loop: multimillion-dollar judgments against providers, brought by a solid industry of trial lawyers devoted to representing mistreated patients, make headlines regularly. These judgments then cause liability insurers to panic, with many refusing to cover health care providers at all. As such, the insurers who have stayed in the medical liability market charge a premium providers increasingly can't afford to pay.

For lawmakers, the issue is a tough one: how do you set a cap on the amount a plaintiff can receive for the preventable death of a loved one? Patient advocates frame the issue as a David-versus-Goliath scenario, charging that the monolithic medical community wants to limit consumers' rights to sue providers for poor care. Meanwhile, as the industry waits for the federal government to come up with a solution, states have begun to tackle the issue themselves by setting their own limits on the amount of money a malpractice judgment can reap for the plaintiff. Voters in the state of Texas, which was listed on the

AMA's liability list, recently approved a constitutional amendment capping awards for non-economic damages at $250,000. (Similar measures are in place in West Virginia and Ohio.) Though these states' actions are a far cry from the national reform physicians and insurers desire, it is at least a start in a definitive direction.

Hot hospitals

In 2006, $607 billion was spent on care in hospitals. Growing demand for hospital services, along with higher rates from private insurers, have led to an increase in capital expended in this area. Among the approximately 5,700 registered hospitals in the U.S., a few tower over the rest. Each year, *U.S. News & World Report* publishes a ranking of the nation's top hospitals, surveying doctors around the country about hospitals' reputations in 16 medical specialties, as well as other factors like staffing, morbidity rates and technology. In 2008, the magazine's list named Baltimore's Johns Hopkins Hospital No. 1 overall—a position the institution has held for 18 years running. The Mayo Clinic came in second, followed by the Ronald Reagan UCLA Medical Center and the Cleveland Clinic.

Nurses, stat

Despite industrywide attempts to improve the quality of care in hospitals that don't make the grade, there may be little rectification of these issues if the current situation of nurses does not improve. As demand for health services in the population increases, there will be a contemporaneous rise in the demand for skilled health workers, particularly nurses, who constitute the bulk of workers in the industry. In 2006, hospitals in the U.S. reported that there were 118,000 unfilled positions for registered nurses. Projections of the shortage of nurses indicate a demand that will balloon to 800,000 vacant positions by 2020. Hospitals, under pressure from insurers and other groups to lower costs, have been hiring fewer nurses; consequently, as their jobs become increasingly stressful and frustrating due to being more thinly stretched, experienced nurses often desert the profession for jobs with higher pay and less aggravating working conditions.

In 2006, a Pittsburgh newspaper reported that there were 118,000 vacancies for registered nurses in the U.S.; however, the article pointed out that there were 500,000 people who had passed the nursing exam in the country who were not currently working in the medical industry. While some may be taking time off to raise children, others left the profession due to the onerous working conditions. In addition, nursing is a notoriously low-paying occupation. The Bureau of Labor Statistics reports that the median income for nurses was a little over $57,000 in 2006, the most recent year for which data was available.

In order to cope with the shortage of qualified workers, many hospitals and nursing facilities are increasing nurses' working hours, driving even more people away from the profession. Many nurses' groups are worried that working 12-hour shifts will render nurses unable to deliver high-quality care due to fatigue and stress. Further complicating the matter is the lack of qualified nursing instructors. While there are plenty of people willing to go to nursing school, for both a chance to care for people and the solid career prospects, many nursing schools are turning away qualified candidates because they cannot find enough instructors.

Where the jobs are

In spite of its daunting complexity, the health care industry has one big upside: it's a reliable producer of jobs. The health services industry, the largest of all industries in 2006, as categorized by the Bureau of Labor Statistics (BLS), employed nearly 14 million people that year. Of the 20 occupations the BLS projects to grow the fastest in coming years, seven are in health services. Furthermore, of new jobs that will be created by 2016, three million) will be in health services, more than in any other industry. The Labor Department predicts an increase of 22.2 percent in nursing jobs by 2014, while physician's assistant jobs will grow by 54 percent, occupational therapist positions by 33 percent and home care opportunities by 66 percent. Fitness trainers and dental hygienists are also expected to be popular professions.

Visit Vault at **www.vault.com** for insider company profiles, expert advice, career message boards, expert resume reviews, the Vault Job Board and more.

VAULT CAREER LIBRARY   267

While the suggestion of working in the health care industry may conjure visions of crushing med school debt and grueling internships, in fact the majority of jobs in the sector require fewer than four years of college education. Graduates of one- and two-year certification programs, for example, can work as medical records and health information technicians. Service occupations abound, including medical and dental assistants, nursing and home health aides and facility cleaning jobs. The BLS predicts particularly strong growth in jobs outside of the inpatient hospital sector, such as medical assistants and home health aides. There is a constant clamor for more nurses, too, as facilities face growing regulatory pressure to meet mandatory staffing levels.

Health Care Management

Health care management, also known as health care administration, encompasses a wide range of jobs in a variety of organizations. Health care managers are involved in the delivery of health care and the development of public policy regarding financing of and access to care. It is a field that has evolved over the last 50 years and continues to evolve as the health care delivery system changes. Health care managers work for organizations and individuals, from physician groups to hospitals, insurance companies and government agencies. Their roles are diverse, as well, ranging from line supervisors to directors and middle managers, to executives.

As the health care field has grown through advances in medicine, new technology and new types of health care facilities, so has the number of disciplines that health care managers oversee. In addition to expanding clinical areas requiring managers, such as imaging centers, ambulatory surgery centers, home care, occupational health, assisted living and adult day care, to name a few, disciplines in need of professional management have developed. These include specialists in the realm of financial management, reimbursement, revenue cycle management, planning, fundraising and development, performance improvement, medical management and business development.

The health care field is one of the most rapidly growing in the United States today. An aging population, longer life expectancy and new technology, treatments and medication are major contributors to this growth. As such, the need for health care professionals, including managers at all levels, will increase. The roles and responsibilities of health care managers may change as the health care system continues to do so. But the primary objective of management will remain constant: creating a work environment within an organization that promotes the accomplishment of goals and objectives.

Roles in the field

Health care managers come from a large number of professions. In addition to the majority of managers who graduate from programs in health care administration, public administration or business administration, there are many different kinds of health care managers. These include clinical managers, financial managers, information systems managers, and public relations and marketing managers. Individuals with undergraduate or graduate degrees in management generally enter the field after the completion of their training with the goal of obtaining a middle management or upper-level management position in a health care organization. Managers in professions, such as finance, often have worked in another field, have developed their skills and can readily transfer these skills to the health care environment. Clinical managers, including nurses and physicians, may work as clinicians for a period of time before entering management.

Entry-level

As in any organization, there are different levels of management in health care. Entry-level management positions are generally referred to as line supervisors. These people supervise the day-to-day activities of a group of employees. Examples of this type of position are a chemistry lab supervisor in a hospital, a nursing supervisor in a nursing home, a food services supervisor in an assisted living facility and a case management supervisor in a managed care company. Many of these individuals are trained in a clinical or technical field, such as X-ray technology, ultrasound or nursing, and have come up through the ranks.

Manager

The next management level is department manager, or department head. These individuals are responsible for an entire department in a hospital, nursing home or other health care organization. An environmental services manager in a nursing home, a health information management (also known as medical records) department head in a hospital, and a project manager in a consulting firm are all at this management level. Many of these individuals have formal management training (a bachelor's or master's degree or other training program) and/or certification in their specific discipline other than management.

Director

The level above department manager is often called director, although some organizations refer to their managers as directors. Director usually implies the management of a broad function in the company, such as director of public relations or director of staff development, who is responsible for their specific area in multiple departments and often for the entire organization. Managers in these roles may have clinical experience (e.g., certified oncology manager or registered record administrator).

In health care systems with corporate structures, like Community Health Systems and Hospital Corporation of America (two national hospital chains), the title of director is often used for individuals with corporate or systemwide responsibility for a function such as the director of materials management who is in charge of this function for all of the hospitals and other facilities in the system. Another example of a corporate director is the director of managed care at a smaller hospital system in the New York area, Atlantic Health.

Physicians

Physicians assume management roles, as well. These include the head of a clinical department in a hospital (e.g., medicine, surgery, obstetrics), the head of a clinical section in a large hospital (e.g., cardiology, urology) and various positions in hospitals that are administrative in nature, including medical director, chief medical officer, director of performance improvement, director of clinical effectiveness and medical director of a managed care organization. Many of these physician-executives obtain management degrees and attend management training courses prior to or after achieving these positions.

Executive-level

There are several designations for executive-level management in health care organizations. One title sequence uses administrator to signify the highest management level. In this scheme, there are associate administrators and assistant administrators. In hospitals and nursing homes that use these titles, the administrator is the highest ranking executive responsible for the entire organization. Associate administrators and assistant administrators report to this individual and are responsible for multiple departments and/or large functional areas. A common variation of this structure is president and chief executive officer, executive and senior vice presidents and vice presidents. For the most part, the roles and responsibilities of these individuals correspond to the first set of titles. Another set of titles designates executive director as the top person, and associate and assistant executive director for the top managers reporting to this individual. Those who hold these positions may have worked their way up through the management ranks and almost always have graduate degrees in health care management, business administration or a similar discipline.

Corporate management

In health systems, multihospital organizations or hospitals operating other facilities, such as nursing homes and ambulatory care centers, there is also a corporate management level. These executives have system responsibilities for the operations and specific functions (e.g., financial management) for the entire organization and usually have the title corporate director or vice

Visit Vault at **www.vault.com** for insider company profiles, expert advice, career message boards, expert resume reviews, the Vault Job Board and more.

VAULT CAREER LIBRARY   269

president. There is also a corporate president or chief executive officer and a corporate chief financial officer. These companies may be regional, national or international and either for-profit or nonprofit. They may be comprised of one type of health care facility, such as a nursing home, or many types, such as hospitals, physician practices and insurance companies. Manor Care, a for-profit chain, for example, operates long-term care facilities throughout the country. Kaiser Permanente is comprised of physician practices, affiliated hospitals and provides various insurance plans.

In an academic setting, deans and university vice presidents often have overall responsibilities for the hospitals and other health care facilities in the organization. The health care executives at the hospital or other health care facilities report to these individuals.

Looking to the future

New roles and positions continue to evolve. Administrators and managers for organizational effectiveness, and managers of clinical effectiveness are two examples.

And there is good reason to believe that as the health care system continues to evolve, new roles for managers will be created. These positions may be in areas of outcomes management, health education, information systems and ambulatory services. As access to health and health care increases via the Internet, people have more information on which to base their health care decisions. This will lead to increased accountability in terms of quality of care and health outcomes. Health information systems managers will be needed to develop ways to compile, store and share the data that is used in diagnosing and treating illness. The promotion of healthy lifestyles has become a high priority and will continue to be driven by health education. The need to control escalating health care costs will continue to result in less health care provided in expensive inpatient settings and more in ambulatory care settings. Alternatives to institutional long-term care will also have an impact. New models for the provision of care to the growing elderly population are being developed and tested. One such demonstration project is PACE (programs of all-inclusive care for the elderly). These programs provide comprehensive primary care, acute care and long-term care services to individuals as an alternative to nursing home admission. An interdisciplinary team develops care plans for program enrollees, and Medicare and Medicaid reimburse services provided on a capitation (pre-determined monthly payment per enrollee) basis.

Government policy and regulation will play a major role in shaping new management positions in a number of ways. Limiting Medicare reimbursement for specific procedures (e.g., surgeries) and treatments, and reporting requirements for infection rates and hospital acquired infections will further stimulate the growth of ambulatory care. Government reporting requirements for infections rates and hospital acquired infections will result in an increase in the number of quality improvement professionals and managers. All of these factors contribute to field that is expected to expand and diversify for years to come.

Physical Therapy Careers

What is physical therapy?

Physical therapy is a growing profession with four areas of practice: examination of individuals with impairment, functional limitation, and disability; treatment of impairment and functional limitation through therapeutic intervention, which includes exercise, patient education and application of modalities; consultation; and research. Physical therapists evaluate ill or injured persons to determine what functional limitations are present. For example, a young man who suffers from spinal cord injury will have strength and flexibility limitations in various muscle groups depending on the level of injury. A young woman with multiple sclerosis may have functional limitations in balance and coordination. Initial evaluations performed by the physical therapist include measurements on a wide battery of abilities.

Physical therapists measure an individual's capability in domains, including strength, endurance, flexibility, coordination, balance, gait, skin integrity and ability to perform simple activities of daily living. After initial evaluation of a patient, the physical therapist will identify a set of problems with physical function and assess how these problems may best be approached through exercise, massage or a modality (treatment applications other than exercise, such as hot/cold packs, ultrasound (healing through deep sound technique) or electrical stimulation).

Physical therapists today also act as consultants through their knowledge of exercise, and those in clinical and academic settings are also involved in research projects to determine whether the treatment interventions they are currently using are grounded in theory and to determine how best to improve upon interventions. In today's health care arena, physical therapists must be patient advocates; that is, balance the dual roles of providing expert information to patients on all types of disease and injuries, allowing the patient to play an active role in choosing options for treatment.

Where do physical therapists work?

Physical therapists work in a variety of settings, including acute care hospitals, rehabilitation centers, fitness centers, nursing homes, schools and private practice.

Acute care

The acute care setting is fast-paced and requires the physical therapist to work as a member of an interdisciplinary team that may include a social worker, doctor, nurse, occupational therapist and speech therapist. As a member of the acute care team, the physical therapist sees patients immediately after acute injury and illness, and often evaluates patients before and after surgery. For instance, an 85-year-old woman suffering from a fracture to the hip may require a total hip replacement. The therapist must evaluate this patient's strength, range of motion, balance and coordination after the injury, before surgery and after surgery. Exercise intervention would be cautious and determined by level of pain and flexibility limitations.

Rehabilitation

Rehabilitation centers focus on returning patients to a way of life that most resembles what life was like prior to injury. Physical therapists will often see patients every day or three times a week, and work over a period of three months or more to enable a spinal cord-injured patient to be able to move from a bed to a chair, or to enable a brain-injured patient to walk 200 feet without falling.

Fitness

When a physical therapist works in a fitness center, his focus is on exercise, either as prevention to illness or as a way to maintain a healthy lifestyle. A physical therapist may also evaluate and treat minor sports injuries that occur as a result of excessive or ill-advised exercise. The fitness center therapist may work with persons with or without disabilities who wish to stay healthy through exercise.

Nursing home

A physical therapist working in a nursing home or skilled nursing facility (SNF) needs to be comfortable with and skilled at working with the old, severely disabled and terminally ill population. The major difference for the physical therapist working in the nursing home or skilled nursing facility is that the patients he or she sees will not be discharged to home. They will stay at the respective facility their whole lives, and this difference can take an emotional toll on the physical therapist, as patients often suffer from depression.

Schools

A physical therapist working in the school system sees the very young client versus the very old. In the United States, and some other parts of the world, children with disabilities are integrated into schools with the non-disabled. The disabled

Visit Vault at www.vault.com for insider company profiles, expert advice, career message boards, expert resume reviews, the Vault Job Board and more.

VAULT CAREER LIBRARY

271

pediatric population needs the services of physical therapists, occupational therapists and often speech therapists. The physical therapist working in the public schools works a September-to-June schedule with summers off, and daily working hours often vary. School systems also require that a physical therapist work as a member of a interdisciplinary team (teacher, parent, student, physical therapist, occupational therapist and speech therapist), but the therapist will have more autonomy than the hierarchy of an acute care hospital allows.

Evaluation by physical therapists

When a physical therapist evaluates a patient (regardless of whether she is working in a direct access or non-direct access state), evaluation is divided into two parts. There is a subjective portion of the evaluation, in which the therapist listens to the patient's history and story of injury or illness, and there is an objective portion, where the therapist conducts a series of tests for strength, flexibility, balance, coordination, skin integrity and more. Physical therapists learn not only to be compassionate and attentive listeners but also to be acute observers of physical strengths and deficits. She is looking to connect a deficit in an area, such as strength or balance, with a "functional" deficit. In other words, a deficit on a quantitative test is connected to what portion of the patient's physical function and quality of life is being affected. Once limitations are found, the physical therapist writes down, or "documents," baseline measures and later compares these with how far the client progressed or improved with treatment.

Academics and clinicians in the field of physical therapy are focused on providing treatment guided by empirical evidence. Compared to the fields of psychology and medicine, for example, the emphasis on empirical evidence to justify treatment is more recent in physical therapy. Progressive resistive exercise (exercise using increasing amount of weight resistance with a specified number of repetitions) has been used to strengthen musculature for at least a century, and consistent systematic reviews of randomized clinical trials to determine whether progressive resistive exercise strengthens muscles more effectively than no exercise have only been conducted in physical therapy over the past 20 years. In today's health care environment, students and practicing physical therapists demand evidence supporting the proven effects of treatments they are using and that such treatments can be verified with published research. Students entering the field of physical therapy today will encounter colleagues who have published, taught, developed a clinical expertise niche or done a little of it all. The possibilities in the field are endless. Today, the American Physical Therapy Association urges all practicing physical therapists to enroll in continuing education classes to keep skills up to date and with a scientific edge. Most professionals do so gladly and are often reimbursed by the sites/programs at which they work.

Physical therapy educational programs strive to provide students with as much about what it is like to have a disability, injury or illness as possible. PT students not only study the anatomy and physiology of the human body but also participate in discussions and courses centering around the psychosocial needs of persons with disabilities. PT programs include sections on the legal ramifications of being disabled and PTs in and out of school must stay up to date on all aspects of health care policy and how it affects their patients through continuing education, referred journals and the media.

Physical therapists must promote the power of exercise, both aerobic and anaerobic. Aerobic exercise (e.g., riding a bike for 15 minutes or more, vigorous walking for 30 minutes, running for 10 minutes, swimming) increases circulation to the heart, improves lung capacity and increases endurance for greater periods of exercise. An individual recovering from a heart attack or stroke with the proper precautions will benefit greatly from aerobic exercise as improved circulation, cardiovascular health and aerobic endurance has been proven to protect against future heart attacks or strokes. Aerobic exercise is beneficial to all ages and for many illnesses. (There is currently an obesity epidemic among America's children and aerobic exercise is directly linked to a healthy weight in children.) Anaerobic exercise is exercise of shorter duration where the emphasis is on force output versus sustained activity. Examples of anaerobic exercise would be a bench press of fewer than three repetitions, jumping from a standing position in basketball, or a wrestler pinning an opponent down in fewer than three minutes. Anaerobic exercise challenges muscles to their ultimate force output and stretches fibers to increase muscle bulk. Physical therapists use anaerobic exercise to increase muscle strength in patients who are weakened through many different illnesses and injury.

Physical therapists "prescribe" exercise for infants, children, young and older adults, and those considered to be very old (85 and up). Public health experts today are calling on physical therapists for advice and consultation on all types of morbidity epidemics, such as childhood obesity, cardiovascular disease and osteoporosis; so, in many cases, physical therapists can augment clinical practice (clinical practice is defined as the evaluation and treatment of patients in need of physical therapy services) with private consultation to companies, nonprofit organizations or schools. Aside from knowing "how much and what kind" of exercise to prescribe, physical therapists should also know all contraindications (when not to prescribe) exercise.

Physical therapists use their hands to work, called "manual therapy" in PT vernacular. All physical therapists have the ability to do manual therapy and are schooled in different techniques of massage and mobilization (moving soft tissue and bones manually). However, some physical therapists find career tracks that take them away from direct contact with the patient. Physical therapists who become teachers and administrators will be less adept at manual therapy techniques because of lack of daily practice than those who evaluate and treat patients for a living. Some physical therapists become famous because of the effectiveness of their manual skills. Ted Corbitt is a renowned manual therapist who gained a national reputation over more than 25 years at the International Center for the Disabled in New York. A long-distance runner, he also created the idea for the New York City marathon with Fred Lebow.

Manual therapy includes techniques for stretching, strengthening and reducing pain. Physical therapists may use massage as a manual technique for reduction of pain. Techniques include: effleurage, a massage technique from Sweden in which broad strokes are used to increase circulation throughout the body; acupressure, which identifies trigger points through deep pressure; and friction massage, quick, brisk movements in the direction opposite fibers' alignment to interrupt neuronal pain signals and increase circulation. Depending on the type of injury, a therapist may choose effleurage to relax tense musculature throughout the body, trigger point massage to release a specific tight muscle (the trapezius, for example, is often tight due to poor posture) or friction massage for an injury like a sprained ankle, in which specific massage at the site of pain can compliment rest, ice and elevation. Physical therapists also perform mobilization techniques, a method by which tissue is moved to reduce pain. There are four grades of mobilization (1-4), from most gentle to more forceful pressure. PTs also perform myofascial treatment (moving the fascia of the body to reduce pain) without instruments, only hands. Myofascial treatment has been proven very effective with chronic pain patients. Craniosacral therapy is another type of manual treatment in which the cranium (the skull) and the sacrum (the portion of the backbone between the coccyx and the low back) are mobilized and massaged to relieve pain. Craniosacral therapy is effective in the reduction of migraine headaches, arthritic pain and many types of chronic pain.

When physical therapists are not treating patients with manual therapy or exercise, they may be providing so-called "modality" treatments, which include use of whirlpools, paraffin treatments (hot wax), electrical stimulation or ultrasound (healing by sound waves). Whirlpool treatment may be used to clean wounds after injury, and also helps decrease swelling. Paraffin is often used for the hands and feet, to relieve arthritis-related joint pain. Electrical stimulation is often used after a neurological injury, such as stroke, to stimulate nerve action potential and regain movement. Ultrasound is used to decrease pain and increase circulation after any injury, and the theory is that sound waves make this possible.

Physical therapists also provide their patients with advice about their physical problems, providing tips for reducing physical stress and strain, options for exercise once at home, as well as counsel on postural alignment, healthy work environments, even the right shoes.

As physical therapy moves from requiring a master's degree to a clinical doctorate, physical therapists are performing not only evaluation but also functional physical diagnosis, as a doctor would. In the past, physical therapists were only expected to evaluate and treat patients, but the increasing number of clinical doctorates in the field is elevating those therapists' role in the treatment process.

Visit Vault at www.vault.com for insider company profiles, expert advice, career message boards, expert resume reviews, the Vault Job Board and more.

VAULT CAREER LIBRARY 273

Not all personnel in the field of physical therapy are licensed to evaluate and treat patients. The two professional rungs in the field of physical therapy are the physical therapist and the physical therapist assistant. A physical therapist assistant (PTA) is an individual who completes a two-year associate's degree undergraduate program and is able to provide treatment only under the direction of a physical therapist; a PTA is not licensed to evaluate patients. Nonprofessional personnel include physical therapy aides, who provide setup, maintenance of treatment area and scheduling services.

To help individuals achieve maximum functional capabilities in order to continue to live as full a life as possible, physical therapists set short-term and long-term goals at the time of evaluation for all patients. An example of a short-term goal for a patient with a low back injury may be to decrease the pain level from a level of 9/10 (extreme pain) to 7/10 (moderate-high level pain). An example of a long-term goal for a patient with low back injury may be to have the patient be able to return to work or school. Physical therapists are trained to write all goals as measurable items, primarily because insurance companies reimburse objective and quantifiable measures. It's important to look for places of employment that allow enough time for documentation of these goals and other note-writing. Increasingly, due to managed care, the complexity of federal and non-federal insurance rules and patient liability issues, there is more and more paperwork required by all professionals working with patients. Daily duties for the physical therapist involve not only evaluating and treating patients but also writing down all findings and treatment in measurable terms carefully and consistently. A good place of employment allows the physical therapist enough time for note-writing so that the copious paperwork stays under control and the therapist does not have to stay late after hours to keep up with it. Many places of employment now encourage PTs to input data into a computer, thus saving time for the therapist and standardizing note-writing across the organization.

While typical diagnoses physical therapists evaluate and treat include orthopedic injuries, such as bone fractures or muscle strains/sprains, neurological conditions, such as stroke and spinal cord injury, cardiovascular conditions, including asthma, and heart conditions, physical therapists treat conditions that affect a myriad of systems in the body. And people often have more than one problem at a time, which is referred to as a dual diagnosis. Increasingly, patients are more knowledgeable about medical conditions largely because of Internet access, so physical therapists often evaluate patients who have researched their own condition. This means that the PT sometimes has to spend time re-educating the patient with accurate information about physical therapy procedures, so it's critical that the PT have a love of lifelong learning to stay abreast of all the changes in health care treatments.

Nursing

Nurses work both inside and outside hospitals. Typical nursing jobs include: medical-surgical nurses caring for hospitalized people, nurse practitioners providing outpatient care for chronic diseases, and RNs (registered nurses) supervising support staff in long-term care facilities. A variety of full-time, part-time and flexible-hours positions are available around the world for nurses educated in the U.S. Demand and salaries for nurses are rapidly growing in the U.S. By 2020, the demand is expected to be nearly double that of 2005.

Nursing is a challenging profession, yet there are many opportunities to advance. Within a given institution, RNs may move from a staff to a management position, often within only a year or two. RNs may specialize and further their careers by taking additional certification or a graduate degree. RNs with flexible schedules may work part time when raising a family, then go to full time. It is very common for RNs to maintain two or more jobs at once, due to the high demand for experienced nurses and the prevalence of part-time flexible work. The career opportunities vary widely with educational preparation and work location.

Nursing specialties

Clinical specialties in nursing correspond with many medical specialties, such as medical-surgical, pediatrics, women's health, geriatrics, family practice, intensive care, home care, long-term care and public health.

Nursing careers are also plentiful in specialties such as informatics, education, administration and research. Nurse informaticists are in great demand for the development and implementation of clinical documentation systems. Nurse educators are needed to educate new nurses to feed the overall strong demand. Nurse administrators are important to guide the work of health care, and nurse researchers are essential to contribute to our knowledge of effective health care.

Basic nursing skills

All nurses must be skilled at working with people and at applying their knowledge of physiology and pathophysiology to patients' potential and actual health problems. Nursing skills include communication, physical examination, diagnosing problems, problem-solving with the patient, intervening with patient education and technical procedures, coordinating care across providers and sites, and advocating for the best care for the patient.

Communication

Communication is the foundation of working with people; nurses learn verbal communication skills, such as reflective listening, repeating, summarizing and clarifying. Good communication facilitates relationship-building with patients, families and other members of the health care team, such as physicians and other therapists. Much communication is written out to document the care given. Nurses must be able to write clearly and concisely to describe the assessment, diagnosis and plan for each patient.

Skilled educators

Nurses must be skilled at educating patients and families. Research shows that the most frequent nursing intervention in most settings is teaching and counseling. The first step in teaching is assessment of the patient's baseline knowledge, so that time is not spent going over information that is already known. Assessment also allows for clarification and correction of any prior inaccurate information. Subsequently, education will fill in gaps in knowledge pertaining to the diagnoses, goals or plan of care. Often, nurses will teach about the normal functions of the body and how disease disrupts them. Recommended treatments can be explained in turn. In addition, after a risk assessment, nurses will teach how to prevent common problems that could complicate recovery and limit years of healthy life. One recommended principle of education is to transmit the teaching in several ways, using pictures and written materials, as well as discussion. For example, to teach a new diabetic, pictures of the pancreas and digestive organs and photos or videos of insulin injection technique will be used along with discussion and written instruction. Nowadays, multimedia and Internet-based presentations are often available for common problems. One evolving aspect of patient education, considered to be an aspect of informatics used by all nurses, is for the nurse to evaluate educational materials and direct patients and families to the most up-to-date and accurate sources.

Case management

Care coordination, or case management, is one of the most important nursing skills for today's complex environment in health care. Many different health care professionals may be involved in this function, but because of their close and frequent patient contact in all health care settings, nurses often take the lead role. Depending on the problems the patient faces, there may be a need for a myriad of health care services, such as social work, medical equipment, medications, transportation, legal advice, housing, nutrition support, housekeeping support, safety and communications support. Nurses are often in a position to serve as "command central" to coordinate these services to preserve and restore health. Indeed, a required part of planning a hospital discharge is to assess the resources and environment where the patient is going next.

Advocacy

Advocacy is a nursing skill useful on both micro and macro levels. An individual patient may benefit from nursing advocacy when, for example, he has no health insurance and little cash to purchase a medication prescribed by a physician. The nurse, knowing the relative costs of equally effective medications, could approach the physician and advocate for a less expensive prescription. On the macro level, nurses belong to professional organizations, such as the American Nurses Association

Visit Vault at www.vault.com for insider company profiles, expert advice, career message boards, expert resume reviews, the Vault Job Board and more.

VAULT CAREER LIBRARY   275

(ANA), which maintain lobbyists to speak up for legislation to benefit the health of all Americans. ANA lobbyists also speak in favor of specific measures to benefit the profession of nursing, such as funding for collegiate nursing education, and state and federal laws pertaining to the licensure of foreign-trained nurses. Over the years, nursing advocacy has been key in making birth control legal and available and improving the health of low-income and vulnerable families.

A Day in the Life: Medical-Surgical Hospital Nurse

Dan Bratton, RN, BSN, works rotating shifts at the medium sized (220 beds) Good Samaritan General Hospital. For two weeks, Dan works 7 a.m. to 3:30 p.m., the next two weeks will be 3 to 11:30 p.m., and the next two weeks will be 11 p.m. to 7:30 a.m. (The 30-minute overlap between shifts gives the nurses that are leaving some time to report to the nurses taking over the important events that pertain to each patient.) Dan graduated six months ago and this is his first position in a medical-surgical unit. Today, Dan is working the day shift, 7 a.m. to 3:30 p.m. The day shift is busy because this is when physicians come in to see their patients and many diagnostic tests and therapies are scheduled.

6:45 a.m. Dan arrives a few minutes early so he can change into his hospital-supplied scrub suit and get himself organized for the day.

7 a.m. Dan's supervisor gives him a list of eight patients to care for. Dan knows two of the patients from his previous shift; six of the patients are new. They range in age from 25 to 85 and their diagnoses include diabetes mellitus, congestive heart failure, two days post-stroke and acute renal failure.

7:05 a.m. Dan listens to the report of all the nurses going off shift, paying particular attention to his eight patients. Because the report is tape recorded, any questions must be asked of the night shift leader.

7:30 a.m. Dan goes to the patients' records to check each care plan, describing tasks and schedules for the day. Each patient's physician will be coming in early to go around to see his/her patients. Dan will check on any discharges scheduled and any therapy or diagnostic testing that requires the patient to travel to another area of the hospital. Then he plans his day around these events and the medication and care schedule for each patient.

8 a.m. Dan accompanies the physicians to report on any changes in the past 24 hours and to gather information on what is next in the physician's plan. He discovers that the diabetic patient is to be discharged to home and he will meet with family members to reinforce the self-care needed to balance treatment for diabetes: exercise, nutrition and medication. Also, one of the post-stroke patients is going to be moved to a rehabilitation facility. Dan talks with those family members to answer questions, provide reassurance and explain the goals of rehab. He shows them a web site, www.medlineplus.gov, where they can find specific information about stroke, appropriate rehabilitation, safety and home care, and any medications that may be prescribed later.

9 a.m. Dan receives and stores the single-dose medications for his patients, which have been brought to the unit by a pharmacy technician. He has to check the physicians' documentation for new orders and authorize them, and set them in motion for each of his eight patients. The day goes very quickly, even without any real crises arising. Medications and treatments must be given before patients go to their therapy with rehabilitation or before they go to have radiology testing or treatments.

10 a.m. Most of the patient discharges occur before noon. The patients who are going home need to have specific discharge instructions, as well as an escort to leave the hospital safely. As soon as one patient leaves, another is admitted, so Dan greets the new patient and completes paperwork setting up a nursing care plan.

11 a.m. Dan "rounds" on his patients again before lunch to check blood pressures and other vital signs, and to keep an eye on everyone.

12 p.m. This is a good day. Dan gets to relax and eat lunch with a colleague. They discuss a continuing education program on diabetes that they will attend over the weekend. According to their state's Board of Nursing regulations, they need 30 hours of continuing education every two years in order to renew their license to practice.

12:30 p.m. Dan and his colleague return to work. He sees that one of his patients has called for help. When he goes to the patient's room, he finds that she became dizzy and has fallen on her way to the toilet. He helps her back to bed and assesses her condition. Fortunately, she appears to have no broken bones and the dizziness has passed. He cautions the patient not to stand up quickly but to give herself a couple of minutes sitting at the bedside before standing and walking. He also encourages her to seek assistance when she wants to get out of bed. After checking the patient's medication list, Dan phones the patient's physician and suggests some medication changes that may decrease the patient's tendency toward dizziness. Dan knows that the circumstances around this event are very important because his hospital is working to decrease the overall rate of falls and patient injuries.

1:30 p.m. By this time, Dan must administer another round of medications and treatments to his patient group. He checks the physician orders to find new IVs, blood tests and referrals were ordered. Dan checks with the unit secretary to see that these were ordered. Dan talks with one of the medical school students about patient falls and how to prevent them.

2:30 p.m. Dan speaks with a nursing school faculty member on the telephone. She is looking for a clinical practice site for students in the summer rotation. He agrees to work with undergraduate student nurses and to recruit fellow staff nurses to take other nurses. He does a final round to check each patient's condition before he leaves for the day.

3 p.m. Dan gives a report to the group of nurses coming on for the next shift. He speaks to his supervisor regarding his preference for next month's schedule that is being planned. (Some hospitals have made self-scheduling available to the nursing staff.) Then, Dan has a few moments to document the care he provided during the past eight hours. He enters data into a computerized record that contains easy templates for routine care. After that, it is time to relax for a moment!

Visit Vault at **www.vault.com** for insider company profiles, expert advice, career message boards, expert resume reviews, the Vault Job Board and more.

VAULT CAREER LIBRARY   277

Employer Directory

Aetna Inc.
151 Farmington Avenue
Hartford, CT 06156
Phone: (860) 273-0123
Fax: (860) 273-3971
Toll free: (800) 872-3862
www.aetna.com

AMERIGROUP Corporation
4425 Corporation Lane
Virginia Beach, VA 23462
Phone: (757) 490-6900
Fax: (757) 222-2330
www.amerigrp.com

Applied Biosystems Inc.
850 Lincoln Centre Drive
Foster City, CA 99404
Norwalk, CT 06856-5435
Phone: (650) 638-5800
Fax: (650) 638-5884
Toll free: (800) 327-3002
www.appliedbiosystems.com

Beckman Coulter, Inc.
4300 North Harbor Boulevard
Fullerton, CA 92834-3100
Phone: (714) 871-4848
Fax: (714) 773-8283
Toll free: (800) 233-4685
www.beckman.com

Beverly Enterprises, Inc.
1000 Beverly Way
Fort Smith, AR 72919-0001
Phone: (479) 201-2000
www.berverlycares.com

Blue Cross and Blue Shield Association
225 North Michigan Avenue
Chicago, IL 60601-7680
Phone: (312) 297-6000
Fax: (312) 297-6609
www.bcbs.com

Boston Scientific Corporation
1 Boston Scientific Place
Natick, MA 01760-1537
Phone: (508) 650-8000
Fax: (508) 650-8910
www.bostonscientific.com

Caremark Pharmacy Services
211 Commerce Street, Suite 800
Nashville, TN 37201
Phone: (615) 743-6600
Fax: (205) 733-9780
www.caremark.com

CIGNA Corporation
2 Liberty Place
1601 Chestnut Street
Philadelphia, PA 19192
Phone: (215) 761-1000
Fax: (215) 761-5515
www.cigna.com

Community Health Systems, Inc.
4000 Meridian Boulevard
Franklin, TN 37067
Phone: (615) 465-7000
www.chs.net

Coventry Health Care, Inc.
6705 Rockledge Drive, Suite 900
Bethesda, MD 20817
Phone: (301) 581-0600
Fax: (301) 493-0731
www.cvty.com

DaVita Inc.
601 Hawaii Street
El Segundo, CA 90245
Phone: (310) 536-2400
Fax: (310) 536-2675
Toll free: (800) 310-4872
www.davita.com

Express Scripts, Inc.
1 Express Way
St. Louis, MO 63121
Phone: (314) 996-0900
www.express-scripts.com

Fresenius Medical Care AG & Co. KGaA
Else-Kröner-Straße 1
61346 Bad Homburg
Germany
Phone: +49-6172-609-0
Fax: +49-6172-608-2488
www.fmc-ag.com

HCA Inc.
1 Park Plaza
Nashville, TN 37203
Phone: (615) 344-9551
Fax: (615) 344-2266
www.hcahealthcare.com

Health Management Associates, Inc.
5811 Pelican Bay Boulevard, Suite 500
Naples, FL 34108-2710
Phone: (239) 598-3131
Fax: (239) 598-2705
www.hma-corp.com

Health Net, Inc.
21650 Oxnard Street
Woodland Hills, CA 91367
Phone: (818) 676-6000
Fax: (818) 676-8591
Toll free: (800) 291-6911
www.healthnet.com

HealthSouth Corporation
1 HealthSouth Parkway
Birmingham, AL 35243
Phone: (205) 967-7116
Fax: (205) 969-3543
Toll free: (888) 476-8849
www.healthsouth.com

Henry Schein, Inc.
135 Duryea Road
Melville, NY 11747
Phone: (631) 843-5500
Fax: (631) 843-5658
www.henryschein.com

Employer Directory, cont.

Hillenbrand, Inc.
1 Batesville Boulevard
Batesvill, IN 47006-7798
Phone: (812) 934-7500
Fax: (812) 934-7613
www.hillenbrandinc.com

Hill-Rom Holdings
1069 State Route 46 East
Batesville, IN 47006-9167
Phone: (812) 934-7777
Fax: (812) 934-8329
ir.hill-rom.com

Humana Inc.
The Humana Building
500 West Main Street
Louisville, KY 40202
Phone: (502) 580-1000
Fax: (502) 580-3677
Toll free: (800) 448-6262
www.humana.com

Johns Hopkins Health System
600 North Wolfe Street
Baltimore, MD 21287
Phone: (410) 955-5000
Fax: (410) 955-0890
www.hopkinshospital.org

Kaiser Permanente
1 Kaiser Plaza
Oakland, CA 94612
Phone: (510) 271-5800
Fax: (510) 267-7524
www.kaiserpermanente.org

Kindred Healthcare, Inc.
680 South 4th Street
Louisville, KY 40202-2412
Phone: (502) 596-7300
Fax: (502) 596-4170
Toll free: (800) 545-0749
www.kindredhealthcare.com

Laboratory Corporation of America Holdings
358 South Main Street
Burlington, NC 27215
Phone: (336) 229-1127
Fax: (336) 436-1205
www.labcorp.com

Magellan Health Services, Inc.
55 Nod Road
Avon, CT 06001
Phone: (860) 507-1900
Fax: (860) 507-1990
Toll free: (800) 410-8312
www.magellanhealth.com

Mariner Health Care, Inc.
1 Ravinia Drive, Suite 1250
Atlanta, GA 30346
Phone: (678) 443-7000
Fax: (770) 393-8054
www.marinerhealth.com

Mayo Foundation for Medical Education and Research
200 1st Street SW
Rochester, MN 55905
Phone: (507) 284-2511
Fax: (507) 284-0161
www.mayo.edu

Medco Health Solutions, Inc.
100 Parsons Pond Drive
Franklin Lakes, NJ 07417-2603
Phone: (201) 269-3400
Fax: (201) 269-1109
www.medco.com

Medical Mutual of Ohio
2060 East 9th Street
Cleveland, OH 44115-1355
Phone: (216) 687-7000
Fax: (216) 687-6044
Toll free: (800) 700-2583
www.mmoh.com

Medtronic, Inc.
710 Medtronic Parkway
Minneapolis, MN 55432-5604
Phone: (763) 514-4000
Fax: (763) 514-4879
Toll free: (800) 328-2518
www.medtronic.com

Quest Diagnostics Incorporated
3 Giralda Farms
Madison, NJ 07940
Phone: (201) 393-5000
Fax: (201) 729-8920
Toll free: (800) 222-0446
www.questdiagnostics.com

Sierra Health Services, Inc.
2724 North Tenaya Way
Las Vegas, NV 89128
Phone: (702) 242-7000
Fax: (702) 242-9711
www.sierrahealth.com

St. Jude Medical, Inc.
1 Lillehei Plaza
St. Paul, MN 55117-9983
Phone: (651) 483-2000
Toll free: (800) 328-9634
www.sjm.com

Stryker Corporation
2825 Airview Boulevard
Kalamazoo, MI 49002-1802
Phone: (269) 385-2600
Fax: (269) 385-1062
www.stryker.com

Sun Healthcare Group, Inc.
18831 Von Karman, Suite 400
Irvine, CA 92612
Phone: (949) 255-7100
Fax: (949) 255-7054
Toll free: (800) 729-6600
www.sunh.com

Employer Directory, cont.

Tenet Healthcare Corporation
13737 Noel Road
Dallas, TX 75240
Phone: (469) 893-2200
Fax: (469) 893-8600
www.tenethealth.com

UnitedHealth Group Incorporated
UnitedHealth Group Center
9900 Bren Road East
Minnetonka, MN 55343
Phone: (952) 936-1300
Fax: (952) 936-1819
Toll free: (800) 328-5979
www.unitedhealthgroup.com

Universal Health Services
Universal Corporate Center
367 South Gulph Road
King of Prussia, PA 19406-0958
Phone: (610) 768-3300
Fax: (610) 768-3336
www.uhsinc.com

WellPoint, Inc.
120 Monument Circle
Indianapolis, IN 46204
Phone: (317) 488-6000
Fax: (317) 488-6028
www.wellpoint.com

High Tech

Industry Overview

It's a tech, tech world

As industries go, the tech sector is a fairly new one, but is revolutionizing the way people conduct themselves socially and in business. Technology has been so rapidly integrated into the fabric of modern life that the semiconductor chip, a device that hardly existed 50 years ago, has become a commonplace part of modern life. The sector is fairly broad, and encompasses companies that manufacture hardware—the guts of the computer—like hard drives, chips, circuit boards and wiring, and software, the programs that run on said chips. Other companies offer their customers some combination of hardware and software—like Hewlett-Packard and Dell, who ship computers with operating systems and programs already installed.

Chips off the old block

Microchips are up there with the wheel and domesticated animals in terms of human inventions that have had a dramatic effect on history. The microchip as we know it—which consists of multiple circuits embedded in a semiconductive substrate—was invented by Jack Kilby, an employee of Texas Instruments, in 1958. The first semiconductors, which only had a handful of circuits, were initially used in highly-funded government projects, like the Apollo Moon mission and in the guidance systems for Minuteman missiles. As the production of chips became less expensive, they began their inexorable move into the realm of consumer goods during the late 1970s and early 1980s. Unlike those first microchips, which combined tens of circuits on a single chip, microchips produced today can have billions of circuits in an area that can fit on a fingertip.

While the first microchips were soldered together by hand in a lab, today's versions are assembled by building up multiple layers of silicon on a chip in clean rooms. Chip manufacturing involves hundreds of steps, which gradually build up the microscopic circuitry on the face of the chip. Chips are built on a substrate of pure silicon, called a wafer. A machine cuts wafers—which are about a millimeter thick—off of an enormous cylindrical crystal of pure silicon. After cutting, the surfaces of wafers are polished; any imperfections in the surface of the wafer will result in chips that do not function properly. As chip manufacturing technology improved, wafers increased in size from about four inches in the 1960s to 12 inches (30 cm) today; some memory chips are still made on smaller wafers. Anywhere from a few hundred to 1,000 can fit on a 30-centimeter wafer. After polishing, the wafer is transferred to a machine that coats the surface with an insulating layer of silicon dioxide a few atoms thick, which, in turn, is coated with a light-sensitive material called a photoresist. The wafer is then exposed to light filtered through a lithographic plate, which allows an acid etch bath to remove the photresist that was exposed to light, as well as some of the silicon underneath it. An atom-thick layer of metal, such as copper or aluminum, can be deposited on these exposed parts of the chip; when the photoresist is removed, only the metal remains to connect the various parts of the chip. Other electrical features can be added to the surface of the chip by implanting the silicon with a smattering of individual atoms, often of boron or arsenic, known as dopants. The boron or arsenic atoms are shot into the crystal structure of the silicon with a particle accelerator. Successive layers of insulating and conducting pathways are gradually built up by repeating these processes, often hundreds of consecutive times.

Since the electrical pathways of modern processor chips are measured in mere nanometers—billionths of an inch—nearly any errant piece of schmutz can short out a circuit. Therefore, chips must be manufactured in what are known as 'clean rooms,' where the ambient level of dust is significantly reduced by filtration. Workers in these environments also wear bunny suits, which protect the wafers from hair or skin cells that they might shed.

Visit Vault at www.vault.com for insider company profiles, expert advice, career message boards, expert resume reviews, the Vault Job Board and more.

VAULT CAREER LIBRARY 281

Bumpy road

The semiconductor industry is highly cyclical, prone to vertiginous highs and astonishing lows. This is partly due to the industry's high cost of entry; a fab or foundry, a plant where microchips are made, can take several years—not to mention $2 billion and change—to build. As the price of chips rises, more fabs are built; as they add their capacity to the marketplace, the price of chips falls. This has already happened several times over the course of the industry's history, notably in the 1980s, when Japanese manufacturers flooded the marketplace with inexpensive chips. The market reached a high in 1999—in time to fuel the tech boom—and again in 2004, in order to power the recovery from the tech bust.

In Soviet Russia, you power your devices

Tech isn't just chips, however—batteries present their own host of problems for designers of computer gadgets. In addition to adding to the size and weight of the product, they are often taxed by the demands of fueling features like bigger, brighter displays—for days at a time. Engineers are nearly at a loss to provide products that can stand up to the rigors of powering zippy processors, big displays and Internet connections between charges. As batteries are pushed to their limits, they can suddenly fail—or worse, explode.

One explosion-free plan for powering the next generation of cell phones would harvest power from the gadgets' human hosts. While this sounds like a premise for a horror movie, it's really quite clever. Carrying a cell phone while walking—having the device jiggling up and down in a purse or pocket—can generate a small charge, which can be stored in a capacitor for later use. Piezoelectric materials, which generate electricity when compressed, can be put beneath buttons to ease the battery's output during those epic games of Brick Breaker.

Giving the customers what they want

Speaking of those power-hungry gizmos, the overwhelming trend in the tech industry is to add more features to products. The scheme is a surefire crowd-pleaser: feature-laden gadgets attract customers and sell at a premium, and adding a chip that turns a cell phone into a music player doesn't contribute much to its manufacturing cost. This process, known as feature creep, has a downside, however. Consumers only spend about 20 minutes on average fussing around with a new product—and if they can't figure out all the bells and whistles in that period of time, they're likely to return it. While it may be easy and cheap to add more features, it's extremely difficult to design an elegant, easy-to-use interface for the device, instead of just adding more menus and buttons.

Tech Workers = Nerds?

When people think of IT workers, especially programmers and engineers, they often think of the ultimate nerd. They may get images of the lone man with a five o'clock shadow, messy hair and a pocket protector, sitting in a dark room and staring at a computer screen all day and night. Or, they may get an image of the espresso junkie who rides a Razor Scooter in the office, playing foosball and starting Nerf gun fights all day long. These stereotypes of IT are becoming less true.

The IT field has come to resemble traditional corporate culture more than it did during the dot-com heyday. IT employees must be able to communicate well and work sensitively with others, they must travel for some jobs, and they must deal with all sorts of environments to succeed.

Instead of wearing pocket protectors and bad hair, most successful tech workers know how to present themselves professionally to managers and non-tech departments. Increasingly, even programmers need to communicate constantly with analysts, business development offices, and other corporate departments.

Rather than work odd hours and obsess over minor code details, successful engineers know how to prioritize their tasks and follow project requirements efficiently. They need to be around during regular business hours in order to coordinate with business departments. They may work long hours, but that is usually to keep up with tight deadlines born from tighter budgets.

In a nutshell, many IT departments no longer have the time or money to accommodate the stereotypical nerd. While some tech offices still have foosball tables and video games in the office, the number of such offices has been dwindling for years. Companies have been downsizing, and employees have had to take on multiple roles. Workers simply cannot afford the time to fool around in the office, much less gain a reputation of doing so. Companies cannot afford to have departments full of antisocial geeks, since so much of business depends on smooth interdepartmental communication. Many companies have even engaged in efforts to make their tech employees more sociable and stronger communicators.

Contrary to the stereotypes, IT employees must often face a workplace higher in stress, higher in its demands and lacking in diversity.

Data, data everywhere

People are also producing more data than ever. Luckily, the cost of data storage is also falling, currently at a rate of around 15 percent every three months. While the cost of data storage has dropped precipitously—from $10,000 per megabyte in 1956 to less than $1 per gigabyte in 2008, the amount of data that people and businesses want to store has increased dramatically. A great deal of this data, especially the portion created by companies—from credit card transactions to funny cat pictures sent to the office via e-mail—must be saved for several years according to regulations like Sarbanes-Oxley. This translates into strong growth for the data-storage products industry, but stand clear of falling margins, since price competition in this sector can be intense.

One laptop per lap

Developing economies are a hot market for tech companies—and not just those who want to manufacture goods there. The wealth of the citizens in these countries is increasing dramatically, pushing people into a growing middle class. Combine that factor with competitive Western markets saturated with products and jaded consumers—and the solutions are obvious. The companies bringing the gospel of the byte to the citizens of growing economies have diverse motives for doing so, from increasing computer literacy among the world's poorest people to seeking profits and gaining market share. Nicholas Negroponte, a former MIT professor, has a plan to bring a $100 laptop (actual cost: $130) to poor people in developing countries. The laptops, whose design is not yet finalized, can be used as an e-book (with a black-and-white screen that can be read in sunlight), laptop or game device—and can also be networked over a wireless connection, just like conventional machines. The laptops run on a version of Fedora Linux, to encourage children to develop their own software, and also to keep prices down. The governments of Egypt and Argentina are particularly interested in the devices, which are expected to ship in the latter half of 2007.

Microsoft is pursuing customers in the developing world, partly in search of profits, and to curb the growth of free operating systems, which can erode the market share of Windows and its Office suite. In 2007, Microsoft announced that it would begin selling PCs aimed at children in India, which has not adopted the laptops for children initiative. The plan is intended to supplement education in areas where public schools may lack such necessities as running water, electricity, teachers and books. Microsoft's computer, which will cost about $500, or $100 more than some of the less expensive models, will come equipped with a Windows operating system, Word, Encarta and programs tailored to help children cram for school exams. The device isn't designed to get poor children up to speed with the Internet, but will help the company gain market share in

Visit Vault at www.vault.com for insider company profiles, expert advice, career message boards, expert resume reviews, the Vault Job Board and more.

VAULT CAREER LIBRARY   283

the growing Indian economy, where it has the potential to lose ground to less expensive machines running Linux—it hopes to grab one billion customers by 2015. Intel is also looking to sell low-cost computers in Asia in 2007. Aimed at middle-class customers, who make around $5,000 per year, the devices will cost about $300. Company officials say that despite the low prices, they are still making a profit.

An Apple a day

Microsoft is seeking new markets because its dominance at home is increasingly coming under threat. Apple—whose computers were once the purview of a small, rabid fringe of computer users—is now the mainstream. In the younger generation, it's hard to find someone who doesn't own some kind of iPod (and have it permanently welded to his ears). The iPhone has been a roaring success, as well—the company reported that it sold 1 million of them four months after the launch, and expects to make it an even 10 million by early 2009. However, the company is not just about spiffy consumer electronics—it's been gaining in the computer race as well. Although it still hangs behind industry behemoths Hewlett-Packard and Dell, its share of the pie has been growing—Apple holds over 20 percent of the U.S. personal computer market, up from single-digits just a few years ago. Industry pundits note that consumers enjoy Apple computers' modern-looking cases, pretty graphics and relative imperviousness to viruses.

The Scope of High Tech Careers

As befits such a large and diverse industry, there are a variety of jobs to please all types—not just shaggy guys with 1970s eyewear who think it perfectly reasonable to wear socks with sandals. Career options include semiconductor design and manufacture, programmers, systems designers, data storage experts and, of course, those much-maligned IT guys, who are a feature of nearly every sizeable business. The Bureau of Labor Statistics says that the tech sector is experiencing a period of rapid expansion, and will grow 40 percent between 2004 and 2014. While many jobs—including some software development and chip manufacturing jobs—are moving overseas, there will continue to be a demand for IT professionals in the U.S.

Prepare for odd questions

Some companies in the tech industry—notably Google—are notorious for their oddball interviewing tactics. Google actively seeks out techy types that have also written books or started their own companies, and has been known to recruit people by putting brainteasers on billboards. Not every company in the industry uses such off-the-wall strategies, however. Insiders report that interviews usually have several rounds—sometimes as many as three phone screens before a face-to-face interview. Interviews for jobs that require specific skills—like programming expertise—generally have a technical component where the job seeker must demonstrate his skills. Common interview questions of the non-brainteaser sort include the standard behavioral questions—"stories about leadership, teamwork, dealing with ambiguity, multi-tasking, project management, conflict management," according to one source at a major hardware company.

Getting your foot in the door

Tech companies frequently hire interns for the summer and during the school year. As the number of CS majors shrinks—down 49 percent from 2002 to 2007—the competition for the top candidates is heating up. In addition to the cachet of a big-ticket name on the student's resume, interns are showered with perks as if the tech bubble never burst. Google interns get free nosh—morning, noon and night—at the company's renowned café, while Microsoft interns can get free housing and transportation to and from work. There are also internship opportunities in the field for electrical and mechanical engineers and IT divisions are frequently in need of younger helpers to patiently teach executives how to send meeting requests in Outlook.

Not moving out, but moving up

Many workers in the tech industry are understandably worried about their jobs moving overseas. An Indian programmer is happy to work for a fraction of the cost of a programmer in Silicon Valley, for instance, and does the same work in about the same period of time. Though tech industry layoffs have slowed from the massive cuts seen in 2006 and 2007, the industry can still be mercurial. And, although some jobs are moving overseas, Americans are moving into positions that can only be done face-to-face—like sales or consulting. IBM uses mixed teams of U.S.-based consultants and programmers in India to design custom software for its consulting projects. The Tata consulting group has even hired 1,000 workers in the U.S., citing the importance of face time with clients. To stay ahead of the outsourcing wave, employees should be flexible and keep their skills up-to-date.

Categories of Tech Professionals

Let's take a look at three major categories of workers: hardware, software and support personnel.

Hardware

Hardware-oriented workers create and maintain electronic communications infrastructures. They build computers, which both businesses and home users buy. They also build large computers called servers, which mostly businesses buy. When businesses buy computers and servers, company hardware employees set up the computers, connecting them to each other and the server. This way, all of the computers have a common set of resources available to them, and all of the computers can communicate with each other. Hardware employees are often the ones who decide the architecture of the computer clusters and the resources they contain.

Software

Software employees create programs that use and manipulate computer infrastructures. Through typing code and commands into the computers, they design the software interfaces between people and hardware. They also use those interfaces to create utilities and applications that perform specific tasks like tracking business records.

Nowadays, they build systems for the Internet and other networks. They make sure that information flows efficiently between computers within an organization, or to and from a web site. At the same time, they keep the information safe, making sure that only authorized people can access sensitive information.

Support

The hardware and software infrastructures at most companies are so large and complex that separate departments must plan them and support them. Support role employees include people in customer care, leadership and managerial roles, and testing departments. Analysts and managers decide the future of business IT infrastructures. Constantly examining new technology and how it can make business more effective, they weigh the costs and benefits to buying new hardware or modifying existing systems. Quality assurance testers make sure that the systems perform as they were designed and planned. Performing tests and discovering the limits of the systems makes sure that the infrastructure investments are worth the cost and effort in the long run. Customer, sales and user support people make sure that company employees know how to use the systems, and that the systems are in good working order. They also help customers use the software, information or hardware that the company distributes.

Visit Vault at www.vault.com for insider company profiles, expert advice, career message boards, expert resume reviews, the Vault Job Board and more.

VAULT CAREER LIBRARY   285

Common Positions for Recent College Grads

Entry-level network employees

Desktop support or customer service workers (more specific information on these positions below) do the most basic network maintenance. These workers sit at their desks, receiving phone calls or e-mails from people who need help using any of the company's software or hardware. Specifically in the network capacity, they provide end user support for network-based applications and perform routine network repairs. Desktop support workers who work exclusively with network matters may be referred to as LAN support workers, or network maintenance workers. These support workers only deal with client machines and cables; they do not touch the server.

If people phone in and report network problems, like if an employee's client computer can no longer communicate with the network, the desktop or LAN support worker recommends solutions to the problem over the phone, such as reconfiguring the client operating system to detect the network. If that does not help, the support worker schedules and performs repairs on the client hardware and software. Such repairs can include: tightening loose network cables attached to the client machines, installing more RAM on client machines or reinstalling client application software. They also go all around the office configuring the individual client computers to communicate with the network.

Entry-level network employees make about $29,000 to $40,000 a year. They usually work regular 40-hour workweeks, although they must work after hours or weekends if the network requires maintenance or repairs at those times. These workers should know the common concepts and procedures of network repair and upkeep, but they usually rely on existing guidelines and instructions, reporting to a project leader or more senior LAN support worker.

In time, which can be as short as a year, the support worker can prove enough network competence and knowledge to become a junior network or systems administrator.

Junior administrators

Junior administrators are task-oriented employees who do basic server work. They do not research, gather data from managers or make planning decisions. Instead, they perform specific tasks given to them by senior admins. However, although they are junior, these admins do not tool with end-user applications or client machine operating systems. Those duties still belong to desktop support personnel. At the junior level, a lot of network and systems duties overlap.

Junior network administrators do basic network configuration and basic network maintenance, such as opening or closing server ports as needed. They also do a lot of the network monitoring. The computer programs that monitor networks produce warning messages if network problems arise, so junior administrators must watch for these messages.

"The junior sys admin also does basic configuration and maintenance," says Greg Land, a junior systems administrator for HotJobs.com. "If there's some kind of network problem, they might replace server memory modules, or replace server CPUs." Also, if the senior system adminstrator determines that a certain number of server resources need to be allocated for something like company e-mail, the junior system adminstrator configures the server software accordingly.

With experience and demonstrated competence, comes seniority. Within about two to four years, junior administrators can attain senior ranks. Both salary and responsibilities increase substantially here. While junior administrators are task-oriented, senior admins are project-oriented.

Junior software engineers

A recent college graduate with little experience could get a job as a junior software engineer. Inexperienced software engineers usually start off supporting existing software. They review and analyze the results of software tests, and they help to implement software by installing the programs or applications. They also debug and modify programs according to the direction of senior engineers.

They sit at their desks, in cubicles or in rooms of several engineers, typing on computer screens that are full of text windows. They use various utilities to map out program designs graphically, and they use many purely text interfaces to install or modify their software projects. Rather than developing entire software packages, they create small dependency programs or functions that the main programs use. Beginner developers may make $55,000 to $87,750 per year.

Good analytical and problem-solving skills are necessary for success here. And, at this point, their biggest asset is programming know-how. There are a lot of parts to the job, all of which involve sitting in front of a computer screen: aiding with small portions of program design, debugging existing portions of software, installing programs or dependencies, documenting and mapping programs, etc. These engineers may look like the typical nerd, with bad haircuts and five o'clock shadows, spending most of their time at text screens and cavorting with other like-minded engineers. Deadlines can be insanely demanding, and software engineers often work over 40 hours a week and on weekends.

Support specialists

Computer support specialists, or technical support specialists/workers, or customer service representatives, or helpdesk workers/technicians provide technical assistance to users over the phone or via e-mail. Using diagnostic programs, they help customers or fellow employees troubleshoot and repair their hardware or software. Support specialists also help users install hardware and software.

These workers sit at their desks taking calls and answering e-mails all day from people having problems using company hardware or software. More technically trained workers go around the office helping users install or repair their client computers. Other experienced ones may take more complicated technical calls from customers. "It's helpful for people entering IT to have experience in helpdesk, because it gives them exposure to a wide variety of issues on any level of an IT product," says Anthony Dickerson, a technical support worker from a proprietary banking software company.

Helpdesk positions also help technical people get used to dealing with customers and building professional relationships. In addition to that, helpdesk often teaches people to stay calm in bad situations. For example, Ingrid Johanns worked in technical support for a health care company. She relates, "The software guys were working on a system that would make automatic calls to patients, to remind them to do something (do an exercise, go to an appointment, etc.). And they screwed up. The system accidentally called people at two in the morning, and it would not stop calling until the recipient had listened to the message fully. Very bad. And my job at the time, being in customer support ... well, they had me call all the patients and apologize for the call. I wanted to kill those software guys. It was their fault—they should have made those TOTALLY AWKWARD calls. Anyway, you really learn how to call people and talk with them about anything. You get over that awkward feeling really fast by overdosing on awkwardness."

Support specialists must often help people who do not know much about computers, and they must typically answer questions that the product manuals often do not. Thus, specialists must communicate carefully with users to diagnose problems and walk the users through solutions. Good communication skills are paramount to advancement here. Good analytical and problem-solving skills are also essential.

Support specialists get different types of questions at different types of companies. Workers at a hardware sales company may get questions about how to manually configure computer components. Workers at an e-commerce site may get questions about how to access personal information through the company's web site.

Visit Vault at **www.vault.com** for insider company profiles, expert advice, career message boards, expert resume reviews, the Vault Job Board and more.

V/\ULT CAREER LIBRARY   287

Specialists also need to understand the various stresses that each business will offer. For instance, specialists at a financial web site may get many frantic phone calls from customers worried about their money. "I've had a customer service job at a credit card company for clients, and I've done customer service at a medical insurance group, Blue Cross/Blue Shield," says Dara Sanderson, who now works at WebMD. "Both of them were different. The one at Blue Cross/Blue Shield was a little less frantic, but the questions you got were more important because you're dealing with people's health. Both of them were the type of job that could be very tedious, and there were days when you would dread having to deal with people. Neither were mentally very difficult to handle, though."

Usually, helpdesk workers only need to work 40 hours a week, although customer service offices must often operate 24 hours a day. Thus, they may work evenings or weekends if the company provides support over extended hours. Also, overtime work may be necessary when unexpected technical problems arise.

The Internet

Today there are few aspects of modern life untouched by the Internet, an interconnected set of computers and networks fused together by copper wires and cables. Most often, albeit inaccurate, when most people today refer to "the Internet," they mean the World Wide Web, an interrelated set of documents, files and data joined together by hyperlinks communicating in standard Internet Protocol (IP). The confusion is understandable, as you don't have to know how the Internet works to use it. And using it is almost essential, as the functions of everyday living are increasingly conducted on this vast, seemingly formless network. Entire lives are lived online—people can fall in love, find a home, pay bills, work a job, manage their retirement funds and eventually arrange for their funerals all from the comfort of their butt, thanks to the Internet.

Much like the days of our lives, business is increasingly conducted online, as well. Indeed, it is difficult to isolate a discrete "Internet industry" as companies of every stripe invest more and more in their online presence—TV networks now offer online videos, retail giants run online stores, insurance companies sign up new members online, magazines "publish" exclusively online and so on. Furthermore, the infrastructure that supports the Internet is a mash-up of telecommunications and technology products, comprised as it is of fiber-optic cables, PCs, mobile phones, satellites and wireless technology. One has to search far and wide to find an American business that has ignored the siren song of the Internet, and the Web's seemingly unlimited real estate continues to provide aspiring entrepreneurs the space to build their dreams upon.

Despite scars that remain from the now-legendary dotcom bubble at the beginning of the century (when the bottom fell out on the skyrocketing dotcom industry), the Internet continues to engage the imagination of businesses, consumers and information junkies across the globe. In fact, business is booming, and the industry is all a-buzz about the concept of Web 2.0—a term coined by O'Reilly Media in 2003 to describe the (perceived) ascendancy of second-generation web-based companies. The popularity of user-friendly and user-generated community sites like craigslist and Wikipedia, along with the rise of entertainment sites like YouTube, is taken as a sign of an increasingly Net-based human existence, which can be translated into dollars and cents for savvy Internet companies.

Better to ask where it isn't

If it's difficult to imagine any American lives untouched by the Internet, it's probably because there aren't all that many. According to the Nielsen/NetRatings, about 70 percent of Americans use the Internet in 2007, up from only 44 percent in 2000. The number is growing—albeit at a slowing pace—as Web access becomes ubiquitous to the point of unavoidable. Today, surfers can access the Web through an array of Internet service providers (ISPs), be it on dial-up telephone lines, landline broadband (via coaxial cable, fiber optic or copper wires), Wi-Fi, satellite or cellular phones. Public places, such as libraries, Internet cafes and airport terminals, offer immediate connection to those without home access and those who find themselves jonesing for the 'Net while away from their personal computer. City governments—like those of Minneapolis, Minnesota and San Francisco—have experimented with blanketing their metropolitan areas with wireless access, with citizens paying a subscription fee to log on from anywhere within the town proper. In August 2006, Google introduced free wireless access to the town it calls home, Mountain View, California.

The days of dialup are coming to a close, with a whimper; witness the dramatic rise and fall of America Online (AOL), a titan of the dialup age that is struggling to keep pace as cable and wireless communications companies capitalize on the advances in broadband and Wi-Fi affordability and ease of use. Broadband, specifically, has emerged as the hot connection of the future, and cable companies like Comcast and TimeWarner have jumped to provide this high-speed access through their existing networks, with phone companies like AT&T and Verizon nipping at their heels.

The rise of broadband comes with its share of controversy, of course. The bone of contention here is the issue of "net neutrality," a term that refers to the level playing field of the World Wide Web, where no site is any more or less accessible than any other. The telephone companies that own the fiber-optic networks across which Internet data flows would like to charge more for their services to high-traffic content providers like Google and Yahoo!, but these companies have fought back, saying broadband ISPs could unfairly discriminate who—and how much—they charge to freeze out competition. The FCC stepped into the fight in May 2007, announcing that it will investigate the divisive issue.

Search and ye shall find

As with any Web, it would be easy to become entangled and lost in the criss-crossing mess of hyperlinks that makes up the Internet, were it not for helpful search engines. Google and its ilk make the Web comprehensible, gathering all the random and disparate web pages into neat listings for those who have lost their way. Launched in 1998, Google became the unmatched leader of search by 2001 (and it remains so-in May 2007, Nielsen/NetRatings reported that 56 percent of Web searches are conducted through Google) and, in perhaps the ultimate brand accomplishment, has become a commonly used verb in the English language. As the king of the search, Google not only points the way to not only your local pizza place, a web site about the history of pizza or an instructional video on how to make pizza, but also to new trends in Internet use, with its various specialized searches and ever-enhanced features for the savvy surfer.

In the last several years, several industry giants have looked to dip into Google's market dominance, as former Google client Yahoo! launched its own search engine in 2004 based on a number of acquired companies and technologies, as did MSN Search, owned by Microsoft, which also relied on other companies to provide its search engine listings in the past. Search engines garner their revenue via ads targeted by keyword and sales of advertising placement to affiliated web sites.

The retail that wags the dog

When the Internet first became widely known in the mid-1990s, pundits predicted that its biggest successes would come from content, or web-based news and information sources. What took some time to figure out, and what is still being debated today, is how companies and web sites are supposed to make money on content that is largely available for free. Throughout its brief existence, the Web has been most profitable in e-commerce and online advertising, though subscription-based content sites have shown some staying power of late, as have fee-based community forums and job boards.

E-commerce drives the popularity and payback potential of the Internet by tapping into the long-ingrained American love for shopping. As a group, Americans spent $114 billion online in 2006, according to the U.S. Census Bureau. Both web-specific retailers, as well as established traditional brands have seen their share of success and failure as Americans become more accustomed to doing their shopping online. Well-publicized failures of companies that existed solely in e-commerce, like those of online grocery delivery services Webvan and Streamline.com, have served as cautionary tales to already-established retailers looking to merge onto the information superhighway; supermarket chains, such as Safeway and Pathmark, took note and began successful e-commerce online delivery shopping options following the demise of their virtual brethren.

Visit Vault at www.vault.com for insider company profiles, expert advice, career message boards, expert resume reviews, the Vault Job Board and more.

VAULT CAREER LIBRARY   289

Revenue continues to rise for online companies of every shape and size, including B2C (business to customer) sites, such as renaissance vendor Amazon.com and DVD-rental titan Netflix, auction sites, such as eBay and B2B (business to business), that use automated processes to link trading partners. Many e-commerce sites combine principles of other forms of Internet business, for instance, travel sites like Orbitz, Travelocity and Priceline, which are operated like search engines that allow users to search for low-priced airfares, travel accommodation and car rental.

The business of keeping in touch

As the Internet-surfing populace grows ever more advertising savvy—and wary—companies trolling for customers have found ways of using social networking sites to generate hype around their brands. Sites like MySpace.com, an online community that allows its members to upload personal music, blogs and pictures (a high-tech incarnation of the standard see-and-be-seen motivation) and Facebook, a sort of MySpace Junior for college and high school students, build up word of mouth around the latest pop culture must-haves. These sites are free to their members and earn revenue through banner advertisements and product placement, including faux-profiles of rock bands and movie characters.

People will also pay to find online what they could get for free in the rapidly passé real world. Fee-based services, such as classmates.com and ancestry.com, hook folks up with former classmates and information about family members, while dating services, such as match.com and lavalife.com, link the lovelorn with potential mates.

You b-log to me

If social networking sites make the web feel like one big cocktail party, then blogs provide the witty (or banal) banter. Short for the now-dated term "weblog," blogs give Internet cruisers the chance to express and disseminate their point of view uncensored and uncut. The blog is representative of a larger Internet trend, wherein the personal is touted over the collective. User-generated content reigns on the Web, and the accumulation of millions of individuals spouting their uniqueness often has the paradoxical impact of a thundering, incoherent cacophony. On the other hand, this kind of mass expression is lauded for leveling the media playing field that has traditionally been stacked in favor of large corporations, and creating the kind of competition that lets the crème de la crème of user-generated content rise to the top.

With at least 24 million blogs in America, every possible subject is likely to be covered, including rhapsodic tributes to favored brands. Public relations firms are seeing these blogs as an immediate window into customer feedback and the opinions of a brand's largest fans provide an unprecedented glimpse into consumer preference. With more and more consumers expressing skepticism about product information provided to them by corporations, marketers see the unbiased opinion (if you call ecstatic fanaticism unbiased) expressed on product-centric blogs filling a niche in high demand.

Playing video games

The rapid growth of vlogs (think a blog in video form) and web sites offering downloadable video podcasts seems to indicate that more and more people have lost interest in commercial television offerings, willing to seek out alternative broadcasting online or make their own programs. Mefeedia.com, which tracks the growth and variety of vlogs, reported more than 20,000 vlogs in January 2007, a staggering increase from just 600 two years previous. Like their text-based cousin, most vlogs tend to be personal diaries and reflections that read as exercises in self-absorption, yet several sites have figured out that money can be made. For example, the daily three-minute fake TV news report *Rocketboom*, shot on digital video and edited on a laptop (costing around $20 an episode), attracts over 300,000 people per day, an audience roughly equivalent of many cable TV news programs, thanks to a deal penned with TiVo in 2005. Toting big viewership, *Rocketboom* garnered $80,000 in February 2006 when the firm sold its first ads on (what else?) eBay.

Newsworthy times

Amid the clamor of Joe and Jane Laptops gushing their opinions in every conceivable form, the voice of traditional journalism has been a little drowned out. Although a growing number of sites have found mixed success providing credentialed reporting to paying subscribers (like the "online magazine" Salon.com and *The New York Times*' short-lived TimesSelect option) the deluge of citizen reporting—and the tendency to trust it as credible news—has many worried about the eroding value of credibility. Bloggers operate without the demands of capital investment, commercial concerns or the traditional ethical restrictions of conventional journalism, which can sometimes lead to triumphs in on-the-spot reporting (the only footage of the Virginia Tech shootings of April 2007 was taken on a cell phone and uploaded to CNN's user-generated web site, iReport) but can also lead to trouble. One example of blogging gone wrong caused a $2.8 billion freak-out on Wall Street in May 2007. After a prank e-mail went out to Apple workers saying that the release of the much-anticipated iPhone would be delayed four months, the fake news quickly found its way onto a popular tech blog, AOL's Engadget. Bad news travels fast; within 10 minutes Apple's market value fell $2.8 billion, with its stock dropping from $107 to $104. Although the stock bounced back by the end of the day, the ordeal serves as a cautionary tale of the risk involved in blogging and its lightning-fast distribution of information.

On the other side of the coin, the blogosphere has also served to keep tabs on the occasional flubs that traditional journalism serves up to believing viewers. CBS in particular learned the hard way about the influence of the blogosphere, when conservative bloggers began vehement criticism of a CBS piece on George W. Bush's military service during the 2004 campaign that relied on documents that could not be authenticated. Hoping to establish their credibility in the midst of bloggers' microscopic (and somewhat ironic) attention for details, certain networks have taken to the Internet to preempt potential criticism. By the end of 2005, all of the major networks had adopted features on their web sites to provide transparency to their editorial and production decisions. The end result is that the making of news on the Web has become more of an exchange of information, rather than a disbursal of it.

Content-ed

The Internet is rapidly turning into the Grand Central Station for all things entertaining, thanks to a widening array of distribution methods that facilitate the creation of web-based entertainment and media content. Some, such as blogs, vlogs and podcasts, came from the underground, were embraced by enterprising individuals and picked up on by global corporations as a channel to new audiences. Others, such as mobisodes (content created for viewing on cell phones) and television episodes to be watched on iPods, take the entertainment technology breakthroughs of the past several years and inject them into a fully corporate, capital-intensive marketing and distribution plan. These emerging channels for distributing content comprise the horse that everyone's betting on—Web 2.0.

Anybody who wants to stay in the Internet game, then, has to get in on the content action. The ever-prescient Google again led the pack when it bought video-sharing web site YouTube.com for $1.6 billion in October 2006. Some analysts say that pairing Google's resources with YouTube's popularity could usher in the future of television; a future where any show comes in several mediums for viewing anywhere, with an accompanying slew of interactive message boards and games, all available via the Web. Even old-hat TV-based television is feeling the crunch to compete with the gotta-have-it-now attitude cultivated by Internet video devotees. Cable companies and phone providers such as Verizon and AT&T that have entered the paid-TV market offer interactive features like on-demand programming, which allows subscribers to download movies whenever they want.

The holy trinity of networks-CBS, NBC, and ABC—has also moved to integrate itself with the new media forms of the Internet. ABC's hit deserted-island drama *Lost* perhaps best illustrates the spreading tentacles of TV on the Web. Fans of the show can catch up on missed episodes online, download it to their iPods through Apple's iTunes store, share their theories with other viewers on message boards, play *Lost*-related games, and download pictures of cast members to their mobile phones-all from ABC's web page. And ABC is not alone in this trend; writers of FX's *Nip/Tuck* have posted blogs on the

Visit Vault at **www.vault.com** for insider company profiles, expert advice, career message boards, expert resume reviews, the Vault Job Board and more.

VAULT CAREER LIBRARY

291

Web community myspace.com for the Carver, the show's resident serial killer, and writers for CBS's *How I Met Your Mother* contribute entries to a character's blog on the network's site. The success of *Prom Queen*, a web-exclusive series of two-minute episodes created by ex-Disney head Michael Eisner, points to the emerging trend toward wholly web-based video content, which is cheaper to make than broadcast series.

Watch that phone!

Part of the Web 2.0 utopian vision is bringing the Internet to screens other than the PC of old. To this end, Apple launched the Apple TV in March 2007, a device that lets users bring iTunes movies, podcasts and such to their TV screens. With the arrival of third-generation mobile phone technology (3G), the broadcasting and viewing of video footage on mobile television screens has become a realistic commercial possibility. 3G enables the transfer of both voice data (a phone call) and non-voice data (downloading information, sending e-mail, instant messaging, etc.). The roll-out of Apple's iPhone in June 2007 was a high point in the dawn of 3G technology—the eagerly awaited and widely hyped gadget offered a Web browser, music player and video player in addition to the usual calling capabilities, all packaged in Apple's signature slick style.

The day the music died

Not everything on the Net is free, and in case anyone forgot that they were tactfully reminded on June 26, 2007, when Internet radio stations across the U.S. shut down for the day to raise awareness of an impending fee hike that could put a serious cramp on their existence. In March 2007, the Copyright Royalty Board (CRB) decided to raise the fees it charges Internet radio stations; the 2005 rate was 7 cents per song per listener, but by 2010, under CRB's decree, it will rise to 19 cents a pop. Additionally, the new fees are retroactive for 17 months, meaning that many Internet radio stations' coffers will be cleaned out the same day the new rules kick in. Said stations argued that their services only helped the music industry by giving exposure to musicians and asked Web radio listeners—which total about 19 percent of Americans over 12, according to a Bridge Ratings & Research poll—to urge their congressfolks to act on their behalf.

The availability of music online is a contentious issue all around, especially as more and more music is downloaded for iPods or desktop music players, rather than bought in record stores. Historically, songs available for purchase online came with digital rights management (DRM) software that limits buyers' ability to copy or transfer the music to a different device. Consumers have been up in arms about DRMs and the limits they impose for some time, and they scored a victory in May 2007 when Apple's iTunes online store began offering music from EMI (the world's third-largest music label) DRM-free. The iTunes store is the most popular digital media download site on the Web, and has sold more than 2.5 billion songs, 50 million TV shows, and two million movies since its inception in 2003. The format change, which now allows buyers to copy their songs as much as they'd like or gleefully transfer them to and fro, is expected to spread throughout the industry, given Apple's tremendous clout and the music industry's growing dependence on Internet sales.

Surf's up!

The Internet is riding a big wave, and with the influx of new technologies that amp up mobile access and video capability, that wave isn't expected to crash against the rocks any time soon. The U.S. Bureau of Labor Statistics predicts that Internet industry will outrun the projected growth of the U.S. economy in the next several years, with 28 percent wage and salary growth from 2004 to 2014.

Startup companies, which pop up like weeds all over the Internet, pose a particular conundrum to the job seeker; as evidenced by YouTube's trajectory from pet project to $1.6 billion company in just a few years, the Web offers great potential to cash in on a good idea. At the same time, small companies pose a risk of failure and even the best ideas can take a long time to find their market. Generally speaking, however, as the Internet becomes more central to conducting business, there will be an ever-rising demand for workers to provide content for the Web, along with a demand for manpower to harness and organize the network.

Working the web

The Internet supports a vast diversity of jobs, from the workers who install the networks along which information passes to the data entry clerks who key in that multitudinous information to the computer technicians who maintain the servers and connections that make up the Web. And that's just the infrastructure—just as beefed-up content has come to the foreground as an Internet trend in recent years, so has the crowd that creates the content grown.

Playing god

Content creation refers to the writers and web producers who create and update the information and material displayed on a web page to entice viewers into repeat site visits. That can include articles, interactive applications, and downloadable and web-streamed music and video. The business model of some content-centered web sites, such as TheOnion.com and DrudgeReport.com, depends entirely on money generated by advertising revenue. Other sites, such as online magazine (webzine) Salon.com, offer Internet surfers the opportunity to pay a subscription fee to avoid advertisements (either embedded or in "pop-up" form) while reading articles. The online content of established "old" media sites, such as *Newsweek* or CNN, contain advertisements but also serve as an elaborate means of branding, bolstering awareness of their traditional product. Regardless of how the business makes its money, content is key to obtaining and keeping an Internet audience, and those who produce that content need a background in writing, marketing or related communications fields.

Marketers work alongside both the sales force and content creators to develop original, cost-conscious and effective ways to promote a web site's content and services. Successful marketing campaigns begin and end with a single-minded focus on return on investment (ROI), looking to come out with more sales than money spent on marketing. As seen in examples above, marketing using new media has become increasingly complex, blurring the line between content and marketing, with faux blogs used to hype shows like *Lost*, consumer blogs dishing news about their favorite brands and TV reruns showing for free. All these various channels are harnessed by the marketer to further awareness of their company and ratchet up traffic on the company site. While those looking to get involved as marketers or content creators might not need to be directly involved in creating web pages, some familiarity with HTML or Photoshop can greatly enhance a job seeker's resume.

Slick site

Web design is arguably content in its own right, as its visual appeal defines the site using it. In fact, web page creation is recognized as an art form among some circles (most prominently by the Webby Awards, which have recognized web sites for their creativity, usability and functionality for 10 years now). There is a high demand for designers trained in newer technologies such as Java programming and Macromedia's Flash programming languages, which facilitate the addition of streaming music and video to online media sites. Naturally, web designers are always learning about new technologies to keep their sites looking as of-the-moment as possible.

Who cares what you think? These guys

One of the truly unique benefits of online media comes from its capacity to provide immediate feedback from consumers. Online media outlets constantly monitor traffic to different parts of their web sites, reader comments and surveys, and discussion boards to understand which portions of their services are popular and which are unappealing. Product researchers cull opinions from these disparate sources to get a read on consumers' reactions to a brand or gimmick. Unlike gauging often

Visit Vault at **www.vault.com** for insider company profiles, expert advice, career message boards, expert resume reviews, the Vault Job Board and more.

VAULT CAREER LIBRARY   293

imprecise television ratings or radio listener audience size, web content providers can immediately read the amount of times content has been downloaded, gaining instant insight into a product's popularity.

Software

The softer side of the industry

A computer without software is merely an expensive paperweight. Software programs tell computers what to do, whether that be creating a spreadsheet, simulating the effect of car crashes to test automotive safety or helping Lara Croft raid tombs. That amounts to a large quantity of indispensable products in this high-tech age. Beyond the necessary, there is the burgeoning field of entertainment software, everything from interactive games to music sharing software. While there's a lot of "free" software out there (either legitimately downloaded from the Internet, pirated or otherwise copied), computer software is a lucrative business.

In the software business, the crucial goal is getting mindshare—making sure that a company's software products are widely used and well known. Economists have proposed a theory of "path dependence," which states that once a software product is installed, a user will tend to buy upgrades and compatible products from the same company. Because of this type of loyalty, the most important thing in the software industry is not necessarily to be best, but to be first and most prominent. Unlike almost every other product-oriented market, software production doesn't stop with a finished program. Customer support, bug fixes, updates and new versions extend the period of a company's responsibility to its products.

Every computer needs an operating system (OS)—an overall control program that schedules tasks, manages storage and handles communication with peripherals, such as printers. The operating system presents a basic user interface, and all applications must communicate with the operating system. There isn't much competition in operating systems, the most divisive sector of the software industry. As of 2007, Microsoft leads the pack with a 90 percent share of the market; Apple trails at around 6 percent, and open-source systems like Linux trail at 4 percent. Despite claims that Linux has better performance, lower cost (most versions are free for download) and broad customization options, it also has a learning curve that few users are willing to climb. Despite its user-hostile reputation, Linux is widely used in the server market due to its customizability and stability, but new graphical user interfaces (GUIs) are making it easier to use. The market share for Linux-based OSes may grow to be a threat to Windows, as many low-cost computers in the developing world are sold with it.

Finding a new platform

The operating system may soon be essentially irrelevant, however. The proliferation of high-speed Internet connections and powerful processors has allowed the development of subscription-based software that can run in a browser window, bypassing all the issues of the program's compatibility with the operating system. In early 2007, Google introduced Google Apps, a basic suite of office programs. In addition to Gmail, Apps includes a basic spreadsheet handler and word processor. The programs are supported either with advertising, or through subscriptions to schools and businesses, for about $50 per person per year—considerably less than it costs to buy Office, and there are no servers to maintain. Google isn't the first one on the scene, however. Salesforce.com introduced the concept with its online, subscription-based customer relations management software in 2002. These programs offer a lot of convenience. Since they aren't tied to a particular computer, users can log in to access their data wherever there's an Internet connection. These programs also offer the companies that distribute them a number of advantages. It's much harder for consumers to steal copies of programs, since the program resides on a remote computer, and the offering company can just cut off access to users who try using it without paying.

Patent medicine

While subscription software may solve some piracy woes, the code itself may still cause headaches. One area of contention in the software industry is the use of software patents. While computer programs are undeniably subject to copyright, whether or not they can be patented is still a murky issue that has not been decisively treated in the courts. The defenders of software patents maintain that licensing code is necessary to promote innovation in the industry and help companies recoup the costs of program development. The proponents of unlicensed, open-source software, whose source code is freely distributed to anyone who might care to tinker with it, aver that software code is not patentable and furthermore, that patents slow the development of the industry, leave businesses open to patent litigation, and encourage companies to sit on portfolios of patents in order to extract licensing fees.

Obviously, the patented software and free software camps have butted heads on numerous occasions. These occasions generally feature a software company claiming that some piece of free software violates one or more of their patents. The free software contingent often reacts by rewriting the offending bits of code, rendering the case moot, but some of these cases have wound up in court, as in SCO v. Novell. In 2006, in a bizarre twist, Microsoft and Novell hashed out a deal in which Microsoft agreed that anyone who purchased licenses to Novell's flavor of Linux was protected from being sued for violating patents that Microsoft allegedly holds on code in the Linux operating system. To further complicate matters, Microsoft won't reveal the nature of the 200-plus patents that the code violates, lest the offending code be excised. Pundits suggest that this is a ploy by Microsoft to extract licensing fees from companies that maintain large servers that run Linux—and several members of the Fortune 500 have already paid up. Novell, despite being party to the agreement, maintains that the code is clean.

This situation is further complicated by the legalities of the distribution of open-source software. Some, but certainly not all, of the free code floating around on the Internet is released under the General Public License (GPL), a copyright-like set of rules maintained by the Free Software Foundation. Unlike a traditional copyright, which limits the ability of the customer to copy or sell the copyrighted material, these rules—the General Public Lisence or GPL—lets users of the product freely use, modify, sell or pass along the intellectual property to which it applies, provided that everyone has access to the source code of said intellectual property. In the summer of 2007, the authors of the GPL released the license's third version, colloquially known as GPLv3. This new version has two notable differences from the earlier version. It states that all Linux users are protected by the Microsoft-Novell patent deal, while enjoining companies from selling products containing open-source software that is designed to break the product when something detects altered code. This change came about due to the use of open-source software with a built-in anti-modification feature in the TiVo. It remains to be seen how the conflict between the GPL and Microsoft will play out.

Going up

The software industry is expected to grow—the Bureau of Labor Statistics tapped it as one of the fastest-growing careers between 2004 and 2014, expected to make gains of 60 percent by 2014. However, this growth may be tempered somewhat by an economic downturn, as well as being affected by the increasing use of outsourced workers. However, given the demand for software updates, upgrades and features, and the proliferation of ever more complex computers in everything from pockets to cars, the demand for code will remain robust.

Work on those soft skills

Interviews at major software employers generally consist of several rounds of interviews—one hire even reported going through seven bouts of evaluations. Programmers should be prepared to code a program or solution to a programming problem on the fly, since many companies test their applicants. Some companies, especially Google, are well known for asking math and logic-based brain-teaser questions of their new hires—even if they're applying for the PR department.

Visit Vault at www.vault.com for insider company profiles, expert advice,
career message boards, expert resume reviews, the Vault Job Board and more.

VAULT CAREER LIBRARY   295

Google also hosts an annual Code Jam, which offers a $10,000 purse to the best programmer in attendance as determined by a competition.

The number of graduates with computer science majors is shrinking, falling 40 percent over the period between 2002 and 2006. This means that the competition for high-quality hires is heating up among software companies. College interns—still wet behind the ears—are being carted off to Google for free food, and get the chance to party with Bill Gates at Microsoft. In addition, both companies keep the little whippersnappers occupied by allowing them to poke around in the code that drives the companies' products. (The interns universally agree that this is the coolest part.)

Not moving out, but moving up

Many workers in the high-tech industry are understandably worried about tech jobs moving overseas. An Indian programmer is happy to work for a fraction of the cost of a programmer in Silicon Valley, for instance, and does the same work in about the same period of time. The U.S. is steadily losing tech jobs—60,000 were eliminated in the first three months of 2007. Although these jobs are moving overseas, Americans are moving into positions that can only be done face-to-face, like sales or consulting. IBM uses mixed teams of U.S.-based consultants and programmers in India to design custom software for its consulting projects. The Tata consulting group has even hired 1,000 workers in the U.S., citing the importance of face time with clients.

Employer Directory

3Com
350 Campus Drive
Marlborough, MA 01752-3064
Phone: (508) 323-5000
Fax: (508) 323-1111
Toll free: (800) 638-3266
www.3Com.com

Adobe Systems
345 Park Avenue
San Jose, CA 95110-2704
Phone: (408) 536-6000
Fax: (408) 537-6000
Toll free: (800) 833-6687
www.adobe.com

Advanced Micro Devices
1 AMD Place
P.O. Box 3453
Sunnyvale, CA 94088-3453
Phone: (408) 749-4000
Fax: (408) 749-4291
Toll free: (800) 538-8450
www.amd.com

Affiliated Computer Services Incorporated
2828 North Haskell
Dallas, TX 75204
Phone: (214) 841-6111
Fax: (214) 821-8315
www.acs-inc.com

Akamai Technologies, Inc.
8 Cambridge Center
Cambridge, MA 02142
Phone: (617) 444-3000
Fax: (617) 444-3001
www.akamai.com

Apple Incorporated
1 Infinite Loop
Cupertino, CA 95014
Phone: (408) 996-1010
Fax: (408) 974-2113
www.apple.com

Applied Materials
3050 Bowers Avenue
Santa Clara, CA 95054-3299
Phone: (408) 727-5555
Fax: (408) 748-9943
www.appliedmaterials.com

CA - Computer Associates
1 CA Plaza
Islandia, NY 11749
Phone: (631) 342-6000
Fax: (631) 342-6800
www.ca.com

Cisco Systems
170 West Tasman Drive, Building 10
San Jose, CA 95134
Phone: (408) 525-4000
Fax: (408) 526-4100
Toll free: (800) 553-6387
www.cisco.com

Dell Incorporated
1 Dell Way
Round Rock, TX 78682
Phone: (512) 338-4400
Fax: (512) 283-6161
www.dell.com

Freescale Semiconductor Incorporated
6501 William Cannon Drive West
Austin, TX 78735
Phone: (512) 895-2000
www.freescale.com

Fujitsu Limited
Shiodome City Center
1-5-2 Higashi-Shimbashi, Minato-ku
Tokyo 105-7123
Japan
Phone: +81-3-62-52-22-20
Fax: +81-3-62-52-27-83
www.fujitsu.com

Hewlett-Packard
3000 Hanover Street
Palo Alto, CA 94304
Phone: (650) 857-1501
Fax: (650) 857-5518
www.hp.com

Hitachi Limited
6-6, Marunouchi 1-chome, Chiyoda-ku
Tokyo 100-8280
Japan
Phone: +81-3-32-58-11-11
Fax: +81-3-32-58-23-75
www.hitachi.com

IBM
New Orchard Road
Armonk, NY 10504
Phone: (914) 499-1900
Fax: (914) 765-7382
Toll free: (800) 426-4968
www.ibm.com

Intel
2200 Mission College Boulevard
Santa Clara, CA 95054
Phone: (408) 765-8080
Fax: (408) 765-3804
www.intel.com

Intuit
2631 Marine Way
Mountain View, CA 94043
Phone: (650) 944-6000
Fax: (650) 944-3699
www.intuit.com

Lenovo Group Limited
1009 Think Place
Morrisville, NC 27560
Phone: (866) 458-4465
Fax: (877) 411-1329
www.lenovo.com

McAfee Incorporated
3965 Freedom Circle
Santa Clara, CA 95054
Phone: (408) 988-3832
Fax: (408) 970-9727
www.mcafee.com

Visit Vault at **www.vault.com** for insider company profiles, expert advice,
career message boards, expert resume reviews, the Vault Job Board and more.

VAULT CAREER LIBRARY

297

Employer Directory, cont.

Microsoft Corporation
1 Microsoft Way
Redmond, WA 98052-6399
Phone: (425) 882-8080
Fax: (425) 936-7329
www.microsoft.com

National Semiconductor Corporation
2900 Semiconductor Drive
P.O. Box 58090
Santa Clara, CA 95052-8090
Phone: (408) 721-5000
Fax: (408) 739-9803
www.national.com

Network Appliance Incorporated
495 East Java Drive
Sunnyvale, CA 94089
Phone: (408) 822-6000
Fax: (408) 822-4501
www.netapp.com

Novell Incorporated
404 Wyman Street, Suite 500
Waltham, MA 02451
Phone: (781) 464-8000
Fax: (781) 464-8100
www.novell.com

NVIDIA Corporation
2701 San Tomas Expressway
Santa Clara, CA 95050
Phone: (408) 486-2000
Fax: (408) 486-2200
www.nvidia.com

Oracle Corporation
500 Oracle Parkway
Redwood City, CA 94065
Phone: (650) 506-7000
Fax: (650) 506-7200
www.oracle.com

QUALCOMM Incorporated
5775 Morehouse Drive
San Diego, CA 92121
Phone: (858) 587-1121
Fax: (858) 658-2100
www.qualcomm.com

Red Hat, Inc.
1801 Varsity Drive
Raleigh, NC 27606
Phone: (919) 754-3700
Fax: (919) 754-3701
www.redhat.com

Samsung
250, 2-ga, Taepyung-ro, Jung-gu
Seoul, 100-742
South Korea
Phone: +82-2-751-7114
Fax: +82-2-727-7892
www.samsung.com

SAP AG
Dietmar-Hopp-Allee 16
69190 Walldorf
Germany
Phone: +49-6227-74-7474
Fax: +49-6227-75-7575
www.sap.com

SAS Institute Incorporated
100 SAS Campus Drive
Cary, NC 27513-2414
Phone: (919) 677-8000
Fax: (919) 677-4444
www.sas.com

Seagate Technology LLC
920 Disc Drive
Scotts Valley, CA 95066
Phone: (831) 438-6550
Fax: (831) 429-6356
Toll free: (877) 271-3285
www.seagate.com

Sun Microsystems Incorporated
4150 Network Circle
Santa Clara, CA 95054
Phone: (650) 960-1300
Fax: (408) 276-3804
www.sun.com

Symantec Corporation
20330 Stevens Creek Boulevard
Cupertino, CA 95014-2132
Phone: (408) 517-8000
Fax: (408) 517-8186
www.symantec.com

Texas Instruments Incorporated
12500 TI Boulevard
Dallas, TX 75243-4136
Phone: (972) 995-2011
Fax: (972) 927-6377
www.ti.com

Toshiba America, Inc.
1251 Avenue of the Americas,
Suite 4110
New York, NY 10020
Phone: (212) 596-0600
Fax: (212) 593-3875
www.toshiba.com

Unisys Corporation
Unisys Way
Blue Bell, PA 19424
Phone: (215) 986-4011
Fax: (215) 986-2312
www.unisys.com

Vmware
3401 Hillview Avenue
Palo Alto, CA 94304
Phone: (650) 475-5000
Fax: (650) 427-5001
www.vmware.com

Hospitality and Tourism

Industry Overview

Hospitality everywhere

The hospitality and tourism industry is made up of a variety of interconnected sectors, including lodging (everything from roadside motels to luxury resorts), recreational activities (cruises, theme parks and the like), rental cars and food services. All of these sectors work in tandem with the transportation industry to bring consumers to the destinations where they'll spend money on the local goods and services. In the industry, this is known as an "upstream" effect: the more likely travelers are to board a plane to get somewhere, for instance, the more in demand the hospitality and tourism industry's services become. According to the American Hotel and Lodging Association (AHLA), spending by overseas and domestic vacationers in the U.S. alone was $654 billion in 2005—about $1.8 billion per day. In the States, after automobiles and food stores, hospitality and tourism is the No. 3 retail industry, and one of the top-three businesses for nearly two-thirds of the 50 states. The World Tourism Organization estimates worldwide growth of travel and tourism in 2007—measured by number of arrivals—at 4 percent.

Lodging, travel agencies and food services are briefly discussed below, followed by an analysis and discussion of opportunities available in the airline industry.

Who wants to go somewhere?

Because of industry's interrelated segments, the aftereffects of the September 11 attacks, along with other turmoil overseas, had a chilling effect from 2001 through 2003. The subsequent dip in the economy also led to slashed budgets for business travel, the bread and butter of the lodging and rental car sectors. But through 2007, a variety of factors—including a perception that the economy is improving, increased confidence about security and lower-cost plane fares—have led to an overall rebound. PKF Hospitality Research predicted hotel revenue (along with costs, unfortunately) would be up for the fourth consecutive year in 2007. Even high gas prices haven't managed to dampen travelers' wanderlust. According to a survey conducted by AAA, 1.7 percent more people took a trip of 50 miles or more over the last weekend of May, 2007 than did the year before. They also noted travelers would economize on food and hotels in order to reduce the sting of high prices at the pump.

Checking into hotels

According to the Bureau of Labor Statistics, nearly 62,000 establishments—including upscale hotels, RV parks, motels, resorts, casino hotels, bed-and-breakfasts and boarding houses—provide overnight accommodation in America, with a staggering 4.4 million rooms on offer each night. These employ 1.8 million wage and salary workers in the process; two-thirds of these work in service occupations, such as housekeeping and food prep. All of this helped the lodging industry earn roughly $133 billion in receipts during 2006.

Hotels fall into several categories: commercial, resort, residential, extended-stay and casino. Some commercial hotels are also classified as conference facilities, with spaces designed to accommodate large-scale meetings and events. In recent years, the industry has seen the most growth in extended-stay properties, accommodating guests for visits of five nights or longer. By eliminating traditional services like lobby facilities, 24-hour staff and daily housekeeping, the sector has been able to reap profits. In addition, during the last few years, properties more commonly tack on charges to the room rate (for facilities fees, energy taxes or wireless charges, for example), regardless of whether the guest has actually used the features in question. Partly for these reasons, average revenue per available room (known in the trade as RevPAR) increased 7.7 percent in 2006.

Visit Vault at www.vault.com for insider company profiles, expert advice, career message boards, expert resume reviews, the Vault Job Board and more.

VAULT CAREER LIBRARY 299

Top hotel corporations include Marriott International, Starwood and the Intercontinental Group. Another hospitality giant is Cendant, considered the world's largest hotel franchiser, with Days Inn, Super 8 and other brands under its roof. In July 2006 Cendant's board voted to divide the company into four parts. Its travel booking services became Travelport, which owns Orbitz; the Cendant name continues to be attached to the company that controls the Avis and Budget car rental firms; and the hotels and timeshares are owned by Wyndham Worldwide. (The Blackstone Group bought Travelport and took it private later that year.) Realogy was created to take over the company's real estate functions. Accor and InterContinental are the segment leaders in Europe.

Inhospitality

If you've had a bad customer service experience in the hospitality and tourism industry, you're not alone—and the industry's trade organizations do care about your plight. The industry has struggled for some time with human resource issues, and "the current bad situation is worsening," says the International Society of Hospitality Consultants (ISHC). The ISHC frets that the "spirit of hospitality is deteriorating," with guest services compromised by staff reductions, high turnover and poorly trained workers.

Other labor issues also dog the industry. As hotels compete with other sectors, like retail and fast food, for unskilled and semi-skilled labor, workers are becoming increasingly demanding of benefits. In addition, for a sector that relied heavily on an immigrant labor population, post-September 11 border tightening has also put strain on the industry. But, according to the ISHC, the challenge that will most affect the lodging industry onward from 2006 is higher operating costs, especially those associated with labor and fuel. Hoteliers must also contend with rising insurance premiums (most notably in areas prone to natural disasters such as hurricanes), escalated competition between accommodations, stiffer "brand standards" and the rising cost of construction and renovation.

Electronic customers

Nearly every portion of the hospitality and tourism industry has adjusted to the increased presence of the Internet in travel planning and spending. Industry analysts predict that, worldwide, 38 percent of travel bookings will be made online by 2011 (amounting to $128 billion in sales); another 33 percent currently use the Internet to research lodging and other travel specifics, but then book by other means. According to a TIA survey in 2007, consumers much prefer the comforting glow of their computer screen to waiting on hold, or, heaven forbid, dealing with someone face-to-face. According to the survey, travel agent bookings were down to a mere 4 percent of all travel booked.

Indeed, across the industry, electronic distribution—a means of allowing travel agencies, consolidators, consumers and other bookers to access available rooms, rental cars, flights and even golf course tee times online—has become the norm. The Internet has had the effect of empowering customers, allowing them to comparison shop for the best deals through so-called "e-mediaries" like Expedia, Orbitz and Travelocity, all of which sell rooms and travel services, such as rental cars, often at discounted rates. Consumers' ability to compare prices before booking has created downward pressure on room rates, which, according to the ISHC, will continue to affect hotels' profitability.

At the same time, hotels have become more reliant on electronic database systems and the Internet to fill rooms, and have upgraded the feel and features of their proprietary web sites. As a result, most people now make their arrangements via specific hotel or brand web sites (as opposed to the e-mediaries), and in 2006, consumers using those online portals were more satisfied with the experience than any other travel site, such as Hotwire, Expedia or Travelocity.

While online hotel and transportation bookings allow customers to minimize large-ticket expenses, travelers who book online do have a tendency to be freer with their pinched pennies once they arrive at their destination. The TIA reported in 2005 that online bookers spent more and participated in more activities while on vacation than those who arranged their trips by phone.

Rock me Amadeus (and Galileo, too)

The electronic distribution trend stems from the global distribution system (GDS) and Internet distribution system (IDS) models that form the inner machinery of the travel industry. The GDS sector arose in the 1960s as a means for airlines to keep track of their schedules, seat availability and prices. Formed by airline leaders such as American (which founded Sabre), the GDSs were installed in travel agencies in the 1970s, marking one of the first successful business-to-business e-commerce ventures. A few decades later, e-commerce travel sites like Expedia and Travelocity, using Sabre and other GDS systems as their information engines, made travel booking available to the connected masses. In addition, the more than 500,000 travel agents operating worldwide now have a wealth of electronic methods to plug into and shop from. Entities that want to survive in hospitality and tourism can't afford to be shut out of these systems.

There are four main GDSs, or booking systems, in the world, allowing access to bookings for airlines, car rentals, hotels and cruise reservations. Known by different names in various parts of the world, the GDSs are familiar to American travel bookers as Amadeus, Galileo (a subsidiary of Travelport), Sabre and Worldspan. According to the Hotel Electronic Distribution Network Association (HEDNA), cost per booking for hotels through a GDS or IDS is less expensive than any other distribution method, including bookings made directly through the property.

Decommissioning agencies

Ironically, what started off as a tool to help travel agents access and sell travel to consumers has now led to the steady erosion of the travel agency business itself, since consumers no longer need to rely on a middleman to purchase airline tickets or travel packages. The segment is now dominated by bigger traditional travel retailers like American Express and Carlson Wagonlit; many smaller shops have gone under in the past decade. E-retailer Expedia held the position of the 2006 market leader.

Airlines, once a steady source of income for travel agencies, also contributed to the downturn in the agency system. Beginning in the mid-1990s, major air carriers, after decades of providing at least a 10 percent commission to agents on sales, slashed or eliminated these commissions entirely. The loss of income drove some agencies out of business, while others consolidated. According to the BLS, the number of travel agents in the U.S. was around 88,000 in 2006, while it was 103,000 just two years earlier. Associations such as the American Society of Travel Agents insist that the industry can continue to thrive by providing the extra attention to detail, insider knowledge and customer service that consumers crave and can't get from electronic sources.

Feeding the masses

In the vast lodging and recreation territory, it can be difficult to deliver food and other sundries to guests cheaply and efficiently—and that's where outsourcing companies enter the picture. With revenue of more than €12.8 billion in 2006, French company Sodexho is the biggest firm providing outsourced food and services to hospitality facilities (as well as a host of other institutions from offices to nursing homes and elementary schools). It ranks fourth in market capitalization among all players in the restaurant industry, coming in behind McDonald's, Starbucks and Yum! Brands. And its effectiveness has been recognized by the International Association of Outsourcing Professionals, which voted it No. 1 in its industry group and fourth overall.

Another global contender is Aramark, which returned to private ownership in early 2007. The company collected $10 billion from its worldwide food service business in 2006 (and another $1.6 billion from rental and sales of uniforms and job apparel). It provides services to colleges, universities and corporations, and operates concession services at entertainment venues and sporting events.

Visit Vault at **www.vault.com** for insider company profiles, expert advice, career message boards, expert resume reviews, the Vault Job Board and more.

VAULT CAREER LIBRARY   301

Hospitality Careers

Tours of duty

The good thing about hospitality and tourism is that there's almost always a job to be found. The BLS reports that jobs in accommodation and food services as a whole are expected to increase more than 17 percent through 2014. There is a wide variety of jobs in the industry for people of all skill sets and education levels, and high turnover means wide availability. Except for the mid- to upper-level positions, compensation levels are on the low side.

Most entry-level jobs in hotels require little training. Housekeeper and janitor positions require the least training and education, and have the fewest opportunities for advancement, though they can be attractive to people who might want seasonal or temporary work. Those who work in guest services as a host or hostess or desk clerk can advance to supervisory positions with sufficient experience. Completion of a program in hotel management will lead to more rapid advancement. Hotels may also need people in the food service industry, such as chefs and restaurant staff. Hospitality involves 24-hour service, and low seniority usually entails working night and weekend shifts, at least initially. Sales positions are usually fast-paced and often require prior experience.

Travel agents need at least a high school diploma, and good sales, research, and computer skills (a BA in geography or travel services helps as well). Currently, 13 states require travel agents to be certified or registered. The Travel Institute offers a downloadable educational course geared toward certification, and the American Society of Travel Agents (ASTA) provides a wealth of information about the industry and working as an agent.

Not always hospitable

It isn't easy working in the hospitality industry—guests can be rude, the holiday rush is nightmarish and some employees work seven days a week. Hotel managers must oversee and synchronize the activities of all the different departments of a hotel, such as housekeeping, dining, recreation, security and maintenance, and make sure both his guest and employees are happy. Hotel managers are also responsible for the behind-the-scenes operations, including accounting, personnel and publicity. They often assume a financial role, overseeing the business side of things, such as budgeting and revenue management.

It takes a team

Every member of a hotel staff, from housekeeping to the hotel manager, is responsible for the seamless operation of the establishment. At smaller hotels and motels, the responsibility for overseeing rooms, food and beverage service, registration, and overall management can fall on the shoulders of a single manager.

Large hotels, such as The Plaza in New York, employ hundreds of workers, and have many different levels of managers. The general manager may be aided by a staff of assistant managers, each with his or her own department to supervise. The hotel manager sets the establishment's standards of operation (within the owners' or executives' guidelines); it is the job of the assistant managers to see that these are executed adroitly. The general manager sets room rates, allocates funds to departments, approves expenditures and establishes standards for service that employees in housekeeping, decor, food quality and banquet operations must offer to guests. Many hotels have resident managers, who live in the hotel and are on hand 24 hours a day for guests and staff (though they usually work a standard eight-hour day).

Hotel Management

Although in the past, most hotel managers have been hired from food and beverage, front desk, housekeeping and sales positions without formal education, employers now give hiring preference to individuals with degrees in hotel and restaurant management. Internships and part-time jobs also give a step up when it comes to getting hired for a management-track position.

Graduates of hotel or restaurant management programs usually start as trainee assistant managers or at least advance to such positions quickly. Another in are leadership training programs, which hire recent graduates to participate. New hotels without formal on-the-job training programs often prefer experienced personnel for higher-level positions.

Leadership-in-training programs

Because hotel managers oversee so many different departments, even the most senior general manager must have an understanding of each one. Like orchestra conductors, they bring together a sea of different departments and employees to perform in harmony. The best way to learn about each part of the hotel team is through hands-on experience. Most hotel chains, such as Hilton Hotels, have leadership development programs for their managers. For example, in Hilton's Leadership-in-Training (LIT) program a trainee rotates through about a dozen different hotel departments in a six- to eight-month period. The central goal of a rotational training program like LIT is to provide trainees with an overview of an organization's operations so that they can best coordinate them.

Vault Q&A: Nancy Vu, Manager of Field Employment and Recruiting, Hilton Hotels

In 2005, Hilton Hotels relaunched its management training program, called the Leader-In-Training (LIT) program. In its first year, the company hired 28 recent graduates for the program. Nancy Vu, manager of field employment and recruiting at Hilton Hotels, took time out from her schedule to talk with Vault from Hilton's corporate headquarters in California.

Vault: I understand that this is a new, or relaunched, management training program. Tell me about the genesis of the program.

Vu: We started in 1999. When Hilton Hotels Corporation acquired Promus Hotels Company, we acquired four new hotel brands—Doubletree, Embassy Suites Hotels, Hampton and Homewood Suites by Hilton—and thousands of additional team members. Prior to the acquisition, we had a management development program called the HPDP [Hilton Professional Development Program] in place. After the merger, we reviewed the program and realized that it really catered to just the Hilton brand, so we had to implement a new program that worked with all of the brands.

Vault: How long was HPDP around?

Vu: Since about 1988. We have directors and VP who came through that program and are still with us.

Vault: So what's new about this program?

Vu: What we've done is taken a look at that old program, and looked at how we can revamp it so we can tie together the various properties, so that if someone's a trainee at a Hilton or a Doubletree, they could eventually become a manager at a Doubletree or any other brand.

Vault: How does the program work?

Visit Vault at **www.vault.com** for insider company profiles, expert advice, career message boards, expert resume reviews, the Vault Job Board and more.

VAULT CAREER LIBRARY

303

Vu: It's a six- to eight-month program. We have six different tracks: sales, food and beverage, revenue management, front office, housekeeping and human resources.

Each trainee is assigned to a training hotel—and this hotel could be a Doubletree, a Hilton or an Embassy. The first three to four months is general rotation in the hotel. A new team member goes through 11 or 12 different areas of the hotel—every major department is covered, including property operations, finance, human resources, engineering, banquets and others.

Vault: What happens after that initial period of rotations?

Vu: The last three to four months, they spend in their area of specialization in the same hotel. After that, they are placed in an entry-level management position. So if you're on the sales track, you'll be a sales manager.

Vault: Do the employees stay with the hotel they were at?

Vu: More than likely, they'll end up staying in their training hotel, but if not, they'll stay in their region. [Hilton has six geographic regions: Northeast, Southeast, Central, West, Hawaii and Focus Service and International.]

Vault: How do you place the trainees?

Vu: The SVP of Operations looks for areas of need in hotels, and then we try to find a win-win situation, where the hotel need matches with the candidate's area of interest. For example, the Hilton New York has a revenue management trainee and a front office trainee this year. So again, using the Hilton New York example, we looked for students specifically interested in the Northeast, and specifically interested in sales or front office. We don't want to put them in a track where they don't want to be.

Vault: What are the requirements for the program?

Vu: You have to have a minimum 2.8 GPA and you have to be enrolled in the hotel program at your college or university. We recruited at 16 schools this past year.

Vault: Why do you have the trainees go through the initial rotation period?

Vu: If you're going to become a general manager one day, you're going to have to understand all the different departments and functions. The more well rounded you are in understanding all of operations, the better you're going to be as a general manager or any executive-level position. We want them to understand how each department links to one another.

Our front office people stay in very close contact with sales, our sales stay in very close contact with revenue management. There's so much interaction within each of the departments—engineering/maintenance are in close contact with housekeeping, because they are the team members who are actually in contact with our customers. We want our trainees to get their feet wet in all these areas. That way, they have a better understanding of what goes on in the rest of the hotel.

That said, not everybody [who goes through the program] wants to become a general manager. Some students go through this training program find they love working in other aspects of the hotel. For example, someone who has an affinity for the front office could start as a director of front office at a 200-room hotel and work their way up to director of front office at a 1,200-room hotel.

Vault: Is there an orientation that starts the program?

Vu: We held a kick-off meeting in mid-June with all of the trainees, where they had an opportunity to meet with each other and start building a network that will serve as a support group while they're in the program. Also, there are many executive committee members at corporate headquarters that attended the meeting and offered support and advice.

Vault: Is there any classroom training as part of the program?

Vu: We conducted a few training courses during the orientation. Within the program itself, in addition to whatever training they have on the job, they are required to attend or participate in specific training courses.

Vault: What sort of courses are these?

Vu: There are diversity training programs, safety training and others. We have those training requirements for any manager that joins Hilton. And if we're grooming people in this program to be managers, then it's our expectation that they're going to take these training courses during their training. Also, as part of the program, they're required to do a project. They thought they were done with projects after graduating, but no.

Vault: What sort of projects do they work on?

Vu: It's determined by what department they work in. For example, in sales, maybe they'd be asked to participate in a sales blitz, a promotion where you're improving the hotel's visibility among all your clients or potential clients. For food and beverage, it could be creating a brand-new menu item for the restaurant.

Visit Vault at **www.vault.com** for insider company profiles, expert advice, career message boards, expert resume reviews, the Vault Job Board and more.

V/\ULT CAREER LIBRARY

305

Employer Directory

Accor
2, rue de la Mare Neuve
91 021 Evry Cedex
France
Phone: +33-1-69-36-80-80
Fax: +33-1-69-36-79-00

Amadeus IT Group SA
Calle Salvador de Madariaga 1
E- 28027 Madrid
Spain
Phone: +34-91-582-0100
Fax: +34-91-582-0188
www.amadeus.com

American Automobile Association
1000 AAA Drive
Heathrow, FL 32746
Phone: (407) 444-7000
Fax: (407) 444-7380
www.aaa.com

American Express Travel Related Services Company, Inc.
200 Vesey Street
3 World Financial Center
New York, NY 10285
Phone: (212) 640-5130
Fax: (212) 640-9365
www.americanexpres.com/travel

Aramark
Aramark Tower
1101 Market Street
Philadelphia, PA 19107
Phone: (215) 238-3000
Fax: (215) 238-3333
www.aramark.com

Avis Budget Group, Inc.
6 Sylvan Way
Parsippany, NJ 07054
Phone: (973) 496-3500
Fax: (888) 304-2315
www.avisbudgetgroup.com

Boyd Gaming Corp.
3883 Howard Hughes Parkway
9th Floor
Las Vegas, NV 89169
Phone: (702) 792-7200
Fax: (702) 792-7313
www.boydgaming.com

Carlson Companies
701 Carlson Parkway
Minnetonka, MN 55305
Phone: (763) 212-1000
Fax: (763) 212-2219
www.carlson.com

Carnival Corporation
3655 NW 87th Avenue
Miami, FL 33178-2428
Phone: (305) 599-2600
Fax: (305) 406-4700
www.carnivalcorp.com

Choice Hotels International
10750 Columbia Pike
Silver Spring, MD 20901
Phone: (301) 592-5000
Fax: (301) 592-6157
www.choicehotels.com

Cintas Corporation
6800 Cintas Boulevard
Cincinnati, OH 45262
Phone: (513) 459-1200
Fax: (513) 573-4130
Toll free: (800) 246-8271
www.cintas-corp.com

Club Méditerranée
11 rue Cambrai
75019 Paris
France
Phone: +33-1-53-35-35-53
Fax: +33-1-53-35-32-01
www.clubmed.com

Compass Group PLC
Compass House
Guildford Street
Chertsey, Surrey KT16 9BQ
United Kingdom
Phone: +44-19-32-57-30-00
Fax: +44-19-32-56-99-56
www.compass-group.com

Darden Restaurants, Inc.
5900 Lake Ellenor Drive
Orlando, FL 32809
Phone: (407) 245-4000
Fax: (407) 245-5389
www.dardenrestaurants.com

Denny's, Inc.
203 East Main Street
Spartanburg, SC 29319-9966
Phone: (864) 597-8000
Fax: (864) 597-8780
Toll free: (800) 733-6697
www.dennys.com

Dollar Thrifty Automotive Group, Inc.
5330 East 31st Street
Tulsa, OK 74135
Phone: (918) 660-7700
Fax: (918) 669-2934
www.dtag.com

Enterprise Rent-A-Car Company
600 Corporate Park Drive
St. Louis, MO 63105
Phone: (314) 512-5000
Fax: (314) 512-4706
www.enterprise.com

Expedia, Inc.
3150 139th Avenue SE
Bellevue, WA 98005
Phone: (425) 679-7200
Fax: (425) 679-7240
www.expediainc.com

Employer Directory, cont.

**Fairmont Raffles Hotels
International Inc.**
Canadian Pacific Tower
100 Wellington Street West
Suite 1600, TD Center
Toronto, Ontario M5K 1B7
Canada
Phone: (416) 874-2600
Fax: (416) 874-2601
www.fairmont.com
www.raffles.com

FirstGroup PLC
395 King Street
Aberdeen, AB24 5RP
Scotland
Phone: +44-1224-650-100
Fax: +44-1224-650-140
www.firstgroup.com

Four Seasons Hotels Limited
1165 Leslie Street
Toronto, Ontario M3C 2K8
Canada
Phone: (416) 449-1750
Fax: (416) 441-4374
www.fourseasons.com

Global Hyatt Corporation
71 South Wacker Drive
Chicago, IL 60606
Phone: (312) 750-1234
Fax: (312) 750-8550
www.hyatt.com

Harrah's Entertainment, Inc.
1 Caesars Palace Drive
Las Vegas, NV 89109
Phone: (702) 407-6000
Fax: (702) 407-6037
www.harrahs.com

Hertz Global Holdings, Inc.
225 Brae Boulevard
Park Ridge, NJ 07656
Phone: (201) 307-2000
Fax: (201) 307-2644
www.hertz.com

Hilton Hotels Corporation
9336 Civic Center Drive
Beverly Hills, CA 90210
Phone: (310) 278-4321
Fax: (310) 205-7678
www.hiltonworldwide.com

IAC/InterActiveCorp
555 West 18th Street
New York, NY 10011
Phone: (212) 314-7300
www.iac.com

InterContinental Hotels Group
67 Alma Road
Windsor SL4 3HD
United Kingdom
Phone: +44-17-53-41-01-00
Fax: +44-17-53-41-01-01
www.ichotelsgroup.com

Intrawest ULC
200 Burrard Street, Suite 800
Vancouver, British Columbia V6C 3L6
Canada
Phone: (604) 669-9777
Fax: (604) 669-0605
www.intrawest.com

Joie de Vivre Hospitality, Inc.
567 Sutter Street
San Francisco, CA 94102
Phone: (415) 835-0300
Fax: (415) 835-0311
www.jdvhotels.com

**Kimpton Hotel & Restaurant
Group, LLC**
222 Kearney Street, Suite 200
San Francisco, CA 94108
Phone: (415) 397-5572
Fax: (415) 296-8031
www.kimptonhotels.com

Las Vegas Sands Corp.
3355 Las Vegas Boulevard South
Las Vegas, NV 89109
Phone: (702) 414-1000
Fax: (702) 414-4884
www.lasvegassands.com

Marriott International
10400 Fernwood Road
Bethesda, MD 20817
Phone: (301) 380-3000
Fax: (301) 380-3969
www.marriott.com

MGM Mirage
3600 Las Vegas Boulevard South
Las Vegas, NV 89109
Phone: (702) 693-7120
Fax: (702) 693-8626
www.mgmmirage.com

**National Railroad Passenger
Corporation**
60 Massachusetts Avenue NE
Washington, DC 20002
Phone: (202) 906-3000
Fax: (202) 906-3306
www.amtrak.com

Omni Hotels Corporation
420 Decker Drive, Suite 200
Irving, TX 75062
Phone: (972) 730-6664
Fax: (972) 871-5665
www.omnihotels.com

Penn National Gaming
825 Berkshire Boulevard, Suite 200
Wyomissing, PA 19610
Phone: (610) 373-2400
Fax: (610) 373-4966
www.pngaming.com

priceline.com, Inc.
800 Connecticut Avenue
Norwalk, CT 06854
Phone: (203) 299-8000
Fax: (203) 299-8948
www.priceline.com

Royal Caribbean Cruises Ltd.
1050 Caribbean Way
Miami, FL 33132
Phone: (305) 539-6000
Fax: (305) 539-4440
www.royalcaribbean.com

Visit Vault at www.vault.com for insider company profiles, expert advice,
career message boards, expert resume reviews, the Vault Job Board and more.

VAULT CAREER LIBRARY 307

Employer Directory, cont.

Sabre Holdings
3150 Sabre Drive
Southlake, TX 76092
Phone: (682) 605-1000
Fax: (682) 605-8267
www.sabre-holdings.com

Six Flags, Inc.
1540 Broadway, 15th Floor
New York, NY 10036
Phone: (212) 652-9403
Fax: (212) 354-3089
www.sixflags.com

Sodexo, Inc.
9801 Washingtonian Boulevard
Gaithersburg, MD 20878
Phone: (301) 987-4500
Fax: (301) 987-4438
Toll free: (800) 763-3946
www.sodexousa.com

Star Cruises Limited
Suite 1501, Ocean Centre
5 Canton Road
Tsimshatsui, Kowloon
Hong Kong SAR
Phone: +852-23-78-20-00
Fax: +852-23-14-38-09
www.starcruises.com

Starwood Hotels & Resorts Worldwide, Inc.
1111 Westchester Avenue
White Plains, NY 10604
Phone: (914) 640-8100
Fax: (914) 640-8310
www.starwoodhotels.com

Travelport Limited
Morris Corporate Center III
400 Interpace Parkway, Building A
Parsippany, NJ 07054
Phone: (973) 939-1000
Fax: (973) 939-1096
www.travelport.com

Trump Entertainment Resorts, Inc.
1000 Boardwalk
Atlantic City, NJ 08401
Phone: (609) 449-6515
Fax: (609) 449-6586
www.trumpcasinos.com

TUI AG
Karl-Wiechert-Allee 4
D-30625 Hanover
Germany
Phone: +49-511-566-00
Fax: +49-511-566-1901
www.tui-group.com

Vail Resorts, Inc.
390 Interlocken Crescent, Suite 1000
Broomfield, CO 80021
Phone: (303) 404-1800
www.vailresorts.com

Viad Corp
1850 North Central Avenue, Suite 800
Phoenix, AZ 85004-4545
Phone: (602) 207-4000
Fax: (602) 207-5900
www.viad.com

Walt Disney Parks and Resorts, LLC
1375 East Buena Vista Drive
Lake Buena Vista, FL 32830-8402
Phone: (407) 828-1750
Fax: (407) 934-8889
disney.go.com/destinations

Wyndham Worldwide Corporation
7 Sylvan Way
Parsippany, NJ 07054
Phone: (973) 753-6000
Fax: (973) 753-7537
www.wyndhamworldwide.com

Wynn Resorts, Limited
3131 Las Vegas Boulevard South
Las Vegas, NV 89109
Phone: (702) 770-7555
Fax: (702) 697-5009
www.wynnresorts.com

Human Resources

Every organization has people, which means every organization needs human resources (HR) professionals. HR helps manage and develop the people in an organization. Sometimes called "personnel" or "talent management," HR is the function in charge of an organization's employees, which includes finding and hiring employees, helping them grow and learn in the organization, and managing the process when an employee leaves. Human resources takes care of people from the time they're interested in the organization to long after they leave.

The History of Human Resources

Now a thriving, growing profession, human resources wasn't always a key part of most organizations—if at all. Until the early 1900s, all human resources functions were typically handled by the workers themselves or their bosses (often called master craftsmen). As more workers were needed, master craftsmen would just go out and find them (talk about the birth of recruiting!).

When the 1900s brought inventions and changes in the workplace, like machines that automated production, human resources began to take shape. The addition of machines made factories run more quickly and smoothly, but also meant that the workers had to learn how to use them, and forced factory managers to introduce rules and procedures on the factory floor.

Frederick Taylor, a businessman and researcher, first introduced the concept of scientific management. Taylor's theory took workplace rules and procedures one step further, declaring that there was only one best way to do a job. He spent years collecting data on the tasks making up specific jobs and then researching the workers who performed each small task. Workers who performed well, following tasks to the letter, remained employed and were paid well. Those who didn't were among the first to hear "you're fired."

Taylor's research was the first to increase worker productivity, but his robotic approach didn't prove to be an effective management tool. Still, his work showed the importance of managing workers to increase a company's success. While Taylor's work focused more on company success than that of the worker, it propelled many companies to begin to personalize the workplace, anticipating the first appearance of HR. One of the earliest HR roles was that of a welfare secretary whose role was to look out for the welfare of the workers. An ancestor of what's now called a benefits manager, welfare secretaries created libraries and recreation areas in the workplace, as well as primitive medical and health programs.

But HR really took shape in the 1930s when a company called Western Electric asked a team of researchers to figure out how to increase workers' productivity at one of their plants in Chicago. The Hawthorne Studies, taking their name after the targeted plant, set out to determine whether changing the lighting in the plant could help the employees work faster. What they found instead was how important it was for plant managers to pay attention to the workers, reward them for a good job and make sure they were satisfied. The idea of happy workers being productive workers took hold and still remains true today. If a company wants to perform well, it has to create and manage a content workforce. HR plays a critical role in making sure that happens.

The Hawthorne Studies fueled the study of worker behavior in organizations, and what was called behavioral science. The growth of behavioral science as a field studied how jobs and the workplace affect workers and how workers affect the performance of a company.

The study of behavioral science reinforced the importance of welfare secretaries. The secretaries' jobs became more and more complex as governments introduced labor laws to keep up with the changing workplace. These laws, restricting the rights of both employers and employees, required the welfare secretaries to keep paper records of employees and their activities. One of the first human resources laws, the Fair Labor Standards Act (FLSA) created a minimum wage, set rules for child labor and required employers to treat employees fairly in regards to wage and hours worked.

Visit Vault at **www.vault.com** for insider company profiles, expert advice, career message boards, expert resume reviews, the Vault Job Board and more.

VAULT CAREER LIBRARY   309

In many industries, workers also began organizing into unions—groups of workers banding together to lobby for rights in the workplace. New laws around union activity also required companies and welfare secretaries to understand and comply with the laws.

Many companies began hiring multiple welfare secretaries—one responsible for hiring employees, another responsible for employee benefits and perhaps another to train employees on the factory floors. These specialty areas evolved into the specialty areas of the human resources profession today.

Human Resources Today

Today, human resources is essential to the success of business. The level of importance HR holds does differ from organization to organization, but businesses consistently rely on HR professionals to help them through high-growth times and periods of turmoil. Regardless of how successful (or not) an organization is, there is always a need for HR staff. The welfare secretary title may be long gone, but the idea of having human resources professionals focus on specific areas of managing and developing a company's workers has remained. Now, in most organizations, there are HR professionals who focus specifically on hiring, training, benefits, labor relations, health and safety and more.

While it's important to like working with people and wanting to help them to be successful in HR, that's definitely not the only skill or attribute you need to be a successful HR professional. HR is about creating systems, processes and environments where employees perform better and are satisfied, and there are many different career paths and opportunities in the profession. For example, HR professionals can take center stage as a recruiter or trainer. In these roles, you're interacting with people all day long, whether conducting interviews or running a training course. But HR professionals can also serve behind the scenes, administering payroll, tracking HR metrics (statistics about company workers) or running an organization's Human Resource Information System (HRIS), technical databases where all employee data is stored and managed.

While HR continues to grow as a function, in many companies it does not carry the importance or value of its colleagues in finance, sales or marketing. Know that as satisfying as an HR career can be, the profession still struggles to gain respect in many places.

What Do HR Professionals Do?

Typical HR responsibilities are focused in major areas such as recruiting and staffing, compensation and benefits, training and learning, labor and employee relations, and organization development. Most HR professionals have experience in one or more of these specialty areas. These areas all deal with helping employees in an organization perform more effectively and satisfactorily on the job.

Recruiting and staffing

You're either in or you're out. When an employee leaves and a job opens up or new jobs are created, HR is usually in charge of the process. Recruiting and staffing is one of the largest areas of HR. Recruiters start the process—working with specific departments to write job descriptions and understand what skills and abilities the new employee should have. Then they're off and running—responsible for finding candidates, determining who might be a good fit, conducting interviews and making job offers. While recruiters involve department employees in the process to interview and make the hiring decisions, it's the recruiters who are usually in charge of finding the talent, managing interview scheduling, negotiating offers and making sure departments have all the information they need to make the best hiring decisions possible.

While recruiters work to find and hire the talent, staffing experts determine who should go where. They strategize with different departments to anticipate hiring needs and help determine where a new employee might best fit in an organization.

Staffing professionals are heavily relied on in high-growth companies to make sure the company is prepared to hire enough new employees to grow the company, and that employees are in the right positions.

Recruiting and staffing professionals are also called upon to help an organization market to prospective employees. This can include creating and managing recruiting events, designing marketing pieces, such as company brochures and commercials, and staffing career fairs to educate prospective employees about open opportunities. Many organizations also have recruiting and staffing professionals dedicated to working with universities. These roles are focused on finding talent on undergraduate and graduate school campuses and can include a great deal of travel and campus presentations.

Compensation and benefits

Finding talent is important, but employees also have to be paid. HR, specifically compensation and benefits professionals, are in charge of making sure new employees are given an appropriate salary and benefits, and current employees continually receive their salary and benefits.

Compensation experts focus on the money. This includes processing regular payroll (making sure that the check is in the mail) and payroll changes, including raises and tax changes. Compensation experts also work closely with an organization's finance department to ensure salaries stay within each department's budget, as well as conducting and researching salary surveys to make sure they're paying the going rate.

Benefits professionals also have to make sure employees are taken care of—they specialize in helping employees with medical and other company benefits. This may include teaching new employees about their medical plan choices, implementing and managing the plans offered by the company, and managing the cost of benefits for the company.

Compensation and benefits professionals are also often tasked with communicating salary and benefits information to employees. This may include marketing and promoting new benefits offerings to a company or managing a company's open enrollment period—a brief period of time where employees can change medical plans and other benefit options.

One-on-one counseling may also be part of the job. If an employee leaves an organization, the benefits manager may counsel the employee on access to health insurance available after departure. Employees also often seek guidance on understanding their compensation packages, making changes to employment tax forms or managing a difficult medical insurance claim.

Training and learning

Part teacher, part manager, part leader—that's a training professional. Helping employees become oriented to a new job or company is just one of the many responsibilities of training and learning professionals. Sometimes called training, or learning and development, it's helping both new and tenured employees develop and grow as professionals both on and off the job.

Training and learning professionals are typically responsible for running programs designed to educate and develop employees. This can include programs for an entire employee population, such as new hire orientation or ethics training, but also includes more specialized programs for different groups of workers within a company, like online training courses, in-class instruction or on-the-job training.

Training managers, for example, are called upon to do everything from registering and tracking training courses, to developing new courses and evaluating the effectiveness of training programs after they happen. This may include designing surveys or determining if newly trained employees perform better than they did before the training. They also may be responsible for providing information to employees on training classes and programs outside the company.

In some organizations, training and learning professionals actually deliver the training courses. They might create a presentation skills course and then send trainers on the road to teach the new course to employees around the country. Since it's often cheaper to train current employees rather than hire new ones, training and learning is becoming increasingly

Visit Vault at www.vault.com for insider company profiles, expert advice,
career message boards, expert resume reviews, the Vault Job Board and more.

VAULT CAREER LIBRARY

311

important in the business world. A company's strong commitment to training and development is also a boost to its workers' morale.

Labor and employee relations

Just like welfare secretaries responded to new laws in the early 1900s, labor and employee relations professionals ensure that anything dealing with employee contracts, rights, responsibilities and complaints is taken care of right quick.

Labor relations is a function typically found in companies whose employees are members of unions. Labor relations professionals are called upon to deal directly with unions, doing everything from interpreting current union contracts to negotiating new ones. They also analyze and monitor union activity and work with unions during organizing campaigns—the time when unions recruit new members.

Employee relations professionals need to be familiar and comfortable with the law; they are also responsible for equal employment opportunity and affirmative action programs. For government agencies or companies that do work for the government, this may include creating reports to demonstrate a company is complying with the law and making an effort to hire and retain employees from underrepresented ethnicities. Other key responsibilities may include counseling or conflict resolution within an organization, helping employees who are dealing with disagreements in the workplace or have issues preventing them from doing their jobs.

Labor and employee relations is not found in every human resources department. Organizations that don't have government contracts or unionized employees may rely on outside attorneys or consultants to deal with any legal issues or employee conflicts that arise.

Organization development (OD)

While developing employees is important, perhaps just as important is developing an organization. A relatively new field, organization development focuses on evaluating how a company is structured and how employees work together to see where improvements can be made. Also referred to as organization effectiveness, this might include helping to restructure the chain of command in a department to helping employees cope with a major change, such as the introduction of a new company-wide technical system.

OD professionals are experts in understanding behavior and psychology. They often act as internal consultants, helping their fellow employees understand how a new company program might affect the employees' behavior.

They often work closely with training professionals to address development needs for the company. OD professionals may develop companywide team-building activities or introduce new programs for leadership development.

OD specialists often manage the performance review process, making sure that employees are evaluated and moved within the organization based on how well they're working. OD specialists may also help companies develop succession plans (determining who is in line to be the next person in a leadership position, such as CEO or CFO) and mentoring programs, making sure less experienced employees can learn from their more experienced comrades. OD professionals may also be called upon to help an employee address individual issues through executive coaching, or a department address a leadership or performance challenge.

Less common OD work may include coaching or career development. Coaches, common at the executive level, help employees overcome poor teamwork or management skills. Many large firms are hiring external coaches, or creating coaching functions in order to help valuable employees deal with singular issues that may prevent them from being promoted.

Health and safety

Factory machines, hazardous chemicals and construction sites are all potentially dangerous situations for workers. This is where health and safety professionals come in. One of the oldest HR specialties, health and safety professionals are responsible for ensuring a safe working environment for all workers—this is more of an issue in industries with risky work settings, such as manufacturing, health care and construction. While all organizations must protect the safety of their employees while at work, it is more complicated in industries that have work sites beyond a typical office environment.

One of the major components of the role of a health and safety professional is to be proactive—assessing a work environment to anticipate where the dangers might be and correcting them before an injury occurs. This might include periodic tours of a work site, or research into the latest workplace safety options.

Health and safety professionals are also responsible for reacting to issues, concerns or problems related to the workplace environment. They might handle a complaint from a worker about a dangerous factory machine or an on-site injury. They work closely with compensation and benefits professionals to handle any injuries and determine how to prevent future injuries from occurring.

Working with an organization's legal team and employee law specialists is also part of the role. Health and safety professionals are responsible for following federal and state rules governing workplace safety, including, in some industries, submitting reports that demonstrate a company's compliance with the law.

Why HR?

While HR professionals have varying degrees of interaction with an organization's employees, all HR people can enjoy the satisfaction of knowing that the work they do has a direct impact on people every day. HR professionals like helping employees navigate through tough problems and get back to normal on the job. Whether it's helping an employee overcome a performance problem or fix an expensive and stressful medical claim, there is an inherent satisfaction in these types of tasks.

They also enjoy the ability to interact with different groups of people; HR professionals may be working with employees in many different parts of the company. Organization development specialists may act like internal consultants helping different departments in a company work better together. This means they might be working with a sales team one week and a product design team the next. So there is a ton of variety in their day-to-day tasks.

In his role at Bank of America, Phil Skeath likes the diversity of projects. "Each time I am on a new project," he says, "I find myself identifying general concepts I learned in my educational experience, adapting them and applying them to a specific issue in the bank."

They also like contributing to the business and bottom line. For example, one of the most common issues CFOs are facing in 2005 (according to *CFO Magazine*) is the rising cost of health care. HR and benefits professionals who analyze how to lower these costs can save a company millions of dollars. Talk about making an impact.

Why not?

For most HR professionals, the positives of working in HR (such as extending a job offer to a very excited job candidate) are enough to outweigh the drawbacks (in the opposite category, downsizing or laying off employees). Otherwise, they wouldn't be there in the first place. But no job is perfect. Even rock stars have to deal with annoying paparazzi and screaming fans. While it's highly unlikely you'll be chased by reporters working in HR, you may be chased by unhappy employees. One of the toughest things about working in HR is providing a service many employees take for granted. No one says, "thanks HR," every time they get a paycheck. But if something goes wrong, if employees don't get paid, if benefits disappear or new employees aren't trained properly, you may end up with a mailbox full of angry callers to contend with.

Visit Vault at **www.vault.com** for insider company profiles, expert advice, career message boards, expert resume reviews, the Vault Job Board and more.

VAULT CAREER LIBRARY 313

Like many professions, starting out in HR, you may also have your fair share of administrative work. Many HR careers begin with processing paperwork for new employees, or entering and maintaining resumes in an online database. This might seem like menial work, especially if you've just received a college degree, but don't walk away too quickly. These roles, while tedious, provide a great learning opportunity and a chance to prove you're ready for more responsibilities. HR also suffers from some common misconceptions, like being a touchy-feely profession or being female-dominated.

Ready to help your colleagues and organization perform better? Before you determine what type of HR role you might best be cast in, it's important to understand that HR as a function isn't the same in every organization.

Human Resource Management

Human resource management (HRM) is the set of traditional HR activities that manage or support the people in the organization, and every working organization has to have at least one person responsible for HRM. The major areas of HRM include:

- Recruiting and staffing
- Compensation and benefits
- Labor and employee relations
- Health and safety

In HRM roles, professionals need to keep the HR motor humming and wheels turning. Imagine if you stopped receiving your paycheck or if your company stopped recruiting altogether. HRM functions are key to keeping organizations running smoothly, and HRM professionals are responsible for preventing any interruption in services that employees expect.

HRM professionals are also responsible to the organization as a whole. Running all of these processes can cost a lot of money, and it is up to HRM professionals to make decisions that help save the company money and make sure employees are well served. In each of the major areas of HRM, professionals are continually evaluating processes and implementing new programs and systems to serve the organization better. Examples include:

- **Recruiting and staffing:** Recruiting management systems (RMS) or applicant tracking systems (ATS) are the latest trend in electronically managing the influx of resumes during busy recruiting times. These systems save organizations money by streamlining the recruiting process and requiring fewer staff members to manage employee records.

- **Labor and employee relations:** Legal training for managers on topics, such as sexual harassment and workplace law, is becoming more and more common, in order to proactively reduce lawsuits related to workplace behavior.

- **Health and safety:** While injuries at plants and hazardous sites are common, HR professionals are also recognizing the increase in office injuries; many health and safety professionals are introducing ergonomically correct office furniture. While these fancy chairs and glare-reducing computer screens may be expensive, such investments can prevent future injuries and their associated costs.

- **Compensation and benefits:** Benefits outsourcing is a popular way to reduce costs and responsibility for an organization. Some compensation and benefits professionals work with outside vendors to manage programs such as an employee stock purchase plan. Since these outside vendors already have the expertise and systems in place to manage these programs, it saves the company the expense of creating them from scratch.

Companies such as the Home Depot are well known for their HR practices, and are consistently looking for ways to ease and automate the function in order to serve customers, and ultimately the organization, better. The Home Depot has become more recently renowned for creatively recruiting veterans who have recently finished their military careers. Since advertising on online job boards can be expensive, finding new channels to recruit prospective employees is an important way to save valuable recruiting dollars.

As a human resources VP for a consulting firm professes, improving the way employees are served is an important part of the job. "In the last five years, over 75 percent of our HR transactions have been automated to better serve our customers. We created a company Intranet and put our benefits elections process online, as well as all of our employee policies and procedures. No more paper!"

HRM professionals are also often charged with reporting HR's return on investment (ROI) to the company through tracking HR metrics (statistics on how a company's employees are performing) and demonstrating the value HR brings to the company. Compensation and benefits professionals might track how much employees are spending on health care costs and seek ways to reduce them. On the other hand, an employee relations professional might track statistics on how many minorities are employed in an organization for an affirmative action report. Measuring such activity is important for HRM professionals to show their commitment to an organization's bottom line.

HR management professionals must continually be thinking about ways to better serve and save a company money at the same time.

Common Human Resource Management Roles

Common HRM roles include:

- Compensation manager
- Senior recruiter
- Health and safety manager
- Employment lawyer
- Labor relations specialist
- Benefits specialist
- HR generalist

Human Resource Development

Human resource development (HRD) is the second part (albeit much smaller) of the HR world. If HRM professionals are keeping the wheels turning smoothly, HRD professionals are helping them turn faster and better. Human resource development refers to the activities in an organization that help develop and grow employees. Many organizations simply refer to HRD as training or learning and development but in reality, it's much more than that. HRD includes:

- Training and learning
- Organization development, which includes:
    - Succession planning (determining who is next in line for a CEO or other senior job)
    - Coaching (helping employees overcome on-the-job problems)
    - Performance management (those pesky performance reviews)

HRD is the area of HR that is growing most quickly as organizations recognize the need to go way beyond simply managing their workforce. While smaller organizations often have HR generalists assume the responsibility for training alongside other HR tasks, large companies, such as Medtronic, Bank of America and Texas Instruments, have entire functions devoted to subsets of HRD such as organization development.

"Organization development is a key part of human resources," says Phil Skeath, a performance improvement consultant at Bank of America. "We are business partners who support our line managers' needs, but we are also an integral part in driving the company's strategy."

Visit Vault at **www.vault.com** for insider company profiles, expert advice, career message boards, expert resume reviews, the Vault Job Board and more.

VAULT CAREER LIBRARY 315

HRD professionals may be responsible for a certain subset of the workforce (such as training the sales force), or may serve as internal consultants working on projects as they arise, such as helping to restructure a department or working on the succession plan for an entire division. Other HRD responsibilities include employee performance evaluations, training new employees and helping companies deal with change as the result of a new program, technology, merger or acquisition.

HRD careers are growing every year. Training and development is one area in which the Bureau of Labor Statistics (BLS) predicts growth in 2005 and beyond. This is due not only to how complex jobs are becoming, but also the aging of the workforce, and the many changes in technology requiring more and more training and development programs for workers. What does this mean for HR professionals? HRD might well be an increasingly popular career path.

Because HRD is not only growing, but is structured very differently from organization to organization, if you see HRD as a viable career path, it's important to research where it fits in specific companies. Organizations that only have a training and learning function may not see as much value in HRD as a company that has a specific organization development function.

Employer Directory

Accord Human Resources
Oklahoma Tower
210 Park Avenue, Suite 1200
Oklahoma City, OK 73102
Phone: (405) 232-9888
Fax: (405) 232-9899
Toll free: (800)725-4004
www.accordhr.com

Administaff
19001 Crescent Springs Drive
Kingwood, TX 77339
Phone: (281) 358-8986
Fax: (281) 348-3718
Toll free: (800) 237-3170
www.administaff.com

ADP Total Source Group
10200 Sunset Drive
Miami, FL 33173
Phone: (305) 630-1000
Fax: (305) 630-2006
www.adptotalsource.com

Adecco SA
Sägereistrasse 10
8152 Glattbrugg
Switzerland
Phone: +41-44-878-8888
Fax: +41-44-829-8888
www.adecco.com

Allegis Group, Inc.
7301 Parkway Drive
Hanover, MD 21076
Phone: (410) 579-4800
Fax: (410) 540-7556
Toll free: (877) 388-3823
www.allegisgroup.com

Automatic Data Processing, Inc.
1 ADP Boulevard
Roseland, NJ 07068
Phone: (973) 974-5000
Fax: (973) 974-3334
Toll free: (800) 225-5237
www.adp.com

Barrett Business Services
8100 NE Parkway Drive, Suite 200
Vancouver, WA 98662
Phone: (360) 828-0700
Fax: (360) 828-0701
Toll free: (800) 494-5669
www.barrettbusiness.com

Buck Consultants
1 Pennsylvania Plaza
New York, NY 10119
Phone: (212) 330-1000
Fax: (212) 695-4184
www.buckconsultants.com

Ceridian Corporation
3311 East Old Shakopee Road
Minneapolis, MN 55425
Phone: (952) 853-8100
Fax: (952) 853-4430
www.ceridian.com

COMFORCE Corporation
415 Crossways Park Drive
Woodbury, NY 11797
Phone: (516) 437-3300
Fax: (516) 396-9528
Toll free: (877) 266-3672
www.comforce.com

Convergys
201 East 4th Street
Cincinnati, OH 45202
Phone: (513) 723-7000
Fax: (513) 421-8624
www.convergys.com

Employco Group, Ltd.
350 East Ogden Avenue
Westmont, Il 60599
Phone: (630) 920-0126
Fax: (630) 920-0157
www.employco.com

Entegee, Inc.
70 Blanchard Road, Suite 102
Burlington, MA 01803
Phone: (781) 221-5800
Fax: (781) 221-4544
Toll free: (800) 368-3433
www.entegee.com

Express Employment Professionals
8516 Northwest Expressway
Oklahoma City, OK 73162
Phone: (405) 840-5000
Fax: (405) 717-5669
Toll free: (800) 222-4057
www.expresspros.com

Hay Group
The Wanamaker Building
100 Penn Square East
Philadelphia, PA 19107
Phone: (215) 861-2000
Fax: (215) 861-2111
www.haygroup.com

Hewitt Associates
100 Half Day Road
Lincolnshire, IL 60069
Phone: (847) 295-5000
Fax: (847) 295-7634
www.hewitt.com

Kforce Inc.
1001 East Palm Avenue
Tampa, FL 33605
Phone: (813) 552-5000
Fax: (813) 254-9640
Toll free: (800) 395-5575
www.kforce.com

Kelly Services, Inc.
999 West Big Beaver Road
Troy, MI 48084
Phone: (248) 362-4444
Fax: (248) 244-4360
www.kellyservices.com

Visit Vault at **www.vault.com** for insider company profiles, expert advice, career message boards, expert resume reviews, the Vault Job Board and more.

VAULT CAREER LIBRARY   317

Employer Directory, cont.

Manpower Inc.
100 Manpower Place
Milwaukee, WI 53212
Phone: (414) 961-1000
Fax: (414) 906-7985
www.manpower.com

Maxim Healthcare Services, Inc.
7227 Lee Deforest Drive
Columbia, MD 21046
Phone: (410) 910-1500
Fax: (410) 910-1515
www.maximhealthcare.com

Meador Staffing Services, Inc.
722 A Fairmont Parkway
Pasadena, CX 77504
Phone: (713) 941-0616
Fax: (713) 941-3582
Toll free: (800) 332-3310
www.meador.com

Mercer LLC
1166 Avenue of the Americas
New York, NY 10036
Phone: (212) 345-7000
Fax: (212) 345-7414
www.mercerHR.com

Medical Staffing Network Holdings, Inc.
901 Yamato Road, Suite 110
Boca Raton, FL 33431
Phone: (561) 322-1300
Fax: (561) 322-1200
Toll free: (877) 676-8326
www.msnhealth.com

Modern Business Associates
9455 Koger Boulevard, Suite 200
St. Petersburg, FL 33702
Phone: (727) 563-1500
Fax: (727) 563-1501
Toll free: (888) 622-6460

MPS Group, Inc.
1 Independent Drive, Suite 2500
Jacksonville, FL 32202
Phone: (904) 360-2000
Fax: (904) 360-2350
www.mpsgroup.com

On Assignment, Inc.
26651 West Agoura Road
Calabasas, CA 91302
Phone: (818) 878-7900
Fax: (818) 878-7930
www.onassignment.com

Paychex, Inc.
911 Panorama Trail South
Rochester, NY 14625-2396
Phone: (585) 385-6666
Fax: (585) 383-3428
www.paychex.com

Paystaff Corporation
7361 Calhoun Place, Suite 510
Rockville, MD 20855
Phone: (301) 340-3800
Fax: (301) 340-3801
Toll free: (800) 776-0076
www.paystaff.com

PDS Technical Services, Inc.
1925 West John Carpenter Freeway
Suite 550
Irving, TX 75063
Phone: (214) 647-9600
Fax: (214) 647-9636
Toll free: (800) 270-4737
www.pdstech.com

Robert Half International Inc.
2884 Sand Hill Road
Menlo Park, CA 94025
Phone: (650) 234-6000
Fax: (650) 234-6999
www.rhi.com

Select Staffing
1511 North Westshore Boulevard
Suite 900
Tampa, FL 33607
Phone: (813) 830-7700
Fax: (813) 830-7029
www.selectstaffing.com

SOI Holdings, Inc.
5260 Parkway Plaza Boulevard
Suite 140
Charlotte, NC 28217
Phone: (704) 523-2191
Fax: (704) 523-2158
Toll free: (800) 572-2412
www.soi.net

Spherion
2050 Spectrum Boulevard
Fort Lauderdale, FL 33309
Phone: (954) 308-7600
Fax: (954) 308-7666
www.spherion.com

Towers Perrin
263 Tresser Boulevard
Stamford, CT 06901
Phone: (203) 326-5400
www.towersperrin.com

Volt Information Sciences, Inc.
560 Lexington Avenue
New York, NY 10022
Phone: (212) 704-2400
Fax: (212) 704-2417
www.volt.com

Watson Wyatt Worldwide
901 North Glebe Road
Arlington, VA 22203
Phone: (703) 258-8000
Fax: (703) 258-8585
www.watsonwyatt.com

Westaff, Inc.
298 North Wiget Lane
Walnut Creek, CA 94598
Phone: (925) 930-5300
Fax: (925) 934-5489
www.westaff.com

Investment Management

Do you enjoy following the financial markets—whether it be reading *The Wall Street Journal*, watching CNBC, or checking stock prices on the Internet? Do you consider yourself to be creative and analytical, opinionated and objective? If that is the case, you may find a career in investment management an appealing option.

Imagine an industry that rewards individuals for working independently, thinking on their feet and taking calculated risks. Additionally, how many industries can you think of that broadly impact households all over the world? Very few. That is one of the many exciting aspects of the asset management industry—with household increasing and the demise of Social Security as a tool for long-term savings, more people than ever before are planning for their future financial needs. As a result, the industry is growing and more visible than ever.

Investment Management vs. Asset Management

A quick note about the terms **investment management** and **asset management**: these terms are often used interchangeably. They refer to the same practice—the professional management of assets through investment. Investment management is used a bit more often when referring to the activity or career (i.e., "I'm an investment manager" or "That firm is gaining a lot of business in investment management"), whereas "asset management" is used more with reference to the industry itself (i.e., "The asset management industry").

More stability

Because of the stability of cash flows generated by the industry, investment management provides a relatively stable career when compared to some other financial services positions (most notably, investment banking). Investment management firms are generally paid a set fee as a percentage of assets under management. (The fee structure varies, and sometimes is both an asset-based fee plus a performance fee, especially for institutional investors.) Still, even when investment management fees involve a performance incentive, the business is much less cyclical than cousins like investment banking. Banking fees depend on transactions. When banking activities, such as IPOs and M&A transactions, dry up, so do fees for investment banks, which translates into layoffs of bankers. This occurred in 2000-2001, with the tech bubble burst, and most recently in late 2007, with the subprime mortgage debacle. In contrast, assets are quite simply always being invested.

History

To better understand why asset management has become such a critical component of the broader financial services industry, we must first become acquainted with its formation and history.

The beginnings of a separate industry

While the informal process of managing money has been around since the beginning of the 20th century, the industry did not begin to mature until the early 1970s. Prior to that time, investment management was completely relationship-based. Assignments to manage assets grew out of relationships that banks and insurance companies already had with institutions—primarily companies or municipal organizations with employee pension funds—that had funds to invest. (A pension fund is set up as an employee benefit. Employers commit to a certain level of payment to retired employees each year and must manage their funds to meet these obligations. Organizations with large pools of assets to invest are called institutional investors.)

These asset managers were chosen in an unstructured way—assignments grew organically out of pre-existing relationships, rather than through a formal request for proposal and bidding process. The actual practice of investment management was

Visit Vault at **www.vault.com** for insider company profiles, expert advice, career message boards, expert resume reviews, the Vault Job Board and more.

VAULT CAREER LIBRARY   **319**

also unstructured. At the time, asset managers might simply pick 50 stocks they thought were good investments—there was not nearly as much analysis on managing risk or organizing a fund around a specific category or style. (Examples of different investment categories include small cap stocks and large cap stocks.) Finally, the assets that were managed at the time were primarily pension funds. Mutual funds had yet to become broadly popular.

ERISA, 401(k) plans and specialist firms

The two catalysts for change in the industry were: (1) the broad realization that demographic trends would cause the U.S. government's retirement system (Social Security) to be under-funded, which made individuals more concerned with their retirement savings; and (2) the creation of ERISA (the Employment Retirement Income Security Act) in 1974, which gave employees incentives to save for retirement privately through 401(k) plans. (401(k) plans allow employees to save pre-tax earnings for their retirement.) These elements prompted an increased focus on long-term savings by individual investors and the formation of what can be described as a private pension fund market.

These fundamental changes created the opportunity for professional groups of money mangers to form "specialist" firms to manage individual and institutional assets. Throughout the 1970s and early 1980s, these small firms specialized in one or two investment styles (for example, core equities or fixed income investing).

During this period, the investment industry became fragmented and competitive. This competition added extra dimensions to the asset management industry. Investment skills, of course, remained critical. However, relationship building and the professional presentation of money management teams also began to become significant.

The rise of the mutual fund

In the early to mid 1980s, driven by the ERISA laws, the mutual fund came into vogue. While mutual funds had been around for decades, they were only generally used by almost exclusively financially sophisticated investors who paid a lot of attention to their investments. However, investor sophistication increased with the advent of modern portfolio theory (the set of tools developed to quantitatively analyze the management of a portfolio; see sidebar below). Asset management firms began heavily marketing mutual funds as a safe and smart investment tool, pitching to individual investors the virtues of diversification and other benefits of investing in mutual funds. With more and more employers shifting retirement savings responsibilities from pension funds to the employees themselves, the 401(k) market grew rapidly. Consequently, consumer demand for new mutual fund products exploded (mutual funds are the preferred choice in most 401(k) portfolios). Many specialists responded by expanding their product offerings and focusing more on the marketing of their new services and capabilities.

Modern Portfolio Theory

Modern Portfolio Theory (MPT) was born in 1952 when University of Chicago economics student Harry Markowitz published his doctoral thesis, "Portfolio Selection," in the Journal of Finance. Markowitz, who won the Nobel Prize in economics in 1990 for his research and its far-reaching effects, provided the framework for what is now known as MPT. The theory quantifies the benefits of diversification, looking at how investors create portfolios in order to optimize market risk against expected returns. Markowitz, assuming all investors are risk averse, proposed that investors, when choosing a security to add to their portfolio, should not base their decision on the amount of risk that an individual security has, but rather on how that security contributes to the overall risk of the portfolio. To do this, Markowitz considered how securities move in relation to one another under similar circumstances. This is called "correlation," which measures how much two securities fluctuate in price relative to each other. Taking all this into account, investors can create "efficient portfolios," ones with the highest expected returns for a given level of risk.

Consolidation and globalization

The dominant themes of the industry in the 1990s were consolidation and globalization. As many former "specialists" rapidly expanded, brand recognition and advanced distribution channels (through brokers or other sales vehicles) became key success factors for asset management companies. Massive global commercial and investment banks entered the industry, taking business away from many specialist firms. Also, mutual fund rating agencies such as Lipper (founded in 1973, now a part of Reuters) and Morningstar (founded in Chicago in 1984) increased investor awareness of portfolio performance. These rating agencies publish reports on fund performance and rate funds on scales such as Morningstar's 5-star rating system.

These factors led to a shakeout period of consolidation. Over the last 20 years, there have been well over 150 mergers in the industry, creating well-established and formidable players such as BlackRock and JP Morgan Asset Management. The top-10 mutual fund firms now control roughly 50 percent of total assets, while the top-20 mutual funds control roughly 65 percent of total assets.

Traditional vs. alternative asset managers

The dominant theme over the past five to 10 years has been the proliferation of alternative asset managers. It is necessary to make the distinction between traditional asset managers and alternative asset managers. Traditional asset managers (such as mutual funds) are highly regulated entities that are governed by strict laws and regulations. The Securities and Exchange Commission (SEC) is the principal governing body and regulates these funds under the Investment Company Act of 1940. The rules governing traditional asset managers are primarily instilled to protect the investors and limit the amount of unnecessary risk-taking. Traditional asset managers have defined investment mandates, which determine what types of securities and strategies they can pursue in a given portfolio.

Alternative asset managers include assets classes such as hedge funds, private equity and venture capital. Their investment strategies and regulation differ from traditional asset managers as they are lightly regulated investment vehicles that do not always have defined investment strategies or risk tolerances. These asset classes are often designed to be uncorrelated with the broad stock and bond markets and seek to provide positive returns in a variety of economic situations. Since alternative investments are very risky, investors need to be deemed "accredited" (which is determined by net worth) in order to invest in these products.

The Industry Today

A robust economy has led to ever-increasing wealth creation, which in turn led to even greater demand for money management services today. Some analysts estimate the total global investable asset universe to be worth around $60 trillion, having grown by roughly 10 percent annually over the past decade. According to Merrill Lynch, there were 9.5 million people across the world with greater than $1 million in financial assets in 2007, up from 8.2 million in 2004. Mutual fund demand has continued to increase; as of 2006, there were 9,000 different funds in the market (up from just 3,000 in 1990). In fact, nearly 50 million households invest in mutual funds, with a total worth of $24 trillion as of June 2007 ($1 trillion as recently as 1990).

As the industry has matured, total assets under management (AUM) in the United States have grown to $60 trillion. Consolidation and globalization have created a diverse list of leading industry players that range from well-capitalized divisions of investment banks, global insurance companies and multinational commercial banks to independent behemoths, such as Fidelity and Capital Group.

Working in the industry, unlike other areas of financial services like investment banking, does not require that you live in a particular region of the country.

Visit Vault at **www.vault.com** for insider company profiles, expert advice, career message boards, expert resume reviews, the Vault Job Board and more.

VAULT CAREER LIBRARY

321

Buy-side vs. Sell-side

If you've ever spoken with investment professionals, you've probably heard them talk about the "buy-side" and the "sell-side." What do these terms mean, what are the differences in the job functions, and how do the two sides of the Street interact with one another?

What's the difference?

The sell-side refers to the functions of an investment bank. Specifically, this includes investment bankers, traders and research analysts. Sell-side professionals issue, recommend, trade and "sell" securities to the investors on the buy-side to "buy." The sell-side can be thought of primarily as a facilitator of buy-side investments—the sell-side makes money not through a growth in value of the investment, but through fees and commissions for these facilitating services. Simply stated, the buy-side refers to the asset managers who represent individual and institutional investors. The buy-side purchases investment products (such as stocks or bonds) on behalf of their clients with the goal of increasing its assets. In this section, we'll take a brief look at the types of jobs on each "side."

What are the differences between buy-side and sell-side jobs?

On the surface, the roles of buy-side and sell-side analysts sound remarkably similar. However, the day-to-day job is quite different. Sell-side analysts not only generate investment recommendations, they also need to market their ideas. This involves publishing elaborate and lengthy investment reports and meeting with their buy-side clients. In contrast, the buy-side analyst focuses entirely on investment analysis. Also, the buy-side analyst works directly with portfolio managers at the same firm, making it easier to focus on the relevant components of the analysis. The sell-side analyst is writing not for a specific team of professionals, but for the buy-side industry as a whole.

Despite these differences in responsibilities, professionals in buy-side and sell-side research analyst positions develop similar skill-sets. In fact, sell-side research and investment banking positions are the most popular training grounds for finance professionals who eventually switch to the buy-side.

How do the buy-side and sell-side interact?

Sell-side firms earn a trading fee every time a security (such as a bond or a stock) is bought or sold in a buy-side firm's portfolio. Because portfolio trades can generate sizeable commissions, sell-side firms (investment banks) have quite an incentive to develop relationships with the asset managers. Through institutional salespeople, investment banks provide asset managers with services such as analyst recommendations and access to firm sponsored IPOs and debt offerings. Additionally, the traders and salespeople who want asset managers' business will often present them with gifts such as expensive dinners and tickets to sporting events. An investment management professional in New York says, "I have been to Yankees games, Knick games, the U.S. Open, a rock concert, and eaten at over a dozen of the city's finest expensive restaurants. It's good to be the client." At the same time, another insider from a major asset management remarks, "It's important to be somewhat conservative. No firm wants to have it known that their guys have a lavish lifestyle and are out partying all night long; it might make it hard to convince the Carpenter's Union that you will do the best job possible managing their money." Most firms today prohibit employees from accepting gifts in excess of $100. So while you may still have dinner at a nice restaurant if you have a business meeting, do not expect to get World Series tickets anytime soon.

Professional Positions in Asset Management

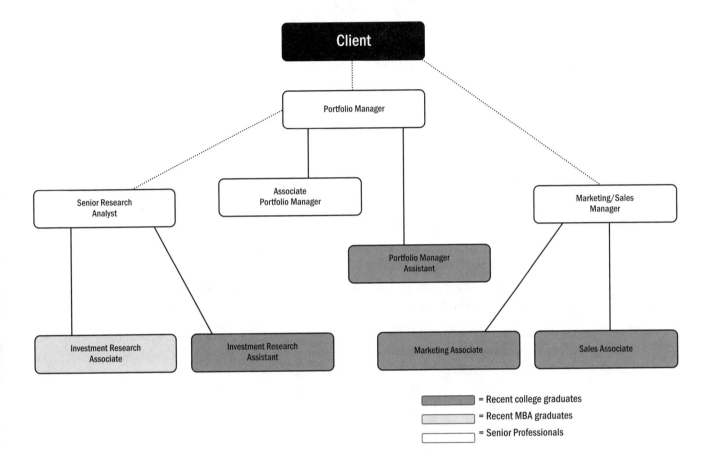

Portfolio Management

The portfolio management segment of the firm makes the ultimate investment decision; it's the department that "pulls the trigger." There are three jobs that typically fall under this component of the firm: portfolio managers, portfolio analysts (or associate portfolio managers) and portfolio manager assistants. Recent college graduates often fill portfolio assistant positions, while individuals with many years of investment experience hold associate and senior portfolio manager assignments. MBAs are not hired as portfolio managers right out of business school, unless they have a ton of experience. Typically, MBAs who wish to pursue a career in portfolio management join investment management firms in their investment research divisions. After several years in research, MBAs will then have a choice: either stay in research or leverage their research experience to move into an associate portfolio manager position or broaden their experience by covering additional sectors.

Visit Vault at **www.vault.com** for insider company profiles, expert advice,
career message boards, expert resume reviews, the Vault Job Board and more.

VAULT CAREER LIBRARY   323

Portfolio Manager Assistant Uppers and Downers

Uppers	Downers
• Broad exposure to the industry • Reasonable working hours • Direct exposure to portfolio managers	• Less formal training process • Some operations work • Repetitive assignments

Portfolio manager assistant

In general, portfolio manager assistants screen for potential investments, monitor portfolio characteristics and assist in client relations. Recent college graduates typically will spend two to four years in this role before returning to business school or migrating to a role in the investment research department.

This position varies among the firms in the industry, and the role itself differs depending on which segment of the firm you work in—mutual fund, institutional or high net worth. For instance, high-net-worth portfolio assistants spend more time working with clients, while institutional assistants spend more time monitoring and analyzing portfolios. Regardless, the general assignment focuses on supporting the portfolio manager.

Portfolio manager assistants are often instrumental in the process of screening for potential investments. Using the general strategy of the investment product—such as market-capitalization, earnings growth, valuation multiples or industry—the assistant screens all available stocks in the market to identify the smaller list that meets the portfolio's criteria. The screened list, for an active portfolio, varies but typically ranges between 100 and 300 securities. Portfolio manager assistants then gather additional research for the portfolio manager to begin the process of fundamentally analyzing the potential investment.

Once investments are made, portfolio manager assistants are responsible for monitoring the reconciliation of the trades. In this role, they work with the operations staff to assure that the portfolio is properly updated and performance records are accurate. Most firms have separate operations departments that reconcile trades and produce monthly client reports. However, many of the smaller firms require their portfolio assistants to perform the operations function as well. You should be aware of this, and clarify the exact job responsibilities when applying and interviewing for the job.

Portfolio assistants also participate in the process of client service, although the proportion of time spent in this area depends on the client type being served. For instance, an analyst to a mutual fund portfolio manager would spend very little time on client service. Institutional and high net worth portfolio managers have fewer clients and they meet with them one to two times a year. Intermittently, their clients require vast and detailed investment reports and market commentaries. While marketing helps prepare these formal presentations, the portfolio manager analyst plays a crucial role in collecting economic and market data for investment commentary and portfolio analysis sections of the report.

The position requires a person who understands capital markets, is capable of meeting deadlines and enjoys working on multiple projects simultaneously. The downside is that the reporting and operational components of the job have a quick learning curve and then become repetitive. Furthermore, it is not the best place to learn how to really value companies. Rather, you are being exposed to the years of experience that the portfolio manager possesses. Most important, portfolio manager analysts receive the benefit of seeing a broad picture of investing money across several industries, whereas research analysts typically get exposure to one component or sector. All in all, in the right setting, the position is a great introduction to asset management and a worthwhile apprenticeship to pursue.

Investment Research

The investment research segment is responsible for generating recommendations to portfolio managers on companies and industries that they follow. Similar to the portfolio management segment, there are several positions in the research hierarchy: senior research analyst, research associate-analyst (or junior analyst) and research associate.

On the sell-side, senior analysts typically have three to five years of post-MBA research experience or six to 10 years of post-college experience (if an MBA was not pursued). On the buy-side, new MBA graduates typically occupy the senior analyst position. The research associate-analyst is typically a sell-side position for recent MBA graduates. These positions are usually occupied for several years or until the candidate is deemed capable of covering his own sector. Both buy-side and sell-side firms employ recent college graduates as research associates. It is typically a two- or three-year program that can lead to a more senior position or result in the associate returning to business school.

Investment research associate

Investment research associates work with senior research analysts (or in some cases, associate-analysts) to help in developing investment recommendations for portfolio managers. Recent college graduates will spend, on average, two or three years in this role before returning to business school. However, some of the most successful associates are often promoted directly to associate-analyst (most of these fast-trackers will have completed their CFA while working as an associate).

The investment research associate is responsible for helping to monitor the industry and changes within companies covered in the industry, and to update financial models accordingly. Associates collect data for industry data services, company conference calls and surveys. For instance, in the previous Apple Computer example, the associate would be collecting data about consumer demand and input prices for semiconductors. Additionally, the associate provides support to the senior analyst in the construction of recommendation reports sent out to the portfolio managers. Specifically, the associate updates charts and modifies numerical sections of the report.

While some of the work is routine and the hours are long, associates are sitting next to, and learning from, the intellectual capital of the firm. If you work for a good analyst they will teach you the ropes, including the intangibles behind analyzing companies, financial valuation and industry knowledge.

The role of investment research associate requires a high level of quantitative knowledge. Primarily, a basic working knowledge of accounting, financial markets, financial analysis and statistics is needed for this position. Aside from a strong quantitative background, research associates need to be detail oriented, analytical problem solvers, diligent, and superior communicators. Generally, firms are looking for finance or accounting majors for these jobs, but engineers and science majors are also coveted for technology and health care related industries.

Investment Research Associate Uppers and Downers

Uppers	Downers
• Great quantitative experience	• Long hours (60+ hours/week)
• Most portfolio managers were once in research	• Lots of independent time in front of the computer
• Gain industry expertise	• Repetitive assignments
• Pays well	
• Typically a collegial environment	

Visit Vault at **www.vault.com** for insider company profiles, expert advice, career message boards, expert resume reviews, the Vault Job Board and more.

VAULT CAREER LIBRARY   325

A Day in the Life: Senior Analyst, Hedge Fund

5:45 a.m. Wake up and check BlackBerry for any news.

6 a.m. Check foreign markets on CNBC from home before I leave for work. (Foreign stock markets and the futures market are a good proxy of how the U.S. markets will open.)

6:30 a.m. Arrive at work. Monitor foreign positions and comb through e-mail, checking for any upgrades or downgrades from sell-side analysts.

7 a.m. Attend morning meeting with the other five members of our portfolio team. We discuss two positions. Company XYZ has doubled in three months and now represents a significant concentration of the portfolio. We decide to trim our position. The other stock has underperformed significantly. Our investment thesis remains intact and we decide to schedule a call with Company XYZ's CFO for later in the day.

8 a.m. Receive phone call from a sell-side analyst that downgraded a stock I have a large position in. He explains his reasoning for the downgrade. I expect the stock to drop significantly and may use the opportunity to purchase more stock.

8:30 a.m. Read the sell side analyst's downgrade report. Revisit my financial model and assumptions. I disagree with certain key conclusions and check the pre-market trading activity. It appears the stock is down 12 percent.

9 a.m. Notify the portfolio manager that I want to purchase more of the stock. He approves the decision.

9:30 a.m. The market opens and the stock is down 15 percent. I contact our trader and let him know I want to purchase an additional 100,000 shares.

9:35 a.m. The trader calls me and confirms he was able to find 100,000 shares and made the purchase.

9:45 a.m. Meet with a colleague on the options desk for coffee. As an analyst covering three industries, I brief him on my industry outlooks. He is trying to devise an options strategy to capitalize on the volatility of one of my industries. I assist by notifying him of upcoming catalysts that will increase volatility in the industry.

11 a.m. Meet with the portfolio manager to further discuss Company XYZ and why the stock is underperforming. He asks extremely detailed questions on the company's inventory levels. I answer most of the questions but need to get back to him on others.

11:30 a.m. Call up several distributors of the company to discuss inventory levels. Determine that inventory remains at all-time low levels. Write the portfolio manager a quick e-mail.

1 p.m. Eat lunch with a sales representative from J.P. Morgan. The purpose of the lunch is to introduce me to a new sell-side analyst the firm has hired and to hear his investment ideas.

2 p.m. Prepare for the conference call with Company XYZ's CFO. Write down five topics I plan on discussing with him.

2:30 p.m. Conference call with CFO of company XYZ.

3:30 p.m. Discuss the call with the portfolio manager. We agree to hold onto the position.

4 p.m. Go through e-mail and return phone calls.

6 p.m. Prepare for earnings releases of three companies for the next day.

7 p.m. Go home.

Marketing and Sales

Increasingly, as the industry grows and matures, investment management companies are focusing on professional marketing and sales as a point of differentiation—especially on the institutional side of the business.

Traditionally, marketing and sales have been more or less an afterthought: much of the marketing and sales work was performed by investment professionals. This is no longer the case, however; and firms are increasingly building teams of dedicated marketing and sales professionals.

Because sales and marketing professionals are typically required to be fluent in all of the investment products, these positions create a great opportunity to learn about the various investment styles that clients demand. This area is a great career opportunity for those who are interested in asset management but don't want to be the investment decision maker.

If your goal is to use sales and marketing as a stepping stone to the investment side, make it a point to network early on with investment professionals and prove yourself at your current job before making it known that you want to make the switch, and work toward developing the quantitative skills needed for the investment positions.

Below is a broad description of the positions that exist in the institutional marketing and sales segment.

Marketing or sales associates

Marketing and sales associates are typically recent college graduates. The positions are quite similar, although they are traditionally segmented by different types of organization.

Marketing associates assist in creating portfolio review presentations and in developing promotional presentations for potential new clients. They are traditionally segmented by investment product type such as equity or fixed income.

Sales associates assist in answering RFPs (request for proposals) issued by institutions seeking to hire new investment managers. Additionally, associates assist senior client servicing officials in maintaining and expanding client relationships. Sales associates are traditionally segmented by client type—public pension funds, corporate pension funds, endowments and foundations.

Marketing or Sales Associate Uppers and Downers

Uppers	Downers
• Broad knowledge of all of the investment products in the marketplace	• Difficult to jump to the investment side
• Great professional atmosphere for people who like the industry but don't want to be the investment decision maker	• Limited focus on building quantitative skills
• Less hierarchical career path than the investment side	• Repetitive assignments
• More entry-level jobs than the investment side	
• Lots of client interaction	

Visit Vault at **www.vault.com** for insider company profiles, expert advice, career message boards, expert resume reviews, the Vault Job Board and more.

VAULT CAREER LIBRARY   327

Employer Directory

AllianceBernstein
1345 Avenue of the Americas
New York, NY 10105
Phone: (212) 969-1000
Fax: (212) 969-2229
www.alliancebernstein.com

Allianz Group
Königinstrasse 28
D-80802 Munich
Germany
Phone: +49-89-38-00-0
Fax: +49-89-38-00-34-25
www.allianz.com

American Century Companies, Inc.
4500 Main Street
Kansas City, MO 64111
Phone: (816) 531-5575
Fax: (816) 340-7962
Toll free: (800) 345-2021
www.americancentury.com

Ameriprise Financial, Inc.
707 2nd Avenue South
Minneapolis, MN 55402
Phone: (612) 671-3131
Fax: (612) 671-5112
Toll free: (800) 386-2042
www.ameriprise.com

Bank of America Corporation
Bank of America Corporate Center
100 North Tryon Street
Charlotte, NC 28255
Phone: (704) 386-5681
Fax: (704) 386-6699
www.bankofamerica.com

Barclays Global Investors, N.A.
45 Fremont Street
San Francisco, CA 94105
Phone: (415) 597-2000
Fax: (415) 597-2171
www.barclaysglobal.com

BlackRock, Inc.
40 East 52nd Street
New York, NY 10022
Phone: (212) 810-5300
Fax: (212) 935-1370
www.blackrock.com

The Blackstone Group L.P.
345 Park Avenue
New York, NY 10154
Phone: (212) 583-5000
Fax: (212) 583-5712
www.blackstone.com

CalPERS
Lincoln Plaza
400 Q Street
Sacramento, CA 95814
Phone: (916) 795-3829
Fax: (916) 795-4001
Toll free: (888) 225-7377
www.calpers.ca.gov

Capital Group Companies
333 South Hope Street, 53rd Floor
Los Angeles, CA 90071
Phone: (213) 486-9200
Fax: (213) 486-9217
www.capgroup.com

Charles Schwab
120 Kearny Street
San Francisco, CA 94104
Phone: (415) 636-7000
Fax: (415) 636-9820
Toll free: (800) 648-5300
www.schwab.com

Credit Suisse Asset Management
11 Madison Avenue
New York, NY 10010
Phone: (212) 325-2000
Fax: (212) 538-3395
www.credit-suisse.com/am/en

D.E. Shaw & Co., L.P.
120 West 45th Street
39th Floor, Tower 45
New York, NY 10036
Phone: (212) 478-0000
Fax: (212) 478-0100
www.deshaw.com

DC Energy
8065 Leeburg Pike, 5th Floor
Vienna, VA 22182
Phone: (703) 506-3901
Fax: (703) 506-3905
www.dc-energy.com

Deutsche Bank
345 Park Avenue
New York, NY 10017
Phone: (212) 454-3600

Theodor-Heuss-Allee 70
60486 Frankfurt
Germany
Phone: +49 69-910-00
Fax: +49 69-910-34-225
www.db.com

Dreyfus Corporation
200 Park Avenue
New York, NY 10166
Phone: (212) 922-6000
Fax: (212) 922-7533
www.dreyfus.com

E*TRADE FINANCIAL
135 East 57th Street
New York, NY 10022
Phone: (646) 521-4300
Fax: (212) 826-2803
www.etrade.com

Edward Jones
12555 Manchester Road
Des Peres, MO 63131
Phone: (314) 515-2000
Fax: (314) 515-2820
www.edwardjones.com

Employer Directory, cont.

Federated Investors, Inc.
Federated Investors Tower
1001 Liberty Avenue
Pittsburgh, PA 15222-3779
Phone: (412) 288-1900
Fax: (412) 288-6446
Toll free: (800) 341-7400
www.federatedinvestors.com

Fidelity Investments
1 Federal Street, 27th Floor
Boston, MA 02109
Phone: (617) 563-7000
Fax: (617) 476-6150
www.fidelity.com

**Franklin Resources, Inc.
(Franklin Templeton
Investments)**
1 Franklin Parkway
Building 970, 1st Floor
San Mateo, CA 94403
Phone: (650) 312-2000
Fax: (650) 312 5606
www.franklintempleton.com

GAMCO Investors, Inc.
1 Corporate Center
Rye, NY 10580-1422
Phone: (914) 921-5100
Fax: (914) 921-5392
Toll free: (800) 422-3554
www.gabelli.com

Goldman, Sachs & Co.
85 Broad Street
New York, NY 10004
Phone: (212) 902-1000
Fax: (212) 902-3000
www.gs.com

HSBC North America Holdings
26525 Riverwoods Boulevard
Mettawa, IL 60045
Phone: (224) 554-2000
Fax: (224) 552-4400
www.hbscusa.com

ING Investment Management
Prinses Beatrixlaan 15
2595 AK The Hague
Netherlands
Phone: +31-70-378-1781
Fax: +31-70-378-1854
www.ingim.com

INVESCO
30 Finsbury Square
London, EC2A 1AG
United Kingdom
Phone: +44-20-76-38-07-31
Fax: +44-20-70-65-39-62
www.amvescap.com

Janus Capital Group
151 Detroit Street
Denver, CO 80206
Phone: (303) 333-3863
Fax: (303) 336-7497
www.janus.com

**J.P. Morgan Chase
Investment Management**
245 Park Avenue
New York, NY 10017
Phone: (212) 270-6000
Fax: (212) 270-2613
www.jpmorgan.com

Lazard Asset Management
30 Rockefeller Plaza, 58th Floor
New York, NY 10112-6300
Phone: (800) 821-6474
www.lazardnet.com

Legg Mason
100 Light Street
Baltimore, MD 21202-1099
Phone: (877) 534-4627
Fax: (410) 454-4923
Toll free: (877) 534-4627
www.leggmason.com

MFS Investment Management
500 Boylston Street
Boston, MA 02116
Phone: (617) 954-5000
Fax: (617) 954-6620
Toll free: (800) 637-2929
www.mfs.com

**Morgan Keegan-Wealth
Management Division**
Morgan Keegan Tower
50 Front Street, 17th Floor
Memphis, TN 38103
Phone: (901) 524-4100
Fax: (901) 579-4406
www.morgankeegan.com

**Morgan Stanley Investment
Management**
1585 Broadway
New York, NY 10036
Phone: (212) 761-4000
Fax: (212) 762-0575
www.morganstanley.com

Northern Trust Corporation
50 South LaSalle Street
Chicago, IL 60603
Phone: (312) 630-6000
Fax: (312) 630-1512
www.ntrs.com

Nuveen Investments
333 West Wacker Drive
Chicago, IL 60606
Phone: (312) 917-7700
Fax: (312) 917-8049
www.nuveen.com

**Pacific Investment
Management Co. (PIMCO)**
840 Newport Center Drive, Suite 100
Newport Beach, CA 92660
Phone: (949) 720-6000
Fax: (949) 720-1376
www.pimco.com

Visit Vault at www.vault.com for insider company profiles, expert advice,
career message boards, expert resume reviews, the Vault Job Board and more.

VAULT CAREER LIBRARY   329

Employer Directory, cont.

Pequot Capital Management
500 Nyala Farm Road
Westport, CT 06880
Phone: (203) 429-2200
Fax: (203) 429-2400
www.pequotcap.com

Putnam Investments
1 Post Office Square
Boston, MA 02109
Phone: (617) 292-1000
Fax: (617) 482-3610
Toll free: (800) 225-1581
www.putnam.com

Raymond James Financial
880 Carillon Parkway
St. Petersburg, FL 33716
Phone: (727) 567-1000
Fax: (727) 567-8915
Toll free: (800) 248-8863
www.rjf.com

Schroders plc
31 Gresham Street
London EC2V 7QA
United Kingdom
Phone: +44-20-76-58-60-00
Fax: +44-20-76-58-69-65
www.schroders.com

State Street Corporation
1 Lincoln Street
Boston, MA 02111
Phone: (617) 786-3000
Fax: (617) 664-4299
www.statestreet.com

T. Rowe Price
100 East Pratt Street
Baltimore, MD 21202
Phone: (410) 345-2000
Fax: (410) 345-2394
www.troweprice.com

TD Ameritrade
4211 South 102nd Street
Omaha, NE 68127
Phone: (402) 331-7856
Fax: (402) 597-7789
Toll free: (800) 237-8692
www.amtd.com

TIAA-CREF
730 3rd Avenue
New York, NY 10017
Phone: (212) 490-9000
Fax: (212) 916-4840
Toll free: (800) 842-2252
www.tiaa-cref.org

UBS Financial Services
1285 Avenue of the Americas
New York, NY 10019
Phone: (212) 713-2000
Fax: (212) 713-9818
www.ubs.com

The Vanguard Group
100 Vanguard Boulevard
Malvern, PA 19355
Phone: (610) 648-6000
Fax: (610) 669-6605
www.vanguard.com

Wellington Management Co., LLP
75 State Street
Boston, MA 02109
Phone: (617) 951-5000
Fax: (617) 951-5250
www.wellington.com

Journalism

Industry Overview

All the news ...

The newsroom as seen on the big screen—think *All the President's Men*, the *Spider-Man* series or *Citizen Kane*—rarely paints an accurate picture these days. Due to a variety of factors (the Internet, paper costs, fewer advertisements), the journalism industry is in the midst of a battle royale for survival, and though "the news" will obviously still be with us years from now, just how it will be delivered is still a matter of some debate. In 1985, newspaper publishers produced 62.8 million copies of their product, their highest total ever. By 2003 however, the Newspaper Association of American measured circulation for the country's 1,456 dailies at 55.2 million, and with an industry circulation shrinkage rate of 2 to 3 percent in the years hence, that number has dropped lower still.

The larger newspaper publishers no longer rely solely on the printed page, of course; over the past few decades, many have started or acquired other forms of broadcast (such as television outlets, radio stations or cable networks) or developed alternative sources of income. Weather networks (The Weather Channel), employment/career web sites (Monster and CareerBuilder), an online vendor of used cars, even a company specializing in ads carried on elevator TV screens have all made their way into the collection of businesses held by publishers. Education is a force, too: The Washington Post Company operates Kaplan, a well-respected source of campus learning and occupational and higher-education test preparation.

Most people would recognize the dozen or so companies with high-profile portfolios, among them Gannett, Tribune Company, The New York Times Company, The Washington Post Company, Dow Jones Corporation, Hearst Newspapers or The McClatchy Company. However, the industry is deeply fragmented, with scores of companies managing a roster of smaller daily, weekly and community publications.

Flippin' pages

The glossy pages generate lots of looks as well. Magazine publishers issue 6,700 titles to consumers around the globe (nearly twice that for trade publications), 80 percent of which have an associated web site. The Magazine Publishers of America, a trade organization servicing the industry, claims as its members more than 240 U.S. companies with 1,400 brands among them.

How to make money

There are two revenue streams that measure the fitness of the news and magazine publishing industry—circulation and advertising sales. The first of these refers to the number of copies sold (and doesn't include free subscriptions or those given away for promotions), and the associated revenue attributed to its two components (subscription delivery or newsstand purchase) can vary. For example, *Reader's Digest*, the magazine with the biggest circulation not based on membership, collects almost 95 percent of its revenue from subscriptions, while another top-10 publication, *People*, amassed more than half of its $533 million in 2006 from issues bought at retailers. Generally, magazine houses collect about 70 percent of their circulation revenue from subscription sales.

However, it's display and classified advertisements—on a national, regional or local level—that comprise most of the revenue for a magazine or newspaper publisher. The New York Times Company, for example, collected 65 percent of its revenue in ad sales in 2006, while ad sources contributed to 72 percent of revenue for the somewhat more diversified Journal Communications. Ad revenue at magazines is somewhat lower at 55 percent (2006). However, an uptick in readers (9 percent

Visit Vault at **www.vault.com** for insider company profiles, expert advice, career message boards, expert resume reviews, the Vault Job Board and more.

VAULT CAREER LIBRARY 331

from 2001 to 2006) is good news for both magazines and the best known corporations. The top-50 advertisers, including companies such as No. 1 Procter & Gamble, PepsiCo. and GM, spent almost $8.5 billion on mag advertising in 2006.

Instead of circulation guarantees, a handful of news publishers have advocated setting "readership" benchmarks for advertisers, which would account for additional readers from papers purchased then passed on to other readers. But that may not help either. The number of readers per copy of a daily paper is at its lowest level (just over 2.1) of the past 15 years, although the figure for Sunday editions remains a relatively robust 2.5, surpassing the rate for all but the two latest of the last 15 years. Others hope to define an advertiser's potential audience by a (non-overlapping) combination of unique readers of print and visitors to a publisher's dedicated web site. The online component is continually refreshed throughout the day/week/month, which generates multiple visits and page-views as readers search for updated information.

It's trickier for book publishers, even with a roster of "star" writers. Breaking unproven authors is challenging at best, and with no consumer polling conducted, the market is, pardon the expression, hard to read. Books that generate heavy interest at auction—when publishers buy the printing rights from an author—don't always translate to huge sales to the public. Any variety of factors can be the culprit in a poor showing: the title, cover art, voice of the book, time of year of the release, marketing plan, word of mouth, book availability, current events, level of consumer confidence in the economy. And again, publishers and editors only have intuition, sales figures of similar titles and a vague sense of what's worked before to go on.

In the financial markets, industry analysts say "past performance is no indication of future results," and this can be true for book publishers as well. *Thirteen Moons,* the latest release by author Charles Frazier, generated an $8 million advance, but fell flat at 250,000 copies, after his previous *Cold Mountain* sold more than 1.5 million. Generally, sales of a title in the 20,000-copy range are considered decent, and a company makes money with perennial sellers and those with 100,000 copies or more in print.

Circulatory problems are serious!

The health of the publishing industry carries a large question mark in the 21st century. A number of factors have converged to threaten the physical production of newspapers and magazines, and while most publishers, including Jann Wenner of Wenner Publications and Time Inc.'s CEO Ann Moore, are confident that the printed page won't disappear, all have recognized just how dire the situation is. Newspaper circulation has eroded considerably from the early part of the decade; one daily, *The Seattle Post-Intelligencer*, reaches 34 percent fewer readers than it did in 1999. According the Audit Bureau of Circulations, for the six-month period that ended in September 2006 (compared to the previous year), 18 of the top-20 papers saw circulation slumps, with seven properties down by more than 5 percent. Over time, figures have shown an average 2 to 3 percent decline per year for the industry. To alleviate the pressure, both *The New York Times* and *The Wall Street Journal* recently raised their home-delivery and newsstand prices.

That dive in circulation translates easily into reduced advertising revenue. Publishers are forced to reduce the guaranteed base for advertisers, which means a smaller rate and smaller total sales. A sharp downturn in the U.S. housing market has resulted in fewer real estate classifieds and display ads, further hampering the situation. According to the Newspaper Association of America, sales of newspaper print advertising amounted to $46.6 billion in 2006, a decline of 1.7 percent from the previous year, but that doesn't begin to illuminate the effects on individual companies. For instance, in just the first three months of 2007, The Washington Post Company found both its ad revenue and profit off by 16 percent.

To stem the trend, in 2006 a dozen newspaper groups—including Cox Newspapers, Belo Corp., The McClatchy Company, Hearst Newspapers and Lee Enterprises—entered into a partnership with Yahoo! However, it's more than just a simple move to increase sales. The arrangement, which affects over 260 newspapers around the country, will serve to control expenditures by maximizing efficiency (the Yahoo! sales force will sell newspaper space to its online advertiser base, and news salespeople will sell Yahoo! space to their advertisers). The companies' news content will also be carried on the Yahoo! Network, and this is expected to pave the way for the distribution of newspaper content via cell phones. In conjunction, publishers are concentrating on developing their presence on the Internet. Despite the large jumps seen in visitors to these companies' web sites (estimated by some at 20 to 30 percent), revenue from online exposure typically comprises only 2 to 6 percent of newspaper revenue at this point.

And now, some input from our readers

Several companies have evaluated their operations and found it no longer makes sense to keep print and online media as separate entities. Gannett presented some major changes to its business model in November 2007—news desks at all of the company's papers (except those at *USA Today*) will be converted into "information centers" by mid-2007, and traditional departments (national, city, lifestyle and sports, for instance) will be reorganized into seven groups: public service, digital, data, community conversation, local, custom content and multimedia. Also, in a practice known as "crowdsourcing," papers will no longer rely solely on reporters and editors to gather the news. Rather, staffers in each of the new groups will actively seek contributions from the readership, and monitor web site blogs for story ideas and public sentiment. (Gannett tested the new strategies in 11 locations during the previous year.) While crowdsourcing has provided viable contributions for the photostock industry and for the online encyclopedia Wikipedia, it invites potential problems of journalistic integrity and fact-checking. And though the process would make the online and print news offerings more vital and timely, if a shift to this type of sourcing became more common in the industry, it could easily lead to further staff reductions and the loss of a news-savvy knowledge base of reporters.

The most successful news publishers appear to be those lacking a large metropolitan daily, whose properties consist of smaller dailies, weeklies or less frequent community papers. Analysts reason that since these contain pieces of more specialized local interest, alternative sources are harder to come by, and readers are less apt to defect. Though these papers are still stagnant or declining in terms of circulation, the percent of declines are smaller, and are deteriorating at a much slower rate than at the big city newspapers. The Journal Register Company, Lee Publications and GateHouse Media, among others, have a policy of clustering, accumulating smaller weeklies or special interest publications, sometimes supplementing them with broadcast stations to amass a mini-monopoly on local information. Though it may seem counterintuitive to generate an audience this way, the companies find that the newspapers direct readers to the stations and vice versa, creating a more comprehensive opportunity for advertisers.

Of course, the last resort option is a sale to another publisher, or worse, an equity partner (that usually maintains its monetary and creative interest for a limited time period). In the latest, largest example of the latter, entrepreneur Sam Zell took the debt-laden Tribune Company private for $8.2 billion in April 2007. The following month, Thomson Corp. agreed to merge with Reuters for upwards of $17 billion, and Dow Jones (with the rest of the Wall Street community) was stunned by an unsolicited $5 billion bid from News Corp. head Rupert Murdoch. The Bancroft family, owners of 64 percent of Dow Jones' voting shares, rejected the enormous offer at first, but later agreed to be snatched up by a mogul known for his hands-on management style and the somewhat less-than-objective leanings of his media properties.

Magazine methods

During 2006 and the first half of 2007, magazine publishers closed or suspended 47 titles due to their poor performance, among them three from Hachette Filipacchi Media (the months-old *Red* and *For Me*, plus *ElleGirl*, *Premiere* and *Shock*), Meredith Corporation's *Child*, Time Inc.'s *Teen People* and Condé Nast's *Cargo*. However, in a few cases, the parent company has chosen to keep the brand alive online, continuing to engage loyal fans while hoping to build traffic (and advertising revenue) for the company's web sites. The online sites are showing large increases in number of visitors, but as with newspaper companies, proceeds from these typically make up a small percentage of revenue. Industry insiders still place a value on owning content (and an Internet site can hold an unlimited amount of it) but the process has to be reconsidered. Time Inc.'s *Sports Illustrated*, for example, has devised a revenue stream by licensing its classic photos.

Visit Vault at **www.vault.com** for insider company profiles, expert advice, career message boards, expert resume reviews, the Vault Job Board and more.

VAULT CAREER LIBRARY   333

It's much more common for companies to sell their underperforming magazines to other publishers than to merge. During 2006 and 2007, more than 110 magazines changed hands, sometimes in groups of 10 or 20. On the other hand, Condé Nast Publications, the Meredith Corporation, Reader's Digest and Hearst Magazines have independently taken similar creative steps to address the problem of diminished sales. Each has created a media division that produces at least some creative work, which may incorporate in-store events, television specials, contests, online or outdoor media in addition to "traditional" ad pages, for its advertisers; some have the capability to provide more intensive marketing and ad evaluation guidance. Since 47 percent of magazine pages are devoted to advertising, this is a great way to generate continual income.

Working in the Industry

A (long) day in the life

Positions in newspaper publishing are largely focused on editorial, production and marketing/ad sales functions. Increasingly, with the intermingling of print and online centers, entrants to the world of journalism are expected to have some sort of familiarity with online sourcing or publishing in addition to an English or journalism degree. Book and magazine houses also need candidates with good editorial skills and expertise in layout and production. Online and print advertising are still the dominant sources of newspaper revenue, so top sales people are always in demand. (This is also true for publishers of periodicals.) Obviously, book publishers have no need for ad sales people, they're only interested in selling the final product. To do so, there's a need for public relations staff and creative individuals who can come up with inventive ways to market a book with media, Internet, mobile or in-store tie-ins.

An editorial position at a magazine or a newspaper publisher would be similar but with more emphasis on meeting deadlines (weekly or daily, as opposed to the more common monthly goals in books), internal organization and leadership. To succeed in one of these capacities, you've got to love to read—editors often take manuscripts home to read after work or on weekends—and look forward to long, sometimes erratic, working hours. To make up for that, companies often have decent-to-excellent diversity and benefit policies, and perks ranging from product discounts to access to special events and such. But depending on who's running the show, the company environment can range from pleasant to horrible.

People who have interviewed at publishers of any type don't report any tricky questions popped during the interview process. As in any industry, for potential sales personnel, the answer to "On a scale of 1 to 10, how motivated are you to go into sales?" must be answered with a confident "10."

Career futures

Magazines, and to a much greater extent, newspapers, look to be ailing. Unfortunately, with the trends of slipping circulation and revenue come staff reductions. Layoffs affected the staff at MediaNews Group's *The Denver Post*, The New York Times Company's *Boston Globe* and *The Washington Post* in 2006 or 2007, and similar actions could conceivably occur at just about any news publisher. In several cases, shareholders unhappy with company performance have pressed for a sale, resulting in consolidation (as was the case with The McClatchy Company acquisition of Knight-Ridder in 2006), or an equity buyout. Tribune Company, for one, landed in private investor hands for the first time. It remains to be seen if ownership by equity partners—industry outsiders—can shake companies like Tribune out of a slow downward spiral.

Magazines

Magazines were the first true national media in America. Newspapers had been a predominantly local medium, but magazines were the first to unite people across the country with the help of the U.S. Postal System as the means of distribution. Magazines edified and entertained people from coast to coast with interests in homemaking, hunting, politics and hundreds of other topics and hobbies.

By 1900, there were over 5,500 magazines in circulation. According to the Magazine Publishers of America, there are now well over 17,000 titles. Magazines like *Cosmopolitan, Atlantic Monthly* and *The Saturday Evening Post* became media fixtures in the American home by the middle of the last century. In 1923 the term "newsmagazine" was coined, with the launch of *Time*, by Henry Luce and Briton Hadden. Today, magazines are facing rising production and distribution costs. Many in the industry believe their survival lies in targeting smaller niche audiences.

What makes magazines unique?

The longer format of magazines allows writers to go deeper into stories or provide more detailed information about a specific topic, whereas newspapers typically offer the latest headlines of the day. Magazines unite people with common interests, like fishing, crafts, gardening or automobiles. In some instances, magazines are saved to be used as reference material in the home or office. For example, many amateur chefs and food enthusiasts save their copies of *Bon Appetit, Cooking Light* or *Food & Wine* for the recipes and cooking tips they find within their pages. While magazines are just as portable as newspapers, they are more likely to be passed around and shared with others, reaching a larger audience beyond just their subscription and newsstand circulation.

What attracts people to work for a magazine?

Overall, there are more aesthetic considerations in the development of a magazine than for a newspaper. Magazines have a personality all their own. Newspapers, on the other hand, are literally black and white, offering few frills beyond getting out the news of the day.

On the content side, many journalists savor the opportunity to sink their teeth into just one story or to stick to a specific content area. For photographers, there are far more creative opportunities in magazines than in newspapers, where photography is primarily limited to capturing images of news as it happens.

On the business side, magazines offer the opportunity to develop direct marketing campaigns to target niche audiences, rather than the one-size-fits-all marketing strategies of broadcast television. Sponsorships are also more focused on national advertisers, rather than local ones, as is common among newspapers.

Is a career in magazines for you?

Stability is not necessarily a feature of working in magazines. Pay is very low as you start out, so it is necessary to move around a lot in order to increase your salary. Increasingly, many jobs in magazines are becoming freelance, especially on the content side, for writers, photographers, designers and illustrators.

The hours can also be crazy, especially when you are trying to meet a deadline, but working for a magazine can be very exciting. Since there always seems to be a new magazine being launched, you will be invited to many different parties. There are some people lucky enough (depending on how you look at it) to plan these posh events as their full-time jobs. As you gain responsibility, there is the potential for travel, as well.

Visit Vault at **www.vault.com** for insider company profiles, expert advice, career message boards, expert resume reviews, the Vault Job Board and more.

VAULT CAREER LIBRARY   335

Desired skills and traits

Research: Due to their longer format and less frequent publication, magazines place a different emphasis on research than do newspapers. Not only is it important to get the facts straight, but far more detailed knowledge of subject matter is required. Research in newspapers tends to be broader, in magazines it's inclined to be more focused.

Writing: A distinct writing style is necessary to capture the brand and personality of the magazine. A more personalized style also guides readers through longer stories commonly found in magazines. On the flip side, there are many magazine features that now require highly creative and "punchy" copy for features that offer readers quick pops of information.

Expertise: As magazines become more and more niche oriented, it is helpful to bring a unique area of expertise to the table, even for more general publications, like *Time* or *Newsweek*. Many writers and reporters for magazines are increasingly freelance, so it is important to begin building a knowledge base in a particular area like health, business or entertainment. As a result, you can write for any magazine, rather than limiting yourself to one magazine title.

Business skills: In such a highly competitive marketplace, where most newly launched magazines fail within the first year, business skills are crucial. Understanding demographic research, database management and direct marketing are a must. Even on the creative side, it doesn't hurt to understand the basics of business and how to better connect with your target audience.

Entrepreneurial spirit: Last year, over 400 new titles were launched in the U.S. While established titles may not champion the entrepreneurial spirit, start-up magazines definitely do. A "can-do" attitude, good organizational skills, creativity and the ability to solve problems are all welcome traits in helping to establish a new magazine title.

TV News

Broadcast television burst forth in the late 1940s, growing out of the tradition of broadcast radio. In fact, it was first regarded as "radio with pictures." It soon developed into a form all its own. It brought groundbreaking events into millions of Americans' living rooms, from Edward R. Murrow's look at the life of migrant workers to Walter Cronkite reporting from the middle of the Vietnam war zone, to the live-television assassination of Lee Harvey Oswald by Jack Ruby.

Since its birth over 60 years ago, television news has grown to become the voice of local communities throughout America, and national broadcasts have helped make our vast country seem smaller. Over the last two decades, the emergence of cable television, led by the pioneering efforts of Ted Turner's CNN in 1980, has grown to deliver news 24/7.

What makes television news unique?

Broadcast television has enabled interview subjects to share their story in their own words. Sometimes moving images speak for themselves without the aid of a professional journalist's words. Broadcast stories have made us swell with pride, shed a tear or bust a gut. Television has enabled a mass audience to witness history first hand—to view news as it happens.

Through the years, television journalism has provided Hollywood with inspiration, ranging from dramas like *Broadcast News* to revealing looks at the industry based on true stories, like *The Insider*, to comedies like *Anchorman*. Why are Americans so fascinated by television news? For the same reason so many people pursue a career in this business—the combination of the star power generated by a visual broadcast medium and the ability of video journalism to capture the raw emotion of a story.

What attracts people to work in television news?

Many television journalists love the rush of reporting live news events and being able to share those images with viewers at home. Video enables journalists to capture the sights, sounds and details of a moment like no other medium.

Most news broadcasts are live, adding to the pressure of the environment and the immediacy with which news is delivered to a mass audience. Television news shares many of the same characteristics of other journalistic disciplines, but it is perceived as the most glamorous. At the national level, your work can be shared with a larger audience than newspapers, magazines or radio can attract.

Network/cable news track

Producing

Production assistant: An entry-level position performing administrative duties that vary from company to company and even from show to show.

Broadcast associate: In charge of gathering basic elements for a broadcast, including archival footage and research for producers.

Booker: Focused on booking guests to be interviewed for live broadcasts. This position is common in cable news, as well as morning broadcasts that have a lot of live guests.

Assistant or associate producer: Depending on the size of the organization, an assistant producer is junior to an associate producer, but they both perform similar functions. Responsibilities include setting up interviews, research, arranging and sometimes supervising shoots and gathering other elements required for a piece.

Segment producer: In charge of one portion of a broadcast, generally in between two blocks of commercials.

Web producer: An increasingly important part of each broadcast and news organization, overseeing the production of various web pages dedicated to a particular show or a specific topic area.

Show producer: Performs similar functions as a producer at the local level. Show producers generally work in cable news and oversee the rundown, script and elements for a show.

Field producer or producer: Oversees the logistics of producing a story or elements for a piece in the field. After seeking approval of the executive producer for a story, they oversee its entire process, from developing an outline to identifying interview subjects to setting up interviews for correspondents; many times they even conduct the interviews themselves.

Senior producer: Works with producers to develop story ideas and to provide editorial guidance and suggestions.

Executive producer: Oversees an entire broadcast. Responsibilities include setting budgets, helping to arrange high-profile interviews, developing story ideas and providing overall editorial direction for the broadcast.

National or foreign editor: Function is similar to that of an assignment editor. Keeps an eye on developing stories on national or international scene. Also coordinates the necessary resources for the coverage of domestic or foreign news events.

Senior executive producer: Within large news organizations, a senior executive producer manages the overall brand of a show, particularly when there are multiple broadcasts under the same name, like *60 Minutes* or *Dateline*. Determines potential revenue opportunities, provides editorial guidance and steers the overall promotion of the broadcast.

Vice president: Oversees a specific operational area, like newsgathering, or a daypart, like primetime broadcasts.

President: Head of the news operation, providing overall editorial, financial and brand direction for organization.

Visit Vault at www.vault.com for insider company profiles, expert advice, career message boards, expert resume reviews, the Vault Job Board and more.

VAULT CAREER LIBRARY   337

On air

Correspondent: Functions much the same as reporters do at the local level, but they have a producer assigned to them, helping them put their video package together. They will write the script, but the producer gathers the elements. In cable news, they will also perform several live shots throughout the progression of a developing story.

For magazine shows or "soft news," correspondents conduct interviews and write the script for their piece. Stories for magazine shows can run as long as 10 minutes, while packages for a hard news broadcast, like the evening news, run only about one and a half minutes.

Anchor: As with local broadcasts, the anchor is the central figure of a show, introducing all the stories and correspondents. They will also conduct interviews on the set and sometimes in the field. Salary varies, depending on the reach of the broadcast.

Local Television News Track

Assignment desk

Desk assistant: An entry-level position at a local station on the assignment desk. Works with assignment editor to answer phones, read the wires, listen to the police and fire department scanners, as well as help coordinate photographers and reporters in the field.

Assignment editor: Manages the assignment desk. Generally there is a dayside assignment editor and a nightside assignment editor. Many stations also have an assignment editor to cover the overnight hours and to help prepare for the early morning newscasts. They pitch story ideas, assign reporters and photographers to stories and gather research to help with the development of stories.

Producing

Production assistant: Another entry-level position to help with administrative tasks and to provide additional support to the assignment desk, reporters, producers, photographers and editors.

Associate producer: After a year or so spent in an entry-level position, this is the next step on the road to becoming a producer. Works with producer(s) on one or two assigned newscasts, the 5 p.m. and 6 p.m. news, for example. Asked to write "readers," copy read by the anchor with no video, as well as introductions for reporter packages. May also edit video on a nonlinear editing system.

Producer: Generally oversees one broadcast, sometimes two. Develops the "rundown," a document that determines the order of the stories in the newscasts and makes sure the entire newscast runs on time. Writes the opening headlines and some readers. Constantly monitors wires and assignment desk for breaking news, as well as the latest developments for existing stories.

Executive producer: Oversees all newscasts. Depending on the market, there may also be a senior producer who works with the executive producer. Works to make sure lead story is consistent throughout all newscasts. Works with producers to maintain editorial and production standards as articulated by the station.

Assistant news director: Works with news director to manage entire newsgathering and production operation.

News director: Oversees all aspects of news gathering operation, from editorial to production, to graphics, making sure the look and feel of all newscasts is consistent with the editorial standards and overall vision of the station.

Photographer: The actual collection of video is gathered by photographers, or "photogs." Many photographers learn their trade on the job or receive special training at a trade school. Like on-air talent and producers, they also move around the country to build their career.

Increasingly, more and more photogs are also wearing the editor's hat, due to shrinking budgets and new technologies that make it even easier to edit. Most photogs at local stations already edit a reporter's package, either back at the station or in a live truck (a vehicle used to broadcast from remote locations).

On air

The "face" of the newsgathering operation is the reporters and anchors of each station, also referred to as "the talent." Becoming an on-air reporter or anchor is very tough. Most people will start out as a general assignment reporter in a very small market and will move around the country every one to two years, jumping to larger markets with better financial compensation.

Some will also have to work less coveted schedules like overnights and weekends just to start building their career and demo tape. It is no longer uncommon for reporters to start out as "video journalists" or VJs. These reporters are virtual one-man bands. They use digital video cameras and laptop editing software, shooting and editing their own video, in addition to producing and writing their own story.

Meteorologist or weatherman: Meteorologists possess a degree in meteorology or atmospheric science, whereas some weathermen do not. Much of today's weather forecasting is left to high-powered computers that offer various models to predict the weather. Weather is one of the most popular segments of local broadcasts. There are both on-air and producing opportunities in weather. Beyond television stations, there are also opportunities on cable at The Weather Channel and local 24/7 weather channels, as well as weather service companies like AccuWeather or WeatherCentral.

Sportscaster or sports anchor: In some cases, a station's lead sports anchor is also referred to as the sports director. There is a growing emphasis within some local television stations on reducing their sports staff and delegating coverage of sports to the news staff, as a result of increasing competition from sports cable networks and web sites. Alternatively, there are more and more opportunities to work in sports cable television, as well as for professional sports organizations and leagues that have recently launched their own networks.

Radio News

Radio was the first electronic mass medium, bringing live news events as they happened into millions of homes for the first time. Still unsure of its impact, Orson Welles duped millions of listeners into thinking martians were invading earth in 1938. Charles Collingwood, Eric Sevareid and Edward R. Murrow brought millions of Americans to the front lines of war, sending back live reports from Europe during World War II.

Radio was quickly adopted by Americans: 90 percent of homes owned one by 1930. In that year, radio personality Lowell Thomas gave birth to radio news when he began reading the news on air. At first, newspapers tried to fight this trend, citing copyright laws, but they were eventually overruled when the courts determined that no one could own the news, and the factual content was part of the public domain. The Golden Age of radio was eclipsed by the advent of television in the 1950s, forcing it to reinvent itself from the primary electronic medium for news and entertainment into a local medium for news, talk and music.

Visit Vault at **www.vault.com** for insider company profiles, expert advice, career message boards, expert resume reviews, the Vault Job Board and more.

V/\ULT CAREER LIBRARY   339

What makes radio unique?

Radio is a mass medium, but it creates a one-on-one relationship between the announcer and the listener. The listener is allowed to visualize a story for themselves, becoming absorbed in their own imagination as they are guided by a storyteller. For this reason, radio has been often referred to as "the theater of the mind."

Radio is probably the least expensive of all media to consume, thereby truly reaching out to a mass audience. The phenomenon of talk radio also promotes a diversity of voices and allows the average man or woman the opportunity to be heard in a public forum. The unique features of radio provide insight in to what is on the minds of Americans. It's no surprise that radio talk show hosts are regularly interviewed by television broadcasters when major news events like the attacks of September 11th occur, in order to understand the common person's perspective.

What attracts people to work in radio?

Like newspapers, every day is different and there is a focus on serving local communities. Radio provides a more personal connection to the audience than print. The nature of the medium promotes a sense of immediacy—getting reaction from the community as news happens. Of course, if you have a voice like velvet, it certainly won't hurt your chances of landing an on-air gig!

On the business side, radio offers a similar opportunity to that of newspapers, in working with local sponsors. Radio also enables advertisers to target niche audiences, and offers greater flexibility to refine their marketing messages than they can in print. Once an ad hits the presses, there's no turning back, but it is technically possible to change a radio spot throughout the course of the day.

Career Track

Content

The primary function of the editorial staff is to gather and report the news. Each morning, they have a meeting to pitch story ideas and to assign resources to stories to be covered that day. They monitor wires, call on their sources and read a variety of print media to find stories.

Much of the content in radio is interview-driven, and because there are no visual elements, a premium is placed on telling a story through the written word. Anchors conduct interviews in the studio by phone, live on the air, with a newsmaker like a local politician, civic leader or another member of the community. Reporters will conduct interviews as part of their stories and will also collect sound bites from "Man on the Street" (MOS) interviews to be used in taped stories or as part of live interview segments.

Desk assistant: For those just getting their start in radio, the desk assistant is a "jack of all trades," helping to research stories, set up interviews and even write copy for news readers. Generally, most start out at smaller stations, where there is an opportunity to gain more hands-on experience than at a station in a larger market.

Writer: Writes copy for announcers and anchors, as well as introductions for packages produced by reporters. Once again, at smaller stations with fewer resources, anchors most likely write much of their own scripts.

Producer: More likely found at larger stations, producers develop the rundown for live broadcasts and book interviews for live interview broadcasts or talk shows.

Assignment editor: Cruises the wires, the fire department and police scanners and consults community sources, looking for stories or breaking news like fires and shootings. The assignment editor will also help write certain stories, particularly those from the wires, as well as copy to introduce reporter packages.

Reporter: Goes out into the community to investigate leads and news tips, gathers information for stories and conducts interviews. Once a reporter has gathered all the elements for his story, he writes a script and produces his package or segment. Reporters also report live from news events.

Anchors: Monitors the wires for stories, writes copy, introduces stories by reporters, provides perspective for breaking news, conducts live interviews and delivers the news to the community of listeners.

Host: Similar to an anchor, but generally associated with a live broadcast made up of in-studio interviews or call-ins from listeners.

Commentators: Provide opinions or editorials about news events or issues facing a local community.

Assistant news director: Manages day-to-day news gathering and production operations.

News director: Provides editorial direction for the station, develops budgets and oversees the assignment of resources for news coverage.

General manager: Provides overall leadership for editorial, sales and promotion for a station. Median salary varies widely depending on the size of the station and market.

Visit Vault at **www.vault.com** for insider company profiles, expert advice, career message boards, expert resume reviews, the Vault Job Board and more.

VAULT CAREER LIBRARY   **341**

Employer Directory

ABC, Inc.
77 West 66th Street
New York, NY 10023-6298
Phone: (212) 456-7777
abcradionetworks.com
Owns more than 70 radio stations.

ABC News
77 West 66th Street, Room 100
New York, NY 10023
Phone: (212) 456-7777
Fax: (212) 456-1424
www.abcnews.com

Advance Publications
950 Fingerboard Road
Staten Island, NY 10305
Phone: (212) 286-2860
Fax: (718) 981-1456
www.advance.net
Owns: The Star-Ledger (New Jersey), Cleveland Plain Dealer

American City Business Journals, Inc.
120 West Morehead Street, Suite 400
Charlotte, NC 28202
Phone: (704) 973-1000
Fax: (704) 973-1001
www.bizjournals.com

American Express Publishing Corporation
1120 Avenue of the Americas
New York, NY 10036
Phone: (212) 382-5600
Fax: (212) 768-1568
www.amexpub.com
Owns: Food & Wine, Travel + Leisure

American Media Inc.
1000 American Media Way
Boca Raton, FL 33431-1000
Phone: (561) 997-7733
Owns: Men's Fitness, SHAPE

The Associated Press
450 West 33rd Street
New York, NY 10001
Phone: (212) 621-1670
Fax: (212) 621-5447
www.ap.org

Belo Corp.
400 South Record Street
Dallas, TX 75202-4841
Phone: (214) 977-6606
www.belo.com
Owns: The Dallas Morning News, The Providence Journal

Bloomberg L.P.
731 Lexington Avenue
New York, NY 10022
Phone: (212) 318-2000
Fax: (917) 369-5000
www.bloomberg.com
Syndicates business reports to 840 affiliates worldwide.

Bonnier Corporation
460 North Orlando Avenue, Suite 200
Winter Park, FL 32789
Phone: (407) 628-4802
Fax: (407) 628-7061
www.bonniercorp.com

CBS News
524 West 57th Street
New York, NY 10019
Phone: (212) 975-4321
www.cbsnews.com

Citadel Broadcasting
7201 West Lake Mead Boulevard
Suite 400
Las Vegas, NV 89128
Phone: (702) 804-5200
Fax: (702) 804-5936
www.citadelbroadcasting.com
Owns more than 200 radio stations.

Clear Channel Communications
200 East Basse Road
San Antonio, TX 78209
Phone: (210) 822-2828
www.clearchannel.com
No. 1 radio station owner in the U.S. It owns, operates, programs or sells airtime for over 1,200 radio stations.

CNBC
900 Sylvan Avenue
Englewood Cliffs, NJ 07632
Phone: (201) 735-2622
moneycentral.msn.com

CNN
1 CNN Center
Atlanta, GA 30303
Phone: (404) 827-1500
www.cnn.com

Community Newspaper Holdings, Inc.
3500 Colonnade Parkway, Suite 600
Birmingham, AL 35243
Phone: (205) 298-7100
Fax: (205) 298-7108
www.cnhi.com

Condé Nast Publications
4 Times Square, 17th Floor
New York, NY 10036
Phone: (212) 286-2860
www.condenast.com
Owns: Allure, Vogue, Wired, Glamour, GQ, The New Yorker, Vanity Fair, Lucky

Consumers Union of the United States, Inc.
101 Truman Avenue
Yonkers, NY 10703
Phone: (914) 378-2000
Fax: (914) 378-2900
www.consumersunion.org
www.consumerreports.org

Employer Directory, cont.

Cox Enterprises, Inc.
6205 Peachtree Dunwoody Road
Atlanta, GA 30328
Phone: (678) 645-0000
Fax: (678) 645-1079
www.coxenterprises.com

Crain Communications
1155 Gratiot Avenue
Detroit, MI 48207-2997
Phone: (313) 446-6000
Fax: (313) 446-1616
www.crain.com
Owns: Advertising Age, AutoWeek, TelevisionWeek

Cumulus Media
14 Piedmont Center, Suite 1400
Atlanta, GA 30305
Phone: (404) 949-0700
Fax: (404) 949-0740
www.cumulus.com
Second-largest owner of radio stations in U.S. with over 300 stations.

Cygnus Business Media
1233 Janesville Avenue
Fort Atkinson, WI 53538
Phone: (800) 547-7377
www.cygnusb2b.com

Daily News, L.P.
450 West 33rd Street
New York, NY 10001
Phone: (212) 210-2100
Fax: (212) 643-7831
www.nydailynews.com

Dow Jones & Company
200 Liberty Street
New York, NY 10281
Phone: (212) 416-2000
www.dj.com
Owns: The Wall Street Journal

The E.W. Scripps Company
312 Walnut Street
Cincinnati, OH 45201
Phone: (513) 977-3000
Fax: (513) 977-3721
www.scripps.com
Owns: Denver Rocky Mountain News, The Commercial Appeal (Memphis)

Emmis Communications Corporation
40 Monument Circle, Suite 700
Indianapolis, IN 46204
Phone: (317) 266-0100
Fax: (317) 631-3750
www.emmis.com
Owns 27 radio stations.

Entercom Communications
401 City Avenue, Suite 809
Bala Cynwyd, PA 19004
Phone: (610) 660-5610
www.entercom.com
Owns more than 100 radio stations.

F+W Publications, Inc.
4700 East Galbraith Road
Cincinnati, OH 45236
Phone: (513) 531-2690
Fax: (513) 531-0798
www.fwpublications.com

Fisher Communications
100 4th Avenue North, Suite 510
Seattle, WA 98109
Phone: (206) 404-7000
Fax: (206) 414-6037
www.fsci.com
Owns 27 radio stations.

Forbes Inc.
60 5th Avenue
New York, NY 10011
Phone: (212) 620-2200
Fax: (212) 620-2245
www.forbesinc.com
Owns: Forbes

Fox News Channel
1211 Avenue of the Americas
New York, NY 10036
Phone: (212) 301-3000
www.foxnews.com

Freedom Communications, Inc.
17666 Fitch Avenue
Irvine, CA 92614-6022
Phone: (949) 253-2300
Fax: (949) 474-7675
www.freedom.com
Owns: The Gazette (Colorado Springs), Orange County Register

Gannett Co.
7950 Jones Branch Drive
McLean, VA 22107-0910
Phone: (703) 854-6000
Fax: (703) 854-2001
www.gannett.com
Owns: USA Today

GateHouse Media, Inc.
350 Willowbrook Office Park
Fairport, NY 14450
Phone: (585) 598-0030
Fax: (585) 248-2631
gatehousemedia.com

Gruner + Jahr AG & Co. (U.S. Office)
375 Lexington Avenue, 10th Floor
New York, NY 10017
Phone: (212) 499-2000
www.guj.de
Owns: Fast Company, Family Circle, Parent, Child, YM

Hachette Filipacchi Media U.S., Inc.
1633 Broadway
New York, New York 10019
Phone: (212) 767-6000
www.hfmus.com

Visit Vault at **www.vault.com** for insider company profiles, expert advice, career message boards, expert resume reviews, the Vault Job Board and more.

VAULT CAREER LIBRARY

343

Employer Directory, cont.

Hearst Magazines
300 West 57th Street
New York, NY 10019
Phone: (212) 649-2000
Fax: (212) 765-3528
www.hearst.com/magazines
Owns: Cosmopolitan, Good Housekeeping, Town & Country, O, The Oprah Magazine, Esquire, Popular Mechanics

Hearst Newspapers
959 8th Avenue
New York, NY 10019
Phone: (212) 649-2000
www.hearst.com/newspapers
Owns: Houston Chronicle, San Francisco Chronicle, San Antonio Express-News, Albany Times Union, Seattle Post-Intelligencer

Hollinger (U.S. Office)
401 North Wabash Avenue, Suite 740
Chicago, IL 60611
Phone: (312) 321-2299
www.hollinger.com
Owns: Chicago Sun-Times

International Data Group, Inc.
1 Exeter Plaza, 15th Floor
Boston, MA 02116
Phone: (617) 534-1200
Fax: (617) 423-0240
www.idg.com

Journal Communications, Inc.
333 West State Street
Milwaukee, WI 53203
Phone: (414) 224-2000
Fax: (414) 224-2469
www.jc.com

Journal Register Company
790 Township Line Road, Suite 300
Yardley, PA 19067
Phone: (215) 504-4200
Fax: (215) 504-4201
www.journalregister.com

Landmark Communications, Inc.
150 West Brambleton Avenue
Norfolk, VA 23510
Phone: (757) 446-2010
Fax: (757) 446-2489
www.landmarkcom.com

Lee Enterprises, Inc.
201 North Harrison Street, Suite 600
Davenport, IA 52801
Phone: (563) 383-2100
Fax: (563) 323-9609
www.lee.net

The McClatchy Company
2100 Q Street
Sacramento, CA 95816
Phone: (916) 321-1846
Fax: (916) 321-1964
www.mcclatchy.com

McGraw-Hill Companies
1221 Avenue of the Americas
New York, NY 10020
Phone: (212) 512-2000
Fax: (212) 512-3840
www.mcgraw-hill.com
Owns: BusinessWeek

Media General
333 East Franklin Street
Richmond, VA 23219
Phone: (804) 649-6000
Fax: (804) 648-6066
www.mediageneral.com
Owns: Tampa Tribune, Richmond Times-Dispatch, Winston-Salem Journal

MediaNews Group
101 West Colfax Avenue, Suite 1100
Denver, CO 80202
Phone: (303) 563-6360
Fax: (303) 894-9327
www.medianewsgroup.com
Owns: The Denver Post, Salt Lake Tribune

Meredith Corporation
1716 Locust Street
Des Moines, IA 50309-3023
Phone: (515) 284-3000
Fax: (515) 284-2700
www.meredith.com
Owns: Better Homes and Gardens, Ladies' Home Journal, MORE

Morris Communications Company LLC
725 Broad Street
Augusta, GA 30901
Phone: (800) 622-6358
Fax: (706) 722-7125
www.morris.com

MSNBC
1 MSNBC Plaza
Secaucus, NJ 07094
Phone: (201) 583-5000
www.msnbc.com

National Public Radio
635 Massachusetts Avenue NW
Washington, DC 20001-3753
Phone: (202) 513-2000
www.npr.org
Owns 680 member stations.

NBC News
30 Rockefeller Plaza
New York, NY 10112
Phone: (212) 664-4444
www.msnbc.com

The New York Times Company
620 8th Avenue
New York, NY 10018
Phone: (212) 556-1234
www.nytco.com
Owns: The New York Times, Boston Globe, International Herald Tribune

National Geographic Society
1145 17th Street NW
Washington, DC 20036-4688
Phone: (202)857-7000
www.nationalgeographic.com
Owns: National Geographic

Employer Directory, cont.

Nice Media LLC
257 Park Avenue South, 5th Floor
New York, NY 10010
Phone: (646) 835-5200
Fax: (212) 780-0003
www.nichemediallc.com

**Omaha World-Herald
Company**
1314 Douglas Street, Suite 1500
Omaha, NE 68102
Phone: (402) 444-1600
www.owh.com

PBS
2100 Crystal Drive
Arlington, VA 22202-3785
Phone: (703) 739-5000
Fax: (703) 739-8495
www.pbs.org

PRIMEDIA
745 5th Avenue
New York, NY 10151
Phone: (212) 745-0100
Fax: (212) 745-0121
www.primedia.com
Owns: Motor Trend, Soap Opera Digest

**The Reader's Digest
Association, Inc.**
Reader's Digest Road
Pleasantville, NY 10570
Phone: (914) 238-1000
Fax: (914) 238-4559
www.rd.com

The Reed Elsevier Group PLC
1-3 Strand
London WC2N 5JR
United Kingdom
Phone: +44-20-79-30-70-77
Fax: +44-20-72-27-57-99
www.reedelsevier.com

Reuters Group PLC
The Reuters Building
South Colonnade, Canary Wharf
London E14 5EP
United Kingdom
Phone: +44-20-7250-1122
www.reuters.com

Rodale, Inc.
33 East Minor Street
Emmaus, PA 18098
Phone: (610) 967-5171
Fax: (610) 967-8963
rodale.com
*Owns: Men's Health, Organic Living,
Organic Style, Men's Health*

Seattle Times Company
1120 John Street
Seattle, WA 98109
Phone: (206) 464-2111
Fax: (206) 493-0883
www.seattletimescompany.com

Stephen's Media Group
111 West Bonanza Road
Las Vegas, NV 89106
Phone: (702) 383-0211
Fax: (702) 383-4676
www.stephensmedia.com

Sun-Times Media Group, Inc.
350 North Orleans Street
Chicago, IL 60654
Phone: (312) 321-2299
Fax: (312) 321-6426
www.thesuntimesgroup.com

Time Out Group Ltd.
Universal House
251 Tottenham Court Road
London W1T 7AB
United Kingdom
Phone: +44-20-7813-30-00
Fax: +44-20-7813-60-01
www.timeout.com

Time, Inc.
1271 Avenue of the Americas
New York, NY 10020-1393
Phone: (212) 522-1212
Fax: (212) 522-0602
www.timeinc.com
*Owns: Time, Entertainment Weekly,
People, Sports Illustrated, Fortune*

Tribune Company
435 North Michigan Avenue
Chicago, IL 60611
Phone: (312) 222-9100
Fax: (312) 222-1573
www.tribune.com
*Owns: Chicago Tribune, The Los
Angeles Times, Newsday*

**The Washington Post
Company**
1150 15th Street NW
Washington, DC 20071
Phone: (202) 334-6000
Fax: (202) 334-4536
www.washpostco.com
*Owns: The Washington Post,
Newsweek*

The Weather Channel
300 Interstate North Parkway
Atlanta, GA 30339
Phone: (770) 226-2609
www.weather.com

Wenner Media LLC
1290 Avenue of the Americas
New York, NY 10104-0298
Phone: (212) 484-1616
Fax: (212) 484-3435
*Owns: Rolling Stone, Men's Journal,
US Weekly*

Westwood One
40 West 57th Street
New York, NY 10019
Phone: (212) 641-2000
www.westwoodone.com
*Broadcasts programming to more than
7,700 radio stations.*

Visit Vault at **www.vault.com** for insider company profiles, expert advice,
career message boards, expert resume reviews, the Vault Job Board and more.

VAULT CAREER LIBRARY   345

Law

Corporate Law Basics

What is corporate law?

A corporation is an artificial legal entity, typically chartered by a state and formed in order to operate a business. Once chartered, the corporation is legally distinct from its owners and is liable for its own debts and must pay its own taxes.

Many, if not most, lawyers deal with corporations, and not all of them call themselves "corporate lawyers." In fact, at this point, you might not have a clear idea of the differences among a litigator who works in-house for a corporation, a tax lawyer who advises corporations from the vantage point of a law firm and a corporate lawyer. If you watch too much television, you might believe that lawyers negotiate deals one day and head to the courtroom for high-profile litigation the next. This is highly unusual in the real practice of law. While both litigators and corporate lawyers deal with corporations, they do so in very different ways.

Litigation vs. transactional law

One of the basic divisions in the practice of law is between litigation and corporate, or transactional, law. Litigation attorneys, or litigators, deal with the judicial process, with civil disputes or criminal cases that may be headed to court. In the realm of criminal law, they are prosecutors, public defenders or private defense attorneys. Those attorneys who handle contract disputes, personal injuries, and other non-criminal matters, are civil litigators. Clients of "commercial litigators" include corporations and businesses.

Note that being a litigator doesn't automatically put you in a courtroom. Public defenders may indeed be in court every week. But litigators who work on corporate or commercial matters might never go to court. They serve their clients by filing motions and briefs and settling conflicts without actually going to trial.

It's a myth that everyone who wants to be a lawyer wants to spend time in a courtroom. Many people don't have any interest in criminal law or personal injury. Many aspiring lawyers would prefer helping create a business venture to suing one. Attorneys who facilitate transactions in the fields of corporate or tax law, intellectual property or employee benefits are considered transactional lawyers. In the world of business, transactional lawyers try to set up deals in a way that will avoid litigation and make clear the rights and responsibilities of all parties in the event that something does go wrong.

The difference between corporate law and commercial litigation is simple. Corporate lawyers craft transactions or deals, and litigators step in when those transactions go wrong. Litigators resolve disputes through the judicial system or through alternative methods such as mediation or arbitration.

Transactional law and corporate lawyers

So, what is a corporate lawyer? Basically, corporate lawyers advise businesses on their legal obligations, rights and responsibilities. Attorneys who call themselves corporate lawyers are usually corporate generalists, lawyers who advise businesses on their legal obligations, rights and responsibilities, provide advice on business structures and evaluate ventures. In order to serve the sophisticated needs of their clients, corporate lawyers also coordinate with fellow transactional lawyers in such specialties as tax, ERISA and real estate.

Many firms use the terms "transactional" and "corporate" interchangeably when describing areas of practice. Corporate lawyers structure transactions, draft documents, negotiate deals, attend meetings and make calls toward those ends. A corporate lawyer seeks to ensure that the provisions of an agreement are clear, unambiguous and won't cause problems for

Visit Vault at **www.vault.com** for insider company profiles, expert advice, career message boards, expert resume reviews, the Vault Job Board and more.

 V\ULT CAREER LIBRARY   347

their client in the future. (Or, are ambiguous in such a way that the client's interests are served.) Corporate attorneys also advise on the duties and responsibilities of corporate officers, directors and insiders.

Not all firms categorize the varieties of corporate practice in the same way. For example, some firms might have separate practice groups for antitrust or mergers and acquisitions, while others include them within their corporate department. The following list, while not exhaustive, outlines some of the areas in which corporate attorneys might spend their time.

Areas of Corporate Practice

Corporate formation, governance and operation

As mentioned above, corporation is a legal entity created through the laws of its state of incorporation. Individual states make laws relating to the creation, organization and dissolution of corporations. The law treats a corporation as a legal "person" that has the standing to sue and be sued, and is distinct from its stockholders. The legal independence of a corporation prevents shareholders from being personally liable for corporate debts. The legal person status of corporations gives the business perpetual life; the death (or, in today's climate, discrediting) of an official or a major stockholder does not alter the corporation's structure, even if it affects the stock price.

A corporate lawyer can help a client create, organize or dissolve a business entity. To form a corporation, attorney drafts articles of incorporation, which document the creation of the company and specify the management of internal affairs. Most states require a corporation to have bylaws defining the roles of officers of the company. Corporate lawyers also deal with business entities in the forms of partnerships, limited liability companies, limited liability partnerships and business trusts; and each form has its own set of legal rights and responsibilities, organizational structure and tax burdens. Attorneys help their clients decide which of these legal forms is best suited for the business they want to run and the relationships the principals want to build with each other.

A corporate lawyer who helps a client form a company might later be called upon for other legal advice related to the startup or management of the business, like reviewing a lease for office space or equipment, or drafting employment contracts, non-disclosure and non-compete agreements. Corporate lawyers might research aspects of employment law or environmental law or consult with another attorney who specializes in that field. Business executives also seek advice from corporate attorneys on the rights and responsibilities of corporate directors and officers.

Mergers & acquisitions

One major corporate practice area is mergers and acquisitions (M&A). Through acquiring (buying) or merging with another company, a business might add property, production facilities or a brand name. A merger or acquisition might also work to neutralize a competitor in the same field. M&A attorneys provide legal counsel about proposed transactions. Typically, to evaluate a proposed venture, a team of corporate lawyers reviews all of the company's key assets and liabilities, meaning financial statements, employment agreements, real estate holdings, intellectual property holdings and any current, pending or likely litigation. This is called due diligence. The lawyer(s) can then assess the situation and raise specific issues with the client—for example, who's responsible for the Environmental Protection Agency investigation of that piece of property the company owns? What happens to the employees of the target company or to the stock options of the company's directors?

M&A lawyers consult with their clients about these questions and together lawyer and client determine which parties should accept current or potential liabilities. The lawyers then draft the merger or acquisition agreement and negotiate in detail the terms of each party's rights, responsibilities and liabilities.

Venture capital

In a venture capital practice, a lawyer works on private and public financings and day-to-day counseling. This means he/she helps new businesses find money for their ventures, organizes their operations and maintains their legal and business structures after formation. In venture capital, as in any corporate law position dealing with emerging companies, lawyers help build and expand businesses. Their responsibilities can include general corporate work, like drafting articles of incorporation and other documents, as well as technology licensing, financing, and mergers and acquisitions.

Some lawyers find this type of work less confrontational than M&A practice because the client is working with other parties toward a common goal. Sometimes, in mergers & acquisitions, the parties see the process as a zero-sum game in which each must get the best deal no matter how it may affect future relations with the other company. This is especially the case in hostile takeovers.

Project finance

The development and construction of power plants, oil refineries, industrial plants, pipelines, mines, telecommunications networks and facilities and transportation systems involve the cooperation of many different entities, many different lawyers and extremely large sums of money. Project finance attorneys specialize in these deals. They form a project entity, a corporation, partnership or other legal entity that will exist for the term of the project, and they draft power purchase agreements and construction contracts and negotiate financial terms with lenders and investors.

Corporate securities

Some corporate lawyers specialize in securities law. On a federal level, the Securities Act of 1933 requires companies who sell securities to the public to register with the federal government. Corporations must follow certain protocols regarding disclosure of information to shareholders and investors depending on the size of the corporation and the type of investor. If shares of a company's stock are traded on a public stock exchange, the company has to file detailed reports with the Securities and Exchange Commission and distribute parts of those reports (the prospectus) to shareholders. The Securities Act of 1934 addresses the obligations of companies traded on a national stock exchange.

To ensure the companies remain in accordance with these laws, corporate attorneys prepare reports for initial public offerings, yearly and quarterly disclosures, and special disclosures whenever something happens that might affect the price of the stock, like impending litigation, government investigation or disappointing financial results. Even if you don't specialize in corporate securities law, the issuance of stock and the creation and distribution of the reports are subject to a whole host of rules with which corporate lawyers must be familiar.

Intellectual property

Corporate lawyers often advise their clients on intellectual property matters. Intellectual property law can include research and analysis of trade secret issues, patent and trademark licensing and protection, software licensing and copyright law.

Non-legal roles

Business clients frequently look to their lawyers for advice directly related to the operation of their business but only tangentially related to the law, such as how to deal with special interest groups, how to respond to concerns about product safety, whether to fire an executive, how to plan for the possibility of adverse media coverage, how to create a business plan, how to cope with a serious ethical lapse, whether to close a factory and what kind of compensation plans should be offered to employees.

Visit Vault at www.vault.com for insider company profiles, expert advice,
career message boards, expert resume reviews, the Vault Job Board and more.

VAULT CAREER LIBRARY 349

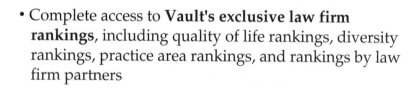

The credit crunch and its aftermath

Healthy economic conditions have a predictable effect on corporate law practices. The boom years of the mid-to-late 90s saw incredible levels of IPO and securities activity, and the record mergers and acquisitions of the last years contributed disproportionately to many a law firm's revenue figures. In 2008, however, the situation is dramatically altered. Credit crunch aftershocks, bank closings, soft markets and low investor confidence directly affect the immediate prospects of corporate law practices. Even optimistically speaking, it will be some time before markets normalize—let alone reach the levels of the last years. Though deals and transactions will always occur, the pace has dropped off considerably, and deals that do come up will fall to a chosen few firms.

A Day in the Life: Junior Corporate Associate

Here's a look at a day in the life of a junior corporate associate at a medium-sized firm.

8:30 a.m. Arrive at the office and proceed directly to an internal training session covering an aspect of the year-end reporting process. This training is part of a six-session series presented by the firm every year to prepare the associates for the upcoming reporting season.

10 a.m. Return to office to pick up file on a private biotechnology client and hurry to a meeting with a senior associate. At the meeting, discuss the list of names and addresses of the client's stockholders (mailing list), which I reviewed the day before in preparation for a Section 228 Notice of Action Taken mailing. Point out to the senior associate which addresses are missing and ask her to obtain these from the client. She also suggests where to look for additional information regarding stockholder addresses.

10:30 a.m. Discuss the upcoming Section 228 Notice of Action Taken with my assistant. This particular mailing will be to nearly 100 stockholders. You have found that if you discuss upcoming large projects with your assistant in advance, she is more likely to clear her schedule of other work and help you complete the project in a timely manner.

10:35 a.m. Take a few minutes to check e-mails from the night before. Most of them discuss various due diligence issues that have been uncovered during document review for a merger. (I am working on a team with a mid-level associate and a partner on a merger of our client with and into another biotechnology company.)

10:50 a.m. Briefly review estimated corporate tax forms from California that need to be forwarded to another client. Draft a cover letter to the client to accompany the tax forms and instructions.

11:15 a.m. Meet with the midlevel associate to discuss various merger diligence issues and the "to-do" list for the day.

11:30 a.m. Proofread the cover letter to be sent with the tax forms and instructions and send the packet to the client.

11:40 a.m. At the request of the mid-level associate, call opposing counsel to discuss a new diligence question. Take notes of discussion. Copy a few documents from the master diligence file for the review of the midlevel associate and bring the copies to her office.

12:10 p.m. Eat lunch in office. Organize e-mails from the previous day while eating. Moving e-mails from the inbox into client-related folders helps you to locate relevant messages quickly.

1 p.m. Revise the mailing list for the Section 228 mailing to incorporate new information provided by the senior associate. Find additional information in a closing binder that the senior associate provided during the morning meeting. Check the mailing list against the stock ledgers to ensure that all stockholders are accounted for. Give the list to assistant so that she can get an early start on preparing mailing labels.

Visit Vault at **www.vault.com** for insider company profiles, expert advice, career message boards, expert resume reviews, the Vault Job Board and more.

VAULT CAREER LIBRARY

351

2:15 p.m. Prepare a first draft of Disclosure Schedule to the Agreement and Plan of Merger. Briefly meet with the mid-level associate to give her a copy of the draft and to share thoughts about further improvement of the draft.

6 p.m. When I return to the office, I find an unexpected voice mail from a public company client regarding the latest edits to an Amendment to Form S-2, which the client plans to file with the SEC the next day. I have been involved with the drafting of the Form S-2, but not with this particular round of edits, which were made by a senior associate. Call the client back and discuss the edits with her, pointing out that she should further discuss a few of the edits with the senior associates the next morning.

6:20 p.m. Prepare and send a long e-mail to the controller of the client involved in a merger asking him to provide some additional information for inclusion in the disclosure schedule and to help with the preparation of a few sections of the schedule.

6:50 p.m. Receive and review e-mail from opposing counsel containing additional questions in connection with her due diligence review of our client's documents.

7 p.m. Call opposing counsel to discuss her due diligence questions. Answer two questions, and promise to follow up on the others and call her back the next day with the answers.

7:15 p.m. Forward the unanswered due diligence questions to the midlevel associate for her review.

7:20 p.m. Revise the draft disclosure schedule to incorporate the comments made by the midlevel associate during our last meeting. Leave a copy of the revised schedule in her office for her review.

8 p.m. Organize files and prepare a tentative to-do list for the next day.

8:15 p.m. Leave the office and hurry to catch an 8:20 p.m. train home.

Litigation Basics

What is litigation?

Litigation is always in the news—from the controversial landmark abortion case, Roe v. Wade, to the O.J. Simpson trials, to the environmental class action lawsuits portrayed in the films *Erin Brockovich* and *A Civil Action*. A litigation is a legal proceeding between two or more parties. A litigator is a lawyer who represents a party in litigation. Because litigation is an adversarial proceeding between opposing parties, most of a litigator's job involves preparing for trial, even if a negotiated settlement is the ultimate goal.

In cases where parties have contracted to resolve their disputes out of court, a mediator can be hired to find an amicable compromise between the parties. This mediation (or, in some cases, arbitration) reduces the number of cases that go to trial so the already crowded courts are not completely overwhelmed.

Criminal proceedings

There are two kinds of litigation: civil and criminal. When someone breaks a state or federal law, he commits an offense against society. The government, on behalf of the community, begins a criminal proceeding to hold the offender responsible. A criminal litigation is therefore between the government and the accused, or defendant. The government is represented by a prosecutor, typically a district attorney (for state prosecutions) or a federal prosecutor (for federal crimes). The defendant is represented by either a private criminal attorney or a public defender appointed by the state. (Occasionally, usually against the advice of both his lawyer and the judge, a defendant chooses to represent himself, or acts pro se.)

Most states divide crimes into misdemeanors and felonies. A misdemeanor is any offense that results in less than one year of jail time. Petty theft, possession of a small amount of drugs, or breaking and entering are some examples of misdemeanors. Many misdemeanors can result in a fine or instead of jail time. Felonies are more serious offenses that virtually always result in prison terms of more than one year and may include a fine, as well as incarceration. Murder, racketeering, rape and kidnapping are all felony offenses. In some states, serious felonies, such as the murder of a policeman or murder with premeditation, are capital offenses, in which cases a criminal defendant might face the death penalty. Any person accused of a crime is presumed innocent until proven guilty beyond a reasonable doubt.

Civil actions

A civil action encompasses virtually any non-criminal court proceeding. It can be a private action between two citizens, a proceeding by one person against the state, a suit by an individual against a corporation or any combination thereof. The party bringing the suit, known as the plaintiff or petitioner, usually is seeking a sum of money (damages) from another party (the defendant or respondent) to compensate her for a claimed injury or loss. Sometimes, the remedy sought involves not money but performance; one party wants the court to compel another either to do something he is obligated to do or to stop doing something that is injurious to one bringing suit. In a civil action, the case turns not on the defendant's guilt but on the issue of liability—a party is found either liable or not liable. The burden of proof required to establish liability in a civil suit is generally a lower threshold than the "guilt beyond a reasonable doubt" required in a criminal trial.

In the case of both criminal and civil litigation, the parties may never actually make it to court; they might come to a mutual compromise before the trial date. Parties to a civil suit might reach a financial agreement or other settlement, while the prosecution and defense in a criminal case might agree to a plea bargain, under which a prosecutor offers a reduced charge or sentence in exchange for the defendant's plea of guilt.

Lawsuits and Trials

A lawsuit is filed at the trial level. A trial might be in front of a jury or just a judge (known as a bench trial). In criminal actions, a defendant has the right to a speedy trial. There is no such right for parties in civil cases, and many civil actions go on for years. Most litigation will never even reach a courtroom—the parties might settle, one side might withdraw from the suit or a judge might dismiss the case before trial.

A trial entails everything you see on television: a judge, a jury, a variety of evidence, opposing lawyers and two parties. During the trial, the jury considers questions of fact: Did Mr. Hughes kill his wife? Was the car crash an accident? Was XYZ Company negligent in manufacturing faulty women's lingerie? Did the wire in the plaintiff's bra actually cause the injury she claims it did? The jury is there to decide these questions, using only the evidence presented in court. Before and during the course of the trial, there are also questions of law to be addressed by the judge: Should photos of Mr. Hughes' bedroom be allowed into evidence? Is the testimony of XYZ's chief designer admissible? Should the fact that juror number three slept through the testimony result in a mistrial?

The judge decides questions of law, usually after both parties have presented their arguments. In making her decision, the judge relies on previous case law and the relevant rules of civil and criminal procedure. (You can see questions of law being decided on *Law & Order* and *The Practice* when the lawyers meet the judge in chambers before trial, usually to request that she exclude a piece of the prosecutor's evidence for one reason or another. In real life, before making such a decision the judge would review lengthy written memoranda from all lawyers involved).

When the trial is over, the losing party often has the opportunity to appeal the decision to an appellate court. The role of the appeals court is not to second-guess the jury's or judge's rulings on the facts; at the appellate level, only questions of law can be reviewed. The appellate court hears from both sides to decide, essentially, if the trial was conducted properly. If the

Visit Vault at **www.vault.com** for insider company profiles, expert advice, career message boards, expert resume reviews, the Vault Job Board and more.

V∧ULT CAREER LIBRARY 353

appeals court concludes that a question of law was not properly decided by the trial judge, it can reverse or overturn the lower court's decision—essentially negating it—or it can remand the case, asking the lower court to reconsider the case in light of the appellate court's opinion. A reversal is often followed by a remand. In the case of Mr. Hughes' murder trial, an appellate court would not decide whether or not Mr. Hughes killed his wife—the jury already concluded that he did—but it can find that the photos of his bedroom were improperly admitted into evidence. The court might then overturn the guilty verdict and remand the case back to the lower court for a new trial in which the jury will not be able to consider those photographs as evidence.

An appellate court is rarely seen on television, but the decisions of appeals courts are very important, not only to the parties involved but also to future litigants in the same jurisdiction.

A Day in the Life: Corporate Litigation Associate

9:30 a.m. Arrive at work. Get coffee, make small talk with office mate, and check e-mails and phone messages with assistant.

10:15 a.m. Return phone calls and e-mails. Call senior associate with question regarding yesterday's research issue. Call duplicating to check on document review on white-collar crime case, and put them in contact with paralegal assigned to the case.

10:40 a.m. Go down to document review room. There are 70 boxes of documents here, but some are out being copied. Review documents with fellow associates, looking for relevant issues.

12:30 p.m. Associate lunch in conference room. Lunch/training session is about witness interviews. Take notes and eat roast beef sandwiches. Schmooze with fellow associates about who's working for the most demanding partner.

1:50 p.m. Return to office. Check e-mails and continue with yesterday's research issue about statute of limitations in federal court for securities fraud cases. Spend most of the time researching the issue on Westlaw and LexisNexis.

4 p.m. Take a break from the computer and go down to the document review room. Go through witness statements, expert testimony, product promotional materials, statistical data and internal memos to look for evidence of intent.

5:15 p.m. Return to office and prepare for meeting with partner and rest of team.

5:30 p.m. Meeting with partner and rest of team. Meeting goes long, but the focus of the research has now changed. Partner would like a memo in 48 hours on this new research issue. Update partner on document review and duplicating process.

6:30 p.m. Speak with senior associate about organization and approach of new memo and how to research new issue. Check with document review room on duplications of documents. Plan out how much more needs to be done and talk with paralegal about organizing document review.

7:30 p.m. If you're feeling really motivated, you can go back to the document review room. Otherwise, leave for home, knowing it will be waiting for you tomorrow!

A Day in the Life: Assistant District Attorney

9 a.m. Arrive at office, check e-mails and get files and paperwork for court.

10 a.m. Arrive at court for multiple issues, including an arraignment for a burglary case, hearings for drug possession cases, money laundering case and attempted murder case. Speak with court clerks while clients arrive and judge hears various issues.

12:15 p.m. Meet opposing counsel for plea bargain agreement for drug possession case.

1 p.m. Quick lunch at desk, looking over e-mails and phone calls. Wait for witness to show up at 2 p.m.

2 p.m. Witness doesn't show. Work on research for motion on attempted murder case involving Fourth Amendment right of seizure.

3 p.m. Brief interview with police officers on felony assault case.

3:30 p.m. Witness for 2 p.m. finally shows up with father and sister. Conduct fact-finding issue on domestic violence case. Witness recants some testimony and father pressures her not to testify against her husband, leaving ADA uncertain as to strength of case.

4:45 p.m. Contact court clerks regarding hearing status of various cases.

5:10 p.m. Review documents for money laundering and call witnesses and corporate officers for interviews in the next few days.

6:15 p.m. Head home.

Paralegal

A mixed lot

From freshly graduated English BAs to document-drafting veterans with training and certification, paralegals are really something of a mixed lot. Some have formal training, while others do not. Some have one of many certifications, while others have none. Paralegals, or legal assistants, as they are sometimes called, come from a great variety of backgrounds and perform a wide range of tasks. As a result, compensation and working conditions vary to a large degree. Further complicating matters is that, while some legal assistants find they enjoy their paralegal careers, many others aspire to law degrees.

Swimming in paper

Generally speaking, much of what paralegals do involves the large mounds of paperwork generated by legal work. Legal assistants may find themselves sifting through these documents, organizing them, analyzing them or even drafting them. In addition, paralegals perform research and prepare reports based upon their findings. To do this, paralegals must have a good understanding of legal terminology and good research skills. When permitted by law, paralegals involved with community service sometimes even represent clients at administrative hearings. In short, paralegals can do everything a lawyer does, except the "practice of law" (i.e., they cannot present cases in court, set legal fees or give legal advice). Paralegals are free to do just about anything else, which is good if it involves using the brain, but numbing if it involves rote clerical work.

Varying pay

Pay for legal assistants reflects the great variety of the work performed. Entry-level workers do not enjoy high salaries, but with increased experience and education, compensation becomes healthier. Paralegals in major metropolitan areas tend to earn more money than those in smaller locales. Similarly, working for a large law firm means higher pay. Major firms may also have perks in the way of bonuses, extra vacation time, and tickets to sports events and the like. At any rate, paralegals can almost always count on hefty overtime hours at the rate of time and a half to boost salaries.

Some feel that obtaining a certification or a degree in paralegal studies can lead to greater compensation and responsibility. Two certifications are available to those in the profession, the certified legal assistant exam (CLA) and the paralegal advanced

Visit Vault at **www.vault.com** for insider company profiles, expert advice, career message boards, expert resume reviews, the Vault Job Board and more.

VAULT CAREER LIBRARY 355

competency exam (PACE). The two-day CLA exam is offered by the National Association of Legal Assistants three times a year. The PACE is affiliated with the National Federation of Paralegal Associations and is administered throughout the year by an independent agency. Once either of these certifications has been obtained, a paralegal may use the title registered paralegal (RP).

In addition to certification exams, many paralegal training programs are available (some are run through colleges and universities, while others are independent). Most of these degrees are either two- or four-year programs. Correspondence courses, which have grown increasingly popular due to the Internet, are also an option. Degrees recognized by the American Bar Association and the American Association for Paralegal Education tend to be the most reputable.

Employer Directory

Akin Gump Strauss Hauer & Feld LLP

Robert S. Strauss Building
1333 New Hampshire Avenue NW
Washington, DC 20036-1564
Phone: (202) 887-4000
www.akingump.com

Allen & Overy LLP

1 Bishops Square
London, E1 6AD
United Kingdom
Phone: +44-20-7330-3000
Fax: +44-20-3088-0088

Arnold & Porter LLP

555 Twelfth Street, NW
Washington, DC 20004-1206
Phone: (202) 942-5000
www.arnoldporter.com

Baker & McKenzie

1 Prudential Plaza
130 East Randolph Drive, Suite 2500
Chicago, IL 60601
Phone: (312) 861-8000
www.bakernet.com

Baker Botts LLP

1 Shell Plaza
910 Louisiana
Houston, TX 77002-4995
Phone: (713) 229-1234
www.bakerbotts.com

Boies, Schiller & Flexner LLP

575 Lexington Avenue, 7th Floor
New York, NY 10022
Phone: (212) 446-2300
www.bsfllp.com

Cadwalader, Wickersham & Taft LLP

1 World Financial Center
New York, NY 10281
Phone: (212) 504-6000
www.cadwalader.com

Cleary Gottlieb Steen & Hamilton LLP

1 Liberty Plaza
New York, NY 10006
Phone: (212) 225-2000

2000 Pennsylvania Avenue, NW
Washington, DC 20006
Phone: (202) 974-1500
www.cgsh.com

Clifford Chance LLP

31 West 52nd Street
New York, NY 10019-6131
Phone: (212) 878-8000
www.cliffordchance.com

Covington & Burling LLP

1201 Pennsylvania Avenue, NW
Washington, DC 20004-2401
Phone: (202) 662-6000
www.cov.com

Cravath, Swaine & Moore LLP

Worldwide Plaza
825 Eighth Avenue
New York, NY 10019-7475
Phone: (212) 474-1000
www.cravath.com

Davis Polk & Wardwell

450 Lexington Avenue
New York, NY 10017
Phone: (212) 450-4000
www.dpw.com

Debevoise & Plimpton LLP

919 Third Avenue
New York, NY 10022
Phone: (212) 909-6000
www.debevoise.com

Dechert LLP

1095 Avenue of the Americas
New York, NY 10036-6797
Phone: (212) 698-3500

Cira Centre
2929 Arch Street
Philadelphia, PA 19104-2808
Phone: (215) 994-4000

1775 I Street NW
Washington, DC 20006-2401
Phone: (202) 261-3300
www.dechert.com

Dewey & LeBoeuf LLP

1301 Avenue of the Americas
New York, NY 10019-6092
Phone: (212) 259-8000
www.deweyleboeuf.com

DLA Piper

1251 Avenue of the Americas
27th Floor
New York, NY 10020-1104
Phone: (212) 335-4500
www.dlapiper.com

Freshfields Bruckhaus Deringer

520 Madison Avenue, 34th Floor
New York, NY 10022
Phone: (212) 277-4000

701 Pennsylvania Avenue NW
Suite 600
Washington, DC 20004
Phone: (202) 777-4500

65 Fleet Street
London, EC4Y 1HS
United Kingdom
Phone: +44-20-79-36-40-00
www.freshfields.com

Fried, Frank, Harris, Shriver & Jacobson LLP

One New York Plaza
New York, NY 10004
Phone: (212) 859-8000
www.friedfrank.com

Visit Vault at **www.vault.com** for insider company profiles, expert advice,
career message boards, expert resume reviews, the Vault Job Board and more.

VAULT CAREER LIBRARY

357

Employer Directory, cont.

Fulbright & Jaworski LLP
1301 McKinney, Suite 5100
Houston, TX 77010-3095
Phone: (713) 651-5151
Fax: (713) 651-5246
www.fulbright.com

Gibson, Dunn & Crutcher LLP
333 South Grand Avenue
Los Angeles, CA 90071-3197
Phone: (213) 229-7000
www.gibsondunn.com

Goodwin Procter LLP
Exchange Place
53 State Street
Boston, MA 02109
Phone: (617) 570-1000
Fax: (617) 523-1231
www.goodwinprocter.com

Hogan & Hartson LLP
555 13th Street, NW
Washington, DC 20004-1109
Phone: (202) 637-5600
www.hhlaw.com

Irell & Manella LLP
1800 Avenue of the Stars, Suite 900
Los Angeles, CA 90067
Phone: (310) 277-1010
Fax: (310) 203-7199
www.irell.com

Jenner & Block LLP
330 North Wabash Avenue
Chicago, IL 60611-7603
Phone: (312) 222-9350
Fax: (312) 527-0484
www.jenner.com

Jones Day
51 Louisiana Avenue, NW
Washington, DC 20001-2113
Phone: (202) 879-3939
www.jonesday.com

King & Spalding LLP
1180 Peachtree Street NE
Atlanta, GA 30309-3521
Phone: (404) 572-4600
www.kslaw.com

Kirkland & Ellis LLP
Aon Center
200 East Randolph Drive
Chicago, IL 60601
Phone: (312) 861-2000
www.kirkland.com

Latham & Watkins LLP
*Although Latham & Watkins is a global
firm without any one particular office
serving as headquarters, for ease of
communications, correspondence can
be sent to:*
335 South Grand Avenue
Los Angeles, CA 90071-1560
Phone: (213) 485-1234
www.lw.com

Linklaters
1 Silk Street
London, EC2Y 8HQ
United Kingdom
Phone: +44-20-7456-2000

1345 Avenue of the Americas
New York, NY 10105
Phone: (212) 903-9000
www.linklaters.com

**Mayer, Brown, Rowe & Maw
LLP**
71 South Wacker Drive
Chicago, IL 60606
Phone: (312) 782-0600
www.mayerbrown.com

McDermott Will & Emery
227 West Monroe Street, Suite 4400
Chicago, IL 60606
Phone: (312) 372-2000
www.mwe.com

**Milbank, Tweed, Hadley &
McCloy LLP**
1 Chase Manhattan Plaza
New York, NY 10005-1413
Phone: (212) 530-5000
www.milbank.com

Morgan, Lewis & Bockius LLP
1701 Market Street
Philadelphia, PA 19103
Phone: (215) 963-5000
www.morganlewis.com

Morrison & Foerster LLP
425 Market Street
San Francisco, CA 94105-2482
Phone: (415) 268-7000
www.mofo.com

Munger, Tolles & Olson LLP
355 South Grand Avenue, 35th Floor
Los Angeles, CA 90071-1560
Phone: (213) 683-9100
www.mto.com

O'Melveny & Myers LLP
400 South Hope Street
Los Angeles, CA 90071
Phone: (213) 430-6000
www.omm.com

**Orrick Herrington & Sutcliffe
LLP**
666 5th Avenue
New York, NY 10103-0001
Phone: (212) 506-5000

The Orrick Building
405 Howard Street
San Francisco, CA 94105-2669
Phone: (415) 773-5700
www.orrick.com

**Paul, Hastings, Janofsky &
Walker LLP**
Park Avenue Tower
75 East 55th Street, 1st Floor
New York, NY 10022
Phone: (212) 318-6000
Fax: (212) 319-4090
www.paulhastings.com

Employer Directory, cont.

Paul, Weiss, Rifkind, Wharton & Garrison LLP
1285 Avenue of the Americas
New York, NY 10019
Phone: (212) 373-3000
www.paulweiss.com

Proskauer Rose LLP
1585 Broadway
New York, NY 10036
Phone: (212) 969-3000
www.proskauer.com

Quinn Emanuel Urquhart Oliver & Hedges LLP
865 South Figueroa Street, 10th Floor
Los Angeles, CA 90017
Phone: (213) 443-3000
www.quinnemanuel.com

Ropes & Gray LLP
1 International Place
Boston, MA 02110
Phone: (617) 951-7000
www.ropesgray.com

Shearman & Sterling LLP
599 Lexington Avenue
New York, NY 10022
Phone: (212) 848-4000
www.shearman.com

Sidley Austin LLP
1 South Dearborn
Chicago, IL 60603
Phone: (312) 853-7000

787 Seventh Avenue
New York, NY 10019
Phone: (212) 839-5300
www.sidley.com

Simpson Thacher & Bartlett LLP
425 Lexington Avenue
New York, NY 10017
Phone: (212) 455-2000
www.simpsonthacher.com

Skadden, Arps, Slate, Meagher & Flom LLP and Affiliates
4 Times Square
New York, NY 10036
Phone: (212) 735-3000
www.skadden.com

Sullivan & Cromwell LLP
125 Broad Street
New York, NY 10004
Phone: (212) 558-4000
www.sullcrom.com

Vinson & Elkins LLP
First City Tower
1001 Fannin Street, Suite 2500
Houston, TX 77002-6760
Phone: (713) 758-2222
Fax: (713) 758-2346
www.velaw.com

Wachtell, Lipton, Rosen & Katz
51 West 52nd Street
New York, NY 10019-6150
Phone: (212) 403-1000
www.wlrk.com

Weil, Gotshal & Manges LLP
767 5th Avenue
New York, NY 10153
Phone: (212) 310-8000
www.weil.com

White & Case LLP
1155 Avenue of the Americas
New York, NY 10036
Phone: (212) 819-8200
www.whitecase.com

Williams & Conolly LLP
725 12th Street, NW
Washington, DC 20005
Phone: (202) 434-5000
Fax (202) 434-5029
www.wc.com

Willkie Farr & Gallagher LLP
787 7th Avenue
New York, NY 10019
Phone: (212) 728-8000
www.willkie.com

Wilmer Cutler Pickering Hale and Dorr LLP
60 State Street
Boston, MA 02109
Phone: (617) 526-6000

1875 Pennsylvania Avenue NW
Washington, DC 20006
Phone: (202) 663-6000
www.wilmerhale.com

Wilson Sonsini Goodrich & Rosati
650 Page Mill Road
Palo Alto, CA 94304-1050
Phone: (650) 493-9300
www.wsgr.com

Winston & Strawn LLP
35 West Wacker Drive
Chicago, IL 60601
Phone: (312) 558-5600
www.winston.com

Visit Vault at **www.vault.com** for insider company profiles, expert advice, career message boards, expert resume reviews, the Vault Job Board and more.

VAULT CAREER LIBRARY 359

Management Consulting

What is Consulting?

Strategy holding steady

2007 marked the consulting industry's third consecutive year of growth. The robust economy had clients interested in implementing improvements—and willing to spend top dollar to get the right advice. Positive economic conditions, such as the boom in private equity, set the stage for clients to focus on profit lines and to find savvy ways to cut costs. Consulting firms also benefited from an all-time high in M&A activity, as strategy shops were called on to help with due diligence projects or postmerger integration. In the U.S., which accounts for almost 50 percent of the worldwide consulting market, revenue hit $160 billion, up from $156 billion in 2006.

Though business was strong throughout most of 2007, by its end, the subprime mortgage crisis had changed the economic climate dramatically. Fallout from years of dubious lending policies motivated corporations across the industry spectrum to rein in their strategy spending. As a result, and in marked contrast to the double-digit growth of previous years, the consulting industry grew modestly in 2007, up just 6 percent for the year. And while analysts aren't yet predicting an all-out crisis for 2008, they are nevertheless forecasting tighter budgets and fewer engagements overall. The credit debacle hasn't meant only doom and gloom for the industry, however: In the short term, it is providing work, as financial services firms look to consultants for help with crisis management and recovery strategies. FTI Consulting, for example, has been especially prosperous of late, seeing a surge in demand in the face of the credit crunch. The firm focuses on services for companies that are facing trouble—whether economic, legal or regulatory—and its forensic accounting division, especially, has shown marked growth since 2007.

Weathering the storm

One thing is for certain—consultancies are better prepared this time around. After the dot-com trauma of the early 21st century, clients became more sophisticated buyers, demanding more value, deeper expertise and targeted solutions. Many now insist that their projects be staffed by senior level consultants—industry experts who really know their sector—rather than fresh-out-of-school generalists. In response to such client selectivity, over the last decade consulting firms have shifted strategies, offering specific industry knowledge and emphasizing quantifiable results. To differentiate themselves in the marketplace, many firms are now focused on niche areas such as economic consulting, security or globalization strategy. And rather than honing in solely on strategy, firms have also started offering a wider range of services, including IT, restructuring and compliance.

Anybody's game

With clients demanding targeted services, more niche firms (many spun off from larger consultancies after the dot-com bust and its ensuing layoffs) have entered the landscape, jousting with the larger, well-established consulting shops for projects. Competition in the consulting world has no doubt gotten tougher, since small firms are often able to undercut the fees of blue-chip houses by keeping overhead and staff expenses low. Smaller firms may also get a foot in the door by accepting projects that aren't as "sexy," such as implementation or data migration, before taking on actual strategy work.

Further heating up competition are the Big Four accounting firms that have re-entered the consulting arena. After the Enron scandal, the Securities and Exchange Commission tightened independence requirements, prompting several of the Big Four to separate their consulting divisions from their audit and accounting wings. 2007 saw the end of the five-year noncompete agreements that Ernst & Young, PricewaterhouseCoopers and KPMG signed with their spin-offs. The companies were

Visit Vault at www.vault.com for insider company profiles, expert advice, career message boards, expert resume reviews, the Vault Job Board and more.

VAULT CAREER LIBRARY   361

effectively released back into the consulting fold, and cranked up their business advisory services and financial and risk consulting divisions accordingly.

The hiatus has not diminished their brand value in clients' eyes, however: In 2007, consulting and advisory services were the fastest growing service lines for all three firms, and all posted impressive financial results. Ernst & Young posted a 29 percent revenue share coming from its transaction advisory services division in 2007, while KPMG's advisory division accounted for 32 percent of revenue and PwC's advisory service line brought in 22 percent. Deloitte, the only of the Big Four firms not to cast off its consulting practice, also enjoyed success in this area, with its advisory and consulting divisions comprising 31 percent of total revenue in 2007.

Servicing financial services

A large part of the past two years' strategy consulting growth was propelled by record-level M&A activity. Strong profits and cheaper debt drove up corporate demand for deals, while private equity firms rife with cash were eager to get in on the action. In 2007, the value of the global M&A market was $4.3 trillion (of which $1.4 trillion came from the U.S.), up 20 percent over 2006, and the frenzy created a new client base for consulting firms. As these transactions increased in value and grew more complex, consultants were called in to evaluate potential deals, analyze markets, conduct due diligence and smooth postmerger wrinkles. Bain & Company's mergers and acquisitions practice, for example, provides acquisition screening, due diligence, integration advisory and other M&A strategies aimed at growth and facilitation. Bain reported that 2007 M&A activity was strongest during the second and third quarters.

In 2008, however, with M&A and private equity activity dropping off, a range of other financial services has pumped demand for consulting services. As the market becomes more dynamic and more global, businesses are placing higher priority on risk management, raising demand for risk and security consulting. Another hot area is regulatory consulting, as banks navigate Basel II requirements and Sarbanes-Oxley compliance issues. Kennedy Information forecasts that financial services consulting spending will increase from $60 billion in 2007 to $74 billion in 2008.

America's got talent

Despite the shaky economic conditions, there are no signs of consulting firms slowing their recruiting plans. According to Kennedy Research, 75 percent of consulting firms plan to hire as many new recruits in 2008 as they did in 2007, when hiring at the junior level was at its peak. This aggressive hiring stance indicates that most firms are confident that the credit crunch won't stifle business growth in the long term. Some companies are also raising target hiring numbers to keep up with the slightly higher turnover that has resulted from competition for experienced consultants. Due to the war for talent, many U.S. firms saw 20 to 35 percent attrition in 2007.

In 2008, top graduates just entering the consulting field will be able to choose from a spectrum of options. Some will no doubt be attracted to the name and prestige of a blue-chip firm or a public entity that can offer stock options. Smaller, niche firms, on the other hand, may appeal to candidates who wish to accrue specialized experience. Although large public companies are typically able to offer higher salaries, smaller or private firms can lure candidates with the promise of more client exposure, faster career progression or profit sharing from an early stage in their career.

Recruiters are also scouring campuses for MBA candidates who have particular industry expertise, rather than a broad, generalist background. As firms seek to add value in a business climate where engagements are more complex and clients are pickier about whom they work with, specialist consultants are in high demand. Candidates with a track record in the public sector, compliance or risk management will likely have their choice of firms. Consultants with a few years' experience are also in demand, as companies seek out hires who can hit the ground running. And even with the financial services industry taking a beating, companies that specialize in this sector, such as Oliver Wyman and The Boston Consulting Group, are still hiring at a steady pace.

Cashing in

Though demand for talent is high, pay levels within the industry—both in terms of base salary and bonuses—have remained relatively flat. Some firms do offer an incentive-based compensation structure, tying bonuses to individual and group performance, and to that of the firm as a whole. As consultancies still aren't able to compete with the lucrative bonuses offered by hedge funds or private equity groups, many are sweetening employment packages with lifestyle perks like flexible schedules, work-from-home options, sabbaticals or part-time career tracks. The strategy seems to be working: Despite the unimpressive salary increases, the consulting industry remains one of the top picks for new MBA grads (and the stream of layoffs in the financial sector has no doubt enhanced the industry's allure for students).

Outsourcing's second wave

Well after the first wave of business process outsourcing projects first took customer service and software development overseas, the BPO market is still providing loads of work. In an ongoing effort to boost efficiency and save money, companies are now outsourcing more complex operations like finance, payroll and human resources. In 2007, the National Outsourcing Association estimated the North American BPO market at over $127 billion—more than half of the $217 billion global market. Consulting firms are getting a piece of this lucrative pie by assisting clients with global sourcing strategies and helping to transform their business operations to a BPO model.

Although the BPO market is still going strong, the business is trending away from the mega-deals ($1 billion-plus engagements) of the past. In North America, total contract value in 2007 dropped, as did contract duration. As *Consulting Times* posits, 2007 was the first time total contract numbers declined—by 12 percent. Part of the drop is due to maturation of the market; businesses are increasingly using several specialist providers, and contracting each for just one piece of the whole BPO project, instead of using a single outsourcing provider for all. According to Gartner Research, the highest demand for BPO services comes from the financial services and multi-process markets.

India and beyond

India continues to be a hot spot for growth, both for outsourcing and for advisory service lines. Between 2005 and 2007, IBM doubled its employee numbers in India to over 53,000, and in 2008, KPMG announced plans to raise headcount in the country from 3,000 to 5,000 by 2010. Accenture has also taken a substantial interest in the Indian market—it employs 35,000 there, more than in any other region, and maintains 12 global delivery centers.

Though most consulting firms are still investing resources in the subcontinent, India's rising labor costs and shortage of talent have firms eyeing China. In fact, according to a 2007 report from research firm IDC, China is expected to overtake India as the top outsourcing destination by 2011. Deloitte aims to have 20,000 employees in China by 2015, up from 8,500 in 2007, and Ernst & Young plans to expand from 8,000 to 30,000 in the country over the next decade, adding two or three new branches in Asia annually within the next few years. Additional areas popping up as prime BPO centers include Vietnam, Singapore and the Philippines. In fact, IDC predicts that the Asia Pacific BPO market as a whole will expand to $14 billion by 2010.

The next big thing

Consulting firms are also seeing business take off in other developing economies, such as Eastern Europe. Outsourcing in the region has been ramping up, thanks to the availability of highly educated, multilingual workers who demand less in salary than their Western European counterparts. The region's outsourcing industry, estimated at $2 billion in 2007, is expected to grow 30 percent by 2010. But Eastern Europe is now more than just an outsourcing destination; it is becoming a strong market for strategy consulting. As more countries in the region meet European Union economic standards, and as formerly

Visit Vault at www.vault.com for insider company profiles, expert advice, career message boards, expert resume reviews, the Vault Job Board and more.

VAULT CAREER LIBRARY   363

state-owned industries—such as telecommunications—deregulate, multinational businesses are establishing a presence in Turkey, Romania, the Czech Republic and Russia. As such, consultants are being tapped by banks, financial services and telecom clients to help them navigate these new markets. Kennedy Information predicts that growth in the $4 billion Eastern European consulting market will outpace that of the Western European market through 2009.

Earthy efforts

Environmental awareness was an emerging focus for the consulting industry in 2007. The pitfalls of global warming prompted a number of firms to adopt long-term initiatives with the stated goal of reducing their carbon footprint—many even hoping to achieve carbon neutrality. L.E.K., Capgemini and A.T. Kearney, as well as others, launched formal green programs in 2007. Among their resolutions are increased use of recycled and recyclable office materials, reduced energy waste in daily operations and minimization of air travel to client sites. These firms and others also spearheaded environmental advisory practice areas, applying the lessons of conservation learned in their own programs toward assisting clients, especially those in industries such as oil and gas, chemicals and energy, that face increasingly stringent compliance standards.

Practice Areas

Operations and implementation

Operations consulting is what puts strategy into action. In years past, operations consulting focused on saving money and increasing efficiency. In the recent booming economy, however, clients were more focused on expansion and profit growth, so operations consulting now revolves around responding to market changes, globalization and customer interaction (though today, with clients taking a cautionary stance toward spending, there has been a slight shift back to earlier conventions). While strategy involves marking out clear goals, operations consulting focuses on the practical means of reaching these goals, which might include allocating resources, shifting value chain priorities, evaluating benefits of outsourcing or examining customer service and distribution—all to help clients alter processes in response to competition or react to shifts in the market. Kennedy Information estimates that the $45 billion operational consulting market will grow at a compound annual growth rate of 7.1 percent through 2010.

Typical engagements may include:

- Evaluating procurement, sourcing and supplier relationships for a manufacturer
- Developing a global financial reporting system for a multinational business
- Implementing a customer loyalty program to help a credit card company attract and retain customers

Human resources consulting

Even with fine-tuned strategies and streamlined operations, businesses won't succeed without the right people in place. HR consulting addresses the issue of maximizing the value of staff and placing the right employees in roles that suit them. HR consulting firms are also hired for organizational restructuring, talent management, HR systems implementation, benefits planning and compensation. This segment is expected to expand in 2008, and to continue growing at a compound annual rate of 83 percent through 2010, according to Kennedy Information. Increased demand for benefits consulting, due to revisions in the U.S. Pension Protection Act and Financial Accounting Standards Board changes to pension plans, is contributing to growth in the market.

An important subsection of HR consulting is HR outsourcing. Increasingly, clients are turning to HR consulting firms to manage their internal HR systems. Kennedy Information reports that the combined global market for HR outsourcing and HR BPO was worth $31 billion at the end of 2007.

Examples of typical human resources consulting engagements include:

- Helping a business devise a leadership development plan for its junior employees
- Evaluating the financial consequences of changing benefits plans
- Developing a retention strategy for a firm that has experienced high turnover

Health care/pharmaceuticals consulting

With a market worth over $20 billion, health care consulting continues to be a core growth area. As the U.S. population and that of other industrialized countries ages, as scientists make further advances in genetic engineering and as patents for blockbuster drugs expire, the health care industry thrives.

The National Coalition on Health Care reports that total U.S. health care expenditures were $2.3 trillion in 2007, and are expected to hit $4.2 trillion by 2016. Furthermore, health spending in the U.S., at 16 percent of GDP, accounts for a larger share of GDP than in any other major industrialized country. With so much cash at stake, the industry is predictably overrun with players. That's where health care and pharmaceutical consulting firms come into play—helping clients, such as life sciences firms, hospitals, HMOs and drug companies, navigate a complicated maze of legislation, tackle competition, manage costs on vendors and equipment, and implement new technology.

Examples of typical health care/pharmaceutical engagements include:

- Developing an electronic medical records system for a hospital
- Analyzing market competition for a new pharmaceutical product
- Helping an insurance company manage reimbursements

Economic consulting

With global economies growing progressively intertwined, businesses in the U.S. are no longer isolated from economic shifts in other parts of the world. Thus, clients often turn to think tank-like economic consulting firms for guidance. These firms, typically loaded with economics PhDs and MBAs, as well as industry experts, investigate the economic factors that help clients resolve competition, antitrust, public policy and regulation issues, both domestic and global. Quantitative analysis, statistical studies and modeling services often form the core of economic consulting engagements.

Examples of typical economic consulting engagements include:

- Helping a client comply with a multitude of tax regulations in the various countries in which it operates
- Projecting the financial impact of a new environmental regulation
- Assessing the implications of a proposed merger

Financial consulting

In 2007, consulting spending by the financial services industry topped $60 billion, and is projected to hit $74 billion by 2011, according to Kennedy Information. Growth in the sector is predicted to remain strong over the long term, despite (and largely due to) current credit woes. The market has gained momentum as consultants step in to assist companies manage crises, deal

Visit Vault at www.vault.com for insider company profiles, expert advice, career message boards, expert resume reviews, the Vault Job Board and more.

VAULT CAREER LIBRARY

365

The Traveling Salesman Problem

A lot of people go into the consulting field with the notion that travel is fun. "Traveling four days a week? No problem! My last vacation to Italy was a blast!" However, many soon find the traveling consultant's life to be a nightmare. Many consultants leave the field solely because of travel requirements.

Here's what we mean by consulting travel. Different consulting firms have different travel models, but there are two basic ones:

- A number of consulting firms (the larger ones) spend four days on the client site. This means traveling to the destination city Monday morning, spending three nights in a hotel near the client site, and flying home late Thursday night. (This will, of course, vary depending on client preference and flight times.) The same firms often try to staff "regionally" to reduce flying time for consultants.

- The other popular travel model is to go to the client site "as needed." This generally means traveling at the beginning of the project for a few days, at the end of the project for the presentation, and a couple of times during the project. There is less regularity and predictability with this travel model, but there is also less overall time on the road.

Here are some variations of these travel modes that pop up frequently:

- International projects involve a longer-term stay on the client site. (Flying consultants to and from the home country every week can get expensive.) For example, the consultant might stay two or three weeks on or near the client site (the client might put you up in a corporate apartment instead of a hotel to save costs) and then go home for a week, repeating the process until the end of the project.

- Then, there is the "local" project that is really a long commute into a suburb, sometimes involving up to two hours in a car. Examples of this include consulting to Motorola (based in not-so-convenient Schaumburg, Ill.) while living in Chicago, or consulting to a Silicon Valley client while living in San Francisco. In these cases, you might opt to stay at a local hotel after working late, instead of taking the long drive home. This is not very different from nonlocal travel, and it can be more grueling, due to the car commute.

You need to ask yourself a number of questions to see if you are travel-phobic. For example, when you pack to go on vacation, do you stress about it? Do you always underpack or overpack? Do you hate flying? Do you hate to drive? Do you mind sleeping in hotel rooms for long periods of time? Are you comfortable with the idea of traveling to remote cities and staying there for three or four nights every week for 10 weeks? If you're married, do you mind being away from your spouse (and children if you have them) for up to three nights a week? Does your family mind? Will your spouse understand and not hold it against you if you have to cancel your anniversary dinner because the client wants you to stay a day later? If you and your spouse both travel for work, who will take care of the pets? Does the idea of managing your weekly finances and to-do lists from the road bother you?

If these questions make your stomach churn, look for consulting companies that promise a more stable work environment. For example, if you work in financial consulting and live in New York City, most of your clients may be local. But because consulting firms don't always have the luxury of choosing their clients, they can't guarantee that you won't travel. Moreover, many large companies build their corporate campus where they can find cost-effective space, often in the suburbs or large corporate parks. (If you absolutely cannot travel, some of the largest consulting firms, such as Accenture, have certain business units that can guarantee a non-traveling schedule—ask.)

Note that travel is common in the consulting field, but not all consultants travel. And not all clients expect you to be on site all the time. It absolutely depends on the firm's travel model, industry, your location and, most importantly, your project.

with global market competition, develop offshore establishments and find new markets and customers. Other financial service areas driving expansion are regulatory compliance, M&A, divestitures, private equity and risk.

Financial consulting firms tend toward two types of service offerings; either they work with financial services firms to enhance their strategies and performance, or they use a specific financial model to enhance client performance. In both cases, the focus is typically on boosting shareholder value.

Examples of typical financial consulting engagements include:

- Applying a proprietary financial model to improve performance
- Helping an investment firm identify a strategy to reach a new target market
- Evaluating liquidity for a private equity firm

Consulting Skill Sets

Consultants focus their energies in a wide variety of practice areas and industries. Their individual jobs, from a macro level, are as different as one could imagine. While a supply chain consultant advises a client about lead times in their production facility, another consultant is creating a training protocol for a new software package. What could be more different?

Despite the big picture differences, however, consultants' day-to-day skill sets are, by necessity, very similar. (Before we go any further: by skill set, we mean "your desirable attributes and skills that contribute value as a consultant." Skill set is a handy, abbreviated way to refer to same.)

Before we talk about the skill sets, keep in mind that there is a big difference between the job now and the job six to eight years from now, if and when you are a partner. We are going to talk about whether you would like the job now, but you should think about whether this might be a good long-term career for you. Is your goal to see it through to partner? If you would rather have an interesting job for six years, you just have to know you have the qualities to be a good consultant and manager. To be a partner, you have to be a persuasive salesperson. You will spend nearly 100 percent of your time selling expensive services to companies who don't think they need help. Your pay and job security will depend on your ability to make those sales.

Do you have the following characteristics in your skill set?

- **Do you work well in teams?** Consultants don't work alone. Not only do they frequently brainstorm with other consultants, but they also often work with employees at the client company, or even with consultants from other companies hired by the client. Consultants also frequently attend meetings and interview potential information sources. If you're the sort of person who prefers to work alone in quiet environments, you will not enjoy being a consultant.

- **Do you multitask well?** Not only can consulting assignments be frenetic, but consultants are often staffed on more than one assignment. Superior organizational skills and a good sense of prioritization are your friends. Would your friends describe you as a really busy person who's involved in a ton of activities, and still able to keep your personal life on track?

- **Speaking of friends, do you like talking to people?** Do you find yourself getting into interesting conversations over lunch and dinner? If you consider yourself a true introvert and find that speaking to people all day saps your energy, you will likely find consulting quite enervating. On the other hand, if you truly relish meetings, talking to experts, explaining your viewpoints, cajoling others to cooperate with you and making impromptu presentations, you've got some valuable talents in your consulting skill set.

- **Did you love school?** Did you really like going to class and doing your homework? There's a high correlation between academic curiosity and enjoyment of consulting.

Visit Vault at www.vault.com for insider company profiles, expert advice, career message boards, expert resume reviews, the Vault Job Board and more.

VAULT CAREER LIBRARY   367

- **Are you comfortable with math?** Consulting firms don't expect you to be a math professor, but you should be comfortable with figures, as well as commonly used programs like Excel, Access and PowerPoint. If you hate math, you will hate consulting. On a related note, you should also relish and be good at analysis and thinking creatively. Consultants have a term, now infiltrating popular culture, called "out of the box thinking." This means the ability to find solutions that are "outside the box"—not constrained by commonly accepted facts.

- **Are you willing to work 70, even 80 hours a week?** Consultants must fulfill client expectations. If you must work 80 hours a week to meet client expectations, then that will be your fate. If you have commitments outside work, for example, you may find consulting hours difficult. Even if you have no major commitments outside work, understand what such a schedule means to you. Try working from 8 a.m. to 10 p.m. one day. Now imagine doing so five days a week for months on end.

- **Last, but certainly not least, are you willing to travel frequently?** (See the next section for a discussion of travel in consulting.)

Be truthful. If you can't answer most of these points with a resounding "yes," consulting is most likely not for you. The point is not just to get the job, but also to know what you're getting into—and to truly want to be a consultant.

Who Hires Consultants, and Why?

Corporations, governments and nonprofit institutions hire consultants for a number of reasons. Every consulting project springs from a client's need for help, or at least the kind of help that short-term, internal hiring can't solve. Some clients, for example, need to overhaul their entire IT infrastructure, yet they're out of touch with the latest back-end systems or don't have the staff resources for such a large project. Other clients may be merging, but lack any experience with post-merger staffing procedures and need a neutral party to mediate. Some clients may need an outsider's perspective on a plant shutdown. Perhaps a client wants to bring in extra industry knowledge.

Consultants get hired for political reasons too. Launching big projects can be very cumbersome, particularly at Fortune 500 companies. In order for a single dollar to be spent on such a project, most companies require senior executive approval. And without a major consultancy brand name attached to the project, approval can be hard to get. But once a consulting firm steps into the picture, everyone involved has plausible deniability in the event that the project fails. There is an old adage: "No one ever got fired for hiring McKinsey" (or a similarly prestigious consulting firm). Some clients still adhere to this as a rule of thumb.

Second, even if a giant project gets the green light, there's no guaranteeing it will be implemented. The reason? Simple bureaucratic inertia. Senior executives lose interest. Direct reports move on to other issues. In short, companies lose their focus. (An insider at a large private global corporation reports that steps from a major consulting report from 1996 were approved but, as of September 2002, had not yet been implemented.) By bringing in consultants to oversee large projects, companies ensure that someone is always watching the ball. In many cases, the correct solution may be quite evident to many, but having it confirmed by an outside party makes implementing a plan easier politically.

In the era of downsizing, consultants have another political use. Companies with an itch to fire a percentage of their workforce often like to bring in consultants. When the consultants recommend a workforce reduction, the company can fire at will, blaming their hired guns for the downsizing.

For some types of consulting (particularly outsourcing or IT), consultants are actually a form of cost-effective labor. It costs the firm less money to hire some outsiders to help them with a project, rather than hire some folks full time at the expense of a competitive salary and benefits package. Consultants may also get the job done faster, not because they are necessarily better, but because the company might not get away with forcing regular employees to adhere to a compressed time frame by staying late hours. By definition, consultants are hired to work not at the pace of the corporation but at a differently prescribed pace. A contingency performance basis makes this an even better deal for the client.

Whatever the reasons for hiring consultants, they're bound to be compelling—because, even despite the cost-effectiveness argument in some cases, consultants are very costly on average. Given travel expenses, hotel bills and actual project fees, hourly prices for consultants can easily climb into the $500 per hour range.

The worker behind the curtain

Consultants are a backroom breed of professional. In joint projects with their clients, they do much of the work and can expect none of the recognition. All consultants must deliver bottom-line value, and often spend countless hours huddled in cramped spaces to do just that. If you do a great job, chances are your client will thank you, but you may never hear about it again. In some cases, you will leave your project before its completion and may never know whether it succeeded or failed.

If you enjoy recognition and completion, you will want to consider the type of consulting firm you join. Does your firm have a history of repeat business? If so, you will have a better chance of seeing the client through different projects and business cycles; you may even work with the same client on different engagements. (Marakon Associates, for example, boasts that 90 percent of its work comes from engagements with previous clients.) Other firms might offer a methodology that isn't as repeatable. If your firm focuses solely on competitive analysis studies, chances are good that, if your client stays in the same industry, you won't need to sell that service to them again.

Economic consulting firms, like Charles River Associates and the Brattle Group, often help law firms with litigation support, including research, economic analysis and testimonies. This can be very interesting work, and since you're supporting one side or the other of a public dispute, you will certainly know how the fruits of your labor will turn out. Depending on the size of the dispute, so might everyone else who follows the business news.

Another example is M&A consulting. Some firms, like L.E.K. Consulting, have practice areas specifically focused on due diligence, company analysis and transaction support. The bad news is that on such projects, you are subject to the even longer and more erratic hours suffered by other M&A professionals. On the bright side, you will eventually read in *The Wall Street Journal* about any triumph enjoyed by your client. Your firm may not be mentioned, but at least you will be able to see the results of your hard work become a reality. (It'll also be easier for you to transition to other financial work in the future, if that is your wish.)

So, think about the level of recognition and completion you need for your work, and look for a firm that does the type of work that suits your level. If you find that you require higher levels of recognition and completion than any type of consulting can offer, then you may want to look into other professions.

Training for Consultants

A career in consulting is attractive for many reasons, but few of these are as important to jobseekers as the amount of training they will receive. Unlike industries, such as consumer products or pharmaceuticals, where companies funnel investment dollars into product design and research and development, the consulting industry's largest expenditure (apart from staff salaries and overhead) is training. Every year, consulting firms allocate as much as 20 percent of their revenues to internal training programs, and consultants reap the benefits. It is not uncommon for a consultant to spend four to eight weeks per year attending firm-sponsored classes, taking computer-based training programs (CBTs), and studying industry-related literature to improve their performance on the job.

The training requirements in consulting are, by any measure, extensive and employees who hail from top-ranked schools and prestigious firms find the ongoing skill development not only to be personally satisfying, but also valuable. Headhunters and recruiters for Fortune 500 companies realize how much training consultants receive, and they are willing to pay top dollar for people who have spent considerable time developing their skills.

Visit Vault at **www.vault.com** for insider company profiles, expert advice, career message boards, expert resume reviews, the Vault Job Board and more.

VAULT CAREER LIBRARY

369

Orientation training

Over the course of their careers, consultants will encounter two general categories of training: orientation and ongoing training. Orientation training begins soon after new hires walk in the door and greet their assigned human resource representatives. In large firms, most of the orientation training actually occurs in a distant location: After new hires fill out reams of paperwork at their home office, they board a plane and fly to the firm's massive training campus. Once they check into their assigned rooms, attend a welcome meeting and spend some time getting to know their "classmates" from around the world, they begin a program that will last anywhere from one to four weeks, depending on the firm.

Orientation training is notoriously rigorous and exhausting. New hires spend most of their days working in teams, meeting with firm executives who pose as clients, attending lectures, learning computer code and completing CBTs. Consulting firms spend millions of dollars each year to prepare new hires for their first few projects and they make sure that, by the end of the training, employees understand just how strenuous consulting can be. Consulting firms do budget in time for rest and relaxation, but such time pales in comparison to the hard work and countless hours of team-based learning. Regardless, most new consultants, despite feeling worn out at the end of each day, find the experience very gratifying. Orientation training may be a rude awakening, but it offers many perks. Where else can recent college graduates work with people from around the world, build lasting friendships and be paid large sums of money to attend class?

Ongoing training

Once consultants get acclimated to living in hotels and working with clients, training requirements re-emerge as part of their ongoing development. Every year experienced consultants complete a curriculum of computer training, industry-specific seminars, management workshops and a host of other training programs designed to complement on-the-job learning.

Aside from making consultants better at what they do, ongoing training also functions as a tool to gauge how ready employees are for promotion. Indeed, many firms will not promote an employee unless he/she first completes the required curriculum for that particular year. Consultants, therefore, have a two-part incentive for completing their ongoing training requirements. Not only do they hope to become better consultants, but they want very much to rise through the ranks, make more money and have greater responsibility.

Employer Directory

A.T. Kearney
222 West Adams Street
Chicago, IL 60606
Phone: (312) 648-0111
www.atkearney.com

Accenture
1345 Avenue of the Americas
New York, NY 10105
Phone: (917) 452-4400
Fax: (917) 527-9915
www.accenture.com

The Advisory Board Company
2445 M Street NW
Washington, DC 20037
Phone: (202) 266-5600
Fax: (202) 266-5700
www.advisoryboardcompany.com

AlixPartners
2000 Town Center, Suite 2400
Southfield, MI 48075
Phone: (248) 358-4420
Fax: (248) 358-1969
www.alixpartners.com

Alvarez & Marsal
600 Lexington Avenue, 6th Floor
New York, NY 10022
Phone: (212) 759-4433
Fax: (212) 759-5532
www.alvarezandmarsal.com

Analysis Group, Inc.
111 Huntington Avenue, 10th Floor
Boston, MA 02199
Phone: (617) 425-8000
Fax: (617) 425-8001
www.analysisgroup.com

Aon Consulting Worldwide
Aon Center
200 East Randolph Street, 10th Floor
Chicago, IL 60601
Phone: (312) 381-4844
Fax: (312) 381-0240
www.aon.com/hcc

Archstone Consulting
4 Stamford Plaza
107 Elm Street, 6th Floor
Stamford, CT 06902
Phone: (203) 940-8200
Fax: (203) 940-8201
www.archstoneconsulting.com

Arthur D. Little
125 High Street
High Street Tower, 28th Floor
Boston, MA 02110
Phone: (617) 532-9550
Fax: (617) 261-6630
www.adlittle-us.com

Bain & Company
131 Dartmouth Street
Boston, MA 02116
Phone: (617) 572-2000
Fax: (617) 572-2427
www.bain.com

**BearingPoint Inc.
Management & Technology
Consultants**
1676 International Drive
McLean, VA 22102
Phone: (703) 747-3000
Fax: (703) 747-8500
www.bearingpoint.com

Booz & Company
101 Park Avenue, 18th Floor
New York, NY 10178
Phone: (212) 697-1900
Fax: (212) 551-6732
www.booz.com

The Boston Consulting Group
1 Beacon Street
Boston, MA 02108
Phone: (617) 973-1200
Fax: (617) 973-1339
www.bcg.com

Cambridge Associates LLC
100 Summer Street
Boston, MA 02110
Phone: (617) 457-7500
Fax: (617) 457-7501
www.cambridgeassociates.com

CRA International, Inc.
John Hancock Tower
200 Clarendon Street, T-33
Boston, MA 02116
Phone: (617) 425-3000
Fax: (617) 425-3132
www.crai.com

Cornerstone Research
353 Sacramento Street, 23rd Floor
San Francisco, CA 94111
Phone: (415) 229-8100
Fax: (415) 229-8199

599 Lexington Avenue, 43rd Floor
New York, NY 10022
Phone: (212) 605-5000
Fax: (212) 759-3045
www.cornerstone.com

Corporate Executive Board
1919 North Lynn Street
Arlington, VA 22209
Phone: (571) 303-3000
Fax: (571) 303-3100
www.executiveboard.com

Deloitte
1633 Broadway, 35th Floor
New York, NY 10019
Phone: (212) 492-4500
Fax: (212) 492-4743
www.deloitte.com

**Diamond Management &
Technology Consultants, Inc.**
John Hancock Center, Suite 3000
875 North Michigan Avenue
Chicago, IL 60611
Phone: (312) 255-5000
Fax: (312) 255-6000
www.diamondconsultants.com

Visit Vault at **www.vault.com** for insider company profiles, expert advice,
career message boards, expert resume reviews, the Vault Job Board and more.

VAULT CAREER LIBRARY

371

Employer Directory, cont.

Ernst & Young LLP

5 Times Square

New York, NY 10036

Phone: (212) 773-3000

Fax: (212) 773-6350

www.ey.com

First Manhattan Consulting Group

90 Park Avenue

New York, NY 10016

Phone: (212) 557-0500

www.fmcg.com

FTI Consulting, Inc.

500 East Pratt Street, Suite 1400

Baltimore, MD 21202

Phone: (410) 951-4800

Fax: (410) 224-8378

www.fticonsulting.com

Gallup Consulting

The Gallup Building

901 F Street NW

Wasington, DC 20004

Phone: (202) 715-3030

Fax: (202) 715-3041

www.gallupconsulting.com

Gartner, Inc.

56 Top Gallant Road

Stamford, CT 06902

Phone: (203) 964-0096

www.gartner.com

Giuliani Partners LLC

5 Times Square

New York, NY 10036

Phone: (212) 931-7300

Fax: (212) 931-7310

www.giulianipartners.com

Hay Group

The Wanamaker Building

100 Penn Square East

Philadelphia, PA 19107

Phone: (215) 861-2000

Fax: (215) 861-2111

www.haygroup.com

Hewitt Associates

100 Half Day Road

Lincolnshire, IL 60069

Phone: (847) 295-5000

Fax: (847) 295-7634

www.hewitt.com

Huron Consulting Group

550 West Van Buren

Chicago, IL 60607

Phone: (312) 583-8700

Fax: (312) 583-8701

www.huronconsultinggroup.com

IBM Global Business Services

New Orchard Road

Armonk, NY 10017

Phone: (914) 499-1900

Fax: (914) 765-7382

www.ibm.com/consulting

IMS Health Incorporated

901 Main Avenue, Suite 612

Norwalk, CT 06851

Phone: (203) 845-5200

www.imshealth.com

Katzenbach Partners LLC

381 Park Avenue South

New York, NY 10016

Phone: (212) 213-5505

Fax: (212) 213-5024

www.katzenbach.com

KPMG LLP

345 Park Avenue

New York, NY 10154

Phone: (212) 758-9700

Fax: (212) 758-9819

www.kpmg.com

Kurt Salmon Associates

1355 Peachtree Street NE, Suite 900

Atlanta, GA 30309

Phone: (404) 892-0321

Fax: (404) 898-9590

www.kurtsalmon.com

L.E.K. Consulting

28 State Street, 16th Floor

Boston, MA 02109

Phone: (617) 951-9500

Fax: (617) 951-9392

www.lek.com

LECG

2000 Powell Street, Suite 600

Emeryville, CA 94608

Phone: (510) 985-6700

www.lecg.com

Lippincott

499 Park Avenue

New York, NY 10022

Phone: (212) 521-0000

Fax: (212) 308-8952

www.lippincott.com

Mars & Co

124 Mason Street

Greenwich, CT 06830

Phone: (203) 629-9292

Fax: (203) 629-9432

www.marsandco.com

Marakon Associates

245 Park Avenue, 44th Floor

New York, NY 10167

Phone: (212) 377-5000

Fax: (212) 377-6000

www.marakon.com

McKinsey & Company

55 East 52nd Street

New York, NY 10022

Phone: (212) 446-7000

Fax: (212) 446-8575

www.mckinsey.com

Mercer LLC

1166 Avenue of the Americas

New York, NY 10036

Phone: (212) 345-7000

Fax (212) 345-7414

www.mercer.com

Employer Directory, cont.

Mitchell Madison Group LLC
17 State Street, 22nd Floor
New York, NY 10004
Phone: (646) 873-4100
Fax: (212) 742-9719
www.mitchellmadison.com

Monitor Group
2 Canal Park
Cambridge, MA 02141
Phone: (617) 252-2000
Fax: (617) 252-2100
www.monitor.com

Navigant Consulting, Inc.
30 South Wacker Drive, Suite 3100
Chicago, IL 60606
Phone: (312) 583-5700
Fax: (312) 583-5701
www.navigantconsulting.com

NERA Economic Consulting
50 Main Street, 14th Floor
White Plains, NY 10606
Phone: (914) 448-4000
Fax: (914) 448-4040
www.nera.com

Oliver Wyman
1166 Avenue of the Americas
New York, NY 10036
Phone: (212) 345-8000
www.oliverwyman.com

The Parthenon Group
200 State Street, 14th Floor
Boston, MA 02109
Phone: (617) 478-2550
Fax: (617) 478-2555
www.parthenon.com

PricewaterhouseCoopers LLP
300 Madison Avenue, 24th Floor
New York, NY 10017
Phone: (646) 471-4000
Fax: (813) 286-6000
www.pwc.com
www.pwc.tv

PRTM
444 Castro Street, Suite 600
Mountain View, CA 94041
Phone: (650) 967-2900
Fax: (650) 967-6367
www.prtm.com

Putnam Associates
25 Burlington Mall Road
Burlington, MA 01803
Phone: (781) 273-5480
Fax: (781) 273-5484
www.putassoc.com

Roland Berger Strategy Consultants
230 Park Avenue, Suite 112
New York, NY 10022
Phone: (212) 651-9660
Fax: (212) 756-8750
www.rolandberger.com

Towers Perrin
One Stamford Plaza
263 Tresser Boulevard
Stamford, CT 06901
Phone: (203) 326-5400
Fax: (203) 326-5499
www.towersperrin.com

Watson Wyatt Worldwide
901 North Glebe Road
Arlington, VA 22203
Phone: (703) 258-8000
Fax: (703) 258-8585
www.watsonwyatt.com

ZS Associates
1800 Sherman Avenue, 7th Floor
Evanston, IL 60201
Phone: (888) 972-4173
Fax: (888) 972-7329
www.zsassociates.com

Visit Vault at **www.vault.com** for insider company profiles, expert advice,
career message boards, expert resume reviews, the Vault Job Board and more.

VAULT CAREER LIBRARY   373

Manufacturing

Industry Overview

Got the motor running ...?

Once the bedrock of the U.S. economy, most segments of the American manufacturing industry are still growing, at least in terms of profits and productivity. But in terms of employment, manufacturing jobs are increasingly moving overseas. The Bureau of Labor Statistics (BLS) reports that, except for Italy, every G-7 nation has shed manufacturing jobs over the last five years (notably, Japan is included among the G-7 countries). And the decline in U.S. manufacturing employment actually dates back even further, as the BLS calculates that employment has declined by an average of 0.2 percent every year since the mid-1950s (with productivity increasing by 3.2 percent every year).

Economists praise manufacturing for the "multiplier effect," which holds that manufacturing creates economic output in other industries by using intermediate goods and services in the production process. According to the National Association of Manufacturers (NAM), every $1 generated by a manufacturing product has created an additional $1.37 in intermediate economic output. Unfortunately, the opposite is true: when manufacturing slows down, so do the complementary industries associated with it. Several manufacturing-related sectors of the U.S. economy have experienced this kind of slowdown in recent years, largely because of rising material costs, notably of oil and steel. The industry didn't suffer as long as consumers were willing to carry the higher costs, but the U.S. housing market collapsed in summer 2007, wiping out a great deal of consumer confidence in the process. The housing crisis was also disastrous for a few manufacturing segments, particularly wood and forest products, which provides house-building materials.

Still, the U.S. manufacturing industry is the largest in the world, with U.S. firms accounting for nearly 25 percent of the sector's worldwide sales and leading in areas such as aerospace, telecommunications and consumer goods. Taken alone, U.S. manufacturing surpasses the GDP of all but six of the world's countries. In addition, it's the No. 2 country in terms of exporting manufactured products, and in total manufacturing output in dollars (close to $1.5 trillion in 2006). The manufacturing and exporting of goods is critical to maintaining a strong currency and economy, so it's no wonder economists pay close attention to manufacturing stats and figures.

The manufacturing industry covers a wide array of businesses, from mineral products, metals, chemicals, plastics, machinery, computers and electronics to motor vehicles, furniture, paper, textiles and clothing. Several of the more important sectors are discussed below; Vault's guide to the consumer products industry addresses food and consumer goods manufacturing and marketing.

Auto manufacturing for the people

Arguably, the first half of the 20th century was the Golden Age of U.S. manufacturing, when Detroit hummed with auto production and Henry Ford ushered in the next phase of the Industrial Revolution with his assembly line production method. Beginning in the 1970s, though, American auto production began a gradual decline in terms of production standards and sales. In 2007, Detroit automaker General Motors managed to hold off Toyota for the title of No. 1 automaker worldwide, but just barely—GM sold 9.37 million vehicles, while Toyota sold 9.36 million.

In the late 1990s, American carmakers were riding high because of consumers' appetite for big trucks and sports utility vehicles (SUVs), as opposed to the typical subcompact made by an Asian company. The new millennium was a different era, though, as rising gas prices and increased environmental awareness exposed many American-made vehicles as gas-guzzling, energy-inefficient dinosaurs. Consumers began preferring the sporty hybrids in which Asian firms specialize (e.g., the Toyota Prius) and U.S. automakers' profit margins were hammered by the high wages and cushy benefits of North American assembly line workers. (Rising steel prices didn't help, as the price per ton more than doubled from $260 in mid-year 2003

Visit Vault at **www.vault.com** for insider company profiles, expert advice, career message boards, expert resume reviews, the Vault Job Board and more.

VAULT CAREER LIBRARY   **375**

to $580 in 2006, and surged by another 40 percent in the first four months of 2007.) All of these factors led to some whopping losses: GM reported a $38.7 billion deficit in 2007, the worst in company and automotive industry history. Not to be outdone, Ford lost $12.7 billion in 2006, the worst annual result in that company's history. Chrysler reported its own $1.5 billion loss in 2007, a figure so bad that parent company Daimler sold it to private equity firm Cerberus Capital Management for $7.4 billion—the first U.S. auto privatization in half a century. Meanwhile, Toyota streaked across the finish line with almost $14 billion in 2007 earnings.

American and international auto firms have similarly opposite fortunes in terms of employment—Chrysler, Ford and GM are cutting back drastically on North American manufacturing. By the end of 2007, membership in Detroit's major union, United Auto Workers, fell below 500,000 for the first time since World War II. Membership peaked at 1.5 million in 1979 and has been in steady decline ever since. The number is sure to grow smaller in future years, as the big three are currently offering buyouts to the majority of North American plant employees. In 2006 alone, over 67,000 workers took buyout offers from Ford and GM, and Chrysler has the stated goal of cutting 21,000 North American jobs by 2009.

While U.S. companies are shrinking North American operations, foreign firms are expanding in the same region. And these companies' new manufacturing facilities are usually not located in Michigan—BMW, Honda, Hyundai and Toyota have all recently built plants in the Southeastern U.S., and in late 2007 Volkswagen said it was ditching Auburn Hills, Michigan, as its U.S. headquarters, in favor of Northern Virginia. Ironically, as these firms increasingly move production to the U.S., some are experiencing similar struggles to the Detroit firms. For instance, as demand weakened in the U.S. during the economic downturn of 2007 and 2008, Hyundai drastically reduced North American production by about 20 percent at its plant in Mobile, Alabama. And in early 2008, Toyota had almost one assembly plant's worth of idle capacity, making cars that wouldn't immediately sell.

As sales continue to slump in the U.S. and the dollar continues to weaken, North American auto-manufacturing is coming to resemble that of Asia: a cheap manufacturing base, from which companies can turn a profit by exporting cars worldwide. And unexpectedly, Detroit's big three are some of the best-positioned automakers to thrive in an export economy, having restructured much of the workforce through 2007's landmark buyouts. The buyout initiatives are still underway, though, and if no employees decide to leave Ford, GM and Chrysler, then forced layoffs will become inevitable in order to increase these firms' bottom line.

To pique public interest, automotive companies are increasingly combining with major electronics manufacturers to provide a variety of in-vehicle add-ons, like satellite radio, crash avoidance systems and iPods; the percentage of electronic content in automobiles is expected to increase to 40 percent by 2010. At the same time, such developments increase automotive warranty costs and the possibility of vehicle recalls. Furthermore, besides the need to develop a hybrid vehicle that will sell well as Toyota's Prius or Honda's Civic, expected changes in regulation of emissions and fuel efficiency are prompting Chrysler, Ford and GM to get with the hybrid program. In 2004, Ford redesigned its Escape SUV as a hybrid, and GM will debut its own hybrid SUV, the Saturn VUE, in 2010. Chrysler doesn't have a hybrid model close to production, but says it is working on developing one.

Steely resolve

Steel is another U.S. manufacturing mainstay, dating back to the days when Pittsburgh magnate Andrew Carnegie co-founded U.S. Steel in 1901. At the time, it was the biggest enterprise in the history of U.S. business, accounting for about 67 percent of American steel production in its first year of operation. U.S. Steel's massive size eventually prompted antitrust prosecution, but the reality of the current steel industry isn't much different. Because of the universal demand for steel, especially as developing countries industrialize, the price of steel has consistently risen for years. Smaller firms are ill-equipped to handle these high material costs, so the industry tends toward consolidation. In 2007, the world's No. 1 steelmaker, Mittal Steel, merged with No. 2 Arcelor to create the giant ArcelorMittal, while a spate of domestic acquisitions left four dominant steelmakers in the U.S., including Nucor and U.S. Steel, profiled in this edition. The statistics tell the story of consolidation: the top-three U.S. steel firms accounted for 35 percent of hot-rolled coil production in 2001, yet were responsible for 60 percent just five years later (according to the steel consultancy First River).

Despite working to meet increasing demand, the U.S. is no longer the center of the steel industry; that distinction now belongs to China, which quadrupled its steel production between 1998 and 2005 and now accounts for about 30 percent of world steel production. Some American firms, like U.S. Steel, are courting acquisition or expansion opportunities in China, while others, like Nucor, are fiercely critical of jobs going overseas. Nevertheless, the steel industry continues to consolidate into larger and more powerful blocs. The industry saw 241 mergers or buyouts in 2006, and another 200 in 2007, according to Bloomberg. U.S. Steel was an active buyer, notably purchasing Lone Star Technologies for $2.1 billion to command the top spot as producer of pipes for gas and oil interests.

In the first half of 2008, one particularly gruesome indicator appeared to show that the U.S. steel industry was working at levels that almost exceeded its present capabilities—the number of deaths on the job. For the first six months of 2008, the number of workers killed at steel mills was 15—one higher than the figure for all of 2006, and almost double the figure for all of 2005, when eight workers were killed. While those numbers in themselves may be compelling, it takes the figures behind them to give an idea of the true scale of the U.S. steel industry, and (perhaps) the reason the death toll has increased.

While the number of workers producing steel has remained constant over the last few years (close to 100,000 in iron and steel mills, according to the BLS), overtime rates in 2008 shot up by around 20 percent in early 2008 as the industry attempted to take advantage of the booming market. It seems that there is a reasonable case to be made that the increased overtime contributes to the number of deaths at work and that the solution is to expand to meet the demand it is facing. The long-term picture, however, is less clear, as the BLS expects automation, consolidation and further technical improvements to lead to further job cuts in the steel industry in future. That leaves U.S. steelworkers—and the industry—in an unusual position, as their increased efficiency and productivity helps meet unprecedented demand for their product, while at the same time shrinking the number of jobs within the industry.

Chemically altered

Besides representing the largest single slice—4 percent—of the manufacturing pie, chemical production is perhaps the most important segment of the industry, since it makes the solvents, dyes and other compounds used in all manner of other manufacturing industries: automobile production, paper processing, pharmaceuticals, electronics and agricultural. (Over 55 percent of manufacturers say that their production is directly dependent on chemicals.)

Chemical firms also make soaps, bleaches and cleaners for consumers. The 2004 and 2005 hurricane seasons in the Southeastern U.S. hurt this segment by destroying a number of factories. Also, high oil prices drove up the cost of many petrochemicalderived products, and rising prices for natural gas, used as part of many manufacturing processes, have added to costs as well. This has resulted in decreased revenue along with an increased drive toward mergers and acquisitions—like BASF's June 2006 purchase of the Engelhard, a manufacturer of pigments and chemical catalysts, for $5 billion. Analysts see specialty chemicals such as these as perhaps the best avenue for growth; manufacturers can keep a competitive edge by producing agents used for highly specific purposes.

Despite estimates of higher production, the BLS expects employment within the chemical manufacturing segment of the manufacturing industry to decline by 14 percent by 2014, due to increased efficiency, production outsourcing and more stringent regulation, among other factors. Three sectors—basic chemicals, other chemical products and synthetics—are projected to be the hardest hit, losing a total of 80,000 workers.

Visit Vault at www.vault.com for insider company profiles, expert advice, career message boards, expert resume reviews, the Vault Job Board and more.

VAULT CAREER LIBRARY   377

Cruising the skies

Aerospace is another sector contributing significantly to U.S. manufacturing. In the commercial sphere, airplane manufacturing is dominated by the American firm Boeing and its European rival, Airbus. Other large aerospace firms provide parts for commercial aircraft, as well as a range of products and services for military use and space travel. Of these, some of the largest are Lockheed Martin, Northrop Grumman and Raytheon, the latter being a specialist in high-tech, electronics-based military products.

Other firms with large aerospace operations are true conglomerates, with a range of manufacturing operations in other industries. Textron, for instance, has leading helicopter and aircraft operations (Bell and Cessna), but also makes golf carts, automotive parts, hydraulics systems and others. Another conglomerate, United Technologies Corp., actually originated as the engine division of Boeing in 1929. Today, the company makes air conditioners through its Carrier subsidiary and elevators through its Otis division, besides other products.

Commercial aircraft production was severely depressed after September 11th, but bounced back in the past several years. According to the Aerospace Industries Association, sales, orders, exports and employment in the segment all increased significantly from 2004 to 2007. The civil aircraft segment, with a 16 percent sales boom, was particularly robust. Total sales in 2006 of $200 billion represented an increase of $11 billion over the previous year, and the AIA's predictions for 2008 remain on the positive side, with another 13 percent surge.

All roads lead to tech

Electronics manufacturing covers companies engaged in manufacturing power distribution equipment, communications devices, semiconductors, industrial electronics and household appliances, among other things. The sector plays a vital role in a number of other industries, including telecommunications, medical and automotive, and is thus inextricably tied to the rise and fall of these dependent industries. Innovative new consumer products and advancing digital technology have opened up new markets and avenues of revenue. Despite this, the BLS expects that employment in this sector will decrease by 7 percent through 2014 due to increased efficiency and jobs being moved overseas. An excellent example is Sanmina-SCI Corp., which makes circuit boards and components for technology firms, and relies on 10 large customers for about 60 percent of its sales.

Production grab bag

Other manufacturing sectors include textiles, apparel, forestry products (furniture and paper), rubber and minerals; together, these hold claim to roughly 22 percent of all U.S. manufacturing output. In the forest sector, employment figures have plummeted in recent years due to a convergence of unfavorable economic conditions and changes in demand due to the new "paperless" business environment, as well as manufacturing techniques for furniture and cabinetry that use less wood.

For a while, the industry expected solid profits due to the increasing demand for lumber driven by a rise in housing and construction activity in the hurricane-damaged Southeast. But the good news didn't last long. A severe depression in the housing market settled in, demand for lumber declined and predictions for new home construction in 2007 came in at a nine-year low. As a result, forestry titans like International Paper and MeadWestvaco began exiting traditional operations. In 2006, IP sold a whopping 5.1 million acres of forestland, the largest private sale of forestland in U.S. history; and in 2005 MeadWestvaco sold 900,000 acres and exited the paper business altogether after 150 years of operating paper mills. Both companies refocused on packaging operations, a higher-margin business that doesn't require as extensive a commitment to owning forestland and maintaining paper mills.

Work hard for the money

Though the industry as a whole enjoys higher wages than private industry (by nearly 25 percent), its component sectors vary wildly. Nonsupervisory workers at apparel manufacturers have average weekly earnings considerably lower ($351) than the average for all manufacturing ($659)—and worse, the textile sector projects a loss of 46 percent of its staff due to imports and technological advancements in the coming years. Steelworkers and workers at autos and aerospace product manufacturers have the highest salaries in the group.

Nonetheless, the industry began experiencing a great deal of pricing pressure in the mid-2000s. The price of natural gas, used in many processes, has jumped, and a combination of higher costs (corporate taxes, insurance and legal costs, pollution abatement fees and employee benefit programs) has put the U.S. at a significant disadvantage. In a report, the NAM and AMR Research calculate that these additional costs "add 31.7 percent to the [price] of doing business in the United States compared to our nine (largest) trading competitors." And, as the proportion of exported manufacturing goods has risen, passing these costs along to the consumer has become extremely difficult. These facts point to possible escalating encroachment on the manufacturing industry by foreign firms, as seen with the success of China's steel companies.

The outlook for 2008 is bad, frankly, as the economic slowdown that began with the housing slump of summer 2007 resulted in fewer investments in manufactured goods and the industry in general. New orders of manufactured products fell 4.7 percent in January 2008 and another 1.7 percent in February, according to the U.S. Commerce Department, and large-scale machinery orders fell by 13.3 percent in February, the largest decline on record. This news was doubly bad as exports had been one of the bright spots of the U.S. economy, considering the declining value of the dollar, and economists actually expected manufacturing orders to grow as exports picked up slightly.

A shifting outlook

Following a boom that spanned most of the 20th century, manufacturing employment declined sharply during the 2001-2003 economic downturn. Despite the economy's general resurgence from 2003 to 2006, industry employment has not kept up, according to the BLS. A number of circumstances led to the slump, including increased oil and energy prices. And like many industries, manufacturing has seen a steady push toward technologies that promise greater efficiency and productivity while reducing the need for manpower.

It's likely that many of the factory jobs lost since the beginning of the century will never return, signaling a fundamental shift in the industry as a whole. The BLS predicts total manufacturing employment will decrease by 0.6 percent through 2014. Statistics from the labor department released in February 2008 showed a decline in manufacturing jobs for the 19th straight month, placing employment at just below 13 million—the lowest total since 1950. Worryingly, productivity began to fall in early 2008 because of the housing market's collapse, turmoil in the credit markets and a general economic downturn. Production was humming along in January 2008, increasing by 0.1 percent, but then unexpectedly fell by 0.5 percent in February, according the Federal Reserve Bank of New York.

None of this means that manufacturing firms aren't looking to hire new employees; instead, it signals that manufacturing's identity as the blue-collar worker's industry of choice is probably gone. According to a 2005 survey conducted by Deloitte and NAM, 90 percent of employers in the industry reported a demand for skilled workers, and 65 percent of that total needed scientists and engineers. At a 2005 trade show, NAM president John Engler said, "The emerging problem in manufacturing is not a shortage of jobs, but rather a shortage of qualified applicants." Another NAM survey found that in 1973, over 50 percent of manufacturing workers had not finished high school and only 6 percent had taken college classes; by 2001, over 50 percent of workers were high school graduates and 25 percent had attended college. Although the shift has been gradual, manufacturing is becoming more of a white-collar industry. Companies and trade groups are developing initiatives (manufacturing certification programs, school and community career information sessions) to address this problem, hopefully before it becomes critical.

Visit Vault at **www.vault.com** for insider company profiles, expert advice, career message boards, expert resume reviews, the Vault Job Board and more.

VAULT CAREER LIBRARY   379

What is the Supply Chain?

Suppliers and vendors

A simple definition of supply chain is the network of vendors that provides materials for a company's products, but in reality, the supply chain is more complicated. There is a stream of flows from supplier to supplier until a product reaches an end user. For example, oil is rigged from the ground, sent to a refinery, plastic is made, an injection molding shop buys plastic pellets, makes plastics components, ships the components to a customer, the customer assembles the plastic parts into their machine, and then sells the machine to their customer. The farther away from the customer, the farther "upstream" a supplier is considered to be.

The network of vendors in a supply chain often includes tiered suppliers (meaning a company does not receive materials directly from the supplier, but is involved in getting materials or parts from an upstream supplier to a downstream supplier). The more complex a product, the more significant the upstream supplier's roles are. From a supply chain manager's perspective, his suppliers are primarily responsible for managing their own supply chain but he should have some involvement.

Oftentimes, a manufacturing facility acts as a supplier to a downstream manufacturing facility. For example, a company could have their manufacturing plant in the U.S. and their assembly plant in Mexico. The U.S. plant would be considered an internal supplier, since it's part of the same company. The transportation of materials throughout the supply chain is often called logistics. This includes air, land and sea shipping, as well as customs processing to allow materials to cross borders. The supply chain does not end until the product reaches the consumer. For this reason, distribution centers, distributors and wholesalers are all part of the supply chain. It is not rare for a supply chain to involve a dozen parties.

The relationship between a supplier and a manufacturing company is not as simple as a supply chain manager ordering parts and the supplier shipping them. There are continuous flows between the supplier and the customer. The Supply Chain Flow Process Chart on page 336 shows these flows in chronological order from top to bottom. (Note that this figure is for an already established supplier and material.) In the case of a new supplier, a supplier audit (a verification that a supplier has the potential to meet the manufacturer's needs) should be conducted first to determine if the supplier is appropriate for the work.

In the case of new material, the customer must first supply the anticipated number of units required, along with all of the drawings and specifications, to the supplier to get a quotation of unit price and lead time. After the quotes are received and a supplier is chosen, a purchase order should be done for the setup costs and samples. Setup costs can be a few hundred to hundreds of thousands of dollars (mostly tooling costs). A supply chain manager should always present the setup costs along with the piece price quote when working with engineers (so manufacturing methods are not specified solely on unit cost). For example, making a simple part by thermoforming would cost about $50 each, whereas making it by injection molding would cost $5 each. However, injection molding requires a $10,000 mold. If you only need 20 pieces annually, you are better off using thermoforming.

Depending on whether prototypes or the component have already been made or not, the samples ordered may be just to verify the ability of the supplier to make the parts, or to verify the design of the finished product. In other words, the supplier may fabricate a part correctly, but a manufacturer's engineering department may determine that the part needs to be redesigned. This would start the process over.

A manufacturing company has to furnish a forecast (usually annually) so the supplier can then go through his supply chain and make sure that all the materials needed (e.g., material, lubricant, machine capacity, labor resources) for the component the supplier provides will be available. A manufacturer then issues a purchase order, which serves as a commitment to purchase a defined number of units. A purchase order must have terms and conditions accompanying it to protect your company. Usually, a customer will not want to receive the entire forecast amount at once. Instead, a manufacturer could issue multiple purchase orders throughout the year, or do what is called a blanket purchase order for a large number and then make releases against that purchase order for small numbers when they actually want it.

College Career Bible • 2009 Edition

Manufacturing

For example, a company uses 1,000 rods of aluminum in a year. They may lock into a price for the entire year (the price of aluminum changes daily), but not take delivery of all 1,000 rods at once. Instead, the supply chain manager would request economic order quantity (EOQ) releases. An EOQ is the optimal balance between taking delivery for the entire 1,000 rods at once and paying for material that will not be used for months, and paying transportation, inspection and transaction costs for receiving frequent smaller shipments. The formula for EOQ is:

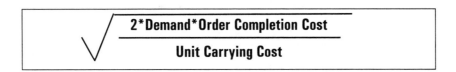

$$\sqrt{\frac{2*\text{Demand}*\text{Order Completion Cost}}{\text{Unit Carrying Cost}}}$$

The Order Completion Cost is the total cost of placing the purchase order, paying for a setup at the vendor (if applicable), and paying the transportation and in-house handling to get the components to the production floor. The unit carrying cost is the cost of holding inventory (insurance, warehouse lease, shrinkage costs, security, cost of capital, etc.).

Customers can do releases to the supplier at specific time intervals or specific inventory intervals. With inventory intervals, when a customer gets to a certain number of rods left, they would issue a release for the next shipment of rods.

A supplier should send a confirmation to the customer acknowledging they have received the purchase order and agreed to the terms and conditions described therein. The supplier sends the material per the purchase order and then sends an invoice for the number shipped. Once the goods have been accepted by the customer, a payment is sent to the supplier equal to the amount of the invoice.

Suppliers

There are basically three types of suppliers. In the first, or most conventional scenario, a company provides a design for what they want the supplier to furnish and the supplier makes it to the company's specifications. The second is the Original Equipment Manufacturer (OEM) supplier. In this case, the company does not specify the design for a custom product, but in fact buys a product that the supplier sells to many customers. These products are called off-the-shelf (a screw is an example of a component that is usually purchased as an off-the-shelf product rather than being custom designed).

Contract manufacturers are the third type of suppliers, in which formal contracts between the supplier (the contract manufacturer) and your manufacturing company are relied upon. The contract manufacturer purchases or makes all of the components, assembles the product, tests it and ships the finished product either directly to the customer or to a warehouse. Companies that want to get out of the manufacturing aspect of their products turn to contract manufacturers. The supply chain manager finds suitable contract manufacturers and manages the relationship after a contract has been signed. A company has to put a huge amount of trust into the contract manufacturer, since the customer does not have the same level of visibility or control over the manufacturing of the product as they do when they are making the product themselves. Contract manufacturing is an option in almost every industry from food processing to semiconductors.

Freight forwarders and transportation providers

Transportation providers and freight forwarders are also controlled by a supply chain management practitioner. Transportation providers pick up product from one location and deliver them to another. Obviously, it is very costly to pick up some cargo in Los Angeles and drive it all the way to New York for delivery. For this reason, these companies consolidate shipments from different places in a departing hub (whether it be a port, a warehouse or an airport), send them to an arriving hub, and then deliver them to their final destination. It is quite common for a transportation provider to hand off a shipment to another company to carry out some or all of the transportation. This is called subcontracting or third-party carriers. Specialty transportation providers also exist (i.e., for transporting explosive materials, refrigerated cargo). Some

Visit Vault at www.vault.com for insider company profiles, expert advice, career message boards, expert resume reviews, the Vault Job Board and more.

VAULT CAREER LIBRARY   381

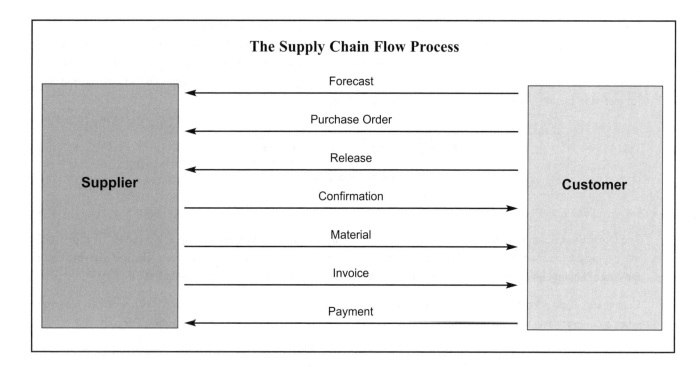

The Supply Chain Flow Process

Supplier ← Forecast ← Customer

Purchase Order

Release

Confirmation →

Material →

Invoice →

← Payment

manufacturing companies have traffic, transportation or logistics departments that take care of most of this work so a supply chain manager can concentrate on suppliers only.

Freight forwarders specialize in transportation across borders. They coordinate the paperwork, book the space with a transportation provider, and track the goods from pickup to delivery. Because of the complexity of customs requirements, tariff codes and language barriers for different countries, it is better to have freight forwarders involved if a company is dealing with more than a few countries or commodities.

Supply Chain Careers

Supply chain management occupations

Below are brief summaries of the duties for supply chain management occupations. Not every organization will have all of these positions and the duties of the positions will not be limited to those described here.

Buyer: Buyers do purchasing just like supply chain managers. The difference is that supply chain managers buy parts and materials for the company's products, whereas buyers purchase everything else. Some examples of items that buyers procure are desktop computers, office supplies and hand tools.

Planner: A planner takes the forecast from marketing/sales and breaks that into a build schedule of what products should be built and when they should be built to meet inventory goals. Planners also work with supply chain managers to control inventory of parts and materials.

Purchasing administrative assistant: A purchasing administrative assistant takes care of the filing of paperwork for the purchasing department. S/he will also coordinate travel arrangements.

Logistics manager: A logistics manager is responsible for the traffic of goods coming to and going from the factory. This encompasses air, land and ocean traffic, both domestic and international.

Supply chain engineer: A supply chain engineer works on technical issues with the supplier. This involves working with suppliers to improve their quality, helping them to analyze failures, and developing new products.

Commodity manager: A commodity manager is similar to a supply chain manager. Some companies separate the ownership of parts and materials for the supply chain managers by product line. For example, if a company makes binoculars, telescopes, cameras and microscopes, and they have four supply chain managers, they might assign one supply chain manager for each product family. Another approach is to distribute the work by commodity. One supply chain manager would be responsible for the optics on all of the product families and one supply chain manager would be responsible for the plastic parts on all of the product families. When this is the case, the supply chain managers can be called commodity managers.

Receiving inspector: A receiving inspector is responsible for checking the quality of the parts and materials that come from the vendor before they get moved to the production floor for consumption and before the supplier gets paid. There are statistics charts that define the number of samples from a shipment that need to be checked to meet the desired confidence level that the entire lot received is acceptable, so a receiving inspector does not check 100 percent of the incoming items.

Procurement manager: A procurement manager is in charge of the buyers and supply chain managers. The procurement manager sets the goals for the department and provides a level of escalation when a supply chain manager is having trouble managing a supplier.

Receiving coordinator: The receiving coordinator processes the parts and materials delivered. This includes doing a receiving transaction in ERP, moving the parts to their location and making sure the paperwork the supplier sends matches what was received.

Receiving supervisor: The receiving supervisor is responsible for the receiving department. Besides supervising receiving department workers, the receiving supervisor is in charge of creating and improving department processes.

Accounts payable coordinator: The accounts payable coordinator works in the accounting department and processes the invoices from the suppliers. After verifying the invoices match what was actually received, the accounts payable coordinator sends a payment to the supplier.

Visit Vault at **www.vault.com** for insider company profiles, expert advice, career message boards, expert resume reviews, the Vault Job Board and more.

VAULT CAREER LIBRARY   383

Employer Directory

AAR Corporation
1100 North Wood Dale Road
Wood Dale, IL 60191
Phone: (630) 227-2000
Fax: (630) 227-2019
Toll free: (800) 422-2213
www.aacorp.com

ABB Limited
Affolternstrasse 44
8050 Zürich
Switzerland
Phone: +41-43-317-71-11
Fax: +41-43-317-44-20
www.abb.com

Airbus S.A.S.
1, Rond point Maurice Bellonte
31707 Blagnac Cedex
France
Phone: +33-5-6193-33-33
Fax: +33-5-6193-49-55
www.airbus.com

Alcoa Incorporated
201 Isabella Street
Pittsburgh, PA 15212-5858
Phone: (412) 553-4545
Fax: (412) 553-4498
www.alcoa.com

Amcor Limited
679 Victoria Street
Abbotsford, VIC 3067
Australia
Phone: +61-3-9226-90-00
Fax: +61-3-9226-90-50
www.amcor.com

Amphenol Corporation
358 Hall Avenue
Wallingford, CT 06492
Phone: (203) 265-8900
Fax: (203) 265-8516
Toll free: (877) 267-4366
www.amphenol.com

Apogee Enterprises Inc.
7900 Xerxes Avenue South
Suite 1800
Minneapolis, MN 55431
Phone: (952) 835-1874
Fax: (952) 835-3196
Toll free: (877) 752-3432
www.apog.com

Armstrong World Industries, Inc.
2500 Columbia Avenue
Lancaster, PA 17603
Phone: (717) 397-0611
Fax: (717) 396-6133
www.armstrong.com

BAE Systems plc
Stirling Square
Carlton Gardens
London, SW1Y 5AD
United Kingdom
Phone: +44-12-52-37-32-32
Fax: +44-12-52-38-30-00
www.baesystems.com

BASF Group
Carl-Bosch-Straße 38
67056 Ludwigshafen
Germany
Phone: +49-621-60-0
Fax: +49-621-60-425-25
www.basf.com

BE&K, Inc.
2000 International Park Drive
Birmingham, AL 35243
Phone: (205) 972-6000
Fax: (205) 972-6651
www.bek.com

Bell Microproducts Inc.
1941 Ringwood Avenue
San Jose, CA 95131
Phone: (408) 451-9400
Fax: (408) 451-1600
Toll free: (800) 800-1513
www.bellmicro.com

BHP Billiton Finance Limited
L 27 180 Lonsdale Street
Melbourne 3000
Australia
Phone: +61-13-00-55-47-57
Fax: +61-3-96-09-30-15
www.bhpbilliton.com

The Black & Decker Corporation
701 East Joppa Road
Towson, MD 21286
Phone: (410) 716-3900
Fax: (410) 716-2933
Toll free: (800) 544-6986
www.bdk.com

BMW Group
Petuelring 130
Munich 80788
Germany
Phone: +49-89-3820
Fax: +49-89-382-258-58
www.bmwgroup.com

Boeing Company
100 North Riverside Plaza
Chicago, IL 60606-1596
Phone: (312) 544-2000
Fax: (312) 544-2082
www.boeing.com

Boise Cascade Holdings LLC
1111 West Jefferson Street
Boise, ID 83702
Phone: (208) 384-6161
www.bc.com

Caterpillar Inc.
100 NE Adams Street
Peoria, IL 61629
Phone: (309) 675-1000
Fax: (309) 675-1182
www.cat.com

Employer Directory, cont.

Chevron Phillips Chemical Company LLC
10001 Six Pines Drive
The Woodlands, TX 77380-1498
Phone: (800) 231-1212
Fax: (800) 231-3890
www.cpchem.com

Chrysler LLC
1000 Chrysler Drive
Auburn Hills, MI 48326-2766
Phone: (248) 576-5741
Toll free: (800) 992-1997
www.chryslerllc.com

Cintas Corporation
6800 Cintas Boulevard
Cincinnati, OH 45262
Phone: (513) 459-1200
Fax: (513) 573-4130
Toll free: (800) 246-8271
www.cintas.com

Commercial Metals Company
6565 North MacArthur Boulevard
Suite 800
Irving, TX 75039
Phone: (214) 689-4300
Fax: (214) 689-5886
www.commercialmetals.com

Cooper Tire & Rubber Company
701 Lima Avenue
Findlay, OH 45840
Phone: (419) 423-1321
Fax: (419) 424-4108
Toll free: (800) 854-6288
www.coopertire.com

Corning Incorporated
1 Riverfront Plaza
Corning, NY 14831-0001
Phone: (607) 974-9000
Fax: (607) 974-8091
www.corning.com

Crown Holdings, Inc.
1 Crown Way
Philadelphia, PA 19154-4599
Phone: (215) 698-5100
Fax: (215) 676-7245
www.crowncork.com

Cummins, Inc.
500 Jackson Street
Columbus, IN 47202
Phone: (812) 377-5000
Fax: (812) 377-3334
www.cummins.com

Daimler AG
Mercedesstraße 137
70546 Stuttgart
Germany
Phone: +49-711-17-0
Fax: +49-711-17-94116
www.daimler.com

Dana Holding Corporation
4500 Dorr Street
Toledo, OH 43615
Phone: (419) 535-4500
Fax: (419) 535-4643
Toll free: (800) 472-8810
www.dana.com

Deere & Company
1 John Deere Place
Moline, IL 61265
Phone: (309) 765-8000
Fax: (309) 765-5671
www.deere.com

Delphi Corporation
5725 Delphi Drive
Troy, MI 48098
Phone: (248) 813-2000
Fax: (248) 813-2670
www.delphi.com

Donaldson Company, Inc.
1400 West 94th Street
Minneapolis, MN 55431
Phone: (952) 887-3131
Fax: (952) 887-3155
www.donaldson.com

The Dow Chemical Company
2030 Dow Center
Midland, MI 48674
Phone: (989) 636-1000
Fax: (989) 989-1556
Toll free: (800) 258-2436
www.dow.com

Dril-Quip, Inc.
13550 Hempstead Highway
Houston, TX 77040
Phone: (713) 939-7711
Fax: (713) 939-8063
www.dril-quip.com

DuPont
1007 Market Street
Wilmington, DE 19898
Phone: (302) 774-1000
Fax: (302) 999-4399
Toll free: (800) 441-7515
www.dupont.com

Eaton Corporation
Eaton Center
1111 Superior Avenue
Cleveland, OH 44114-2584
Phone: (216) 523-5000
Fax: (216) 523-3787
www.eaton.com

Ecolab Inc.
370 Wabasha Street North
St. Paul, MN 55102
Phone: (651) 293-2233
Fax: (651) 293-2092
www.ecolab.com

Emerson Electric Co.
8000 West Florissant Avenue
St. Louis, MO 63136
Phone: (314) 553-2000
Fax: (314) 553-3527
www.gotoemerson.com

Visit Vault at www.vault.com for insider company profiles, expert advice, career message boards, expert resume reviews, the Vault Job Board and more.

VAULT CAREER LIBRARY   385

Employer Directory, cont.

Federal-Mogul Corporation
26555 Northwestern Highway
Southfield, MI 48034
Phone: (248) 354-7700
Fax: (248) 354-8950
www.federal-mogul.com

Foamex International Inc.
1000 Columbia Avenue
Linwood, PA 19061-3997
Phone: (610) 859-3000
Fax: (610) 859-3035
Toll free: (800) 776-3626
www.foamex.com

Ford Motor Company
1 American Road
Dearborn, MI 48126-2798
Phone: (313) 322-3000
Fax: (313) 845-6073
www.ford.com

General Dynamics Corporation
2941 Fairview Park Drive, Suite 100
Falls Church, VA 22042-4513
Phone: (703) 876-3000
Fax: (703) 876-3125
www.gd.com

General Motors Corporation
300 Renaissance Center
Detroit, MI 48265-3000
Phone: (313) 556-5000
www.gm.com

Georgia Gulf Corporation
115 Perimeter Center Place, Suite 460
Atlanta, GA 30346
Phone: (770) 395-4500
Fax: (770) 395-4529
www.ggc.com

Georgia-Pacific Corporation
133 Peachtree Street NE
Atlanta, GA 30303
Phone: (404) 652-4000
Fax: (404) 749-2454
www.gp.com

Goodrich Corporation
Four Coliseum Centre
2730 West Tyvola Road
Charlotte, NC 28217-4578
Phone: (704) 423-7000
Fax: (704) 423-5540
www.goodrich.com

The Goodyear Tire & Rubber Company
1144 East Market Street
Akron, OH 44316-0001
Phone: (330) 796-2121
Fax: (330) 796-2222
www.goodyear.com

Hamilton Sundstrand Corporation
1 Hamilton Road
Windsor Locks, CT 06096
Phone: (860) 654-6000
www.hamiltonsundstrandcorp.com

Handy & Harman
555 Theodore Fremd Avenue
Rye, NY 10580
Phone: (914) 921-5200
Fax: (914) 925-4496
www.handyharman.com

Harley-Davidson, Inc.
3700 West Juneau Avenue
Milwaukee, WI 53208
Phone: (414) 342-4680
Fax: (414) 343-8230
www.harley-davidson.com

Herman Miller, Inc.
855 East Main Avenue
Zeeland, MI 49464-0302
Phone: (616) 654-3000
Fax: (616) 654-5234
www.hermanmiller.com

HNI Corporation
408 East 2nd Street
Muscatine, IA 52761-0071
Phone: (563) 272-7400
Fax: (563) 272-7655
www.hnicorp.com

Honeywell International Inc.
101 Columbia Road
Morristown, NJ 07962-1219
Phone: (973) 455-2000
Fax: (973) 455-4807
Toll free: (800) 601-3099
www.honeywell.com

Hyundai Motor America
10550 Talbert Avenue
Fountain Valley, CA 92728-0850
Phone: (714) 965-3000
Fax: (714) 965-3149
www.hyundaiusa.com

Ingersoll-Rand Company Limited
Clarendon House
2 Church Street
Hamilton HM 11
Bermuda
Phone: (441) 295-2838
www.irco.com

International Paper Company
6400 Poplar Avenue
Memphis, TN 38197
Phone: (901) 419-7000
Fax: (901) 214-9682
Toll free: (800) 223-1268
www.ipaper.com

Jaguar Cars Limited
Browns Lane, Allesley Coventry
West Midlands CV5 9DR
United Kingdom
Phone: +44-24-76-40-21-21
Fax: +44-24-76-20-21-01
www.jaguarvehicles.com

Johnson Controls, Inc.
5757 North Green Bay Avenue
Milwaukee, WI 53209
Phone: (414) 524-1200
Fax: (414) 524-2077
www.johnsoncontrols.com

Employer Directory, cont.

Lockheed Martin Corporation
6801 Rockledge Drive
Bethesda, MD 20817-1877
Phone: (301) 897-6000
Fax: (301) 897-6704
www.lockheedmartin.com

MeadWestvaco Corporation
11013 West Broad Street
Glen Allen, VA 23060
Phone: (804) 327-5200
Fax: (804) 897-6383
www.meadwestvaco.com

Monsanto Company
800 North Lindbergh Boulevard
St. Louis, MO 63167
Phone: (314) 694-1000
Fax: (314) 694-8394
www.monsanto.com

Moog Inc.
Plant 4, Jamison Road
East Aurora, NY 14052
Phone: (716) 687-4567
Fax: (716) 687-5969
www.moog.com

National Oilwell Varco, Inc.
7909 Parkwood Circle Drive
Houston, TX 77036
Phone: (713) 346-7500
Fax: (713) 435-2195
Toll free: (888) 262-8645
www.natoil.com

Northrop Grumman Corporation
1840 Century Park East
Los Angeles, CA 90067-2199
Phone: (310) 553-6262
Fax: (310) 553-4561
www.northropgrumman.com

Nucor Corporation
1915 Rexford Road
Charlotte, NC 28211
Phone: (704) 366-7000
Fax: (704) 362-4208
www.nucor.com

OSRAM SYLVANIA Inc.
100 Endicott Street
Danvers, MA 01923
Phone: (978) 777-1900
Fax: (978) 750-2152

Owens Corning
1 Owens Corning Parkway
Toledo, OH 43659
Phone: (419) 248-8000
www.owenscorning.com

PACCAR Inc.
777 106th Avenue NE
Bellevue, WA 98004
Phone: (425) 468-7400
Fax: (425) 468-8216
www.paccar.com

Parker Hannifin Corporation
6035 Parkland Boulevard
Cleveland, OH 44124
Phone: (216) 896-3000
Fax: (216) 896-4000
www.parker.com

Pella Corporation
102 Main Street
Pella, IA 50219
Phone: (641) 628-1000
Fax: (641) 628-6070
Toll free: (800) 374-4758
www.pella.com

Pitney Bowes Incorporated
1 Elmcroft Road
Stamford, CT 06926-0700
Phone: (203) 356-5000
Fax: (203) 351-7336
www.pb.com

Plum Creek Timber Company, Inc.
999 Third Avenue, Suite 4300
Seattle, WA 98104-4096
Phone: (206) 467-3600
Fax: (206) 467-3795
Toll free: (800) 858-5347
www.plumcreek.com

PolyOne Corporation
33587 Walker Road
Avon Lake, OH 44012
Phone: (440) 930-1000
Fax: (440) 930-3799
Toll free: (866) 765-9663
www.polyone.com

PPG Industries, Inc.
One PPG Place
Pittsburgh, PA 15272
Phone: (412) 434-3131
Fax: (412) 434-2011
www.ppg.com

Quanex Building Products Corporation
1900 South Loop West, Suite 1500
Houston, TX 77027
Phone: (713) 961-4600
Fax: (713) 439-1016
Toll free: (800) 231-8176
www.quanex.com

Rayonier Inc.
50 North Laura Street
Jacksonville, FL 32202
Phone: (904) 357-9100
Fax: (904) 357-9101
Toll free: (800) 243-2590
www.rayonier.com

Raytheon Company
870 Winter Street
Waltham, MA 02451-1449
Phone: (781) 522-3000
Fax: (781) 522-3001
www.raytheon.com

Rockwell Automation, Inc.
1201 South Second Street
Milwaukee, WI 53204-2496
Phone: (414) 382-2000
Fax: (414) 382-4444
www.rockwellautomation.com

Visit Vault at www.vault.com for insider company profiles, expert advice, career message boards, expert resume reviews, the Vault Job Board and more.

VAULT CAREER LIBRARY   387

Employer Directory, cont.

Rolls-Royce plc
65 Buckingham Gate
London, SW1E 6AT
United Kingdom
Phone: +44-20-72-22-90-20
Fax: +44-20-72-27 91-78
www.rolls-royce.com

Sanmina-SCI Corporation
2700 North 1st Street
San Jose, CA 95134
Phone: (408) 964-3555
Fax: (408) 964-3636
www.sanmina-sci.com

Shanghai Automotive Industry Corporation (Group)
489 WeiHai Road
Shanghai, 200041
China
Phone: +86-21-22-01-16-88
Fax: +86-21-22-01-11-188
www.saicmotor.com

Shaw Industries, Inc.
616 East Walnut Avenue
Dalton, GA 30722
Phone: (706) 278-3812
Toll free: (800) 441-7429
www.shawfloors.com

The Sherwin-Williams Company
101 Prospect Avenue NW
Cleveland, OH 44115-1075
Phone: (216) 566-2000
Fax: (216) 566-2947
www.sherwin-williams.com

The Stanley Works
1000 Stanley Drive
New Britain, CT 06053
Phone: (860) 225-5111
Fax: (860) 827-3895
www.stanleyworks.com

Tenneco Inc.
500 North Field Drive
Lake Forest, IL 60045
Phone: (847) 482-5000
Fax: (847) 482-5940
www.tenneco.com

Textron Inc.
40 Westminster Street
Providence, RI 02903-2591
Phone: (401) 421-2800
Fax: (401) 457-2220
www.textron.com

Toyota Motor Corporation
1, Toyota-cho
Toyota, Aichi
Japan
Phone: +81-565-28-21-21
Fax: +81-565-23-58-00
www.toyota.co.jp
www.toyota.com

TRW Automotive Holdings Corp.
12001 Tech Center Drive
Livonia, MI 48150
Phone: (734) 855-2600
Fax: (734) 855-2999
www.trw.com

Tyco International Ltd.
9 Roszel Road
Princeton, NJ 08540
Phone: (609)720-4200
Fax: (609) 720-4208
www.tyco.com

United States Steel Corporation
600 Grant Street
Pittsburgh, PA 15219-2800
Phone: (412) 433-1121
Fax: (412) 433-5733
www.ussteel.com

United Technologies Corporation
One Financial Plaza
Hartford, CT 06103
Phone: (860) 728-7000
Fax: (860) 565-5400
www.utc.com

Universal Forest Products, Inc.
2801 East Beltline Avenue NE
Grand Rapids, MI 49525
Phone: (616) 364-6161
Fax: (616) 361-8302
Toll free: (800) 598-9663
www.ufpi.com

The Valspar Corporation
1101 Third Street South
Minneapolis, MN 55415-1211
Phone: (612) 332-7371
Fax: (612) 375-7723
www.valspar.com

Vitro America Inc.
965 Ridge Lake Boulevard
Memphis, TN 38187
Phone: (901) 767-7111
Fax: (901) 682-3062
Toll free: (800) 238-6057
www.vitroamerica.com

Volkswagen AG
Brieffach 1849
Wolfsburg 38436
Germany
Phone: +49-53-61-9-0
Fax: +49-53-61-92-82-82
www.vw.com

Vulcan Materials Company
1200 Urban Center Drive
Birmingham, AL 35242
Phone: (205) 298-3000
Fax: (205) 298-2960
www.vulcanmaterials.com

Employer Directory, cont.

W.L. Gore & Associates, Inc.
555 Papermill Road
Newark, DE 19711
Phone: (410) 506-7787
Fax: (410) 996-8585
Toll free: (888) 914-4673
www.gore.com

Walter Industries, Inc.
4211 West Boy Scout Boulevard
Tampa, FL 33607-2551
Phone: (813) 871-4811
Fax: (813) 871-4399
www.walterind.com

Weyerhaeuser Company
33663 Weyerhaeuser Way South
Federal Way, WA 98003
Phone: (253) 924-2345
Fax: (253) 924-2685
Toll free: (800) 525-5440
www.weyerhaeuser.com

Worthington Industries, Inc.
200 Old Wilson Bridge Road
Columbus, OH 43085
Phone: (614) 438-3210
Fax: (614) 438-7948
www.worthingtonindustries.com

Visit Vault at **www.vault.com** for insider company profiles, expert advice,
career message boards, expert resume reviews, the Vault Job Board and more.

VAULT CAREER LIBRARY   389

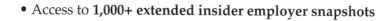

Media and Entertainment

The Industry

Star power

The media and entertainment universe is dotted with veritable galaxies of companies, from multibillion-dollar diversified conglomerates to small, independent movie studios and production facilities. Taking the astronomical metaphor one step further, these galaxies are populated by stars—the talented cadre of actors, actresses, singers, musicians, writers, directors and famous-for-being-famous types that dazzle the public eye.

But let the twinkly associations end there, because the entertainment industry isn't only the cosmic glamourama it's cracked up to be. Albeit populated by heavenly bodies (in the form of sculpted hunks and damsels), the media world also requires a lot of down-to-earth man- and womanpower to keep functioning. High school dropouts and PhDs in philosophy, MBAs and computer programmers, septuagenarians and 20-somethings, all work cheek by jowl to bring creative endeavors to life, to grow sustainable billion-dollar franchises like *Spider-Man* and *Harry Potter*, and to create new ways to keep the American public amused while spending its money on leisure.

Digital technology, increasingly implemented to enhance consumers' experience, now affects every aspect of the entertainment world, widening the array of customer choices and simplifying product distribution. From video-on-demand (VOD) television, which delivers programming to sets à la carte, to digital music downloads to digital satellite radio and even to digitally filmed movies, the smorgasbord of digitized delights grows every year.

As with any revolution in consumer choice, the dawning of the digital entertainment era has disrupted old business models and formerly dominant companies. The most obvious example is the music industry, which had no answer for the Napster music sharing service, save to render it illegal. More recently, the rise of Apple's iTunes music-selling software has caused a dearth in CD sales, forcing the industry to re-evaluate the value of the good old record store. Similarly, the proliferation of TV products like TiVo, which allow viewers to easily record shows and watch them later, skews tried-and-true Nielsen ratings, leaving networks desperate to find an accurate way to measure real viewership for worried advertisers.

Motion Pictures

You oughtta be in movies

Movies are by far the biggest segment of the media and entertainment industry, not only because of their prominence within the American cultural landscape, but also because of a successful motion picture's ability to sell products in other channels as well (also known as ancillary revenue streams). As demonstrated by Lucasfilm, a hit movie (or better yet, a hit movie franchise) can move lots of product in home video, international distribution, TV rights and so on. Each of the eight major film studios releases about 20 to 30 films each year, with the average studio release costing about $30 million.

In a nutshell

Once a movie is "green-lit" and a plan of action mapped out, production starts. Filming sometimes happens on a soundstage on a film studio's property, which are usually located in sunny and temperate Los Angeles, precisely for reasons of weather. Movies with larger budgets also often shoot "on location" anywhere from New York City to somewhere halfway around the world, like New Zealand, where *Lord of the Rings* was shot.

Visit Vault at **www.vault.com** for insider company profiles, expert advice, career message boards, expert resume reviews, the Vault Job Board and more.

VAULT CAREER LIBRARY   391

After all the raw footage has been filmed, it is taken to an editing studio, where the director works with professional film editors, sound effects artists and, sometimes, special effects wizards to pull a movie together into a cohesive whole. This is also the stage when music, titles and credits are added and when the film preview (or "trailer") is created and sent to movie theaters.

The creative side

The creative arm of the motion picture industry—where the movies are actually made—gets to have all the fun. Production companies, the "homes" of producers, receive hundreds of (mostly unsolicited) scripts every year from famous, semi-famous, unknown and possibly insane aspiring screenwriters, from which promising projects are culled. In the ensuing development phase of a project, producers, screenwriters, agents and studio executives sketch out a blueprint for a film. The latter stage of development is also often called preproduction. This is everything that transpires just before filming starts—location scouting, casting and the hiring of the crew, etc.

The creative side is the where the movies are actually made. There are a few key divisions on the creative side of the movie business:

• **Development:** The key players in the development stage are producers, screenwriters, agents and studio executives. Production companies, the "homes" of producers, start with a script. Every year, these companies are delivered hundreds of scripts (mostly unsolicited) from famous, semi-famous and unknown writers. The executives at each of the production companies then sort through the scripts (written by both new and established screenwriters), negotiate with agents to purchase interesting ones, and then bring together key players (e.g., a director, lead actors, other producers) who will commit to starring in or making the film if a studio finances it. A studio is then "pitched" the idea and if the film is approved, the film then gets a "green light" to go into production. The latter stage of development is also often called pre-production.

• **Pre-production:** This is everything that happens to get a movie rolling just before filming starts—location scouting and the casting and hiring of the crew, for instance.

• **Production:** Once a movie is "green lit," production starts. To use an analogy, if the screenplay is the blueprint, production is when the movie is built by the cast and crew. Filming sometimes happens on a soundstage on a film studio's property, but often it occurs "on location," at an out-of-studio venue.

• **Post-production:** After all the raw footage has been filmed, it is taken to an editing studio, where professional film editors and the director work together with sound effects artists and special effects wizards (if necessary) to pull a movie together. This is also the stage when music, titles and credits are added and when the film preview (called a "trailer" in industry-speak) is created and sent to movie theaters.

It's a bird, it's a plane ... no, it's computer-generated imagery

Digital technology is changing the movie-making game, mostly in the shape of computer-generated imagery (CGI) effects, the increasing complexity of which are changing the very possibilities for making films. With the special effects services of companies like LucasFilm's Industrial Light and Magic (ILM) and Pixar increasingly finding their way into action-heavy summer blockbusters and kid-friendly computer animated features, what was once physically impossible (like, say, swinging from skyscraper to skyscraper on threads of web shot from your own wrist) looks possible.

Some recent movies, like the 2007 animated feature Oscar-winner *Happy Feet*, are one huge special effect. Other popular franchises, like *Harry Potter* and *Transformers*, are effects-crazed to the point of rendering the tangible world inadequate. For those who lament the days of hand-drawn cartoons and spaceships hanging by strings, a backlash is already in the works. When the much-awaited movie version of *The Simpsons* opened in the summer of 2007, advertisements played up its gloriously low-tech 2-D imagery. Disney, meanwhile, announced plans to diss its Pixar subsidiary by making an animated feature the old-fashioned way, with real live human animators. Slated to appear in 2009, *The Frog Princess* will be Disney's first full-on hand-drawn, 2-D feature since 2004's *Home on the Range*. In the interim, the company plans to hire old-school animators to collaborate with the current computer-centric ranks at the happiest place on earth.

The business side

Beyond the creation and perfecting of the film product comes the business end of the movie industry, which deals with ancillary revenue streams and creative vehicles (e.g., theme parks, licensed products, home video). In other words, it's where the suits step in to figure out how to translate all the creativity into money.

Because many of the most successful movies of all time are franchises—*Star Wars*, *Indiana Jones*, *Lord of the Rings*, etc.— the business side works to exploit the enormous revenue opportunities that come with leveraging those properties. They do so through DVD and pay-per-view sales that bring movies to little screens across the country.

Movie characters live on as action figures, T-shirt imagery and bedspread motifs long after their movie has left theaters, thanks to licensing deals with consumer products companies. Large destination parks (like Disneyland and Universal Studios), with attractions based on popular movies, further fan the flames of fantasy, giving movie lovers some live-action bang for their buck.

As the business side has come to generate billions of dollars in recent years, movie studios have grown into diversified conglomerates with many different business arms. The main divisions are:

- **Home video:** Tapes and DVDs are the second phase of a movie's life cycle, bringing films into the homes of consumers after its life in the box office has run its course.

- **Consumer products:** All filmed properties and characters with commercial appeal are further exploited by other companies that pay licensing fees for the rights to use images and names.

- **Retail:** Virtually all major film studios sell customized items directly to customers either through stores, catalogs or direct mail, some in larger endeavors than others (e.g., The Disney Stores, Warner Brothers Studio Stores).

- **Theme parks:** Large destination parks (e.g., Disneyland, Universal Studios) provide the opportunity to further leverage a film's appeal to consumers in an exciting, live-action setting.

A bunch of exhibitionists

Vital in the movie business is the relationship that studios have with movie theaters, or exhibitors, as they are called in the industry. Before 1948, under the "studio system," film production studios and exhibitors functioned as different arms of the same company, with one arm providing the content that the other would show. It was a pretty stable business model, but also one that tended towards consolidation and a handful of studios—Paramount, Metro-Goldwyn-Mayer, Warner Brothers— came to account for virtually all of the industry's business. In 1948, the U.S. Department of Justice ruled that such large companies were illegal monopolies, and forced the companies to split their production and distribution businesses. It was a shake-up of the industry similar to digital technology's current affect on record labels, and neither movie studios nor movie theaters were ever the same.

After 1948, the power of studios over box offices weakened, leaving them more exposed to the whims of consumer preference. Also, the lure of television sets in people's living rooms didn't work in studios' favor. Movie theaters, separated from their production brethren, needed to work harder to court audiences and began building theater complexes with multiple screens (naturally called multiplexes) in the 1960s, showing a wider array of movies in one location. The movie studios followed suit, and began producing more varied types of films, which ultimately led to the proliferation of movie niches and independent films produced on small budgets.

Visit Vault at **www.vault.com** for insider company profiles, expert advice, career message boards, expert resume reviews, the Vault Job Board and more.

VAULT CAREER LIBRARY   393

Despite the twee comforts of indie films, studios and theaters' favorite genre remained the blockbuster, which re-emerged with a vengeance with *Star Wars* in the late 1970s. Over the course of the 1980s and 1990s, these films were designed to draw as wide an audience as possible on their opening weekends. Megaplexes started popping up in the 1990s, taking the multiplex to the next level with more screens than ever, stadium seating and fancy pants sound.

But despite the womb-like comfort offered by their movie theaters, exhibitors have been hurting in recent years, largely due to the advances in TV technology that have turned the humble family room into a high-tech multimedia paradise. Additionally, the length of time between a movie's theatrical release and its DVD release is contracting as VOD technology grows in popularity, allowing folks to skip the lines, expensive concessions and distractions of movie theaters and still see movies within weeks of their release. Exhibitors Regal Entertainment, AMC and Cinemark have sought salvation through digitization, setting aside competitive gripes to form an industrywide group, Digital Cinema Implementation Partners, entrusted with the job of making its founders' theaters fully digital by 2011.

Television

The box that talks

Often playing second fiddle to the much-lauded motion picture industry comes television—witness the barely concealed scoffs that often follow the phrase "made-for-TV movie." Still, with televisions in the homes of over 99 percent of the U.S. population, film's low-art cousin is arguably the most powerful media vehicle in the entertainment industry. TV's "studio system" moment—when the industry's business model started to change dramatically—came gradually over the course of the 1970s and 1980s, as cable television stations started to mature. Governmental influence and technology were both crucial to this development, as cable companies' deregulation prompted rapid expansion and subsequent advances in increased bandwidth in distribution (with digital cable) allowed them to become widespread and affordable.

The result has been a lot more TV, which has led to new and exciting programming but also a glut of channels targeting ever-narrower niches, from golfers to do-it-yourselfers to *Leave It to Beaver* enthusiasts. Still, several cable channels—such as E!, ESPN, Lifetime, USA, Comedy Central and MTV—have gradually strung together enough good programming and cultivated their respective niches to erode the once-dominant share of the networks (ABC, CBS, NBC).

The TV industry is structured somewhat differently from the film biz. One of the key differences is that TV is full of sales and marketing positions, since most networks make money on advertising. If a show is particularly successful, it can make even more money by being sold into syndication (everybody still loves *Everybody Loves Raymond*), by being made into a movie (like TV's favorite dysfunctional cartoon family, *The Simpsons*) or by launching spin-offs (witness the second life of *Cheers*' elitist psychiatrist, Frasier).

Typically, networks don't make much money from the actual development of shows; those spoils go to shows' creators and production companies. Advertising, therefore, is all the more critical for networks. While the bulk of ad revenue comes in at the national level, the major networks have bodies of network affiliates throughout the country that have individual sales forces selling local advertising, which comprises most of the remaining portion of overall company revenue. In addition to ad sales, affiliates also manage some content creation, primarily local news production.

The production of television programming follows a similar trajectory as that of motion pictures. However, because of the unique challenges presented by the faster-paced television broadcast industry, steps have been built into the creative process, which allow broadcasters to tweak their shows for maximum audience draw. Once a show is on the air, its performance is closely monitored in the Nielsen ratings, which track the specific demographics of who is watching it. Networks provide comments on scripts to develop shows with the most promising audience appeal, reconfigure schedules to improve performances and cut shows when they fail to build a loyal audience. Shows with low ratings that also attract the much-sought-after 18- to 34-year-old audience are often kept on the schedule.

TV networks

Here are some key divisions of television networks:

• **Development:** The television industry parallels the film industry in that scripts for new television shows are constantly sought out and studied in the hopes of creating the next *Friends* or *ER*. Job positions within TV development are typically divided into the different types of programming that appears on TV—sitcoms, dramas, miniseries, specials and daytime. Network executives are "pitched" ideas by production companies and writers. If the executive likes an idea, a "green light" is given for the show's pilot, the introductory episode. If the pilot is successful, it then becomes a series.

• **Production:** Because television typically calls for shorter production cycles, television studios are often fully equipped soundstages where TV shows are filmed and edited and where final cuts are put into post-production.

• **Programming:** Once a show is on the air, it is watched carefully to see how it performs. Programming executives closely monitor Nielsen ratings, provide comments on scripts to develop shows with the most promising audience appeal, reconfigure schedules to improve performances and cut shows when they fail to build a loyal audience.

• **Network affiliates:** While the bulk of ad revenues come in at the national level, the major networks have bodies of network affiliates throughout the country that have individual sales forces to sell local advertising, which comprises most of the remaining portion of overall company revenues. In addition to ad sales, affiliates also manage some content creation, primarily local news production.

From boob tube to YouTube

Recently, television networks have struggled to keep up with the delectable video offerings on the World Wide Web and have, accordingly, hustled to keep advertisers from taking their money to the Internet. In addition to maintaining web sites, cable channels and networks have taken to offering games and message boards to generate buzz for their shows, along with creating web-specific programming in the form of "webisodes" to ensure continued site traffic.

The explosive popularity of the Google-owned YouTube web site, which allows any Joe with a hookup to upload homemade videos for all the world to see, has prompted TV channels to embrace—sometimes awkwardly—user-generated content as well. ABC announced in May 2007 that it will produce a news show featuring submitted video, called i-Caught. VH1, a child of the Viacom cable family, launched a series of interactive comedy shorts under the title Acceptible.tv early in 2007, allowing viewers to submit their own shorts and vote for their favorites online.

Playing games

What to do in the rare event that there's nothing to watch on TV? Luckily, the big box has another use—video games. The term "video game" has become something of a misnomer, as the industry is ever-evolving to new, higher tech generations of digital fantasy-making that render the term "video" sadly outdated. Making great technological strides in the past couple of decades, and thereby relegating the simplistic graphics of Pong and Pac-Man to the nostalgia heap, the gaming industry creates increasingly realistic (if outlandish) virtual worlds for joystick-wielding enthusiasts.

And the games aren't limited to TV screens, either. Souped-up mobile phones increasingly offer game-like activities, and computer-based games have allowed for greater interactivity among players on the Internet. Through licensing deals, video games also provide another commercial outlet for big screen characters; gamemaker Activision released multiple games starring Spider-Man and Shrek when the third installments of their signature films hit theaters in 2007.

Visit Vault at **www.vault.com** for insider company profiles, expert advice, career message boards, expert resume reviews, the Vault Job Board and more.

VAULT CAREER LIBRARY

395

The industry supports both the artists who create, design and flesh out game characters and their various missions but also the techies who program in all the neat effects that make gamers drool. As advancing technology permeates every facet of the media and entertainment industry, of course, those who can combine skills in creating content and translating it into a digital format will remain in high demand.

Music

Hear that?

Enough with feasts for the eyes, let the public's ears have their treat as well. Churning out the hits and duds that range from top-40 pop to obscure avant-garde instrumental experiments, the music industry gets the tunes to our ears through the combined efforts of several arms—there are divisions that discover new artists, there are those that develop and produce music with mass appeal, and there are the promoters and marketers. And now, in the age of the Internet, there are lots of people hired to make sure that the record labels do not get fleeced by music freeloaders who find ways to acquire and disseminate the product for free, or to figure out how to create profitable businesses distributing or marketing music through the Internet.

Record companies, most of which are owned by the "Big Four" mega-music corporations—EMI, Sony BMG, Universal and Warner—promote, disseminate and control the rights to recorded music of artists under contract to them. The artists, meanwhile, get their cut of the cake through royalties or up-front payments in exchange for copyrights. These artists are vetted by the A&R folks—the talent scouts that listen to demo tapes, attend shows, troll music lovers' blogs and keep an ear to the ground to understand new trends and uncover the voices that best bring those trends to life. Once an act has been signed onto a record label, the producers perfect the music to make it commercially palatable for radio stations, critics and consumers. The packaging of the CD and creation of the artist's image are also finalized in this stage. Once an album is ready to debut, PR and marketing reps step in to get airplay on radio stations, get the music video shot and (ideally) aired, drum up television and press coverage, and generally put the artist in the public eye

After years of fighting the easy transfer of music files over the Internet—during which time CD sales have not-coincidentally plummeted—the music industry has recently shown signs of giving in to the digital age. In April 2007, industry big boy EMI announced it would begin offering songs free of antipiracy software through Apple's iTunes music store, effectively giving consumers the freedom to copy and share music to their hearts' content, once they pay a slightly higher fee than usual for access to a song. EMI's top-dog brethren are expected to follow in its footsteps.

Music careers

That said, for job seekers, the most promising opportunities continue to be in A&R, distribution and marketing.

• **A&R:** These are the talent scouts who listen to demo tapes, attend shows, travel and keep their ear to the ground to understand new trends and to uncover fresh voices that best bring those trends to life.

• **Production:** Once an act has been signed onto a record label, the producers perfect the music to make it commercially palatable for radio stations, critics and consumers. The packaging of the CD and creation of the artist image is also finalized in this stage.

• **PR/Marketing:** This is the group that toils to get airplay on radio stations, gets the music video shot and hopefully aired, leverages television and press coverage and puts the artist in the public eye. Arbitron ratings, essentially Nielsen ratings for radio, let both radio stations and record labels know what consumers are listening to, what is working and what is most popular.

- **Distribution:** This group specifically deals with getting the CDs into record stores and venues where consumers can purchase them.

- **Concerts:** Concerts and live performances that are able to attract large numbers of consumers are increasingly underwritten by large corporate sponsors to defray expenses (e.g., Pepsi sponsoring a Britney Spears concert tour).

The biggest media companies (e.g., AOL Time Warner, Viacom, The Walt Disney Company) span across all of these industries (and then some).

Radio days

Through stations both airwave- and Internet-based, the music industry has long relied on the radio medium to publicize and build up an audience for its latest releases. Arbitron ratings—essentially the Nielsen ratings of radio—let both radio stations and record labels know what consumers are listening to. Despite the influx of technologies that have relegated traditional AM/FM radio to antiquated status, radio play in all its forms remains integral to the success of recording artists; a June 2007 Arbitron study reported that 232 million Americans listen to radio a week.

Radio, too, has gone the way of all media, finding a second home in digital formats that are free of traditional radio's much-maligned static buzz. Big name talk show hosts, like ex-CBS bad boy Howard Stern, have been drawn to digital satellite radio for the freedom it offers from the obscenity regulations of the Federal Communications Commission (FCC). Digital satellite radio requires users to subscribe to the service, much like digital TV, and is currently dominated by two as yet unprofitable firms, XM and Sirius; the two companies plan to merge, if the FCC will allow it. FM giant Clear Channel is hoping America's ears will tune in to high-definition (HD) radio, which provides clarity of sound minus subscription fees (for all its freedom from regulation, satellite radio doesn't offer the best sound). Clear Channel plans to convert all of its 700 radio stations to HD technology by 2008.

Pay per play

As the forms of radio have multiplied, so have the complications of tracking the music they play and collecting payment for it. The music industry, looking to make up for losses in CD sales, is increasingly devising new ways to extract payment from radio companies. In March 2007 the Copyright Royalty Board (CRB) decided to raise the fees it charges Internet radio stations. The CRB's 2005 rate was 7 cents per song per listener, but it will rise to 19 cents a shot by 2010. Internet stations argued that their services only helped the music industry by giving exposure to musicians and asked web radio listeners— which total about 19 percent of Americans over 12, according to a Bridge Ratings & Research poll—to urge their Congressional representatives to act on their behalf.

That "free exposure" argument is falling on deaf ears, as the music industry is also moving to overturn legislation that allows traditional radio stations to play music without paying royalties to music labels. Following a 2007 study published by economics professor Stan Liebowitz, which argued that radio play impeded sales of CDs and digital recordings by giving music away for free, organizations within the music industry—including the clout-wielding Recording Industry Association of America—joined forces as the musicFIRST coalition with the goal of making traditional radio pay the fees already shelled out by satellite and Internet radio.

Visit Vault at **www.vault.com** for insider company profiles, expert advice, career message boards, expert resume reviews, the Vault Job Board and more.

VAULT CAREER LIBRARY 397

The Big Conundrums

There are two broad subcategories within media and entertainment: creative and business. The creative side makes the content, employing the efforts of producers, studio engineers, musicians, cinematographers, directors, Foley (sound) artists, animators, on-camera talent, on-air personalities, cue-card holders, costume designers, makeup artists, and on and on. The business side sells the content through marketing reps, promoters and salespeople, while talent agents funnel opportunities to their clients. Legal- and business-minded worker bees also take on the tangled mess of copyrights and royalties while managing the growth of a media company. This also includes the corporate high-level strategy groups, the divisions (a/k/a business units) that work in the trenches of a specific operation and the standard overarching business functions evident in every company (like accounting, legal, human resources and IT departments).

Many positions in the entertainment ranks don't require a college degree per se, but it doesn't hurt to have a theatrical or communications educational background, and to keep creative skills honed through workshops and classes. Technical degrees can help job seekers land positions in film crews and at TV and radio stations. Much of the work in the industry is project-based, meaning that creative workers live a freelancer's lifestyle, with down periods that can take a toll on savings accounts and peace of mind. While radio and television operate through affiliates scattered all over the country, much of the music and film industries are centered in the twin hubs of New York City and Los Angeles. These are the go-to places to find the most opportunities in entertainment.

The perks are undeniable: access to the latest and greatest in pop culture, including occasional face time with America's vaunted celebrity elite. Also, there's the thrill that comes from contributing to high-profile projects. But one source warns that the glitter can wear off, revealing an industry that is essentially "materialistic and shallow." Also, because pretty much everybody dreams, at some point, of a glamorous job in the entertainment industry, those going for the gold in this field can expect serious competition. The Bureau of Labor Statistics reports that the competition is tightest, not surprisingly, for positions offering a stab at celebrity status—writers, actors, directors and producers—while behind-the-scenes positions like editors and engineers offer better prospects.

The role of education

The role of education in the success of Hollywood players remains an enigma. Insiders often say that their degree was worthless in landing their job. Many positions in the entertainment ranks don't require a college degree per se, but it doesn't hurt to have a theatrical or communications educational background, and to keep creative skills honed through workshops and classes. Technical degrees can help job seekers land positions in film crews and at TV and radio stations. In general, the creative side does not reward MBAs. On the business side, however, a graduate degree is often a critical success factor. Furthermore, entry into the business side of entertainment comes to many only because of an MBA—there are executive training programs at many top media companies (e.g. Bertelsmann, Sony, Disney, Random House) that recruit at many leading business schools. While these are competitive and coveted positions, there is enough to go around for the truly committed. One recent MBA graduate from a top program said, "I just moved to Los Angeles without a job and had interviews with everyone I knew for a month straight—informationals, job interviews, anyone who would talk to me." She eventually landed a promising manager-level position in television distribution.

On the creative side, there is a slew of hot directors and other moviemakers who hail from the ranks of the film school elite— New York University, the American Film Institute, UCLA, USC and others. While these schools offer strong alumni networks and thorough training, they are costly investments. In addition to the annual tuition of the program, there is the additional expense of creating one's final project—a film that will likely cost at least $20,000. There are many success stories of talented people who saved money by taking classes at local community colleges, rented cheap equipment and made their way to festivals like Sundance.

Choosing an industry

The decision on what industry to pursue depends on one's interests and passions. The industries are all similar—personalities drive the business, egos are enormous, attitudes are bad and expectations are high. There are important differences, however. Film and TV generally allow more transition between the two (writers, actors, directors, even producers switch between the two media), but for the most part, it is much harder to transition out of music or publishing.

Survival Skills for Creative Assistants

While widely regarded as the bottom, the legendary dregs of the pool, the creative assistant (CA) position is the starting point for any career launch into the creative side of the industry. Cynics say assistants are there to feed the egos of self-important creative executives, but others assert that it is a rite of passage to the brotherhood (and sisterhood) of entertainment, not to mention a good training ground for the next generation of creative executives.

The typical job of a creative assistant is to do everything from fetching coffee to kids from one's boss' day care, answering hundreds of calls on a daily basis and making dinner reservations for one's manager, to occasionally, if there is time, reading scripts and writing coverage.

Being an assistant is the first rung up the entertainment ladder. Here are some tips for getting and keeping these jobs—and setting yourself up to move up beyond the assistant level.

Getting in

While assistants are the proverbial low men on the creative totem pole, they are nonetheless difficult positions to land because there is a fixed number of spots and openings are rare. A position becomes available only when people are promoted, fired or quit. Furthermore, it is the starting place for everyone, so the competition is quite tough. Even experienced business executives with MBAs who want to transition to the creative side are unable to avoid becoming a CA. Throughout the media and entertainment world are countless former attorneys, accountants and other aspiring professionals.

The most popular way of breaking into an assistant position is through referrals. Others break in through cold calls. Still others penetrate the ranks by making friends with other assistants and then patiently trolling for the next job opening. Some CAs migrate from a low-status boss to a higher-status boss, remaining in the assistant ranks for many years.

Managing your boss

The position of assistant encompasses such duties as secretary, butler, chauffer, mother and confidante. For all the books ever written on management skills, they are all but irrelevant in the entertainment industry. Rarely will you aggregate a larger group of individuals who care less about developing others. One executive described the junior ranks as "suckling on the teats of wolves."

The most important traits of successful assistants are:

- **Flexibility.** Many assistants are required to juggle and reprioritize their own lives in order to accommodate their managers. One assistant tells of missing a flight for a vacation because the manager called inquiring about some small bit of information that the assistant was supposed to have had.

- **Patience**. Many assistants report countless evenings of waiting around in the office long after the boss had left to a leisure dinner with "business partners." Many managers often tell their underlings to wait until they they are told to go home. Usually the request is legitimized by the (flimsy) guise of receiving a phone call that must be immediately patched through.

Visit Vault at www.vault.com for insider company profiles, expert advice, career message boards, expert resume reviews, the Vault Job Board and more.

VAULT CAREER LIBRARY

399

- **Resourcefulness**. Often, it is the assistant's responsibility to unearth obscure tidbits of information or to seek out some difficult-to-find object. Whether it reservations at 8 p.m. on a Friday night for the most popular restaurant in town or a rare edition of an out-of-print book, assistants are often expected to find ways to make difficult things happen.

- **Indulgence**. The assistant is also expected to be kind and proactive—remembering birthdays and special occasions, congratulating successes and commiserating failures. The best assistants are known for anticipating special requests, accommodating the quirks of their managers, before the manager asks. "I'll try to get my boss his favorite latte every morning if he's unable to pick one up for himself," says one assistant at a prominent Hollywood talent agency.

- **Eagerness**. Cheerfulness and a positive attitude, even in the face of adversity, is vital in the profession. The grumpy are quickly replaced with those more eager and willing.

Making the most of low wages

Assistants make anywhere from $20,000 per year to above $45,000. Usually, the higher paid assistants are in the coveted positions of working at a studio in a unionized position. The majority of assistants earn a salary near the lower end of the spectrum. In order to sustain a viable lifestyle, most assistants resort to the usual manners of making ends meet—sharing living expenses with roommates in modest neighborhoods, limiting indulgences on food (ordering in on the company's dime whenever possible), cutting back expenses on clothing and entertainment, investing in cheap transport, borrowing funds from parents. Despite the low salaries, there are often perks to the profession that should not be overlooked. Some engage in supplementary income sources, such as teaching on weekends, in order to increase their cash flow.

Getting promoted

If you stick it out long enough in a CA job, you'll probably move up. The hard part is waiting it out, often over the course of several years, sacrificing late nights, while making the right connections and waiting for a lucky break. While there are things that can be done—meeting lots of people, keeping your ears and eyes open to opportunities, jumping to a lesser-known company in order to make a transition out of the assistant ranks—promotion ultimately boils down to timing, persistence and good fortune. Good assistants quickly learn to build networks with other assistants, to share information on what's hot in order to give their bosses the extra edge, to religiously listen in on phone calls and to constantly look out for their own best interests.

Employer Directory

ABC, Inc.
77 West 66th Street
New York, NY 10023-6298
Phone: (212) 456-7777
Fax: (212) 456-1424
www.abc.com

Activision
3100 Ocean Park Boulevard
Santa Monica, CA 90405
Phone: (310) 255-2000
Fax: (310) 255-2100
www.activision.com

AMC Entertainment Holdings, Inc.
920 Main Street
Kansas City, MO 64105
Phone: (816) 221-4000
Fax: (816) 480-4617
www.amctheatres.com

Bad Boy Entertainment
1710 Broadway
New York, NY 10019
Phone: (212) 381-1540
Fax: (212) 381-1599
www.badboyonline.com

Bertelsmann AG
Carl-Bertelsmann-Strasse 270
33311 Gütersloh
Germany
Phone: +49-52-41-80-0
Fax: +49-52-41-80-96-62
www.bertelsmann.com

Black Entertainment Television
One BET Plaza
1235 West Street NE
Washington, DC 20018
Phone: (202) 608-2000
Fax: (202) 608-2589
www.bet.com

Bloomberg L.P.
731 Lexington Avenue
New York, NY 10022
Phone: (212) 318-2000
Fax: (917) 369-5000
www.bloomberg.com

British Broadcasting Corporation
Broadcasting House
Portland Place
London, W1A 1AA
United Kingdom
Phone: +44-20-75-80-44-68
Fax: +44-20-76-37-16-30
www.bbc.co.uk

Cable Satellite Public Affairs Network
400 North Capitol Street NW
Suite 650
Washington, DC 20001
Phone: (202) 737-3220
Fax: (202) 737-6226
www.c-span.org

CBS, Inc.
51 West 52nd Street
New York, NY 10019
Phone: (212) 975-4321
Fax: (212) 975-4516
www.cbs.com

Clear Channel Communications
200 East Basse Road
San Antonio, TX 78209
Phone: (210) 822-2828
Fax: (210) 822-2299
www.clearchannel.com

Comcast Corporation
1500 Market Street
Philadelphia, PA 19102-2148
Phone: (215) 665-1700
Fax: (215) 981-7790
www.comcast.com

Cox Communications, Inc.
1400 Lake Hearn Drive
Atlanta, GA 30319
Phone: (404) 843-5000
www.cox.com

Creative Artists Agency
2000 Avenue of the Stars
Los Angeles, CA 90067
Phone: (424) 288-2000
Fax: (424) 288-2900
www.caa.com

The DIRECTV Group, Inc.
2230 East Imperial Highway
El Segundo, CA 90245
Phone: (310) 964-5000
Fax: (310) 535-5225
www.directv.com

Discovery Communications, Inc.
1 Discovery Place
Silver Spring, MD 20910
Phone: (240) 662-2000
Fax: (240) 662-1868
www.discovery.com

DreamWorks Animation SKG Inc.
1000 Flower Street
Glendale, CA 91201
Phone: (818) 695-5000
Fax: (818) 695-9944
www.dreamworksanimation.com

Electronic Arts
209 Redwood Shores Parkway
Redwood City, CA 94065
Phone: (650) 628-1500
Fax: (650) 628-1422
www.ea.com

EMI Group plc
27 Wrights Lane
London, W8 5SW
United Kingdom
Phone: +44-20-77-95-70-00
Fax: +44-20-77-95-72-96
www.emigroup.com

Visit Vault at **www.vault.com** for insider company profiles, expert advice, career message boards, expert resume reviews, the Vault Job Board and more.

VAULT CAREER LIBRARY

401

Employer Directory, cont.

Fox Entertainment Group
10201 West Pico Boulevard
Building 100, Suite 3220
Los Angeles, CA 90035
Phone: (310) 369-1000
Fax: (310) 969-3300
www.fox.com

Gannett Company, Inc.
7950 Jones Branch Drive
McLean, VA 22107-0910
Phone: (703) 854-6000
Fax: (703) 854-2046
www.gannett.com

Group Televisa SA
Avenida Vasco de Quiroga, No. 2000
Colonia Santa Fe
Delegación Álvaro Obregón
01210 México, D.F.
Mexico
Phone: +52-55-5261-2445
Fax: +52-55-5261-2494
www.televisa.com

Home Box Office (HBO)
1100 Avenue of the Americas
New York, NY 10036
Phone: (212) 512-1000
Fax: (212) 512-1182
www.hbo.com

International Data Group, Inc.
1 Exeter Plaza, 15th Floor
Boston, MA 02116-2851
Phone: (617) 534-1200
Fax: (617) 423-0240
www.idg.com

Liberty Media
12300 Liberty Boulevard
Englewood, CO 80112
Phone: (720) 875-5400
Fax: (720) 875-5401
www.libertymedia.com

Live Nation, Ltd
9348 Civic Center Drive
Beverly Hills, CA 90210
Phone: (310) 867-7000
Fax: (310) 867-7001
www.livenation.com

Lucasfilm Limited
1110 Gorgas Avenue
San Francisco, CA 94129
Phone: (415) 662-1800
Fax: (415) 448-2495
www.lucasfilm.com

Martha Stewart Living Omnimedia, Inc.
11 West 42nd Street
New York, NY 10036
Phone: (212) 827-8000
Fax: (212) 827-8204
www.marthastewart.com

Metro-Goldwyn-Mayer Inc.
10250 Constellation Boulevard
Los Angeles, CA 90067
Phone: (310) 449-3000
Fax: (310) 449-8857
www.mgm.com

MTV Networks Company
1515 Broadway
New York, NY 10036
Phone: (212) 258-8000
Fax: (212) 258-6175
www.mtv.com

NBC Universal
30 Rockefeller Plaza
New York, NY 10112
Phone: (212) 664-4444
Fax: (212) 664-4085
www.nbcuni.com

News Corp.
1211 Avenue of the Americas
8th Floor
New York, NY 10036
Phone: (212) 852-7000
Fax: (212) 852-7147
www.newscorp.com

Nintendo of America, Inc.
4820 150th Avenue NE
Redmond, WA 98052
Phone: (425) 882-2040
Fax: (425) 882-3585
www.nintendo.com

Paramount Pictures Corporation
5555 Melrose Avenue, Suite 121
Hollywood, CA 90038
Phone: (323) 956-5000
www.paramount.com

Pixar Animation Studios
1200 Park Avenue
Emeryville, CA 94608
Phone: (510) 922-3000
Fax: (510) 922-3151
www.pixar.com

Public Broadcasting Service
2100 Crystal Drive
Arlington, VA 22202-3785
Phone: (703) 739-5000
Fax: (703) 739-8495
www.pbs.org

Reed Elsevier Group PLC
1-3 Strand
London, WC2N 5JR
United Kingdom
Phone: +44-20-79-30-70-77
Fax: +44-20-71-66-57-99
www.reedelsevier.com

Reed Elsevier NV
Raderweg 29
1043 NX Amsterdam
The Netherlands
Phone: +31-20-485-2222
Fax: +31-20-618-0325
www.reedelsevier.com

Employer Directory, cont.

Reuters Group Limited
The Reuters Building
Canary Wharf
London, E14 5EP
United Kingdom
Phone: +44-20-72-50-11-22
Fax: +44-20-75-42-40-64
www.reuters.com

Regal Entertainment Group
7132 Regal Lane
Knoxville, TN 37918
Phone: (865) 922-1123
Fax: (865) 922-3188
www.regalcinemas.com

Sirius Satellite Radio Inc.
1221 Avenue of the Americas
36th Floor
New York, NY 10020
Phone: (212) 584-5100
Fax: (212) 584-5200
www.sirius.com

Sony BMG Music Entertainment
550 Madison Avenue
New York, NY 10022-3211
Phone: (212) 833-7100
Fax: (212) 833-7416
www.sonybmg.com

Sony Corporation of America
550 Madison Avenue
New York, NY 10022
Phone: (212) 833-6800
Fax: (212) 833-6938
Toll free: (800) 556-3411
www.sony.com

SourceMedia
One State Street
27th Floor
New York, NY 10004
Phone: (212) 8030-8200
www.sourcemedia.com

Take-Two Interactive Software, Inc.
622 Broadway
New York, NY 10012
Phone: (646) 536-2842
Fax: (646) 536-2926
www.take2games.com

Time Warner
1 Time Warner Center
New York, NY 10019
Phone: (212) 484-8000
www.timewarner.com

Universal Music Group
1755 Broadway
New York, NY 10019
Phone: (212) 841-8000
Fax: (212) 331-2580
www.umusic.com

Univision Communications Inc.
1999 Avenue of the Stars, Suite 3050
Los Angeles, CA 90067
Phone: (310) 556-7665
Fax: (310) 556-7615
www.univision.com

USA Network, Inc.
30 Rockefeller Plaza
New York, NY 10112
Phone: (212) 664-4444
Fax: (212) 664-6365
www.usanetwork.com

Viacom Inc.
1515 Broadway
New York, NY 10036
Phone: (212) 258-6000
Fax: (212) 258-6464
www.viacom.com

Virgin Group, Ltd.
120 Campden Hill Road
London W8 7AR
United Kingdom
Phone: +44-20-72-29-12-82
Fax: +44-20-77-27-82-00
www.virgin.com

Vivendi SA
42 avenue de Friedland
75380 Paris Cedex 08
France
Phone: +33-1-71-71-10-00
Fax: +33-1-71-71-10-01
www.vivendiuniversal.com

The Walt Disney Company
500 South Buena Vista Street
Burbank, CA 91521-9722
Phone: (818) 560-1000
Fax: (818) 560-1930
disney.go.com

Warner Music Group Corp
75 Rockefeller Plaza
New York, NY 10019
Phone: (212) 275-2000
Fax: (212) 757-3985
www.wmg.com

William Morris Agency
1 William Morris Place
Beverly Hills, CA 90212
Phone: (310) 859-4000
Fax: (310) 859-4462
www.wma.com

Visit Vault at **www.vault.com** for insider company profiles, expert advice, career message boards, expert resume reviews, the Vault Job Board and more.

VAULT CAREER LIBRARY 403

Nonprofit

Imagine what it might be like to say:

"Today at work I helped to provide a safe place for 100 teens in my community to go after school to receive tutoring and homework assistance."

"This year at work I raised a million and a half dollars to fund a program that promotes better early education for young children."

"Throughout the course of my career I helped to clean up my city's most depressed neighborhoods and developed hundreds of new affordable homes for disadvantaged families."

If being able to do this type of work in the course of your career appeals to you, you may want to consider a career in the nonprofit/philanthropy world. It won't be easygoing, though. In recent years, and especially since the September 11 terrorist attacks, the U.S. has seen a jump in its number of registered charitable organizations. All of these organizations are in need of strong leaders as many in the sector are concerned that our country is not prepared to financially support this recent influx of newly registered charities. It is clear that only the strongest and savviest organizations are certain to survive.

This need for more and better trained nonprofit administrators is fueling the development of many well-respected degree programs at universities and colleges nationwide. At the same time, more people, particularly college age and recent graduates, are showing an interest in pursuing a career in nonprofit administration.

The rewards can be quite satisfying for professionals who succeed. Such positions come with, at times, a tremendous amount of prestige and respect, interactions with a broad array of people from all class levels and at executive levels, a satisfying salary. Many organizations represent the lifeblood of their communities and are in the daily eye of the local, and sometimes national, public and media.

Many Choices

While work in the nonprofit world can be characterized in certain general ways, such as the ones above, the sector is hugely diverse, both in terms of types of organizations and types of positions available. Nonprofits can be huge organizations, employing thousands of paid workers coordinated through a well-defined organizational structure (for example, regional chapters). They can just as easily be tiny—many nonprofits are comprised of only a paid executive director and volunteers.

Moreover, the missions of nonprofits vary widely. The type of organization most commonly associated with the term "nonprofit" is the community-based organization, frequently referred to as a CBO. CBOs represent a tremendously important group of service providers, implementing their programs on the "front lines" of direct service. These organizations are seen as diligent, tireless workers, often responding to very basic, unmet needs that exist within a community. Typical examples of CBOs would be homeless shelters, "meals-on-wheels" programs and job placement nonprofits.

CBOs aren't the only type of nonprofit, of course. On a larger scale, the IRS, U.S. Bureau of Labor Statistics and numerous universities and think tanks that study the sector do lump nonprofit organizations into several different categories largely based on approach and purpose. The most common categories used are health, education, social and human services, religious, civic and advocacy, international relief and development, arts and culture and funders. It's a crude kind of taxonomy and definitely not infallible, since many nonprofits fall into more than one category. (The IRS and Bureau of Labor Statistics use a more complicated classification system to capture specific information about the number and kinds of nonprofits; for instance, they try to determine how many community hospitals there are or how many nonprofit theater groups.) But organizations that exemplify one category or another do share with one another characteristics in size, infrastructure and, to some extent, the kinds of people who work there.

Visit Vault at **www.vault.com** for insider company profiles, expert advice, career message boards, expert resume reviews, the Vault Job Board and more.

VAULT CAREER LIBRARY   405

Here's a bit more information about the kinds of groups in each category that might help you make some decisions about where you would like to work. Again, the descriptions here are very general and cannot be applied to every organization in any particular category. Moreover, no one kind of nonprofit has cornered the market on efficiency and dynamic leadership, nor mismanagement and dysfunction.

Health organizations

Health organizations—such as hospitals, clinics, nursing homes, hospice facilities and drug rehabilitation centers—take up the largest piece of the nonprofit pie, in terms of revenue, expenses and the number of people they employ. According to the latest version of the Nonprofit Almanac published by the Urban Institute, more than half the revenue earned by or contributed to the entire nonprofit sector goes to organizations providing health services. Perhaps because of their relative wealth, or the demands of physicians, salaries at health organizations (especially hospitals) tend to be among the highest in the nonprofit world. Along with healing the sick, health organizations nurture extensive bureaucracies to deal with stringent state and federal regulations, concerns about patient privacy and the need to navigate complicated health insurance programs—including Medicare and Medicaid—which provide the lion's share of revenue. So as a fundraiser, you are just as likely to work with a hospital administrator of some sort as you are a doctor or nurse. In some health organizations, politics may go hand in hand with treatment of the sick; hospital associated with universities will have interns, residents and researchers vying for the best residencies, teaching and administrative positions. You may also see different departments at a hospital competing with one another for funding, especially for clinical research. Facilities focused on community health (including hospice care and community hospitals) are known to have warmer, friendlier environments. It's important to remember that even if you are squirreled away in the administrative offices as a fundraiser, sickness and death will be a part of your everyday existence. Some find that fulfilling; others find it depressing.

Educational institutions

Primarily universities, colleges, and private, independent schools (meaning those that are not part of the system of public schools), educational institutions are the second-largest category based on revenue and employment. For the most part, universities and schools rely heavily on tuitions, as well as funding from individuals, foundations, and state and federal agencies. Schools are also among the oldest American nonprofit institutions; indeed Harvard University, which was founded in 1638, is considered to be the first nonprofit in the U.S. Thus many schools have a strong sense of history which staff and alumni are rather proud of. There is, however, a big difference in the size, infrastructure and organizational culture between a university and an independent school. Universities are large (employing hundreds of people), hierarchical and extremely political places, exacerbated by the fact that professor/scholars tend to have strong personalities. Associate professors jockey for tenure, tenured professors squabble among themselves about their scholarly pursuits and publishing opportunities and different departments fiercely compete for dollars. Given their size and the myriad demands for resources, universities maintain large fundraising programs with well-paid staff. Independent schools—ranging from Montessori to Catholic to boarding—are considerably smaller. Some mimic universities in style and structure, but most are far less formal. Fundraising teams are also small with as little as two staff. Salaries are also considerable smaller than at universities. Many independent schools have religious affiliations, which as an employee you may be expected to uphold. Both universities and independent schools focus most fundraising activities on alumni, and there may be opportunities to meet distinguished former students who have gone on to Hollywood or politics. Most fundraisers for schools and universities find interactions with students, parents and alumni to be the best part of their jobs.

The social or human service category

This category encompasses a broad array of groups that provide resources and services for the disabled and disenfranchised, including legal aid societies, housing assistance programs and homeless shelters, soup kitchens, job training centers, child welfare groups, day care operations, immigrant assistance organizations, rape crisis centers, and mental health counseling facilities, among many, many others. While this class of nonprofits places third in terms of total revenue for the sector, the sheer number of such groups far exceeds any other category. As a result, many scholars in the nonprofit field describe social service agencies as the face of the nonprofit world, the kind of group that most people think of when they hear the word "nonprofit." The size and scope of work for these organizations is extraordinarily diverse, ranging from The Salvation Army's multi-faceted programs for the poor to a soup kitchen. Most social service operations heavily rely on state and federal funding, either through grants or contracts and are therefore subject to myriad regulations from those for food preparation to client privacy. Social service agencies must also wrestle with establishing rigorous and somewhat cumbersome self-evaluation processes, since many government agencies and private foundations award contracts and grants based on performance. This is an issue that the entire nonprofit sector contends with, but it's a particular challenge for social service groups because of their heavy reliance on public funding. Moreover, the United Way (a major funder for social services groups) also requires that its beneficiaries establish benchmarks and performance outcomes. Aside from organizations like the Salvation Army, Catholic Charities or the YMCA, most social services groups are small and lean without much of infrastructure beyond what is required of them by state agencies and the federal government. As a result, fundraising teams are often small and are not paid top dollar. As a fundraiser, you are most likely to work with social workers and clinicians, who are generally a compassionate and caring bunch. However, they are not necessarily very educated about or interested in fundraising.

The category of religious organizations

Congregations of various religious sects (Christian, Muslim, Jewish, Buddhist, etc.) and any denominations or associations under which congregations may organize constitute the category of religious organizations. There are many hospitals, schools, social services agencies and advocacy groups with religious affiliations (such as the Salvation Army or Catholics for Free Choice), but these organizations fall under the category of the cause that they serve or the assistance they provide. The primary purpose of a congregation is to offer religious guidance and education to the individuals that belong to it, while denominations are regional or national associations that provide additional leadership and support services to individual congregations. It is important to note that a congregation in any given community may be completely independent from a particular denomination. While there are a few large congregations with several paid staff (including fundraisers), most are very small and run entirely by volunteers, aside from the priest, pastors, ministers, rabbis, etc. providing religious instruction. Likewise, any social services that a congregation provides (such as clothes or housing to the needy) are almost entirely volunteer operations. And as you would expect, congregations are almost entirely reliant on donations from its members. There are therefore few opportunities to work for a congregation or denomination as a professional fundraiser. However, there are many opportunities with other nonprofit organizations with religious ties. As you would expect, the character of congregations and denominations is determined by the structure and culture of the faith, the religious leadership and the individual members.

Civic and advocacy organizations

These organizations comprise a relatively small (in terms of revenue and number of people they employ) category of nonprofits focused on changing policies around a particular issue or problem. Such prominent groups as the Sierra Club, National Organization for Women, American Civil Liberties Union, National Association for the Advancement of Colored People, American Association of Retired People and the Christian Coalition fall into this category, as well as a range of smaller groups focused on specific issues in their communities. Generally these groups engage in four basic activities: (1) educating and organizing people to engage their local policy-makers (county commissioners, state agencies, Members of Congress, etc.); (2) generating interest in an issue with the media; (3) analyzing changes in policy and educating the general public on their impact; and (4) directly advocating for policy changes with local, state and federal officials. Many of these groups are centered in major metropolitan areas near seats of government. As you would expect, the largest groups have

Visit Vault at www.vault.com for insider company profiles, expert advice, career message boards, expert resume reviews, the Vault Job Board and more.

VAULT CAREER LIBRARY   407

headquarters in Washington, D.C. Advocacy organizations are not political action committees or private lobbying firms, and as public institutions are subject to strict regulations regarding direct lobbying of policy-makers. Most receive very little support from government agencies. Rather the major sources of funding are individuals, corporations and foundations (although foundations have requirements on what kind of advocacy activities they can support). The largest advocacy groups will pay top-dollar for experienced fundraisers; smaller groups in communities often employ one fundraiser who relies heavily on program staff for assistance, especially in foundation relations, proposal development and report writing. Core staff at advocacy groups is usually comprised of some combination of lawyers, public relations and communications specialists, and organizers who tend to be passionate, driven and somewhat aggressive. The pace at advocacy groups can be more intense, especially when Congress and state legislatures are in session. Some find it energizing, while others quickly burn out.

International relief and development groups

Known abroad as non-governmental organizations (NGOs), international relief and development groups focus on activities to improve the quality of life for communities outside of the United States, primarily in developing countries. Groups like the American Red Cross and Oxfam provide immediate, direct relief in the wake of war and natural disasters, while other groups devote time and energy to education and building local economics. This category of nonprofits also includes organizations who do not provide direct assistance to communities but peripherally impact quality of life—environmental organizations like the Ocean Conservancy and Conservation International are examples. Most groups also have a dual focus on direct relief activities and advocacy. According to the Nonprofit Almanac, more than 5,000 such groups are incorporated in the United States. The majority of the United Nation's and U.S. government's humanitarian relief funds are funneled through these international groups, which usually have headquarters in Washington, D.C. or New York (to connect more directly to the United Nations), as well as field offices in the countries where they work. Fundraising teams usually work from headquarters with opportunities to travel abroad. Like advocacy groups, the largest of the international relief agencies will pay their fundraising staff well. Since there's a heavy reliance on government funding, there's also a heavy focus on proposal and report writing, so fundraisers are usually strong writers. The rest of the staff is usually comprised of policy experts from the U.S. and abroad with field staff who are largely from the country in which they are working. The work is rewarding, exciting, dangerous and stressful. In some countries, field staff are at considerable risk from terrorism and civil strife, and most are used to living without much luxury. With a truly global workforce, cultural difference is a challenge, especially in navigating different communication styles.

The category of "arts and culture" organizations

These organizations include community and professional theaters, dance companies, nonprofit art galleries and museums, orchestras and symphonies, literary and cultural magazines, as well as a range of arts appreciation groups. While there are almost as many arts groups in the country as there are in health care, the arts community is far less wealthy. Revenue to health care groups is in fact 25 times greater than what goes to the arts. Salaries are therefore considerably smaller at arts organizations, although there are many cases where a development director is paid more than the artistic director. Most revenue comes from ticket sales, so marketing and audience development is an important concern and a constant challenge. Arts groups in fact are always looking for ways to engage new constituents, especially the Generation Xers who have accumulated some wealth by now (largely through the dot-com boom). Art organizations also tend to work in close partnership with schools to support arts education programs. They also try to foster relationships with corporate interests that see a variety of opportunities to elevate their profile through the arts. Most arts groups struggle to keep qualified and experienced administrative staff because of the lower salaries, long hours (especially when working for a performance group) and the strong temperament of artistic directors and boards. It is not at all unusual for highly public and bitter fights to break out between boards and organizational leadership over the artistic direction of an organization. That said, the passion, dedication and talent of artists involved with these organizations is intoxicating.

Grant-giving organizations

Like private foundations and federated charities, grant-giving organizations fall into the "funders" category. These groups generally do not engage in any other activity other than giving away money, although there are exceptions, such as the Pew Charitable Trusts, which provides grants and is also involved in advocacy work. While private foundations like the Ford Foundation are the most commonly known, there are in fact a variety of nonprofit organizations that function as grant givers. Federated charities are organizations that collect donations from individuals and distribute them to a chosen group of nonprofit organizations. Those charities that wish to receive funds usually go through an application process to demonstrate that they are legal and viable nonprofits. Most people are familiar with the United Way, but there are other such groups, such as Jewish federations and societies that raise funds for research and treatment of diseases—an example is the Leukemia and Lymphoma Society. Investment firms can also establish donor-advised funds that are registered as nonprofit organizations. These funds are comprised of donations from wealthy individuals and are managed by a financial advisor who may either follow the instructions of the donor on which charities to support or may make those decisions on their own. Most community foundations also create donor-advised funds to help donors in any given location be effective in their philanthropy. Like other nonprofit organizations, a board of directors (usually known as the board of trustees) oversees the general direction of grant-giving. A professional staff of financial advisors, policy experts and those with expertise in nonprofit management make day-to-day decisions about how to wisely invest the pool of funds and how to distribute grants. Like the rest of the nonprofit sector, there are far more small family foundations and donor-advised funds run by one or two staff than large, professional foundations run by many. The larger foundations and federated charities generally pay well and provide rather generous benefits. Jobs at foundations are among the most competitive in the fundraising and philanthropic giving field.

Nonprofit Uppers and Downers

Uppers

Many of the positive aspects of working in a nonprofit/philanthropy career apply to many different organizations.

- The work a nonprofit staff member goes beyond simply executing a role in the general pursuit of making someone more money, or as much money as possible. The job that a staff member does can positively impact the lives of sometimes thousands of people, or change or improve some negative aspect of our society for future generations, or create new, affordable homes for disadvantaged families, or teach a mentally disabled person a trade and help him achieve financial independence. Nothing can measure up to the feeling at the end of the day when you realize that every call you made, letter you wrote, bill you reconciled, staff meeting you sat through, paper you filed or decision you made could benefit someone who needs your organization's help.

- Nonprofits are generally more family-friendly than the corporate world. Many are more casual, offer better vacation and work hours, and have a more liberal approach to lifestyle choices. However, this is not universal—so check before making the assumption.

- Because there are never enough people to do the work, working in a nonprofit can give you the opportunity to do a variety of tasks outside of your job description.

Downers

Downers in nonprofit careers tend to depend on the organization. However, there are certain unattractive qualities that many share.

- Staff members often do the equivalent of more than one person's job for often lower salaries (overstaffed and underpaid).

Visit Vault at www.vault.com for insider company profiles, expert advice, career message boards, expert resume reviews, the Vault Job Board and more.

VAULT CAREER LIBRARY

409

- There are few, if any, company perks of the sort offered by employers in the corporate world (gym memberships, entertainment tickets, etc.). Perhaps more importantly, in recent years, standard benefit packages (health care plans and so on) have also been shrinking.

- Success is often difficult to determine. For example, say a local advocacy organization implements a community education campaign promoting parents to read more to their children. Is it possible to achieve a truly accurate determination of the campaign's success and to what degree parent behavior changed? Quite possibly, there is simply not enough funding that would be needed to design a community survey, or, at best, conduct adequate focus groups.

- Success is often tied to bringing in money/fundraising. While you may reap greater satisfaction from working at an organization whose overriding goal is not to make money, don't think that you're escaping the importance of money altogether.

- Working at certain nonprofits can mean continually seeing unhappy, indigent people—or worse. For example, employees at women's domestic abuse shelters see a steady daily stream of battered women and their children. The shelter's staff often faces depression and burnout.

- High academic standards—many nonprofits require a master's degree, and some require PhDs for senior positions. Many also require hands-on experience with target beneficiaries before being taken seriously.

Nonprofit Doesn't Mean Money Doesn't Matter

Today's nonprofit organization is a very different institution than it was only a decade ago. In a nutshell, the nonprofit corporate culture has become more professional. An increased emphasis on efficient management has enhanced the sector's approach to program implementation or problem solving through the development of better, more cost-effective strategies for providing services. Just as important, nonprofit organizations have also greatly improved their approach to cultivating and accessing stronger financial support. Many unpredictable variables impact our national economy and subsequently philanthropic donations to nonprofits. The nonprofit/philanthropy field is learning how to protect itself from financial fluctuations.

One common approach to this challenge is to diversify funding sources. An extreme example of this is a church in Jamaica, N.Y. that is running and staffing its own charter bus company, essentially running its own for-profit venture and "donating" the income to the church's operational funds. More commonly, however, nonprofits are branching out into other areas of service in hopes of attracting new donors. This is programmatically justified as a way of making a more comprehensive impact on a single area of service or issue.

Other nonprofits are developing entirely new competencies in hopes of introducing the organization to an entirely new pool of supporters. One example of this is an early education advocacy group, Child Care Action Campaign, which has served as a facilitator and communicator of research and best practices for 20 years. Recently, however, it developed and implemented an early literacy child care provider training program, sending trainers out into neighborhoods to teach providers how to encourage literacy with the young children in their care. This decision was responsible for nearly $300,000 in new support from donors who only fund "direct service" programs (nonprofits that work directly with those it seeks to serve, rather than just training workers who work with them or conducting research), essentially opening a door to a new revenue stream. In this instance, the organization jumped into community or direct service while continuing its work in advocacy and research.

Development Work and Organizations

From large development organizations and banks, such as the IMF and the World Bank, funding giant multi-decade projects, to small NGOs (nongovernmental organizations) organizing grassroots projects, to volunteer agencies providing everything from fence builders to business consultants, global development has become a huge industry.

There is a wide range of opportunities under the "development" umbrella, and just as wide of a variety of people working in this industry. Development gurus range from top-level senior executives to junior volunteers straight out of college. Opportunities run from micro-finance to building bridges, from environmental work to helping democracy take hold in remote corners of the world. Many development organizations focus on economic development and financial skills. While there are certainly still opportunities to help villagers build houses, more and more opportunities focus on small business development, nurturing local entrepreneurship and providing sustainable business skills.

Types of "development" organizations

Development is such a broad term, but the following groups of organizations are generally included under this umbrella:

- **Public multinationals:** Huge organizations like the UN, the World Bank and the ADB (Asian Development Bank)

- **Multinational NGOs:** Large non-government organizations, such as Amnesty International, CARE, Doctors without Borders and the World Wildlife Fund (WWF)

- **Smaller NGOs:** Hundreds of locally based, often grassroots organizations devoted often to one particular issue or problem, be it women's health, micro-finance or political education

- **Volunteer organizations:** Organizations that rely on volunteers, though they may pay a stipend

There are also private companies involved in development work and branches of private companies that work as a nonprofit on development-related issues. For example, many of the major consulting and tax consulting companies have arms dedicated to the issues of development, privatization and economic development. Their clients are mainly governments and the public multinationals.

Volunteering for development work

Volunteering is often the first step for many people to get involved in development work, though volunteering can be an attractive option even if you don't envision a long-term career in development. Volunteering, either on a long-term (up to two years) or short-term (a few months) basis, is a great way to experience another culture while making a difference.

There are thousands of volunteer opportunities out there, offering you the chance to get involved in whatever your particular passion or geographic preference is. The most famous organization for Americans is the Peace Corps, but there are numerous other organizations and agencies that offer opportunities for committed volunteers.

Most volunteer assignments are just that: volunteer, meaning you won't be drawing a salary. In some cases, though, you may draw a stipend. A stipend is a living allowance to cover basic necessities, so that while you might not be saving any money, you won't be out of pocket either. Some programs will cover airfare and housing. When evaluating whether or not volunteering is feasible for you, consider loan-forgiveness—many universities have loan-forgiveness programs for graduates who choose to work in the nonprofit sector.

Many volunteer opportunities require you to pay the organization for the opportunity to volunteer. Think seriously about these types of opportunities, especially for "volunteer" programs that are for teaching English. While it is great to have the support these programs offer, you could easily be paid for doing the same work.

Visit Vault at **www.vault.com** for insider company profiles, expert advice, career message boards, expert resume reviews, the Vault Job Board and more.

VAULT CAREER LIBRARY   411

A Day in the Life: Peace Corps Volunteer, Senegal

Mark is a Peace Corps Volunteer in Senegal, West Africa.

6:30 a.m. Thwunk! Thwunk! The sound has been creeping into my sleep for about an hour now, and I finally wake up and acknowledge it. Outside my hut, the women of the village have been up [forever] pounding millet.

7:15 a.m. I dress—no shower now, but one later. With no electricity or running water, a shower in the morning would be a luxury. Plus, I know I'm going to get dirty today, so what's the point?

7:45 a.m. Time for a leisurely breakfast in the family compound. We all sleep in our own huts, and meet in the middle for meals and socializing. I sit on a raised dais and drink the local coffee—bitter but good. As I drink, I think about what I have to do today: the upcoming meeting, the state of my motorcycle—do I have enough gas?

8 a.m. I wave goodbye to my host family—the men are heading out to the fields and the women are cooking or going out on water runs. I hop on my motorcycle—with 50 villages in my area of responsibility, good, reliable transport is a major concern. Luckily this little guy hasn't let me down yet.

8:30 a.m. I drive along the dusty roads and wave to the occasional villager I see. After two years here, they all know me, and I know most of them.

9:15 a.m. I arrive at my target village, dusty and hot. Even though it's still relatively early, the sun seems impossibly high in the sky, like it's been every day. Senegal is one of the hottest places on earth. Sometimes, I feel like I spend every day just sweating.

9:30 a.m. The women of the village are slowly gathering in one of the central compounds around me. Today is our fifth meeting, and we're actually going to get started on the project we've been talking about for two months now: planting a fruit orchard. The women will use the fruit to supplement their family's diets, or to sell for some surplus cash at the market.

10 a.m. All the women have finally arrived. Time is a different concept here: having everyone together an hour after the meeting was scheduled is actually great. Heck, I was even 10 minutes late! I explain what we're going to be doing today, and then we all head down to the field that's designated to be the orchard.

10:45 a.m. We're hard at work in the future orchard, carefully preparing the fruit seedlings in little bags of soil and lining them up in the ground. As we work, the women chatter and tease me. They all want to know when I'm going to bring my girlfriend to live in the compound. The fact that I don't have a girlfriend doesn't seem to stop them! They also ask about my family, and tell me about theirs.

12 p.m. A good morning's work, and time to get out of the sun. I have lunch at one of the compounds and share news with the men of my host family. Then a short nap, a quick play with some of the smaller kids, and then it's time to be off. I'll be back next month when the seedlings start to sprout.

1:30 p.m. I head towards the nearest town, realizing I've actually got a free afternoon. This is a rarity—with the number of villages I'm responsible for, I usually have two or even three meetings in a given day. This is good—I've got some shopping to do, not to mention getting some more gas for the motorcycle ...

2:30 p.m. Fuda is the central town around here, a hub for all the villages in the area. I wander through the market, picking out some vegetables for my family. They don't receive a stipend for hosting me, so I try to help out in other ways. Buying some vegetables to add to the family's cooking budget and (I've got to admit—bring some changes in my diet!) is a good way to help out.

3:30 p.m. Potatoes, tomatoes, onions, a couple of delicious looking oranges, gas for my motorcycle and a new shirt for myself. All in order. I've still got time and some energy, so I stop by a local bar. I hope to see one or both of the other Peace Corps volunteers that serve in the area, but I'm out of luck.

4 p.m. I down a local beer—like the coffee, it's bitter but good! I chat with the owners of the bar and a couple of men who have sought refuge on the cool patio. They all know me by now, and after studying the local language fairly intensively during my first year I'm now comfortable enough to talk about anything.

4:30 p.m. No more beer, I have a long drive ahead of me back to my village. I leave a note for the other PCs, telling them I'll be back on Saturday, and telling them to look for me. Then it's back on the motorcycle and the dusty roads.

6 p.m. My favorite time of the day. The work is over, I've had my shower, and the heat is slipping away as the sun starts to set. All around the village people are drifting between compounds, talking and catching up on the news of the day. We have plenty of visitors over at our house. I relax on our dais in the middle of the compound, trying to forget about the busy day I have ahead of me tomorrow. It'll take care of itself.

8 p.m. Supper is prepared by my eight-year-old "niece," who is just learning to cook. Tonight it's chicken and a rice mixture that we eat with our hands. The sun is setting now, and after eating we lie back on the dais, staring up at the sky. We talk about astronomy and the stars, then listen to the BBC on the radio for a while. After, we discuss international politics and the state of the world. The villagers are very interested in the world outside, and since I've come to live here I've become much more aware of world events, too. Funny to think that in a tiny village on the edge of Africa the people are more informed than in some of the biggest cities back home.

10 p.m. My host dad wakes me gently. I've drifted off to sleep outside on the dais, and now it's time to go to my hut and my real bed.

Grant Writers

According to the perception perpetuated by the often money-strapped nonprofit community, the grant writer is the one person who can keep the organization afloat, or at least allow staff to embark on that next exciting project. However far from the truth this may be—and in fact it is, since foundation grants account for only 12 percent of all charitable giving in the United States—the myth persists each time a sizable grant is awarded to an organization.

True-life, fairy-tale stories about life-saving (or organization-saving) grants abound. Richard Linklater received a $2,300 grant from a Texas-based nonprofit supporting independent film to complete *Slackers*, the film that established his career. On the other end of the scale, Conservation International—one of the largest conservation organizations in the world—received a $261 million grant from the Betty and Gordon Moore Foundation for a range of special projects to protect biological diversity worldwide; this is the largest grant ever awarded to an environmental group. Such stories of a single grant that makes a dream project possible only lend power to a certain mythology around grant fundraising.

So who gives out these grants? For the most part, the primary focus of institutional fundraising is foundations, which are in fact another kind of legally recognized nonprofit organization established for the purpose of distributing funds to worthy causes. Like other nonprofits, foundations will have a governing board, usually known as the board of trustees, and an executive director or president, all of whom are usually involved in making decision about who to fund.

So what do grant writers do every day? Whether they work as in-house grant writers or freelancers, grant writers aren't just writers, they're also correspondents, researchers, financial managers and active participants in the program side of nonprofits.

And when they finally sit down to write the grant proposal, they bring everything together to make sure it best represents the nonprofit program.

Visit Vault at **www.vault.com** for insider company profiles, expert advice, career message boards, expert resume reviews, the Vault Job Board and more.

VAULT CAREER LIBRARY

413

There is much more to the grant-writing profession than cranking out well-written grant proposals. There are four fundamental ongoing responsibilities of a grant writer:

- Writing or managing the process of writing grant proposals and reports on current grants
- Identifying prospective foundation, corporate and government grant makers and devising strategies for initiating or strengthening relationships with these funders
- Maintaining regular correspondence and contact with current and prospective funders
- Maintaining a calendar of proposal submission and reporting deadlines and coordinating staff involvement in meeting those deadlines

These activities fall under the rubric of institutional fund raising, referring to the range of institutions that give grants—foundations, corporations and government agencies.

Asker of the hard questions

The grant writer is often the first person to document all aspects of a program or project and therefore plays an important role in helping flesh out that program. It is often the grant writer who asks the most difficult questions about the program, knowing that the grant maker will ask the same tough questions. The grant writer is therefore a crucial player in program planning for the organization, and can often lead this process.

Unlike other fund-raisers (particularly major gift and planned giving officers), grant writers are less likely to work directly with funders, although there are opportunities to interact with staff at foundations, government agencies and corporations with grant-making programs. Most of the time, grant writers collaborate closely with a nonprofit's leadership—primarily the executive director, but also with other managers—and with program staff on building relationships with foundations and corporations.

Most foundation officers want to hear the inside scoop on any issue from those on the front lines, or they want the executive director to show up for a meeting to demonstrate how important the foundation is to the grant-seeking organization. The grant writer is therefore scheduling meetings with foundations (depending on the size of the nonprofit, this administrative task may be delegated to the executive director's assistant or to a development coordinator) and helps staff prepare for these meetings, rather than attending them.

The grant writer also drafts most correspondence to grant makers, from thank you notes to informal updates on program activities. A good grant writer is also reminding program staff to regularly send information on to funders, from news articles in which the nonprofit is cited, to legislation that a program person helped draft.

Researcher

Research is another key activity. In addition to interviewing program staff, grant writers are on the Internet, reviewing news articles on the issues on which the nonprofit focuses and on grant makers' activities. Grant writers are often asked to provide detailed briefings to the executive director on potential funders, including information on current assets, stock prices of corporations with foundations, latest grants awarded, staff changes at the foundation, and any intelligence on grant makers' program planning processes.

A good grant writer will also work with the executive director on any pitch for a new project, whether on paper or for a meeting with a foundation officer. In this capacity, the grant writer coaches the executive director or program staff on buzz words or jargon that will strike a chord with a particular foundation's staff (capacity building, leveraging funds and partnerships are popular terms among foundations, for example), and on how to position a project as strongly matching the foundation's interests.

Financial manager

A grant writer is also a financial manager of sorts, working closely with a nonprofit's accountant or director of administration to develop budgets for projects and programs, and also with program staff on how they spend grants. At larger nonprofits, a finance department may produce financial documents for grant makers and employ a grants manager to oversee expenditures to grants; but more often than not, the grants writer is as knowledgeable as the organization's leadership and financial officers about program expenses and how a particular grant ought to be spent. So number crunching is a part of the job, as are Excel spreadsheets. However, budgets and financial reports can be a welcome distraction from writing.

A Day in the Life: In-house Grant Writer

This is the day in the life of a fictional grant writer who works for a $5 million regional nonprofit organization with a mission to expand respite care services for families with mentally ill children.

9 a.m. Come into the office, turn on the computer in your cubicle and scan your e-mail. The executive director has sent a message asking for the latest stock report for a well-known retail company. He is meeting tomorrow with the company's owner, who has an autistic child and who recently established a small family foundation with a focus on improving services for the mentally ill.

9:15 a.m. Search the MSN Money web site for the monthly closing prices of the retail company's stock. You print a chart of stock prices, an article announcing a recent stock split and the foundation's proposal submission guidelines posted on the foundation's web site. You consult with your boss, the director of development, on what additional information to provide. She suggests that you remind the executive director that he was going to speak with the company's owner not only about a personal gift, but also about approaching the foundation to fund a new project, a web site for families needing respite care for mentally ill children. You dash off a quick note to the executive director to accompany the packet you have pulled together.

10:15 a.m. Start on your main project for the day: a draft proposal to a large foundation describing your organization's biggest, most complex program—a state-wide outreach and education initiative for low-income families with mentally ill children. You have a lot of questions about how a new lecture series at local community centers will build upon a number of outreach events the organization sponsored last year, including a poorly attended lecture series at local libraries. You review your notes from a recent meeting with program staff, and call the director of community outreach to discuss how these new lectures will be different from the previous ones and how she hopes to encourage greater attendance.

12:30 p.m. Run out and grab some lunch from the deli across the street. You bring it back to your desk so that you can continue to work through the proposal draft.

1:30 p.m. Look up at the clock and see that you have a half-hour to finish preparing for the monthly meeting of the public policy team. You finalize a short presentation on the status of existing foundation funding for a campaign to lobby the state legislature for greater health care coverage for respite care. You add a summary of the history, interests and submission deadlines for three foundations you and the director of development have identified from prospect research. You stick your head into your boss' office to see if she will be joining the meeting. She is on the phone with the chair of the board discussing the elements of the next fundraising report and presentation to for the next board meeting. You quickly make a note to yourself to provide her with a quick summary of grants that have come in this month.

2 p.m. Join the policy meeting. The director of public policy starts a discussion about whether to partner with a regional mental health center with strong connections to state officials. You remind the team that one of the foundations you have identified as a prospect is also funding the center. You also ask a number of questions about this partnership and how the two organizations would work together to engage officials at the state's department of mental health.

Visit Vault at **www.vault.com** for insider company profiles, expert advice, career message boards, expert resume reviews, the Vault Job Board and more.

VAULT CAREER LIBRARY   415

3:15 p.m. Return to your desk and resume drafting the proposal. You complete the section on the lecture series and turn your attention to creating the budget. You recall a conversation in the hallway with the director of administration, who mentioned that rent would be going up next year. You call the director to figure out if you should adjust the percentage added to the program expenses for overhead.

4:30 p.m. Finish a draft of the budget and e-mail it to the program director and the director of administration for review. The executive director calls to thank you for the stock information and to ask what he should highlight about the new project in his meeting tomorrow. You go over with him the overall structure of the web site and remind him that there will be a chat room devoted to parents with autistic children.

5:15 p.m. Turn your attention back to the draft proposal. People are starting to leave the office, so it's quieting down. You figure if you can plow through another 45 minutes, you can complete the draft.

6:05 p.m. Look up from a completed draft and see that it is time to go. You quickly look over the draft and see that there are a lot of questions highlighted in yellow. You decide to review it one more time tomorrow before sending it out to program staff for comment. Your boss is still around and you ask if she wants to see the draft before or after program staff have reviewed it. She opts for after the program staff review and asks that you flag for her any remaining program questions that remain unanswered. You turn off the computer.

6:15 p.m. Just as you are about to head out the door, the executive director calls again. The program officer at another large foundation contacted him. She said that she reviewed the proposal describing the health care coverage campaign and is recommending to the foundation's board an increase in funding by $50,000. The executive director compliments you on your work on the proposal, adding that he can now hire a new outreach person to enlist psychiatrists and pediatricians in the campaign. You make a note to write a thank you to the foundation officer tomorrow. As you close the door, you think about asking your boss to hire a freelance grant writer to help with three proposals due next month.

Social Work

According to NASW, there are over 600,000 professional social workers in the U.S. And according to the U.S. Bureau of Labor Statistics, in 2004 social workers held approximately 562,000 jobs, and employment is expected to rise faster than the average for all occupations through 2014, with hospitals, substance abuse, schools and private practice seeing the most increase. As people live longer, but not necessarily better quality lives, there will be a continued need for social workers to provide casework, advocacy, individual and family therapy.

Generally, social work positions are divided into two main areas, professional and paraprofessional social work. A paraprofessional is generally classified as a case aide, a technician or a peer. These positions tend to rely more on personal attributes, like life experience and personality, than level of education. Persons in these positions usually perform basic counseling or provide concrete services that do not require clinical skills.

Family and children services

Social workers in this role work to improve the social and psychological functioning of children and their families to maximize the family's well-being. Some social workers assist single parents in locating child care and dealing with parenting alone; they may arrange adoptions for people who want to adopt and for those who want to have their children adopted; and they help find foster homes for neglected, abandoned or abused children.

In addition to abuse and neglect services, these social workers also focus on areas, such as family communication, adjustment to changes within families, like divorce or marriage, and they can also provide marriage counseling to couples.

School social work

Public and private schools from elementary through to college employ social workers to address issues such as truancy, teenage pregnancy, suicide and mental illness. They may be called upon to advise teachers on coping with disruptive students, and they also teach workshops to classes on topics, such as self-esteem, sexuality and violence in the home. Parents and social workers combine efforts when family life disruptions, such as death, divorce or even the birth of a new sibling, has an effect on the student's learning.

Medical social work

Medical social workers provide individuals and families with the psychosocial support needed to cope with chronic, acute or terminal illnesses, such as Alzheimer's, cancer, AIDS and other medical conditions that cause a disruption to regular life. They also advise family caregivers on the prognosis of the ill person's condition and how best to care for the person at home, or they'll recommend a nursing home or hospice care when necessary. They provide counseling to patients on what to expect as their condition progresses, to alleviate some of the anxiety of not knowing what will happen next. And social workers help plan for patients' needs after discharge from hospitals or rehabilitation centers by arranging for at-home services, from meals-on-wheels to oxygen equipment.

Mental health

Mental health social workers work in inpatient settings such as psychiatric hospitals, or outpatient services in the community at therapeutic centers or community mental health programs that provide counseling and medication monitoring for patients outside of the hospital. Social workers in these centers often work closely with other providers, medical doctors, case managers and family members to ensure that each is aware of the client's treatment and their cooperation in the treatment.

Substance abuse

Social workers in the substance use and addiction field are trained to treat clients holistically, taking into account a person's physical environment, family support system, spiritual beliefs and cultural attitudes, along with the addiction. Traditionally, substance use counseling was handled by people with CASAC certification (credentialed alcoholism and substance abuse counselor), but more recently social workers have been filling these roles because of their more specialized training and holistic approach to treatment. This field is a good example of how the diverse and flexible skills of social workers can adapt to a number of different issues.

Clinical social work

Clinical social workers rely on a variety of therapeutic theories and tools to help individuals, couples, families and groups with mental, behavioral and emotional disorders, from eating issues to depression, to personality disorders. Unlike other areas of practice, clinical social workers are defined more by how they work than where and for whom. For instance, clinical social workers practice in schools, mental health agencies, private practice and community-based organizations, whereas those who practice school social work are only found in schools or school-based settings.

According to NASW, clinical social workers are the largest group of professionally trained mental health providers in the United States, supplying more than half of counseling and therapy services.

Visit Vault at www.vault.com for insider company profiles, expert advice, career message boards, expert resume reviews, the Vault Job Board and more.

VAULT CAREER LIBRARY   417

Where do social workers work?

Local, state and federal governments offer many opportunities for social workers to engage directly with clients as well as indirectly though policy work, research and program administration. Government services cover a wide range of issues, including public health, child and family services, homelessness, mental health, poverty and the law. For the most part, these programs focus on meeting the basic needs of people such as food, shelter, safety and medical care by administering public welfare benefits (food stamps and cash assistance), coordinating entrance to homeless shelters and determining eligibility for Medicaid or Medicare health insurance.

Nonprofit refers to an organization established for purposes other than profit making. Major nonprofit employers of social workers include agencies like Good Shepherd Services, Salvation Army, UNICEF, the Boys and Girls Club, the YMCA and the American Red Cross, where social workers range in position from the highest-level management to the person greeting you at the door. Most social service agencies that are not government-administered are nonprofits. The mission of most nonprofits is to alleviate or ameliorate some social ill, such as homelessness, poverty, hunger, violence or disease.

Local, state and federal governments, as well as nonprofit and private businesses, hire policy social workers as lobbyists, analysts, evaluators and researchers to determine causes of certain social ills and propose possible remedies, much like research-oriented social workers we'll discuss later. Social workers in this field address problems, such as child abuse, homelessness, substance abuse, poverty, mental illness, violence, unemployment and racism, working to improve systems to better conditions for the people affected. Social workers analyze policies, programs and regulations to determine which solutions are most effective for a given problem. They identify social problems, study needs and related issues, conduct research, propose legislation and suggest alternative approaches or new programs. They may foster coalitions of groups with similar interests and develop interorganizational networks. On a daily basis, this often means analyzing census data and legislation, drafting position papers, testifying at public hearings, working with the media, talking with policy-makers, and lobbying elected and appointed officials. Their tasks may also involve raising funds, writing grants or conducting demonstration projects. Often, social workers are the directors of organizations that do this work.

All hospitals have social workers on staff, especially specialized hospitals and rehabilitation centers. These include hospitals for special surgery such as orthopedics, hospice centers and short- or long-term rehabilitation centers in which social workers counsel patients on their diagnosis, recovery issues, adjustment back to normal life, or coping with the loss of a family member.

KPMG, Deloitte & Touche and Ernst & Young are a few of the corporate consulting companies winning contracts from government and nonprofit organizations for technical assistance in improving the delivery of social services, through team-development, training and administration. These companies look to hire master's level social workers to develop and deliver training on topics including organizational development, conflict resolution, help with technology solutions, policies and procedures tailored to the agencies' specific needs, and clinical guidance to other social workers. Because of social workers' specialized educational and experiential training in terms of the staff, clients and issues nonprofits face, they give these companies a unique edge in this type of setting, which increases the effectiveness of the training. To be successful in this field, it is important to have good analytical, strategic planning, presentation and writing skills. Seeking internships in corporations is an important step in acquiring this kind of position upon graduation.

Growth areas

There is expected to be a strong demand for substance abuse social workers over the next 10 years and more, as drug users are increasingly being placed into treatment programs instead of being sentenced to prison. The criminal justice and correctional systems are increasingly requiring substance abuse treatment as a condition of sentencing or probation. As treatment programs become more widespread, demand will increase for social workers who can assist drug users on the road to recovery.

Another area where growth is expected is among social workers and employers who focus on the elderly or in the area of gerontology. Although hospitals are keeping patients for shorter periods of time, home health care is growing, in keeping with the increased demand of seniors who can live at home, but need additional support to do so. Additionally, the growing number of nursing homes, retirement communities and assisted living facilities is creating a wealth of opportunities for social workers in this field.

A Day in the Life: Social Work Case Manager

Cynthia works in Boston as a case manager with homeless clients, helping them with securing public assistance, housing subsidies and other needs to maintain that housing. She has a bachelor's degree in social work and has been in the field for two years. Her salary is $32,000.

9 a.m. Check voicemail; complete case notes from the previous day; write schedule.

10 a.m. Meeting with client, but client does not show up for appointment.

10:30 a.m. Unscheduled meeting with client; complete housing subsidy paperwork; phone call to local shelter to secure bed for the night; provide a meal voucher.

11:45 a.m. Intake interview with potential client, but after half an hour realize client is not eligible because he has the option of staying with family outside of city.

12:30 p.m. Eat lunch while on the phone with public assistance to advocate for several clients to receive their rent checks on time to move into apartments by the first of the month.

2 p.m. Home visit with client.

3:45 p.m. Supervision with program coordinator, review of current cases and suggestions on how to proceed.

4:30 p.m. Review of files for correct and up-to-date paperwork.

5 p.m. Write and mail four letters to clients without contact for two weeks or more.

Visit Vault at **www.vault.com** for insider company profiles, expert advice, career message boards, expert resume reviews, the Vault Job Board and more.

VAULT CAREER LIBRARY   419

Employer Directory

AARP
601 E Street NW
Washington, DC 20049
Phone: (202) 434-2277
Fax: (202) 434-6548
www.aarp.org

American Cancer Society, Inc.
1599 Clifton Road NE
Atlanta, GA 30329
Phone: (404) 320-3333
Fax: (404) 982-3677
www.cancer.org

American Civil Liberties Union (ACLU)
125 Broad Street, 18th Floor
New York, NY 10004-2400
Phone: (212) 549-2500
Fax: (212) 549-2646
www.aclu.org

American Heart Association, Inc.
7272 Greenville Avenue
Dallas, TX 75231
Phone: (214) 373-6300
Fax: (214) 706-1191
www.americanheart.org

American Red Cross
2025 E Street NW
Washington, DC 20006
Phone: (202) 303-4498
www.redcross.org

American Society for the Prevention of Cruelty to Animals (ASPCA)
424 East 92nd Street
New York, NY 10128-6804
Phone: (212) 876-7700
Fax: (212) 423-9813
www.aspca.org

AmeriCares Foundation, Inc.
88 Hamilton Avenue
Stamford, CT 06902
Phone: (203) 658-9500
Fax: (203) 966-6028
www.americares.org

America's Second Harvest
35 East Wacker Drive, Suite 2000
Chicago, IL 60601
Phone: (312) 263-2302
Fax: (312)263-5626

AmeriCorps
1201 New York Avenue NW
Washington, DC 20525
Phone: (202) 606-5000
www.americorps.org

Amnesty International USA
Five Penn Plaza
New York, NY 10001
Phone: (212) 807-8400
Fax: (212) 627-1451
www.amnestyusa.org

Big Brothers Big Sisters of America
230 North 13th Street
Philadelphia, PA 19107
Phone: (215) 567-7000
Fax: (215) 567-0394
www.bbbsa.org

The Bill & Melinda Gates Foundation
1551 Eastlake Avenue East
Seattle, WA 98102
Phone: (206) 709-3100
Fax: (206) 709-9180
www.gatesfoundation.org

The Boy Scouts of America
1325 West Walnut Hill Lane
Irving, TX 75015
Phone: (972) 580-2401
Fax: (972) 580-2413
www.scouting.org

Boys & Girls Clubs of America
1275 Peachtree Street NE
Atlanta, GA 30309
Phone: (404) 487-5700
Fax: (404) 487-5705
www.bgca.org

Carnegie Corporation
437 Madison Avenue
New York, NY 10022
Phone: (212) 371-3200
Fax: (212) 754-4073
www.carnegie.org

Corporation for Public Broadcasting
402 Ninth Street NW
Washington, DC 20004
Phone: (202) 879-9600
Fax: (202) 879-9700
www.cpb.org

The Ford Foundation
320 East 43rd Street
New York, NY 10017
Phone: (212) 573-5000
Fax: (212) 351-3677
www.fordfound.org

Girl Scouts of the United States of America
420 Fifth Avenue
New York, NY 10018
Phone: (212) 852-8000
Fax: (212) 852-6514
www.girlscouts.org

Goodwill Industries International
15810 Indianola Avenue
Rockville, MD 20855
Phone: (301) 530-6500
Fax: (301) 530-1516
www.goodwill.org

Habitat for Humanity International
121 Habitat Street
Americus, GA 31709
Phone: (229) 924-6935
Fax: (229) 924-6541
www.habitat.org

Employer Directory, cont.

Human Rights Watch
350 5th Avenue, 34th Floor
New York, NY 10118-3299
Phone: (212) 290-4700
Fax: (212) 736-1300
www.hrw.org

The Humane Society of the United States
2100 L Street NW
Washington, DC 20037
Phone: (202) 452-1100
Fax: (202) 778-6132
www.hsus.org

March of Dimes Foundation
1275 Mamaroneck Avenue
White Plains, NY 10605
Phone: (914) 428-7100
Fax: (914) 428-8203
www.marchofdimes.com

Médecins Sans Frontières
Rue de la Tourelle, 39
1040 Brussels
Belgium
Phone: +32-2-280-1881
Fax: +32-2-280-0173
www.msf.org

National Women's Law Center
11 Dupont Circle NW, Suite 800
Washington, DC 20036
Phone: (202) 588-5180
www.nwlc.org

Open Society Institute
400 West 59th Street
New York, NY 10019
Phone: (212) 548-0600
Fax: (212) 548-4679
www.soros.org

The Peace Corps
1111 20th Street NW
Washington, DC 20526
Phone: (202) 692-2230
Fax: (202) 692-2901
www.peacecorps.gov

Planned Parenthood Federation of America, Inc.
434 West 33rd Street
New York, NY 10001
Phone: (212) 541-7800
Fax: (212) 245-1845
www.plannedparenthood.org

The Rockefeller Foundation
420 Fifth Avenue
New York, NY 10018
Phone: (212) 869-8500
Fax: (212) 764-3468
www.rockfound.org

Rotary International
1 Rotary Center
1560 Sherman Avenue
Evanston, IL 60201-3698
Phone: (847) 866-3000
Fax: (847) 328-8281
www.rotary.org

The Salvation Army
615 Slaters Lane
Alexandria, VA 22313
Phone: (703) 684-5500
Fax: (703) 684-3478
www.salvationarmyusa.org

Smithsonian Institution
1000 Jefferson Drive SW
Washington, DC 20560
Phone: (202) 633-1000
Fax: (202) 786-2377
www.si.edu

Teach for America, Inc.
315 West 36th Street, 7th Floor
New York, NY 10018
Phone: (212) 279-2080
Fax: (212) 279-2081
www.teachforamerica.org

UNICEF
3 United Nations Plaza
New York, NY 10017
Phone: (212) 326-7000
Fax: (212) 887-7465
www.unicef.com

United Nations
First Avenue at 46th Street
New York, NY 10017
Phone: (212) 963-1234
Fax: (212) 963-3133
www.un.org

United Way of America
701 North Fairfax Street
Alexandria, VA 22314
Phone: (703) 836-7100
Fax: (703) 683-7840
national.unitedway.org

YMCA of the USA
202 North Wacker Drive
Chicago, IL 60606
Phone: (312) 977-0031
Fax: (312) 977-9063
www.ymca.net

Visit Vault at **www.vault.com** for insider company profiles, expert advice, career message boards, expert resume reviews, the Vault Job Board and more.

VAULT CAREER LIBRARY 421

Pharmaceuticals and Biotech

What's in a Name: Big Pharma, Big Biotech and Biopharma

Small molecules and large companies

Strictly speaking, the term "pharmaceuticals" refers to medicines composed of small, synthetically produced molecules, which are sold by large, fully integrated drug manufacturers. The largest of these players—companies like Pfizer, GlaxoSmithKline and Merck—as well as a handful of others are known as "Big Pharma" because they are huge research, development and manufacturing companies with subsidiaries around the globe. Indeed, Big Pharma is where most of the industry's sales are generated. During 2007 the industry racked up $712 billion in global sales and that number is predicted to grow to $735 billion in 2008, a five to six percent uptick from 2007.

A profitable business

According to the Kaiser Family Foundation, from 1995 to 2002, the pharmaceutical business was the most lucrative industry in America. Pharmaceutical manufacturers didn't fare as well in later years, however. In 2003, the pharmaceutical industry ranked third; and in 2005, it ranked fifth. However, in 2006, the pharmaceutical industry ranked second in the country.

From aspirin to Herceptin: a brief history of the industry

Many of today's big pharmaceutical firms have roots that go back to the late 19th or early 20th century. Not all of these companies started out as drug manufacturers. For instance, Frederich Bayer founded Bayer in Germany in 1863 to make synthetic dyes. In the 1920s and 1930s, scientists discovered miracle drugs such as insulin and penicillin, and pharmaceutical companies began to market researchers' life-saving inventions. During the 1950s and 1960s, companies started to mass produce and market new drugs, such as blood-pressure medications, birth control pills and Valium. Pharmaceutical companies researched and developed new cancer treatments, including chemotherapy, in the 1970s. The modern biotech business was born when Herbert Boyer and Robert Swanson founded Genentech, which would eventually make breast cancer biologic Herceptin. In the 1980s, drug companies faced new environmental and safety regulations and mounting economic pressures. For Big Pharma, the 1990s was a time of turmoil. There were lots of mergers and acquisitions in the industry during that decade, and pharmaceutical companies also began to use contract research organizations for more of their R&D efforts.

Big Pharma

In 2006, large pharmaceutical companies launched several high-profile products, including the HPV vaccine, Gardasil; oral diabetes drug, Januvia; and cancer treatment, Sutent.

Big Pharma is responsible for all those television commercials urging us to contact our doctors if we suspect we suffer from restless leg syndrome or social anxiety disorder. Yet despite life-saving, cancer-fighting drugs and significant corporate philanthropy, Big Pharma's recent product recalls and concerns over drug safety have made it the industry many people love to hate. In 2007, diabetes medication Avandia made the headlines after researchers found it increased patients' risk of heart attack.

Before we help you chart a career in the industry, we should point out that both the scope of players and the types of products the industry produces are moving targets. This is because the pharmaceutical and biotech industries are gradually integrating into one industry.

Visit Vault at **www.vault.com** for insider company profiles, expert advice, career message boards, expert resume reviews, the Vault Job Board and more.

V/\ULT CAREER LIBRARY   423

Most of the largest Big Pharma players are either gobbling up small biotechs through outright acquisitions or, alternatively, are entering licensing agreements. For example, in 2006, AstraZeneca acquired small biotech firm Cambridge Antibody Technology Group and Merck purchased GlycoFi and Abmaxis. In 2008, U.K. pharma stalwart GlaxoSmithKline forked over $1.65 billion to purchase privately-held specialty pharmaceutical company Reliant, the maker of Lovaza, a heart drug that is the only prescription omega-3 med approved by the FDA to treat very high triglyceride levels. This trend is likely to continue throughout the rest of this decade, since it's increasingly difficult to find innovative new drugs through traditional science.

In fact, innovation is the industry's biggest current challenge. Companies are using acquisitions and alliances to round out their product pipelines and meet investor expectations. Big drug manufacturers can now claim to research, manufacture and sell both types of drugs: synthetic small molecules (or old chemistry) and injectable large molecules (or biologics).

Big Pharma

In 2006, large pharmaceutical companies launched several high-profile products, including the HPV vaccine, Gardasil; oral diabetes drug, Januvia; and cancer treatment, Sutent.

Big Pharma is responsible for all those television commercials urging us to contact our doctors if we suspect we suffer from restless leg syndrome or social anxiety disorder. Yet despite life-saving, cancer-fighting drugs and significant corporate philanthropy, Big Pharma's recent product recalls and concerns over drug safety have made it the industry many people love to hate. In 2007, diabetes medication Avandia made the headlines after researchers found it increased patients' risk of heart attack.

Before we help you chart a career in the industry, we should point out that both the scope of players and the types of products the industry produces are moving targets. This is because the pharmaceutical and biotech industries are gradually integrating into one industry.

Most of the largest Big Pharma players are either gobbling up small biotechs through outright acquisitions or, alternatively, are entering licensing agreements. For example, in 2006, AstraZeneca acquired small biotech firm Cambridge Antibody Technology Group and Merck purchased GlycoFi and Abmaxis. In 2008, U.K. pharma stalwart GlaxoSmithKline forked over $1.65 billion to purchase privately-held specialty pharmaceutical company Reliant, the maker of Lovaza, a heart drug that is the only prescription omega-3 med approved by the FDA to treat very high triglyceride levels. This trend is likely to continue throughout the rest of this decade, since it's increasingly difficult to find innovative new drugs through traditional science.

In fact, innovation is the industry's biggest current challenge. Companies are using acquisitions and alliances to round out their product pipelines and meet investor expectations. Big drug manufacturers can now claim to research, manufacture and sell both types of drugs: synthetic small molecules (or old chemistry) and injectable large molecules (or biologics).

The Global Pharmaceutical Industry

Three major market segments dominate the global industry. North America is the largest and comprises about 46 percent of the total market, Europe is second with some 31 percent. Japan comes in third at about 9 percent in 2007 sales. Although these combined markets account for nearly 86 percent of global sales, the remaining emerging market segments—other Asian countries, Africa, Australia and Latin America—are growing rapidly. According to IMS Health, Inc., a health care research and information company, sales in Asia, Africa and Australia were $62 billion in 2007, a 13.1 percent increase from 2006. Global pharmaceutical sales in Latin America in 2007 were $32 billion, a 12 percent increase from the previous year.

Although a handful of super-large companies rake in most of the pharmaceutical industry's revenue, the global industry is actually highly fragmented. More than 2,000 pharmaceutical and biotech companies exist worldwide. In the top tier are the large, multinational companies that dominate the market, or Big Pharma. In the middle tier are the specialty companies.

Many large companies have tended to absorb second-tier companies before they can grow enough to pose a competitive threat. That trend has a contracting effect on the number of firms. The opposite happens on the third and lowest tier, which is composed of an ever-increasing group of startups mostly focused on discovery research.

According to IMS Health, Inc., as recently as 1999, the global pharmaceutical market was valued at $334 billion. By 2007, total global sales had nearly doubled to $663 billion, or more than half a trillion dollars! (IMS derived this figure from retail sales in major global markets.) This astonishing growth reflects the increasing role of pharmaceuticals as a first-line treatment option for many disease conditions in the developed world. The term "first-line" means that physicians opt to prescribe a pharmaceutical first in lieu of a more invasive procedure, such as surgery. In some cancers, physicians now have the option of recommending a tumor-shrinking drug, for example, before surgery to minimize the level of invasiveness to the body.

In the U.S.

The U.S. pharmaceutical industry is comprised of approximately 100 companies—according to the Pharmaceutical Research and Manufacturers of America (PhRMA), a leading industry trade and lobbying organization—with the top 10 companies referred to as Big Pharma. According to the Biotechnology Industry Organization (BIO), there were also 1,452 biotech companies in the United States at the end of 2006.

The U.S. has not only the largest pharmaceutical market in the world but also the only one without government price controls. This is a consequence of the privately-owned system prevalent in the U.S. and a strong industry lobby, which has resisted government incursions into its market-based pricing. On the other hand, developed economies with universal health care access (European Union, U.K., Japan) exert stringent controls on the prices companies can charge. A big consequence is that, with thin profit margins, the incentive for innovation is curbed, and former leaders, especially in the EU (German and French companies, in particular) lost the lead in innovation in the 1990s. Standard & Poor's expects the U.S. to continue to be the largest of the top 10 pharmaceutical markets for the foreseeable future, as well as the fastest growing.

Although pharmaceutical companies are scattered throughout the continental United States, the industry is geographically concentrated in the Mid-Atlantic states, New York, New Jersey and Pennsylvania, and on the West Coast in California. A handful of companies can also be found in Massachusetts, Illinois and North Carolina. New Jersey is the heart of the industry and has by far the largest number of companies within a single state. According to the California Healthcare Institute, roughly a quarter of U.S. biotech jobs are in sunny California.

Medicare change boosts drugs sales

Before January 1, 2006, Medicare, the federal health program for the disabled and elderly, didn't pay for outpatient prescription drugs. The Medicare Prescription Drug, Improvement and Modernization Act—known as Part D—gave Medicare beneficiaries the option to enroll in private drug plans. Due to the changes, Medicare became the country's largest public customer of prescription medications in 2006. The change to Medicare helped boost prescription sales in the United States in 2006, but the U.S. Department of Health and Human Services doesn't think it will have a huge impact on drug spending in the future.

Growth in generics

In 1984 the passage of the Drug Price Competition and Patent Term Restoration Act, also called the Hatch-Waxman Act, increased generic drug manufacturers' access to the marketplace. One recent trend in the industry has been a boom in generic drug sales. The biggest generic drug manufacturers, such as the Israeli firm Teva and U.S.-based companies Mylan and Barr, have thousands of employees and boasted more than a billion dollars in revenue in 2006. According to the Kaiser Family

Visit Vault at www.vault.com for insider company profiles, expert advice, career message boards, expert resume reviews, the Vault Job Board and more.

VAULT CAREER LIBRARY   425

Foundation, in 2006 more than 60 percent of prescriptions dispensed and 20 percent of prescription drug sales were generics, and sales of generic drugs grew 22 percent from 2005 to 2006.

In the United States, managed health care has contributed to the rise in generic drugs. Managed care programs such as HMOs often ask their doctors to prescribe generic drugs in place of more expensive brand-name products. Recent changes to the Medicare program in the United States are also likely to lead to an increase in generic drug sales. Under Medicare Part D, through "multitiered pricing," plans can charge patients more for brand-name drugs than generics. In addition, plans can ask doctors to fill out prior authorization forms in order for patients to obtain branded drugs.

The expiration of patents on branded pharmaceuticals has also increased generic drug companies' revenues. As more brand-name drugs go off patents in coming years, generic drug manufacturers' profits are likely to increase. Big pharmaceutical companies that make brand-name drugs usually attempt to extend their drugs' exclusivity and prevent generic competition. They do this in various ways, including litigation. Some big pharmaceutical companies have responded to generic competition by entering into licensing agreements with generic drug manufacturers.

To complicate things further, not all pharmaceutical companies make just generics or only branded drugs. For example, Novartis has a generics division, called Sandoz. Due to strong growth and two major acquisitions in 2005, Sandoz is currently the second-largest generics company in the world based on sales after Teva. Sandoz raked in $7.2 billion in pharmaceutical sales in 2007 alone. Some generic companies also sell branded pharmaceuticals. For instance, generic drug manufacturer Barr's subsidiary Duramed Pharmaceuticals develops, makes and sells the firm's proprietary pharmaceuticals, mostly female healthcare products, such as Seasonale and Seasonique oral contraceptives.

Generic drug companies are also branching out into generic versions of biologic drugs. In 2005, Barr Pharmaceuticals announced a deal to license Croatian pharmaceutical company Pliva's version of Neupogen, a white-blood-cell booster made by Amgen. In 2006, Barr and Iceland's Actavis Group battled for Pliva. Barr outbid Actavis, and—in a deal worth $2.5 billion—the company acquired Pliva. The Croatian company is working on a copycat version of Amgen's Epogen, a protein that boosts red blood cells. Barr has also broken ground on a $25 million biotech factory in Croatia.

A rise in CROs

Increasingly, pharmaceutical companies have been outsourcing drug research and development. As a result, contract research organizations (or CROs) have been on the rise. In 2005, a survey by Cambridge Healthtech Advisors found that 45 percent of pharmaceutical companies expected to outsource at least 60 percent of their clinical development work by 2008. Examples of CROs include New Jersey-based Covance and North Carolina's Quintiles Transnational Corporation. In 2006, Covance worked with more than 300 biopharmaceutical companies, ranging from small and startup organizations to the world's largest pharmaceutical companies. Quintiles has helped develop or commercialize the world's 30 best-selling drugs.

Departments in a Pharmaceutical Company

According to the Bureau of Labor Statistics, about 28 percent of jobs in the pharmaceutical and medicine manufacturing industry are in professional and related occupations. Most of these positions are for science technicians and scientists. Some 13 percent of professionals in the industry work in offices as administrative support, and three percent are employed in sales. About a quarter of jobs in the pharmaceutical and biotech business are in manufacturing and production.

The major departments of a conventional pharmaceutical company include R&D, operations, quality control, clinical research, business development and finance and administration. Each department houses several functional groups or specific, logically related areas of activity. At generic drug companies, departments are similar. They might include administration, business development, finance, human resources, information technology, legal and intellectual property, manufacturing, marketing and sales. At most generic drug companies, researchers don't spend years trying to discover the next big thing. Instead, researchers in the companies' labs reverse-engineer compounds that already exist to find bioequivalent compounds.

As you think about a career in the pharmaceutical industry, it's useful to identify the general area(s) where your primary interests and aptitudes lie. Let's take a look at the different departments.

Research and development

The research and development (R&D) department is responsible for discovering promising drug candidates. The three major functions include discovery research, bioinformatics and animal sciences. The discovery research function is responsible for performing experiments that identify either targets on the cell or potential drug candidates. The animal sciences function provides cell cultures, grows microorganisms and manages the care of animals used in discovery research. The extensive data generated from experiments is analyzed with the assistance of the bioinformatics function, which assists discovery research in identifying the most biologically active compounds.

Because the pharmaceuticals business is a research-intensive industry, there are many jobs in R&D. In 2004, about 14 percent of medical researchers were employed in pharmaceutical and medical manufacturing. These researchers' median salary was $76,800.

Clinical research

Once a drug candidate is identified as a potentially viable treatment R&D, the clinical research department takes over and becomes responsible for shepherding the drug through the FDA approval process. The clinical research function sets up and manages the clinical trials needed to determine a drug's safety and effectiveness or "efficacy." The regulatory affairs function ensures that all FDA reporting requirements are completed and submitted in a timely manner. Finally, the medical affairs/drug information function is responsible for overseeing all the information related to a drug candidate.

Operations

The operations department is responsible for making commercial quantities of a candidate drug available. Once a promising drug candidate has been identified, the process/product development function determines how to "scale up" quantities of a product to make enough available for clinical trials, since laboratory-size quantities are usually very small. When a product successfully emerges from clinical trials successfully, the manufacturing and production function creates the final product—complete with packaging and labeling—that we see on the shelves of pharmacies and drugstores. Also housed under the operations umbrella is the environmental health and safety function, which assesses the environmental impact of a potential product.

Quality

The FDA has strict safety regulations for factories that make pharmaceuticals and biologics. If the FDA suspects a vaccine or other drugs might be contaminated, the agency can close manufacturing plants. Among other things, a pharmaceutical company's quality department makes sure the firm follows government regulations. The department has groups focusing on quality control, quality assurance and validation. These groups ensure that products are manufactured along rigorous, consistent standards of quality. This usually entails that well-defined and documented procedures are followed when producing a product either for clinical trials or as an end product.

Visit Vault at **www.vault.com** for insider company profiles, expert advice, career message boards, expert resume reviews, the Vault Job Board and more.

V/\ULT CAREER LIBRARY

427

Finance and administration

The finance and administration department contains these two functional areas as well as information systems and legal. All activities relating to the financial management of the company, its legal relationships to investors, creditors, employees and government regulators are housed in this department. The companywide computer systems—separate from computing specifically directed at analyzing research data—are also managed here.

Business development

The business development group is typically responsible for identifying prospective new alliance partners and managing existing alliances. The marketing function studies markets, identifies target customer bases, and sets pricing and promotion strategy. The sales function actually meets with potential customers in the field—usually specialist physicians in targeted areas of specialization (e.g., cardiologists, endocrinologists, urologists).

Project management

Finally, many pharmaceutical companies also have a separate project management department, which is responsible for ensuring that work requiring the collaboration of several internal departments is discharged smoothly and efficiently. This department oversees special projects that don't naturally fit into any of the traditional formal functions but that require cross-functional collaboration. Unlike general managers, who work on companies' overall operations, project managers tend to focus on specific ventures. A project manager might help launch products, develop marketing programs, run annual sales meetings or manage clinical trials.

To Lab or Not to Lab?

Given the breadth of choices in the pharmaceutical industry, you might well wonder how to focus your own career aspirations. You may be turned on by science while in college enough to earn a major in a scientific discipline but not be sure you want to make research your life-long career. That's fine, as long as you have a sense of how to manage the critical early years of professional experience. To help you get a wide-angle view of the major career paths available, we have found it helpful to think in terms of two fundamental paths: laboratory research oriented and non-laboratory research oriented. Within each path are several different career tracks.

Laboratory research-oriented career paths are found in the R&D department. This area is also called "discovery research" because the work involves discovering new processes, drugs and technologies. These careers involve "bench work," referring to a laboratory bench, where scientists set up experiments generate data.

Non-research oriented career paths include everything else. Several functions—operations, manufacturing and quality—have an engineering bent and are primarily focused on the applications of science. Others, like clinical research, include all the jobs needed to set up and manage clinical trials and oversee submissions to regulatory agencies. Note that the "clinical research" function includes all the jobs needed to set up and manage clinical trials. They are put here rather than in the research-oriented path since they require knowledge of medicine and occur in clinical settings, such as hospitals or clinics. Still others are business-oriented and include support functions, such as finance, administration, legal, IT, business development and sales/marketing. Finally many companies have a project management function that helps coordinate projects that overlap among several internal functions.

The common denominator is that careers in most of these functions require at least an undergraduate foundation in a life science. This includes the more generic business functions. Many careers require advanced training in science in addition to education in a functional area. For example, attorneys specializing in intellectual property often also have advanced degrees in the sciences. Business development people typically have either a bachelor's or a master's degree in a scientific area in addition to an MBA. The industry sets these educational prerequisites for employment outside the lab because business people need a thorough grounding in the vocabulary of genetics, an orientation to the basic concepts behind the products and a familiarity with the issues and challenges facing the industry. The bottom line is this: if you are up and coming in the educational system, you are joining a limited pool of qualified talent competing for the available jobs. That's good news if most of your career is still ahead of you.

Laboratory Research Careers

Discovery research

At smaller companies, many jobs are in discovery research. Discovery researchers can range from protein chemists to geneticists, to biochemists, to many other disciplines in the life sciences. There are jobs at all levels. With a bachelor's degree, you can get an entry-level job as a research associate and work for several years, though you will need an advanced degree for more senior jobs. Most responsible positions, however, require a PhD. You can definitely break into the industry after undergraduate studies. Entry-level research positions will get your feet wet and give you a chance to experience the culture of research first-hand before committing yourself to advanced studies. The salary range for a research associate is from $40,000 to $70,000. The scientist job is the more senior researcher position in R&D. For the scientist track, the salary range is typically $60,000 to $130,000. Scientific managers can earn salaries in the range of $100,000 up to more than $175,000. As discussed earlier, many pharmaceutical companies have contracted out research to contract research organizations (CROs), so researchers also should consider working for CROs.

Non-Laboratory Research Careers

Non-laboratory research careers encompass a large range of functions, including engineering, careers in medical and clinical settings, administrative/support functions and sales and marketing.

When a product has been demonstrated to be safe in animals, it's ready to be tested on a small sample of humans and be submitted as a candidate for a new drug to the FDA. These activities occur in clinical settings, involve interpretation of massive amounts of clinical data and require extensive documentation to the regulatory body. Two basic paths exist: clinical research and regulatory affairs. Jobs in these functions are usually grouped together in most companies.

Clinical research

First, let's clarify the term "research" in clinical research. Clinical researchers are physicians, nurses and data management professionals who administer and interpret the reactions of patients who have been enrolled in clinical trials. Often, these patients suffer from the disease condition targeted and need to pass a set of qualification criteria set by specialist physicians, who must ensure that their overall health status is sufficiently stable to participate in testing the experimental drug. Once a drug is administered to an enrolled patient, the patient is carefully monitored for reactions to the drug. These include desired effects and other adverse or undesired effects. Both sets of data are captured both manually and electronically. Sometimes, manual data has to be transferred to electronic form. All data eventually becomes housed in computer databases, where physicians and database managers interpret the overall effects of the drug on the total population of patients enrolled in the study. These activities thus constitute research in a clinical setting using clinical data.

Medical knowledge at all levels is required for careers in clinical research—physicians identify prospective patients and interpret clinical data; nurses administer drug candidates and help monitor patient reactions; even database specialists need

Visit Vault at **www.vault.com** for insider company profiles, expert advice, career message boards, expert resume reviews, the Vault Job Board and more.

VAULT CAREER LIBRARY   429

to have some understanding of the type of data the medical professionals generate in order to collaborate with physicians in interpreting it. With the hundreds of biotech drug candidates in the pipeline, clinical research jobs are expected to continue to be plentiful.

Regulatory affairs

Regulatory affairs is the other clinically-oriented track. Jobs in this function involve dealing with all aspects of the regulatory environment surrounding drug approval, including submitting New Drug Applications (NDAs), preparing submissions to the FDA summarizing clinical trial results, keeping up with legislation affecting regulatory policy, ensuring the drug company meets new regulations, and working with the marketing function to make sure the message sent to consumers is consistent with federal compliance requirements. Careers in this function often require extensive reading and writing skills, as well as enthusiasm toward activities that protect both the company and the consuming public.

Biopharma Sales and Marketing

Most companies consider sales and marketing to be one function, but with two basic areas of activity. Within the sales function, you can typically find three career tracks: field sales, sales management and managed markets. A fourth track, sales training, is closely associated with sales and is distinct from the broader training and development function, which is usually associated with human resource departments. Sales training groups bridge the sales and marketing function: in some companies, they are considered part of marketing support; and hence, part of the marketing function.

Within the marketing function are two main areas of activity: marketing management and marketing support. Marketing management is responsible for introducing products and managing product life cycles. Marketing support is an umbrella-like term that incorporates several distinct groups, some of which are quite large, but all of which serve essentially the same purpose: to provide support services for marketing managers. Depending on the size of the company, the distinction between the two areas may be either blurred or nonexistent. Typical marketing support groups include training and development, advertising and promotion, market analysis, customer call center, e-business, and commercialization and strategic planning.

Fully integrated Big Biotech companies have their own sales and marketing infrastructure and essentially the same job classifications with the same responsibilities. Unlike some of their Big Pharma cousins, biotech sales reps are specialty reps, who market products to specific and highly defined patients groups. For example, biotech sales reps promote specialty injectable protein products to specialist physicians (such as oncologists), who are treating a narrowly defined condition. This focus contrasts sharply with those Big Pharma reps promoting traditional pharmaceuticals to non-specialist physicians (primary care doctors, internists) providing general medical care to the mass market.

Most companies require some experience in pharmaceutical sales before permitting someone to move into specialty sales. That's a significant factor in charting your career. Both Big Pharma companies as well as biotechs can have specialty products. The distinction is that biotech products are exclusively specialty products, whereas Big Pharma—which has a broader product offering—has products targeted at primary care physicians and products aimed at specialists.

This is a good time to think about a career in biopharmaceutical sales and marketing, since more biotech-based drugs are moving through the development pipeline. In addition, roles in business development often require a foundation in sales (as well as experience in several other functions). Once hired, many companies encourage valued employees to gain such experience, and incorporate lateral moves in annual career development plans. This is important to know at the outset, since it will help you evaluate the opportunities available in sales and marketing.

Field sales

A position in field sales is the entry-level job in the sales function. The main purpose of the field sales force is to promote the company's products to customers—typically solo or small-practice groups of physicians—within an assigned geographic territory. Reps are carefully selected, trained rigorously and equipped with detailed product information. They should know their products inside out and work hard to understand the medical science on which those products are based. Within field sales are two areas, territory sales and specialty sales.

The entry-level field sales positions are pharmaceutical sales representative and territory sales representative. The next rung is medical specialist or hospital specialist. Specialty sales representatives are the most experienced, often with several years of direct sales under their belt. This job exists in both Big Biotech and Big Pharma companies. The responsibilities of a pharmaceutical sales rep are well defined across the industry and fall into three distinct areas of activity. Selling is the main responsibility, and requires reps to sell the company's products within the assigned territory, make product presentations, arrange educational meetings for physicians, and co-promote products (when the company has made co-marketing deals with another company).

Administrative responsibilities require reps to manage the selling process (i.e., prioritize their physician and pharmacy customer lists, take notes on call outcomes, prepare reports to district manager), attend company meetings, manage time effectively by working out optimal sales call schedules, work out territory logistics with team members, maintain expense logs, arrange for catering for lunchtime seminars with medical specialists, organize promotional materials and drug samples, and maintain the company car.

Professional development responsibilities require reps to learn features, benefits and basic medical science of assigned products; learn about competing products and their advantages or disadvantages relative to the company's own product; attend professional development training sessions; complete required online training programs; and master selling process and continually refine selling skills.

Generally speaking, cash compensation comprises salary plus bonuses. Total cash compensation for entry-level sales reps typically ranges from roughly $44,000 to $73,000.

Marketing management

Marketing management is where marketing strategy is formulated and implemented, new products are introduced, and existing-product lifecycles are managed. Until recent years, the marketing function was vertically integrated, meaning that a single-ladder existed for reaching senior positions. It was theoretically possible to begin a career as an entry-level marketing associate, and several decades later, achieve senior executive VP for marketing. Some Big Pharma companies are still organized this way.

Yet with Big Pharma companies merging into mega-companies, some companies have opted to organize therapeutic areas and their associated products into separate business units, so that marketing management decisions get made with fewer layers of oversight and with closer contact with customer physicians and targeted patient groups. In this organizational model, therapeutic areas (e.g., oncology drugs, cardiovascular drugs, anti-hypertensives) and the products associated with them become wholly integrated business units. Most Big Biotech companies have opted to follow the second model, since their more-targeted products are best delivered via smaller organizations.

The main job title in marketing management (consistent throughout the industry) is product manager. A product manager's responsibilities fall into two main categories, management and administration. The product manager must develop and manage the short term product strategy and marketing plans for assigned products, oversee development of business plans, specify the positioning of a product among its competitors, monitor those competitors' products, acquire both a quantitative and intuitive feel for customer needs, and act as an in-house champion for a product or brand. Administratively, product

Visit Vault at www.vault.com for insider company profiles, expert advice, career message boards, expert resume reviews, the Vault Job Board and more.

VAULT CAREER LIBRARY   431

managers must develop budgets, maintain records of expenses, and manage and develop entry-level support staff (e.g., market research analysts, marketing associates, undergraduate interns and co-op students).

In companies where therapeutic areas and associated products are organized as business units, product managers effectively become mini-CEOs, involved in virtually every aspect of getting a product to market. Product managers should also have substantial communication and negotiation skills, as they are required to interact with professionals from every part of the organization. Total compensation for marketing product managers ranges from $62,000 to $109,000, depending on the manager's level of experience.

Interviewing at pharmaceutical companies

Regardless of their position and department, most employees at pharmaceutical companies say they endured several rounds of interviews. Typically, people have more interviews for higher-level positions than entry-level ones. Interviewers usually ask a combination of questions about applicants' backgrounds, interests and why they want to work at the company. Applicants for research jobs are sometimes asked to give a presentation of their past work. For some positions, applicants have tests in addition to interviews.

Most pharmaceutical company employees say interview questions tend to be straightforward. An employee at Bayer says the interview included queries like "why are you looking?" and "what can you do for Bayer?" One insider at Bristol Myers Squibb says, "The interview questions asked most are typical. What was your greatest achievement? What are your strengths and weaknesses? What do you like least about the company and what do you like the most? Where can you see yourself in five years?" Scenario-based questions are also common. For example, the employee at BMS was also asked to talk about handling a difficult situation. Another BMS insider says the most memorable question was "Describe three features you like about yourself the most and the least." One scientist at J&J says, "Questions were about my personality, what were my qualities, examples of situations where I helped in the solution of problems, how I dealt with pressure and examples. Also, there were questions about my education and experience: specific skills and knowledge."

If you're applying for a sales job, also be ready to talk about the company's products. One Amgen insider says, "I was asked what I thought I could contribute to the Amgen team, and what specific knowledge I had of Amgen products." Sometimes interviewers will also want to see you in action. One sales rep at Eli Lilly explains, "It isn't uncommon for someone to pick up something off the desk and ask you to sell it to them."

The future of pharmaceuticals

Many pharmaceutical companies have downsized, especially in areas such as sales, during recent years. In early 2007, Pfizer CEO Jeffrey Kindler said the company was cutting 10,000 positions worldwide. A month later, AstraZeneca announced that it would cut that firm's global workforce by more than 4 percent. As discussed above, many pharmaceutical companies are outsourcing research and development to CROs, and this trend is likely to continue in coming years.

Overall, however, things bode well for people who are interested in working for pharmaceutical companies. The U.S. Department of Health and Human Services expects prescription drug spending to increase to $497.5 billion by 2016, a 148 percent increase from 2005, when prescription drug spending in the U.S. was about $200 billion. Moreover, the U.S. Bureau of Labor Statistics projects that the number of jobs in pharmaceutical and medicine manufacturing will increase by about 24 percent between 2006 and 2016. This makes it one of the fastest growing manufacturing industries. The bureau adds that, even if there's an economic downturn, the market for pharmaceuticals is likely to remain strong. The Bureau of Labor Statistics also projects that employment for medical researchers will grow much faster than other occupations.

Life on the Job: Pharma Sales Rep

The sales rep profiled here promotes general therapeutic products and has been on the job long enough to have earned at least one promotion. Note the nursing degree and how, combined with communication skills, it translates into an attractive base salary.

Name of position	Pharmaceutical Executive Sales Representative
Function	Sales
Education level	Hospital Diploma RN; BS, Communications
Company type and size	Large, public, international pharmaceuticals company
Typical number of hours per week	45-50 hours
Salary range	$60K to $120K base; bonus: based on meeting and exceeding market share goals (from $5K per quarter); bonuses are uncapped.
Perks	Stock options, tied to bonus structure—top 10 percent will be rewarded with extra stock; each year the top 25 percent of sales reps are part of the Winner's Circle, get special prizes and vacations; company car and associated expenses (insurance and mileage)

Responsibilities

I am responsible for maintaining and growing the market share of my products. I'm given a list of target physicians in my territory and am expected to see eight to 10 physicians per day. Through data provided by the marketing department, I know exactly what an MD is prescribing before going in to see him. I do both pre- and post-call planning. I am also expected to do business analysis—i.e., to maintain lists of market growth forms to figure out where our growth is and where our growth potential is.

I work in a team—there are two other reps at my level. Three geographies work for the same district sales manager—that's a total of nine reps and one or two specialty reps. I have to coordinate with teammates to determine the tactics for approaching an MD. Our team works out a routing schedule, with three-week rotations. So, for any given week, I know exactly where to go. I schedule lunches in the week where I'm going to be in that town.

I am also expected to go to two pharmacies per day—to see what they have back-ordered and what continuing education they have. I usually do a pharmacy call in the morning, since the pharmacist is not likely to be busy during that time frame. That knocks one call out of the way. It also kind of gets your mouth in gear.

I also do a lot of continuing education, much of which happens over lunch. We usually have two or three lunches per week. We provide lunch for the entire staff, since they receive the education. Finally, we have special projects—such as arranging dinner meetings with physicians, nurses and other health care professionals to provide forums where specialists can talk with each other.

Success criteria

The most important success criteria are being flexible and being able to get along with people. Don't get crushed when they say no. See it as an opportunity to work on the problem—to let the situation evolve. So good people skills is a crucial asset.

You also have to have an ability to grasp medical knowledge—to be able to talk to a doctor. If he/she switches gears and talks about an area outside the product's field, you have to be able to converse with him/her.

Being a nurse, I've learned to figure out what a physician really needs, instead of what he says he needs. You have to be perceptive, to learn to read people. I can sense when a very nice physician is tense or not in a position to talk to me. It's not

Visit Vault at www.vault.com for insider company profiles, expert advice, career message boards, expert resume reviews, the Vault Job Board and more.

VAULT CAREER LIBRARY   433

about my agenda, but theirs. Then I just say, "This doesn't seem like a good time to talk. I'll be back another day and we can talk then." They're usually very appreciative and positively disposed to talk to me the next time I call on them.

A typical day

7:45 a.m.	Leave home; drive to first call; do pre-call planning
8:45 a.m. to 12 p.m.	Pharmacy visit Physician office visits
12 p.m. to 2 pm	Offices closed; lunch with staff and/or physicians; great chance to talk to them; catch up on computer work; file reports. Call in specialist to an office to talk about important issues (e.g., latest post-launch data on adverse effects or ongoing clinical results for drugs in development)
2 p.m. to 5 p.m.	Pharmacy visit Physician office visits
5 p.m. to 6:30 p.m.	Evening event set up; usually one per month: this involves making sure the meeting room is ready (e.g., slide projector, easel for note pad, writing implements, refreshments)
6:30 p.m. to 9 p.m.	Host evening event: this involves introducing the speaker(s), moderating the meeting, and making a presentation of how my company's product fits into the disease state that the physician experts are discussing
9 p.m.	Follow up on the computer at home to complete post-call planning (e.g., write up notes, document questions and responses, identify outstanding issues and queries, special needs)

Uppers and downers

Uppers	Downers
• It's not a 9-to-5 job. It's an independent lifestyle. • We all carry the same products and the same compensation, so that makes teamwork and collaboration very easy. • We're very well taken care of. We stay in nice places and the bonus structure adds incentives to our work.	• It can be lonely. You don't have an office to go to. It's pretty much you driving around all day. You don't have that office camaraderie except when we have big meetings, and that can be kind of weird. The people at the physician offices can become your family. Sometimes I bring Christmas party food and share it at a doctor's office. There are some physicians with whom you develop great rapport. • Getting organized enough can be hard for some people. Some companies have networked computers that can keep track of when you are making your calls, so if you don't get started until late, that could become a problem. • Access is difficult; a lot of physicians don't have a lot of time. Five minutes apiece and 15 reps a day can add over an extra hour to the physician's day!

Advice for job seekers

Get sales experience, especially in consumer products. Develop an understanding of the industry and its foremost issues to show the interviewer that you understand the challenges you will be facing. Also research the job and practice your responses to anticipated questions out loud. That will help you understand where you need to become more polished.

Employer Directory

Abbott
100 Abbott Park Road
Abbott Park, IL 60064
Phone: (847) 937-6100
Fax: (847) 937-1511
www.abbott.com

Acambis PLC
Peterhouse Technology Park
100 Fulbourn Road
Cambridge CB1 9PT
United Kingdom
Phone: +44-12-23-27-53-00
Fax: +44-12-23-41-63-00
www.acambis.com

Allergan, Inc.
2525 Dupont Drive
Irvine, CA 92612
Phone: (714) 246-4500
Fax: (714) 246-4971
www.allergan.com

Amgen, Inc.
One Amgen Center Drive
Thousand Oaks, CA 91320-1799
Phone: (805) 447-1000
Fax: (805) 447-1010
www.amgen.com

Amylin Pharmaceuticals, Inc.
9360 Towne Centre Drive
San Diego, CA 92121
Phone: (858) 552-2200
Fax: (858) 552-2212
www.amylin.com

Applera Corporation
301 Merritt 7
P.O. Box 5435
Norwalk, CT 06856-5435
Phone: (203) 840-2000
Fax: (203) 840-2312
www.applera.com

AstraZeneca PLC
15 Stanhope Gate
London, W1K 1LN
United Kingdom
Phone: +44-20-73-04-50-00
Fax: +44-20-73-04-51-83
www.astrazeneca.com

Barr Pharmaceuticals, Inc.
223 Quaker Road
Pomona, NY 10970
Phone: (845) 362-1100
Fax: (845) 362-2774
www.barrlabs.com

Baxter International, Inc.
1 Baxter Parkway
Deerfield, IL 60015-4625
Phone: (847) 948-2000
Fax: (847) 948-2016
www.baxter.com

Bayer AG
Bayerwerk, Gebäude W11
Kaiser-Wilhelm-Allee
51368 Leverkusen
Germany
Phone: +49-214-30-1
Fax: +49-214-30-66328
www.bayer.de

Becton, Dickinson and Company
One Becton Drive
Franklin Lakes, NJ 07147-1880
Phone: (201) 847-6800
Fax: (201) 847-6475
www.bd.com

Biogen Idec Inc.
14 Cambridge Center
Cambridge, MA 02142
Phone: (617) 679-2000
Fax: (617) 679-2617
www.biogenidec.com

Boehringer Ingelheim corporation
Binger Strasse 173
55216 Ingelheim
Germany
Phone: +49-6132-770
Fax: +49-6132-720
www.boehringer-ingelheim.com

Celgene Corporation
86 Morris Avenue
Summit, NJ 07901
Phone: (908) 673-9000
www.celgene.com

Cephalon, Inc.
41 Moores Road
Frazer, PA 19355
Phone: (610) 344-0200
Fax: (610) 738-6590
www.cephalon.com

Charles River Laboratories International, Inc.
251 Ballardvale Street
Wilmington, MA 01887-1000
Phone: (978) 658-6000
Fax: (978) 658-7132
www.criver.com

Covance
210 Carnegie Center
Princeton, NJ 08540
Phone: (609) 452-4440
Fax: (609) 452-9375
Toll free: (888) 268-2623
www.covance.com

Eli Lilly and Company
Lilly Corporate Center
893 South Delaware
Indianapolis, IN 46285
Phone: (317) 276-2000
Fax: (317) 277-6579
www.lilly.com

Visit Vault at **www.vault.com** for insider company profiles, expert advice,
career message boards, expert resume reviews, the Vault Job Board and more.

VAULT CAREER LIBRARY   435

Employer Directory, cont.

Exelixis, Inc.
170 Harbor Way
South San Francisco, CA 94083
Phone: (650) 837-7000
Fax: (650) 837-8300
www.exelixis.com

Forest Laboratories
909 3rd Avenue
New York, NY 10022
Phone: (212) 421-7850
Fax: (212) 750-9152
www.frx.com

Genentech, Inc.
1 DNA Way
South San Francisco, CA 94080
Phone: (650) 225-1000
Fax: (650) 225-6000
www.gene.com

Genzyme Corporation
500 Kendall Street
Cambridge, MA 02142
Phone: (617) 252-7500
Fax: (617) 252-7600
www.genzyme.com

Gilead Sciences, Inc.
333 Lakeside Drive
Foster City, CA 94404
Phone: (650) 574-3000
Fax: (650) 578-9264
www.gilead.com

GlaxoSmithKline
980 Great West Road, Brentford
London, TW8 9GS
United Kingdom
Phone: +44-20-80-47-50-00
Fax: +44-20-80-47-78-07
www.gsk.com

Hospira, Inc.
275 North Field Drive
Lake Forest, IL 60045
Phone: (224) 212-2000
Fax: (224) 212-3350
Toll free: (877) 946-7747
www.hospira.com

Human Genome Sciences, Inc.
14200 Shady Grove Road
Rockville, MD 20850
Phone: (301) 309-8504
Fax: (301) 309-8512
www.hgsi.com

ImmunoGen, Inc.
128 Sidney Street
Cambridge, MA 02139
Phone: (617) 995-2500
Fax: (617) 995-2510
www.immunogen.com

Incyte Corporation
Experimental Station
Route 141 & Henry Clay Road
Building E336
Wilmington, DE 19880
Phone: (302) 498-6944
Fax: (302) 425-2707
www.incyte.com

Infinity Pharmaceuticals, Inc.
780 Memorial Drive
Cambridge, MA 02139
Phone: (617) 453-1000
Fax: (617) 453-1001
www.ipi.com

Inspire Pharmaceuticals, Inc.
4222 Emperor Boulevard, Suite 200
Durham, NC 27703-8466
Phone: (919) 941-9777
Fax: (919) 941-9797
www.inspirepharm.com

Invitrogen Corporation
1600 Faraday Avenue
Carlsbad, CA 92008
Phone: (760) 603-7200
Fax: (760) 602-6500
www.invitrogen.com

Johnson & Johnson Inc.
1 Johnson & Johnson Plaza
New Brunswick, NJ 08933
Phone: (732) 524-0400
Fax: (732) 524-3300
www.jnj.com

King Pharmaceuticals
501 Fifth Street
Bristol, TN 37620
Phone: (423) 989-8000
Fax: (423) 274-8677
www.kingpharm.com

Laboratory Corporation of America Holdings
358 South Main Street
Burlington, NC 27215
Phone: (336) 229-1127
Fax: (336) 436-1205
www.labcorp.com

Lexicon Pharmaceuticals, Inc.
8800 Technology Forest Place
The Woodlands, TX 77381-1160
Phone: (281) 863-3000
Fax: (281) 863-8088
www.lexpharma.com

McKesson Corporation
1 Post Street
San Francisco, CA 94104
Phone: (415) 983-8300
Fax: (415) 983-7160
www.mckesson.com

Merck & Co., Inc.
One Merck Drive
P.O. Box 100
Whitehouse Station, NJ 08889
Phone: (908) 423-1000
Fax: (908) 735-1253
www.merck.com

Millennium Pharmaceuticals, Inc.
40 Landsdown Street
Cambridge, MA 02139
Phone: (617) 679-7000
Fax: (617) 374-7788
www.mlnm.com

Employer Directory, cont.

Monsanto Company
800 North Lindbergh Boulevard
St. Louis, MO 63137
Phone: (314) 694-1000
Fax: (314) 694-8394
www.monsanto.com

Mylan Inc.
1500 Corporate Drive, Suite 400
Canonsburg, PA 15317
Phone: (724) 514-1800
Fax: (724) 514-1870
www.mylan.com

Novartis AG
Lichtstrasse 35
CH-4056 Basel
Switzerland
Phone: +41-61-324-1111
Fax: +41-61-324-8001
www.novartis.com

Novo Nordisk A/S
Novo Allé
2880 Bagsværd
Denmark
Phone: +45-4444-8888
Fax: +45-4449-0555

Nuvelo, Inc.
201 Industrial Road, Suite 310
San Carlos, CA 94070-6211
Phone: (650) 517-8000
Fax: (650) 517-8001
www.nuvelo.com

Perrigo Company
515 Eastern Avenue
Allegan, MI 49010
Phone: (269) 673-8451
Fax: (269) 673-9128
www.perrigo.com

Pfizer Inc.
235 East 42nd Street
New York, NY 10017
Phone: (212) 573-2323
Fax: (212) 573-7851
www.pfizer.com

Quintile Transnational Corp.
4709 Creekstone Drive, Suite 200
Durham, NC 27703
Phone: (919) 998-2000
Fax: (919) 998-9113
www.qtrn.com

Roche Group
Grenzacherstrasse 124
CH-4070 Basel
Switzerland
Phone: +41-61-688-1111
Fax: +41-61-691-9391
www.roche.com

Sanofi-Aventis
174 Avenue de France
Paris 75013
France
Phone: +33-1-53-77-40-00
Fax: +33-1-53-77-42-96
www.sanofi-aventis.com

Schering-Plough Corporation
2000 Galloping Hill Road
Kenilworth, NJ 07033
Phone: (908) 298-4000
Fax: (908) 298-7653
www.schering-plough.com

Shire PLC
Hampshire International Business Park
Chineham, Basingstoke
Hampshire RG24 8EP
United Kingdom
Phone: +44-1256-894-000
Fax: +44-1256-894-708
www.shire.com

Takeda Pharmaceutical Company Limited
1-1, Doshomachi 4-chome
Chuo-ku, Osaka 540-8645
Japan
Phone: +81-6-6204-2111
Fax: +81-6-6204-2880
www.takeda.com

Teva Pharmaceutical Industries Limited
5 Basel Street
Petach, Tikva 49131
Israel
Phone: +972-3-926-7267
Fax: +972-3-923-4050
www.tevapharm.com

UCB S.A.
60 Allée de la Recherche
B-1070, Brussels
Belgium
Phone: +32-2-559-9999
Fax: +32-2-559-9900
www.ucb-group.com

Vectura Group PLC
One Prospect West
Chippenham, Wiltshire SN14 6FH
United Kingdom
Phone: +44-12-4966-7700
Fax: +44-12-4966-7701
www.vectura.com

Verenium Corporation
55 Cambridge Parkway
Cambridge, MA 02142
Phone: (617) 674-5300
www.verenium.com

Watson Pharmaceuticals, Inc.
311 Bonnie Circle
Corona, CA 92880
Phone: (951) 493-5300
Fax: (973) 355-8301
www.watsonpharm.com

Wyeth
5 Giralda Farms
Madison, NJ 07940
Phone: (973) 660-5000
Fax: (973) 660-7026
www.wyeth.com

Visit Vault at www.vault.com for insider company profiles, expert advice, career message boards, expert resume reviews, the Vault Job Board and more.

VAULT CAREER LIBRARY   437

Public Relations

What is PR?

It's hard to give an all-encompassing definition of public relations because it is practiced in so many different ways for various people and organizations. Merriam-Webster's dictionary defines public relations, also known as PR, as "the business of inducing the public to have understanding for and goodwill toward a person, firm or institution." PR includes publicity, press agentry, book publicity, propaganda (for the government), corporate communications, crisis management and advertising.

Like advertising, the concept of "public relations" existed long before today. Socrates is said to have remarked that "the way to a good reputation is to endeavor to be what you desire to appear." In "Ecclesiastes," the *Bible* says, "Have regard for your name, since it will remain for you longer than a store of gold." But the business as we know it today was born at the end of World War I. In a nutshell, PR is chiefly concerned with image management, and it is meant to help individuals, corporations, governments and other organizations communicate effectively with the public.

The term "public" can suggest many different groups. For a corporation, it can mean employees, shareholders, environmental groups or the government. For an individual, it could mean voters, fans or an entire community. PR professionals deal with perception, representation and effective communication. For example, they help employers communicate with employees, customers to understand the companies that serve them and citizens to understand the politicians who serve their communities. At the same time, PR agents analyze trends—they study existing social attitudes and advise their clients about how they can win the support of the "publicis." In some cases, the PR agent tries to shape the attitudes of the general population so that they will respond in a positive way. At its best, PR presents a true image of reality to the public, and facilitates an effective, honest dialogue. But at the core of it all, PR professionals' job is to present their clients to the public in a favorable light, which is why people tend to associate PR with "spin."

Public Relations History

A little background

Though publicity and press agentry (essentially getting clients' names into newspapers) were common in the 19th century, PR as we know it is generally considered to be a 20th century phenomenon. It was born during a period of increasing hostility toward big business. Early in the 20th century, investigative reporters began exposing the rampant corruption of corporate America. Among the most popular of these journalists' exposes were Ida Tarbell's *History of the Standard Oil Company* and Upton Sinclair's *The Jungle*. The honors depicted in the latter sparked the creation of the Federal Food and Drugs Act in 1906. In response to the scrutiny, corporations began taking steps to improve their reputations. Several railroad companies retained ex-journalists and ex-press agents to handle publicity issues. The Publicity Bureau, founded in 1900, was retained by railroad companies and other businesses that feared they were next in line for legislation. Soon thereafter, a few other publicity agencies popped up, and several organizations, including the United States Marine Corps and the University of Pennsylvania, set up their own publicity offices.

During World War I, the government began using PR extensively. In 1917, President Wilson endorsed the creation of the Committee on Public Information (CPI). Led by George Creel, the CPI was staffed by several budding architects of the PR industry, including Edward Bernays and Carl Byoir. There they learned, according to the Museum of Public Relations, that "words could be used as weapons." To gain public support for the war effort, encourage enlistment and sell Liberty Bonds, the CPI organized public rallies, reached out to non-English speaking men eligible for the draft and created newsreel announcements to urge people to contribute to the war effort.

Visit Vault at **www.vault.com** for insider company profiles, expert advice, career message boards, expert resume reviews, the Vault Job Board and more.

VAULT CAREER LIBRARY 439

The "Father of Spin"

Many of today's major PR firms began in the period directly following the war, and the founders of those firms laid the basic groundwork of the industry. The business as we know it was largely the brainchild of Edward Bernays, the fabled "Father of Spin." The nephew of Sigmund Freud, Bernays is said to have inherited the famed psychoanalyst's knack for understanding human behavior. He also possessed a trait critical to the PR business—the ability to anticipate changes in public opinion. Early in his career, he worked as a press agent for the theater. As a member of the CPI, he helped sell the war as an effort to "Make the World Safe for Democracy." In 1919, Bernays set up shop in New York, calling himself a "public relations counselor," and handled communications and marketing-related "persuasion projects" for clients, including the U.S. War Department and the American Tobacco Company.

The "Father of Spin" published the first book on the PR profession, *Crystallizing Public Opinion*, in 1922. Bernays felt that the average man was an intellectually limited, conformist creature, so it was up to the intellectual elite to mold public opinion. He believed that the so-called "intelligent few" were essentially social scientists who could guide the masses and influence history by applying the theories of mass psychology to corporate and political agendas. Not surprisingly, both Adolf Hitler and Spain's Francisco Franco approached Bernays for counsel (he turned both down). An Austrian-born Jew, Bernays reportedly lamented the fact that Joseph Goebbels, the notorious Nazi, kept a copy of *Crystallizing Public Opinion* on his desk.

Bernays pioneered the practice of promoting corporate agendas through social causes. In his own words, he helped his clients "create events and circumstances from which favorable publicity would stem." To that end, he developed "public service" agendas for unnamed corporate sponsors. After WWI, for example, he was called upon to help an ailing hair net company. Bernays urged labor commissioners to require women who worked with machinery to wear hair nets for their safety and waitresses to wear them in the interests of hygiene. He never named the hair net company, but sales improved. To help sell another client's bacon, he published a survey of 5,000 doctors who agreed that Americans should eat big breakfasts. He later orchestrated the "Light's Golden Jubilee," a global media event in celebration of the invention of the lightbulb, which General Electric ghost-sponsored.

Further growth

After WWII and throughout the Depression, the PR industry continued to grow. The National Association of Public Relations Counsel (NAPC) was founded in 1936, and the American Council on Public Relations (ACPR) formed in 1939. In 1948, the NAPC and ACPR merged to form the Public Relations Society of America (PRSA), which still exists today. Just as it did during WWI, PR grew considerably during WWII. The federal government created the Office of War Information in 1942 and used PR to develop, support and distribute information. The division was later renamed the United States Information Agency (USIA), which was folded into the State Department in 1999.

In the 1940s and 1950s, Bernays continued to help political leaders use mass persuasion to their advantage. During this period, he wrote the famous *Engineering of Consent*, in which he explained, among other things, the particular usefulness of visual symbols to influence the masses. And while universities and journalism schools had been offering PR courses since 1920 (the first to offer a PR curriculum was the University of Illinois), Boston University created the first school wholly dedicated to public relations in 1947.

Hidden PR professionals

Few people outside the industry have ever heard of Bernays, largely because he was a staunch believer in the hidden yet omnipresent PR professional. For him, the PR counselor is ever the strategist, never the voice. This attitude underlies another of Bernays' innovations—the front organization. For example, in the late 1940s and late 1950s, a newly elected government in Guatemala threatened to take over some of the plantations owned by the United Fruit Company and divide them among the peasants. When Bernays was called in, he set up the Middle America Information Bureau, which was financed by—you guessed it—United Fruit. The bureau disseminated information to American newspapers about communist influences in Guatemala, and soon a CIA-backed rebellion toppled the Guatemalan government.

If you think such tactics are a thing of the past, think again. In the early 1990s, several PR firms became embroiled in ethics controversies. For example, Hill and Knowlton drummed up support for the war against Iraq by creating a group called "Citizens for a Free Kuwait." What became clear later was that the $11 million account was more than 99 percent funded by the exiled Kuwaiti government. More recently, PR firm Edelman formed an organization called Working Families for Wal-Mart. The aim of the organization was to counteract criticisms by groups such as Wal-Mart Watch. A blog called Wal-Marting Across America detailed the travels of a couple named Laura and Jim, who parked their RV for free in the store's parking lots across the country. Everywhere Jim and Laura went, they found happy Wal-Mart employees. In October 2006, *BusinessWeek* writer Pallavi Gogoi revealed that Wal-Mart had paid for the couple's RV and gas, and that it had also paid the pair to write the blog. Although there was a Working Families banner on the site, nowhere did it mention that Wal-Mart had financed Jim and Laura's trip.

Entertainment PR

Henry Rogers, known as the master of entertainment PR, created the industry by launching his own publicity firm in 1936. Rogers is credited with setting many ethical and creative standards for the PR profession, and he is often recognized for bringing respect to the industry. In 1939, he helped make the then-unknown Rita Hayworth a household name by convincing a magazine editor to do a story on her. In 1945, Rogers launched the first full-scale Oscar publicity blitz, which helped Joan Crawford win the award for Best Actress. That campaign set a standard followed by studios and actors to this day. Within five years, Rogers became one of the most successful independent PR agents in Hollywood. In 1950, he teamed up with Warren Cowan to create Rogers and Cowan, the largest entertainment PR agency in the world. Now a division of the Interpublic Group, R&C later expanded to serve corporate clients as well as motion picture, television and recording stars.

Creating an industry

From the 1950s on, PR has built upon the foundation laid by Bernays, Rogers and a few other PR notables. Daniel Edelman founded his eponymous Chicago-based firm in the 1950s, as did Harold Burson and Bill Marsteller (today their firm is one of the largest in the business). By the late 1980s, there were more than 2,000 PR agencies in the U.S. alone, and many more around the world. All the major U.S. agencies have foreign outposts, most of which are staffed and run by local residents. Currently, many PR firms are expanding into Europe and Asia, especially China and India, and seeing great growth in these areas. Edelman, for example, saw a 32 percent revenue increase in China during 2006. In May 2007, Fleishman-Hillard opened an office in Mumbai, India. Ogilvy recently bought a firm in Düsseldorf, and GolinHarris opened an office in Jakarta.

PR has essentially created a distinction between reality and what is presented by the media. Most people don't realize that many of the stories presented in newspapers, magazines and on TV are essentially planted by PR people. Reporters don't just go out every day and look for the news—they find much of their information in press releases prepared by PR professionals. PR agents spend a lot of time brainstorming ideas that relate to their clients and calling up journalists to pitch them. And usually, when journalists review products, it's because publicity agents send them samples and hope to get a story or a mention. Some PR firms even create video news releases (VNRs) and send them to television stations. Media outlets often broadcast portions of VNRs or just don't use them at all. In March 2005, however, The New York Times criticized television networks' affiliates for running VNRs from various government agencies without editing them or telling the public the source of the information.

Not surprisingly, the image-making industry has a negative reputation of its own. Even though many PR professionals are ex-journalists, press releases are considered the stepchildren of journalism. This may change, however, as more journalism

Visit Vault at **www.vault.com** for insider company profiles, expert advice,
career message boards, expert resume reviews, the Vault Job Board and more.

VAULT CAREER LIBRARY   441

and communications graduates choose to pass on lower newspaper and magazine salaries in favor of better-paid gigs in PR. Additionally, PR offers greater management potential, the chance to learn business skills and the opportunity to apply those skills to other industries.

The Publication Relations Society of America has established a code of ethics for the organization's members. The society says the core values of public relations include advocacy, honesty, expertise, independence, loyalty and fairness. PRSA members promise to "serve the public interest by acting as responsible advocates" of those they represent.

While PR professionals uphold the fact that their major objective is to merge the client's interest with the public interest, it's important to remember that in the end the clients are writing the checks. Even Bernays, by the end of his life, believed that the PR business had taken a turn for the worst. PR professionals constantly cite the need to uphold ethical standards within the industry, and PR gaffes from none other than the leading figures in the industry have caused the industry to continue to suffer from image problems.

The greening of public relations

During the fall of 2007, two large PR firms—Fleishman-Hillard and GolinHarris—announced "worldwide sustainability practices." Other large PR agencies including Edelman, CGI Group, Weber Shandwick and Ogilvy, have also set up practices focusing on sustainability. In addition to publicizing other companies' green initiatives, some PR firms have also made efforts to improve their own environmental practices. For example, in March 2007, MWW Group announced that it was launching an agencywide campaign to make MWW a "green company." The campaign includes initiatives to conserve energy and reduce waste. MWW also partnered with Carbonfund.org, a nonprofit organization, to contribute to projects that will offset the firm's carbon footprint. Weber Shandwick's London headquarters recently received ISO 14,001 environmental certification in recognition of the firm's procedures and policies. The agency's London office has done things like set printers so that the default is double-sided, which helps save paper. It also switched to a taxi company that offsets carbon emissions.

PR 3.0

PR firms' public relations efforts are no longer confined to print media and television. Today many PR professionals also utilize online media. For example, a September 2007 article in *The New York Times* describes how book publicists are increasingly using blogs for author "appearances." And book publicists aren't the only PR professionals who are using blogs and other forms of digital media. For example, Edelman is involved in a public relations effort for the city of Des Moines, Iowa, which attempts to get more people to "give Iowa a try." The campaign uses campy video clips, which are posted on sites such as YouTube and AOL Video, to try to reach younger audiences.

Candice Huang, a PR professional with a technology PR firm in California, says, "In my company, lots of people use social networking sites, such as LinkedIn, to build and expand contacts. Sometimes we find new business leads there and invite people who we already established relationships with to the site to continue dialogues in a timely manner." Huang adds, "People in tech PR seem to be pretty comfortable new social networking tools." Andrew Careaga, director of communications at Missouri University of Science and Technology, says that public relations and marketing people at colleges and universities have also been trying to do some things in online media. Careaga explains, "Everyone is trying to figure out how to use social networking to get the word out."

In 2007, a survey of the Council of Public Relations Firms' members found that 84 percent of firms were "actively engaged in the blogosphere on behalf of clients," and PRWeek says that one of the biggest trends in the industry is a rise in social media. As is the case in the advertising industry, public relations professionals have been using online communities such as Second Life, Facebook and YouTube more frequently. Social media capabilities have come to be viewed as a necessity, and expertise in digital media gives agencies a competitive advantage in pitches. Many PR firms have started to use digital practices more regularly. Brodeur now uses blogs with more of the firm's clients, and some of the larger agencies—including

Edelman, Weber Shandwick and Fleishman—have social media shops. *PRWeek* adds, "Both smaller and larger firms essentially are both identifying and establishing, officially or unofficially, a core group of staffers to serve as futurists to track social and digital media innovation."

Breaking Down Public Relations

Public relations practitioners are advocates for business, nonprofits, governments and other organizations to help those entities better communicate with the public. Their primary role is to understand the world around them, anticipating trends that will affect their clients or the organization they represent. Those attracted to the industry are generally strategic thinkers who enjoy the challenge of crafting a message to meet the communications goals of an organization. Of course, there's no denying that schmoozing is a must in this industry; convincing journalists to write about your client is a talent unto itself.

In public relations, careers generally follow one of two tracks. People can work at either a public relations firm or in PR for a company or nonprofit organization. The federal and local government, as well as colleges and universities, also hire lots of PR people. Many people who work in public relations for government agencies or nonprofits believe strongly in the mission of the organization or agency. Careaga says of higher education marketing, "It's not necessarily the highest paying, but you get to tell stories about creative, eccentric people. And it's energizing to work in an institution that has a mission of education."

It's more common now for PR professionals to shift back and forth between firms and in-house PR over the course of their careers. On the agency side, or internally at a company, public relations professionals help organizations better understand how the marketplace perceives them, and how to best relate to its various shareholders, including its employees, customers, stockholders and anyone else with a vested interest in the company. Developing and maintaining a wide variety of relationships is another crucial responsibility of a public relations professional.

Breaking into PR

Agencies: The most common route into the public relations field is to join a public relations firm. Firms pitch their communication services to clients ranging from corporations to nonprofit organizations to government agencies. These services include organizing press events, writing press releases, launching new products, publishing, providing "damage control" for corporate missteps or miscommunication, as well as a variety of other strategic support.

Corporate Communications: Also referred to as the "client side" in the public relations world. There are two primary corporate communications roles, media relations and investor relations. Media relations focuses on relationships with media outlets like newspapers and television stations. Investor relations focuses on those shareholders with a financial stake or interest in the company, like stockholders, financial analysts and potential investors. Some senior executives in this field develop and maintain the overall corporate communications strategy.

Publicists: A public relations function in which the communications needs of a single individual, such as an author or other celebrity, is served. One well-known publicist is Stephen Huvane, who has represented clients such as Jennifer Aniston, Helen Hunt, Liv Tyler, Demi Moore and Gwyneth Paltrow. In politics, publicists are referred to as press secretaries. Publicists manage all relations with the media, promote their client's activities (or downplay them in some cases) and manage their public schedule.

So how do you break into the PR biz? Says one top publicist: "Get some internship experience to really understand how PR works and what the job entails. Every type of PR is different, whether it's consumer PR, tech PR, entertainment PR, etc."

Visit Vault at **www.vault.com** for insider company profiles, expert advice, career message boards, expert resume reviews, the Vault Job Board and more.

VAULT CAREER LIBRARY   443

The day-to-day

The public relations industry has grown vastly in scope in the past couple of decades. It has moved beyond simply drafting press releases for the launch of a new product or doing damage control for a corporate entity, tasks most commonly associated with the profession. The practice of public relations has become more and more sophisticated as the media world has grown in complexity. Public relations is not only about generating buzz or maintaining an image, but also about complex strategic communications. Once regarded as "practitioners" crafting communications and messages for press releases, public relations professionals have now widened their scope. Huang says, "PR is becoming a very vital part in any corporation or organization. I like to think of PR professionals as strategists or think tanks. They help identify the current, important issues to the clients and watch for any crisis or significant trends that their clients should know of. For example, Green IT is becoming really big, and it's PR people's job to help their clients understand what it's really all about."

With a growing focus on the business and strategic impact of communications, the industry's role grows more important with every passing day. Careaga from Missouri University of Technology and Science says that, during a typical day, he responds to media requests and works on brochures, but he has lots of meetings with people from different academic departments. He explains, "It's important to touch base with different departments and know what's going on." In addition, the public relations people at the university try to figure out how to promote science and engineering as "fun and exciting."

The most striking difference of public relations, when compared with other sectors of information media, is its lack of a designated distribution channel for its content. In fact, it is dependent on all of the available media outlets to help spread the information it has gathered on behalf of its clients. Public relations practitioners work with journalists at television stations, magazines, newspapers, web sites and radio stations to get their message out. However, while public relations information is gathered to help develop and implement a communications strategy on behalf of a paying client, journalists gather information to be shared with the communities they serve.

So is a PR career for you?

Take a look at the main job responsibilities/skills you'll need for a career in public relations.

Staying Informed: If you have an insatiable appetite for news, you'll love this career. Reading a variety of newspapers every day is a must. Consume information from any and all sources as it relates to your clients or the organization you represent, including the mainstream press, trade magazines, web sites, chat rooms, discussion boards, online newsletters and industry conferences.

Organization: As they say, the devil is in the details! With the massive amount of information you will need to organize, every bit of information is vital, and you will always need to have it at your fingertips. You will also be responsible for organizing meetings, press conferences, panel discussions and other major events.

Communications: The majority of your time will be spent communicating in writing or verbally. There is no better place to learn the art of a well written memo than in public relations. At the very least, a stint in public relations will greatly enhance your communication skills. Huang says, "Writing is essential. Some PR agencies look at your writing samples before they look at your resume. Not everyone is a good writer, so you want to be that really good writer who everyone can go to and count on."

Listening: Probably the most overlooked part of great communications skills. More often than not, misunderstandings can easily be averted by listening first, saving you time and money.

Anticipation: The bulk of public relations used to be focused on reacting to a situation and then developing a response, referred to as "spinning." More and more public relations has now shifted towards thinking ahead and analyzing trends; reducing surprises and developing more effective communication strategies.

A booming business

So what are typical salaries among people in the industry? According to the Public Relations Society of America (PRSA), during 2006, a survey found that the overall median annual salary among public relations professionals was $71,480. The median salary for people working in small companies was $64,460. Employees at medium-sized companies typically earned $66,800, while the median salary for individuals working at larger firms was $82,300. Senior or executive-level employees reported a median salary of $94,800, and managers' median wages were $71,600. In comparison, account executives/PR specialists earned $47,500 and associate/entry-level folks made just $26,000.

Visit Vault at **www.vault.com** for insider company profiles, expert advice, career message boards, expert resume reviews, the Vault Job Board and more.

VAULT CAREER LIBRARY   **445**

Employer Directory

APCO Worldwide Inc.
700 12th Street NW, Suite 800
Washington, DC 20005
Phone: (202) 778-1000
Fax: (202) 466-6002
www.apcoworldwide.com

Brodeur Partners
855 Boylston Street
Boston, MA 02116
Phone: (617) 587-2800
www.brodeur.com

Burson Marsteller
230 Park Avenue South
New York, NY 10003
Phone: (212) 614-4000
www.bm.com/pages/home

Cohn & Wolfe
292 Madison Avenue
New York, NY 10017
Phone: (212) 798-9700
www.cohnwolfe.com

Edelman
200 East Randolph Drive, 63rd Floor
Chicago, IL 60601
Phone: (312) 240-3000
Fax: (312) 240-2900
www.edelman.com

Euro RSCG Worldwide, Inc.
350 Hudson Street
New York, NY 10014
Phone: (212) 886-2000
Fax: (212) 886-2016
www.eurorscg.com

Fleishman-Hillard Inc.
200 North Broadway
St. Louis, MO 63102
Phone: (314) 982-7725
www.fleishman.com

Golin/Harris International
111 East Wacker Drive, 10th Floor
Chicago, IL 60601
Phone: (312) 729-4000
www.golinharris.com

Hill & Knowlton, Inc.
909 3rd Avenue
New York, NY 10022
Phone: (212) 885-0300
Fax: (212) 885-0570
www.hillandknowlton.com

Ketchum Inc.
1285 Avenue of the Americas
New York, NY 10019
Phone: (646) 935-3900
Fax: (646) 935-4499
www.ketchum.com

Manning, Selvage & Lee
1675 Broadway, 9th Floor
New York, NY 10019
Phone: (212) 468-4200
www.mslpr.com

Ogilvy Public Relations Worldwide
825 8th Avenue
World Wide Plaza
New York, NY 10019
Phone: (212) 880-5200
Fax: (212) 370-4636
www.ogilvypr.com

Porter Novelli, Inc.
75 Varick Street, 6th Floor
New York, NY 10013
Phone: (212) 601-8000
Fax: (212) 601-8101
www.porternovelli.com

Publicis Consultants Worldwide
133 Avenue des Champs Elysées
Paris Cedex 8
France
Phone: +33-1-44-43-70-63
Fax: +32-1-44-43-75-11
www.publicis-consultants.com

Qorvis Communications, LLC.
8484 Westpark Drive, Suite 800
McLean, VA 22102
Phone: (703) 744-7800
Fax: (703) 744-7840
www.qorvis.com

Rowland Communications Worldwide, Inc
1675 Broadway, 3rd Floor
New York, NY 10019-5820
Phone: (212) 527-8800
www.rowland.com

The Ruder Finn Group
301 East 57th Street
New York, NY 10022
Phone: (212) 593-6423
www.ruderfinn.com

Schwartz Communications, Inc.
230 Third Avenue
Waltham, MA 02451
Phone: (781) 684-0770
Fax: (781) 684-6500
www.schwartz-pr.com

Waggener Edstrom Worldwide, Inc.
Civica North Tower
225 108th Avennue NE, Suite 700
Bellevue, WA 98004-5737
Phone: (425) 638-7000
Fax: (425) 638-7001
www.wagged.com

Weber Shandwick Worldwide
919 3rd Avenue
New York, NY 10022
Phone: (212) 445-8000
Fax: (212) 445-8001
www.webershandwick.com

Publishing

Industry Overview

Bowker's Books In Print, the authority on book publishing statistics, counted more than 276,649 new titles issued in 2007, and a total of 6.5 million books in print from 72,000 publishers in the U.S. The larger printing houses operate numerous imprints, or labels. Simon & Schuster, for example, has more than 20 between its children's and adult divisions. Furthermore, some publishers are highly specialized, only releasing limited-edition graphic novels, for instance, or books on hotel interiors, and others only issue a handful of volumes per year.

Paperback promotion

Publishers sold 3.1 billion books in 2007, and the market is generally not affected by wide swings in readership. But sales erosion has occurred over time for hardcover books, and best sellers are often less "best" than in the 1990s.

Book publishers now offer a wider range of products than ever before, and do so in a more calculated way. Television and radio spots are created for new books by noted authors like Patricia Cornwell or James Patterson, and nonfiction tomes are visibly promoted on the morning and late-night talk show circuits. Publishers' web sites often contain original content, encourage the development of a community of book-lovers that share their experiences (via blogs and fan reviews), and hook avid bibliophiles with author interviews and special member-only content. Since 2000, audio books are a standard part of many a new release's package, and despite the fact they're about 50 percent more expensive than the print version, have accumulated 5 percent of the "book" market.

The insanely popular teen wizard series from J.K. Rowling continues to drive the children's/young adult market, and the July 2007 release of *Harry Potter and the Deathly Hallows* came with an initial print run of 12 million (10 percent more than the last installment). It comprimises a large part of the estimated 6.5 percent growth in sales (and 9 percent of revenue) for the juvenile segment during the year. Unfortunately for its publisher Scholastic, this will be the last volume in the saga.

For any book that doesn't have "Harry Potter" in its title, bad publicity is often the best publicity. When it was discovered that author James Frey fictionalized most of his best seller, the "nonfiction" autobiographical *A Million Little Pieces* (Doubleday), he appeared on the Oprah Winfrey show in January 2006 to atone (along with his editor, Nan Talese), but sales of the book remained healthy. Oh, and having Oprah Winfrey endorse a book to the devoted members of her book club is nothing less than a surefire way for both author and publisher to strike it rich—no matter if the book is a new title or buried in the back catalog. After all, she gave her stamp of approval to Frey's book just months earlier, bumping its profile and goosing sales on the way to a global total of 3.5 million.

Publishing operations are an eclectic mix of multinational conglomerates, private firms, associations and educational institutions. Below is a list of the industry's largest book publishing employers in the U.S.

Visit Vault at **www.vault.com** for insider company profiles, expert advice, career message boards, expert resume reviews, the Vault Job Board and more.

VAULT CAREER LIBRARY   447

Trade Books	Parent Company and Sales ($mil.)
Random House	Bertelsmann (Germany) $2,649
The Penguin Group	Pearson (UK) $139.7
HarperCollins Publishers	News Corp. (Australia) $165.2
Simon & Schuster	CBS Corporation (US)
Hachette Book Group USA	Lagardère (Fr)
FSG/St. Martin's/Macmillan/Henry Holt	Holtzbrinck (Germany) $170.3
Educational/Professional	
Thomson Reuters	(Canada/UK) $7,296
Reed Elsevier	(UK) $4,584
McGraw-Hill	(US) $6,772.3
Pearson Education	Pearson (UK) $5,073.7
Wolters Kluwer	(Netherlands) $4,872.2
Houghton Mifflin	(US)
John Wiley & Sons	(US) $1,673.7
Children's	
Scholastic	(US) $2,205

*Sources: Hoover's Inc.; corporate web sites   * Includes newspaper and other non-book publishing holdings*

As you can see, ownership is heavily international, with European, Australian and Canadian firms controlling the majority of the well-known American publishing companies. The largest U.S. publishing operations are often units of even larger multinational media conglomerates. Each of these firms has many divisions, and within each of these divisions, there are a number of imprints (sometimes called "lines" or "lists"), which are the publicly used "brand" names for groups of books in a given market, format, and/or genre.

No matter what types of books they produce, however, you'll see the same types of publishing professionals at all of these organizations—editors, marketers, salespeople and production specialists—performing very similar tasks.

Operating units/imprints

The operating units or divisions of book publishing companies are typically organized around their "imprints"—the brand names given to particular product lines. Often imprints specialize in certain genres or areas of interest and have names that reflect their focus. Other times, the imprints are the names of companies that were acquired and have a publishing reputation that the acquiring company wishes to keep alive.

Here are some examples of the nation's largest trade book publishers and the imprints within them.

Trade Book Publishers	Imprints
Random House	Bantam, Doubleday, Dell; Pantheon; Knopf; Ballantine; Fodor's; Crown; Vintage
The Penguin Group	Putnam; Viking; Dutton; Puffin; Dorling Kindersley; Rough Guides
HarperCollins Publishers	HarperCollins; Avon; Perennial; Quill; Zondervan; Ecco; William Morrow
Simon & Schuster	Pocket Books; Free Press; Scribner; Atria Books; Howard Books
Hachette Book Group USA	Little, Brown; Grand Central Publishing; Faith Words; Center Street

Breaking into the Industry

Landing a job as an editorial assistant—also called "starting at the bottom"—is considered the best way into one of these industries. (It's better still to enter publishing and make industry connections via a college or graduate school internship.) It establishes an applicant's dedication to the field, and with the variety of tasks and contacts involved, provides a good method for evaluating possible career paths.

During a typical day at a book publisher, an assistant may handle incoming mail, deal with author contracts, schedule meetings, format manuscripts, track the progress of a book's development and contact book reviewers (academics or other professionals who may read through titles, evaluate the book's potential space in the marketplace, and offer notes on content). An associate- or senior-level editor would be more directly involved with the manuscripts (i.e., read them to find viable projects) and authors (throughout the life of the project, from contract negotiation to book design). And there's always the editing, both for content and for grammatical structure.

Throw some paper up in the air, and see where it lands

It takes a lot of hard work, long hours and dedication to make it in publishing and journalism, but the challenges these industries currently face make personal success a more slippery outcome than at any other time. Book publishers are the least affected by business and technology cycles, but their products do smack up against the widening range of entertainment propositions competing for consumers' time. The more leisurely, thoughtful pursuit of pleasure reading surely pales for some compared to ever-louder movie blockbusters, video games, Internet surfing, mega-feature cell phones and iPods. For all those reasons, advertising for new books needs to be more creative to stand out amongst the noise, and has for some projects—notably the 2006 release of Stephen King's *Cell* (with an elaborate mobile tie-in of ads, audio and original content).

A (long) day in the life

Positions in newspaper publishing are largely focused on editorial, production and marketing/ad sales functions. Increasingly, with the intermingling of print and online centers, entrants to the world of journalism are expected to have some sort of familiarity with online sourcing or publishing in addition to an English or journalism degree. Book and magazine houses also need candidates with good editorial skills and expertise in layout and production. Online and print advertising are still the dominant sources of newspaper revenue, so top sales people are always in demand. (This is also true for publishers of periodicals.) Obviously, book publishers have no need for ad sales people, they're only interested in selling the final product. To do so, there's a need for public relations staff and creative individuals who can come up with inventive ways to market a book with media, internet, mobile or in-store tie-ins.

Visit Vault at www.vault.com for insider company profiles, expert advice, career message boards, expert resume reviews, the Vault Job Board and more.

VAULT CAREER LIBRARY 449

Landing a job as an editorial assistant—also called "starting at the bottom"—is considered the best way into one of these industries. (It's better still to enter publishing and make industry connections via a college or graduate school internship.) It establishes an applicant's dedication to the field, and with the variety of tasks and contacts involved, provides a good method for evaluating possible career paths. During a typical day at a book publisher, an assistant may handle incoming mail, deal with author contracts, schedule meetings, format manuscripts, track the progress of a book's development, and contact book reviewers (academics or other professionals who may read through titles, evaluate the book's potential space in the marketplace, and offer notes on content). An associate- or senior-level editor would be more directly involved with the manuscripts (i.e., read them to find viable projects) and authors (throughout the life of the project, from contract negotiation to book design). And there's always the editing, both for content and for grammatical structure. An editorial position at a magazine or a newspaper publisher would be similar but with more emphasis on meeting deadlines (weekly or daily, as opposed to the more common monthly goals in books), internal organization and leadership. To succeed in one of these capacities, a person's got to love to read—editors often take manuscripts home to read after work or on weekends—and look forward to long, sometimes erratic, working hours. To make up for that, companies often have decent-to-excellent diversity and benefit policies, and perks ranging from product discounts to access to special events and such. But depending on who's running the show, the company environment can range from pleasant to horrible.

People who have interviewed at publishers of any type don't report any tricky questions popped during the interview process. As in any industry, for potential sales personnel, the answer to "On a scale of 1 to 10, how motivated are you to go into sales?" must be answered with a confident "10."

Employer Directory

Bantam Doubleday Dell
1540 Broadway
New York, NY 10036
Phone: (212) 354-6500
www.randomhouse.com/bantamdell

Bauer Publishing U.S.A.
270 Sylvan Avenue
Englewood Cliffs, NJ 07632
Phone: (201) 569-6699
Fax: (201) 569-5303
www.bauerpublishing.com

Bonnier Corporation
460 North Orlando Avenue, Suite 200
Winter Park, FL 32789
Phone: (407) 628-4802
Fax: (407) 628-7061
www.bonniercorp.com

Chronicle Books LLC
680 Second Street
San Francisco, CA 94107
Phone: (415) 537-4200
Fax: (415) 537-4460
www.chroniclebooks.com

Condé Nast Publications Inc.
4 Times Square, 17th Floor
New York, NY 10036
Phone: (212) 286-2860
Fax: (212) 286-5960
www.condenast.com

Cygnus Business Media
1233 Janesville Avenue
Fort Atkinson, WI 53538
Phone: (800) 547-7377
www.cygnusb2b.com

F+W Publications, Inc.
4700 East Galbraith Road
Cincinnati, OH 45236
Phone: (513) 531-2690
Fax: (513) 531-0798
www.fwpublications.com

Hachette Filipacchi Media U.S., Inc.
1633 Broadway
New York, New York 10019
Phone: (212) 767-6000
www.hfmus.com

HarperCollins Publishers, Inc.
10 East 53rd Street
New York, NY 10022
Phone: (212) 207-7000
Fax: (212) 207-7145
www.harpercollins.com

Harvard Business School Publishing
300 North Beacon Street
Watertown, MA 02472
Phone: (617) 783-7400
Fax: (617) 783-7664
www.harvardbusiness.org

The Hearst Corporation
300 West 57th Street
New York, NY 10019
Phone: (212) 649-2000
Fax: (212) 649-2108
www.hearst.com/magazines

Houghton Mifflin Company
222 Berkeley Street
Boston, MA 02116-3764
Phone: (617) 351-5000
Fax: (617) 351-1105
www.hmco.com

Ingram Book Group
1 Ingram Boulevard
La Vergne, TN 37086
Phone: (615) 793-5000
Fax: (615) 287-6990
www.ingrambook.com

John Wiley & Sons, Inc.
111 River Street
Hoboken, NJ 07030
Phone: (201) 748-6000
Fax: (201) 748-6008
www.wiley.com

L.M. Berry and Company
3170 Kettering Boulevard
Dayton, OH 45439
Phone: (937) 296-2121
Fax: (937) 296-2011
www.lmberry.com

Lee Enterprises, Inc.
201 North Harrison Street, Suite 600
Davenport, IA 52801
Phone: (563) 383-2100
Fax: (563) 323-9609

The McGraw-Hill Companies, Inc.
1221 Avenue of the Americas
New York, NY 10020
Phone: (212) 512-2000
Fax: (212) 512-3840
www.mcgraw-hill.com

Pearson PLC
1330 Avenue of the Americas
New York, NY 10019
Phone: (212) 641-2421
Fax: (212) 641-2521
www.pearson.com

The Penguin Group
375 Hudson Street
New York, NY 10014
Phone: (212) 366-2000
Fax: (212) 366-2666
us.penguingroup.com

R.R. Donnelley & Sons Company
111 South Wacker Drive
Chicago, IL 60606
Phone: (312) 326-8000
Fax: (312) 326-7156
www.rrdonnelley.com

Rand McNally & Company
8255 North Central Park Avenue
Skokie, IL 60076
Phone: (847) 329-8100
www.randmcnally.com

Employer Directory, cont.

Random House, Inc.
1745 Broadway
New York, NY 10019
Phone: (212) 782-9000
Fax: (212) 302-7985
www.randomhouse.com

**The Reader's Digest
Association, Inc.**
Reader's Digest Road
Pleasantville, NY 10570
Phone: (914) 238-1000
Fax: (914) 238-4559
www.rd.com

Rodale, Inc.
33 East Minor Street
Emmaus, PA 18098
Phone: (610) 967-5171
Fax: (610) 967-8963
rodale.com

Scholastic Corporation
557 Broadway
New York, NY 10012
Phone: (212) 343-6100
Fax: (212) 343-6934
www.scholastic.com

Simon & Schuster, Inc.
1230 Avenue of the Americas
New York, NY 10020
Phone: (212) 698-7000
Fax: (212) 698-7099
www.simonsays.com

The Thomson Corporation
Metro Center, 1 Station Place
Stamford, CT 06902
Phone: (203) 539-8000
Fax: (203) 539-7734
www.thomson.com

Time Out Group Ltd.
Universal House
251 Tottenham Court Road
London W1T 7AB
United Kingdom
Phone: +44-20-78-13-30-00
Fax: +44-20-78-13-60-01
www.timeout.com

Time, Inc.
1271 Avenue of the Americas
New York, NY 10020-1393
Phone: (212) 522-1212
Fax: (212) 522-0602
www.time.com

**Verlagsgruppe Georg von
Holtbrinck GmbH**
Gänsheidestraße 26
70184 Stuttgart
Germany
Phone: +49-711-2150-0
Fax: +49-711-2150-100
www.holtzbrinck.com

W.W. Norton & Company
500 Fifth Avenue
New York, NY 10110
Phone: (212) 354-5500
Fax: (212) 869-0865
www.wwnorton.com

Real Estate

A concrete business

Real estate is tangible. It's a piece of land and any building or structures on it, as well as the air above and the ground below. Everyone comes into direct contact with real estate; the places where we live, work, vacation, shop and exercise are all assets to be bought, sold and rented. The real estate industry is usually considered one of the most dynamic sectors in the American economy—people may sell their stocks, but they always need a place to buy groceries and somewhere to sleep.

Yes, it's for real

The real estate sector depends on a number of economic factors; small shifts can turn trends significantly. For example, the technology industry boom helped the real estate industry in Silicon Valley in the 1990s. There was more demand for space—both commercial and residential—and asset values skyrocketed. The subsequent technology bust had a dramatic effect on some parts of the sector, too. Commercial real estate firms that deal with office and retail development projects found the market glutted with available space, driving prices down. Residential is affected by economic swings as well, in addition to changes in the federal interest rate (which affects mortgage interest rates) and the unemployment rate (which affects both consumer confidence and buying power). In turn, these have effects on mortgage lenders and housing construction companies (such as Lennar, Pulte Homes, Beazer Homes and KB Homes).

Most residential real estate offices are small and focus on properties in their immediate location. But their brand names come from just a few industry leaders. Realogy, a 2006 spin-off of Cendant, has several big names in its stable, including Sotheby's International, ERA, Century 21 and Coldwell Banker. The company claims it was involved in one in four U.S. residential real estate transactions in 2007. During that year, Apollo Management acquired Realogy, and the company signed a licensing deal with Meredith Corporation to use the Better Homes and Gardens brand. Realogy's competition includes RE/MAX and HomeServices of America. Firms that only handle commercial real estate are frequently larger and employ more brokers and salespeople than residential firms; they may also manage properties or administer real estate investment trusts (REITs). Most of the residential companies also deal in commercial sales.

Real estate rollercoaster

In the early part of the decade, the topic of real estate frequently popped up in the news media, as housing prices on both coasts and in urban areas skyrocketed. The reasons for this were numerous: following the market crash of 2000, the Federal Reserve rolled back interest rates from 6.5 percent to 1 percent over a three-year period, and a loosening of lending regulations made getting money to buy a house easier than ever. The influx of cheaper money fueled the boom: housing prices on the coasts shot up 55 to 100 percent, accounting for inflation, in five years. According to an article in *BusinessWeek*, in the first half of 2005, real estate accounted for 50 percent of the growth of the GDP; in less overheated markets it usually accounts for a tenth of that amount.

Since then, the sales market has fallen hard—and fast. Newly-constructed properties, which had been built up rather optimistically over those five years, began to be offered cheap to fill up empty units. By June 2006, the National Association of Realtors said the annual rate of residential sales was down nearly 9 percent compared to a year before. One year later, that figure was down another 10 percent to just under six million, the lowest seasonally-adjusted total in four years. The number of homes listed for sale at that point (4.4 million, the largest amount since 1992) was enough to last almost nine months at current sales rates. The situation in Florida was especially bad, compounded by huge property taxes, the hurricanes of 2004 and 2005 and the resultant spiral in insurance costs.

Visit Vault at **www.vault.com** for insider company profiles, expert advice, career message boards, expert resume reviews, the Vault Job Board and more.

VAULT CAREER LIBRARY   453

Prices leveled off, and then inched down for 10 straight months, dropping a total of 4 percent since October 2005. In a June 2007 article in *The New York Times*, Mark Zandi (chief economist at Moody's Economy.com) indicated that price declines were occurring in over 40 percent of metro areas in the United States, some by 8 to 12 percent. After the housing bubble burst, the subprime mortgage crisis emerged as a problem in 2007 and 2008, when borrowers started having trouble making payments on adjustable-rate loans with interest rates that had shifted upwards. To make matters worse, many people's homes were now worth less than what they had paid for them. Foreclosure filings increased because homeowners couldn't resort to options such as selling their homes or taking out other loans.

From bad to worse

The situation became more abysmal in 2008, when banks and other financial institutions suffered huge losses related to increasing mortgage payment defaults and falling real estate values. The Housing and Economic Recovery Act of 2008, which attempted to restore confidence in the U.S. mortgage industry, was passed in July 2008. The act lets the Federal Housing Administration guarantee as much as $300 billion in new 30-year fixed rate mortgages for homeowners with subprime loans. In addition, during 2008 the federal government bailed out mortgage lenders Fannie May and Freddie Mac, and the Fed also made massive loans to fund J.P. Morgan Chase's acquisition of Bear Stearns and to keep massive insurance firm AIG solvent.

After investment bank Lehman Brothers filed for bankruptcy, stock markets plummeted on September 15, 2008, a day the news media dubbed "Meltdown Monday." The following week, Federal Reserve Chairman Ben Bernanke and Treasury Secretary Henry Paulson urged Congress to pass a $700 billion bailout package, which would let the federal government purchase bad mortgages and other assets. While testifying on Capitol Hill, Bernanke said that the world's financial markets were under "severe stress." Bernanke added, "Action by Congress is urgently required to stabilize the situation and avert what otherwise could be very serious consequences for our financial markets and for our economy."

Some opponents to the legislation say the government (and, hence, the taxpayer) shouldn't be bailing out private companies. Other individuals approve of the plan but think it needs to include adequate safeguards, such as requiring that troubled financial firms don't give "golden parachutes" and big bonuses to executives. The National Association of Realtors has said that it supports the government's attempts to stabilize the financial markets.

Next on the real estate horizon

The subprime mortgage crisis has had an obvious impact on residential real estate, but it's also creating problems in the commercial real estate market. In August 2008, the National Association of Realtors said it expected poor economic conditions to have an impact on commercial real estate over the coming six to nine months. In New York, the financial crisis is expected to slow big construction projects such as Atlantic Yards in Brooklyn and the World Trade Center, and office buildings might have trouble renting out space if companies downsize.

If the economic downturn continues for an extended time, the results would be horrendous; bringing to mind the last time housing prices took a large fall: the Great Depression of the 1930s. Even if the economy and the real estate market recover, it's unlikely that housing prices will hit the historic highs that they saw in 2005 any time soon.

Working in the Industry

How to be real

During 2007, the real estate and construction business employed more than nine million people in the United States. These numbers have started to fall, however, as the real estate market has tanked. Individuals in the mortgage business have been casualties of the downturn, and in 2007 Tucson-based American Home Mortgage laid off 7,000 employees. Real estate agents, who were rolling in cash just a couple years ago, have started leaving the business as it becomes harder to make a living in the profession. In the St. Louis area, there were 8,625 real estate agents in August 2008 compared to 9,441 in August 2007. Moreover, fewer folks are entering the industry. For example, in Kentucky, 1,406 sales agents became licensed during the Kentucky Real Estate Commission's 2008 fiscal year, down from 1,880 in 2007.

Those who work in this sector often enjoy greater flexibility in job responsibilities than people in other industries. Drawbacks include low-paying entry-level positions, competitive co-workers and long, irregular hours when starting out. Furthermore, once established in an area, relocation can be detrimental to your career—success in a new place requires a solid base of geographically-specific knowledge (i.e., the quality of local schools, business zoning issues, community concerns, etc.). According to the National Association of Realtors, the median gross income for all realtors in 2008 was $42,600, a decrease from $47,700 in 2006 and $49,300 in 2004.

In order to sell real estate services, you must be a licensed professional in the state where you do business. To become a realtor, all states require a person to pass a written exam focused on real estate law and transactions and be affiliated with a broker. Most states require you to be at least 18 years old and a high school graduate, and to have completed a minimum number of classroom hours. Some states waive the classroom requirements for active attorneys or offer correspondence course credit options in lieu of the classroom hour requirement. The license fee varies, but runs around $100 to $200 for the exam and $400 for the classes. In addition, realtors must pay for their own errors and omissions insurance (around $500 a year) and annual dues to Realsource, an organization that manages the MLS (Multiple Listing Service), which contains the details of all properties for sale in a given market. State licenses need to be renewed annually or every other year, and some states have continuing education requirements for renewals.

Look both ways

The Bureau of Labor Statistics predicts that over the next 10 years the demand for brokers and sales agents will increase 11 percent. A growing population will result in a steadily increasing demand for housing. There is relatively high turnover in the industry, which results in a fairly constant demand for new entrants. Impediments to growth include the increased use of the Internet, which allows people to search for properties that suit their criteria without consulting a professional (much like how the regular consumer has bypassed travel agents in the tourism industry). The industry is very sensitive to fluctuations in interest rates and to the overall health of the economy, and demand for employees can drop precipitously in the face of a sluggish economy or high interest rates.

This may not be the best time to enter a field that is, in polite economic terms, experiencing a "correction." Property sellers (reluctant to unload at a loss) and buyers (looking for a deal in the current environment) are finding little common ground, and realtors have time, but little commission, on their hands.

Visit Vault at **www.vault.com** for insider company profiles, expert advice, career message boards, expert resume reviews, the Vault Job Board and more.

V∧ULT CAREER LIBRARY   455

Residential Real Estate Brokers

Residential real estate agents help buyers and sellers in the process of obtaining or getting rid of residential property. Some agents work with buyers, helping them find places to live and negotiating with sellers, while others work with the sellers. Agents rarely represent both parties, as this is perceived as a conflict of interest. There are about half a million real estate brokers and agents in the United States.

Agents are usually independent sales professionals who contract their services to sponsoring real estate brokers in exchange for a commission-sharing agreement. The commission on a home sale varies by market but is normally 5 to 6 percent of the sale price. This commission is split four ways: between the seller's agent, the buyer's agent, and the sponsoring brokers with whom each agent is associated. Many agents work solely on commission and don't get much in the way of benefits or monetary help with the overhead necessary to perform their jobs.

Although there are different organizations through which you can receive your classroom instruction, the state government issues and oversees licenses. If you visit the National Association of Realtor's web site at www.realtor.org, you can find information about residential real estate as well as licensing requirements for each state and locations of authorized real estate classes.

This industry attracts all types of personalities. There's a potpourri of career switchers, from lawyers to housewives, who end up in residential real estate. If you like being your own boss and interacting with people, being a realtor can be very rewarding.

Tenant Representation

A tenant representation agent, commonly known as a "tenant rep," acts on behalf of companies and other corporate clients looking to lease or buy either a portion of a property or an entire real estate asset. A large part of the job involves business development: because tenant reps are often responsible for building their own book of business, prospecting for new clients is a big part of the job. Although there's some direction by the broker and senior tenant reps in the office, for the most part tenant reps use cold-calling to drum up business.

Tenant representation is very competitive, even cutthroat, since one not only has to compete against outside reps but also those inside one's own office. In fact, some tenant rep brokers see the competition inside as being worse than outside the shops. Often there are disputes about who is entitled to chase what business—though usually the senior brokers win out.

When the time comes for one of his or her clients to buy, sell or lease, the tenant rep finds a list of choices in the market, then handles the accompanying negotiations. Tenant reps usually work in teams to spread the work. Often the team is composed of one senior and one junior broker. The junior broker will make the cold calls and set up meetings with prospective clients. At the meetings the senior broker will take the lead and try to win the business. Once the process begins, the junior broker will do the legwork for market alternatives and examine options with the senior broker. All possible alternatives are presented to the client for review. The senior broker generally handles the lease or sale negotiations. This mutually beneficial system gives the senior broker a "cold caller" and provides a training platform for the junior broker. Junior brokers should expect to work at least 50 to 60 hours per week; senior brokers' hours fluctuate based on deal flow.

Once junior brokers have surpassed certain earning requirements, they're promoted to senior brokers. They still make cold calls to get leads, though not nearly as often as junior brokers. The company relies on its senior brokers to win business and handle transactions from start to finish. Sometimes, senior brokers help create and execute management policy and even have equity at smaller firms.

Property Management

Real estate owners commonly employ professional property managers, who are charged with the day-to-day management of real estate assets. They ensure that tenants are satisfied, the building is in good condition, rent is paid and that rents reflect market conditions. Property managers get a solid general introduction to real estate, as they deal with a wide variety of issues including leasing, construction, tenant relations and market analysis.

A good manager can save an owner a great deal of money by operating the asset efficiently and keeping the tenants happy. The property manager plays a crucial role in expense control, as the owner relies on him to manage any and all operating expenses at the building. Property management also requires good interpersonal and analytical skills because tenants sometimes can be difficult and expect things to be resolved immediately. While leasing agents do much of the lease negotiations, property managers are involved in the process as well.

Visit Vault at **www.vault.com** for insider company profiles, expert advice, career message boards, expert resume reviews, the Vault Job Board and more.

VAULT CAREER LIBRARY   **457**

Employer Directory

AMB Property Corporation
Pier 1, Bay 1
San Francisco, CA 94111
Phone: (415) 394-9000
Fax: (415) 394-9001
www.amb.com

Apartment Investment and Management Company
4582 South Ulster Street Parkway
Suite 1100
Denver, CO 80237
Phone: (303) 757-8101
Fax: (303) 759-3226
Toll free: (888) 789-8600
www.aimco.com

Archstone
9200 East Panorama Circle, Suite 400
Englewood, CO 80112
Phone: (303) 708-5959
Fax: (303) 708-5999
www.archstonesmith.com

AvalonBay Communities, Inc.
2900 Eisenhower Avenue, Suite 300
Alexandria, VA 22314
Phone: (703) 329-6300
Fax: (703) 329-1459
www.avalonbay.com

Beazer Homes
1000 Abernathy Road, Suite 1200
Atlanta, GA 30328
Phone: (770) 829-3700
Fax: (770) 481-2808
www.beazer.com

Boston Capital Corporation
1 Boston Place
Boston, MA 02108-4406
Phone: (617) 624-8900
Fax: (617) 624-8999
www.bostoncapital.com

Boston Properties, Inc.
111 Huntington Avenue
Boston, MA 02199-7610
Phone: (617) 236-3300
Fax: (617) 536-5087
www.bostonproperties.com

Brookfield Properties Corporation
BCE Place, 181 Bay Street, Suite 330
Toronto, Ontario M5J 2T3
Canada
Phone: (416) 369-2300
Fax: (416) 369-2301
www.brookfieldproperties.com

Catellus - A ProLogis Company
4545 Airport Way
Denver, CO 80239
Phone: (303) 567-5700
www.catellus.com

CB Richard Ellis Group, Inc.
100 North Sepulveda Boulevard
Suite 1050
El Segundo, CA 90245
Phone: (310) 606-4700
Fax: (310) 606-4701
www.cbre.com

CBL & Associates Properties
2030 Hamilton Place Boulevard
Suite 500
Chattanooga, TN 37421-6000
Phone: (423) 855-0001
Fax: (423) 490-8390
Toll free: (800) 333-7310
www.cblproperties.com

Centex Corporation
2728 North Harwood Street
Dallas, TX 75201-1516
Phone: (214) 981-5000
Fax: (214) 981-6859
www.centex.com

Century 21 Real Estate LLC
1 Campus Drive
Parsippany, NJ 07054
Phone: (877) 221-2765
Fax: (973) 496-7564
www.century21.com

Coldwell Banker Real Estate Corporation
1 Campus Drive
Parsippany, NJ 07054
Phone: (973) 407-2000
Fax: (973) 496-7217
Toll free: (877) 373-3829
www.coldwellbanker.com

Day & Zimmermann Group
1500 Spring Garden Street
Philadelphia, PA 19103
Phone: (215) 299-8000
Fax: (215) 299-8030
www.dayzim.com

Developers Diversified Realty
3300 Enterprise Parkway
Beachwood, OH 44122
Phone: (216) 755-5500
Fax: (216) 755-1500
www.ddrc.com

Duke Realty Corporation
600 East 96th Street, Suite 100
Indianapolis, IN 46240
Phone: (317) 808-6000
Fax: (317) 808-6794
Toll free: (800) 875-3366
www.dukerealty.com

Equity Office Properties Trust
2 North Riverside Plaza, Suite 2100
Chicago, IL 60606
Phone: (312) 466-3300
Fax: (312) 454-0332
www.equityoffice.com

Employer Directory, cont.

Equity Residential
2 North Riverside Plaza, Suite 450
Chicago, IL 60606
Phone: (312) 474-1300
Fax: (312) 454-8703
www.equityresidential.com

FelCor Lodging Trust Incorporated
545 East John Carpenter Freeway
Suite 1300
Irving, TX 75062
Phone: (972) 444-4900
Fax: (972) 444-4949
www.felcor.com

Forest City Enterprises, Inc.
1100 Terminal Tower 50 Public Square
Cleveland, OH 44113-2203
Phone: (216) 621-6060
Fax: (216) 263-4808
www.forestcity.net

General Growth Properties, Inc.
110 North Wacker Drive
Chicago, IL 60606
Phone: (312) 960-5000
Fax: (312) 960-5475
www.generalgrowth.com

Heitman LLC
191 North Wacker Drive, Suite 2500
Chicago, IL 60606
Phone: (312) 855-5700
www.heitman.com

Hilton Hotels Corporation
9336 Civic Center Drive
Beverly Hills, CA 90210
Phone: (310) 278-4321
Fax: (310) 205-7678
www.hiltonworldwide.com

Hines
Williams Tower
2800 Post Oak Boulevard
Houston, TX 77056-6118
Phone: (713) 621-8000
Fax: (713) 966-2053
www.hines.com

Hospitality Properties Trust
400 Centre Street
Newton, MA 02458
Phone: (617) 964-8389
Fax: (617) 969-5730
www.hptreit.com

Host Hotels & Resorts, Inc.
6903 Rockledge Drive, Suite 1500
Bethesda, MD 20817
Phone: (240) 744-1000
Fax: (240) 744-5125
www.hosthotels.com

Hovnanian Enterprises, Inc.
110 West Front Street
Red Bank, NJ 07701
Phone: (732) 747-7800
Fax: (732) 747-7159
www.khov.com

HRPT Properties Trust
400 Centre Street
Newton, MA 02458-2076
Phone: (617) 332-3990
Fax: (617) 332-2261
www.hrpreit.com

Jones Lang LaSalle
200 East Randolph Drive
Chicago, IL 60601
Phone: (312) 782-5800
Fax: (312) 782-4339
www.joneslanglasalle.com

KB Home
10990 Wilshire Boulevard, 7th Floor
Los Angeles, CA 90024
Phone: (310) 231-4000
Fax: (310) 231-4222
www.kbhome.com

Kimco Realty Corporation
3333 New Hyde Park Road
New Hyde Park, NY 11042-0020
Phone: (516) 869-9000
Fax: (516) 869-9001
www.kimcorealty.com

Menard, Inc.
4777 Menard Drive
Eau Claire, WI 54703
Phone: (715) 876-5911
Fax: (715) 876-2868
www.menard-inc.com

TheMcCormick Group
1440 Central Park Boulevard
Suite 207
Fredericksburg, VA 22401
Phone: (540) 786-9777
Fax: (540) 786-9355
www.mccormickgroup.com

MetroList, Inc.
7100 East Belleview Avenue
Englewood, CO 80111-1632
Phone: (303) 850-9576
www.metrolistmls.com

Morgan Stanley Real Estate
1585 Broadway
New York, NY 10036
Phone: (212) 761-4000
www.morganstanley.com/realestate

Murdock Holding Company
10900 Wilshire Boulevard, Suite 1600
Los Angeles, CA 90024
Phone: (310) 208-3636
Fax: (310) 824-7756
www.castlecooke.net

NRT Incorporated
339 Jefferson Road
Parsipanny, NJ 07054
Phone: (973) 240-5000
Fax: (973) 240-5241
www.nrtllc.com

Visit Vault at www.vault.com for insider company profiles, expert advice,
career message boards, expert resume reviews, the Vault Job Board and more.

VAULT CAREER LIBRARY   459

Employer Directory, cont.

Parkway Properties, Inc.
1 Jackson Place
188 East Capitol Street, Suite 1000
Jackson, MS 39201-2195
Phone: (601) 948-4091
Fax: (601) 949-4077
Toll free: (800) 748-1667
www.pky.com

ProLogis
4545 Airport Way
Denver, CO 80239
Phone: (303) 567-5000
Fax: (303) 567-5605
Toll free: (800) 566-2706
www.prologis.com

Public Storage, Inc.
701 Western Avenue
Glendale, CA 91201-2349
Phone: (818) 244-8080
Fax: (818) 553-2376
www.publicstorage.com

Rayonier Inc.
50 North Laura Street
Jacksonville, FL 32202
Phone: (904) 357-9100
Fax: (904) 357-9101
www.rayonier.com

RE/MAX International, Inc.
5075 S. Syracuse Street
Denver, CO 80237-2712
Phone: (303) 770-5531
Fax: (303) 796-3599
Toll free: (800) 525-7452
www.remax.com

RREEF America L.L.C.
875 N Michigan Avenue
Chicago, IL 60611-1803
Phone: (312) 266-9300
www.dbrealestate.com/rreef

Tishman Speyer Properties
45 Rockefeller Plaza
New York, NY 10111
Phone: (212) 715-0300
Fax: (212) 895-0326
www.tishmanspeyer.com

Trammell Crow Residential
2 Buckhead Plaza
3050 Peachtree Road NW, Suite 500
Atlanta, GA 30305
Phone: (770) 801-1600
Fax: (770) 801-1256
www.tcresidential.com

The Trump Organization
725 5th Avenue
New York, NY 10022
Phone: (212) 832-2000
Fax: (212) 935-0141
www.trump.com

URS Corporation
600 Montgomery Street, 26th Floor
San Francisco, CA 94111
Phone: (415) 774-2700
Fax: (415) 398-1905
www.urscorp.com

USG Corporation
550 West Adams Street
Chicago, IL 60661-3676
Phone: (312) 436-4000
Fax: (312) 436-4093
www.usg.com

Vornado Realty Trust
888 7th Avenue
New York, NY 10019
Phone: (212) 894-7000
Fax: (212) 894-7070
www.vno.com

Walton Street Capital L.L.C.
900 North Michigan Avenue
Suite 1900
Chicago, IL 60611
Phone: (312) 915-2800
Fax: (312) 915-2881
www.waltonst.com

Weyerhaeuser Company
33663 Weyerhaeuser Way South
Federal Way, WA 98003
Phone: (253) 924-2345
Fax: (253) 924-2685
Toll free: (800) 525-5440
www.weyerhauser.com

Retail

Industry Overview

A shop on every corner

Unless you happen to be living under a rock, chances are you've had at least one interaction with the retail industry today. From the corner drugstore to the online bookstore, retail—the business of selling things made by others—is an inescapable presence in American life. The National Retail Federation says that during 2007 the retail industry had sales of $4.5 trillion, a huge percentage of the U.S. gross domestic product. It's no surprise, then, that it also employs the most people. According to the Bureau of Labor Statistics (BLS), about 11.6 percent of American employees, or some 15 million in 2005, the most recent year from which data was available, work in retail. Most of these people are employed as retail salespersons in department or clothing stores, but opportunities exist wherever goods are sold. Retailers also hire lots of employees to work in their headquarters in fields such as human resources, public relations, finance and marketing.

Putting the "eco" in economy

The retail sector, given its size as well as the necessity of charming the pants off consumers on a regular basis, supports a number of trends. Perhaps the most prevalent one that's surfaced is the shift towards more ecologically friendly products. While there's some backlash against these products from members of the hardcore environmental movement—who argue that companies overstate their green credentials, and that the best strategy for the planet involves not buying unnecessary items— the public is unlikely to be deterred from buying things left, right and center.

Increased awareness of the effects of carbon emissions on global warming have led consumers to seek out more environmentally-friendly alternatives to the products they usually buy. Of course, retailers are stepping up to the plate and providing consumers with a slew of green options. Home Depot, the second-largest retailer in the U.S., promotes a line of more than 2,500 environmentally friendly products under the Eco Options name. IKEA, one of the world's largest home furnishings retailers, emphasizes making its products from wood from sustainable forests, and it manufactures goods from recycled materials. In 2007, IKEA started charging five cents for plastic bags in its U.S. locations, in order to convince consumers to use fewer of them. Proceeds from the sale of bags will be donated to an environmental charity. And, in early 2008, Whole Foods also announced that it was sacking disposable plastic shopping bags. Instead, Whole Foods will offer free paper bags produced from recycled paper, reusable bags made from recycled plastic bottles that will cost 99 cents each and canvas bags priced between $6.99 and $35.

Retailers aren't just flaunting their green credentials to be altruistic. Aside from the savings that can be reaped by using less fuel in the supply chain, stores can save lots of money on energy costs by reducing consumption of electricity. Clothing company American Apparel, for example, installed a solar electric system on the rooftop of its warehouse in 2006. The firm expects that using solar energy will trim its electric bill by at least 20 percent per year. In addition, the solar power system will help protect American Apparel against quickly rising electricity prices. In September 2007, supermarket chain Safeway announced that it would install solar power in some California stores. And in January 2008, Safeway announced that the company was converting its entire fleet of delivery trucks so that the vehicles will run on biodiesel fuel.

Bricks vs. clicks

Low prices were once the domain of online retailers, though data from 2007 shows that growth in this area is slowing. During the torrid days of the dot-com era, it was widely predicted that online retailers would shortly put brick-and-mortar stores out of business. How could a store that had to pay for costs like utilities and salespeople possibly survive against a dot-com that could summarily undercut them on prices? The tidal wave of consumers opting for an online shopping experience—sales

Visit Vault at **www.vault.com** for insider company profiles, expert advice, career message boards, expert resume reviews, the Vault Job Board and more.

VAULT CAREER LIBRARY 461

grew 25 percent in 2004—made traditional retailers quake in their boots. Data released in early 2008, however, reveals that Internet retail need not fear its imminent demise. Data from the previous year showed that sales in the sector were beginning to cool down. This is partly due to saturation and partly due to brick-and-mortar retailers' creating more enticing environments for shoppers. While online retail sites frequently have awkward layouts, retail stores can beguile customers with customized experiences, not to mention instant gratification and a lack of $10 in shipping charges for a $3 item.

This trend in retail has led to a number of extensions. Apple's sleekly designed stores offer tech-support counters, seminars and group discussions on the company's latest gear, all of which add value to its products—and can't easily be replicated by an online merchant. Lifestyle retailing is another emerging trend. These stores display disparate items—like books, décor and clothing—close together, on the assumption that a customer will come in for a clothes item and leave with a mug, set of drawer handles and notepaper in a similar design vein. Companies like Urban Outfitters have achieved a great level of success with the strategy, and some high-end grocery stores, like the Food Emporium, have started displaying cookware alongside their edibles.

Location, location, location

During the rise of the big box stores, doomsayers predicted the death of the small, local store, subsumed by gigantic, homogenous shops that sold virtually everything. The local retail scene is proving to be more resilient than these pundits initially thought, however. In Texas, Minyard, a grocery-store operator, has had great success with its Carnival markets. Aimed at the rapidly growing Latino population near Dallas-Fort Worth, the stores feature more than a dozen types of chilies, fresh fruit juices and hot corn tortillas. Other amenities include check cashing, money transfer and Latin American brands of cleaning supplies. The stores are so successful that the operating company is putting its weight behind the concept, and expanding them throughout the area. Similarly, British retailer Tesco has introduced Fresh & Easy Neighborhood Markets in select cities in the United States. The firm describes Fresh & Easy as "neighborhood sized stores" that are "easily accessible and offer everything from everyday staples to gourmet items." Other companies, such as Circuit City, are also adding smaller shops to the mix, and Wal-Mart is testing new, smaller-format grocery/convenience stores.

Another rarified realm that chain stores have yet to penetrate in appreciable numbers is New York City, home to flocks of discerning foodies. It would be foolhardy to think that Wal-Mart's offerings could ever satisfy those finicky palates. Several local grocery chains, however, have been catering to this group's need for top-quality meats, specialty chocolates and cheeses, fine preserves and foods like pates. In 2007, the Food Emporium, a local grocery chain, refurbished its location under the 59th Street Bridge to emphasize gourmet products. While the store still sells mundane essentials, like paper towels, its product line focuses on providing delights such as ducks and other game, aged beef and homemade cream cheese.

The price is right

The face of retail in America may be about to change. In April 2007, a revisionist U.S. Supreme Court ruled that manufacturers were allowed to set minimum prices for their products. What does this mean for consumers? According to the ruling, a manufacturer will be able to negotiate a deal with a store (or distributor) to sell its products for a minimum price, preventing the store from marking the product down. Economists predict that the ruling might force smaller discount stores to raise their prices, and hence diminish their high-volume low-markup business model. (Large discount stores, like Wal-Mart or Target, probably have sufficient clout to circumvent these agreements.) On the other hand, the ruling could give a lift to smaller manufacturers, who can arrange to receive more money for their products. Luxury brands will probably see a boost, as they can sell their goods in a wider variety of stores with less brand dilution due to price competition. Of course, this will lead to stores being more selective about what they sell, lest they be left with gobs of terminally-undiscountable summer merchandise in December. The ramifications of this ruling have yet to be fully banged out in the marketplace, let alone the lower courts.

Over there, over there

Retail is rapidly expanding from Western economies into those of the developing world. Faced with mature markets in their home countries, large retailers are intrigued by the opportunities presented by expanding middle classes and swiftly growing economies in Asia. The early 2000s saw significant expansion from retailers like Best Buy, Carrefour and Wal-Mart into China. The latest trend in retail there, however, is outlet malls, which are proving to be popular on both sides of the Pacific. As of 2007, builders were putting up outlet malls near Shanghai featuring brands like Versace and Louis Vuitton.

In January 2008, Sears showed interest in expanding into India, where Wal-Mart is rolling out a cash-and-carry business with partner Bharti Enterprises. Although India is opening up its market to foreign retailers, companies don't necessarily foresee the hurdles they'll have to jump in order to succeed there. The country is still largely rural, and the roads are iffy. While the middle class has 300 million members who may be champing at the bit for the sort of goods doled out by Wal-Mart, 85 percent of the population doesn't qualify as middle class, and 25 percent is under the poverty line. While the lot of this group will improve in the future as India's economy continues to grow, for the present they're unable to afford imported goods. In addition, the country is notorious for its obstructionist bureaucracy—some 40 permits must be obtained in order for construction to start on a supermarket. These factors explain why only about 5 percent of the $280 billion per year retail market is controlled by chain stores. However, the retail sector in the country will see $30 billion invested by 2010.

Struggling through an economic slump

Retailers experienced weaker sales than they'd hoped for during the 2007 holiday season. Even sales of women's clothing— usually a mainstay of the holiday shopping season— plunged, in part due to fears of a recession and high energy prices. And, in January 2008, a report on consumer prices found increases in charges for apparel, suggesting that higher costs may have helped lower retail sales during the holidays. Companies that sell items for homes and home improvement retailers such as Lowe's have also experienced weak sales following the subprime mortgage crisis. The National Retail Federation anticipated a meager increase in sales (just 3.5 percent) for 2008.

The general state of the industry is so bad that a wide range of retailers have either curtailed their expansion plans or shuttered scores of shops—or both. After a wave of bankruptcies in the first quarter of 2008 (among them Lillian Vernon and the Sharper Image), companies announced other changes along with their withering financials. Well-known chains announced a total of 1,000 store closings; shopping malls could host empty storefronts as Charming Shoppes, Foot Locker and Ann Taylor shut a total of 410 outlets among them. Home Depot, hit especially hard by the housing downturn as well, said it would not only close 15 warehouses, but also drop plans for 50 new locations. Kohl's and J.C. Penney will also cut back on openings. Trade group International Council of Shopping Centers forecast almost 5,800 store closings for 2008—a sickening 25 percent more than in 2007.

Although high-end retailers typically fly above economic turmoil, even the luxury market started to show signs of a slowdown in early 2008. During a period when consumers are trying to spend less, discount stores could do well as shoppers "trade down." Supermarket chains such as Safeway are also better positioned than many retailers to weather a recession; consumers concerned about the economy tend to eat at home more than dine out. Some shoppers are also buying more products online to avoid spending money on gas to drive to the mall (and besides, there's often free shipping). Retailers are hopeful that the government's $168 billion economic-stimulus package, which includes tax rebates, could boost consumer spending.

Visit Vault at www.vault.com for insider company profiles, expert advice, career message boards, expert resume reviews, the Vault Job Board and more.

VAULT CAREER LIBRARY

463

Working in the Industry

You don't have to sell out

Retail jobs vary widely in level of compensation and necessary skills. Most retail positions involve standing for long periods and talking to lots of people. A natural sales ability is an asset, especially if salespeople are paid on commission. Salespeople who sell pricey items like cars, jewelry and home appliances are frequently on commission, while employees in grocery or big-box stores are paid an hourly wage. With experience, salespeople can advance to manage groups of workers, or even their own stores, but advancing may require changing jobs.

Just sell yourself

Interviews for retail positions can range from an informal chat to a more formal interview. Generally, stores selling more expensive merchandise will vet potential employees more carefully, and chain stores typically have a more standardized hiring procedure, which may involve personality tests. Survey respondents report between one and five rounds of interviews.

The Bureau of Labor Statistics reports that the retail industry is expected to grow at a rate of 9 to 17 percent between 2004 and 2014. Because turnover is relatively high, the sector offers an abundance of job opportunities for people of all ages and educational levels, making it a leading creator of entry-level jobs. Life in retail isn't always easy: while employees generally get discounts on merchandise, they must be courteous and patient at all times, even with demanding customers, and work nonstandard hours, particularly during the peak holiday season.

The health of this sector varies enormously based on the time of year and robustness of the economy. The sector is unique in that it has high turnover and most positions require few specialized skills; many people's first jobs are in retail, and some return to the industry when in need of short-term or supplementary income.

Retail Careers in Fashion

Retail covers the sale of apparel and related goods and services in small quantities directly to consumers. In the rush for fashion jobs, the retail sector has emerged as a promising contender. Some larger retailers have established training programs. The Gap hires recent college graduates for its retail management program. The program is based in San Francisco over a seven-month period. New hires gain experience in merchandising, planning and production. After successfully completing the program, the graduates have an opportunity to work full-time in the brand (i.e., Old Navy, Banana Republic, Gap Baby, etc.) in which they are trained—and are placed based on Gap's needs, as well as each graduate's skills and interests.

Jobs

Retail clerk: Assists the consumer in the purchase of products and services.

Store manager: Manages the store operations and supervises the clerks.

Marketing: Works on store advertisements and catalogs.

Inventory planner: Sets monetary limits on the retail buyers' purchasing power based on historical and market analysis.

Asset protection: Minimizes store losses and tracks fraud and theft.

Logistics: Works with stores and buyers to optimize supply-chain.

Real estate: Manages stores that vary in size, location and layout to keep stores new. Responsibilities may include construction and building services management.

The scoop

Many people have a less-than-positive view of retailing. "I didn't spend four years in college to work in a store!" is a frequent gripe. This negative reaction belies the fact that retail is a good place to start or build a fashion career. Because jobs selling fine design can be extremely lucrative, retail is becoming more attractive to college graduates. Larger stores are often the best places to start since some offer standardized training programs. Comments an insider: "One of retail's biggest problems is that there is no standard training pattern. Many retailers wait for people to get on-the-job training elsewhere and then cannibalize their competitors." Despite the problem of unstructured training, retail has one indisputably stellar element: almost anyone is eligible. "We look for employees with bachelor's degrees," says an industry source. "School isn't very important. Major isn't very important. Many people who specialized in business, finance or liberal arts will do just fine."

On the corporate side of fashion, opportunities exist in retail buying, planning, merchandising and product development. College grads typically start out as trainees and work their way up, following established or somewhat meandering career paths. Talented and dedicated new hires, especially in large companies or department stores, can expect regular promotions— up to divisional management roles. There are also opportunities in store management, finance and human resources. More creative jobs in retail include catalog production (graphics and copywriting) and window and display design.

Image

While some insiders laud department stores, others attest to the value of small designer companies. "Department stores are out," declares one adamant source. "Smaller, more prestigious retailers—CK, Armani, Tommy Hilfiger—are the way to go. Department stores are stuffy and they convey a feeling of being 'average.' The people I know working on the selling floor of department stores want to get out." Underlying this comment are issues of prestige and class, two prominent—although seldom discussed— aspects of retail. Fashion—and retail in particular—is an image-conscious sector in which an attractive appearance, up-to-date style, impeccable grooming and an air of affluence are important. "High-end retail is a glamour job," says an insider. "The positions are high-profile and low-paying. The people who work in retail are often highly educated and parentally subsidized. The job becomes a lifestyle of fashionable wardrobes, cocktail parties, elite crowds and making the right friends." If you detect an edge of superficiality, insiders confirm it. "High-end retail jobs are often aimed at high-class young women," says a source. "They deal with a wealthy and prominent clientele. Some of the girls are old school—out to find a rich husband."

Employees may have to invest thousands of dollars on a wardrobe to wear to work. In fact, most high-end retailers require their employees to wear only their label. One contact at Ralph Lauren says she must have her work apparel approved by the company, a cumbersome and expensive process. "For a job that pays by the hour," explains a contact, "you may have to invest quite a bit of money." This dress can be very expensive, even though employees receive discounts and supplementary commissions.

Fortunately, selling takes on new meaning when employees are dealing with celebrities and high-powered execs with money to burn. Those who excel in retail know how to build relationships with their customers—"setting aside" new arrivals or sending cards and little gifts (paid for by the company, of course). Wealthy clients may need pampering, but the insiders say the money compensates for the labor. "We're talking about people who walk into a store and buy the same outfit in five different colors," says an insider.

Visit Vault at **www.vault.com** for insider company profiles, expert advice, career message boards, expert resume reviews, the Vault Job Board and more.

VAULT CAREER LIBRARY   465

Inventory Planning and Buying

While the retail industry offers professional opportunities in functions common to all other industries (accounting, information technology and human resources), it offers two major professional paths unique to the industry: inventory planning and buying.

Inventory planners are responsible for making sure that the company's stores are stocked with the appropriate products. At first glance, this may not seem too demanding, but consider that many major retailers operate thousands of stores, and that these stores may carry different product mixes because of the customers they serve. Then, consider that retailers stock different products for different seasons and promotions—think about all of the "Back to School" promotions and holiday products you see at a major retailer. At many retailers, the inventory planning department is also responsible for making sure that the actual "Back to School" signs and product displays are shipped to the stores.

Inventory planning roles are very quantitative and detail-oriented. Professionals in these jobs must learn inventory tracking systems and software that their companies have developed or purchased. Planners generally work out of the company's corporate headquarters or major offices.

While planners are responsible for making sure that the stores are stocked, buyers are responsible for deciding what products the stores should sell. Faced with a surplus of companies all making the case that their products will be the next big thing, buyers must judiciously choose the products they believe will "sell through" to customers.

How do buyers decide? They stay on top of trends, talk with professionals in their industry to try to pick up on any "buzz" surrounding a particular product, evaluate the products' quality and appeal themselves. Then, combining all of this knowledge and the knowledge of who their store's customers are (and what they are willing to pay for certain types of items), the buyers make decisions on what products to stock. Unlike planners, buyers travel a great deal in order to meet with vendors.

Both buyers and planners are organized by the category of product they focus on: think "sporting goods" or "toddler toys" or "women's casual shoes." Inventory planning roles can be entry-level positions, while buying jobs generally require a few years' experience in retail (usually in a planning role).

Employer Directory

Alliance Boots plc
361 Oxford Street, 4th Floor
Sedley Place
London, W1C 2JL
United Kingdom
Phone: +44-11-59-50-61-11
Fax: +44-20-74-91-01-49
www.allianceboots.com

Ahold
Piet Heinkade 167-173
1019 GM Amsterdam
The Netherlands
Phone: +31-20-509-51-00
Fax: +31-20-509-51-10
www.ahold.com

Amazon.com
1200 12th Avenue South, Suite 1200
Seattle, WA 98144-2734
Phone: (206) 266-1000
Fax: (206) 266-1821
www.amazon.com

Arcadia Group
Colegrave House, 70 Berners Street
London, W1T 3NL
United Kingdom
Phone: +44-20-76-36-80-40
Fax: +44-20-79-27-05-77
www.arcadiagroup.co.uk

AutoZone, Inc.
123 South Front Street
Memphis, TN 38103
Phone: (901) 495-6500
Fax: (901) 495-8300
Toll free: (800) 288-6966
www.autozone.com

Barnes & Noble, Inc.
122 Fifth Avenue
New York, NY 10011
Phone: (212) 633-3300
Fax: (212) 675-0413
Toll free: (800) 422-7717
www.barnesandnobleinc.com

Best Buy
7601 Penn Avenue South
Richfield, MN 55423
Phone: (612) 291-1000
Fax: (612) 292-4001
www.bestbuy.com

BJ's Wholesale Club
1 Mercer Road
Natick, MA 01760
Phone: (508) 651-7400
Fax: (508) 651-6114
www.bjswholesale.com

Blockbuster Inc.
1201 Elm Street
Dallas, TX 75270
Phone: (214) 854-3000
Fax: (214) 254-3677
www.blockbuster.com

Borders Group, Inc.
100 Phoenix Drive
Ann Arbor, MI 48108
Phone: (734) 477-1100
Fax: (734) 477-1965
www.bordersgroupinc.com

Cabela's
One Cabela Drive
Sidney, NE 69160
Phone: (308) 254-5505
Fax: (308) 254-4800
www.cabelas.com

Costco Wholesale Corporation
999 Lake Drive
Issaquah, WA 98027
Phone: (425) 313-8100
Fax: (425) 313-8103
www.costco.com

CVS/Caremark Corporation
One CVS Drive
Woonsocket, RI 02895
Phone: (401) 765-1500
Fax: (401) 766-9227
Toll free: (888) 607-4287
www.cvs.com

Delhaize
Square Marie Curie 40
1070 Brussels
Belgium
Phone: +32-2-412-21-11
Fax: +32-2-412-21-94
www.delhaizegroup.com

Dillard's, Inc.
1600 Cantrell Road
Little Rock, AR 72201
Phone: (501) 376-5200
Fax: (501) 399-7831
www.dillards.com

Dollar General Corporation
100 Mission Ridge
Goodlettsville, TN 37072
Phone: (615) 855-4000
Fax: (615) 855-5252
www.dollargeneral.com

**Euromarket Designs, Inc.
(Crate and Barrel)**
1250 Techny Road
Northbrook, IL 60062
Phone: (847) 272-2888
Fax: (847) 272-5366
www.crateandbarrel.com

Foot Locker, Inc.
112 West 34th Street
New York, NY 10120
Phone: (212) 720-3700
Fax: (212) 720-4397
www.footlocker-inc.com

Forever 21
2001 South Alameda Street
Los Angeles, CA 90058
Phone: (213) 741-5100
Fax: (213) 741-5161
www.forever21.com

GameStop
625 Westport Parkway
Grapevine, TX 76051
Phone: (817) 424-2000
Fax: (817) 424-2002
www.gamestop.com

Visit Vault at **www.vault.com** for insider company profiles, expert advice,
career message boards, expert resume reviews, the Vault Job Board and more.

V\ULT CAREER LIBRARY 467

Employer Directory, cont.

The Gap Inc.
2 Folsom Street
San Francisco, CA 94105
Phone: (650) 952-4400
Fax: (415) 427-2553
Toll free: (800) 333-7899
www.gap.com

H&M
Regeringsgatan 48
SE-106 38 Stockholm
Sweden
Phone: +46-8-796-5500
Fax: +46-46-0-820-8094
www.hm.com

Hallmark Cards
2501 McGee Street
Kansas City, MO 64108
Phone: (816) 274-5111
Fax: (816) 274-5061
Toll free: (800) 425-5627
www.hallmark.com

The Home Depot, Inc.
2455 Paces Ferry Road NW
Atlanta, GA 30339-4024
Phone: (770) 433-8211
Fax: (770) 384-2356
Toll free: (800) 430-3376
www.homedepot.com

Hy-Vee
5820 Westown Parkway
West Des Moines, IA 50266-8223
Phone: (515) 267-2800
Fax: (515) 267-2817
www.hy-vee.com

The IKEA Group
Olof Palmestraat 1
NL-2616 LN Delft
Sweden
Phone: +46-42-267-100
Fax: +46-31-15-215-38-38
www.ikea.com

J.C. Penney Corporation, Inc.
6501 Legacy Drive
Plano, TX 75024-3698
Phone: (972) 431-1000
Fax: (972) 431-1362
www.jcpenney.com

J.Crew
770 Broadway
New York, NY 10003
Phone: (212) 209-2500
Fax: (212) 209-2666
www.jcrew.com

J. Sainsbury
33 Holborn
London, EC1N 2HT
United Kingdom
Phone: +44-20-76-95-60-00
Fax: +44-20-76-95-76-10
www.j-sainsbury.co.uk

John Lewis Partnership
171 Victoria Street
London
United Kingdom
Phone: +44-20-78-28-10-00
www.johnlewis.com

Kohl's Corporation
N56 W17000 Ridgewood Drive
Menomonee Falls, WI 53051
Phone: (262) 703-7000
Fax: (262) 703-6143
www.kohls.com

The Kroger Co.
1014 Vine Street
Cincinnati, OH 45202
Phone: (513) 762-4000
Fax: (513) 762-1160
www.kroger.com

L.L.Bean, Inc.
3 Campus Drive
Freeport, ME 04033
Phone: (207) 552-3028
Fax: (207) 552-3080
Toll free: (800) 441-5713
www.llbean.com

Limited Brands, Inc.
3 Limited Parkway
Columbus, OH 43216
Phone: (614) 415-7000
Fax: (614) 415-7440
www.limitedbrands.com

Lowe's Companies, Inc.
1000 Lowe's Boulevard
Mooresville, NC 28117
Phone: (704) 758-1000
Fax: (336) 658-4766
Toll free: (800) 445-6937
www.lowes.com

Macy's, Inc.
7 West 7th Street
Cincinnati, OH 45202
Phone: (513) 579-7000
Fax: (513) 579-7555
Toll free: (800) 261-5385
www.federated-fds.com

Marks & Spencer
Waterside House, 35 N. Wharf Road
London, W2 1NW
United Kingdom
Phone: +44-20-79-35-44-22
Fax: +44-84-53-03-01-70
www.marksandspencer.com

McDonald's Corporation
2111 McDonald's Drive
Oak Brook, IL 60523
Phone: (630) 623-3000
Fax: (630) 623-5004
Toll free: 9800) 244-6227
www.mcdonalds.com

Neiman Marcus Group, Inc.
1 Marcus Square
1618 Main Street
Dallas, TX 75201
Phone: (214) 741-6911
Fax: (214) 573-5320
Toll free: (888) 888-4757
www.neimanmarcus.com

Employer Directory, cont.

Nordstrom Inc.
1617 Sixth Avenue
Seattle, WA 98101-1742
Phone: (206) 628-2111
Fax: (206) 628-1795
Toll free: (800) 282-6060
www.nordstrom.com

PETCO Animal Supplies, Inc.
9125 Rehco Road
San Diego, CA 92121
Phone: (858) 453-7845
Fax: (858) 677-3489
Toll free: (888) 824-7257
www.petco.com

Publix Super Markets, Inc.
3300 Publix Corporate Parkway
Lakeland, FL 33811
Phone: (863) 688-1188
Fax: (863) 284-5532
www.publix.com

RadioShack Corp.
300 RadioShack Circle
Fort Worth, TX 76102
Phone: (817) 415-3011
Fax: (817) 415-2647
www.radioshack.com

Retail Ventures
3241 Westerville Road
Columbus, OH 43224
Phone: (614) 471-4722
Fax: (614) 254-7268
www.retailventuresinc.com

Rite Aid Corporation
30 Hunter Lane
Camp Hill, PA 17011
Phone: (717) 761-2633
Fax: (717) 975-5871
Toll free: (800) 748-3243
www.riteaid.com

Ross Group PLC
Brunel Road, Totton
Hampshire, SO40 3YS
United Kingdom
Phone: +44-23-80-67-55-00
Fax: +44-23-80-67-55-55
www.ross-group.co.uk

Royal Ahold
Piet Heinkade 167 - 173
1019 GM Amsterdam
The Netherlands
Phone: +31-20-509-51-00
Fax: +31-20-509-51-10
www.ahold.com

Safeway, Inc.
5918 Stoneridge Mall Road
Pleasanton, CA 94588-3229
Phone: (925) 467-3000
Fax: (925) 467-3321
www.safeway.com

Saks Incorporated
12 East 49th Street
New York, NY 10017
Phone: (212) 940-5305
www.saksincorporated.com

Sears Holdings
(Sears, Roebuck & Co. and Kmart Corporation)
3333 Beverly Road
Hoffman Estates, IL 60179
Phone: (847) 286-2500
Fax: (847) 286-8351
www.searshc.com

Sherwin-Williams Company
101 Prospect Avenue NW
Cleveland, OH 44115-1075
Phone: (216) 566-2000
Fax: (216) 566-2947
www.sherwin-williams.com

Signet Group
15 Golden Square
London, W1F 9JG,
United Kingdom
Phone: +44-20-73-17-97-00
Fax: +44-20-77-34-14-52
www.signetgroupplc.com

Staples, Inc.
500 Staples Drive
Framingham, MA 01702
Phone: (508) 253-5000
Fax: (508) 253-8989
Toll free: (800) 378-2753
www.staples.com

Starbucks Corporation
2401 Utah Avenue South
Seattle, WA 98134
Phone: (206) 447-1575
Fax: (206) 447-0828
Toll free: (800) 782-7282
www.starbucks.com

SUPERVALU INC.
11840 Valley View Road
Eden Prairie, MN 55344
Phone: (952) 828-4000
Fax: (952) 828-8998
www.supervalu.com

Trader Joe's Company
800 South Shamrock Avenue
Monrovia, CA 91016
Phone: (626) 599-3700
Fax: (626) 301-4431
www.traderjoes.com

Target Corporation
1000 Nicollet Mall
Minneapolis, MN 55403
Phone: (612) 304-6073
Fax: (612) 696-5400
www.target.com

Visit Vault at **www.vault.com** for insider company profiles, expert advice,
career message boards, expert resume reviews, the Vault Job Board and more.

VAULT CAREER LIBRARY

469

Employer Directory, cont.

Tesco PLC
Tesco House, Delamare Road
Cheshunt
Hertfordshire, EN8 9SL
United Kingdom
Phone: +44-19-92-63-22-22
www.tesco.com

TJX Companies
770 Cochituate Road
Framingham, MA 01701
Phone: (508) 390-1000
Fax: (508) 390-2828
www.tjx.com

Toys "R" Us, Inc.
1 Geoffrey Way
Wayne, NJ 07470-2030
Phone: (973) 617-3500
Fax: (973) 617-4006
www.toysrus.com

Tractor Supply
200 Powell Place
Brentwood, TN 37027
Phone: (615) 366-4600
www.tractorsupplyco.com

Wal-Mart Stores, Inc.
702 SW 8th Street
Bentonville, AR 72716
Phone: (479) 273-4000
Fax: (479) 277-1830
www.walmartstores.com

Walgreen Co.
200 Wilmot Road
Deerfield, IL 60015
Phone: (847) 914-2500
Fax: (847) 914-2804
www.walgreens.com

Whole Foods Market
550 Bowie Street
Austin, TX 78703
Phone: (512) 477-4455
Fax: (512) 477-1301
www.wholefoodsmarket.com

Technology Consulting

The State of Technology Consulting

IT services surge

For the past few years, the technology consulting industry has seen an upswing in spending. After a period of stagnation resulting from the stock market downturn of 2000 and 2001, the economy started to pick up again in 2004. The positive economic environment encouraged companies to invest in IT improvements to help boost profits and spur business growth. Over 2006 and 2007, tech consulting firms experienced a return to prosperity, thanks to clients with ample IT budgets. In addition, a wave of regulatory changes—like Basel II and China's State Administration of Foreign Exchange in 2006—opened up significant opportunities in the financial services and banking sectors, driving up demand for tech consulting services.

Cautious clients

Though work has remained steady at most consulting firms, a mild recession after 2007's subprime mortgage crisis once again put businesses in a precarious position. Sluggish economic growth and fears of a crash are forcing companies to be more cost-conscious about spending on "nonessentials" like upgraded data systems. In the short term, industry analysts estimate a slight year-over-year decline in the demand for IT services from 2007. Analysts also predict that more conservative budgets and the ability of providers to broaden their service offerings may push fee levels down in 2008.

Over the long term, however, the outlook is more favorable. Globalization, a growing postmerger integration market and increasing industry deregulation around the world are helping to keep demand for tech consulting consistent. The industry is expected to increase globally at a compound annual growth rate of 5.2 percent through 2010, according to research firm IDC. Consulting projects that support core business operations, such as infrastructure or regulatory requirements, are areas that will likely remain in high demand. Security consulting, custom application development and web services consulting are also promising areas for tech consultants.

Change is good

Facing a market that's sensitive to economic shifts, tech consulting firms must continually adapt their strategies to suit the current marketplace. With the gradual recovery of the consulting industry since 2004, clients have become more sophisticated and have specific demands relating to their industry sector, forcing consulting firms to really prove their worth. Clients also tend to be more price-sensitive, and want to know what the bottom-line savings will be before projects begin. As a result, consultancies have had to concentrate on services that add tangible value and boost profit margins. To protect profits, consulting firms have been aiming for short-term projects that require less labor and expense, like implementation, as well as higher profit margin services, like taking over a client's entire business processes in HR or finance.

In addition, consulting firms have gone to greater lengths to differentiate their services, positioning themselves as specialists on the cutting edge, rather that as generic software implementers. Adding new information technologies to their portfolio also helps larger firms extend their target client base. Instead of investing time and money into expensive R&D, consultancies can acquire smaller firms with a niche technology specialty. For example, in 2007, Accenture purchased California-based defense firm Maxim Systems to bulk up its services in that area. Cisco has proven to be a master of this maneuver, having snapped up over 120 smaller companies in its 24-year history.

Visit Vault at **www.vault.com** for insider company profiles, expert advice, career message boards, expert resume reviews, the Vault Job Board and more.

VAULT CAREER LIBRARY   471

EMEA takes the lead

The tech consulting client makeup is also undergoing a geographic shift. Today, the Europe, the Middle East and Africa region has emerged as a promising market, with the rate of demand quickly eclipsing that of North America. Industry observers predict that by 2009, EMEA will outpace the Americas as the largest IT services market in the world—in 2007, the region had already jumped ahead of the Americas in outsourcing activity.

Asia is also rising in prominence as a major market for tech consulting services. Springboard Research forecasts that the Asia Pacific IT services market will grow annually at 10.5 percent over the next five years, hitting $55 billion by 2011.

Outsourcing's steady climb

Outsourcing remains a core service offering that helps keep profit margins buoyant. While overall demand for IT consulting may slow, the need for IT outsourcing is expected to increase 9 percent in 2008, according to Forrester Research. When outsourcing took off in the late 1990s, these services revolved around cheap call centers and low-cost data services for clients that needed to find a way to cut costs. Now, outsourcing is an almost $400 billion industry, accounting for a major chunk of overall IT consulting revenue, and often involves more complex projects, such as supporting a company's entire IT infrastructure from an offshore location. Since 2006, consulting firms are also getting a boost from a second round of work resulting from mature outsourcing projects. Business process outsourcing is the fastest-growing services sector in the market, with clients also demanding applications development and maintenance.

Although the outsourcing industry is still expanding globally, 2007 saw a decrease in U.S. total contract value for the first time in five years, a result of both smaller contracts and the slowdown of outsourcing business from the Americas.

India dominates

Since the outsourcing craze began, India has dominated the market as the go-to location for lower cost labor. A McKinsey Global Institute report indicates that India's outsourcing industry revenue will expand to $60 billion by 2010. The country's skilled labor market and large English-speaking population have given India a distinct advantage over other developing countries, and American consulting firms continue to pour resources and talent into it to capitalize on the well-established market. In 2007, IBM announced its intention to invest $6 billion in India over the next three years, and in 2008, Cisco announced plans for a talent development program there, aiming to increase its staff in the country six-fold to 360,000 in the next five years. Currently, IBM has almost one-fifth of its employees—about 73,000—in the country, and Accenture has over 37,000 staff there, making India home to its largest workforce. EDS currently has about 32,000 employees in India, thanks in part to its acquisition of Bangalore-based BPO firm MphasiS in 2006.

The country's BPO market is still growing steadily, keeping tech consulting firms supplied with a stream of engagements. NASSCOM predicts that the BPO market will soar to $50 billion from its current $11 billion by 2012. But over the past few years, India has developed beyond its former reputation as strictly a BPO and call center location; recently, the country has experienced a surge in M&A activity, and has started to become a player in international acquisitions. In 2007, Indian firms made over 75 foreign acquisitions, creating a stream of postmerger work in the financial services sector for consultants.

Where will they go next?

While the labor market in India matures, salaries are inching upward at a rate of 15 percent per year, making it more expensive for consulting firms to hire local staff—at this rate, analysts say the country may soon price itself out of the offshoring market. In addition, India faces an impending shortage of workers with IT skills. A 2007 report from Dun & Bradstreet estimated that the country will need half-a-million more tech workers by 2009 to meet expected demand. China, which has also risen recently as an outsourcing hotspot, is facing a similar deficiency in skilled labor.

As such, Western firms have started looking beyond India and China, eyeing other emerging countries for outsourcing opportunities. Indonesia, Vietnam, the Philippines and Eastern European nations are gaining popularity as viable outsourcing centers. In fact, industry observers identify Vietnam as the real up-and-comer, and predict that the country will surpass India and China as a premier outsourcing site by 2012. Thanks to recent economic deregulation and access to the World Trade Organization, companies are now more able to take advantage of Vietnam's skilled labor and low costs.

The race to the States

As consulting firms compete for the most lucrative engagements, those that were once outsourcing shops are making inroads into the high-end IT consulting market. Outsourcing firms looking to move into higher-profit services are heading to the U.S. and Europe to gain regional and industry traction, and to get closer to their customers. Tata Consultancy Services recently increased its U.S. presence with a new development center in Cincinnati, Ohio, opened in March 2008. The firm has not been shy about its intention to steal business from the traditional consulting giants—like EDS and BearingPoint Inc. Management & Technology Consultants—and already has 50 U.S. offices and a headquarters in New York. In August 2007, India-based Wipro acquired U.S. infrastructure management vendor InfoCrossing. The firm also plans to recruit about 500 employees for a new development center in Atlanta, Ga., and it has two more U.S. development centers in the works. Satyam has also been hunting for acquisitions in the U.S., since about 60 percent of its business already comes from North America.

For the most profitable tech engagements, there's no doubt that American firms have the longstanding relationships it takes to establish client trust—which gives them a distinct advantage over newcomers. This could soon change as competitors willing to undercut these firms' prices establish a stronger presence in the West.

Software, strategy and more

Another rising trend in the tech consulting world is the merging of business consulting and IT services. Many companies are wising up to the fact that technology plays an essential role in meeting strategic goals; in searching for solutions to business problems, clients are increasingly turning to consulting firms that can offer nontechnical solutions as well as IT systems. To expand into business consulting, tech firms often acquire a strategy consulting firm. EDS was one of the first firms to start this trend when it purchased A.T. Kearney in 1995 (and subsequently sold it in a management buyout in January 2006). And until IBM took over PricewaterhouseCoopers' strategy consulting practice in 2002, it had focused primarily on systems integration.

Likewise, strategy firms are recently embracing services like outsourcing, formerly considered the domain of software implementers and tech shops. Bain, considered a strategy-heavy house, now offers IT business alignment and outsourcing. The firm also publishes research on technology trends to get the word out about its IT expertise. Even McKinsey, long established as an exclusive strategy player, is vying for a piece of the lucrative tech market by offering outsourcing, IT architecture and other business technology services. Though niche firms have their place in the technology industry, the biggest players have a leg up in winning clients who wish to deal with a firm that can seamlessly weave customized IT solutions and software into business strategy.

Tempting talent

Against the backdrop of a shaky economy, the IT consulting industry is moving forward with aggressive hiring—a clear sign of optimism that the demand for IT services will remain steady. Tech talent is in short supply, and new graduates with the right background are finding that they have their pick of the consulting litter. In many cases, employers competing for new MBAs have had to boost salary offers and relocation payouts, in addition to signing bonuses.

Visit Vault at www.vault.com for insider company profiles, expert advice, career message boards, expert resume reviews, the Vault Job Board and more.

VAULT CAREER LIBRARY   473

Though demand for talent is high, salary increases to are moderate, averaging about 4 to 5 percent. To compensate for these moderate bumps in compensation, consulting firms are becoming more competitive and creative with traditional benefits packages. And in an era of fewer IPOs than in previous decades, applicants are more concerned with overall compensation than with earning shares in a company. Employee-friendly options such as flexible work schedules or on-site conveniences (such as Tata's on-campus laundry service and gym) help win over the best candidates.

Realistic recruiting online

Consulting firms are also getting more creative in their recruiting practices to reel in the cream of the crop. Recently, the digital media world Second Life has become an outlet for firms to conduct "virtual recruiting," hold information sessions and even "meet" and interview candidates (or their avatars). PA Consulting Group implemented Second Life recruiting in 2007, and plans to increase its virtual recruiting presence in the future. IBM Global Services also uses Second Life in its recruiting efforts, as well as for new-hire training and orientation. Firms appreciate that Second Life broadens the candidate pool and provides a low-cost way to interact with potential new hires all over the world.

The combo candidate

While it is a job-seeker's market, IT consulting firms are very choosy about picking hires with the right set of skills. Particularly desirable candidates are those with experience in web development, database management, wireless networking and applications engineering. Firms are also more concerned now about applicants' business savvy, as the line between IT services and business consulting is becoming increasingly blurred. Candidates with a deep understanding of business concepts as well as IT skills are the top picks for the most selective consulting firms.

Practice Areas

Systems integration

This is one of the key functions of an IT consultant, and an area of expansion as companies add increasingly complex IT systems to update their business operations. Systems integration work involves integrating computers and other instruments to be able to share data and information. When two companies merge, or a single company wants to implement new hardware or software, systems integration consultants make all functions compatible. Sometimes, this is a simple matter of installing upgrades. More often, it's a long and arduous process of writing new code to force all the machines and existing software to play nicely together.

Outsourcing

Business process outsourcing continues to be a solid growth area for tech consulting firms, even at a time when growth in overall IT services demand is slowing. Clients are often able to cut costs and reduce management responsibilities by handing over core IT processes to a third party. Consultants, in effect, become the client's IT department. They may handle claims processing for an insurance company or payroll for an HR department. Often, BPO work involves maintaining servers and running help desk operations. Almost every large corporation or public-sector organization is a BPO client these days, from Fortune 500 companies to the U.S. Department of Homeland Security. In April 2008, Computer Sciences Corporation won a multiyear outsourcing deal with Chrysler LLC to provide mainframe, server and storage services for all operations. And in February 2008, EDS signed an eight-year, $1 billion contract with the Infocomm Development Authority of Singapore to help it achieve a standard desktop, network and messaging/collaboration environment across the public sector.

Enterprise solutions

The 2002 passage of the Sarbanes-Oxley Act was a wake-up call for many companies that initially considered themselves capable of managing the technological aspects of compliance on their own. After a couple of years, SOX-compliance consulting contracts became common as companies found they didn't have the data management or security systems in place to maintain confidentiality of the reams of financial information produced. Nor did they have the capacity to facilitate the required audit, tracking and reporting. Sarbanes-Oxley compliance is one of many types of consulting that falls under the "enterprise solutions" category.

Enterprise resource planning is another huge portion of the enterprise solutions consulting business. ERP solutions help companies respond to marketplace strategies and might also combine front- and back-office processes. These solutions might involve product planning, customer service, order tracking, finance or HR processes. As part of an ERP solution, consultants may implement SAP, Oracle or another packaged software. Currently, applications development and maintenance—the creation of custom applications and software services for companies—is a hot growth area within ERP.

Customer relationship management (CRM) systems stormed the tech world in the late 1990s, only to be hit hard by an economic downturn that meant even the most technologically sophisticated customer management system wasn't going to grow sales. Now that spending on tech services has recovered, CRM engagements are on the rise again. These projects focus on helping clients gain a competitive edge with customers through sales intelligence, analyzing customer information or establishing customer care portals. CRM engagements often involve creating a complex software solution for collecting, storing and retrieving large amounts of customer data.

IT strategy

IT consulting engagements that cover the strategic side of the client's business or high-level technology decisions are referred to simply as "consulting" or "strategy" projects, and often involve using IT to support a company's overall business strategy. Most of the large, brand-name management consulting firms have technology strategy practices: Oracle's consulting services group, HP's IT strategy and architecture group, and Accenture's strategic IT effectiveness (SITE) group. These technology strategy consulting groups are often managed by industry specialists (e.g., financial services, pharmaceuticals) who are deeply familiar with the specific information challenges that clients face.

Some IT strategy engagements fall into the business process management (BPM) category. BPM projects center around improving all processes within an organization, all to help the client save money through improving efficiency and effectiveness. Changing processes often means automating or semi-automating a process that has been performed manually, so BPM projects usually involve implementing a new software suite. Over the past few years, the market for BPM software services has exploded. Gartner estimates the worldwide market for BPM suites to more than double from 2006 levels, hitting $2.6 billion in 2011.

Another much-hyped area within IT strategy is service oriented architecture (SOA). SOA is a way of connecting disparate IT systems to help align strategy and IT goals. It involves designing a complete set of independent and changeable business services that make up an end-to-end process. Through SOA, businesses can more quickly update and streamline one process without making changes to an entire system. IDC predicts that the market for SOA, including software, services and hardware, will reach $14 billion annually by 2009.

Web services

In the last decade, web services primarily covered web site design and hosting, and the work was carried out by specialist firms in Silicon Alley (New York's tech center). Today, web services has become more complex, and includes any automated services that are conducted over a network—most commonly, the Internet. Web services consulting now often involves

Visit Vault at www.vault.com for insider company profiles, expert advice, career message boards, expert resume reviews, the Vault Job Board and more.

VAULT CAREER LIBRARY   475

helping a company optimize use of Web 2.0, through knowledge sharing, social networks, blogging, wikis and RSS feeds. These projects may also cover e-commerce implementation and other secure-transaction work. Web services consulting is a high-demand area for a lot of the big tech players like IBM and HP Services. Gartner predicts that more than 60 percent of the $527 billion IT services market will be based on web services, and IDC estimates that spending on web services will reach a whopping $15 billion by 2009.

Security

Security consulting became a booming area for IT firms after the September 11 terrorist attacks, when businesses and residents raised their awareness of threats to U.S. security. IT businesses have capitalized on increased vigilance in the business climate by developing a wider range of advanced security and fraud prevention methods for the financial services and government sectors, as well as for other industries. Businesses hire security consultants to protect them from hackers and viruses, and government agencies use these services to protect their national transportation, infrastructure and public spaces against terrorism. Biometrics (the science of identifying a person via retina patterns, voice, fingerprints and other unique biological characteristics), access control, data encryption and other types of secure communications are growing areas within the industry today.

Research and development

Some consultants are actually full-time researchers, creating new hardware and software to solve problems. Currently, "innovation" is the buzzword in the IT world, and undoubtedly the firms that come with the most cutting-edge applications can turn those into major profits. A large portion of this work focuses on developing new proprietary products (i.e., semiconductors and analysis software) to help a consulting firm sell its services and complete engagements. Consultants might also carry out this type of work for a specific client's use (contract R&D).

A Day in the Life: IT Consultant

Kristine is a consultant at a major consulting firm with many IT consulting engagements. Her role is team leader of the design and developer for eight web-based training modules. She has five analysts on her team.

4:30 a.m. It's Monday morning. Time to wake up. There's time for a shower this Monday morning—such luxury!

5:30 a.m. I am in a cab on the way to the airport, making a mental list of anything that could have been forgotten. I ask the cabbie to tune the radio to NPR.

6:10 a.m. At the airport I go up to the self check-in kiosk. I take the boarding pass and head down to the security line, laptop and small carry-on in hand.

6:25 a.m. At security, I remove my laptop from my bag and place it on the tray. I move through security quickly. No alarms beep.

6:35 a.m. After a quick stop at Starbucks, I arrive at the gate. I say hello to three other members of my project and check out the other passengers I see every week on this Monday morning flight. I board early along with the other premier fliers—one of the perks of being a frequent traveler.

7 a.m. The flight departs on time. Yay! I relish my window seat close to the front of the airplane.

8 a.m. The beverage cart wakes me up. I ask for coffee and scan *The Wall Street Journal* as I drink.

9:30 a.m. I arrive at my destination and share a ride with my fellow consultants to the project site.

10:30 a.m. At the project site. As I crawl underneath my desk to hook my laptop to the client LAN connection, one of my team members informs me that he still hasn't received feedback from his client reviewer. That's not good news.

11 a.m. After checking and responding to e-mail, I call my team member's client reviewer. The reviewer agrees to send me the team member feedback on the training material by noon tomorrow.

11:15 a.m. I remind the team of the 1 p.m. status meeting. I've got to start it on time—I have a meeting downtown at 3:15 p.m. I start to review the content outlines for the training modules.

12 p.m. I scurry, along with two teammates, to get sandwiches at a nearby eatery. Mine is turkey and cheddar.

12:20 p.m. Back at my desk, I get a call from the project manager, who is working at a client site in another state. He tells me that clients in the training department are nervous about their job security and asks that the entire team be sensitive to how the training changes may affect the training positions in the organization.

1 p.m. The team holds a status meeting. I pass on the message from the project manager. Each member discusses what has been completed and what he or she expects to complete that week. Two other team members are having difficulty obtaining feedback from their client reviewers. We all brainstorm ideas on how to obtain the feedback.

2 p.m. I finish up the meeting and get directions to my meeting downtown.

2:40 p.m. Off to the 3:15 p.m. meeting.

3:15 p.m. I meet the head of the training department to discuss the training courses. He calls in a close associate who has opinions on how the courses should be organized. The associate wants to add several more web-based training modules. I politely suggest that part of the additional subject matter could be covered in the modules that have been agreed to in the scope of the project. We all sketch out the course structure on a white board.

4:45 p.m. Back at the project site. I check in with my team members via e-mail.

5:45 p.m. I complete a draft of the course flow in PowerPoint and send it to the client and my manager for review.

7 p.m. I have reviewed 50 percent of the course outlines. It's time to head back to the hotel. I stop by a local diner for a quick dinner.

8:30 p.m. Time for a workout in the hotel gym.

9:15 p.m. I'm ready for bed. Clothes for the next day are hanging in the closet. The alarm clock is set to 6:30 a.m.

10:30 p.m. I go to sleep.

Visit Vault at **www.vault.com** for insider company profiles, expert advice, career message boards, expert resume reviews, the Vault Job Board and more.

VAULT CAREER LIBRARY 477

Employer Directory

Accenture
1345 Avenue of the Americas
New York, NY 10105
Phone: (917) 452-4400
Fax: (917) 527-9915
www.accenture.com

Affiliated Computer Services, Inc. (ACS)
2828 North Haskell Avenue
Dallas, TX 75204
Phone: (214) 841-6111
Fax: (214) 821-8315
www.acs-inc.com

Ajilon Consulting
210 West Pennsylvania Avenue
Suite 650
Towson, MD 21204
Phone: (410) 821-0435
Fax: (410) 828-0106
www.ajilonconsulting.com

Alliance Consulting Group
Six Tower Bridge
181 Washington Street, Suite 350
Conshohocken, PA 19428
Phone: (610) 234-4301
Fax: (610) 234-4302
www.allianceconsulting.com

Atos Origin
5599 San Felipe, Suite 300
Houston, TX 77056
Phone: (713) 513-3000
Fax: (713) 403-7204

Tour les Miroirs - Bat C
18, avenue d'Alsace
92926 Paris La Défense 3 Cedex
France
Phone: +33-1-55-91-20-00
Fax: +33-1-55-91-20-05
www.atosorigin.com/en-us

BearingPoint, Inc., Management and Technology Consultants
1676 International Drive
McLean, VA 22102
Phone: (703) 747-3000
Fax: (703) 747-8500
www.bearingpoint.com

Booz Allen Hamilton
8283 Greensboro Drive
McLean, VA 22102
Phone: (703) 902-5000
Fax: (703) 902-3333
www.boozallen.com

BT Global Services
350 Madison Avenue
New York, NY 10017
Phone: (646) 487-7400
Fax: (646) 487-3370
www.btglobalservices.com

Bull
296 Concord Road
Billerica, MA 01821
Phone: (978) 294-6000
Fax: (978) 294-7999
www.bull.com

Capgemini
623 Fifth Avenue, 33rd Floor
New York, NY 10022
Phone: (212) 314-8000
Fax: (212) 314-8001
www.us.capgemini.com

Place de l'Étoile
11 rue de Tilsitt
75017 Paris
France
Phone: +33-1-47-54-50-00
Fax: +33-1-47-54-50-25
www.apc.capgemini.com

CGI
4050 Legato Road
Fairfax, VA 22033
Phone: (703) 267-8000
Fax: (703) 267-5111

1130 Sherbrooke Street West
Montreal, Quebec H3A 2M8
Canada
Phone: (514) 841-3200
Fax: (514) 841-3299
www.cgi.com

CIBER, Inc.
5251 DTC Parkway, Suite 1400
Greenwood Village, CO 80111
Phone: (303) 220-0100
Toll free: (800) 242-3899
www.ciber.com

Cisco Systems, Inc.
170 West Tasman Drive
San Jose, CA 95134
Phone: (408) 526-4000
Toll free: (800) 553-NETS
www.cisco.com

Cognizant Technology Solutions
500 Frank W. Burr Boulevard
Teaneck, NJ 07666
Phone: (201) 801-0233
Fax: (201) 801-0243
www.cognizant.com

Computer Sciences Corporation
2100 East Grand Avenue
El Segundo, CA 90245
Phone: (310) 615-0311
www.csc.com

Covansys Corporation
32605 West Twelve Mile Road
Farmington Hills, MI 48334
Phone: (248) 688-2088
Fax: (248) 488-2089
www.covansys.com

Employer Directory, cont.

CTG
800 Delaware Avenue
Buffalo, NY 14209
Phone: (716) 882-8000
Fax: (716) 887-7464
www.ctg.com

Deloitte LLP
1633 Broadway, 35th Floor
New York, NY 10019
Phone: (212) 492-4500
Fax: (212) 492-4743
www.deloitte.com

Detica
Surrey Research Park
Guildford ,Surrey
GU2 7YP
United Kingdom
Phone: +44-14-83-81-60-00
Fax: +44-14-83-81-61-44
www.detica.com

**Diamond Management &
Technology Consultants, Inc.**
John Hancock Center
875 North Michigan Avenue
Suite 3000
Chicago, IL 60611
Phone: (312) 255-5000
Fax: (312) 255-6000
www.diamondconsultants.com

EDS
5400 Legacy Drive
Plano, TX 75024
Phone: (972) 605-6000
Toll free: (800) 566-9337
www.eds.com

Getronics
290 Concord Road
Billerica, MA 01821
Phone: (978) 625-5000
www.getronics.com

GFI Informatique
15, rue Beaujon
75008 Paris
France
Phone: +33-1-53-93-44-39
Fax: +33-1-53-93-44-91
www.gfi.fr

Fujitsu Consulting
343 Thornall Street, Suite 630
Edison, NJ 08837
Phone: (732) 549-4100
Fax: (732) 632-1826
www.fujitsu.com/us/services/consulting

HP Services
3000 Hanover Street
Palo Alto, CA 94304
Phone: (650) 857-1501
Fax: (650) 857-5518
www.hp.com/hps

**IBM Global Technology
Services**
New Orchard Road
Armonk, NY 10504
Phone: (914) 499-1900
Fax: (914) 765-7382
www.ibm.com/consulting/services

Infosys Consulting Inc.
6607 Kaiser Drive
Fremont, CA 94555
Phone: (510) 742-3000
Fax: (510) 742-3090
www.infosysconsulting.com

**Interactive Business Systems,
Inc.**
2625 Butterfield Road
Oak Brook, IL 60523
Phone: (630) 571-9100
Fax: (630) 571-9110
www.ibs.com

Keane, Inc.
210 Porter Drive, Suite 315
San Ramon, CA 94583
Phone: (925) 838-8600
Fax: (925) 838-7138
Toll free: (877) 88-KEANE
www.keane.com

Lockheed Martin Corporation
6801 Rockledge Drive
Bethesda, MD 20817
Phone: (301) 897-6000
Fax: (301) 897-6704
www.lockheedmartin.com

Logica
10375 Richmond Avenue, Suite 1000
Houston, TX 77042
Phone: (713) 954-7000
Fax: (713) 785-0880
www.logicacmg.com

McKinsey & Company
55 East 52nd Street
New York, NY 10022
Phone: (212) 446-7000
Fax: (212) 446-8575
www.mckinsey.com

Oracle Consulting
500 Oracle Parkway
Redwood Shores, CA 94065
Phone: (650) 506-7000
www.oracle.com/consulting/index.html

PA Consulting Group
4601 North Fairfax Drive, Suite 600
Arlington, VA 22203
Phone: (571) 227-9000
Fax: (571) 227-9001

123 Buckingham Palace Road
London, SW1W 9SR
United Kingdom
Phone: +44-20-77-30-90-00
Fax: +44-20-73-33-50-50
www.paconsulting.com

Visit Vault at **www.vault.com** for insider company profiles, expert advice,
career message boards, expert resume reviews, the Vault Job Board and more.

VAULT CAREER LIBRARY   479

Employer Directory, cont.

Perot Systems
2300 West Plano Parkway
Plano, TX 75075
Phone: (972) 577-0000
Fax: (972) 340-6100
Toll free: (888) 31-PEROT
www.perotsystems.com

The Revere Group
An NTT DATA Company
325 North LaSalle Street, Suite 325
Chicago, IL 60610
Phone: (312) 873-3400
Fax: (312) 873-3500
www.reveregroup.com

SAIC
10260 Campus Point Drive
San Diego, CA 92121
Phone: (858) 826-6000
www.saic.com

Sapient
25 First Street
Cambridge, MA 02141
Phone: (617) 621-0200
Fax: (617) 621-1300
www.sapient.com

Satyam Computer Services Ltd.
8500 Leesburg Pike, Suite 201
Vienna, VA 22182
Phone: (703) 734-2100
Fax: (703) 734-2110
www.satyam.com

Siemens IT Solutions and Services, Inc.
101 Merritt 7
Norwalk, CT 06851
Phone: (203) 642-2300
www.usa.siemens.com/it-solutions

Smartronix, Inc.
22685 Three Notch Road
California, MD 20619
Phone: (301) 737-2800
Fax: (301) 866-0528
www.smartronix.com

Tata Consultancy Services
101 Park Avenue, 26th Floor
New York, NY 10178
Phone: (212) 557-8038
Fax: (212) 867-8652
www.tcs.com

Telcordia
One Telcordia Drive
Piscataway, NJ 08854
Phone: (732) 699-2000
www.telcordia.com

Unisys
Unisys Way
Blue Bell, PA 19424
Phone: (215) 986-4011
www.unisys.com

Wipro Ltd.
Doddakannelli Sarjapur Road
Bangalore, Karnataka 560 035
India
Phone: +91-80-844-0011
Fax: +91-80-844-0256
www.wipro.com

Telecommunications

Industry Overview

We're all connected

In simpler times, the word "telecommunications" might have conjured up an image of a telephone—and not much else. These days, though, the telephone is less the shining symbol of the industry and more an antiquated relic of its humble beginnings. Telecom today is high-tech and mobile, encompassing wireless communication, broadband Internet access, and cable and digital TV; it's also (for now) landline phone service for those who have yet to enter the 21st century.

These varying forms of modern communication aren't even distinct services anymore. The lines have blurred considerably, so while your cell phone downloads the latest music video, you can call your best friend across the country (sans long distance charges) with a PC and an Internet connection. Due to this growing interrelation among telecom products, the sector's main players have spread their reach into Internet and digital television to offer bundled "triple-play" phone, Internet and cable TV subscription packages to customers.

A big (and broad) industry

According to the Telecommunications Industry Association (TIA), in the U.S., total telecom spending rose more than 8 percent during 2007 (to about $1 trillion), and the global telecom market is expected to reach $4.9 trillion by 2011. Much of this growth comes thanks to the ascendancy of the Internet and the accompanying need for high-speed connections. Big Telecom (namely, the three largest telecommunications firms: AT&T, Verizon and Sprint Nextel) holds the trump card with its control of the fiber-optic network that brings broadband and other services into millions of homes.

The sector also includes cable companies (Comcast, Cablevision, et. al.), mobile and network equipment manufacturers (Cisco, 3Com and Black Box, to name a few) and local telephone service providers, but other firms play less obvious roles in helping people share information electronically. Corporations like Loral Space & Communication make the satellites that are used for military communications as well as for broadcasting radio and TV. Other firms, such as Trimble Navigation, focus on GPS technology, which is increasingly being incorporated into mobile phones and other devices.

The bell tolls for AT&T

Established in 1877 as American Bell, AT&T enjoyed the largest share of the telecom industry pie for nearly a century, thanks to the government's belief that the utility constituted a "natural" monopoly. That monopoly crumbled in 1969, when the Federal Communications Commission (FCC) allowed other companies—such as MCI—to play in Ma Bell's sandbox. But monopolies don't disappear overnight. To encourage competition in the long-distance market, the Department of Justice followed up with an antitrust suit against AT&T in 1974, which resulted in the company's division into a long-distance retailer and seven regional Bell operating companies (RBOCs) that competed in the local call market as independent LECs, or local exchange carriers. Originally, these so-called "Baby Bells" consisted of Ameritech, Bell Atlantic, BellSouth, NYNEX, Pacific Telesis, Southwestern Bell (later SBC) and U.S. West. The dissolution of the "old" AT&T was completed in 1984.

The industry thrived after the breakup, exploding into hundreds of smaller competitors, lowering the cost of long-distance calling dramatically. AT&T, which held about 70 percent of the market in 1984, controlled only a third in 2005. (The company bounced back, however, to become the biggest kid on the playground as the "new" AT&T after its buyout by SBC in 2005 and subsequent union with Bell South and Cingular Wireless in 2006.)

Visit Vault at **www.vault.com** for insider company profiles, expert advice, career message boards, expert resume reviews, the Vault Job Board and more.

VAULT CAREER LIBRARY   481

Untangling the wires

As the long-distance market diversified, the local exchange market remained relatively homogenous. The Telecommunications Act of 1996 aimed to change that by deregulating entry into local markets and requiring that the Baby Bells, or incumbent local exchange carriers (ILECs), offer their network elements to smaller competitors (CLECs). The incumbents were required to unbundle their networks for reasonable prices, with the goal of decentralizing the system into a "network of networks." The act also temporarily blocked an RBOC from entering the long-distance market until it could prove sufficient competition in its local territory.

Another provision of the Telecom Act, which granted RBOCs the right to sell cable television services and phone equipment, proved to be a boon. Thanks to those services and the entry of the Baby Bells into long distance, the Act actually had the opposite of its intended effect, allowing the strongest RBOCs to solidify their positions and dominate the market through mergers and acquisitions. Today, just three RBOCs—Verizon, AT&T and Qwest—dominate both local phone service and the DSL (digital subscriber line) market. Until recently there were five such companies, but the market contracted with AT&T's SBC and BellSouth deals.

Meltdown on Wall Street

As mergers and acquisitions activity heated up, Wall Street took notice: investors poured $1.3 trillion into telecom companies in the five years following passage of the Telecom Act, according to Forbes magazine. But with this activity came increased scrutiny and risk. Ultimately, the industry was subject to the same meltdown that hit the rest of the tech sector beginning in late 2000. Again according to Forbes, the industry's market value plummeted by $1 trillion after the Dow took its dive. Mergers also fell by the wayside: in July 2000, a proposed merger between Sprint and WorldCom fell through when the Justice Department filed a lawsuit that attempted to block the deal.

Compounding the gloom, a number of major telecoms had high-profile problems in their accounting departments. About a half-dozen other providers of telecom services began Chapter 11 bankruptcy proceedings in 2002, dumping customers and employees as they went. The biggest by far was WorldCom. The company filed for the largest bankruptcy in U.S. history in July of that year, racking up $41 billion in debt and an estimated $11 billion in fraudulent expenses—leading to a $100 billion loss to shareholders. Even as the company attempted a rebound, it had to contend with scores of class-action lawsuits. Former CEO Bernard J. Ebbers also faced a growing list of federal fraud and conspiracy charges. Accounting firm Citigroup, which had conspired with WorldCom, announced in May 2004 that it would pay $2.65 billion to investors for its role in the scandal. In March 2005, Ebbers was found guilty on all counts and sentenced to 25 years in prison. A year after that, the beleaguered company was virtually disappeared, having been gobbled up by Verizon in a deal worth $8.5 billion.

For its part, in 2003, Sprint reorganized into separate business and consumer units in an effort to save itself $1 billion.

Honing in on each other

Competition that got rolling when telecom firms entered the cable game following the Telecommunications Act has only gained momentum since. In recent years, it's gotten downright ugly, with each industry reaching into the other's picnic basket of products to get at the goodies. Because of the onward and upward march of technology, the wires and signals that bring you cable TV can just as easily bring you phone service, and vice versa. Throw Internet access into the mix and you've got a subscriber feeding frenzy, with phone and cable companies all vying to sell consumers the same services.

In December 2006, the FCC stepped in to referee the melee. In a ruling that handed advantage to the phone companies, the FCC limited to 90 days the amount of time local municipalities could take to grant phone companies a video franchise in their area. Previously, local governments had historically been slow to grant approval of phone companies entering the cable television game.

Neutral tones

The FCC has also stepped into the ring on the issue of "net neutrality," a term that describes the indiscriminate nature of the web, where no sites are more readily accessible than others. The crux of the issue is whether or not broadband access providers (namely, telephone companies) can charge higher rates to certain Internet content providers—creating a toll-lane on the information superhighway and potentially favoring certain sites over others. The FCC launched an inquiry into the issue in May 2007, specifically looking to see if broadband companies had adhered to the "open Internet" principles laid out by the federal organization in 2005. The debate about "net neutrality" continues. In early January 2008, the FCC said it would launch three inquires into the blocking of certain text messages on cellular phone networks, the slowing of P-to-P (peer-to-peer) traffic and what constitutes acceptable broadband traffic management.

Can you hear me now?

It's practically a social norm that every person in possession of even a modest amount of spending money must have a cell phone. The wireless market outpaced long distance for the first time in 2003, according to TIA number crunchers (LD posted $78 billion in spending to the $89 billion spent on wireless services), the same year that the number of wireless users was estimated to be above one billion worldwide. By December 2007, industry analysts reckoned that 84 percent Americans had wireless phones, and it is projected that 100 percent of the adult population will tote cell phones by 2013. During 2007, total wireless revenue was nearly $139 billion, an increase from $113.5 billion the previous year. Americans used 2.1 trillion cell phone minutes in 2007, and they sent 363 billion SMS text messages. And more than 13 percent of U.S. households were wireless-only in 2007, up from 8.4 percent in 2006.

The wireless boom touched off renewed corporate activity within the industry. Competition began to sizzle in late 2003, as the first phase of a federal law allowing "portability"—aka, letting consumers retain their mobile phone numbers when switching carriers—took effect. One notable event was Cingular's $41 billion purchase of rival AT&T Wireless, announced in February 2004, following a fierce bidding war with Vodafone. Deals kept perking right along as Sprint merged with Nextel in August 2005, when the companies were, respectively, the No. 3 and No. 5 wireless carriers.

Down to the wire

Wireline companies have also been involved in M&A activity during recent years. One Communications was born in July 2006 through a merger between three telecom companies—Choice One, CTC and Conversent. And, in December 2006, the FCC approved a merger between AT&T and RBOC BellSouth. But while landlines were once seen as a source of dependable revenue and a way to spread risk, wireless companies have recently spun off their local phone units to function as independent companies. Sprint cleaved off its wireline business in May 2006 under the name Embarq, while Alltel, after beefing up its stock by acquiring Valor Communications, divested the landline unit under the name Windstream in July 2006. This may have something to do with conventional wisdom (and statistics, of course) that says consumer wireline business is on its way out, the victim of wireless cell phones which are convenient, practical, and for some, ultra fashionable. As evidence, Embarq saw its store of access lines shrink by 416,000 (6 percent of its total) in its first year of life, and the scenario has played out similarly over the past few years with scores of companies. While "wireline" companies are now fully invested in selling cable and wireless as well, they'll try to hold onto those customers as long as they can, either by rolling out new ways for home and mobile phones to interact, or by making a bundled package too affordable to pass up.

Off the hook and on the 'Net

Cell phones aren't the only way consumers are making calls these days—Voice over Internet Protocol (VoIP) service, offered by companies like Vonage and Skype, allows any user to turn a personal computer into a telephone by sending "packets" of voice data over a broadband connection, much the same way that other data is sent online. Growth in the VoIP market has

Visit Vault at www.vault.com for insider company profiles, expert advice, career message boards, expert resume reviews, the Vault Job Board and more.

VAULT CAREER LIBRARY   483

been exponential: in 2005, the number of Internet phone subscribers in the U.S. went from a mere 1.3 million to 4.5 million, according to industry research group TeleGeography. (The think tank also predicts that by 2010, about 19 million talkers will use VoIP on a regular basis.)

Bypassing questions of local and long distance networks entirely, VoIP providers allow complete number portability—a subscriber in Iowa, for instance, could have a Manhattan area code. (She would be all set if only the Chinatown restaurant with the good kung pao chicken would deliver that far.) The technology is also advantageous in terms of cost. Thanks to the FCC, VoIP is exempt from some of the taxes and regulations with which regular phone carriers are saddled. But—of course—the major telecoms petitioned Capitol Hill, trying to level the playing field.

In June 2005 the FCC ruled that VoIP companies had to contribute, just like any other phone company, to the Universal Service Fund (USF). The program disburses the funds as subsidies to carriers for providing service in rural and low-income areas where costs are high; needless to say, carrier fund contributions are mostly passed on to consumers. (The USF itself has been the source of some controversy—industry watchers note that the program has collected billions of dollars, but its subscriber gains are achieved quite inefficiently.) A panel of the U.S. Court of Appeals for the D.C. Circuit in June 2007 ordered cable companies that offer VoIP service to start paying up—specifically, 64.9 percent of their income is subject to the USF tax, which is usually around 10 percent.

Predators or prey?

During the past five years especially, many telecom firms have grown through acquisitions. In August 2006, Oregon-headquartered Integra purchased competitor Electric Lightwave, making Integra a West Coast powerhouse. Integra got even bigger when the company acquired Eschelon Telecom for $710 million in August 2007. That purchase turned Integra into one of the biggest CLECs in the United States.

At the same time, telecoms have become possible targets. Some analysts have suggested that the next step for Internet biggies such as Microsoft or Google could be the acquisition of telephone businesses (possible regulatory complications notwithstanding). For example, in late 2007 rumors circulated that Google could pick up Sprint Nextel to gain control of WiMax networks. Additionally, companies outside the U.S. have started to express an interest in American telecom businesses. In early 2008, for instance, after Motorola announced plans to spin off its mobile devices division, Videocon, an Indian manufacturer of appliances and electronics, expressed interest in Motorola's handset unit.

Mergers on the rise?

In late May of 2008, Verizon Wireless announced that it would buy Alltel for $5.9, and that it would also pick up $22.2 billion in debt. The merger will make the company the largest mobile phone operator in the United States. The deal is expected to be completed by the end of 2008. Other mergers might be in the works as well, as U.S. mobile phone carriers scramble for a greater share of the cell phone market. The Verizon-Alltel deal makes a merger between Sprint Nextel and TMobile USA more likely. Outside of the United States, Deutsche Telekom agreed to acquire Hellenic Telecommunications, which owns mobile assets in the Balkans, in May 2008. In addition, France Télécom and TeliaSonera, a Swedish-Finish telecom company, have talked about teaming up to form the fourth-largest mobile operator in the world.

Will the credit crunch hurt telecoms?

It's unclear how 2007's subprime mortgage mess will affect the sector. According to Deloitte & Touche's Telecommunications Predictions Report, a wide-reaching economic slowdown may have a negative impact on the industry during 2008 if consumers and businesses reduce tele-spending. However, the document adds that the impact of the subprime correction will likely vary from company to company. Individuals and enterprises may put off buying telecom equipment, but they probably won't stop buying Internet or voice services. Moreover, some businesses may actually invest more in telecommunications as a way to improve productivity. Pre-paid services—in the form of mobile phones and calling cards that are the domain of providers such as MetroPCS, Leap Wireless and IDT Corporation—is one segment of the telecom industry that could thrive during the tough times. The group already caters to lower-income consumers, whose ranks may grow if the economic downturn persists.

Working in the Industy

A job market roller coaster

The numbers are intimidating: telecom seems to thrive on sudden booms and equally rapid readjustments. By some estimates, the industry slashed 300,000 jobs during the troubled period beginning in late 2000. Telecom firms have started to cut jobs again during the recent economic slump. In January 2008, struggling Sprint Nextel announced that the company would close 125 retail stores and cut 4,000 jobs, some 7 percent of its workforce. Companies also feel compelled to trim excess fat when they merge—the 2006 MCI-Verizon merger, for example, resulted in the elimination of some 7,000 positions. Even with increased demand for telecom services, the U.S. Department of Labor's Bureau of Labor Statistics (BLS) says that employment in the industry is expected to grow by just 5 percent over the period between 2006 and 2016, compared with an 11 percent increase for all industries put together.

But there's still plenty of work out there. According to the BLS, telecom accounted for nearly one million wage and salary jobs in 2006, the latest year for which statistics are available. Of these employees, nearly two-thirds worked in office and administrative support or sales, while most of the rest toiled in maintenance, installation and repair. In 2006, wireline telecommunications carriers accounted for 49 percent of all telecommunications positions. Another 21 percent of jobs were with wireless carriers, and 15 percent were with cable companies and other program distributors. The rest were primarily with satellite telecommunications businesses and equipment and service resellers. The BLS insists that having a diverse and flexible skill set (and keeping it up to date) is crucial in this rapidly changing industry.

Talk the talk

Not surprisingly, excellent communication skills are necessary throughout the telecommunications industry. Customer service agents have to field calls from agitated subscribers with grace and good humor. Technicians have face-to-face contact with customers when installing or fixing network equipment in the field. And then there are the sales reps that pass out smiles and handshakes with aplomb in pursuit of corporate accounts. Communication serves workers well within the office, too, say insiders, because front-line field and call-center workers often serve as an intermediary between subscribers and management.

While job outsourcing continues to be a factor—customer service positions can be handled as easily in New Delhi, India as in Dayton, Ohio—many telecom positions are here to stay. Because all the industry's networks are based on some sort of physical component, whether its cell phone towers or fiber-optic cables, telecom companies will always need a staff to expand, update and maintain those networks. Accordingly, technical positions abound for those toting undergraduate or advanced degrees in electrical engineering and related fields.

Tough sell?

While call-center jobs are ubiquitous and open to those without college degrees (and can offer commission income on top of salary) insiders say there is no upward mobility for people entering the company from this route. Instead, those looking for a sales position in the telecom industry are encouraged to start with an internship after completing their degree. Once your foot is in the door, our sources stress, networking is crucial to rising through a company's ranks. In fact, networking is

Visit Vault at **www.vault.com** for insider company profiles, expert advice, career message boards, expert resume reviews, the Vault Job Board and more.

V∧ULT CAREER LIBRARY   **485**

important throughout the telecom world, regardless of your position. As one consultant in the industry puts it, "networking has to be built into your system because that man in the blue suit at that official gathering could well be your next lead for a $1 million consulting engagement."

Work free

In addition to the obvious perks involved with working in the telecom industry (free cable TV, anyone? How about free Internet access and cell phone service while we're at it?), many workers report that flexible scheduling is a valued attribute of their jobs. Salespeople, marketers and managers alike are allowed to budget their time as they see fit. As long as they're doing their part to push the company forward, no one in management usually bats an eye at those extra-long lunches or midday golf sessions. Additionally, telecommuting has become more and more acceptable throughout the industry—perhaps because it's these companies' products that are facilitating web conferences and work-from-home options for the rest of the business world.

Employer Directory

Alcatel-Lucent
54, rue La Boétie
75008 Paris
France
Phone: +33-1-40-76-10-10
Fax: +33-1-40-76-14-00
www.alcatel-lucent.com

Alltel Corporation
1 Allied Drive
Little Rock, AR 72202
Phone: (501) 905-8000
Fax: (501) 905-5444
www.alltel.com

AT&T Incorporated
175 East Houston Street
San Antonio, TX 78205-2233
Phone: (210) 821-4105
Fax: (210) 351-2187
www.att.com

AT&T Mobility LLC
Glenridge Highlands Two
5565 Glenridge Connector
Atlanta, GA 30342
Phone: (404) 236-6000
Fax: (404) 236-6005
www.wireless.att.com

BellSouth Corporation
1155 Peachtree Street NE
Atlanta, GA 30309-3610
Phone: (404) 249-2000
Fax: (404) 249-2071
www.bellsouth.com

BT Conferencing
11400 Westmoor Circle, Suite 225
Westminster, CO 19406
Phone: (303) 448-7800
Fax: (303) 448-7803
Toll free: (800) 843-3666
www.wireone.com

BT Group plc
BT Centre
81 Newgate Street
London, EC1A 7AJ
United Kingdom
Phone: +44-20-73-56-50-00
Fax: +44-20-73-56-55-20
www.btplc.com

Cablevision Systems Corporation
12405 Powerscourt Drive, Suite 100
St. Louis, MO 63131
Phone: (314) 965-0555
Fax: (314) 965-9745
www.cablevision.com

Cellco Partnership
1 Verizon Way
Basking Ridge, NJ 07920
Phone: (908) 559-2000
www.verizonwireless.com

CenturyTel, Inc.
100 CenturyTel Drive
Monroe, LA 71203
Phone: (318) 388-9000
Fax: (318) 388-9064
Toll free: (800) 833-1188
www.centurytel.com

Charter Communications Inc.
12405 Powerscourt Drive, Suite 100
St. Louis, MO 63131-3660
Phone: (314) 965-0555
Fax: (314) 965-9745
www.charter.com

Cincinnati Bell Inc.
221 East 4th Street
Cincinatti, OH 45202
Phone: (513) 397-9900
Fax: (513) 397-5092
www.cincinattibell.com

Comcast Corporation
1 Comcast Center
Philadelphia, PA 19102
Phone: (215) 665-1700
Fax: (215) 981-7790
Toll free: (866) 281-2100
www.comcast.com

Corning Incorporated
1 Riverfront Plaza
Corning, NY 14831-0001
Phone: (607) 974-9000
Fax: (607) 974-5927
www.corning.com

Cox Communications Incorporated
1400 Lake Hearn Drive
Atlanta, GA 30319
Phone: (404) 843-5000
Fax: (404) 843-5975
www.cox.com

CSC Holdings, Inc.
1111 Stewart Avenue
Bethpage, NY 11714
Phone: (516) 803-2300
Fax: (516) 803-3134
www.cablevision.com

The DIRECTV Group, Inc.
2230 East Imperial Hightway
El Segundo, CA 90245
Phone: (310) 964-5000
Fax: (310) 535-5225
www.directv.com

DISH Network Corporation
9601 South Meridian Boulevard
Englewood, CO 80112
Phone: (303) 723-1000
Fax: (303) 723-1999
www.dishnetwork.com

Dycom Industries, Inc.
11770 US Highway 1, Suite 101
Palm Beach Gardens, FL 33408
Phone: (561) 627-7171
Fax: (561) 627-7709
www.dycomind.com

Visit Vault at **www.vault.com** for insider company profiles, expert advice, career message boards, expert resume reviews, the Vault Job Board and more.

VAULT CAREER LIBRARY

487

Employer Directory, cont.

Frontier Communications Company
3 High Ridge Park
Stamford, CT 06905
Phone: (203) 614-5600
Fax: (203) 614-4602
www.czn.com

Insight Communications Company, Inc.
810 7th Avenue
New York, NY 10019
Phone: (917) 286-2300
Fax: (917) 286-2301
www.insight-com.com

Level 3 Communications, Inc.
1025 Eldorado Boulevard
Broomfield, CO 80021
Phone: (720) 888-1000
Fax: (720) 888-5085
Toll free: (877) 585-8266
www.level3.com

MasTec, Inc.
800 South Douglas Road
Coral Gables, FL 33134
Phone: (305) 599-1800
Fax: (305) 406-1960
www.mastec.com

Mediacom Communications Corporation
100 Crystal Run Road
Middletown, NY 10941
Phone: (845) 695-2600
Fax: (845) 695-2699
www.medicomcc.com

Motorola, Inc.
1303 East Algonquin Road
Schaumburg, IL 60196
Phone: (847) 576-5000
Fax: (847) 576-5372
Toll free: (800) 262-8509
www.motorola.com

NII Holdings, Inc.
10700 Parkridge Boulevard, Suite 600
Reston, VA 20191
Phone: (703) 390-5100
Fax: (703) 547-5269
www.nii.com

Nortel
195 The West Mall
Toronto, Ontario M9C 5K1
Canada
Phone: (905) 863-7000
www.nortel.com

Orange PLC
50 George Street
London, W1U 7DZ
United Kingdom
Phone: +44-87-03-76-88-88
Fax: +44-20-79-84-16-01
www.orange.co.uk

Puerto Rico Telephone Company, Inc.
1515 FD Roosevelt Avenue
Guaynabo, PR 00968
Phone: (787) 792-6052
Fax: (787) 282-0958
Toll free: (800) 781-1314
www.telefonicapr.com

Qwest Communications International
1801 California Street
Denver, CO 80202
Phone: (800) 899-7780
Fax: (303) 992-1724
www.qwest.com

Scientific-Atlanta, Inc.
5030 Sugarloaf Parkway
Lawrenceville, GA 30044-2689
Phone: (770) 236-5000
Fax: (408) 526-4545
Toll free: (800) 433-6222
www.sciatl.com

Sprint Nextel Corporation
6200 Sprint Parkway
Overland Park, KS 66251
Phone: (703) 443-4000
Toll free: (800) 829-0965
www.sprint.com

T-Mobile USA, Inc.
12920 SE 38th Street
Bellevue, WA 98006
Phone: (425) 378-4000
Fax: (425) 378-4040
Toll free: (800) 318-9270
www.t-mobile.com

TDS Telecommunications Corporation
525 Junction Road
Madison, WI 53717
Phone: (608) 664-4000
Fax: (608) 664-4035
www.tdstelecom.com

Telephone and Data Systems, Inc.
30 North LaSalle Street, Suite 4000
Chicago, IL 60602
Phone: (312) 630-1900
Fax: (312) 630-1908
www.teldta.com

Telephone Electronics Corporation
236 East Capitol Street, Suite 500
Jackson, MS 39201
Phone: (601) 354-9070
Fax: (601) 352-8830
www.tec.com

Time Warner Cable Inc.
One Time Warner Center, North Tower
New York, NY 10019
Phone: (212) 364-8200
Fax: (203) 328-0604
www.timewarnercable.com

Employer Directory, cont.

United States Cellular Corporation
8410 West Bryn Mawr, Suite 700
Chicago, IL 60631
Phone: (773) 399-8900
Fax: (773) 399-8936
Toll free: (888) 944-9400
www.uscc.com

Verio Inc.
8005 South Chester Street, Suite 200
Englewood, CO 80112
Phone: (303) 645-1900
Fax: (303) 792-5644
www.verio.com

Verizon Business
1 Verizon Way
295 North Maple Avenue
Basking Ridge, NJ 07920-1002
Phone: (908) 559-4000
www.verizonbusiness.com

Verizon Communications
140 West Street
New York, NY 10007
Phone: (212) 395-1000
Fax: (212) 571-1897
Toll free: (800) 621-9900
www.verizon.com

Verizon New York Inc.
140 West Street
New York, NY 10007
Phone: (212) 395-2121
Fax: (212) 398-0951
www.verizon.com

Viatel
Wick Road
Egham, Surrey
TW20 0HR
United Kingdom
Phone: +44-17-84-49-42-00
Fax: +44-17-84-49-42-01
www.viatel.com

Virgin Media Inc.
909 Third Avenue, Suite 2863
New York, NY 10022
Phone: (212) 906-8440
Fax: (212) 397-5943
www.virginmedia.com

Vodafone Group plc
Vodafone House
The Connection
Newbury, Berkshire RG14 2FN
United Kingdom
Phone: +44-1635-33-251
Fax: +44-1635-45-713
www.vodafone.com

Vonage Holdings Corporation
23 Main Street
Holmdel, NJ 07733
Phone: (732) 365-1328
Fax (732) 231-6783
www.vonage.com

Windstream Corporation
4001 Rodney Parham Road
Little Rock, AR 72212
Phone: (501) 748-7000
www.windstream.com

XO Communications
11111 Sunset Hills Road
Reston, Virginia 20190-5327
Phone: (703) 547-2000
www.xo.com

Visit Vault at **www.vault.com** for insider company profiles, expert advice, career message boards, expert resume reviews, the Vault Job Board and more.

VAULT CAREER LIBRARY   489

Transportation Services

Industry Overview

Planes, trains and automobiles

Transportation is a vast and dynamic business sector in which time and accuracy—getting people and products where they're going when they need to be there—are two of the crucial factors affecting success and failure. While it's tempting to view the industry as a collection of modes of transport (train, truck, plane and so on), there is much more happening within the sector than mere haulage or people-moving, and it pays to keep an eye on not only the movers, but the shakers (or facilitators) in the industry as well. Where, for example, would boats be without ports, trains without tracks, or planes without airports? Then, of course, there are the companies that merely facilitate transport for others—logistics groups, non-asset based shipping companies and the like, an industry by itself estimated to be worth over $300 billion. And last, but certainly not least, there is the individual to consider. The person who can't afford—or doesn't want—to pay someone else to move their possessions from one place to another but who is willing to do it themselves, given a big enough rental truck. According to Ryder, a firm most well-known for renting trucks to do-it-yourselfers, the U.S. commercial fleet leasing and rental market is worth over $25 billion annually. The case is clear, then; whichever way you turn in transport, from hauling your couch across town to routing a shipment of semiconductors across three continents by several modes of transport, there's money in this game. Squeezing out a profit margin may be getting harder (see below), but for the company that can manage all the variables, the rewards will be there for as long as stuff has somewhere it needs to be. In an increasingly globalized world, with more stuff finding more places to get to, that's shaping up to be a very long time indeed.

Legislating openness

In the last 50 years, there have been two major developments at a political level that have affected the transportation industry—or at least the portion of it that's dedicated to moving freight. Loosely summed up, those developments are deregulation, and NAFTA.

Between 1978 and 1986, the U.S. government passed a series of deregulation legislation (try saying that three times fast) that opened the skies, the railroads and the interstates to country-wide competition, sparking a series of acquisitions, mergers and a pattern of growth across the industry. Trucking companies such as J.B. Hunt found themselves perfectly positioned to take advantage of a glut of new routes, and swiftly established themselves as leading players in the field.

With the new routes, however, came increased logistical concerns, with companies hauling more freight further and further afield, and relying on an ever-increasing number of rigs and drivers to do the hauling—an option that didn't come cheap. Thus, the industry found itself faced with the challenge of finding a more (cost and time) effective way of doing business—by arranging, for example, larger shipments to regional hubs, which could then be distributed on a local basis by trucks. The answer to the conundrum lay in the railroads, and their ability to transport much larger volumes of cargo on a single train than the most ambitious trucker could think about hauling in their rig. A great deal of work lay in conquering the suspicion that naturally arose between two competing modes of transport, but once conquered, the concept of intermodal shipping began to take over from mere trucking alone, with several companies—again including J.B. Hunt—forming partnerships with privately-owned railroads around the company. The next step in the chain, obviously, was shipping and plane cargo to help with international delivery, and pretty soon there were companies that could arrange to ship something pretty much anywhere in the world, utilizing several modes of transport, and never have it leave their possession. That's where companies like the Hub Group and UTi Worldwide come in, posting 2007 revenues of $1.7 billion and $1.5 billion respectively from the logistics sector alone, living proof that there's more to haulage than point A to point B.

Visit Vault at **www.vault.com** for insider company profiles, expert advice, career message boards, expert resume reviews, the Vault Job Board and more.

V/\ULT CAREER LIBRARY 491

The NAFTA effect

As mentioned above, the passage into law of the North American Free Trade Agreement in 1994 had a significant effect on the U.S. transportation industry. Despite being a controversial piece of legislation (which brought fears that U.S. companies would pack up and head south to take advantage of lower labor rates), the agreement has been—broadly speaking— advantageous for the transportation industry. The increase in cargo rolling across both the Canadian and Mexican borders was a boon to U.S. haulage and logistics firms, some of whom partnered with, acquired, or set up firms in the other North American countries to achieve a cohesive transportation network. Schneider is an example of that, having set up a U.S-based operations center just north of the Mexican border, and partnered with a Mexican firm with a similar facility south of the border, in order to ensure smooth passage of goods between the two nations.

At the time of writing, there is a weighty debate raging at Congressional level about the future of a cross-border pilot program—launched in late 2007—that gives Mexican trucks access to U.S. roads and vice versa. The program, which could further streamline trade between the two nations, has met with some vociferous opposition, most notably in the form of Senator Byron Dorgan (D-N.D.), who has called for it to be abandoned, citing safety concerns. Fuel was added to the fire in the early days of 2008, as Congress voted to block funding to set up a program but did not include language that prevents funding for the current program from continuing. Mexico, meanwhile, has threatened to block U.S. imports if the program is halted, reasoning that the U.S. would be in violation of NAFTA if it did so.

Going private

Of all the trends in all the industries, one of the most notable has been the number of private equity buyouts of transportation firms in the last few years. As *Transport Topics* magazine pointed out midway through 2007, private equity firms acquired 16 for-hire carriers in just the first five months of 2007. Most notable among these was perhaps Swift Transportation's buyout by its founders for $2.7 billion—a deal that saw the largest publicly-traded trucking firm in the U.S. relinquish that title. Later in the year, meanwhile, the industry lost another publicly-traded firm, as $3 billion-a-year U.S. Xpress was taken private by its founders. *Transport Topics* notes that the private-equity moves are likely to increase the amount of capital flowing to those firms, which will in turn increase their competitiveness and market share—crucial factors as economic conditions point to slowdown (with recession a distinct possibility), and a likely short-to-medium term decrease in haulage volume. Those looking for a precedent for the carnage that can be wrought on the industry by a back-sliding economy need look no further than the losses and job cuts that followed the economic downturn at the start of the millennium.

Any port in a storm

Should the slowdown continue, it's not only the haulage companies that will suffer. While recession leading to fewer jobs leading to less spending is a fairly simple cycle that obviously affects consumers and producers, it can easily be extrapolated to less goods being shipped. Again, bad news for haulage companies, easy to identify, but the effect on the facilitators of the transportation industry shouldn't be overlooked either.

While airports such as Houston, Atlanta and LAX have spent heavily over the past few decades to keep up with the pace of change, and ports such as Boston and New York are routinely dealing in millions of tons of cargo every year, their respective balance sheets may also be affected by a downturn in trade—and without the luxury enjoyed by the haulage firms of expansion into emerging markets. Having said that, Dallas-Fort Worth Airport has begun increasing the number of passenger routes it serves, marketing the area in Central America as it seeks to increase its share of the aviation market.

Ordinary Joe

Of course, the beating heart of the transportation industry—its raison d'être—is the ordinary man and woman in the street. Without their (and our) needs, there would be no goods being shipped. No reason for all those trains and planes and trucks. Or public transportation, for that matter—one industry segment that is almost certain to ride out a recession with no loss of customer base. In fact, recession—coupled with rising oil prices and a desire for greener forms of transport—may even see ridership of subways and buses going up as more and more people resort to a cheaper method of getting around. This is great, as long as urban mass transit networks can handle the influx of passengers. New York's MTA, for example, has been running at capacity on some lines for quite some time, and yet is still several years away from opening its long-awaited (some would say mythical) Second Avenue line.

The Road Ahead

In its most recent report on the transportation and warehousing industry, the Bureau of Labor Statistics projected an increase in jobs of some 11.9 percent between 2004 and 2014, compared to 14.8 percent across all industry sectors. Of those jobs, more than 40 percent were held by truck drivers—a figure that represents the labor intensity of the industry. While technological advances may have increased miles per gallon, infrastructure and many other factors within the industry, the fact remains that one driver can still only cover so many miles per day.

At the end of 2007, mention anything to do with fuel consumption, and two elephants suddenly appear in the room, begging for attention. The first of these is the ever-increasing price of oil, which has consistently stayed at over $100 a barrel in during 2008. The second, of course, is the environment or—more specifically—CO_2 emissions, which global warming hawks claim are in large part responsible for the phenomenon. As one of the major users of gas, and therefore a major producer of CO_2, the transportation industry sits astride both problems, and under considerable pressure to find solutions to them. While many companies have made efforts to introduce more fuel-efficient machines and energy-efficient buildings, the greening of business practices is a long-term investment with high initial costs that may not be realized as savings on the balance sheets for some time to come.

Overall, the outlook for the industry is something of a mixed bag—slower anticipated job growth than other industries and a vulnerability in an uncertain economic climate come set against continued globalization, with many companies expanding into developing markets to keep the balance sheets ticking over. But that's the nature of the industry—be it people, cargo or the times, it just keeps moving.

Visit Vault at **www.vault.com** for insider company profiles, expert advice, career message boards, expert resume reviews, the Vault Job Board and more.

VAULT CAREER LIBRARY 493

Employer Directory

ABF Freight System, Inc.
3801 Old Greenwood Road
Fort Smith, AR 72903
Phone: (479) 785-6000
Fax: (800) 599-2810
Toll free: (800) 610-5544
www.abfs.com

AMERCO
(U-Haul International, Inc.)
1325 Airmotive Way, Suite 100
Reno, NV 89502
Phone: (775) 688-6300
Fax: (775) 688-6338
www.amerco.com

Arkansas Best Corporation
3801 Old Greenwood Road
Fort Smith, AR 72903
Phone: (479) 785-6000
Fax: (479) 785-6004
www.arkbest.com

BAX Global Inc.
440 Exchange
Irvine, CA 92602
Phone: (714) 442-4500
Fax: (714) 442-2900
Toll free: (800) 225-5229
www.baxworld.com

BNSF Railway Company
2650 Lou Menk Drive
Fort Worth, TX 76131
Phone: (800 795-2673
www.bnsf.com

Carrix, Inc.
1131 SW Klickitat Way
Seattle, WA 98134
Phone: (206) 382-4490
Fax: (206) 623-0179
Toll free: (800) 422-3505
www.carrix.com

Caterpillar Logistics Services, Inc.
500 North Morton Avenue
Morton, IL 60661
Phone: (312) 664-7200
www.catlogistics.com

C.H. Robinson Worldwide, Inc.
8100 Mitchell Road
Eden Prairie, MN 55344-2248
Phone: (952) 937-8500
Fax: (952) 937-6714
www.chrobinson.com

Chicago Transit Authority
567 West Lake Street
Chicago, IL 60661
Phone: (312) 664-7200
www.transitchicago.com

Con-way Inc.
2855 Campus Drive, Suite 300
San Mateo, CA 94403
Phone: (650) 378-5200
Fax: (650) 357-9160
www.con-way.com

CSX Corporation
500 Water Street, 15th Floor
Jacksonville, FL 32202
Phone: (904) 359-3200
Fax: (904) 359-2459
www.csx.com

DHL Holdings (USA)
1200 South Pine Island Road
Plantation, FL 33324
Phone: (954) 888-7000
Fax: (954) 888-7310
www.dhl.com

EG&G
200 Orchard Ridge Drive, Suite 100
Gaithersburg, MD 20878
Phone: (301) 258-6554
Fax: (301) 721-2202
www.urscorp.com/EGG_division

Enterprise Rent-A-Car Company
600 Corporate Park Drive
St. Louis, MO 63105
Phone: (314) 512-5000
Fax: (314) 512-4706
www.enterprise.com

Estes Express Lines, Inc.
3901 West Broad Street
Richmond, VA 23230
Phone: (804) 353-1900
Fax: (804) 353-8001
www.estes-express.com

Expeditors International of Washington, Inc.
1015 3rd Avenue, 12th Floor
Seattle, WA 98104
Phone: (206) 674-3400
Fax: (206) 682-9777
www.expeditors.com

FedEx Corporation
942 South Shady Grove Road
Memphis, TN 38120
Phone: (901) 818-7500
Fax: (901) 395-2000
www.fedex.com

FedEx Freight Corporation
1715 Aaron Brenner Drive, Suite 600
Memphis, TN 38120
Phone: (901) 346-4400
Fax: (901) 434-3118
www.fedex.com/freight

FirstGroup PLC
395 King Street
Aberdeen, AB24 5RP
Scotland
Phone: +44-12-24-65-01-00
Fax: +44-12-24-65-01-40
www.firstgroup.com

Employer Directory, cont.

Hertz Global Holdings, Inc.
225 Brae Boulevard
Park Ridge, NJ 07656-0713
Phone: (201) 307-2000
Fax: (201) 307-2644
www.hertz.com

Houston Airport System
16930 JFK Boulevard
Houston, TX 77032
Phone: (281) 233-1800
Fax: (281) 233-1859
www.fly2houston.com

J.B. Hunt Transport Services, Inc.
615 J.B. Hunt Corporate Drive
Lowell, AR 74745
Phone: (479) 820-0000
Fax: (479) 820-3418
Toll free: (800) 643-3622
www.jbhunt.com

Kansas City Southern
427 West 12th Street
Kansas City, MO 64105
Phone: (816) 983-1303
Fax: (816) 983-1108
www.kcsi.com

Metropolitan Transportation Authority
347 Madison Avenue
New York, NY 10017
Phone: (212) 878-7000
Fax: (212) 878-0186
www.mta.info

Massachusetts Port Authority
One Harborside Drive, Suite 200S
East Boston, MA 02128
Phone: (617) 428-2800
www.massport.com

National Railroad Passenger Corporation (Amtrak)
60 Massachusetts Avenue NE
Washington, DC 20002
Phone: (202) 906-3000
Fax: (202) 906-3306
www.amtrak.com

Norfolk Southern Corporation
3 Commercial Place
Norfolk, VA 23510-2191
Phone: (757) 629-2600
Fax: (757) 664-5069
www.nscorp.com

Pacer International
2300 Clayton Road, Suite 1200
Concord, CA 94520
Phone: (925) 887-1400
Fax: (925) 887-1503
Toll free: (877) 917-2237
www.pacer-international.com

Port Authority of New York and New Jersey
225 Park Avenue South
New York, NY 10003
Phone: (212) 435-7000
Fax: (212) 435-6670
www.panynj.gov

RGIS, LLC
2000 EastTaylor Road
Auburn Hills, MI 48326
Phone: (248) 651-2511
Fax: (248) 656-6628
Toll free: (800) 551-9130
www.rgisinv.com

Roadway Express, Inc.
1077 Gorge Boulevard
Akron, OH 44310
Phone: (330) 384-1717
Fax: (330) 258-2597
www.roadway.com

Ryder
11690 NW 105th Street
Miami, FL 33178
Phone: (305) 500-3726
Fax: (305) 500-3203
www.ryder.com

Sabre Holdings Corp.
3150 Sabre Drive
Southlake, TX 76092
Phone: (682) 605-1000
Fax: (682) 605-8267
www.sabre-holdings.com

Safe Ride Service, Inc.
2001 West Camelback Road
Phoenix, AZ 85015
Phone: (602) 627-6705
Fax: (602) 627-6751
Toll free: (800) 320-1805
www.saferideservices.com

Schneider National, Inc.
3101 South Packerland Drive
Green Bay, WI 54306
Phone: (920) 592-2000
Fax: (920) 592-3063
Toll free: (800) 558-6767
www.schneider.com

SSA Marine
1131 SW Klickitat Way
Seattle, WA 98134
Phone: (206) 623-0304
Fax: (206) 623-0179
Toll free: (800) 422-3505
www.ssamarine.com

Swift Transportation Co., Inc.
2200 South 75th Avenue
Phoenix, AZ 85043
Phone: (602) 269-9700
Fax: (623) 907-7380
Toll free: (800) 800-2200
www.swifttrans.com

Visit Vault at www.vault.com for insider company profiles, expert advice,
career message boards, expert resume reviews, the Vault Job Board and more.

VAULT CAREER LIBRARY

495

Employer Directory, cont.

Werner Enterprises, Inc.
14507 Frontier Road
Harrison, AR 72601
Phone: (870) 741-9000
Fax: (870) 741-7325
Toll free: (800) 874-4723
www.werner.com

WIS International
9265 Sky Park, Suite 100
San Diego, CA 92123
Phone: (858) 565-8111
Fax: (858) 492-2751
Toll free: (800) 888-8210
www.wisint.org

UAL Corporation
77 W. Wacker Drive
Chicago, IL 60601
Phone: (312) 997-8000
www.united.com

UniGroup, Inc.
1 Premier Drive
Fenton, MO 63026
Phone: (636) 305-5000
Fax: (636) 326-1106
www.unigroupinc.com

Union Pacific Corporation
1400 Douglas Street
Omaha, NE 68179
Phone: (402) 544-5000
Fax: (402) 271-6408
www.up.com

United Parcel Service, Inc.
55 Glenlake Parkway NE
Atlanta, GA 30328
Phone: (404) 828-6000
Fax: (404) 828-6562
Toll free: (800) 874-5877
www.ups.com

United States Postal Service
475 L'Enfant Plaza SW
Washington, DC 20260-3100
Phone: (202) 268-2500
Fax: (202) 268-4860
www.usps.com

U.S. Xpress Enterprises, Inc.
145 Hunter Drive
Wilmington, OH 45177
Phone: (937) 382-5591
Fax: (937) 383-3838
www.usexpress.com

Wabash National Corp.
1000 Sagamore Parkway South
Lafayette, IN 47905
Phone: (765) 771-5300
Fax: (765) 771-5474
www.wabashnational.com

Werner Enterprises, Inc.
14507 Frontier Road
Omaha, NE 68145
Phone: (402) 895-6640
Fax: (402) 895-6640
www.werner.com

Yellow Transportation, Inc.
10990 Roe Avenue
Overland Park, KS 66211
Phone: (913) 344-3000
Fax: (913) 696-6122
www.myyellow.com

YRC Worldwide Inc.
10990 Roe Avenue
Overland Park, KS 66211
Phone: (913) 696-6100
Fax: (913) 696-6116
Toll free: (800) 846-4300
www.yrcw.com

APPENDIX

COLLEGE
CAREER
BIBLE

About the Editor

Vault Editors

Vault is the leading media company for career information. Our team of industry-focused editors takes a journalistic approach in covering news, employment trends and specific employers in their industries. We annually survey 10,000s of employees to bring readers the inside scoop on industries and specific employers.

Much of the material in *The College Career Bible* is excerpted from Vault titles to specific industries or career titles. Vault publishes more than 100 titles for job seekers and professionals. To see a complete list of Vault titles, go to www.vault.com.

Visit Vault at **www.vault.com** for insider company profiles, expert advice,
career message boards, expert resume reviews, the Vault Job Board and more.

VAULT CAREER LIBRARY 499

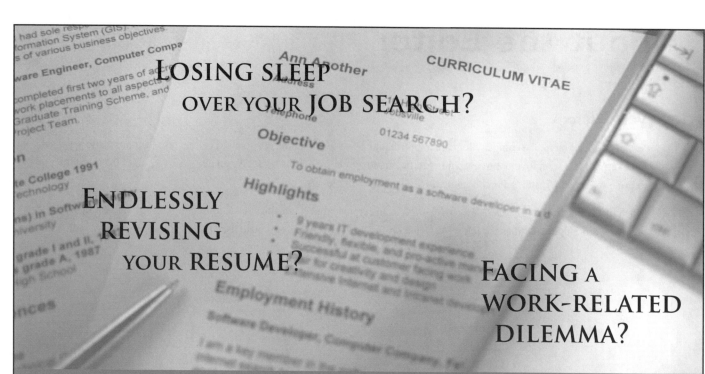

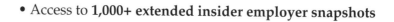